# Entrepreneurship and Knowledge Exchange

"This book introduces and summarizes the fine work being done on the important inter-section between higher education and entrepreneurship. It will be an indispensable tool for students of entrepreneurship, instructors and administrators, and government policymakers – all those interested in how entrepreneurship education can help entrepreneurs and entre-preneurship in a region."

—*David Ahlstrom, Chinese University of Hong Kong*

Over the last several decades there has been a growing interest in the relation-ship between entrepreneurship and university–industry collaboration, namely how such cooperation can benefit entrepreneurship development at individual, national and regional levels. While there are several refereed journal articles on different aspects of university–industry cooperation, most studies dwell primar-ily on instruments such as spin-offs, incubators and graduate entrepreneurs. This collection offers the first book-length compendium of international comparative perspectives on university–industry cooperation.

*Entrepreneurship and Knowledge Exchange* explores insights from a wide variety of countries of relevance to researchers as well as policy and decision makers, especially those working in developing economies. Seminal contributions from top academics in the field, such as Allan Gibb, Peter Scott and Mary Walshok, are included. The issues of knowledge transfer, entrepreneurship and regional/national economic regeneration have inspired countless programs and initiatives at national and regional levels, and the chapters in this book examine these initia-tives, providing both a reference work and a record of practical experience.

**Jay Mitra** is Professor of Business Enterprise and Innovation and Director of the International Centre for Entrepreneurship Research at Essex Business School, University of Essex, UK. His most recent book is *Entrepreneurship, Innovation, and Economic Development* (Routledge, 2012).

**John Edmondson** is Director of IP Publishing Ltd, a publishing house specializing in academic journals, and serves as Senior Enterprise Fellow at Essex Business School, University of Essex, UK. He is Editor-in-Chief of the journal *Industry and Higher Education* and has contributed many articles and reviews to magazines and journals, including business and higher education issues and literature.

# Routledge Studies in Entrepreneurship

**Edited by Susan Marlow and Janine Swail (University of Nottingham, UK)**

This series extends the meaning and scope of entrepreneurship by capturing new research and enquiry on economic, social, cultural and personal value creation. Entrepreneurship as value creation represents the endeavours of innovative people and organisations in creative environments that open up opportunities for developing new products, new services, new firms and new forms of policy making in different environments seeking sustainable economic growth and social development. In setting this objective, the series includes books which cover a diverse range of conceptual, empirical and scholarly topics that both inform the field and push the boundaries of entrepreneurship.

# Entrepreneurship and Knowledge Exchange

**Edited by Jay Mitra and
John Edmondson**

Routledge
Taylor & Francis Group

LONDON AND NEW YORK

First published 2015
by Routledge

2 Park Square, Milton Park, Abingdon, Oxfordshire OX14 4RN
711 Third Avenue, New York, NY 10017

*Routledge is an imprint of the Taylor & Francis Group, an informa business*

First issued in paperback 2018

*Library of Congress Cataloging-in-Publication Data*

Entrepreneurship and knowledge exchange / edited by Jay Mitra and
    John Edmondson.
      pages cm. — (Routledge studies in entrepreneurship ; 7)
    Includes bibliographical references and index.
  1. Academic-industrial collaboration.    2. Technological
innovations.    3. Research, Industrial.    4. Business and
education.    5. Entrepreneurship.    I. Mitra, Jay.
    LC1085.E58 2015
    378.1'035—dc23        2014037574

ISBN: 978-0-415-75038-7 (hbk)
ISBN: 978-1-138-61703-2 (pbk)

Typeset in Times New Roman
by Apex CoVantage, LLC

The Editors are grateful to the corresponding authors for their approval of the
inclusion of their respective papers in this project.

This book is dedicated to two of its contributors, Jo Lorentzen and Eugene Luczkiw, who are no longer with us. Their work, as their inclusion in this volume testifies, lives after them.

# Contents

## Part II: Creating the Culture: Educating Entrepreneurially

## Part III: Gearing Cooperation and Entrepreneurship for Regional Growth

## Part IV: Gearing Cooperation and Entrepreneurship for National Growth

# Introduction: looking back to look ahead

## Jay Mitra and John Edmondson

As primary institutions of higher education provision, universities shape and influence thought and action among young and old and across different domains of learning and subject disciplines, through research, teaching and knowledge exchange (the latter in popular university parlance is often referred to as 'knowledge transfer' and/or 'technology transfer').[1] The necessary and optimum combination of these three missions of the university has attracted much attention in most countries around the world. Questions of 'relevance' shift the argument about the value of university research and education from the sacrosanct notions of the 'public good' to considerations of economic impact, as evinced in jobs and business development.

Universities are the main custodians of codified learning and especially of 'higher' forms of learning for their students and staff. Intellectual curiosity, in-depth enquiry, original findings, the transcription and dissemination of knowledge through teaching, publications and outreach work with external organisations are not circumscribed by either geography or narrow concerns of immediate or contingent relevance predicated on purely economic considerations. They create a learning context full of global, national and regional/local ramifications, and it is essentially in the exchange of knowledge among educators, researchers, students and the wider body of business, governmental and social stakeholders that they create economic, social, cultural and personal value. This learning nexus helps to obtain opportunities for the growth and development of individuals, organisations and the wider environment.

The loftiness of the role of knowledge creation and its dissemination by universities can sometimes lead to the practical meaning of these activities getting lost in paralysing analysis or too much high-mindedness. It is important to remain anchored to the realities of a functioning university – exemplified by the first Chancellor of the University of Berkeley, Clark Kerr, as making arrangements for car parks for the staff, the sex lives of students and sports for the alumni. The Kerr philosophy helps to lighten the debate about the value and purpose of higher education, but there is also something in his statement that indirectly reminds academics of the need to translate the wonders of the abstraction of serious thought and enquiry into conduits and instruments of application for the daily lives of people.

This collection of articles provides a modern historical overview of the relationship between universities and the wider community of learning. What happens between the two is a form of what we refer to as 'knowledge exchange', a deliberate variation of the popular term 'knowledge transfer'. 'Knowledge exchange' presupposes a varied set of producers of knowledge (of which the university is one, albeit a distinctive one of higher learning) – a society or a marketplace for knowledge in which different agents of knowledge exchange know-how, concepts, methods, techniques, research outcomes or practitioner-based findings. 'Knowledge transfer', on the other hand, is redolent of a benefactor–beneficiary relationship, with the benefactor (the university) transferring its expertise to a supplicant beneficiary (industry or other organisation). The linear flow of that construct has long been forgotten (see Kline and Rosenberg, 1986) with the widespread recognition of the facts that:

a) new knowledge can be sourced as much from the ivory tower of blue-sky research as from the hard grind of factories and offices;
b) in common with developments of technology, new knowledge can emerge at various points in the learning process that is involved in its production; and
c) knowledge creation, especially in the world of new technology, demands a constant shuttling of ideas, resources and talent from and between different types of organisations.

# Universities and knowledge creation and exchange: a brief history

September 2014 is a historical landmark because it marks the revival of the oldest university in the world – the Nalanda University in Bihar, India. Institutions such as universities emerge to reflect the time and place in which they are situated, which suggests a natural relationship with the wider environment based on the imparting and absorption of knowledge and learning. Being the first of its kind in ancient Magadha, where an extraordinary intellectual explosion of Buddhist and non-Buddhist heritage marked the times, it became a unique haven of learning affording multiple levels of discourse and analysis. The notion of embracing knowledge and seeking critical insights into developments at the time was a direct contribution to the affiliation of the university with its surrounding environment. Nalanda's long and remarkable existence for 800 years from the 5th to the 12th century CE was characterised by its internationalisation, scholarship and embedding in the learning environment of its times. More than 10,000 students and more than 2,000 teachers were located in this residential seat of learning. Scholars and other visitors from China, Korea, Japan, Tibet, Mongolia, Turkey, Sri Lanka, Singapore and other parts of South East Asia, studying religion, law, history, linguistics, medicine, public health, architecture, metallurgy, pharmacology, astronomy and sculpture, created an Asian heartland of knowledge and value creation. Its high walls, parks and lakes, eight different compounds, 10 temples, meditation halls and nine-storey library might attract the envy of many a modern university. But what distinguished Nalanda's environment was the exchange of knowledge between its students and scholars and the cultural currency of its times. Two attempts by the Huns and Gaudas at its destruction in the 5th and 7th centuries led only to its restoration, until the Turkish invasion during the 12th century ended seven centuries of unique intellectual endeavour (Nalanda University website and Wikipedia, 2014).

It was not until the 10th century that the world was introduced to Al Azhar University in Cairo, with Bologna following in the 11th century (1088 CE) and Oxford in the 12th century (1167 CE). The independent, self-governing institutions of the European Middle Ages were recognised by both the local governments and the church till the 18th century, once again suggesting the necessary external validation and prospective use of the university's activities.

To obtain an understanding of the real modern value of higher education institution (HEI)–industry links, we need to explore developments in Germany and especially the emergence of the *Technische Hochschulen* in the late 19th century. Education in Germany evolved from the classical humanist tradition of *Bildung* in the *Gymnasium* and the university. The pragmatic or utilitarian curricula of science, technology and modern languages were available in the *Realgymnasium*. The *Technische Hochschulen* recruited students from the latter and, together with the *Technische Mittelschulen* (local, small training institutes), they offered diverse, 'pliable, transverse structures' of technical education and learning, enabling industry to recruit new employees in response to changing technology and economic opportunities (Shinn, 1998). As Cahan (1989) notes, the indirect research carried out in the *Physikalisch-Technische Reichsanstalts* (specialising in technology) also helped to establish German-based technological standards and carry out significant work in the field of instrumentation.

Realisation of the significance of time and place becomes significant when we note that innovation in terms of new product development, new technology standards, new supply-side measures (as in education and training) and the creation of new forms of intellectual and human capital were critical factors for the second industrial revolution and for first German and then European industrial growth.

Developments in the machinery of the state led to higher levels of control over public university systems in much of Continental Europe, notably France and Germany, as well as in Japan. Britain and the USA, however, carved out their own paths in much the same way as they managed their broader economic models. US universities in particular retained great autonomy in their administrative policies. According to Rosenberg (2000) and Ben-David (1968), it was this autonomy that drove American universities to be more 'entrepreneurial' and their research and curricula to be more responsive to changing socio-economic demands than their European counterparts (Mitra, 2012).

Two post–World War scenarios provide insights into diverse approaches to university–industry linkages or, indeed, their absence. After the First World War, very few French firms had any research capacity of note – nor did France's educational system provide for any applied research development. After the Second World War, the USSR boasted a significant fundamental and applied research community, larger even than that of the USA, but Soviet industry hardly grew at all. French industry, however, made advances despite restrictive innovation acquisition practices during the First World War (Shinn, 1998).

A key development in the 1980s, the passing of the Bayh–Dole Act, was the harbinger of economic value creation of academic research in the USA. The act gave US universities a right to claim ownership of promising discoveries, including cancer-fighting molecules or better algorithms, even if the research was carried out using public funds. Since then, we have witnessed some amazing outcomes. Stanford earned $336 million from selling its stake in Google in 2005 while, on the East Coast, New York University has earned more than $650 million since the mid-2000s because of the science underpinning Remicade, the arthritis drug. Two other notable examples are those of Northwestern University in Evanston, Illinois, earning $192 million and Carnegie Mellon University in Pittsburgh, Pennsylvania, being awarded $1.2 billion by a federal jury when it found that a semiconductor firm had found easy passage with the university's inventions, forgetting the small business of first seeking permission. The two major public universities in Utah – University of Utah and Utah State University – have raised $100 million of public funds from the state since 2007 to develop the Utah Science Technology and Research Initiative (USTAR) and build its state-of-the-art laboratories and start-up packages in fields such as biomedicine, nanotechnology and energy. Since then, the standing of the University of Utah has shot up in the Shanghai Jia Tong world rankings (to 82 in 2012) of research universities in the world (Science, 2013).

Much of the buzz around 'technology transfer' has been due to the obvious attractions of Mammon and the flow of money from patenting and licensing. Other 'softer' ways of making industries interact with universities are harder to identify or quantify, partly because of the difficulty in tracking the mutuality of knowledge flows. Eight different routes to knowledge transfer and exchange have been identified, as shown in Table 1.

**Table 1. Routes to knowledge transfer and knowledge exchange.**

| Jobs | Research publications | Public dissemination | Industry sponsorship | Collaborative projects | Consulting | Entrepreneurship | Licensing |
|---|---|---|---|---|---|---|---|
| Transfer of skills and ideas through jobs in industry, government and non-profit sectors | Both refereed and general journals and magazines, including trade magazines | Dissemination of ideas and research at refereed and public conferences, seminars, workshops | Project managed by academic sponsored by industry, sometimes involving students | Groups of businesses, government agencies and university academics in cooperative research projects | Academics consulting individual or groups of companies | Researchers involved in new ventures without involvement of university intellectual property | University licenses IP to private business/spin-off or start-up |

*Source:* Adapted from Science, 2013.

The routes identified in Table 1 allow for a wider, more holistic approach that captures a fuller rage of transfer and exchange activities. Consequently, they allow for the development of metrics that can evaluate different services offered by universities and multiple pathways for industry to connect with universities. University associations in the USA and the UK are, for example, working on the creation of additional metrics with which to quantify the number of occasions a university academic is 'hired' by local firms or public organisations for advice and support. In the UK, a scheme run by a local authority in the East of England uses the University of Essex and its International Centre of Entrepreneurship Research to identify selected students on short research or problem-solving projects for local businesses, where students can test their own learning drawn from lectures by applying and validating them through these projects. The scheme is a local counterpart to one of the country's most successful knowledge transfer programmes, KTP (or Knowledge Transfer Partnerships), which brings together a graduate student, an academic and a local firm to solve a business research problem. Similarly, the University of Maryland in the USA runs, among many initiatives, 'entrepreneur hours' hosted by the Maryland Technology Institute, in which experts provide advice to anyone with an interest in commercialising their ideas. Other initiatives of similar import and purpose abound.

Acknowledging the range of knowledge exchange possibilities helps us to obtain a holistic view of the interactions between different university activities and industry interest. A holistic approach is essential for the development of an ecosystem for entrepreneurship enabled by university–industry relationships. For both universities and industries to benefit, a region needs such an ecosystem, with many different kinds of interests engaged and supported, far more than one or two spectacular commercialisations.

## Universities, the nation state and national innovation systems

Implicit in the previous discussion has been the relative importance of universities to national economies. After all, as seats of learning, their productive efforts are best realised through the innovations they create. For this reason, they are widely referred to as a critically important institutional actor in national innovation systems.

Any review of such a system places much emphasis on the importance of robust connections between various institutions in improving national innovative and competitive performance, with universities playing a major role. Some models of university research activity that impact the development of national innovation systems can be identified from the literature, as shown in Table 2.

**Table 2. University research models and national innovation systems.**

| Models | Source | Scope | Critiques |
|---|---|---|---|
| The linear model | Bush, 1945 | Expanding public funding critical to innovation and economic growth; universities were most appropriate institutional locus for basic research; based on 'market failure' rationale for funding basic academic research developed by Nelson (1959) and Arrow (1962). | Critiques offered by Kline and Rosenberg (1986) pointing to curvilinear approach; reference to growth of industrial Japan and evidence of non-essential requirement of basic research; technology being considered to be more useful than science for economic growth. |
| Academic Research v Industrial Research | Dasgupta and David, 1987; David, Foray and Steinmueller, 1999; Branscombe, et al, 1999 | Cultural differences between academic and industrial research. Academic research concerned with original insights and discoveries and critical methodologies plus prompt, refereed publication. Industrial research is dependent on sponsorship, secrecy, problem-solving issues. | Differences can be overstated. Pharmaceutical research relies heavily on publications, for example. Many academic researchers combine 'pure' work and 'applied' work, which support each other, especially in new technology areas. |
| Mode 2 Research (see above) | Gibbons et al, 1994 | Holistic, interdisciplinary approach linked to networked institutions; different from past and associated with post-modern economic environment and scale and diversity of knowledge inputs required from various sources for modern forms of production. | Does not imply decline in value of HEIs in producing knowledge and in the contribution of such knowledge to economic growth. |
| Triple Helix | Leydesdorff and Etzkowitz, 1996; Leydesdorff, 1997; Etzkowitz, 2002 | As in Mode 2, emphasising increased interaction among institutions, and quite importantly each institution taking on some of the roles of others (universities creating firms; firms taking on more academic research, etc.). | Emphasis on 'industrial' component of academic research obscures limited scope of such an approach; lack of sufficient empirical evidence. |

*Source:* Adapted from Mitra, 2012.

## An entrepreneurial approach to knowledge exchange

What is relatively new is the encouragement of the study and practice of entrepreneurship.

'As protectors of the "higher learning realm", higher education institutions (HEIs) across the world have taken up the challenge of entrepreneurship. HEIs support entrepreneurship education and training and indulge in a variety of knowledge transfer activities which promote entrepreneurship directly (as in academic spin-offs) or indirectly through research, training and education. Increasingly much of this "indulgence" occurs at the regional level where HEIs enter into different relationships with other stakeholders pursuing economic growth and competitiveness' (Mitra, 2012, p 186).

'Entrepreneurship' refers to the identification and realisation of opportunities for new products and services made possible by the mobilisation of resources and the creation of new organisations. In other words, the exchange mechanism is not limited to the mere transfer of new knowledge to industry agents but includes the joint creation of new firms with which to use the new knowledge in the economy. The best of universities are able to overcome the limitations of knowledge transfer by means of recognising a mutuality of purpose in knowledge creation and implementation by both parties involved in the exchange process.

## Beyond the helicopter view

Different countries and regions offer varied and interesting contexts for discussion of the topic of HEIs and their relationship with other knowledge-absorbing stakeholders. Cities, for example, are often considered to be the main spatial platforms of higher learning. Universities, in common with the railways, the telegraph, the telephone and the Internet backbone – all major channels of knowledge creation and diffusion – tend to cluster around cities, leaving many of their rural counterparts in unforgiving isolation. Their city locations enable them to interact more effectively with industry, especially services, the government and financial enclaves that seldom function outside urban conurbations. Since the relationship between industry and higher education institutions is predicated on new knowledge formation and its dissemination, it is not difficult to infer why the environment, the institutional factors that provide the necessary rules and constraints for entrepreneurial activity and higher education involvement and the organisational capabilities of both firms and universities need to be part of an entrepreneurial network of knowledge creation and exchange.

HEIs contribute to the national economic output and the social well-being of different economies. In developed nations, the legendary status of institutions such as Harvard, Yale, Oxford and Cambridge often defines the advancement of the countries that harbour them. They do so as a collective of learning institutions producing scientists, engineers, philosophers, artists, businesspeople and even politicians. They advise on government policy matters, and academic stars are often called upon to interact with other governments, industry and non-governmental agencies from different parts of the world. Most leading institutions acquire their status as a result of attracting students and staff from across the globe. Despite their global reach, most universities are locally based, with their names representing the region in which they are located – as, for example, the University of Essex in the UK, the University of Chicago in the USA, and the University of Tokyo in Japan. Producing future world leaders does not preclude universities from making a measurable contribution to economic development in their regions through the academic and administrative jobs they provide, the consumption levels of staff and students and the capital stock of land, buildings and laboratories. These features of the economic impact of universities are deemed integral to regional economic development. What is less well understood is the real and potential worth of the dynamic forms of knowledge exchange that occur, such as links with industry, and that often need better utilisation and informed evaluation.

## Regions of knowledge exchange

The locations of certain universities, business entities, government agencies and social organisations in particular regions have a bearing on the nature, scope and outcome of those regions. The nexus and strength of relationships are often a barometer of the state of the economy, the propensity of firms to absorb knowledge from universities and the willingness of universities to learn from the wealth of practice in knowledge implementation. The relationship expresses itself in the form of student placements in other organisations, consultancy and industry placement of academic staff, three-way partnerships in problem-solving activities involving students, an academic supervisor and a business, the creation of new spin-off firms to commercialise research carried out by academic researchers and industry–university conferences and workshops.

The relationships forged are not always dependent on technology-based or business projects. A good example of a potentially long-term initiative is the project developed by the mayor of Jersey City and his alma mater, NYU Stern. The vision of the mayor, Steven Fulop, at the beginning of his term in 2013 was to create the best mid-sized city in the USA and make it a unique attraction for entrepreneurs and start-ups involving young talent. Given numerous constraints, Mayor Fulop could have turned easily to the likes of Bain and McKinsey for help with the challenges he faced (large parts of the city with high crime rates, low-income neighbourhoods, underperforming schools and public budget cuts). Instead, he commissioned MBA students from NYU Stern to rethink the mission of the Economic

Development Corporation (EDC) and its working relationship with the city government. Following 10 weeks of research, the students suggested that the EDC should add more public–private partnerships with a focus on social improvement and an 18-month implementation plan to restructure the working relationship between the EDC and the mayor's office. They also recommended future projects for Stern students (Bond, 2014).

Businesses that interact with HEIs tend to make use of their local institutions, although this is difficult to achieve in locations where there is either an absence of suitable HEIs or where the range of relevant expertise is limited (Storey, 2003). This understandable dichotomy and possible mismatch between demand and supply makes the learning context of knowledge creation and exchange all the more important.

## The learning context of knowledge creation and exchange

When we refer to the learning context, we can conceptualise three linked but different types of capital that are necessary for investment in knowledge creation – intellectual, human and social. These three types of capital inform the mission of most universities:

a) the generation of new knowledge (research and intellectual capital);
b) the passing of this knowledge to future generations (teaching and the generation of human capital); and
c) serving the needs of industry, commerce (Goddard *et al*, 1994) and the wider social community (the Triple Helix network and the generation of social capital).

But Goddard's view of the third strand separates it from the other two without an appreciation of their interconnectedness. We contend that the real value of knowledge exchange is obtained in all three strands. The test of knowledge creation through research lies in its relevance now or in the future. The 'relevance test' is not governed by laws of immediacy. It could be an evolutionary process in which the research findings bear commercial and other fruit many years after their original discovery. This is the legacy of Nalanda today.

Where research has helped to generate new knowledge, we find a range of subjects that appear to have made a contribution to relevant industrial benefits. A Yale University survey as long ago as 1987 found that biology, for example, had direct relevance for the cultivation of animal feed, drugs and processed food or vegetables. Mathematics, physics and computer science had direct benefits for optical instruments, electronics and logging/sawmills and paper machinery, while materials science had made direct contributions to the production of synthetic rubber and non-ferrous metals. Medical science not only produces doctors but also supports the development of surgical instruments, pharmaceutical drugs and coffee (Mowery and Sampat, 2005). The production and value of human capital through teaching are manifest in the graduate premium which allows university graduates to earn higher salaries than their non-university educated counterparts. Here too, the involvement of practitioners in teaching, together with student placements in industry, government or non-governmental organisations, has become part of the norm of university education.

Widespread and rapid technological and structural change in most economies since the latter part of the 20th century has inevitably influenced universities and other HEIs. This influence has been felt most in terms of funding and resources and different forms of learning (traditional and technological, institutional relationships, etc.), affecting the way HEIs contribute to the production and dissemination of knowledge and their roles and responsibilities in the creation and sustainability of national systems of innovation (Gibbons *et al*, 1994; Howells *et al*, 1998). If these influences matter, and by all accounts they do, then:

a) How do HEIs interact with the wider community of learning?
b) What steps do they take to establish institutions of good practice that identify different forms of learning and knowledge production both within HEIs and in communication with other organisations?
c) Can these interactions be used to generate innovation, new enterprises, jobs and economic development?

## The Triple Helix

In attempting to answer these questions, researchers have invoked the idea of a 'Triple Helix' of relationships between HEIs, industry and government (Leydesdorff and Etzkowitz, 1996). The connection between the three helices is made possible through research and consultancy links, private or public funding for the commercialisation of research, intellectual property management, direct spin-off activities and property-led developments, such as science parks, links to teaching and staff support and funding. Making it possible for these helices and the functional elements to work effectively are the three forms of capital described earlier: intellectual, human and social capital.

The Triple Helix model suggests that not only is a response in different forms of education necessary to generate varied capabilities, but so also is the need to develop and capture other forms of learning and their use in traditional educational institutions and in other 'centres of learning' outside HEIs. As Etzkowitz noted in a recent talk (Etzkowitz, 2014) at the University of Surrey in the UK, this was what he found happening in Silicon Valley and at Stanford when he first started to explore the nature of new knowledge creation and its implementation. We argue that this approach to diversity recognises the need for accelerated learning and innovation that cut across traditional disciplinary lines, which Gibbons *et al* (1994) refers to as Mode 2 science.

In Mode 2, scientists, engineers, technicians and managers seize on industrial and societal problems for their work, and researchers include an intellectually and institutionally flexible group transferring from one problem domain to another as and when opportunities arise, independent of their organisations. Ideas of convergence have gradually become the norm in project-based industrial production activity, with networks of firms across the world often connecting with complementary or feeder technologies, locally based knowledge capabilities and value chain–based functions (Marsh, 2012; Prahalad and Krishnan, 2008). Despite the advent of the MOOCS (massive, open, online computer systems), universities are a long way from such globally networked systems of practice. This asymmetry between a form of new knowledge creation by universities and new developments in the implementation of knowledge in industrial practice raises questions about the ability, or otherwise, of universities to inform practice with significant and relevant learning.

But there could be a bigger problem. In devising new ways of practising knowledge, industry players are also creating new knowledge based on interactive technologies, the coming together of ideas across multiple cultures, techniques for solving problems in real time and generating new possibilities for business growth and development. To understand the phenomenon of network-based production activity and to 'make sense' in Weick's terms, the abstraction cannot be separated from the praxis.

## What prevents university–industry linkages?

It is argued that an absence of diversity in education systems and provision impugns effective and entrepreneurial partnerships between universities and industry. In universities, notions of high-minded science and anti-utilitarian values have had a strong influence on academic staff and their normative rebellion against connections with industry. Back in 1970, an OECD report described the tensions that arise when academic staff activity and its evaluation are based on an implicit understanding that staff may be distracted from their main academic functions by industry-directed work.

The most recent Research Excellence Framework (REF) in the UK in 2013, for example, was noted for its strong reinforcement of the critical value of research to academic progression, especially in terms of publications, and also for researchers' collective angst over the idea of an 'impact factor' in the RAE that attempted to measure the wider economic or social impact of research. The fact that the exercise could not or did not find varied ways of measuring research value beyond rarefied publications – such as consulting, the making of new products or new firms, the public dissemination of new knowledge, citizenship-based research – has less to do with the angst of researchers than with the dearth of imagination in its design.

As Howells *et al* (1998) noted, the best relationships between academia and industry are founded on the former doing what it is best able to do – that is, 'pursuing excellence in research and teaching, rather than attempting to duplicate the functions of industry. The necessary cultural shift comes in terms of being able to understand the needs of industry and provide an interface which allows the swift and effective flow of knowledge and people to their most productive use' (Howells *et al*, 1998, p 7).

## The key test

The real test of the value of knowledge exchange for universities is whether it enhances the student and staff experience and whether such an exchange can make a 'good' university. For industry, the value metrics stretch from calculations about increased profitability to innovation and even corporate social responsibility. The best of research-intensive universities, such as Stanford University in Palo Alto, California, also harbour multi-billion–dollar businesses. There is no apparent conflict between the two, and there is growing evidence that, especially in the USA, universities regard technology or knowledge transfer as an essential prerequisite for attracting top faculty and the most talented set of students, raising research funding and sometimes generating a return from the sale of highly lucrative inventions and the companies formed to develop them.

The idea does not often square with the reality, as 'technology transfer' in most universities loses money for the institution because of unrealistic expectations of the value of commercialisation. There is often a gentler encouragement to spread the knowledge without thinking about its financial return. This reality is partly explained by the fact that different universities have very different budgets, endowments,

cultures and goals of research (NRC, 2010). Various analysts claim that fewer than 15 of the 100 major US universities can account for more than 50% of all commercialisations and that only a 'handful of universities and a small fraction of all inventions are responsible for a large fraction of the revenues received' (NRC, 2010).

An ecosystem of entrepreneurship and economic development creates opportunities for a wider community of interests to benefit mutually from technological, commercial and social innovations. A gradual layering of exchange among a variety of organisations and institutions over time enables the creation of such an ecosystem, and it was in the desire to develop an understanding of how that occurs in many parts of the world that we conceived this book.

## And so to the chapters that follow. . . .

One of the temptations that researchers and policy makers often fall for is to identify a universal, context-free and time-free model for a project (in this case a model for university–industry knowledge exchange). Pieces of research examining projects of the past miss the premium of 'current knowledge' of the period in which the project took place. Discerning meaning from what resources and knowledge were available at a historical point in time is like taking snapshots when they matter most, not 20 years after. While research techniques and hindsight improve, the *Titanic* sinks.

All of the individual chapters that follow are unique pieces of modern history of the evolution of knowledge exchange in different places and at different times. The majority of the chapters are reproductions of work published in one of the few international journals dedicated to the wealth of interactions between industry (in its widest sense) and higher education institutions across the world – *Industry and Higher Education* (IHE). These pieces capture the essence of the times in which they were written. We would not have a painting by Chagall exhibited in any other way! While, unlike curators in art galleries, we have not done restoration work on these articles, we have chosen our papers carefully to cover the latitude of geography together with the spread of time while capturing a variety of experiences of universities working with different organisations. To that we have added some new stories and our own overviews of specific issues that have dominated the debate and discussions on the subject.

The route map for our readers takes them across four distinctive terrains (or themes) of university–industry interaction. We begin the journey with a critical review of the history of the development of interactions and the peculiar challenges that emerged over time. Six chapters by Terry Shinn, Peter Scott, Jo Lorentzen, Jay Mitra, Marina Ranga and Henry Ektowitz and Giancarlo Lauto and colleagues identify some of the building blocks of the relationships between industry and higher education. They seek to obtain a critical understanding of the impact of research and education and industry, the growth of society in which knowledge is created, the local learning that informs international experiences of different forms of interactions, the specific development of entrepreneurship education and training as a vehicle for change for universities and economic development and the overarching 'genetic' framework of the Triple Helix that helps us to better locate the networks of knowledge creation.

The terrain then shifts to culture and especially to the entrepreneurship culture and training that help to realise personal and economic values of research and education through new business formation. Here, Allan Gibb, Mary E. Varghese and colleagues, Nathalie Duval-Couetil and Scott Hutcheson, Eugene Luczkiw and Laurens Hessels and colleagues explore ecosystems and environments conducive to learning and entrepreneurship and test the instruments of student placements and internships in specific institutions.

The focus shifts again in the third terrain to the particular economic landscapes of the rich OECD countries and specific regional, urban or rural environments in which unique experiences are found and forged by local actors. Jonathan Potter and Maria Sole Brioschi and Lucio Cassia cover the larger sweeps of the OECD and EU countries, while Mary L. Walshok and colleagues, Perttu Vartiainen and Arto Viiri, and Dave Chapman and colleagues investigate very specific and disparate local environments in San Diego in the USA, Joensuu in Finland and London in the UK.

The final leg of our journey covers the geography of nations. We do not draw any conclusions as to why some nations fail while others succeed, because perspectives that lead to such conclusions are always limited by their assertions of what works and what does not in different spaces at particular times. We offer instead individual analyses from Singapore, South Africa, Colombia, Mexico and the Netherlands, almost ensuring a trip around the world in five chapters.

As editors and contributors to this volume, we took a calibrated interest in reproducing these articles. Specialist journal articles remain specialist and lose the value of wider readership and absorption, which is part of what we believe knowledge exchange is about. Our purpose is to re-convey the messages of the past so that they resonate in the present. While many of the facts and situations in these articles cannot be replicated, there is much to be obtained from an understanding of what was known at certain points in time in recent history. Our question for our readers and for ourselves is, 'Have things moved on from where they were?' We are not convinced that the nature, scope and direction of universities sharing knowledge with industry have changed substantively. We still have the same problems of IP ownership despite the emergence of the Commons. Universities' involvement with industry remains suspect. Industry's engagement with universities is quite often confined to the niceties of corporate social responsibility and the milk rounds of best (and often the same, stereotyped) corporate fit. Our collaborative and funded projects are too often stifled by bureaucratic pressures, top slicing of income first and value creation later and loose metrics of impact. Technology beckons us to act differently, but we often use it to enhance our safe enclaves. We,

therefore, need to examine what we know, re-learn what we missed and build new platforms for interaction for the future.

We hope that we shall capture the imagination of our readers not least because of the depth and quality of the insights provided by the articles that we have chosen. In helping us to do this, we cannot thank enough the team at Routledge. First, Laura Stearns held us together with considerable encouragement for the initial period of idea development and gestation. Then Lauren Verity, David Varley and Denise File offered patience and gave us the appropriate nudge to help us complete this endeavour.

## Acknowledgements

Over the years, a good deal of our interest and insight into the subject of university–industry interaction has been influenced in a variety of ways by many thinkers, writers and practitioners. I (Jay Mitra) owe much of what I know and question to Sergio Arzeni at the OECD for his infectious enthusiasm, knowledge and understanding of policy; to Mike Cooley in the early days for his lyrical approach to the understanding of the role of technology in knowledge creation and implementation; to Roger Jinkinson for an irreverent acknowledgement of the limitations of codified knowledge and institutions; to Zoltan Acs for knowing the real difference between innovation and entrepreneurship; and to David Storey for the art of engaged and analytical scholarship. No inspiration could ever be found in such loving quantity as that obtained from Gill, my wife, and seldom do I find a sense of wonder as I do when being questioned by my son, Daniel.

We thank also all the contributors to this volume for their work and for their cooperation in giving us permission to include their studies in our collection.

We lost two friends and colleagues in the last decade who gave us much to learn, enjoy and rethink. We have, therefore, dedicated this book to the memory of Eugene Luczkiw and Jo Lorentzen.

## Notes

[1] 'Knowledge transfer' and 'technology transfer' are commonly used terms for university–industry interaction. Some, however, point to the distinction between the two by referring to technology transfer as constituting commercial activity with the prospect of generating profits, while they regard knowledge transfer as more about helping society to benefit from the discoveries and skills of faculty members and students without paying too much attention to the finances. We use the term 'knowledge exchange' to cover both knowledge and technology transfer and also to stress that the transfer process is not just a one-way street. Much is learnt by universities from their involvement with industry that enables their staff and students to validate theories and concepts to make better sense of the world.

## References

Arrow, K. (1962). "Economic welfare and the allocation of resources for invention", in R. R. Nelson (ed.), *The Rate and Direction of Inventive Activity*. Princeton: Princeton University Press, pp 609–626.

Ben-David, J. (1968), *Fundamental Research and the Universities*, Paris: OECD.

Bond, S. (2014), "A mayor with a vision and a touch of MBA knowhow", *Business Education, Financial Times,* Monday 26 May, p 12.

Branscombe, L. M., Kodama, F., and Florida, R. (1999), *Industrializing Knowledge: University–Industry Linkages in Japan and the United States*, Cambridge, MA: MIT Press.

Bush, V. (1945), *Science, the Endless Frontier: a Report to the President (on a Program for Postwar Scientific Research)*, Washington, DC: US Government Printing Office.

Cahan, D. (1989), *An Institute for an Empire: the Physikalisch-Technische Reichsanstalt, 1817–1918*, Cambridge: Cambridge University Press.

Dasgupta, P., and David, P. (1987), "Information disclosure and the economics of science and technology", in Feiwel, G. (ed), *Arrow and the Ascent of Economic Theory*, New York: New York University Press.

David, P., Foray, D., and Steinmueller, W. E. (1999), "The research network and the new economics of science: from metaphors to organizational behaviours", in Gambardella, A., and Malerba, F. (eds), *The Organization of Economic Innovation in Europe*, Cambridge: Cambridge University Press.

Etzkowitz, H. (2002), "Incubation of incubators: innovation as a Triple Helix of university–industry–government networks", *Science and Public Policy,* Vol 29, pp 115–128.

Etzkowitz, H. (2014), Comment as part of keynote speech "Innovation in innovation: the entrepreneurial university in a Triple Helix" at Conference on "Entrepreneurial University, Engaged Industry and Active Government", University of Surrey, Guildford, 29–30 May.

Gibbons, M., Limoges, C., Nowotny, H., Schwartzman, S., Scott, P., and Trow, M. (1994), *The New Production of Knowledge*, London: Sage.

Goddard, J., Charles, D., Pike, A., Potts, G., and Bradley, D. (1994), *Universities and Communities*, London: Committee of Vice Chancellors and Principals.

Howells, J., Nedeva, M., and Georghiou, L. (1998), *Industry–Academic Links in the UK*, London: Higher Education Funding Council for England.

Kline, S., and Rosenberg, N. (1986), "An overview of innovation", in Landau, R., and Rosenberg, N.R. (eds), *The Positive Sum Strategy*, Washington, DC: National Academy Press, pp 275–305.

Leydesdorff, L. (1997), "The new communication regime of university–industry–government relations", in Etzkowitz, H., and Leydesdorff, L. (eds), *Universities in the Global Economy: a Triple Helix of University–Industry–Government Relations*, London: Cassell Academic.

Leydesdorff, L., and Etzkowitz, H. (1996), "Emergence of a Triple Helix of university–industry–government relations', *Science and Public Policy,* Vol 23, No 151, pp 279–286.

Marsh, P. (2012), *The New Industrial Revolution: Consumers, Globalization and the End of Mass Production*, New Haven, CT: Yale University Press.

Mitra, J. (2012), *Entrepreneurship, Innovation and Regional Development*, London and New York: Routledge.

Mowery, D., and Sampat, B. (2005), "The Bayh–Dole Act of 1980 and university–industry technology transfer: a model for other OECD countries?", *Journal of Technology Transfer*, Vol 30, No 1–2, pp 115–127.

Nalanda University (2014), www.nalandauniv. edu.in (last accessed 8 August 2014); see also http://en.wikipedia.org/wiki/Nalanda_ University (last accessed, 8 August 2014).

Nelson, R. R. (1959), "The simple economics of basic scientific research", *Journal of Political Economy*, Vol 67, pp 297–306.

NRC (2010), *Managing University Intellectual Property in the Public Interest*, Washington, DC: National Research Council.

OECD (1970), *Innovation in Higher Education: Three German Universities,* Paris: Organisation for Economic Co-operation and Development.

Prahalad, C. K., and Krishnan, M. S. (2008), *The New Age of Innovation: Driving Co-Created Value Through Global Networks*, New York: McGraw-Hill.

Rosenberg, N. (2000), "American universities as endogenous institutions", in *Schumpeter and the Endogeneity of Technology: Some American Perspectives*, London: Routledge, ch 3.

Science (2013), 'The many ways of making academic research pay-off', *Science*, Vo1 339, No 6121, 15 February.

Shinn, T. (1998), "The impact of research and education on industry: a comparative analysis of the relationship of education and research systems to industrial progress in six countries", *Industry and Higher Education*, Vol 12, No 5, pp 270–289.

Storey, D. (2003), "Entrepreneurship, small and medium-sized enterprises and public policies", in Acs, Z. J., and Audretsch, D. B. (eds), *Handbook of Entrepreneurship Research,* Boston, MA: Kluwer, pp 473–511.

# PART I: HISTORY, CONTEXT AND CHALLENGE

# The impact of research and education on industry

## A comparative analysis of the relationship of education and research systems to industrial progress in six countries

**Terry Shinn**

*This paper provides a comparative analysis of the relationship of science and technology research capacity and the development of education systems to industrial performance. In an exploration which maps developments over the last 150 years, the author takes as his subjects for study six countries – three with outstanding industrial achievement (Germany, Japan and the USA) and three whose growth has been less impressive (England, France and Russia/USSR). Although, the author argues, industrial performance is on the whole not linked directly either to research or education, he finds a strong association between economic development and the ways in which various policies and systems have allowed research and education to interact with industry. The analysis points up what have historically proved to be either positive or inhibiting mechanisms in the promotion of industrial innovation. The paper concludes by placing this analytical review in the context of the future development of industry–research–education interactions and a critical summary of key contemporary theories concerning the sociology of innovation.*

*Terry Shinn is with the Groupe d'Etude des Méthodes de l'Analyse Sociologique (GEMAS), CNRS, La Maison de Sciences de l'Homme, 54 Boulevard Raspail, 75006 Paris, France. Tel: +33 1 49 54 21 53.*

This paper explores the impact of science and technology research capacity and educational change on industrial performance in the century and a half since 1850. Analysis covers three countries remarkable for their industrial achievement (Germany, the USA and Japan) and three countries whose growth has often been relatively less impressive (England, France and Russia/USSR). Research and education are both residual factors of economic behaviour. Unlike monetary, fiscal and investment factors, labour and material costs, and market forces, residual elements are not amenable to rigorous quantitative treatment. While residual properties like research and education may be quantified, nevertheless, qualitative considerations and interpretation are paramount.

Today, most scholars agree that education (as a general phenomenon) does not constitute a linear, direct determinant of industrial growth.[1] For example, Fritz Ringer has shown for the 19th and early 20th centuries that, although German and French education had numerous parallels, such as per capita size of cohorts, the economic development of the two nations was indeed extremely different.[2] Peter Lundgreen, who has compared the size of France's and Germany's engineering communities and the character of training, has come to much the same conclusion.[3] Robert Fox and Anna Guagnini, in a comparative study of education and industry in six European countries and the USA for the decades before the First World War, demonstrate that, although nations had contrasting rates of industrial growth, it was the case that their educational policies and practices nevertheless frequently converged.[4]

The existence of a direct and linear connection between research and industry is also today viewed as doubtful. Two instances exemplify the complexity of the relationship. During the decades immediately preceding and following the First World War, very few French firms possessed any research capacity, and with scant exception, neither was applied research present inside the educational system. Still, France's industry advanced at a steady albeit slow pace, largely thanks to alternative innovation acquisition practices such as patent procurement, licensing and concentration on low-technology sectors.[5] In large measure, France's industrial capacity was derivative, often depending on the importation of technology from abroad.[6] By contrast, on the morrow of the Second World War, the USSR boasted an immense fundamental and applied research community, in the 1960s and early 1970s surpassing in size that of the USA.[7] In spite of this, Soviet industry grew very slowly – even catastrophically so!

In this essay, I will argue that while industrial performance is rarely coupled directly either to research or to education, it is nevertheless the case that economic development is strongly associated with a bi-modal factor of research/education. Only when interacting in a particular fashion does their potential to promote industrial innovation emerge. I will furthermore suggest that in order to be effective, research must be vested with specific structural attributes that enable industry to benefit and that the same holds for science and technical education. A range of historically positive and inhibiting mechanisms will be set forth. I will conclude with a twin discussion of contemporary theories of science/industry change (the 'new production of knowledge' and the 'triple helix' model) and of human capital theory as regards the industry–research–education triad.

## Heterogeneity and uniformity: Germany versus France

Scholars agree that the final third of the 19th century saw a sharp change in the relations of capitalistic industrial production; in effect, the birth of the 'capitalization of knowledge'.[8] Systematic and formalized learning emerged as a crucial component of industrial processes, alongside the existing key elements of capital, equipment, labour and investment. Before the mid-century, technical training had largely taken the form of apprenticeship. The elaboration of industrial novelty had been left to chance and frequently originated in sources exogenous to industry. With the capitalization of knowledge, however, scientific and technical capacity acquired the guise of formal learning, which assumed a central role within firms; and appropriately differentiated education arose which offered the required concepts, technical information and skills. Similarly, industrial innovation was no longer left to isolated, private inventors. Applied research was increasingly promoted inside firms, and government and academia also sponsored applied science- and engineering-related investigations.

By all accounts, Germany was the first nation to move toward the capitalization of knowledge, and accordingly, it developed a range of well-adapted educational sites and research establishments.

In the half century before the First World War, German industrial performance was truly staggering on numerous counts. It suddenly moved ahead of England and France in the middle of the century. Germany spearheaded the second industrial revolution; and in doing so it set historical record after record for economic growth. But precisely how contingent was this impressive achievement on education- and research-associated elements? The renowned *Technische Hochschulen* are often portrayed as the linchpin of German educational service to industry in the later 19th and early 20th centuries, and beyond this as an exemplar of what education–industry relations can achieve.[9] Between 1870 and 1910, three new schools were added (Aachen, Danzig and Breslau) to eight previously established institutions in Prussia and the other *Lander* (Berlin, Karlsruhe, Munich, Dresden, Stuttgart, Hanover, Braunschweig and Darmstadt).

They provided technical education in science, engineering and applied research to tens of thousands of industry-minded men. By around 1900, instruction at the *Technische Hochschulen* had become four pronged: (1) deduction of technical rules from industrial activities; (2) deduction of technical rules from natural laws; (3) adaptation of sometimes abstruse calculating techniques for industrial needs; (4) systematic research into materials and processes applicable to industry. Between 1900 and 1914 alone, the *Technische Hoschchulen* graduated over 10,000 exceptionally qualified students who flooded an already saturated labour market. Alumni became engineers in manufacturing firms in areas associated with chemistry, electricity (and later also electronics), optics and mechanics. Many rose to positions of top management, and some became directors of firms. *Technische Hoschchulen* offered five to seven years of instruction, after 1899 optionally leading to a doctorate degree. The right to grant this diploma was hard won and achieved only after a 20-year bitter struggle against the nation's well-entrenched universities. Until the end of the century, the German university enjoyed an uncontested monopoly over doctoral education. The victory of the *Technische Hochschulen* was singularly important, for it was emblematic of the newly acquired high status of engineering and technical learning and represented tacit admission of the crucial position of industry in the rapidly modernizing German social order.

*Integration – structural and fortuitous*

The late-19th-century emergence of Germany's highly acclaimed *Technische Hochschulen*, whose reputation was totally entwined with industrial success, was part of a broader educational and cultural transformation. Until the mid-century, classical humanistic education, *Bildung*, had comprised the foremost

and almost uncontested form of education in Germany. Classical learning was the hallmark of the educated, traditional bourgeoisie, and such learning was acquired in the very exclusive *Gymnasium* and universities. Humanistic training alone had conferred social legitimacy. After 1850, however, a measure of 'modern' learning began to penetrate Germany's educational system. *Realgymnasium*, which stressed pragmatic/utilitarian curricula such as science, technology and modern languages, began to rival the humanistic *Gymnasium*, and it was from these schools that the *Technische Hochschulen* recruited their students. During the latter decades of the century, the students enrolled in modern secondary schools far outnumbered those in *classical Gymnasium*, and the employment opportunities linked to the modern technological and industrial stream were growing rapidly both in number and prestige. In the latter third of the 19th century, then, science- and technology-related learning had come to occupy a place near the summit of the educational hierarchy alongside erstwhile humanistic learning. Industrial technology had become a mechanism for achieving considerable social and political legitimacy.[10]

However, recent historiography has cast doubt on the causal character of the *Technische Hochschulen* in late 19th-century German industrial performance. Wolfgang Konig claims that before 1900 it was not highly advanced technical learning that spurred industry but instead intermediate technical skills. The *Technische Hochschulen* played a less central role in German economic growth than is generally considered to be the case. Their primary objective was competition with the traditional universities, as they sought to climb in the educational hierarchy. To achieve the desired end, it had been necessary to demonstrate competence in relatively academic, as opposed to more utilitarian, industrial fields of teaching and research. It was only after 1900, when the *Technische Hochschulen* had successfully challenged the universities, that they turned their full attention to concrete industrial development, and they did so with remarkable success.[11]

Konig insists that before 1890, it was not the *Technische Hochschulen* but rather a range of mixed, somewhat lower-level institutions of technical education which drove the expansion of Germany's economy; namely, the *Technische Mittelschulen*. This constellation of schools prospered particularly in the 1870s and 1880s. The constellation was composed mainly of innumerable local, small training institutes that had flourished in the many *Lander* along the entirety of the century. Unlike the *Technische Hochschulen*, during this critical period the *Technische Mittelschulen* catered specifically and exclusively to industry, and Konig claims that their graduates (and often not those of the *Technische Hochschulen*) temporarily comprised the key source of technical innovation in the traditional domain of mechanics, as well as the science- and technology-intensive domains of chemistry and electricity. They offered full-time instruction in eminently practical topics. The duration of courses was generally 12 to 18 months, after which graduates immediately entered industrial employment. They were acknowledged as high-quality technicians, and many became a sort of in-house engineer. Their worth lay in the rare capacity to combine skill and utilitarian knowledge. Significantly, Konig's conclusions complement the argument of Ringer, who sees in the *Oberrealschulen* and their like – higher primary education – the bulwark of Germany's modernization process.[12]

Regarding the end of the century, however, there is complete agreement that it had patently become the *Technische Hochschulen* which supplied much of the scientific and technological knowledge entailed in the continuing growth of industry; and the *Technische Hochschulen* continued to perform this role until late into the inter-war era. Since 1945, the topography of higher German technical learning has changed relatively little. Today, the *Technische Hochschulen* still furnish firms in advanced and traditional technology with armies of highly trained engineers. To this cluster of schools must be added a new group – the Technical Universities – which arose in the 1960s. The latter perform the same cognitive and professional functions as the *Technische Hochschulen*, and they constitute the German university's strategic reaction to a situation in which it was losing a growing number of talented students. Another cluster of technical institutions arose in the 1960s, the *Fachhochschulen*.[13] These schools have taken the place of the former *Technische Mittelschulen*. They offer an only moderately long cycle of instruction, four years compared to the six or seven years in *Technische Hochschulen*. The German technical education system continues to be characterized, however, not only by its remarkable heterogeneity but also by the existence of relatively supple boundaries between institutions. It is therefore quite possible for students in the lower-level *Fachhochschulen* to transfer without penalty either to the higher-status *Technische Hochschulen* or to a university. In sum, pliable transverse structures underpin heterogeneity, while re-definable hierarchic structures guarantee its perpetuation. The result is that German industry, since the middle of the 19th century, has had an immense diversity of institutions of technical education from which to draw. Such diversity has allowed high industrial performance, as firms can recruit new employees in response to changing technology and shifting economic opportunities.[14] But the might of 19th- and 20th-century German industry has not been solely based on scientific and technical training. The capitalization of knowledge in the modern economic order also requires innovation through research. In the person of Justus Liebig (1803–73), Germany possesses a progenitor of modern university–industry research and knowledge relations. Even in the first half of the 19th century, the Fatherland could boast exceptional industrial performance in agricultural chemistry and pharmacy, thanks to linkage between academic and entrepreneurial research. Numerous historians have convincingly shown that during the last 150 years, German chemistry has owed

much of its incontestable successes to a combination of endogenous and exogenous applied science.[15] As early as 1890, Bayer possessed a full-time staff of industrial research chemists and a well-equipped laboratory that was totally integrated into the giant firm's complex bureaucratic structure.[16] From the mid-century onward, the Zeiss Jena optics works thrived completely on the basis of massive in-house research and on research imported from Germany's universities and *Technische Hochschulen*. The same held for the nation's expanding electrical and electro-mechanical sector.

The Empire's industrial performance also benefited from indirect research contributions. The *Physikalisch-Technische Reichsanstalt's* second section, specializing in technology, assisted enterprise in two strategic fashions.[17] Research carried out there paved the way for German-based technological standards, which sometimes prevailed in world competition. Equally important, the second section undertook research in the field of instrumentation. Many of the resulting instrument systems served industrial production and some set the stage for commercial innovations. The Imperial Observatory, Meteorological Office and Oceanographic Station also each had instrumentation sections that generated devices beneficial to economic growth. Finally, as of the last third of the 19th century, Germany spawned a sizeable, active and effective research-technology community specializing in the invention of generic devices for use by business, science, the military and government. This instrumentation-research community continued into the 20th century. Its innovations and progress are testified to in the highly important *Zeitschrift für Instrumentenkunde*. In some respects, high-level instrumentation research, which fully integrates technology and science and industry and education, symbolizes German industrial might and how it was won.[18]

### Rigid compilation

In comparison with Germany, French industry developed more slowly and less cyclically. Over the span of the 19th century, the economy grew at about 1.5% annually, while that of its neighbour rose by an additional 50%, sometimes attaining a growth rate of over 5%. Germany has continued to outstrip France during most of the present century as well.[19] France's relatively gradual expansion has been ascribed to a range of factors, such as banking policy, savings patterns and problems in raw materials, as well as to certain mental, ideological and cultural inclinations. These considerations are clearly relevant to France, but much of the country's sluggish development is also associated with educational institutions of a particular configuration and with particular structures connected with applied research. France's system of higher scientific and technical education is doubtless the most segmented, stratified and hierarchic of all economically advanced nations. Structural rigidities in education, and also in firms, long generated awkward and often impenetrable boundaries. Until recently, public research agencies had turned their back on enterprise. This state of affairs is historically underpinned by a deep cleavage between, on the one hand, a form of social and political legitimacy bound to anti-utilitarian, high-minded science and esoteric high mathematics and, on the other hand, much lower-status, gritty, empirical, manual skills linked to economic matters.

France's system of higher scientific and technical education contains four acutely differentiated strata: the traditional *Grandes Écoles*, the lower *Grandes Écoles*, the national engineering institutes which have historically been connected to the science faculties and the new *Grandes Écoles*.[20] While each strand possesses educational virtues, and certain potential for industry, the specific clusters stand isolated. For technical students, transverse and vertical movement is precluded. Nor, historically, has any form of educational or institutional hybridization occurred.

The traditional *Grandes Écoles* were established during the course of the 18th century (the *École des Mines*, the *École des Ponts-et-Chaussées*, the *École d'Artillerie*, the *École de Génie Militaire* and lastly the *École Polytechnique*, set up in the midst of the 1789 Revolution). The explicit function of this constellation of schools was to secure and protect the prerogatives and powers of the French state. Although the schools trained *ingénieurs*, these were not engineers in either the German or Anglo-American sense of the term! Alumni were guardians of the state's interests, becoming either top-ranking military officers or high civil servants. Civil servants were planners and supervisors in areas related to infrastructure development, exploitation of mineral resources and the like. Military officers constituted the cadre of the French armed forces. Traditional *Grandes Écoles* graduates thus became 'social engineers' rather than industrial personnel and direct actors in the process of economic growth.[21] This was fully consistent with their training in mathematical analysis, a narrowly deductive epistemology, Greek and Latin. Indeed, it was not until well into the 20th century that the modern scientific subjects of mechanics, electricity and the like penetrated the École Polytechnique and that research became a priority.

By virtue of the links between the French state and Ecole Polytechnique–brand learning, deductive reasoning and non-utilitarian subject-matter came to represent intellectual legitimacy. Esoteric mathematics and high science were synonymous with success, prestige and influence. Alternative forms of cognition, namely instrumental varieties of mathematics, the experimental approach to science and applications of knowledge to concrete problems, had the reputation of inferior forms of learning. The gulf between the state *ingénieur* and the industrial engineer was consequently broad and frequently proved impossible to bridge.[22]

France nevertheless required technical personnel to man its nascent industries. Pragmatic technical education emerged in the early 19th century with the foundation of the *Écoles des Arts et Métiers*.[23] Established by Napoleon for the

orphans and sons of soldiers, these schools provided short-term training in fields like woodcraft, metalworking, plumbing, mechanics, etc. Quickly, however, the number of institutions in the constellation grew, courses became more advanced and students were drawn from the *petite bourgeoisie* and lower middle classes. Instruction developed into a two-year programme that included elementary mathematics and elementary science. The thrust of learning was consistently practical. By the end of the 19th century, recruitment was regulated through a national *concours*. Graduates went into industry with few exceptions, where they became technicians, production foremen and engineers. Some rose to administrative positions in firms, but this was relatively infrequent. Throughout much of the 19th and 20th centuries, graduates of the *Écoles des Arts et Métiers* thus comprised the middle-level technical cadre of French enterprise.

While the services rendered by this cluster of schools and their graduates has proven crucial to France's industrial performance, the contributions of the *Écoles* have been shackled. The schools were created in an age of mechanics, and the institutions proved very slow to evolve into new technical sectors such as chemistry, electricity and electronics.

Moreover, *Écoles des Arts et Métiers* failed to incorporate research into their programme or to consider engineering as a science. The approach of the schools and their alumni has been pragmatic yet not exploratory. Innovation has never become a component of practice or thought. Reflecting in some respects the fragile position and status of these schools, it was not until the eve of the First World War that they were permitted to award the title of industrial *ingénieur* to their alumni. From another perspective, though, this constituted an important victory, for it marked the point at which an educational cluster managed to embrace officially the same nomenclature as the non-industrial (anti-industry?) traditional *Grandes Écoles*. While industrial education and science continued to lack the immense legitimating advantages conferred by the *École Polytechnique* and by esoteric mathematics and high science, a measure of social status and influence was nevertheless slowly accruing to technology. Despite this, the achievement pales when compared to the 1899 victory of the *Technische Hochschulen*, which simultaneously raised the academic status of industrial knowledge and prepared the way for much more effective relations with enterprise.

A second stream of relatively low-level technical learning arose during the period 1875 to 1900 – the dawning of republican science. When in 1871 the Second Empire succumbed to Prussia and the Third Republic was established, intellectuals and university professors figured among the ranks of the victorious republicans. A succession of governments revitalized the science faculties, providing them with new buildings, comfortable laboratories and large staffs and recruiting an unprecedented number of students. Research thrived. For the first time, industry was authorized to invest in the science faculties, and the latter were permitted to become involved in local industrial activities. It was in this context that strong university–industry ties came about.[24]

In fewer than 25 years, the re-galvanized faculties set up almost three dozen institutes of applied science. Their function was twofold: (1) to assist regional industry to solve pressing technical problems – this was frequently accompanied by academic research in applied science; (2) to offer training at technician level – courses ran between one and two years – for the offspring of the provincial lower middle classes interested in taking employment with expanding local firms. The institutes covered technical areas as diverse as brewing, wine-making, food, paints and lacquers, photography and photometry, electricity and electro-mechanics, organic and inorganic chemistry, etc. It is to be noted that the birth and rise of the science faculty-related technical schools took place against the backdrop of a profound economic recession. Between roughly 1875 and 1902, the usually stable French economy experienced difficulties. If viewed from a purely economic perspective, this period was one of low demand by industry for technical manpower and for new products and processes. Despite this fact, industry participated actively in the rise of the new technical institutes. Why? It may have been motivated more by political factors than economic ones. In this case, structural integration between learning, industry and research may have been more apparent and ephemeral than real and consequential.

Between 1875 and the explosion of August 1914, these institutes educated many thousands of technicians. In industry, they supplied the low-level cadre required for manufacture. In some important respects, alumni formed the backbone of France's second industrial revolution. But three serious problems quickly impaired the operation of these institutions. First, on the eve of the 1914–18 war, a growing number of enterprises distanced themselves from the faculties and their applied science institutes. Industry investment in them declined.[25] Second, on the morrow of the war, with the exception of Strasbourg, France's faculties crumbled,[26] and the institutes were the first bodies to be disbanded or cut back. In the two decades 1920 and 1930, they constituted little more than a shadow of their former selves – few graduates, no more research, disinterest on the part of business. Third, from about 1900 to the 1930s, a spate of very small, private engineering schools appeared in France, as well as innumerable correspondence courses for engineering.

By the late 1920s, the engineering market had become glutted by a mass of people possessing a variety of training (much of it poor), and this rapidly provoked an acute crisis in the engineering profession.[27] Who exactly was an engineer, and what institutions had the right to confer the title? Schools and graduates battled bitterly with each other. In 1934, a state commission convened to regulate the profession. As in the case of the rapid educational expansion of the 1870s and 1880s, the flurry of activity did not coincide with a phase of industrial growth and demand for technical expertise. Once again, the salients of questions of technical education and

certification were not synchronous with economic growth. The French technical community turned in on itself rather than facing outward in the direction of enterprise. By contrast, in Germany engineers identified themselves with the *Verein Deutscher Ingenieur*, which negotiated with educational institutions on one side and with firms on the other, in order to strengthen the technical profession and to form a cohesive national technical/industrial system. In France, however, engineering professional associations were numerous, often small, fragmented and weak. The identity of engineers lay principally with the schools that formed them. Their logic was often first that of their alma mater, second that of their technical occupation and only thirdly the logic of enterprise.

Finally, the new *Grandes Écoles*, established in the three decades preceding the First World War (the *École Supérieure de Physique et de Chimie*, the *École Supérieure d'Electricité* and the *École Supérieure d'Aeronautique*) have been France's equivalent to Germany's *Technische Hochschulen*. Each of the establishments was fathered by eminent scientists and engineers, whose intellectual and professional trajectories included both academic endeavours and industrial involvement. In the decades immediately following their foundation, the new *Grandes Écoles* provided instruction in elementary mathematics, applied science and engineering. Soon, however, the curriculum became more advanced and complex.

Higher applied mathematics, pure science and applied science and engineering were taught. This greater mathematization of learning drew students from ever-higher social classes, and it also raised the position of the schools in the formal national educational hierarchy.[28]

From the outset, the new *Grandes Écoles* engaged in research, and after 1945, research increasingly became a focal point of the teaching programme. In the case of the *École de Physique et de Chimie*, the Curies did all of their pioneering work in radioactivity at the school, and the *École* became associated with industrial uses of radiation. The three schools making up this constellation figured centrally in the research and advanced engineering of most of the post–1945 industrial achievements in electricity and electronics, aeronautics, synthetic chemistry and technical sectors linked to classical macroscopic physics such as fluid mechanics. It is impossible to exaggerate the contribution in engineering and research of these institutions.[29]

Until the 1960s and 1970s, openness to research within industry was rare, and even fewer were the firms which possessed a research capacity. French industry was singular for its indifference, or even hostility, to science. In a survey of over two dozen of France's technically leading firms in the 1920s, only a quarter had a significant research capacity. The other companies depended on the purchase of patents and licensing for innovation.[30] In the 1890s, several companies had temporarily opened small research laboratories, but they were quickly abandoned. It was not before the post–Second World War era that an authentic groundswell in favour

of industrial research developed, and it was precisely at this juncture that the new *Grandes Écoles* intensified their mixture of high engineering and experimental research orientation.

To palliate deficiencies in applied research, government intervened. France was pressured by the events of the First World War to coordinate extant research and to finance fresh projects for national defence. But for all practical purposes, this project did not survive the war. As indicated above, after 1918, France's science faculties had largely collapsed, and with them much of the country's research potential. Government belatedly recognized this and grew concerned in the late 1920s. Throughout the 1930s, the need to reinforce the nation's war-making technical potential, as well as pure science, led it to found a series of research agencies. These were poorly funded, yet they did offer scholarships to promising young scientists and provided some funding for laboratories. The discourse underpinning the agencies emphasized a mix of industrial knowledge and basic exploration. The *Centre National de Recherche Scientifique Appliquée* was founded in 1938, with the express aim to assist French enterprise and to help prepare for eventual war with Germany. In 1939, it was superseded by the *Centre National de Recherche Scientifique*, which today remains France's premier research institute. After the Second World War, other national research institutes were revitalized or established – the *Commissariat à l'Énergie Atomique*, the *Institut National de la Santé et de la Recherche Médicale*, etc. The state's goal always consisted of both technological and pure knowledge. Despite this, technology, applied science and the engineering sciences have generally been marginal, with very little integration with technical education and with little involvement in enterprise. While research in fundamental science prospered, up until the 1970s, France had failed in numerous economic sectors to formulate a systematic multi-component innovation programme capable of enhancing industrial capacity.[31]

# Over-determination and under-determination: Russia/USSR versus England

Centralization and rigid planning are frequently cited in explanation of the relatively poor performance of the Russian and, more particularly, the Soviet economy.[32] Within limits, however, when the triangle of education–research–industry is inspected closely, in the USSR the first two components proved relatively viable; so why not also industry? Indeed, the three components were intended to function as an intensely integrated system. If industrial performance proved starkly inadequate, it was in some measure because the system was faulty – and not necessarily the internal operations of all of its constituent elements. Although part of the problem surely relates to centralization and planning, in the case of USSR industry–research–education relations, a far deeper defect resided in the extreme over-determination of the relations governing the interface

between the elements comprising the system. The precise generic objectives of industry, of research and of education were etched in stone and, more significantly, so were the exchanges between them. In the USSR and also Russia, over-determination precluded flexibility, and it undercut the potential for efficacious linkage mechanisms.

## A procrustean heritage

Russian research and education were largely imposed from the centre. Impressed by Western European science, and particularly by that of France, Peter the Great decided in 1725 to establish his Russian Academy of Science. Unfazed by the lack of Russian savants, he settled on importing scientists and engineers – mainly from France. Very slowly, the Russian empire developed a clutch of endogenous scholars who came to occupy the St Petersburg Academy. This was facilitated over time by the foundation of numerous universities: Moscow (1755), Derpt (1802), Vilen (1803), Kazan (1804), Kharkov (1805), St Petersburg (1819), Odessa (1865), Tomsk (1888), Yuriev (1893), Saratov (1909), Perm (1916) and Tartu (1918).

Again taking his cue from France, which at that time boasted the largest number and best organized technical schools, Peter the Great and successive tsars founded engineering institutes along French lines, such as the School of Mining, the School of Civil Engineering and the School of Naval Engineering. Exactly as in France, these institutions' graduates served the state, during the 18th and 19th centuries designing and supervising the construction of a good network of roads, canals and rails and organizing the search for and exploitation of mineral resources. The government set up a state engineering corps modelled on that of France.

Engineers were to serve the state, not to assist the development of the country's nascent industries. In much the same vein, the government insisted that the Imperial Academy of Science limit itself to the study of nature. It was discouraged from turning its attention to applied science or technology.[33]

The organization of technical education and research introduced after 1917 by the Bolsheviks was on the whole consistent with that of the former regime. In the late 1920s and 30s, and once again in the 1950s and 60s, innumerable technical schools were opened for the training of engineers and technicians. Nevertheless, a sort of dichotomy existed between university education, reserved for academic science, and the various technical institutes which were mandated to prepare mainly industry-related personnel. By the late 1970s, the USSR had over 180 engineering and technical schools. A hierarchy existed. Institutions located near the major cities such as Leningrad and Moscow tended to train engineers, while low-level and low-prestige technician schools were to be found in remote corners of the Soviet empire. This first dichotomy also extended to the professional profiles of the graduates of USSR higher scientific and technical education. Alumni of the universities found it possible to enter the USSR Academy of Science, where they became full-time researchers in fundamental science. By contrast, those who left the myriad technical institutes took employment with the ministry of industry.

A deep-seated professional hierarchy reinforced this bifurcation. In the 1950s and early 60s, the USSR Academy of Science possessed a moderately sized yet active engineering section. But this was ill tolerated by the purist academicians, and in the mid-60s the engineering section was all but eliminated. The breach between fundamental and industrial science was very profound. In the Soviet republics, matters were somewhat different, however. Each republic had its own academy of science, and several of the latter enthusiastically embraced industrial science.[34] This was particularly the case of Ukraine. In the 1950s, it had already built a strong reputation for its tolerance of industrial science, and its efforts to link technical education, research in the applied sciences and industrial manufacture. This propensity carried on into the 1970s and 80s and has persisted since the collapse of the USSR.[35] Overall, though, for over half a century, hostility and discontinuity characterized dealings between pure scientists and their training and research and industrial engineers and technicians and their training and activities.

The magnitude of the USSR science and technology apparatus became truly impressive in the era following the Second World War. In the 1950s and early 60s, the number of Soviet scientists equalled or exceeded that of the USA, and the number of

Soviet engineers was also impressive. There were in excess of 800,000 scientists in all disciplines combined, and many times this quantity of engineers and formally trained technicians. Quantitatively speaking, Soviet technical education proved effective. Moreover, very advanced practical as well as theoretical learning was frequently available. Research occurred at all of the best institutions, and students received training in it; and research involvement constituted an important role model. Why then did Soviet industry perform so indifferently, and in particular, why was innovation often lacking to such a dramatic extent?[36]

In the late 1920s and early 30s, the so-called 'Industrial Party' sprang up in the Soviet Union. It consisted of a few renowned academicians, scientists involved in industrial research and numerous engineers. Their interest was the rationalization of industry, and for them, this entailed the systematic development of industrial research. They called for Taylorite reforms in manufacturing processes; integration between education, industry and research was central to their scheme.[37] Stalin and his faction violently opposed the Industrial Party. First, its members were accused of harbouring bourgeois ideas and sympathy toward the bourgeoisie. Stalin attacked them as dangerous partisans of the Bukharin clique. When the self-styled 'technocrats' protested their good faith and loyalty to the Communist philosophy, arguing that their ideas were analytical, rational and not linked to the bourgeois class, Stalin retorted that they were too theoretical, an intellectual throw-back and anti-proletarian. In the mid-1930s, the group's key members were arrested and imprisoned. After a hasty show-trial, several were executed and many others died in concentration camps. The Stalinist segment of the Communist Party had severe misgivings over applied research. It was in part viewed as a Western import. But its greater danger lay in the drive of its advocates to use it as a linking mechanism that would thereby connect education, science, technology and industrial production. Such a central integrating mechanism would by its very nature become immensely powerful. Applied research might thus emerge as a challenge to the authority of the constituted Party.

All Soviet production was organized under the Ministry of Industry with a subdivision for each industrial sector. Depending on the moment, there were about 35 ministries of industry; for example, for food, electrical products, civilian electronics, light, synthetic and heavy chemicals, light and heavy machinery, metrology and instrumentation, clothing, etc. Each particular ministry held responsibility for plants and manufacture; it was also in charge of the applied research relevant to the sector. But a gulf stretched between these two functions. Each of the two categories of operation possessed its special bureaucracy and work sites (often separated by hundreds or thousands of miles) and had its specific incentive systems. In manufacturing, plants received bonuses for respecting or surpassing production quota. Evaluation was based exclusively on the quantity of output. As the introduction of novelty was frequently accompanied by production slow-downs due to the need to adapt products or procedures, innovation hampered output and thus constituted a risky production strategy.[38]

Ministerial research agencies were in turn responsible for the conception and design of innovation and for transforming new ideas into prototypes. Scientists and engineers were paid uniquely for such endeavours. They did not get a bonus for the introduction of their ideas into plants.[39] The latter would require scientists to invest time and energy in a sphere outside their realm of jurisdiction. Furthermore, the time thus taken might diminish their innovation output, and thereby earnings. In illustration of this segmentation, while in the 1950s, Soviet engineers in applied science were among the first in the world to develop the oxygen system of steel production, the approach spread only very slowly inside the USSR. Even within the same ministry, the mandate of each organizational department was so over-determined that inter-penetration and linkage proved almost impossible. Of course, Party mandarins were highly aware of this defect. Yet it nevertheless proved intractable as a system. It was institutionally entrenched. Also, as seen by Stalin and his followers, the integrating capacity of applied research might destabilize an already fragile balance of internal power inside the Soviet system.

This does not signify, however, that nothing was done to improve matters. Mention has already been made of the efforts inside Ukraine. The central

Soviet authorities also responded. In the 1980s, a science–industry experiment was set up in Siberia. The government established a big, rich, multidisciplinary Academy of Science complex. Surrounding it was a belt of high-technology firms (the Stanford University Park model). But despite policy and efforts to the contrary, only two networks of communication developed. The Academy laboratories worked closely with other Academy colleagues throughout the USSR. Each of the high-technology firms communicated with its ministry and sometimes with other firms. Yet almost no exchanges arose between manufacturing and Academy science. The history, politics and values of over-determination were not to be so easily effaced.

*A jigsaw landscape*

Of the six countries discussed in this paper, the operation of English research and technical education is doubtless the historically most indefinite case. The ambiguity and inconclusiveness are tied to three considerations: (1) the remarkable industrial performance of England in areas of mechanics-related production in much of the 18th and early 19th centuries (textiles, pumping of mines, railways, etc.) suggests to some analysts that the country possessed an adapted programme of technical education in the field and perhaps some research capacity; (2) for the late 19th and 20th centuries, England exhibits a considerable number and variety of initiatives in technical training and investigation, which are sometimes regarded as evidence of achievement; (3) since England and the USA are associated culturally and industrially, it is sometimes inferred that because England developed certain initiatives derived from those of America, the English counterpart functioned as effectively as the US programmes.

Fritz Ringer states that England only acquired a fully integrated universal primary and secondary school system in the early 20th century. The Education Act of 1902 established effective compulsory education for all social classes. A range of curricula was offered, extending from the classics to modern science and technology and to more immediately practical training. For the first time, the country could boast a quality system beyond the 'ancient nine' very outstanding 'public schools' that had traditionally prepared the social and political elites and that had for some opened the way to Oxbridge.[40] Indeed, until the establishment in 1836 of University College London, which offered instruction in science and modern topics, Cambridge and Oxford constituted the sole universities in England.

While comprehensive schooling is perhaps not entirely a prerequisite to an efficacious research and technology training programme, it is nevertheless an immense benefit.[41] The fact that both Germany and France introduced strong and differentiated public education systems roughly 50 years ahead of England almost certainly gave the two nations an edge, at least in general literacy, and by dint of this, also in technical literacy.

Ringer goes on to say that it was not until 1963, with the Technical Education Act, that England organized a coherent system of higher technical education which linked secondary schooling to higher education, that permitted some movement of students within various constellations of higher training and, finally, that established important areas of differentiation inside higher formal learning with a measure of legitimacy for technology and industry.[42] Indeed, it was not until after the Second World War that England's university capacity began to expand commensurate with that of other nations. In the 1880s and 90s, a few new universities came into being – among them Birmingham, Leeds and Bristol. During the entire inter-war era, only one new university was opened – Reading, in 1926. By contrast, after 1945, English higher education expanded rapidly. Five former university colleges were transformed into universities: Nottingham, Southampton, Hull, Exeter and Leicester. Seven entirely new universities were set up: Sussex, York, East Anglia, Lancaster, Essex, Kent and Warwick. The year 1963 may be regarded as the emblematic date for the systematization and integration of English industry-related education and for the full social recognition and legitimization of technical learning – as was the date 1899 for the German *Technisch Hochschulen* and 1934 for the French engineering community. Again, English achievement came late when compared to other industrially advanced nations.

From the 1820s onward, England, more than any other country, boasted a host of mechanics institutes located in a large number of provincial industrial sites. The schools at Manchester are the best known and most fully studied.[43] Thousands of English technicians passed through such schools in the course of the 19th century.[44] But in substantive terms, what were these mechanical institutes? First, according to all accounts, they recruited their students from the lower social classes – classes whose level of primary education was very modest. The kind of instruction offered was often haphazard – a little arithmetic, design, work with motors and mechanisms, etc. While the level of training varied considerably from institute to institute, it was by and large rather low. Perhaps most important of all, the vast majority of those who entered mechanics institutes did not remain for the full programme.[45] Some students attended courses for a few months or a year. Many others attended only night courses and then disappeared from the school registry. This unstructured and intermittent mode of training contrasts with France and Germany in the domain of mechanics. France's *Écoles des Arts et Métiers* comprised a two-year coherent programme of full-time instruction. The German *Technische Mittelschulen* drew students who already had a sound higher primary education and then gave them an additional 12 to 18 months of full-time training on the job. Until the eve of the First World War, on-the-job experience and apprenticeship in England prevailed over formal learning in mechanics. It was only after 1900 that industrial technology and formal technical learning began to gain in status.

The field of industrial chemistry (that is, autonomous, academic, industrially relevant science) also emerged rather late, in specific arenas even after the Second World War. This was much later than in Germany, and France too had already developed considerable expertise by this time. But the situation in England proved extremely complex, characterized by multiple tentative projects and by confused and sometimes contradictory currents.

The Royal College of Chemistry opened in London in 1845, but its mandate remained ambiguous – chemical analysis versus descriptive data. According to R. Bud and G. K. Roberts, the battle between pure chemistry and pragmatic chemistry was fought between the 1850s and 80s, and the conflict was settled in favour of the former.[46] During this period, English science colleges represented abstract knowledge and the polytechnics represented utilitarian chemistry. The battle was resolved in 1882 with the opening of the Kensington Normal School, where applied chemistry was taught but whose status was lower than that of pure chemistry. While historians agree about the lower status of applied chemistry, disagreement persists over its position in academia and over academia–industry relations.

Some historians point to the multi-faceted aspects of English applied chemistry and to the contradictions of chemistry teaching. Although pure chemistry reigned inside the university, attitudes of staff toward applied studies and research and toward industry were often heterogeneous and thus difficult to define. Universities, like the University of Leeds, provided instruction in fundamental chemistry, and some staff clearly stated that applied chemistry was important to graduates who would become teachers at normal schools and polytechnics – the task of which was to prepare industrial personnel. It is implicit that, although the university did not legitimate applied learning, it was nevertheless open to teaching it – graduates could thereby take up careers that demanded pragmatic knowledge. Academia's distance from application was protected by the fact that in England, it was not a university diploma in chemistry that legitimated an employee in the eyes of an employer but rather the certificate accorded by the Institute of Chemistry – a professional body. Finally, as late as 1911, it was neither the university system nor the professional Institute of Chemistry which sought to establish standards of industrial chemistry. Instead, the Association of Chemical Technologists, an industry body, struggled to impose its will. Here, the landscape of actors, interests and institutions was varied, often dispersed and tangled – a jigsaw landscape! There existed no system and no integration.[47] It is as if initiatives were consistently under-determined, lacking extension and provisions that would enable them to interlock with other projects.[48]

The problematic uncertainty and industry–research–education mismatch seen here in applied chemistry persisted into the 1930s and beyond. In 1939, the whole of England could claim only 400 students training in chemical engineering.[49] For the same year in the USA, there were more than that number enrolled in the discipline at MIT alone. But the fundamental difference between the two countries was not that of scale but rather the organizational structures of industry, research and learning. The English chemical engineering community, striving to develop, struggled to persuade both business and academia of the importance of fostering their speciality. It had to make industry grasp that chemical engineering procedures had far more profit potential than traditional applied chemistry. It had to convince academia to replace, at least in part, learning in traditional industrial chemistry. While both before and after the Second World War there existed some scattered backing for chemical engineering in academia and enterprise, support long remained desultory. There was no driving force capable of consolidating interest or capable of bringing groups together. Enterprise and education were each isolated and sometimes mutually alienating. In the case at hand, the initiatives of a professional applied chemistry body very gradually brought the two forces (business and universities) into alignment. It is not as if no initiatives arose in behalf of chemical engineering. They were abundant. The difficulty lies in the fact that efforts were hit and miss, often of short duration and rarely coordinated.

A final instance of the often under-determined character of English industry, research and educational dynamics: in the late 18th century and first decade of the 19th, England designed and manufactured the finest precision instruments. Twenty years later, it was superseded by France, which built the most precise devices until about mid-century. After that date, Germany became predominant, England ranking a poor third after France.[50] Precision instruments were important not only for scientific research but also increasingly for industrial production. While several English instrument firms, some scientists and a few individuals in politics strove at century's end to upgrade the national precision industry, little of lasting worth was accomplished.

In the first decade of the 20th century, the London City Council set up a plan for the training of technicians in precision instrumentation. Formal learning was to be furnished as a complement to in-house apprenticeship programmes. However, a complementary programme was not envisaged for the training of instrument scientists or engineers, whose job was innovation! The City Council effort fell short of its objectives. Most young people and their small-company employers were content to operate within the well-established, traditional apprentice system. But conditions continued to worsen, and in 1911 Imperial College opened a more complete programme. It was to function on two levels. First, advanced courses inside the university were to be offered to interested scientists and engineers. A chair in optical technology was established for this purpose. Secondly, in an annex, elementary instruction for workers was offered. After initial interest by some firms, this scheme too collapsed. It was not until the 1920s that an intermediate-level programme in technical optics was successfully

created at the Northampton Polytechnic, which catered mainly to technicians.

During the First World War, the depths to which English instrumentation had fallen became glaringly apparent. In 1917, the newly created Department of Scientific and Industrial Research, which was intended to coordinate war-time work and to sponsor fresh technical research,[51] organized a special instrumentation section. Precision instruments constituted one of the Department's primary concerns. After the war, the Department tried to convince instrument firms to develop their research potential – it was not sufficient just to manufacture devices. For complex reasons (the small size of firms and an often conservative company culture), most businesses proved intractable. Although before the conflict the instrument industry had organized a trade association, it was largely dormant and mostly concerned with sponsoring favourable protective legislation. The Department of Scientific and Industrial Research nevertheless managed to push firms to participate with it in organizing a precision instrument research group, the British Scientific Instrument Research Association. Firms moved grudgingly but ultimately acquiesced.

The Department of Scientific and Industrial Research would pay half the costs of research – the research association would be responsible for the remaining percentage. This proposal was explicitly intended to stimulate research towards innovation.[52] But in many areas, photometry for example, the results were meagre.[53] In spite of a myriad of initiatives in the domains of research and of technical, engineering and scientific education, little was achieved. Each programme, albeit rich in itself, often failed to embrace a comprehensive vision. When such a vision did arise, it was practice that proved too fragile and fragmented. The fundamental problem of English under-determination, though, was the failure to arrive at 'extension'; that is, the capacity for one sub-scheme to move beyond its narrow base, to transcend and to inter-mesh with other schemes.

## Polymorphism and opportunity: the USA and Japan

While Germany was the first nation to fully organize the capitalization of knowledge, the USA quickly followed. Before the First World War, the performance of numerous US industries depended on the rational organization of innovation in the form of endogenous and exogenous research on the one hand and, on the other hand, on a strong and finely structured convergence between industry's growing requirement for technical and scientific learning and a 'suitable orientation' of America's universities. In effect, the conscious and careful orchestration of extant and fresh knowledge had become a crucial component of the US capitalistic economic and social order. Technical knowledge, as labour before it, had become an entity for investment, surplus value, profit and exploitation.

The historiography of late 19th- and 20th-century US industry, research, and education relations falls into three families. (A) Some historians argue that US corporate capitalism has long possessed both the power and organizational capacity to shape the cognitive focus and norms of the technical professions and has had the foresight and influence to determine the intellectual and vocational policies and practices of universities. In this view, corporate requirements, logic and structures have successfully dictated university and professional activities. (B) The American university landscape has long been extremely varied, particularly with respect to the balance between engineering, applied science and fundamental science. While engineering and applied science sometimes prevail, they do not enjoy hegemony. Government, philanthropy and autonomous currents committed to fundamental science frequently resist the logic and influence of applied learning and research. (C) The technical professions in the form of engineering and science societies, jealous of their autonomy and potential for a key position in American society, have negotiated effectively both with the university, which trains and certifies them, and with industry, which cannot function without their specialist skills. According to this interpretation, it has been professional demands, even more than industry, which have shaped university and business operations.

Although on many levels and at first blush these three historiographies certainly appear divergent and even contradictory, Nathan Rosenberg and Richard Nelson propose a synthesis which offers at least a measure of reconciliation.

*Interests, institutions and culture*

Between 1890 and 1920, many of America's biggest chemical and electrical companies became large and complex corporations. Internal organization was increasingly bureaucratic and rationalized. This trait extended to labour, equipment, the acquisition of raw resources, investment, management, manufacture and markets. The organization of scientific and technical knowledge also soon succumbed to this logic, and by necessity the organization of innovation was rationalized. No longer was invention to be left to circumstance; it was to be subjected to the control and laws of enterprise.[54] According to David Noble, this bureaucratization of learning and ever-growing ability to institutionalize and integrate research inside firms constituted outcomes of the American corporation's hegemony over higher scientific and technical education and over the conduct of the technical professions in the early 20th century.[55] Symptomatic of this, companies like General Electric (1900), Westinghouse (1903), American Telephone and Telegraph (1913), Bell Telephone (1913), Dupont (1911), Eastman-Kodak (1912), Goodyear (1908), General Motors (1911), US Steel (1920), Union Carbide (1921), etc., set up big, well-organized research laboratories.[56] The purpose was twofold: first, to compete effectively with other firms through developing novel products or more efficient manufacturing methods, and secondly, to patent new products or methods but without putting them on the market, thereby blocking

competitors from gaining in their turn a market advantage. By the 1920s, each of the laboratories had staffs in the hundreds. The phenomenon of corporate research continued to expand during much of the inter-war era, and, according to a business poll taken in 1937, over 1,600 firms possessed a research unit. But what was the source of the science and engineering personnel required by these laboratories and the source of the technicians responsible for the ever-more-specialized tasks of manufacture?

Antebellum American colleges perceived their principal role to be teaching in philosophy, moral rectitude and civic responsibility. They prepared the nation's social and political elites. To the extent that natural philosophy figured in the curriculum, it was taught in the spirit of a 'liberal arts education' and not as technology or experimentation.[57] However, indifference to experimental science, engineering and technology was not everywhere the rule in early 19th-century America. In the first half of the century, two Hudson Valley institutions, the West point Academy and Rensselaer Polytechnic, specialized in engineering and technology. The Massachusetts Institute of Technology (MIT),[58] founded in 1862, soon followed, and on its heels Yale University set up an engineering department. The 1862 Landgrant Act directly involved state government in sponsorship of the applied sciences and teaching at the newly created state universities – first in agriculture and then quickly thereafter in mechanics, chemistry and electrical technology. By the end of the century, America had some 82 engineering schools. Yet even this proved insufficient to sate corporations' need for scientists and engineers.

Business consequently initiated two strategies. In the 1890s, and to a diminishing degree in the next decade, firms introduced company schools. They thereby sought to train their own technical personnel. Big corporations like General Electric and Bell provided scientific and engineering instruction for new employees and offered some advanced courses to older staff. There was also to be a second pay-off. Through a company school, it was hoped that the firm could inculcate its own special corporate culture, thereby moving toward the solution of certain managerial problems as well as technical ones. Yet this scheme was short lived. Companies could not span the breadth of required courses. Business soon admitted that industrial training was best carried out inside America's colleges and universities.[59] To push university educators in the appropriate direction, business, some colleges and a few engineering groups founded the Society for the Promotion of Engineering Education in 1893. The society's goal was threefold: (1) to promote a liberal arts college education; (2) to lobby on behalf of science courses that were adapted to engineering rather than pure knowledge; and (3) to ensure that engineering instruction genuinely addressed current industrial issues. The goal here was not just to transform American universities into docile institutions of applied learning sensitive to the changing

demands of enterprise, however. The university was also intended to become an annex of the industrial research laboratory. Firms quickly grasped that not all research should or could be done inside the company. Universities possessed special expertise and equipment that could also be harnessed to entrepreneurial innovation. Again, according to this view, although the Society for the Promotion of Engineering Education included some professional engineering groups, these were little more than a passive intermediary body intended to further pressure educators. At bottom, the society was most definitely a corporate pressure group whose aim was to bend US higher scientific and technical learning to business' particular ends. Here then, in the 20th century the American university became by and large a research university and to a considerable degree a university of applied research.[60]

Developments at MIT are frequently invoked to demonstrate how technology and applied science have become all pervasive. On the eve of the First World War, a young but highly talented chemist, A. A. Noyes, became professor of chemistry at MIT and soon emerged as head of the department. His and the department's experimental and theoretical research results soon achieved prominence in the USA and beyond. Four years later, a second young chemist, William Walker, joined the MIT chemistry department staff – his speciality was in applied chemistry. The paradigm of Noyes was basic research, while that of Walker was exclusively industrial science. Due to corporate thirst for chemical engineers, Walker rapidly acquired a considerable following, both in business and inside MIT. The technical demand sparked by the war further reinforced his influence.[61] On the morrow of war, conflict between the two men and their respective paradigms flared. When Walker demanded a new, separate applied chemistry facility, Noyes threatened to resign. He insisted that any university in which applied science fully eclipsed basic research and learning was starkly incomplete and did not deserve the title 'university'. MIT accepted Noyes's resignation. The latter transferred to Cal Tech, where he set up that institution's chemistry department.

This victory of corporate technology over fundamental science at MIT set the context for a second important development. In the 1930s, the economy of the Boston region slumped not simply because of the depression but also because of a more general, structural flight of capital. Firms closed and unemployment rose. However, immediately after the Second World War, local financiers and industrialists, working closely with administrators and scientists at MIT, strove to reverse this threatening current through the establishment of a new category of knowledge–enterprise relationship. A form of partnership was proposed between the science expertise of the university and the entrepreneurial expertise of local businessmen. In this spirit, in 1946 the MIT–based American Research and Development Corporation was founded. Its purpose was to solicit technically and economically viable projects from regional groups

(businessmen or scientists) to help organize the venture and to provide limited seed money. The MIT American Research and Development Corporation served entrepreneurial interests by inter-meshing knowledge and capitalistic projects. It was the progenitor of the modern venture capital system.

*Alternative perspectives*

Though a sizeable portion of US university research and teaching is inarguably linked to enterprise, John Servos insists that any claim suggesting that corporate interests totally drive university activities is wrong minded, for it disregards key features of the American knowledge system. Servos's study of the emergence of chemical engineering at MIT in the early decades of the 20th century nuances the interpretation that corporate imperatives proved unconditionally victorious. Indeed, Walker and applied chemistry took over much of MIT chemistry, and Noyes was forced to leave. However, this did not spell the closure of fundamental scientific research and instruction at the university. In order to balance the influence of corporations, university administrators looked to non-business sources of funding. In particular, philanthropic organizations, like the Rockefeller Foundation, were contacted and invited to contribute grants expressly for basic science. (This was crucial not least because during the Great Depression, corporate contributions to MIT fell sharply.) Here, then, an institution admittedly committed to industrial applications nevertheless decided on a multi-pronged strategy which enabled it to succeed both with industry and in areas of fundamental knowledge.[62]

On a complementary register, the workings of professional bodies in engineering and science are seen by some scholars as constituting an additional key factor in the triangle of industry–research–education relations in America and sometimes as comprising a check on corporate hegemony. Various American engineering societies have in the course of the last century pursued independent lines of action that have not always coincided with corporate objectives – 'the revolt of the engineers'.[63] The American Physics Society constitutes another instance. In this century, the society expanded from just a few hundred members to over 10,000. Some practitioners have been employed in industry, but many others have held academic positions. On certain occasions, a cleavage has arisen between entrepreneurial and university demands, and more often than not, the American Physics Society has jealously protected what it regarded as its specific professional prerogatives and the ideals of independent academic research.[64] There thus exists a number of decisive historical cases in which the logic of professional autonomy has countered enterprise rather than functioning either as an agency for the execution of business policy or as a relay mechanism between corporations and education.

Finally, in a highly thoughtful article, Nathan Rosenberg and Richard Nelson have presented an argument that helps align what are often divergent analyses of the dynamics between American industrial performance, research capability and the evolution of technical education. Rosenberg and Nelson accept the claim that since late in the 19th century, American science and academic life have been coloured by a concern with utility. But the authors are equally quick to point out that a broad, cultural propensity toward utility does not necessarily signify that education and research are all applied and organized to serve enterprise. Indeed, Rosenberg and Nelson suggest that in American culture, the dichotomy is not between applied learning and anti-applied learning. A consensus exists in favour of utility. The relevant cleavage lies between short-term research and long-term research. Short-term research is carried out either in the corporate setting or inside academia but in connection with business. Long-term research, say Rosenberg and Nelson, is not the purview of enterprise. It is conducted within academia. Its practitioners are not opposed to the eventual application of their findings – on the contrary. However, academic practitioners of long-term science require a special intellectual and social climate and possess a set of expectations and a value system (and sometimes also need special kinds of resources) not available outside academia. Rosenberg and Nelson thereby make a plea for a division of intellectual labour, but the distinction is not one of utility versus nonutility but instead a long-term time scale and strategy versus short-term response to immediate entrepreneurial demand.[65]

*Innovation: an interstitial phenomenon?*

The traits of polymorphism and opportunity which underpin the American constellation of industry–research–education also characterize Japan, although their expression differs. While pre-Meiji Japan was under-industrialized when compared to several Western countries, the culture was nevertheless craft intensive along two dimensions. Production, be it in agriculture or manufacture, was often strongly tied to high skill and to formal and carefully transmitted knowledge. Moreover, the social and productive systems acknowledged technical innovation, and they were sufficiently flexible to enable its bearers to assert themselves and their novelties. Hence, Tokugawa Japan possessed a cultural trait of receptivity to technology and technical transformation.[66]
This capacity for and appreciation of technology survived inside the highly static Tokugawa political and economic order, otherwise marked by fragmented feudal authority, severe commercial and manufacturing regionalism and the absence of trans-regional infrastructures – all resulting in restricted contact and communication. The latent propensity for mobility and change of Tokugawa Japan is exhibited in the Meiji rapid achievement of quasi-universal literacy. In the last three decades of the 19th century, the literacy rate in the country rose to well over 95%, thereby matching or even exceeding the literacy rate of Germany – Europe's most advanced society in the domain. Japan's accomplishment grew out of the government's construction of thousands of new elementary schools; it was similarly a consequence of a long-standing pre-Meiji high regard for formal learning and the existence of an already established system of lower education. Many specialists of Japanese industry have emphasized the importance of this extremely swift progress in literacy for the country's economic future.[67]

Japan's initial steps toward industrialization in the 1870s, 80s and 90s involved a rapid and massive import of European products, technology and technical experts. Military projects and the development of an infrastructure received first priority. France sold naval ships to Japan and was then invited to design and construct ships inside Japan. Several huge shipyards were set up by the French, employing tens of thousands of men and entailing the establishment of vocational schools, a sound local infrastructure, the development of needed raw materials and manufactured goods and a capacity for organizational integration. Schools in engineering developed under this programme as well. Similar contact was established with the British to build up the railway and telegraph systems, and German companies introduced electricity and the electrical industry. In certain military spheres and also some civilian areas, however, the Japanese government was unwilling to accept anything beyond very short-term dependence on foreign powers. Where feasible, Japanese experts and enterprise rapidly replaced non-Japanese concerns and advisers. As it had been decided to modernize the nation, so society should press swiftly toward industrialization and by this means become free from outside influence and intervention. Within 30 years, Japan had become one of the world's premier military powers and in several key areas had diminished reliance on foreign countries, their technology and production.

Two additional orientations require mention.

Between the 1870s and 1900, scores of talented young Japanese craftsmen and students sojourned in Europe and America. Some pursued formal university instruction. Many more, however, worked as technical apprentices in big, technology-intensive firms or operated as technical visitors. While such ventures were frequently government policy, as often as not they were a result of initiatives taken by some of Japan's growing industrial consortia in chemistry, electricity or mechanics. On returning to their country, these young engineers and technicians were sometimes able to introduce industrial changes – some emulated those encountered in Europe and others were fully original. The second important orientation was totally endogenous. Although Japan based its industry on the West, it rarely sought to reproduce Western technology. The nation's industrialization entailed adaptation, not emulation. This called for a particularly active and energetic variety of national technology. Two examples are illustrative of this. In the late 19th century, primarily British technology was imported to comprise the foundations of the new national textile industry. Yet it immediately became clear that British equipment was inadequate. The short-fibre, tough cotton of east Asia was poorly suited to European machinery. It became urgent for Japan's engineers to frame the appropriate technologies. The same thing occurred in steel production. In order to attain acceptably low impurity levels in smelting on the basis of readily available Japanese fuels, it was necessary to redesign both the brick interiors and venting systems of European blast furnaces.[68] This form of on-site, technology-intensive knowledge and skill persists today. In 1954, Austrian technologists invented the pure oxygen system of steel production – a technique which produced such pollution and did such damage to the furnaces that it was abandoned! However, Japanese engineers quickly grew interested in it, and by novel waste-gas treatment methods and with new furnace design, the oxygen approach soon yielded unprecedented quantities of very high-grade steel.[69]

Throughout the long Tokugawa era, a strong tie existed between 'scientific knowledge' and the regional state bureaucracies. In the late 19th century and during the 20th century, this connection gradually eroded, and it has above all become far more complex. Bureaucratic relations constitute one cornerstone of Japan's polymorphous system of higher scientific and technical education, research and industry.[70] Before 1900, the country possessed a very modest infrastructure in higher scientific and technical education, particularly when measured against its growing industrial base. The Imperial Universities of Tokyo and Kyoto enjoyed a tradition of forming a literary or bureaucratic elite. However, involvement in science and technology occurred only in the two decades before the First World War. The development of Okinawa and Hokkaido Universities in areas of technology took place only in the years just preceding and following the 1914–18 conflict. Moreover, the position of research, as opposed to the diffusion of extant learning, was complicated and hotly debated during this time.

In the years before 1914, the Japanese public health laboratory was seen as performing poorly, to the detriment of the entire nation. University professors and the Education Ministry wanted the laboratory to be placed under university jurisdiction so that research could be conducted. But the supervisors of the laboratory, the Ministries of Agriculture and Commerce, objected, as did private pharmaceutical concerns. The university lobby prevailed, but transfer to the university's jurisdiction proved catastrophic. University professors showed little capacity to do research, to manufacture vaccines or to carry out good management. The laboratory was hence removed from its control and placed in the hands of private ventures – yet closely supervised by government. The significance of this episode lies in the grave doubts that arose over precisely what areas of endeavour were legitimate for Japan's universities and could be effectively pursued by them – particularly with respect to research and especially technical research.

In the years bracketing the war, 38 industrially crucial laboratories were set up having some connection with universities, yet the linkage was always tenuous. In 1900 the Japanese army and navy opened an institute for lighter-than-air flight research, and in 1908–09 this was transformed into an Institute for Aeronautic Research, associated with Tokyo University. Several university professors taught at the Institute, but its strongest links were with the military and the nation's nascent aeronautic industry. Many students were, moreover, not enrolled at the University but were instead either active military officers, industrial personnel or enrolled in private engineering schools. Institutes for physics and chemistry similarly developed at the university during this time. The scenario was the same. Serious doubt existed over the capability of university staff for applied research. Thus, while the university was marginally involved, a broad mix of extra-university interests generally predominated. The so-called university institutes did not in reality belong to the university; they operated under the aegis of enterprise and government. Linkage with the university was helpful, however, as universities provided access to specialized knowledge, special equipment, connections with foreigners and developments abroad and sometimes access to students interested in a particular subject matter and in a particular vocation. Even after the First World War, when Japanese universities became more involved in research, it was the government which established the Japanese Research Council through which many programmes and doctoral projects were coupled to applications. Here again was an instance of relatively balanced triangular relations between the government ministries, industry and education – although the latter admittedly still lay on the margin.

Preceding the First World War, there existed only a handful of private universities, which functioned alongside the national universities. But in the 1920s, Japan boasted 165 private universities, and the number continued to climb rapidly. After the Second World War, the Japanese system of higher education grew immensely, by the 1980s counting over 500 private universities, 95 national public universities, 65 prefectural and local universities and over 400 two-year short-term colleges.[71] The quantity of per-capita engineers trained and employed in these decades surpassed that in the USA, and the amount of technical research was 60% above that of America when related to GNP. In the 1980s and 90s, an extremely high number of doctorates were awarded, which today has resulted in a record quantity of post-doctoral staff conducting research in academic, industry and government laboratories and in hybrid institutes.

While many scholars of Japanese industry–research–education relations concede that in the realm of technological investigations, entrepreneurial imperatives often outweigh those of the university, they nevertheless insist that with respect to the entire national industry–research– education system, it is government that constitutes the foremost element. Indeed, since the 1950s, the Ministry of International Trade and Industry (MITI), whose official role has been the supervision, the coordination and sometimes the control of industrial developments, has seriously sought to steer the economy. Yet in spite of the MITI's prerogatives and intentions, enterprise often manages to operate as a relatively independent agent in its strategies in the arena of research.

Twentieth-century Japan provides many examples of successful industrial resistance to the will of government. Prior to the First World War, the Commerce Ministry opposed the development in Japan of a synthetic silk industry, arguing that traditional, home-grown natural silk comprised Japan's true path. After the 1914–18 conflict, however, industry strongly pressed government to admit a new orientation in textiles, it being the only strategy capable of saving the nation's textile sector. Moreover, several firms announced to the Ministry of Commerce and of Agriculture that they had pursued unauthorized, confidential research inside their laboratories since 1910 on new dyeing procedures that could give Japan a competitive edge. Here, industry subtly out-flanked government. Two outstanding additional instances of this occurred in the 1950s and 60s. In the early 1950s, Sony requested government approval to purchase new semiconductor technology from the USA. Permission was denied. Nevertheless, Sony moved forward with its project, attempting to enter a highly profitable market through the purchase of technology and through important improvements introduced by Sony scientists.[72] In the 1960s Honda asked the MITI to authorize the firm to add an automotive branch to its existing mechanical product lines. The ministry refused, wishing to limit the number of Japanese players in the transportation sector. Honda chose to ignore the MITI and to invest in the production of cars, which quickly led to innovation and to handsome profits. In the cases of semiconductors and automotive design, Japanese research constituted a key element in company success.

In sum, a salient feature of Japan's industry, research and education system lies in its polymorphism and its capacity to seize opportunities. It often appears that key decisions and actions arise and unfold in the interstices between erstwhile institutions and interests. The existence in the country of multiple entrepreneurial, research, and training niches is admittedly wasteful, as many projects fail – for example, as happened with the national aeronautic ventures. Yet it has also historically proven impossible to determine in advance precisely which educational formulae, which manufacturing orientation, which organizational or strategic option and which balance of research are most suitable. Pluralism and elasticity comprise one way of dealing with the kinds of uncertainties associated with some aspects of the contemporary capitalization of knowledge.

## Looking ahead

My theme here, the impact of education and research on industry, is specifically addressed by three currently prominent, highly interesting theories in the sociology of innovation: (1) human capital theory; (2) the hypothesis concerning a 'new production of knowledge'; (3) the 'triple helix' model. Of these theories, the human capital theory is the oldest,

the most empirically grounded and the most predictive – hence the most robust. This model focuses on a spectrum of qualities embedded in individuals – among them motivation, loyalty, flexibility, training and skills.[73] The truly exceptional sociological research of Peter Blau on the survival capacity of firms (Blau studied over 160 New Jersey businesses at an interval of 15 years) shows a strong correlation between the ability of companies to survive and levels of technical training among personnel.[74] Does this finding invalidate the doubts expressed by Ringer, Fox and others that the link between education and industrial performance is acute, linear or direct? Certainly not. Rather, it suggests that a distinction has to be made between education *per se* and specifically technical education and that further questions have to be raised about exactly what technical training can and cannot accomplish. Indeed, the connection between education and affirmative industrial effects may sift across time and may also prove sector dependent. While technical training imparts specific skills, in the case of Blau, the more relevant observation appears to be that it also induces relatively higher levels of flexibility. It is this added flexibility in firms that provides an advantage in a rapidly evolving industrial environment. In Blau's work, the correlation between survival and research is less definite. However, when taken together, the elements of training and research emerge as a particularly potent predictor of company survival. This tends to validate the position taken in the present paper that when examining industry–education linkage, it is highly productive to reason in terms of an education–research tandem.

An intriguing and influential book published in 1994, *The New Production of Knowledge*, configures education and research and their impact on industry in a very different way. According to the study, contemporary science is radically different from its 19th- and early 20th-century predecessors (or is at least in an already advanced state of becoming so!).[75] According to the book's authors, erstwhile, *depasse* science (Mode 1 science) was university bound, was additionally bounded by disciplinary separations, was governed by blinkered inward-looking norms and expectations and was remote from social and economic demand and opportunity. Such science had relatively little relevance for industrial innovation. By contrast, contemporary science (Mode 2 science) is represented as increasingly independent of academia and as free from narrow, confining professional considerations and rigid disciplinary restrictions. It is portrayed as ever-more-tightly integrated into economic and social dynamics and opportunity.

Here, scientists, engineers, and technicians are represented as seizing on industry and societal problems as the basis of their research. Researchers comprise a markedly intellectually and institutionally flexible and mobile group, transferring from problem-domain to problem-domain as opportunities arise, quite autonomous of university constraints. In Mode 2 science, research, like education, is ubiquitous, having no stable locus. Research and training become integrated and non-localized components of industry to such an extent that they are no longer seen as comprising cognitively or institutionally differentiated entities. But there are grave problems with this perception – a perception which, in the enthusiastic pen of its authors, becomes a set of policy and action recommendations.

First, in view of the prediction of the contraction and likely ultimate disappearance of universities, precisely where will new training take place, and how can quality be certified? Since universities ensure reproduction in cognition and skills, what will emerge as the new locus of continuity? Secondly, with respect to the research function, is it realistic to think that novelty can be sustained in an environment of urgent industrial demand? Moreover, can the research perspective be maintained if constantly co-mingled with other concerns? While research never operates in a vacuum, perhaps, as indicated in this article, its effective partner is education – and not as in Mode 2 science, an undefined mix of constantly changing, economically driven filaments. Yet despite the gravity of these reservations, it must nevertheless be granted that the education–research–industry matrix is indeed in transformation; and to one extent or another, new alliances between the three agencies are being formed. That the outcome is broad and total cognitive and institutional de-differentiation seems to me unlikely.

Lastly, the so-called 'triple helix' model offers an alternative picture of what industry–education–research relations are allegedly becoming.[76]

The central idea is once again, as with the new production of knowledge thesis, that contemporary material and intellectual production (industry and education research) diverge from former patterns. The 'triple helix' refers to the three entities of firms, universities and government. According to this view, the erstwhile loose interaction between them is today being replaced by a very different mode of dynamics. The three strands are entwining in a historically unique fashion.

Unfortunately, though, the authors of this model constantly side-step the issue of whether the triple helix (a) comprises a new mix but one which nevertheless leaves intact the fundamental, traditional components; or (b) comprises an unprecedented institutional arrangement – in effect, a new variety of differentiation (neo-differentiation). Although never adequately clear on this key point, it appears to me that they point in the direction of a new differentiation! If this interpretation is correct, it would signify the emergence of a completely fresh nesting of industry–education–research. The linkage would supposedly be tighter than hitherto has been the case, and it would be organic in character. This unprecedented nesting would, furthermore, occur largely exogenously to extant institutions and relations between industry and education; and it would likewise mean that the new dynamics and organizational arrangements would develop at the expense of long-established ones. Again, erstwhile university structures are a liability. Still, by contrast to the new production of knowledge vision, here there exists a measure of latitude for accommodation – as the triple helix model is definitely an evolutionary one.

When viewed from the historical perspective and in terms of comparative sociology, education's and research's impact on industry falls into numerous patterns – and even then, the patterns prove difficult to systematize. Moreover, latent and current transformations in contemporary industry and their relations with education and research further complicate matters. This study has demonstrated that there exists a plurality of effective industry–education–research paths. While certain positive components (heterogeneity, interstitial spaces, fluidity and moderately, but only moderately, strong linkage) seem to operate as positive constants, nevertheless no system for success emerges. In light of this, is pluralism not perhaps the best avenue to follow? This does not signify *laissez-faire* liberalism, however. Such a path would almost certainly quickly preclude numerous potentially affirmative directions of development due to a lack of in-hand, short-term profit. Instead, the highest likelihood for innovation lies in a multiple approach to industry–education–research relations, an approach that guarantees simultaneous ongoing experiments. Since it cannot be predetermined precisely which strategy and formula will prove best adapted to a changing environment, a maximum of experience and trajectories should be played out and preserved as a part of our organizational and cognitive cultural heritage.

# Notes and references

1 This with respect to cohort size, the social composition of those educated, and the degree to which the curriculum is science and technology intensive ('modern' as opposed to 'traditional').

2 Fritz K. Ringer, *Education and Society in Modern Europe*, Indiana University Press, Bloomington, IN, 1979, pp 230–231 and p 237.

3 Peter Lundgreen, 'The organization of science and technology in France: a German perspective', in Robert Fox and George Weisz, eds, *The Organization of Science and Technology in France, 1808–1914*, Cambridge University Press, Cambridge, 1980, pp 327–330.

4 Robert Fox and Anna Guagnini, *Education, Technology and Industrial Performance, 1850–1939*, Cambridge University Press, Cambridge, 1993, p 5.

5 Terry Shinn, 'The Genesis of French industrial research – 1880–1940', *Social Science Information*, Vol XIX, No 3, 1981, pp 607–640.

6 Robert Fox, 'France in perspective: education, innovation, and performance in the French electrical industry, 1880–1914', in Fox and Guagnini, *op cit*, Ref 4, pp 201–226, particularly pp 212–214.

7 Ronald Amann, 'Technological progress and Soviet economic development: setting the scene', in Ronald Amann and Julian Cooper, eds, *Technological Progress and Soviet Economic Development*, Basil Blackwell Ltd, Oxford, 1986, pp 5–30, especially pp 17–19.

8 H. Braverman, *Labor and Monopoly Capital: The Degradation of Work in the Twentieth Century*, Monthly Review Press, New York, 1974.

9 Lundgreen, *op cit*, Ref 3; Ringer, *op cit*, Ref 2, pp 21–54; Peter Lundgreen, *Bildung und Wirtschaftswachstum im Industrialisierungsprozess des 19. Jahrhunderts*, Berlin Colloquium, 1973, pp 128–149, 157; Karl-Heinz Manegold, *Universitat, Technische Hochschule und Industrie*, Duncker & Humblot, Berlin, 1970.

10 Ringer, *op cit*, Ref 2, pp 73–76.

11 Wolfgang Konig, 'Technical education and industrial performance in Germany: a triumph of heterogeneity', in Fox and Guagnini, *op cit*, Ref 4, pp 65–87.

12 Ringer, *op cit*, Ref 2, pp 21–64.

13 B. B. Burn, 'Degrees: duration, structures, credit, and transfer', in Burton

R. Clark and Guy Neave, *The Encyclopedia of Higher Education*, Pergamon Press, Oxford, 1992, Vol 3, pp 1579–1587.

14 *Between Elite and Mass Education: Education in the Federal Republic of Germany*, State University of New York Press, Albany, NY, 1992, Vol 1, chapter 1.

15 Ludwig F. Haber, *The Chemical Industry: 1900–1930: International Growth and Technological Change*, Clarendon Press, Oxford, 1971.

16 Georg Meyer-Thurow, 'The industrialization of invention: a case study from the German chemical industry', *Isis*, Vol 73, 1982, pp 363–381.

17 David Cahan, *An Institute for an Empire: The Physikalisch-Technische Reichsanstalt, 1871–1918*, Cambridge University Press, Cambridge, 1989.

18 Terry Shinn, 'Crossing boundaries: the emergence of research-technology communities', in H. Etzkowitz and L. Leydesdorff, eds, *Universities and the Global Knowledge Economy: A Triple Helix of University–Industry–Government Relations*, Cassell Academic Press, London, 1997, pp 85–96.

19 Rondo E. Cameron, 'Economic growth and stagnation in France, 1815–1914', *The Journal of Modern History*, Vol 30, 1958, p 170.

20 Terry Shinn, 'Enseignement, epistemologie et stratification', in Ch. Charle et R. Ferre, *Le Personnel de l'enseignement superieur en France au XIXe et XXe siecles*, Editions du CNRS, Paris, 1985, pp 229–237.

21 Terry Shinn, *Savoir scientifique et pouvoir social; L'ecole polytechnique, 1789–1914*, Presse de la Fondation Nationale des Sciences Politiques, Paris, 1980.

22 Terry Shinn, 'From "corps" to "profession": the emergence and definition of industrial engineering in modern France', in Robert Fox and George Weisz, eds, *The Organization of Science and Technology in France, 1808–1914*, Cambridge University Press, Cambridge, 1980, pp 183–208.

23 Charles R. Day, *Les écoles des arts et métiers: l'enseignement technique en France, XIXe–XXe siecle*, Belin, Paris, 1991.

24 Mary Jo Nye, *Science in the Provinces: Scientific Communities and Provincial Leadership in France, 1870–1930*,

University of California Press, Berkeley, CA, 1986; Terry Shinn, 'The French science faculty system, 1808–1914: institutional change and research potential in mathematics and the physical sciences', *Historical Studies in the Physical Sciences*, Vol X, 1979, pp 271–332.

25 Shinn, *op cit*, Ref 24.

26 Dominique Pestre, *Physique et physiciens en France 1918–1940*, Éditions des Archives Contemporaines, Paris, 1984, see chapters 1 & 2.

27 Andre Grelon, *Les ingénieurs de la crise: Titre et profession entre les deux guerres*, Editions de l'École des Hautes Études en Sciences Sociales, Paris, 1986.

28 Terry Shinn, '*Des sciences industrielles aux sciences fondamentales: la mutation de l'École supérieure de physique et de chimie*', *Revue francaise de Sociologie*, Vol XXII, No 2, 1981, pp 167–182.

29 France's 1989 and 1991 Nobel prize laureates in physics, Pierre Degenes and Georges Charpak, are both based at the *École de Physique et de Chimie*.

30 Shinn, *op cit*, Ref 5.

31 Fox, 'Electrical industry', *op cit*, Ref 6, p 212.

32 During the era following the Second World War, the USSR stood far behind the USA in many industrial sectors – quality steel, pipe, pharmaceuticals, fine chemicals, semiconductors machine tools, heavy machinery, etc. See Ronald Amann, 'Some approaches to the assessment of Soviet Technology: its level and rate of development', pp 1–34, and R.W. Davies, 'The technological level of Soviet industry: an overview', pp 35–66, both in Ronald Amann, Julian Cooper and R.W. Davies, *The Technological Level of Soviet Industry*, Yale University Press, New Haven, CT, 1977.

33 Y.M. Rabkin, 'Academies: Soviet Union', in Clark and Neave, *op cit*, Ref 13, pp 1049–1055.

34 Julian Cooper, 'Innovation in Soviet industry', in Ronald Amann and Julian Cooper, *Industrial Innovation in the Soviet Union*, Yale University Press, New Haven, CT, 1982, pp 453–513, especially pp 470–471.

35 Paul R. Josephson and Igor Egorov, 'The deceptive promise of reform; Ukrainian science in crisis', *Minerva*, forthcoming.

36 It is very important to point out that not all of Soviet industry was ineffective. In the areas of space, rocketry, military aviation, and tanks, USSR industry performed extremely well. However, these were domains selected by the government for special treatment. They benefited from the allocation of extravagant material and economic resources. They also functioned under operating rules very different from those that regulated most of the nation's industry–research–education triangle. Ronald Amann, 'Industrial innovation in the Soviet Union: methodological perspectives and conclusions', in Amann and Cooper, *op cit*, Ref 34, pp 1–38, especially p 6 and pp 13–14.

37 Kendall E. Bailes, 'The politics of technology: Stalin and technocratic thinking among Soviet engineers', *American Historical Review*, April 1974. By the same author: 'Alexei Gastev and the Soviet controversy over Taylorism, 1918–1924', *Soviet Studies*, Vol XXIX, No 3, July 1977, pp 445–469.

38 Joseph Berliner, *The Innovation Decision in Soviet Industry*, MIT Press, Cambridge, MA, 1976, pp 33–39 and 96–103.

39 Amann, *op cit*, Ref 36, pp 9 and 16.

40 Ringer, *op cit*, Ref 2, pp 208–210.

41 J.-J. Salomon and A. Lebeau, *Mirages of Development: Science and Technology for the Third World*, Lynne Rienner Publishers, Boulder, CO, 1993.

42 Ringer, *op cit*, Ref 2, p 220.

43 Colin Divall, 'Fundamental science versus design: employers, and engineering studies in British universities, 1935–1976', *Minerva*, Vol 29, 1991, pp 167–194.

44 By the 1880s, there were nine fully established programmes in England, four of them in London. In 1892, the tripos in mechanics was set up at Cambridge.

45 Anna Guagnini, 'Worlds apart: academic instruction and professional qualifications in the training of mechanical engineers in England, 1850–1914', in Fox and Guagnini, *op cit*, Ref 4, pp 16–41.

46 R. Bud and G.K. Roberts, *Science Versus Practice: Chemistry in Victorian Britain*, Manchester University Press, Manchester, 1984.

47 J.F. Donnelly, 'Representations of applied science: academics and chemical industry in late nineteenth-century England'. *Social Studies of Science*, Vol 16, 1986, pp 195–234.

48 Donnelly argues that at least part of the difficulty in establishing autonomous academic industry-relevant learning lies in the lack of endogenous industrial research. He associates such research with an elaborate corporate organization, which came to England relatively late. In his impressive study of British industry and education, Sanderson declares that by the end of the 19th and early 20th centuries, over a hundred firms had developed research laboratories. The question nevertheless remains, what functions were performed by these laboratories, and how representative were they? Michael Sanderson, *The Universities and British Industry, 1850–1970*, Routledge & Kegan Paul, London, 1972.

Sanderson has also indicated that English universities were sometimes deeply involved in industrial research. Once again, how representative was this? Even more important, did interlocking mechanisms exist to bring the university and enterprise together on a regular basis? 'The professor as industrial consultant: Olivier Arnold and the British steel industry, 1900–1914'. *Economic History Review*, Vol 31, 1978, pp 585–600.

49 Colin Divall, 'Education for design and production: professional organization, employers, and the study of chemical engineering in British universities, 1922–1976', *Technology and Culture*, Vol 35, 1994, pp 258–288, and especially pp 265–266.

50 Mari E.W. Williams, *The Precision Makers. A History of the Instruments Industry in Britain and France, 1870–1939*, Routledge, London, 1994, particularly chapter 1.

51 Ian Varcoe, *Organizing for Science in Britain*, Oxford University Press, Oxford, 1974.

52 Williams, *op cit*, Ref 50, pp 155–161.

53 Sean F. Johnston, *A Notion or a Measure: The Quantification of Light to 1939*, PhD dissertation, Leeds University, 1994, chapters 7 & 8.

54 Alfred D. Chandler, *The Visible Hand: The Managerial Revolution in American Business*, The Belknap Press of Harvard University Press, Cambridge, MA, 1977.

55 David Noble, *America by Design: Science, Technology, and the Rise of Corporate Capitalism*, A.A. Knopf, New York, 1977, pp VI and XXII–XXI.

56 *Ibid*, pp 110–116; Leonard S. Reich, *The Making of American Industrial Research: Science and Business at GE and Bell, 1876–1926*, Cambridge University Press, Cambridge, 1985.

57 Arthur Donovan, 'Education, industry, and the American university', in Fox and Guagnini *op cit*, Ref 4, p 255–276; Paul Lucier, 'Commercial interests and scientific disinterestedness: consulting geologists in antebellum America'. *Isis*, No 86, 1995, pp 245–267.

58 Henry Etzkowitz, 'Enterprises from science: the origins of science-based regional economic development', *Minerva*, Vol 31, 1993, pp 326–360.

59 Noble, *op cit*, Ref 55, pp 212–219. Donovan, *op cit*, Ref 57.

60 Roger L. Geiger, *To Advance Knowledge: The Growth of American Research Universities, 1900–1940*, Oxford University Press, New York, 1986. By the same author: *Research a Relevant Knowledge: The American Research Universities Since World War II*, Oxford University Press, Oxford, 1993.

61 Etzkowitz, *op cit*, Ref 58.

62 John W. Servos, 'The industrial relations of science: chemical engineering at MIT, 1900–1939', *Isis*, Vol 71, 1980, pp 531–549.

63 Edwin T. Layton, Jr, *The Revolt of the Engineers: Social Responsibility and the American Engineering Profession*, Johns Hopkins University Press, Baltimore, MD, 1986 (originally published by Case Western University Press, Cleveland, OH, 1971).

64 Daniel Kevles, *The Physicists: the History of a Scientific Community in Modern America*, A.A. Knopf, New York, 1978.

65 Nathan Rosenberg and Richard Nelson, 'Universities and technical advance in industry', *Research Policy*, Vol 23, 1994, pp 323–347.

66 Tessa Moris-Suzuki, *The Technological Transformation of Japan, from the Seventeenth to the Twenty-First Century*, Cambridge University Press, Cambridge, 1994, pp 19–72.

67 Hiroyuki Odagiri and Goto Akira, *Technology and Industrial Development in Japan, Building Capability by Learning, Innovation and Public Policy*, Clarendon Press, Oxford, 1996.

68 Moris-Suzuki, *op cit*, Ref 66, pp 61–72.

69 Odagiri and Akira, *op cit*, Ref 67, pp 42–47; also pp 148–152.

70  James R. Bartholomew, *The Formation of Science in Japan: Building a
Research Tradition*, Yale University
Press, New Haven, CT, 1989, pp
268–271.

71  Justin L. Bloom, *Japan as a Scientific
and Technological Superpower*, Technology International Inc, Potomac, 1990, pp
2–7.

72  Odagiri and Akira, *op cit*, Ref 67, pp
165–169.

73  Gary Becker, *Human Capital*, Chicago
University Press, Chicago, IL, 1975.

74  Peter Blau *et al*, 'Technology and organization in *manufacturing*', Administrative Science Quarterly, Vol 21, 1976, pp 20–40;
Jerald Hage *et al*, 'The impact of knowledge in the survival of American manufacturing plants', *Social Forces*, 1993.

75  M. Gibbons *et al, The New Production of
Knowledge*, Sage, London, 1994.

76  Henry Etzkowitz and Loet Leydes-
dorff, *Universities and the Global*
*Knowledge Economy: A Triple Helix
of University–Industry–Government
Relations*, London, Cassell Academic,
London, 1997.

The original draft of this paper was prepared as a thematic contribution to the
conference 'A Triple Helix of University–
Industry–Government Relations: The
Future Location of Research', held at the
State University of New York on 7–10
January 1998. It has been revised and
developed for publication in *Industry and
Higher Education* with the kind agreement of the conference Convenors. The
Conveners wish to acknowledge the
support of the European Commission,
the Fundação Coppetec in Brazil, the
CNRS in France, the Netherlands Graduate School for Science, Technology and
Modern Culture, and the State University
of New York in helping them to disseminate the results of the meeting.

# The knowledge society and the production of knowledge

## Peter Scott

**Abstract:** *Both 'knowledge' and 'learning' have become fuzzy domains. Knowledge is not only produced in new places, new formats and new modes but is suffused throughout society through the action of information and communication technology and the proliferation of global cultures, images and 'brands'. Learning no longer takes place predominantly in formal education settings such as schools, colleges and universities but in the community and, crucially, in the workplace. But work has also become a fuzzy domain, as linear careers have been succeeded by portfolio careers. This article discusses prospects for the even closer integration of learning and work, in these contemporary – and much wider – senses.*

**Keywords:** *knowledge society; new production of knowledge; work-based learning*

*Professor Scott is Vice-Chancellor of Kingston University, River House, 53–57 High Street, Kingston-upon-Thames KT1 1LQ, UK. E-mail: p.scott@kingston.ac.uk*

The title of the conference at which the original version of this paper was presented was 'Towards a Knowledge Society: Integrating Learning and Work'. It highlighted a key characteristic of the knowledge society: the growing fuzziness of boundaries between once-discrete domains with their own distinctive systems and institutions, norms and practices (such as learning on the one hand and work on the other). This fuzziness is easy to observe. More learning is now work based rather than classroom based and more employers are redefining their companies as 'learning organizations'. In the 19th and 20th centuries the overarching trend in society was towards a separation of functions, based on divisions of expert labour underpinned by specific processes (and codes) of professionalization and embodied in special-purpose institutions. The 21st century may witness of a reversal of this trend – or, perhaps, a regression to older modes of pre-industrial pre-professional society in which the separation between the sacred and the secular, the public and the personal and learning and work was less pronounced.

In fact, 'transcendence' may be a better word than 'regression', because the post-industrial order will be very different from the pre-industrial order. The processes of specialization and segmentation have not been thrown into reverse; rather, they have accelerated to such a degree that they have become unstable, volatile and ambiguous. The challenge for the new century, therefore, is both to transcend and to integrate such 19th- and 20th-century categories as work and learning. It has become necessary not only to promote learning more than ever before, but to promote it outside as well as inside formal educational systems (just as it has become necessary to promote health outside traditional healthcare systems). Similarly, it has become necessary to regard work not as a stage that follows formal learning (or, in the context of continuing education and continuing professional development, that proceeds alongside it), but as an arena in which learning takes place as a matter of routine through both formal and informal processes.

Four topics are covered in this article. The first is an exploration of what is meant by the 'knowledge society' – considering it not just as a 'market' or technological phenomenon, but rather as a new kind of society, even a new culture. The second is an examination of changing patterns in the production of knowledge. The intention is not to argue for or against particular conceptualizations of these new patterns but simply to assert that it is now generally accepted that knowledge is generated in new places, new formats and new modes. The third topic is an analysis of the impact of the knowledge society, as a new socio-cultural formation as well as a market and techno-phenomenon, and these new modes of knowledge production on how society is conceived and organized and, in particular, their implications for systems, policies and even institutions. The fourth and final topic comprises a discussion of the theme of the original conference – prospects for the closer integration of learning and work – and a consideration of the implications for research (which are not as straightforward as they appear at first sight) and for higher education in terms of courses and qualifications (which are not straightforward at all).

## Knowledge society

In practice the idea of a knowledge society is difficult to separate from another fashionable idea, that of globalization. Key to both is the effective 'abolition' of time and space, which can now be manipulated (almost) at will. This manipulation of time and space enables novel and global configurations of production and consumption to be developed; it is also at the root of the almost infinitely pliable social and personal identities that characterize the late-modern (or post-modern) world. It is very important to adopt holistic rather than reductionist accounts of the knowledge society and globalization. Sometimes the term 'knowledge society' is used simply to signify the information and communication technology (ICT) revolution (just as 'globalization' is used to describe the triumph of free-market capitalism on the world stage). But it is not the ICT revolution in itself that is crucial; it is the multiple revolutions – economic, social, cultural and political – that the ICT revolution has enabled (Castells, 1996–99). In fact the knowledge society is a much more complex, and reflexive, phenomenon. For this very reason, Nico Stehr (1994) prefers to talk in the plural, of knowledge societies. Anthony Giddens links the development of a knowledge society to the ideas of post-modernity or, as he prefers to put it, 'late-modernity' (Giddens, 1990).

A few key trends can be identified in this context. The first are acceleration and, closely linked, complexity. It has become a cliché to say that change is now remorseless; every year when we expect things to calm down they speed up. But great care needs to be taken in assessing the significance of this trend. As has already been pointed out, it is a mistake to regard acceleration and change as, first, essentially technological and economic phenomena (the impact of ICT and the

triumph of the 'market') and, second, as linear and predictable (exemplified by the proliferation of planning and forecasting, foresight exercises, risk management and the rest). On the contrary, acceleration is a scientific, intellectual and cultural phenomenon. Also it is often, in a real sense, directionless. Everything is in flux.

The second trend is uncertainty, or risk – because alongside the knowledge society is its 'other', the risk society (Beck, 1992). Uncertainty has two distinct aspects. The first, which has received the most attention both in the academic literature and in wider political discourse, is dark and sombre – the downside of economic growth and social change in the form of environmental pollution and family breakdown. But the second, more positive aspect is that successful science is (and always has been) a generator of uncertainty; one problem is solved only for another to appear. At one time this uncertainty was confined within the comparatively safe intellectual sphere. Now it has flooded out into society and the economy at large. As a result, uncertainty is intimately linked to potential, which in turn is a key element in producing innovation. So – risks can be managed, but they cannot and should not be eliminated. Similarly, we must try to reach out, reflexively and imaginatively, to grasp the implications rather than simply foresee the implications of science.

The third trend ('dimension' may be a better term in this case) is that the knowledge society is contested terrain – in two rather different senses. First, as has already been emphasized, its impact is not confined to economic man and woman, but is more keenly felt by us as social animals. Our daily lives are textured by brands (which are themselves sometimes localized or even 'Creole-ized'); life-chances, once raw data for the economic calculus of 'market' right and 'socialist' left alike, have been superseded by lifestyles, even life-brands. In a very real sense, the knowledge society takes us 'beyond the market'. Secondly, the knowledge society and in particular globalization are highly ideological. It would be a great mistake to succumb to the triumphalism of the 'End of History', to quote the (naive) title of Francis Fukuyama's book of a decade ago (Fukuyama, 1990) or to believe that the nation – or welfare – state is being superseded by the 'market' state in some great historical shift (Bobbitt, 2002). Half a century ago, during the so-called post-war settlement, a very different politico-economic environment, the high noon of the welfare state, there was also a lot of talk about the 'end of ideology' (Bell, 1960).

It is important to recognize that globalization embraces not simply the advance of democratic capitalism – animated more often today (sadly) by neo-liberal values than by social democratic ones – but also other less obvious phenomena. One of these is global resistance to free-market globalization. In this respect, the Greenpeace organization is just as much a 'global brand' as Coca-Cola – and, to a significant extent, attitudes to free-market globalization have become substitutes for the traditional left–right party political divisions in developed countries. Another phenomenon is the rise of movements,

often dubbed 'fundamentalist', that are directly opposed to so-called 'Western' values. However unpalatable it may be, al-Quaida is also a creature of globalization – at least in terms of the techniques and technologies it employs. This apparent contradiction, the globalization of the anti-global, is reminiscent of the old contrast between modernity, the secular and rational values of the Enlightenment, and modernization, the technologies and their social analogues that have created the contemporary world. It was once assumed that it was impossible to have the latter without the former – freedom was a precondition of prosperity. One of the consequences of globalization is that this link is no longer so certain.

## The new production of knowledge

The second topic covered in this article is new patterns in the production of knowledge ('generation' is perhaps a better word than 'production'). This is not the place to argue for or against any particular interpretation of the changes taking place in how knowledge is generated. The author, along with other colleagues, has discussed these changes in terms of a shift from 'Mode 1' research, undertaken within a relatively autonomous scientific system, to 'Mode 2' knowledge production, which is much more contextualized and more widely distributed (Gibbons *et al*, 1994; Nowotny, Scott and Gibbons, 2001). But there are equally valid accounts – notably the idea of a 'triple helix' of university, state and industry (Eztkowitz and

Leydesdorff, 1997). There has been a sustained debate about which of these conceptualizations offers the most satisfactory account (Shinn, 2002). Nevertheless, a number of empirical trends suggest that far-reaching changes are underway not just in the production or generation of knowledge but also, it is argued, in its constitution.

The most significant of these trends are familiar to policy makers and institutional leaders and to researchers themselves (although they are not necessarily congenial to the last group). The first trend is a shift from reactive to proactive research funding regimes. Governments are now less interested in simply funding excellent science as defined by scientists themselves; instead, they want to harness basic research to wider science and technology policies (which in turn are elements within wider-still innovation and economic development policies). Thus we have seen the emergence of larger-scale research programmes organized around over-arching themes. At the same time, of course, there is more space for the ingenuity of researchers to be exercised within the interstices of these larger-scale programmes – which themselves have to be defined in broad-brush terms and to be allowed to develop reflexively.

The second trend is the growing emphasis on the commercialization of research findings – but also what might be termed the 'socialization' of research, because this is more than simply a 'market' phenomenon. In a way this is inherent in the idea of a knowledge society – in two main senses. First, 'Big Science' is the new great power politics: although governments continuously emphasize applied science and technology transfer, they still want 'world-class' universities – unconsciously revealing that they still have an essentially linear view of science, beginning with 'pure' science. What armies and fleets were to the 19th and 20th centuries, 'world-class' universities are to the 21st century. Second, a knowledge society is by definition a society that is suffused by science (although it may not always be very sophisticated science, the growing emphasis on evidence-based policy and practice is a good example of this). The knowledge society is not just about the global management of massive data flows. But, just as society is suffused by science, so science is suffused by society.

The third trend is the emergence of new scientific communities distributed across time and space. It is not simply that advances in ICT now make it possible to create global research teams; these teams have new players (for example, management consultants or activist groups) and they are much less well defined (and perhaps more volatile and ephemeral). Within these broader scientific communities it becomes more difficult too to assign clear roles, or distinguish between primary 'producers' and secondary 'users' of research. At an empirical level this has been obvious for some time. For example, senior professors spend as much, or more, of their time constructing bids, orchestrating research teams, managing user expectations as they do actually undertaking research – or, to put it another way, all these other activities, once regarded as secondary or subordinate to the basic creative process, are now part of research.

The fourth trend is the increasing emphasis on responsiveness and the drive towards greater accountability. This can be observed from a number of different perspectives. One is the drive to 'excellence', the emphasis on assuring scientific quality. This creates few problems because discrimination based on peer review is fundamental to the management of science (although concerns may arise if funding for research becomes over-concentrated). But other perspectives emphasize the perceived relevance of research, value-for-money or ethical sensitivity. These other perspectives may lead to greater difficulties because they tend to compromise the autonomy of the scientific process.

It can be argued that the cumulative effect of these empirically observable changes has been to transform the research process. Two examples may serve to illustrate this transformation. First, it has become more difficult to make meaningful distinctions between 'pure' and 'applied' research, because these distinctions relied on the contingent empirical 'external' conditions described above as much as on any inherent 'internal' differences. Of course, it is still possible to distinguish between 'pure' and 'applied' science at both ends of the spectrum – cosmology is different from cosmetics. But more and more research inhabits that difficult-to-define middle ground. The second example is the growing impact of accountability or, more accurately, social interventions in research. For example, it has been argued that public controversies – about such issues as GM food or nuclear power – have a galvanizing and ultimately creative impact on research (rather than, as is commonly assumed, a restrictive influence).

However, the role of controversies in research is to promote conflict rather than consensus, thus rendering science more 'open' than ever (satisfactory closure has become almost impossible to achieve in some areas). Another effect of increasing social intervention in research has been the destabilization of traditional forms of peer review (already under threat because of specialization and reductionism). As a result, it has become necessary to devise different regimes of quality control.

## Domains and systems, policies and institutions

The third topic in this article is the impact of these changes on how we categorize social, economic and political institutions; how systems are planned and managed; and how strategy is developed and policy made. If the broad analysis offered earlier is accepted – that the knowledge society is a complex, fractured, even contested phenomenon, and that fundamental changes are taking place in the way that knowledge is produced – it follows that the typologies typical of the modern world are likely to undergo a process of transformation. This process can be analysed from three perspectives.

The first approach is to examine the basic building blocks (both conceptual and organizational) of the modern world – categories such as the 'state', the 'market', 'culture', 'science' and 'society' itself. Phillip Bobbitt's (2002) concept of a 'market state' is just one example of attempts to re-conceptualize (and re-operationalize) the nation state, which in the course of the 20th century grew into a welfare state (although with different degrees of intensity). The state as regulator, even customer, has replaced the state as guardian and provider. It may be symptomatic of what is happening that Bobbitt combines two hitherto discrete categories – the market and the state. States are behaving more like corporations as they encourage market or quasi-market approaches to public policy, while corporations are behaving more like states as they place greater emphasis on ethical governance and social responsibility. The overall impression is of the transgression of traditional categories with the emergence of hybrid forms – intermediate institutions that are both volatile and ephemeral.

The second approach is to look at systems. It is ironic that, at a time when it appears to be generally accepted that the grand narratives, the meta-discourses, that emerged over the past 250 years (some very grand indeed, like the idea of Enlightenment; others a little less grand, such as Marxism or Freudianism) have been, in different degrees, discredited, many people continue to think and act as if these or other over-arching intellectual frameworks still existed. Systems and institutions are still conceptualized in terms of and constructed on the basis of particular political and economic theories or social analyses (even if the tendency is to be less explicit about such theories and analyses).

If anything, the emphasis on system building has intensified. The belief in the possibility of 'planning', so prevalent in the 1960s, is far from dead. Successive waves of privatization should not be allowed to conceal the fact that most governments are seeking to control the future in greater and greater detail, as their obsession with targets, performance indicators and evaluation regimes indicates. Here, then, are some real dilemmas. How can systems be constructed when their boundaries are highly permeable and there is no agreement about their scope and extent (which may now be, inherently, open ended)? And how is it possible to plan for the future under conditions of increasing uncertainty and instability?

The third perspective is that of policy and strategy. The very nature of policy is being transformed. Once policy was composed of a set of rational instruments; today it is often essentially symbolic (the sound bite is the symbol, to coin a phrase). Policies now have shorter and shorter lifecycles and are dominated by issues of presentation. At the same time institutions are becoming increasingly permeable (and even transgressive), and this makes it increasingly difficult to operate tough top-down strategy-making and policy-implementation regimes. Also, the key actions are no longer the responsibility of single institutions or even of single sectors, but reside in networks of institutions (public and private, large and small) spread across several sectors (education, employment, social security and so on). We may be at the beginning of an important shift away from national governments and their bureaucracies and relatively independent institutions or organizations (whether universities or companies), up to now the two poles of policy making, to much more hybrid intermediate arenas, often with a strong regional focus. What are now demanded of high-level policy makers and institutional leaders are visioning skills, which rely more on intuition and empathy, to address the double challenge of coping with uncertainty and maintaining the integrity of their core values. But this revolution in the policy culture has barely begun.

## Learning and work

The fourth and final part of this article is the integration of learning and work. In fact, neither 'learning' nor 'work' is an entirely satisfactory category: both are too narrow, too reductionist, particularly in the context of a discussion about their integration (although 'transgression' may be a better word for what is happening, because 'integration' implies an orderly and planned process). For a start, it may be better to talk of 'life' rather than simply 'work'. Just as learning and work have become more difficult to separate, so work and life can no longer be so sharply distinguished in a post-industrial age, in contrast to an industrial age with its massed battalions both corporate and proletarian.

Of course, there is a danger that the novelty of this theme will lead to its exaggeration. The worlds of education and employment have always overlapped. Schools and universities may have played a key role in the socialization of the masses and of élites respectively, and in building national identities. But the key dynamic was always the rising demand for skills within a constantly evolving division of labour, which was itself powered by technological change which, in turn, owed a great deal (but not everything) to basic science.

This close articulation of learning and work has been particularly true of higher education in two senses. First, in a general sense, the emergence of the modern university in the second half of the 19th and the early part of the 20th century was very much aligned with the development of an expert, professional society. The ideal of the Humboldtian university may have served as an elegant foundation-myth, but the reality was shaped by increasingly close links with the emerging professions characteristic of an industrial and urban society (and, to be fair to von Humboldt, his own university reforms were very much part of a wider scheme of modernization). The classic case remains the land-grant universities of the USA, established to realize the immense (largely agricultural) potential of the American West and now the academic powerhouses of our modern age.

Second, in a more specific sense, modern higher education systems now comprise other institutions apart from the classical universities (which are not as 'classical' as they appear, of course). The HBO schools in the Netherlands (described in English as Universities of Professional Education), *fachhochschulen* in Germany and the former polytechnics in England are good examples. All these institutions have emphasized an even closer engagement between learning and work – for example, in cooperative education programmes, work-based learning, courses leading to professional qualifications and large numbers of part-time students.

Thus it is misleading to imagine that there is only limited integration between learning and work: the opposite is true. Moreover, that integration is intensifying year by year. The situation in the UK offers an interesting case study. As recently as 10 years ago, activities such as technology transfer (outside a few very expert fields) and community outreach (except as part of higher education's social and cultural responsibilities) were still regarded as essentially peripheral. Today, these activities have moved much closer to the mainstream. Not so long ago, graduate education and lifelong learning were regarded as quite separate – the former led to research careers or providing entry into the élite professions and the latter was concerned with lower-level skills updating or recreational learning. Today, they have come together. There are now many examples of MA and MSc programmes based on 'learning contracts', usually projects undertaken in the workplace. In the UK the new two-year 'Foundation Degrees' are work-based qualifications and require universities to have industrial partners. There are similar examples in most other European countries.

It is interesting to speculate on why universities have changed their behaviour in these ways, and why they have embraced collaboration with industry and business and communities – an engagement that not so long ago would have been regarded with some suspicion as a threat to traditional academic values.

One reason for the change is that politicians now expect universities to establish closer links with the economy and with society, and so funding regimes have been modified to provide the appropriate incentives. But this now-pervasive political rhetoric itself reflects the new contours of the knowledge society, in which skills and research are regarded as primary economic outputs. Another reason is that universities believe that they can profit from such collaboration (although this is not necessarily the case). Again, this is an important consideration at a time when public universities can no longer rely so absolutely on the state for their income. This shift towards mixed public–private funding regimes is itself of great significance; it reflects the growing permeability of sectors and organizations discussed earlier in this paper.

The most important reason, therefore, for the more intense engagement between universities and industry, between learning and work, is the emergence of a knowledge society and the accompanying changes in knowledge production (Scott, 1999). In terms of research, the impact is straightforward. Research has become a pervasive and also a hybrid activity, heavily dependent for its success on effective networks. The impact on higher education, or teaching, is, however, just as great. The whole notion of expertise (and more specifically of academic authority) has become more problematical – more sharply contested in some contexts and more widely (and confusingly?) distributed in other contexts. It no longer resides so categorically in certain institutions and in certain people. So work-based education has become not a secondary activity, indulged in for largely 'external' reasons (to cut costs, enhance relevance or please politicians), but a primary activity justified by 'internal' reasons (because expertise and authority are now shared across the learning–work divide).

If this analysis is correct, it is likely that the integration between learning and work will continue to intensify. However, it would be misleading to regard this process as essentially one way, a process by which academic learning has to accommodate itself to the world of work. The converse is equally important: the workplace has itself become a learning arena, which may have radical implications for traditional forms of industrial organization.

# References

Bell, Daniel (1960), *The End of Ideology: on the Exhaustion of the Political Ideas of the Fifties*, reissued, with *The Resumption of History in the New Century*, 2000, Harvard University Press, Cambridge, MA.

Beck, Ulrich (1992), *Risk Society: Towards a New Modernity*, Sage, London.

Bobbitt, Phillip (2002), *The Shield of Achilles: War, Peace and the Course of History*, Allen Lane, London.

Castells, Manuel (1996–1999), *The Information Age: Economy, Society and Culture*, 3 vols, Blackwell, Oxford.

Etzkotwitz, Henry, and Leydesdorff, Loet, eds (1997), *Universities and the Global Knowledge Economy: a Triple Helix of University–Industry–Government Relations*, Pinter, London.

Fukuyama, Francis (1990), *The End of History and the Last Man*, Penguin, Harmondsworth.

Gibbons, Michael, Limoges, Camille, Nowotny, Helga, Schwartzman, Simon, Scott, Peter, and Trow, Martin (1994), *The New Production of Knowledge: the Dynamics of Science and Research in Contemporary Societies*, Sage, London.

Giddens, Anthony (1990), *The Consequences of Modernity*, Polity Press, Cambridge.

Nowotny, Helga, Scott, Peter, and Gibbons, Michael (2001), *Re-Thinking Science: Knowledge and the Public in an Age of Uncertainty*, Polity Press, Cambridge.

Scott, Peter (1999), 'Decline or transformation? The future of the university in a knowledge society', in Baggen, Peter, Telling, Agnes, and van Haaften, Wouter, eds, *The University in the Knowledge Society*, Concorde Publishing House, Bemmel.

Shinn, Terry (2002), 'The triple helix and the new production of knowledge: prepackaged thinking in science and technology', Social Studies in Science, Vol 32, No 4, August, pp 599–614.

Stehr, Nico (1994), *Knowledge Societies*, Sage, London.

# Local learning and international experiences in higher education–industry relationships

## Apples and oranges?

**Jo Lorentzen**

**Abstract:** This article focuses on the sense and nonsense of comparing higher education–industry relationships across countries. It discusses the conditions under which international benchmarking leads to potentially deleterious policy conclusions and underlines the importance of context specificity. It argues for more attention to the dynamics of local learning, taken here to mean the absorptive capacities of a range of economic actors. It concludes by showing how research into the conditions of local learning can shed light on how regions or countries might make it easier for economic actors 'to learn how to learn' or, in other words, to bridge the gap between lessons from elsewhere and their own absorptive capacities.

**Keywords:** higher education–industry relationships; business–science relationships; international benchmarking; absorptive capacities; South Africa

Jo Lorentzen is with the Research Programme on Human Resources Development, Human Sciences Research Council, 69–83 Plein Street, Cape Town 8000, South Africa. E-mail: jlorentzen@hsrc.ac.za He is also affiliated to the Department of International Economics and Management at the Copenhagen Business School and the School of Development Studies at the University of KwaZulu-Natal.

Forget hammer and nails. Muscle and sweat as engines of economic progress, too, are a relic of a long-gone era in which noisy machines and men and women in clothes soiled with grease and dirt dug underground for the earth's resources, laid railway tracks, built power stations and produced lawn mowers. Today our capital is ideas and the 'nerds' that come up with them. We still need to tap with our fingers to participate fully in the global flow of information, but widespread voice activation promises to eliminate cappuccino-flooded keyboards as the principal culprits of occasional productivity lapses. What little we manufacture in an economy dominated by services helps to navigate our vehicles from the entertainment complex formerly known as the greengrocer to the wellness-cum-genetic-refreshment retreat formerly known as the soccer pitch on the objectively calculated, satellite-monitored shortest possible route. In short, we live in the knowledge society and ours is the Age of the Internet.

Of course, this is nonsense. Most people on the planet work the soil for a living or toil on the squalid fringes of urban congregations. They worry about whether they will have clean water and enough food. Perhaps they hope for electricity and a job that will pay enough to send their children to school. They probably pray to be spared from disease. And they most definitely do not think about how wireless-access protocols would grant them a place in the sun in the global village.

This does not mean that the relationships between science and industry – or more particularly the ways in which suppliers and users of knowledge interact to bring about technological innovation – have no bearing on the poor, especially insofar as the results of these processes improve their lives. What it does mean, however, is that the conditions under which innovation does or does not take place are context specific. They differ across and even within countries. Hence the wholesale adoption of some global best practice, crowned by more or (often) less careful benchmarking, is not on the cards. Yet it is certainly feasible for one country to look at insights gained from the innovation experiences of another, to compare lessons both good and bad, and to try to make them useful for its own learning processes. That is what this article is about.

More specifically, the article focuses on higher education–industry relationships (HEIRs) and discusses their relative importance to innovation. It goes on to describe international experiences with HEIRs and associated attempts to compare them across countries, especially with a view to improving international competitiveness. These are then contrasted with the dynamics of 'local learning', taken here to mean the absorptive capacities of a range of economic actors.

The concluding section suggests how research into the conditions of local learning can shed light on how regions or countries might make it easier for economic actors 'to learn how to learn', or in other words to bridge the gap between lessons from elsewhere and their own absorptive capacities. This is the point at which sound policy will begin, but much needs to be understood before developing or latecomer countries reach it.

## HEIRs in the knowledge economy

It is easy to establish why, in principle, higher education matters for economic growth and development. Economic growth depends prominently on the creation and exploitation of knowledge. Universities are repositories of knowledge. They also advance science and create new technologies that, especially if transferred to the business sector, help firms to innovate. Firms, in turn, are the most important agents of technological innovation. Of course, the private sector has always commercialized science, albeit to varying degrees depending on sector, country and historical period (Nelson, 1993). Firms have sometimes pioneered technological developments without much interaction with university scientists. However, it is beyond doubt that higher education–industry relationships have grown in importance over the last 25 years or so. There has been a rise in the share of new products and processes in a wide range of industries developed in reference to recent academic research, along with a decline in the time lag between academic research results and their commercial offspring (Mansfield, 1998; see also Furman, Porter and Stern, 2002; OECD, 2004a, Figure 3). Industry has been funding a growing share of public R&D, which in OECD countries averages just above 5% (OECD, 2004b, p 17). It was not only in the natural and engineering sciences that academics made themselves useful to industry. For example, research undertaken in

business schools helped firms as early as the 1950s and 1960s with linear programming for production planning, with conjoint analysis for the prediction of market acceptance of new product characteristics and with other analytical tools (Phillips, 1998).

The division of labour among researchers in universities, public institutes and industry is less clear-cut than in the past. It has become more difficult to distinguish between basic and applied research. The blurring between curiosity in academia, mission orientation in the public sector and profit orientation in industry – exemplified by fields such as structural genomics – complicates the interface between science systems and industrial innovation and has given rise to much soul searching regarding the design and expected benefits of science and innovation policy (OECD, 2004a).

Figuring out the dynamics of HEIRs presupposes an understanding of the changing characteristics and interests of the various actors involved in innovation (see Agrawal, 2001, for a good overview of the literature; see Bozeman, 2000, for a review of the US experience). First, in the presence of increased competition and more rapid product life cycles – along with the standard market failures that bedevil R&D – innovative firms succeed best if they can focus their own research competence and access and exploit external knowledge, possibly in conjunction with other firms. Benefits accrue to research synergies that manifest themselves in cost savings or improved R&D productivity, R&D cost sharing and keeping up to date with major technological developments. In short, thanks to cooperative R&D, firms learn, make better products and employ better processes (Caloghirou *et al,* 2001). Especially in view of the tacit nature of much of the transferable knowledge concerned, the connection to the open science community is important for the utilization of university research (Cockburn and Henderson, 1998).

Second, although many knowledge-transfer channels between universities and public research organizations on the one hand and industry on the other continue to be informal, formal technology alliances between higher education institutions and firms are on the rise, as are spin-off companies run by academic entrepreneurs – all this in the context of generally accommodating intellectual property regimes and expanding markets for technology. Lee (2000) reports that in the USA these relationships are sustainable because academics and managers allow the partners to pursue their own interests while also contributing to the mutual goal. Conversely, when academics fear that working with industry – regardless of whether this happens independently or in the context of reduced public funding – may impact negatively on education, research and general university integrity, they are less willing to support cooperation (Lee, 1996).

These alliances have undoubtedly changed the face of universities, although concerns about a shift to more applied at the expense of basic research seem, at least on the whole, unfounded. The explanation for the growth in licensing patented inventions originating in academic research lies rather with an increased inclination of the inventors to patent and of firms to outsource R&D (Thursby and Thursby, 2000). This question cannot be solved theoretically; more empirical research is needed to assess the possibly deleterious effects of HEIRs on the quality and quantity of fundamental science, the research infrastructure or the relative freedom from restrictions on research uses by peers (Poyago-Theotoky *et al,* 2002; OECD, 2004a).

Third, apart from the direct relationship between higher education and industry, the spatially concentrated knowledge spillovers associated with it influence the location of innovative activity (Audretsch and Feldman, 1996). Smart regions are more likely to benefit from smart investments, although it would be naive to believe that university–industry–government links would always be more than the sum of their parts (Hagen, 2002). Nonetheless, this implies that those regions and countries most in need of innovative activity do not stand much of a chance to get it at all.

Finally, regions once characterized by a record of innovative activity may lose their edge. Best and Forrant (2000) recount the attempts by the University of Massachusetts Lowell to stem and reverse the decline of the Merrimack Valley by imbuing both university labs and supplier firms that had traditionally only read and executed blueprints with a sense of strategic direction. Absorptive capacities, or the process of learning, thus matter both for the realization of and the possible gains from HEIRs. Clearly this has implications for developing countries (see the section below on local learning).

## Benchmarking HEIRs internationally: apples and oranges?

It is natural for countries to evaluate their innovation record against their competitors. For example, in 2000 Taiwanese engineers ranked 10th in terms of the number of papers published in the Engineering Index, up from 13th place in 1993. Taiwanese inventors also registered more patents in the USA than any other country except the USA, Japan and Germany. Yet the majority of critical components and manufacturing technologies used in the country are imported. In view of fiercer competition from China and other parts of Southeast Asia (Mohd Yunos and Mod Ghazali, 2002), this raises the question as to why an impressive R&D performance does not translate into more much-needed, widespread improvements in technological capabilities among Taiwanese firms and to what extent the interaction between industry, universities and public research institutes is at fault (Chang and Hsu, 2002). In sum, both the successes and the shortcomings of innovation performance are relative measures that make little sense when looked at in isolation.

Depending on a country's level of development, its knowledge infrastructure has more or less sophisticated systemic features, with various layers of education, training and investment in research. Learning 'happens' within this knowledge infrastructure, and it is both the quality of the structure and the degree and the rate of absorption of the existing stock of knowledge and additions to it that influence a country's technological trajectory. A talented scientist, a committed manager and a motivated child in elementary school are obviously more valuable assets than their dumb, indifferent and negligent counterparts. What really matters and needs to be understood, however, are the curricular instruments through which the scientist 'speaks' to the child, the pathways into the labour market that the child finds upon graduating and the ways in which firms exploit both younger and more experienced human capital across a range of skills and competences.

In theory, the rationale behind comparisons of HEIRs is twofold. First, we want to find out about the relative efficiency of the interaction in meeting the aims and objectives of the concerned stakeholders.

Thus governments are interested in the social return on public investment in research and expect HEIRs to address systemic failures in economy-wide knowledge generation and diffusion. Universities hope for financial support beyond core funding and aim to ensure promising employment prospects for their graduates. Firms, in turn, are keen on well-trained human capital and useable scientific knowledge. Second, we want to tie observable differences in performance to observable characteristics of HEIRs (OECD, 2002, p 21). In principle this should allow one to conclude that one type of HEIR is better than another.

In practice, though, this runs the risk of becoming an apple-and-orange exercise. There is no sound case for the existence of one best innovation practice – perhaps the single most important reason for benchmarking (Kastrinos, 2001). Global pressures on innovation do provide a common motivation in favour of science–industry collaboration, which over time may well lead to similar manifestations of knowledge management and indeed break down select barriers to cross-border knowledge sharing. However, HEIRs are part of larger innovation systems, and we know that despite – and in some sense because of – globalization the constituents and characteristics of these systems continue to differ in major ways across countries. This applies *inter alia* to the managerial, organizational and technological makeup of firms and how they respond to incentives for innovation, the public institutions that perform and fund R&D, the trends driving funding and performance patterns of R&D, and also the scientific disciplines in which countries are historically specialized in the first place (Carayannis *et al,* 2000; OECD, 2002, p 31).

Hence it is undoubtedly possible to compare select inputs and outputs of innovation systems. Nevertheless, it is far from certain that the resulting crude indicators lead to insights that lend themselves to formulating sound and sensible policy. This is because the ratio of one output variable among many (for example, scientific publications or patents) over one input variable among many (for example, public spending on basic research), as frequently used for measuring differential productivity levels of countries, flies in the face of the complexity of interactions that make up an innovation system. In an entertaining mockery of an official British attempt to establish the superior efficiency of public research spending in the UK compared to France, Barré (2001) debunked the claim that the publication of 19 articles per million pounds sterling by the UK in 1996, captured in the Science Citation Index (SCI), compared to France's nine, suggested a differential by a factor of more than two. He restricted public spending measures to those institutions that actually produced publications (and hence excluded

military research), controlled for the propensity to publish in SCI journals by discipline (which is highest for clinical medicine, for example), included the social sciences and the humanities (which are not covered by the SCI), accounted for linguistic biases whereby in all but the most internationalized disciplines, native speakers have an advantage because most SCI journals are in English, discounted the role of publications resulting from non-public spending and managed to produce a ratio slightly in favour of France's efficiency. The contextualization of the indicator is intuitively convincing. Obviously, a recent PhD teaching hordes of undergraduates from the crack of dawn until after sunset is unlikely to be as productive as a peer who is given the opportunity to reconcile the teaching load with the opportunity to turn the dissertation into publications. If these two entry points into academic careers are country specific, then we may safely infer that the two countries have different aims and objectives regarding their respective higher education systems, and thus relative efficiency would need to encompass more parameters to be a reliable measure.

For a start, to be valid any relative measure requires that one compare like with like. A pharmaceutical company in country A may be as inclined to explore patentable molecules as a rival in country B. However, if country A excels in rocket science while country B is a society of poets and sopranos, a comparison of overall patent productivity would have little or no heuristic value. In other words, since R&D intensity varies from sector to sector, and industrial specialization varies from country to country, aggregate comparisons of R&D

intensity are meaningful only up to a point. Similarly, if a pharmaceutical firm manages to commercialize a new drug derived from a biodiverse region in developing country C while failing to do so in developing country D, a whole host of explanations might apply. Only one of these explanations relies on an institutional framework more conducive to innovation activities in country C. Others could be that country D is better at protecting its resources against biopiracy by foreign firms or that commercialization is based on indigenous knowledge whose traditions contradict the requirement that a patentable product be 'new' or, finally, that there is a strong public interest against affording the product in question temporary monopoly rights. In other words, country preferences matter, as do the regulatory frameworks through which they are mediated, both nationally and multilaterally.

In sum, the existence of systematic differences among firms, sectors and countries must be acknowledged. Comparisons must be sensitive to the conceptual and data problems this raises. A good comparative analysis will attempt to look at systems as a whole and will not discount but will focus on their heterogeneity (Smith, 2001). Contextualization is imperative. Only then are comparisons likely to yield meaningful and useful lessons about the underlying dynamics among actors that ultimately account for innovation.

Yet this is easier said than done. Developing input and outcome metrics is an exercise fraught with conceptual problems, even if the unit of analysis under observation is technology-transfer activities between science and industry in one country. Counting

instances of technology transfer is one thing, establishing process metrics and measuring outcome metrics quite another, and there is no generally agreed theoretically satisfactory standard (Carayannis and Alexander, 1999). Shifting the unit of analysis to countries compounds the difficulties. Roughly a decade into research of national systems of innovation (NSIs), Patel and Pavitt (1994) called for an improvement of the empirical basis for evaluating these systems, including a better understanding of the dynamics of technological learning. Another 10 years on, this challenge rings just as true (see also Carlsson *et al, 2002*).

The most promising work in this area combines a conviction that much can be learned about different systems by comparing them, with a willingness to assemble data that are, at least in part, hard to get, as well as a healthy dose of caution with respect to the level of generalization their analysis permits. In a benchmarking study commissioned by the European Commission and the Austrian Federal Ministry of Economy and Labour, Polt *et al* (2001) evaluated what they termed 'industry–science relations' (ISRs) – defined as institutionalized forms of learning that provide a specific contribution to the stock of economically useful knowledge. They looked at three dimensions: the nature and relative channels of interaction, the characteristics of the main actors and the demand and supply they represent on the knowledge market and the framework conditions (replete with incentive structures) that provide the setting for the knowledge market. Table 1 illustrates the mass of data used to describe the three dimensions. Yet while the researchers suggest that levels of ISRs may indeed inform the knowledge-production structures of countries varying from high-technology specialization (for example, Finland) via cumulative development along traditional technology trajectories (for example, Germany) to fast-follower strategies aimed at technology diffusion in traditional industries (for example, Italy), they caution against concluding that a higher level of ISR necessarily translates into a better innovation system. Obviously, firms can exploit other avenues of knowledge acquisition. For example, a low level of ISRs could go hand in hand with intensive intra-industry R&D cooperation (Polt *et al,* 2001, p 252).

All the countries covered in the study by Pohl *et al* are advanced OECD economies with complex innovation systems. It makes sense to study HEIRs, or any other subsystem for that matter, in the context of the broader knowledge infrastructure. The focus on scientific knowledge is warranted insofar as these countries embody knowledge-intensive production. What happens within their HEIRs is likely to affect large and increasing parts of the national economy. By the same token, the dynamics of HEIRs are likely to be relevant to consumers and producers regardless of the extent of their direct exposure to them. In short, analyses of HEIRs are justified in high-income countries simply because what goes on in these relationships matters for how most people live and work.

The picture is much more complicated when we look at developing countries. At the bottom of the technological ladder, the emphasis on science and R&D is meaningless. In countries where most people cannot read and write, scientific knowledge is not the most important source of innovation, much as intellectual property is obviously not the most important right in need of legal protection. Without incorporating local and traditional knowledge, one cannot hope to grasp the dynamics of innovation in societies where, say, the preparation and therapeutic use of a plant-based ointment with palliative properties is passed on from mother to daughter while its molecular structure is not just unknown but also beyond the realm of anyone's curiosity. This presents a challenge for NSI research because its subject – advanced industrial economies – introduces a bias in favour of scientific knowledge that influences its heuristic focus and attendant methodologies. It is clearly easier to study the interaction between foreign technologies and local knowledge when both can be talked about in the language of scientific discovery. For example, although lean management was pioneered by Japanese car makers, industrial and production engineers in the USA and Europe were able to analyse its processes and implement its features in their own automotive plants. When a bioprospector from a pharmaceutical firm in the North hires mother and daughter to discover the leaves they collect for their herbal medicine, what happens complicates the interaction conceptually and raises problems of empirical verification that the national system of innovation (NSI) framework is only beginning to appreciate (Arocena and Sutz, 2000; Lundvall *et al,* 2002). The continuing relevance of the NSI approach will depend on how successfully it addresses these issues.

Table 1. Data used in the Polt *et al* (2001) benchmarking study on ISRs in select European Union countries, the USA and Japan.

| Type | ISR indicators — Indicator | Knowledge-production structures — Variable | Knowledge-production structures — Indicator | Institutional settings — Type | Institutional settings — Indicator |
|---|---|---|---|---|---|
| Contract and collaborative research | R&D financing by industry for HEIs in % of HERD; R&D financing by industry for PSREs in % of GOVERD; R&D financing by industry for HEIs/PSREs in % of BERD | R&D expenditure | BERD in % of GDP; HERD in % of GDP; GOVERD (incl. non-profit private) in % of GDP; Change in GERD as % of GDP | Institutional structure of public research | Universities; Polytechnics and HE colleges; Primarily transfer oriented PSREs; Large research centres with strategic missions; PSREs specialized in basic research |
| | | Size, structure and ownership of firms | Share of enterprises > 10,000 employees in BERD in %; Share of BERD carried out by domestic firms in % | | Departmental PSREs, others |
| Faculty consulting with industry | Significance of R&D consulting with firms by HEI researchers; Significance of R&D consulting with firms by PSRE researchers | R&D activities by innovative SMEs | Share of continuously R&D performing small manufacturing firms (20–50 employees); Share of continuously R&D performing medium-sized manufacturing firms (50–249 employees) | Governance of public research | Competition-based financing in HEIs; Competition-based financing in PSREs; Third mission of universities; Technology transfer as part of evaluation in HEIs |

# Table 1. (Continued)

| | ISR indicators | Knowledge-production structures | | | Institutional settings |
|---|---|---|---|---|---|
| **Type** | **Indicator** | **Variable** | **Indicator** | **Type** | **Indicator** |
| Cooperation in innovation projects | Innovative manufacturing firms that cooperate with HEIs (%) | Patent activities by innovative SMEs | Share of small manufacturing firms having applied for a patent | | Relevance of private HEIs |
| | Innovative manufacturing firms that cooperate with PSREs (%) | | Share of medium-size manufacturing firms having applied for a patent | | Thematically specialized PSREs with transfer mission |
| | Innovative service firms that cooperate with HEIs (%) | | | | Industry representatives on advisory boards, etc., of PSREs |
| | Innovative service firms that cooperate with PSREs (%) | | | | |
| Science as information source for industrial innovation | Innovative manufacturing firms that use HEIs as information source in innovation (%) | High-tech orientation | Share of BERD performed in high tech in % | Intermediary infrastructure | Technology transfer offices in HEIs |
| | Innovative manufacturing firms that use PSREs as information source in innovation (%) | | Share of BERD performed in medium to high tech in % | | Commercialization enterprises, transfer in HEIs |
| | Innovative service firms that use HEIs as information source in innovation (%) | | Share of BERD performed in IT services, private R&D, in % | | Science parks and incubators in HEIs |
| | Innovative service firms that use PSREs as information source in innovation (%) | | Number of high-tech patents per million of population | | Intermediaries at level of industry associations etc. |
| | | | Triad patents per million of economically active population | | (Semi-) public technology and innovation consultants for SMEs |
| | | | Share of firms in total basic research performance in % | | Regional consulting networks |
| | | | | | Information service |

(Continued)

**Table 1. (Continued)**

| | ISR indicators | Knowledge-production structures | | | Institutional settings |
|---|---|---|---|---|---|
| Type | Indicator | Variable | Indicator | Type | Indicator |
| Mobility of researchers | Researchers at HEIs moving to industry per year in % Researchers at PSREs moving to industry per year in % HE graduates at industry moving to HEIs/PSREs per year in % | Disciplinary orientation of science | Share of natural sciences in total HERD in % Share of engineering in total HERD in % Share of NSE in total R&D personnel at PSREs in % | | provision for technology transfer Significance of private intermediaries Joint industrial research networks at sector level |
| Training and education | Income from vocational training at HEIs in % of R&D expenditure Vocational training participation at HEIs per R&D employee at HEIs Share of students carrying out practices at firms during their study in % | Excellence of science | Impact factor of scientific publications in natural sciences (citations per publication) Impact factor of scientific publications in engineering sciences (citations per publication) | | |
| Patent applications by public science | Patent applications by HEIs (and individual HEI researchers) per 1,000 employees in NSEM at HEIs Patent applications by PSREs (and individual PSRE researchers) per 1,000 employees in NSEM at PSREs | Financing of R&D | Share of HERD financed outside GUF in % Direct government funding of BERD in % of GDP Venture capital invested in % of GDP | | |

**Table 1. (Continued)**

| ISR indicators | | Knowledge-production structures | | | Institutional settings |
|---|---|---|---|---|---|
| Type | Indicator | Variable | Indicator | Type | Indicator |
| Royalty incomes by public science | Royalties in % of total R&D expenditure at HEIs<br>Royalties in % of total R&D expenditure at PSREs | Market dynamics in new technologies | Turnover at ICT markets in % of GDP<br>Diffusion of Internet in % of population<br>Share of new products in turnover in % (manufacturing only)<br>Mobile telephone users in % of population | | |
| Start-ups from public science | Technology-based start-ups at HEIs per 1,000 R&D personnel<br>Technology-based start-ups at PSREs per 1,000 R&D personnel | | | | |
| Informal contacts, personal networks | Significance of networks between industry and HEIs<br>Significance of networks between industry and PSREs | | | | |

*Notes:* HERD = higher education R&D expenditure; GOVERD = government R&D expenditure; BERD = business R&D expenditure; HEI = higher education institution; PSRE = public-sector research establishment; NSEMs = natural sciences, engineering (including agricultural sciences) and medicine.

*Sources:* Polt *et al* (2001, Tables A1 -2), OECD (2002, Table 10).

In advanced latecomer countries, universities and other science institutions exist alongside industrial firms, and it is instructive to analyse how efficiently they contribute to the production and use of knowledge (see, for example, Passos *et al,* 2004). Behind this, presumably, lies part of the explanation for the above-average growth rates of patent registrations at the European Patent Office (EPO) and the United States Patent and Trademark Office (USPTO) by firms from developing countries as diverse as Argentina, Romania and South Africa (OECD, 2003, Table A.12.2). However, the degree to which HEIRs directly or indirectly contribute to human livelihoods is arguably more important. In very unequal or dualist societies, HEIRs often contribute at best to isolated pockets of excellence. For example, analyses of the pharmaceutical sector in Brazil or India are woefully inadequate if they ignore indicators such as infant mortality or, more generally, access to the gains from HEIRs in the domestic market. Both countries commit roughly 1% of gross domestic product (GDP) to R&D, and are important manufacturers of generic drugs. However, only Brazil provides HIV-positive people with free anti-retrovirals. To the extent that science and industry rely on a broad-based knowledge infrastructure across a range of simple skills and advanced competences, HEIRs may account for disjointed instances of learning among privileged knowledge producers and users whose interaction has little bearing on the economy at large and thus constitute at worst just another cathedral in the desert.

In sum, international comparisons of HEIRs need not be an apples-and-oranges exercise. They can be very instructive, provided that the indicators used are contextualized and sufficiently comprehensive to capture the idiosyncratic production of different kinds of knowledge across diverse social, political and economic realities.

## Local learning

The experience of HEIRs or innovation systems in OECD economies is relatively well documented. We know a lot less about the knowledge infrastructure in developing countries. This is not to diminish important contributions in this field, irrespective of whether they are couched in the language of innovation systems, focused on HEIRs or treat learning only implicitly (Amsden, 1989; Wade, 1990; Correa, 1995; Radosevic, 1999; Lall and Pietrobelli, 2002; Viotti, 2002). Yet, on balance, our understanding of the dynamics of innovation in the South, especially in Africa, is only beginning (Arocena and Sutz, 2000; Lundvall *et al,* 2002).

There is also an imbalance between the existence of indicators – inspired by the work of the OECD – on S&T, R&D and innovation on the one hand and the absence of research to contextualize them on the other. For example, thanks to the adoption of surveys following OECD methodologies by latecomer countries, we know that business-funded R&D of higher education and government research in Turkey is twice as high as in Hungary and three times higher than the European Union (EU) average and that patents registered in the USA by Czech firms on average cite twice as many scientific articles as the OECD average and eight times as many as Japanese firms (OECD, 2004b, Table A.10). Furthermore, foreign ownership of domestic inventions is around 50% in both Argentina and Romania, but Argentine ownership of foreign inventions is 26 times lower than Romania's (OECD, 2003, Table A.12.2). Finally, in 2000, Thailand graduated twice as many students from advanced research programmes as China, and in 2001, Lithuania had twice as many researchers as neighbouring Latvia but only half as many working in industry (OECD, 2003, Table A.12.3; for information on South Africa, see DST, 2004, or NACI and DACST, 2002).

Thanks to efforts undertaken by the government to rationalize the national system of innovation and to gain a better understanding of its performance relative to the rest of the world, this type of information is now also increasingly available for South Africa (see Table 2 – the left column illustrates 'what we know' while the right column suggests 'what we don't know'). However, as with the other countries referred to above, this information tells us at best which questions to ask – namely, why is that so and what difference does it make? At worst, it leads to pointless comparisons and untenable conclusions. For example, the first South African innovation survey concluded that, because most firms were engaged in 'merely' incremental rather than radical innovation for which they made use of foreign technology, the country was in essence a technological colony of its European masters (Oerlemans *et al*, 2003). It also reported that, for innovative firms, universities and research institutes were the least important external partners, and what little cooperation did take place was primarily with foreign institutions. Therefore, it concluded, '. . . knowledge resources available in South Africa's knowledge infrastructure do not meet the needs of South African industry' (Oerlemans *et al*, 2003, p 81). While that may be the case, it would take much more analysis to justify this conclusion. For a start, 'imitation', far from being a second-rate activity, involves learning about the nature, the uses and the limits of a foreign technology. Insofar as imitation is about understanding, it harbours the seeds of improvement, which in turn can lead to innovation proper. One does not need to go to East Asia to find illustrations for this; examples of technological upgrading also exist in South Africa (Lorentzen and Barnes, 2004).

**Table 2. Indicators of South Africa's knowledge infrastructure and performance, 1999–2001.**

| Select indicators | Conditions of learning |
|---|---|
| *Education* | • Skill match: supply versus demand |
| Population with no formal education, 19% | • Pathways of learners into the world of work |
| Population with at least a high school degree, 3% | |
| Functional literacy, 64% | |
| Bottom-ranked in TIMSS (8th grade) | |
| Lowest average score in numeracy in MLA (4th grade) | |
| Students with pass rates in maths and science with university exemption, 5% | |
| SET students in HE, 27% | |
| *Science and HE system* | • Nature of research activities |
| 21 universities | • Linkages to global knowledge flows and science communities |
| 15 technikons | • Relationship to industry |
| 8 science councils | • 'Innovation chasm'? |
| 35 SETIs and related | • Incentive systems for researchers |
| 45 commercial labs and related | • Budget pressures |
| > 80 research NGOs | |
| Researchers per 1,000 labour force, 1.88 | |
| *Funding* | • Efficiency of public funding |
| GERD/GDP 0.76% | • Effectiveness of public funding |
| Basic research/GDP, 0.19% | • Synergies from joint project funding |
| Industry/R&D, 54% | |
| HE/R&D, 25% | |
| Government/R&D, 20% | |
| Firms that accessed innovation funds, 7% | |

*Technological change*

Sources of product technology:

In-house, 57%

Local, 24%

Foreign, 22%

R&D intensity:

Firms with 0% investment in R&D, 51 %

Firms with > 6% investment in R&D, 7%

(Very) important information sources for firms:

Universities, 13%

Research labs, 9%

Group, 24%

Buyers, 37%

Suppliers, 43%

Competitors, 50%

Principal location of research partners:

Europe, SADC TAI (Finland 0.74, Mozambique 0.07), 0.34

- Relationship between productive capacity and technological capability
- Imitation versus innovation
- Imitation + innovation
- Technology diffusion
- Role of foreign technology
- Nature of supply chain
- South–South cooperation

*Notes:* TIMSS = Third International Mathematics and Science Study – achievement test in mathematics and science in 8th grade, administered by the OECD in some 40, mostly developed countries; MLA = Monitoring Learning Achievement – achievement test in numeracy, literacy and life skills in 4th grade, administered by UNESCO/UNICEF; University exemption = high school (matriculation) score sufficiently high to enrol in tertiary education; SET = science, engineering, technology; HE = higher education; SETI = SET institution; GERD = gross expenditure on R&D; SADC = Southern African Development Community; TAI = Technology Achievement Index as computed by UNDP.

The number of HE institutions is subject to change due to ongoing consolidation.

*Sources:* NACI and DACST (2002); DST (2004); Kraak (2004, Table 11).

Although the inflationary use of the term whereby everything under the sun qualifies as innovation is unhelpful, a definition that has withstood the test of time allows for 'processes by which firms master and get into practice product design and manufacturing processes *that are new to them,* if not to the universe and even to the nation' (Nelson and Rosenberg, 1993, p 4, emphasis added). That this definition was coined for a volume dealing with advanced economies is testimony to the fact that innovation does not always push the technology frontier and that learning happens in relation to – but not only at – the frontier, that it involves not only so-called high-tech sectors and that developing countries do not require such a watered-down definition as to render the concept meaningless.

In short, for the increasingly widely available indicators on knowledge production to contribute to fruitful comparisons of national innovation systems more generally and HEIRs in particular, they must be contextualized. This requires attention to how demand for knowledge, especially by firms, is actually articulated in discrete national and regional contexts.

Learning takes place when firms identify, absorb and exploit relevant knowledge. The object of learning can be process innovations, product innovations or pre-commercial knowledge. Learning is a purposeful act in that it aims at doing things differently – mastering technical change is an example. In this definition, 'learning by doing' is merely an improvement of static efficiencies and not strictly a form of learning. Prior knowledge that, depending on industry characteristics, may be rather costly to accumulate, facilitates learning. R&D also stimulates learning insofar as it helps firms to stay abreast of technological change and decide on the most relevant knowledge to absorb and adapt. R&D is therefore not only – and often not even primarily – about generating new information.

Learning is also a by-product of manufacturing operations. Solving production problems allows firms to identify new information relevant to a product market. Finally, advanced technical training creates skills that make learning easier. Firms that are good learners have a high absorptive capacity, which makes it more likely that they will appreciate emerging technological opportunities. Conversely, those with underdeveloped absorptive capacities risk ending up in technological *cul de sacs* (Cohen and Levinthal, 1989, 1990). Firms must walk a fine line between potential and realized absorptive capacity; a beautiful idea that never makes it to the market is no good (Zahra and George, 2002).

The institutional milieu within which firms operate influences the modalities by which they internalize knowledge. Opportunistic suppliers or buyers, mismatched skill sets from the education sector, an indifferent science sector and a regulatory and trade environment that errs on the side of either too little or too much competition are not conducive to investing in knowledge acquisition. Likewise, structural mismatches between the various constituents of the knowledge infrastructure may bedevil a virtuous interaction. When scientists, engineers and managers do not speak the same language, and when they cannot rely on an institution that helps them to communicate about new information and its operationalization and eventual marketability, then individually successful instances of learning by any one actor are unlikely to translate into the collective mastery of innovation that drives the technological trajectory of countries.

Unfortunately, there is as yet no generally agreed notion of national absorptive capacity aggregated upwards from firm-level competences. However, it would be possible systematically to link absorptive capacities of firms with formal and informal skill profiles and with higher-order knowledge production in the tertiary education and science sector. Stage-based models of development that offer tentative conjectures about how a country moves from a lower to a higher level of technological activity, by conceptualizing the import of both internally generated and foreign knowledge, would provide a useful framework (Narula and Dunning, 2000).

## Future research

HEIRs are but one part of national or regional innovation systems. This article has argued that the study of HEIRs must be embedded in more comprehensive assessments of knowledge creation and use in a society. This is especially pertinent in the South African context, in which relevance 'to the real needs of society' – the *cui bono* of technological progress – is part of the official definition of innovation. In particular, it needs a micro-foundation of the dynamics of learning that involves the absorptive capacities of all actors and organizations that matter to the system – *inter alia* in schools, firms, colleges, universities and other science institutions. If, how and why they interact, what hinders their communication, and to what extent linkages – including to foreign sources of knowledge – between them produce more or less desirable outcomes, and for whom, must inform the research question. In other words, while networked practices may emerge from the analysis, they should never be the point of departure.

The creation of internationally comparable indicators is welcome as long as country rankings do not substitute for proper policy analysis and advice. There is an alternative to introspective navel gazing that ignores positive experiences beyond the rim of one's own teacup and nonsensical bean counting. Much more relevant than South Africa's relative position in the global R&D charts is the difference that R&D expenditure makes to the country's hoped-for catching up, at what cost, to whose benefit and with what time horizon. Once these issues become clearer, relating one's own practice to international practice can become a learning experience from which lessons may be derived for better policy at home and perhaps elsewhere. Comparing indicators critically allows us to understand not just *how* but also *why* two or more innovation systems differ. Arguably, *the fact that* Taiwan registers more patents than South Korea is less interesting than *why* this is so. Once the answer to the latter question emerges with some degree of clarity, enlightened science and technology policy becomes possible.

The consequences of the uncritical adoption of alleged best global practices may be deleterious. However, the good news is that there is a strong emerging interest in the functioning of national innovation systems in developing and latecomer countries. Hence there is a growing body of knowledge to draw on, and research into absorptive capacities is likely to benefit from comparing research designs and results and perhaps from aligning methodologies. It will take some time before our understanding of technological learning in the South catches up with the attendant literature on the North. On the other hand, it took only some two decades to move from initial formulations of the innovation system concept to a broadly accepted and influential body of knowledge concerning advanced economies. If the catch-up logic applies to academic research, the low level of research productivity on learning and innovation in developing countries should translate into higher rates of productivity growth, with a resulting cottage industry of analyses of learning and innovation in developing countries.

# References

Agrawal, Ajay (2001), 'University-to-industry knowledge transfer: literature review and unanswered questions', *International Journal of Management Reviews.* Vol 3, No 4, pp 285–302.

Amsden, Alice H. (1989), *Asia's Next Giant: South Korea and Late Industrialization,* Oxford University Press, New York.

Arocena, Rodrigo, and Sutz, Judith (2000), 'Looking at national systems of innovation from the South', *Industry and Innovation,* Vol 7, No 1, pp 55–75.

Audretsch, D. B., and Feldman, M. P (1996), 'R&D spillovers and the geography of innovation and production', *American Economic Review,* Vol 86, No 3, pp 630–640.

Barré, Rémi (2001), 'Sense and nonsense of S&T productivity indicators', *Science and Public Policy,* Vol 28, No 4, pp 259–266.

Best, Michael H., and Forrant, Robert (2000), 'Regional industrial modernization programmes: two cases from Massachusetts', *European Planning Studies,* Vol 8, No 2, pp 211–223.

Bozeman, Barry (2000), 'Technology transfer and public policy: a review of research and theory, *Research Policy,* Vol 29, pp 627–655.

Caloghirou, Yannis, Tsakanikas, Aggelos, and Vonortas, Nicholas S. (2001), 'University–industry cooperation in the context of the European framework programmes', *Journal of Technology Transfer,* Vol 26, No 1–2, pp 153–161.

Carayannis, Elias G., and Alexander, Jeffrey (1999), 'Secrets of success and failure in commercializing US government R&D laboratory technologies: a structured case study approach', *International Journal of Technology Management,* Vol 18, Nos 3/4, pp 246–269.

Carayannis, Elias G., Alexander, Jeffrey, and Ioannidis, Anthony (2000), 'Leveraging knowledge, learning, and innovation in forming strategic government–industry (GIU) R&D partnerships in the US, Germany and France', *Technovation,* Vol 20, pp 477–488.

Carlsson, Bo, Jacobsson, Staffan, Holmén, Magnus, and Rickne, Annika (2002), 'Innovation systems: analytical and methodological issues', *Research Policy,* Vol 31, pp 233–245.

Chang, P-L., and Hsu, W.-S. (2002), 'Improving the innovative capabilities of Taiwan's manufacturing industries with university–industry research partnerships', *International Journal of Advanced Manufacturing Technology,* Vol 19, pp 775–787.

Cockburn, I., and Henderson, R. (1998), 'Absorptive capacity, coauthoring behaviour, and the organization of research in drug discovery', *Journal of Industrial Economics,* Vol 46, No 2, pp 157–182.

Cohen, Wesley M., and Levinthal, Daniel A. (1989), 'Innovation and learning: the two faces of R&D', *Economic Journal*, Vol 99 (September), pp 569–596.

Cohen, Wesley M., and Levinthal, Daniel A. (1990), 'Absorptive capacity: a new perspective on learning and innovation', *Administrative Science Quarterly*, Vol 35, No 1, pp 128–152.

Correa, Carlos (1995), 'Innovation and technology transfer in Latin America: a review of recent trends and policies', *International Journal of Technology Management*, Vol 10, Nos 7/8, pp 815–845.

DST (2004), *South African National Survey of Research and Experimental Development (R&D) (2001/02 FiscalYear)*, Department of Science and Technology, Pretoria.

Furman, Jeffrey L., Porter, Michael E., and Stern, Scott (2002), 'The determinants of national innovative capacity', *Research Policy*, Vol 31, pp 899–933.

Hagen, Roulla (2002), 'Globalization, university transformation and economic regeneration: a UK case study of public/ private sector partnership', *International Journal of Public Sector Management*, Vol 15, No 3, pp 204–218.

Kastrinos, Nikos (2001), 'Contribution of socio-economic research to the benchmarking of RTD policies in Europe', *Science and Public Policy*, Vol 28, No 4, pp 238–246.

Kraak, Andre (2004), *An Overview of South African Human Resources Development*, HSRC, Cape Town.

Lall, Sanyaya, and Pietrobelli, Carlo (2002), *Failing to Compete: Technology Development and Technology Systems in Africa*, Edward Elgar, Cheltenham.

Lee, Yong S. (1996) ' "Technology transfer" and the research university: a search for the boundaries of university–industry collaboration', *Research Policy*, Vol 25, pp 843–863.

Lee, Yong S. (2000), 'The sustainability of university–industry research collaboration: an empirical assessment', *Journal of Technology Transfer*. Vol 25, pp 111–133.

Lorentzen, Jochen, and Barnes, Justin (2004), 'Learning, upgrading, and innovation in the South African automotive industry', *European Journal of Development Research*, Vol 16, No 3, pp 463–495.

Lundvall, Bengt-Ake, Björn Johnson, Eseben Sloth Andersen and Bent Dalum (2002), 'National systems of production, innovation and competence building', *Research Policy*, Vol 31, pp 213–231.

Mansfield, Edwin (1998), 'Academic research and industrial innovation: an update of empirical findings', *Research Policy*, Vol 26, pp 773–776.

Mohd Yunos and Mohd Ghazali (2002), 'Building an innovation-based economy: the Malaysian technology business incubator experience', *Journal of Change Management*, Vol 3, No 2, pp 177–188.

NACI and Department of Arts, Culture, Science and Technology (DACST) (2002), South *African Science and Technology: Key Facts and Figures 2002*, National Advisory Council on Innovation, Pretoria.

Narula, Rajneesh, and Dunning, John H. (2000), 'Industrial development, globalization and multinational enterprises: new realities for developing countries', *Oxford Development Studies*, Vol 28, No 2, pp 141–167.

Nelson, Richard R., ed (1993), *National Innovation Systems*, Oxford University Press, Oxford.

Nelson, Richard R., and Rosenberg, Nathan (1993), 'Technical innovation and national systems', in Nelson, Richard R., ed (1993), *National Innovation Systems*, Oxford University Press, Oxford.

OECD (2002), *Benchmarking Industry– Science Relationships*, Organization for Economic Co-operation and Development, Paris.

OECD (2003), *STI Scoreboard: Creation and Diffusion of Knowledge*, Organization for Economic Co-operation and Development, Paris.

OECD (2004a), *Science and Innovation Policy*, Organization for Economic Co-operation and Development, Paris.

OECD (2004b), *Science and Technology Statistical Compendium*, *Organization for Economic Co-operation and Development, Paris.*

Oerlemans, L.A.G., Pretorius, M.W., Buys, A. J., and Rooks, G. (2003), *Industrial Innovation in South Africa 1998–2000*, Department of Arts, Culture, Science and Technology, Pretoria.

Passos, Carlos A. S., Cantisano Terra, Branca Regina, Furtado, André T., Vedovello, Conceigâo, and Plonski, Guilherme Ary (2003), 'Improving university–industry partnerships – the Brazilian experience through the scientific and technological support program (PADCT IN)', *International Journal of Technology Management,* Vol 27, No 5, pp 475–487.

Patel, Parimal, and Pavitt, Keith (1994), 'National innovation systems: why they are important, and how they might be measured and compared', *Economics of Innovation and New Technology,* Vol 3, pp 77–95.

Phillips, Fred (1998), 'University–industry partnerships in management research', *Technological Forecasting and Social Change,* Vol 57, pp 257–260.

Polt, Wolfgang, Rammer, Christian, Gassler, Helmut, Schibany, Andreas, and Hartinger, Doris (2001), 'Benchmarking industry–science relations: the role of framework conditions', *Science and Public Policy,* Vol 28, No 4, pp 247–258.

Poyago-Thoetoky, Joanna, Beath, John, and Siegel, Donald S. (2002), 'Universities and fundamental research: reflections on the growth of university–industry partnerships', *Oxford Review of Economic Policy,* Vol 18, No 1, pp 10–21.

Radosevic, Slavo (1999), 'The Eastern European latecomer firm and technology transfer: from "muddling through" to

"ccatching up"', in Bugliarello, G., Pak, N. K., Alferov, Z. I. and Moore, J. H., eds, *East–West Technology Transfer,* Kluwer, Dordrecht.

Smith, Keith (2001), 'Comparing economic performance in the presence of diversity', *Science and Public Policy,* Vol 28, No 4, pp 267–276.

Thursby, J. G., and Thursby, M. C. (2000), *Who Is Selling the Ivory Tower? Sources of Growth in University Licensing,* Working Paper No 7718, NBER, Cambridge.

Viotti, Edoardo (2002), 'National learning systems: a new approach on technological change in late industrializing economies and evidence from the cases of Brazil and South Korea', *Technological Forecasting and Social Change,* Vol 69, pp 653–680.

Wade, Robert (1990), *Governing the Market: Economic Theory and the Role of Government in East Asian Industrialization,* Princeton University Press, Princeton, NJ.

Zahra, Shaker A., and George, Gerard (2002), 'Absorptive capacity: a review, reconceptualization, and extension', *Academy of Management Review,* Vol 27, No 2, pp 185–203.

# Consider Velasquez
## Reflections on the development of entrepreneurship programmes

**Jay Mitra**

**Abstract:** *This paper is concerned with 'ways of seeing' entrepreneurship. The study of entrepreneurship is compared to a painter's study of his or her subject. The detail lies in the values and symbols, which inform the portrait or the landscape in which the entrepreneur evolves. The detail also informs the conceptualization and implementation of the programmes for a variety of audiences. The paper outlines some of the conceptual underpinnings for entrepreneurship programmes across the world and how such programmes emerge in different contexts, especially within higher education institutions. The pursuit of entrepreneurship education poses certain challenges both for the higher education system and the student, and the author discusses these issues and how they have influenced the development of a postgraduate programme in entrepreneurship in his university.*

**Keywords:** *entrepreneurship; process; evolution; higher education institutions; seeing, learning, context*

*Professor Mitra is Director of the Enterprise Research and Development Centre and Chair in Enterprise and Economic Development, Business School, University of Central England, Perry Barr, Birmingham B42 2SU, UK. Tel: +44 121 331 6440. Fax: +44 121 331 7780. E-mail: jay.mitra@uce.com*

Consider Velasquez. The 17th century's 'amazingly mysterious painter' saw and painted the whole Hapsburg court in all its melancholy, uncertainty and paradox, as he did the depth of the individual. He celebrates the authority of Philip IV and his spiritual loneliness and ordinariness in *La Tela Real [The Royal Enclosure]*, 1632–1637. In this work, the grandness of the court and the self-knowledge of mortality reveal a study of both the leader and his environment.

And the latter is brushed with more insight through the portraits of jesters and dwarfs, the customary features of Renaissance and baroque courts. In them, Velasquez saw both the 'freakish' isolation of the individual and the ordinariness of his or her refusal to appear subjugated (Jones, 2002). Through these portraits, these individual units of aesthetic analysis, Velasquez identifies the tragedies of both king and dwarf and reflects on the Hapsburg world. He explores the contradictions in, for example, a man trapped in a child's body (the dwarf) and offers a perspective on what constitutes an in-depth study of the individual (the king or the dwarf), the organizational context (the court) and the wider environment of human melancholy (the Hapsburg Empire).

In considering Velasquez, there is insight to be gained into the study of entrepreneurship, the new subject that is engaging the minds of government, business schools, technologists and others. While there may be no melancholy in their vision, advocates for the study of entrepreneurship are seriously concerned about the need to devise new ways of coping with uncertainty and complexity brought about by technological, demographic, organizational and structural change. There are pressures on individuals to generate creative solutions to work-related or social change through new venture creation; on organizations to change the way they respond to greater uncertainties through innovative new projects, products, processes and management methods; and on policy makers and government to create more facilitating infrastructures and environments for the understanding and accommodation of change.

This article reviews the process by which entrepreneurship has emerged as a subject of study at the postgraduate level in a particular higher education institution. The main objective is to review the important issues involved in the decision to pursue the establishment of such a course. To meet this objective, the paper is organized into the following parts:

- an overview of the importance of entrepreneurship and the reasons for its adoption as a field of study;
- a discussion of the conceptual issues underpinning the relationship between entrepreneurship and small business management and the extended scope and purpose of entrepreneurship as exemplified in the study of entrepreneurial people, entrepreneurial organizations and the entrepreneurial environment;
- a further discussion on learning processes and styles; and finally
- the form of development at the UK's University of Central England.

## Valuing entrepreneurship

The growing value of entrepreneurship as a subject of study is predicated on the following key factors:

- the growing importance of small and medium-sized enterprises

(SMEs) and the evolution of large firms in a rapidly changing international economic environment;

- the challenge to higher education to meet the demands of economic and social change through relevant, professionally oriented, new academic provision at the postgraduate levels – the need for greater attention to entrepreneurship in university business education was cited some time ago by Porter and McKibbin (1988);
- the increased quantity of academic research, suggesting that new knowledge, based on empirical evidence, has been developed to demonstrate the differences between start-up ventures and mature organizations; that a common core of knowledge is being established through an accumulation of studies; and that the quality of writing and research has legitimized the subject within academia (Hills and Morris, 1998);
- the need for graduates, mature students, working professionals, managers and other employees, to acquire and develop a wide array of up-to-date entrepreneurial skills, competencies, and a knowledge base; to be 'entrepreneurial' in both business and non-business settings; to take advantage of 'downshifting' and 'spin-off' opportunities; to consider non-traditional career alternatives in a rapidly changing economic and social environment; and to inform policy

and decision making by up-to-date knowledge of critical issues in entrepreneurship and regional development; and

- the growing attention to cross-disciplinary and cross-functional integration in education provision coupled with industry demands, which have also been associated with the emphasis on the notion that the qualitative, subjective and applied elements of study are as important as the quantitative, conceptual and analytical forms (Ivancevich, 1991).

## Entrepreneurship and SME development

Much of the advocacy of entrepreneurship has manifested itself in its equation with small and medium-sized enterprise (SME) development. In part, such an equation is the result of the recognition of the value and importance of small businesses to any economy and of the changing forms of business organization, as large firms organize their activities in smaller, autonomous units, emulating the entrepreneurial management styles of successful smaller companies.

Since the recession of the 1970s and 1980s, worldwide interest in SME development has centred around the primary economic consideration of job creation. Instrumental in the increasing value of SMEs as a critical area of academic research and focused policy making has been the recognition that SMEs represent 99.8% of the 17.9 million formal businesses in the European Union (ENSR, 1997), that they account for between 66% and 68% of total employment and that they generate between 56.2% and 63% of private-sector business turnover (Coehlo-Rodriguez, 2001; TACIT, 1997). The seminal Birch report (Birch, 1979), which identified their potential as employment generators in the USA, has been complemented by their role in the strategic adjustment of the economies of various developing countries (Gibb, 1996).

The conditions that most favour SME development – the processes of externalization, which also allow for better networking and clustering and consequent competitive advantage for smaller firms through flexible specialization, economies of scale and scope, and agglomeration – have also risen quickly in the research and policy agendas (Mitra, 2000; Pyke *et al*, 1990). A focus on the broader, thematic concepts of innovation and learning has highlighted the distinctive characteristics of SMEs in terms of economic growth and the managerial capabilities required to generate such growth (Matlay and Mitra, 2002).

Recognition and consideration of these issues have made a critical impression on policy making and management education. There is a growing and varied interest in questions about the type of people who make things happen ('enterprising people'), the types of organizations in which such people thrive or ways in which organizations can be designed to effect change in turbulent times ('entrepreneurial organizations') and the wider environment in which enterprising people and organizations evolve ('entrepreneurial environment').

## Entrepreneurship, SMEs and change

It is well recognized that fundamental structural changes have affected the economies of most nations over the past two decades. Reduced labour needs have gone hand in hand with the rationalization of corporations, the demise of long-term career opportunities, the outsourcing of many activities, the growth in self-employment, and increasing opportunities for new ventures. The effects of change are also seen in the growth of the new information economy, e-commerce, growth in portfolio work, the need of organizations to engage people with flexible and dynamic skills and the increasing autonomy of the professional 'knowledge worker' who can generate his or her entrepreneurial work schedule in different environments.

Rapid change and new developments often leave 'learning deficits' among people, in terms of both process (enabling learning to take place) and content (issues and knowledge relating to new developments, which cut across traditional disciplines).

Much of the change that is taking place is being borne or led by small organizations or by larger ones evolving as assemblies of smaller, dynamic and autonomous units. SMEs have, therefore, become a symbol of dynamic change as well as cynosures of research, policy making and further study. Organizational evolution has also gone hand in hand with personal development, especially with the emergence of greater uncertainty, portfolio employment, and greater reliance on individual motivation and creativity (Christensen and Overdorf, 2000).

While the prevailing orthodoxy of the 1960s ruled out the relevance of support for small firms (Stanworth and Gray, 1991), the 1980s (supply-side led) and 1990s (demand led) have seen a strong shift in emphasis in favour of SMEs, so that they have become a plank of economic development. SMEs are important because of their flexible and adaptive nature, their ability to compete with large firms (Storey *et al*, 1998), their ability to innovate (Rothwell and Dodgson, 1989), their contribution to employment growth (Stanworth and Gray, 1991) and new technology push-and-pull factors. For these reasons alone, SMEs have become an important focal point of study with considerable implications for research and education at all levels.

## Entrepreneurship and other organizations

The generation of new knowledge based on an interest in entrepreneurial SMEs and the factors contributing to their growth has almost inevitably spilled over into other organizational domains. 'Entrepreneurship' is a leaky concept, and the notion of smallness and flexibility applies equally to other organizations looking at ways to redesign their structures.

Thus when Pinchot (1985) refers to 'intrapreneurship' as the valorizing of entrepreneurial behaviour within a large organization, he is identifying changes in organizational culture and structures that call for decentralization and the operation of small, flexible, autonomous units of operation.

Handy's (1984) reference to the entrepreneurial worker of the future also draws from ideas relating to the small business entrepreneur, with such a worker managing a range of portfolio jobs as he or she seeks economic and social opportunities.

References to the need for entrepreneurial public-sector organizations to replace traditional bureaucratic monoliths that hinder change are commonplace in various UK government and European Union reports. Only entrepreneurial public agencies are deemed to be able to provide for a facilitating policy environment and support infrastructure for new, dynamic forms of economic and social progress. The spillover has also affected the way non-governmental organizations (NGOs) operate, as reduced public funding and sponsorship have forced them to respond to external pressures for the introduction of different organizational dynamics.

## Entrepreneurship evolving and the value creation process

A cursory observation of the issues referred to above would show that certain common features, such as smallness, flexibility, new opportunity realization, innovation, uncertainty reduction and proactiveness, underline entrepreneurship in any type of organization. These features tend, therefore, to acquire greater significance than questions of the size of organization, the traits of entrepreneurs and life-cycle considerations. A sense of organizations evolving in particular contexts, varying, selecting and retaining different features and values and struggling for a place in the economy (Aldrich, 1999) provides for a better understanding of what entrepreneurship is. In the search for a definition of entrepreneurship that incorporates these dimensions, consideration might be given to that of Stevenson *et al* (1985). These authors define entrepreneurship as 'the process of creating value by bringing together a unique package of resources to exploit an opportunity'. Process, rather than static features, suggests a wide range of activities in different contexts for different types of organization.

In arguing that entrepreneurship is not simply about business (corporate or small businesses), business planning and life skills, Gibb (2000) suggests that entrepreneurship is more about 'behaviours, skills, attributes applied individually and collectively to help individuals and organizations, of all kinds to cope with, enjoy (and indeed sometimes create) high levels of uncertainty and complexity as a means of personal fulfilment'.

## Challenge to higher education

Entrepreneurship evolving (with apologies to Howard Aldrich), poses some problems for its study. Sitting, as it has to date, within the jurisdiction of management education, entrepreneurship provides a challenge to:

- the development of different types of managers in various organizations;
- the notion of a fixed marketplace for management education;
- the different forms of learning for different types of learners;
- the orthodoxy of research modes and methods; and
- the organization of effective delivery platforms.

Education and training organizations have responded in a variety of ways to the growing demand for self-employment and small-business–oriented career options for graduates and professionals, the need to develop entrepreneurial skills of self-sufficiency, team working, adaptability, and so on. The challenge to higher education is considerable, and certain activities are beginning to indicate the benefits that can accrue to HEIs and their stakeholders, including the wider community, from entrepreneurship programmes. Typical initiatives in the UK include:

- a growth in the number of undergraduate and postgraduate courses on entrepreneurship, small businesses, enterprise development, etc;
- the development of Centres for Entrepreneurship whose main focus is on the promotion of entrepreneurial activity through research, consultancy and education (based mainly on the Science and Enterprise Challenge initiative of the UK government);
- the embedding of entrepreneurial activity and mindset within the

culture and structure of higher education;

- the growth in the number of specific units dedicated to university-wide entrepreneurial activity to support teaching and research; and
- the growing demand for flexible learning formats for both graduates and working people to pick up specific higher-level skills, competencies and knowledge to meet the challenges referred to earlier.

Table 1 locates these initiatives in terms of a possible set of objectives.

While it is not within the scope of this article to assess the different

approaches to entrepreneurship development, it is nevertheless obvious that the value and weight of these initiatives lies in a consideration of the variety of pedagogic and learning styles, learner groups, use of research and outcomes. These issues are addressed below under the three headings of 'target learner groups', 'learning issues' and 'learning forms and the learning context'.

The phrase 'target learner groups' refers to the different types of learners that higher education can be involved with as part of the development of entrepreneurship programmes. 'Learning forms' and research issues are considered together in view of their symbiotic relationship in the exploration (as opposed to or together with exploitation) of knowledge (Noteboom, 2000), and the 'learning context' identifies the role of HEIs in providing entrepreneurship education as one of the stakeholders in the promotion of entrepreneurial activity.

**Table 1. HEI–based initiatives and objectives.**

| Initiative | Objective |
| --- | --- |
| Undergraduate and postgraduate courses | Meeting demand, responding to different political and economic agendas |
| Centres for Entrepreneurship | Industry–HEI interaction through research, consultancy, management development, training |
| Embedding of entrepreneurial activity and growth in specific units university-wide | Culture change and curriculum development |
| Demand for flexible learning formats | Innovative approaches to learning and response to demand, including lifelong learning issues |

## Target learner groups

Entrepreneurship learner groups are various, and some degree of prioritization is a necessity for HEIs. Hills and Morris (1998) identify types of learners, stretching from undergraduate and MBA, PhD students through to pre-start entrepreneurs, non-business students, existing business owners, acquisition and turnaround specialists, all seeking:

- intellectual enrichment;
- evaluation of career alternatives;
- meeting entrepreneur support interest; and

- possibilities for corporate entrepreneurship.

Catering to such a disparate group of interests would require an understanding of previous business education/experience and an analysis of demographic, psychographic, industry and other characteristics (Hills and Morris, 1998). What is also of crucial importance is the recognition that HEIs face the challenge of developing the competencies and confidence of different cohorts of people attempting to realize both organizational and personal objectives. The learner groups have personal agendas, for example, for starting up a business or leading new ventures in existing organizations at the individual level. These objectives can be coupled with organizational needs for better creative and networking skills in paradoxical situations and under conditions of uncertainty.

An increasing number of surveys of employers' needs and the labour market have identified a dearth of flexible working, interpersonal, adaptability, team-working, project management, change management, innovation and related skills, all of which are considered central to work in the new economy. These skills are also relevant to the setting up and running of a small business. The common theme is that of entrepreneurship and the learning and use of entrepreneurial skills in paid employment and in running a business. The acquisition of these skills alongside accepted cognitive and pedagogic skills is deemed to be central to the process by which

graduates can best be prepared for the world of work. In the UK, the recent government-led push for graduates, especially science and engineering graduates (through the Science and Enterprise Challenge), to absorb entrepreneurial skills and for institutions to promote the commercialization of their research-based inventions and discoveries, is part of the recognition of the learning deficit within higher education.

The issues raised are also endorsed by the findings of the most recent National Household Survey (a bi-annual survey published by the UK government). The survey shows that one in three people across England is currently running or considering starting a business. The survey of 6,000 people also shows that 86% of them admire entrepreneurs and 76% would encourage their friends or relatives to start their own enterprise.

Learner groups are, therefore, emerging from various points of interest. Whether a behaviouralist approach, such as that of Stevenson *et al* (1985), Gibb (2001), is appropriate enough for understanding the motivation of these groups is perhaps questionable. Do they want to become entrepreneurs or are they driven by the political and economic necessity to augment their success in survival positions? Answers to such questions are unlikely to be simple, as each group (budding entrepreneurs wanting to start up, executives 'downshifting', executives being required to be part of an organizational change process, etc) will demand a variety of possibilities for learning not necessarily offered by a course in entrepreneurship. What matters in this context is whether the menu on offer meets the needs of different learner groups.

## Learning issues

Shifting the focus to what is on offer to learner groups raises questions about the viability of taught provision in the subject. For example, 'Can entrepreneurship be taught?' seems a vacuous question, in the same category as plastic arguments over whether entrepreneurs are born or made. What matters is what they do. And if what entrepreneurs do matters, then the advocacy of any study exploring what they do and why they do what they do is a legitimate topic for scholarly investigation. Hence, the key question arises, 'How can entrepreneurship courses be taught and delivered for a wide range of learners with disparate profiles and needs?'

Hills and Morris (1998) identified three conceptual models for entrepreneurship programmes – the 'business plan', the 'business life cycle' and the 'business functions' models. Each is distinctive, in that the 'business plan' model attempts a creation and realization of specific business objectives in particular contexts, the 'business life cycle' model emphasizes different stages of business activity and the 'business functions' model extends the scope of management studies. In essence, these models can be said to relate entrepreneurial behaviour – and associated skills and attributes – to the distinctive organizational characteristics and task environment of the small firm as well as to

personal attributes. As such, they have their roots in the contingency, congruence and environment fit schools of organizational behaviour (Lawrence and Lorsch, 1969; Nadler and Tushman, 1983; both referred to in Gibb, 1996).

Others (Ronstadt, 1985; Timmons and Stevenson, 1985) have also raised the threshold of programme content by citing the need for studying issues ranging from ambiguity, creativity, ethical assessment to the particular need for undoing the risk-averse bias of many analytical techniques and encouraging entrepreneurial drive. The emphasis here is on the need to respond to change processes and for entrepreneurship education to provide an alternative learning path to meet a variety of objectives. The development of entrepreneurship programmes around the world reflects 'convergence' and 'divergence' in the approaches to entrepreneurship research, education and training, as the proceedings of the International Entrepreneurship Forum (IEF – Mitra and Haynes, 2001) show.

Who learns and the nature of the learning objectives are driven by the individual context, even if there are common 'push' factors of employment creation, economic regeneration driving institutional responses in complex environments. The IEF discussions, involving representatives from nine countries and their institutions, demonstrated different critical concerns centred around various learner groups, despite the common goals of developing a market culture (especially in developing countries, addressing confusing policy imperatives, developing SMEs from start-up to growth and upskilling community needs). Table 2 shows the critical issues that learner groups identified in different environments.

Further examination of the learning issues involved in the study of entrepreneurship, and indeed in the interests of various learner groups, suggests that the content of such study is concerned with the production of novelty or exploration. According to Noteboom (2000),

> Thus there must be relation between entrepreneurship and the cycle of discovery. There is a variety of notions of entrepreneurship . . . and different types of entrepreneurship may be seen as belonging to different stages in the cycle types of discovery . . . different notions of entrepreneurship emphasise different things in different combinations . . .

- innovation (Bentham, Thuen, Schumpeter and perhaps Says);
- creative destruction through novel combinations (Schumpeter);
- the identification and utilisation of possibilities for consumption and production (Cantillon, Smith, Menger, Mises, Hayek, Kirzner);
- the configuration and management of production factors for efficient production (Say, Marshall, Mises);
- the provision of capital.

It is not simply the theoretical underpinnings linking different types of entrepreneurship with different stages in the cycle of discovery that are under consideration in Noteboom's analysis, but also the practical forms and the types of issues that inform the interests of different learner groups in different learning contexts. Therefore, in identifying and describing learning content, the core elements include the realization of potential in the cycle of discovery and a whole range of types of entrepreneurship

**Table 2. Learner issues in different learning contexts.**

| Country | Learning issues in context | Learning objective |
| --- | --- | --- |
| USA | Curriculum development issues and mindset changes | Breaking the mould, continuously |
| Latvia | Developing enterprise in difficult, changing times | High levels of education attainment to lead by example |
| India | Institutional capacity building for government and HEIs | Education not instruction |
| Italy | Academic spin-offs and the knowledge economy | Ascertain whether study is needed for spin-outs and enterprise development |
| Australia | Paradox of freedom and uncertainty | Respond to the need for an 'ambidextrous' university |
| Canada | Linking the classroom and the community | Building social capital |
| Romania | Global pressures and local sustainability | Creating enterprise in difficult times |

*Source*: Adapted from Mitra and Haynes (2001).

corresponding with the different stages of discovery. Noteboom (2000), referring to Rothwell's (1985) idea of 'dynamic complementarity' suggests that these types are not alternatives but are complementary and build on each other, which requires the study of different types of organizations fulfilling different entrepreneurial roles. The subjects (people, organizations and the environment) and the processes (types of entrepreneurship) together have a stake in entrepreneurial churn leading to what can be referred to as a 'stakeholding' approach to entrepreneurship (Matlay and Mitra, 2002).

Grappling with a variety of interests, the education provider needs to consider appropriate forms for its adequate provision. In considering appropriate forms and pedagogy, the context in which these forms are shaped and developed also attracts interest.

## Learning forms and contexts

Accommodating diversity, disparity and stakeholding requires a holistic approach to the study of entrepreneurship and the delivery of entrepreneurship programmes. In developing an entrepreneurial, holistic management approach, the basic task is to encourage managers and other students to learn in a variety of ways and from different sources. Entrepreneurs who may need to be taught pose a different challenge. Style, content and form all require a different, creative and adaptive approach from the traditional reductionist and analytical one espoused by management studies.

Entrepreneurship programmes worldwide have played with different forms of delivery. The involvement of entrepreneurs in delivery, for example, has sometimes been considered more important than traditional lectures and readings. Similarly, the development of the business plan, as a proxy for the formulation of a whole programme, the development of product prototypes and live business creation cases with the availability of restricted venture funding have also found pride of place in courses. The use of workshops, unstructured 'events' and related pedagogy inform the experiential thrust of courses. Behind the formulation of such approaches is the belief that they cater to the practical, flexible and entrepreneurial intentions of learners, as is the debate between qualitative and quantitative approaches to research into and the study of entrepreneurship.

In designing the curriculum and the form of delivery, essentially in the context of management education, the prevailing view is that the form and content will help the learner (the start-up entrepreneur and/or the innovative manager will find answers to problems which they will then apply in practice). The locus of such thinking is the positivist epistemology of practice, or the model of 'technical rationality' (Schon, 1999), which states that professional activity consists in instrumental problem solving made rigorous by the application of scientific theory and practice. Within the framework of technical rationality, the study of entrepreneurship can be fitted into a Schien (1973) schemata that provides for three components to professional knowledge: an underlying discipline or basic science component, an applied science component and a skills and attitudinal component. This would be in keeping with the forms of higher learning in universities, committed, as they are to a particular epistemology, a view of knowledge that fosters selective inattention to practical competence and professional artistry (Schon, 1999).

In attempting to make concessions to 'practical pedagogy' and alternative experiential methods of delivery, entrepreneurship programmes address only part of the challenge of entrepreneurship education. This is because of the need to generate entrepreneurial professionals who cannot be expected to look at artistic ways of coping with phenomena that fall outside the scope of naming and framing, or problem solving and problem setting. The frequent consequence is the dilemma of rigour and relevance, as the 'trained professional' is expected to avoid the messy bits that fall outside the scope of technical solution.

Given the constraints faced by most business/management schools, as they form their particular capabilities around functional approaches and related problem solving, the study of entrepreneurship continues to face considerable odds. A high volume of public exposure to the need (political and economic) to value entrepreneurship generates limited outcomes. Academic credibility needs to be attached to 'reflection and reflecting in action', 'knowing in action' and 'reflecting in practice' (Schon, 1999), modes of learning that allow for:

- a major focus on process delivery;
- ownership of learning by participants;
- the teacher as facilitator and fellow learner;
- flexible and responsive learning sessions;
- negotiation of learning objectives;
- multidisciplinary approaches;
- creative problem setting, problem solving and reflecting;
- intuitive decision making;
- networking;
- holistic management of new business projects and ventures; and
- internationalization

(adapted from Gibb, 2001 and 1996).

A proactive approach on the part of institutions means providing for multiple learning environments that both inform and rejuvenate the learning process. The learning context provides for entrepreneurial succour when appropriate use is made of people, technology and other resources. Creating an international forum for interaction at all levels (student, practitioner and academic) for a variety of activities (such as information sharing, joint publications, refereeing, review of content and processes, the development of international case studies), setting up local fora for stakeholders (businesses, the non-business community of creative people, other faculty students and staff), establishing a portfolio of research, which is best monitored through the way it feeds into the development of curriculum, all form part of the proactive approach. Having a focal point in the form of a Centre for Entrepreneurship, established on the basis of research, development and teaching expertise, entrepreneurial income generation, self-sufficiency and links with the wider international economic community can help considerably in this process.

Universities now have the opportunity to articulate the debate surrounding entrepreneurial education through the development of undergraduate and postgraduate courses in entrepreneurship. This could help meet the demand for up-to-date business and personal development programmes. In addition, courses on entrepreneurship can attract a wider range of students paying full-cost fees and can prepare them for entrepreneurial careers including self-employment, employment in SMEs, work in large organizations and support services. The development of conceptually and academically robust qualifications in entrepreneurship is, therefore, a distinct opportunity for HEIs.

Any progress down the opportunity road helps to overcome the barriers of alleged incompatibility between entrepreneurial and HEI activities. It should also help to overcome the negative view that entrepreneurial activity is somehow peripheral to the learning process at postgraduate level and that entrepreneurship may not fit into a single-discipline model.

By accumulating the relevant, interdisciplinary pedagogic input as part of the study of entrepreneurship, appropriate recognition can be given to the need to harness learning skills in preparation for the real world – which, by definition, is multidisciplinary! In addition, by augmenting the learning process with 'enterprise research' and/ or 'learning by doing', students can be given the opportunity to recognize, adapt from and contribute to multiple forms of learning.

## The market and course development at UCE

The development of the postgraduate entrepreneurship course reflects the thought processes and the working environment referred to above. Recent pronouncements by the UK government's Competitiveness White Paper *Building the Knowledge Economy* and its particular reference to entrepreneurship also help to focus attention on proactive involvement in this sphere of education activity. In addition, the reorganization of business support services in the UK and the emergence of the Small Business Service and the Learning and Skills Councils have opened up a raft of opportunities for professional development opportunities requiring postgraduate-level accreditation.

In 1999 the Business School at the University of Central England established the Enterprise Research and Development Centre (ERDC). This was the first step in recognizing the value of entrepreneurship in the academic portfolio of the school. Starting with a focus on research and development activities and concentrating on key themes that view entrepreneurship development in terms of people, organizations and the wider environment, the ERDC has generated a three-year portfolio of activities that includes:

- A healthy revenue stream of income from a variety of sources (private firms, European funds, research body grants).

- The identification of key underpinning themes for entrepreneurship research with an emphasis on qualitative outcomes (to date – innovation, organizational learning, clusters, e-management and social responsibility). The choice of these themes is based on the view that innovation is symbiotic to entrepreneurship through the study of people and organizations, and lately regional innovation policies. Innovation also underpins the study of clusters, in that it is concerned with cross-organizational forms of new venture creation and innovation. Similarly organizational learning is closely linked to innovation in that the learning process is part of the development of new products and processes, and social responsibility offers both social and economic opportunities for all types of business. The topicality of these themes in the economic and political agenda of local, national and international organizations was consciously taken on board as part of the selection process.
- The nurturing of gifted, young researchers both to work on and 'own' the topics alongside their own research interests.
- The involvement of local firms and representative organizations in the design, development and delivery of programmes (to date programmes of activity have involved over 250 firms).
- The involvement of support service agencies as partners, as beneficiaries of new knowledge drawn from research, and as participants in field research.
- The creation, implementation and delivery of short- course programmes based on the research themes, testing and developing the plan for a Masters programme, and the market for diverse groups. This has been further augmented by substantive research programmes, under the European Structural Funds ('Technology, Information, Innovation and Learning Transfer' or TIILT, and the 'Entrepreneur Development Programme' or EDP), which have specifically sought to assess ways in which small firm owner-mangers, business support service agency staff, policy makers and others best link in with academic initiatives related to entrepreneurship. These major programmes have demonstrated the need for innovative actions, delivery methods, timetabling, types of involvement and action learning based participation, all of which inform the form and content of this proposed Masters programme.
- The development of an MBA Core Unit and an elective/pathway in entrepreneurship.
- The creation and establishment of an International Entrepreneurship Forum for the exchange of ideas, joint programme (research and teaching) development, and dissemination activities. Two major conferences have been held to date to promote the Forum and to explore international research work linking entrepreneurship with learning. A third conference on 'Entrepreneurship and Regional

Development' is to be held in Beijing, China, in September 2002.

These developments have provided the necessary spur, as has the growing amount of anecdotal evidence from UCE students and those from other universities concerning the attractiveness of an entrepreneurship programme.

In addition, UCE has subscribed to the West Midlands Science and Enterprise Challenge Programme (through participation in The Mercia Institute of Enterprise) and specifically under Cornerstone 3b to the promotion and development of entrepreneurship education and research. The development of the MSc programme is of special interest to the Mercia Institute and its constituent universities because this is seen as the first programme of its kind at Masters level on the subject of entrepreneurship, which responds directly to the demands for such courses in the policy, business and academic marketplaces.

Evidence of the demand for a structured programme at the postgraduate level for home students stems from the growing call for standardized, accredited, modular programmes for support service providers. A plethora of support provision has led at best to unbalanced and mixed-quality provision. The need for quality standards demands not only management standards but relevant and appropriate content reflecting business development and learning needs.

While such evidence addresses issues related to support service providers, increasing calls from graduates of various disciplines point to the need for proper introductions and advanced programmes on entrepreneurship and small business management. These courses could help to develop a range of skills normally omitted from higher education curricula together with suitable content. Institutions, such as Strathclyde University, which have successfully piloted such programmes are now building new programmes catering to full-time interest in the subject.

As stated earlier, a solid body of evidence is also emerging from the newly established Mercia Institute of Enterprise, in which UCE, through the ERDC, is an active member. A recent submission for a range of postgraduate provision has been approved, and it is now incumbent on partner institutions to develop their own initiatives to facilitate participation in these developments.

### The proposed degree

*Scope and purpose.* The degree is designed to provide a sound academic base for the understanding and future practice or support of enterprise creation, enterprise management, entrepreneurial behaviour and entrepreneurial activity in all types of organizations but with a particular emphasis on new business ventures. The course will have three critical dimensions – theoretical and research inputs, inputs on functional areas and an action learning (research-based) business and personal development planning route.

The Masters programme will have a strong research focus, which will highlight the following features:

- Critical resolution of organizational problem setting and solving in the context of new business opportunities, including the development of new products and services, new organizational modes, methods and functions, new market opportunities, and related personal development (based on an an existing business or a new business opportunity);
- study and use of research methods from an early stage of the programme;
- research into critical areas affecting new venture creation – from practice to policy development, and the critical resolution of policy-oriented problems; and
- a research-based business plan for an organization or a traditional dissertation.

Students will be made aware of the key economic, technological, social and cultural factors that affect the processes of new venture creation and development, will consider social entrepreneurship issues and will obtain a portfolio of personal skills through a range of traditional inputs, workshops, presentations by entrepreneurs and research inputs. The course units have been modelled on a business plan with sound academic and theoretical underpinnings drawn from economics, sociology, management, art and design, literature and technology management. The course will be a microcosm of business start-up and entrepreneurial activity and will provide for a community of learning in which individual students are motivated to achieve their full entrepreneurial potential.

*Aims and objectives*. The programme aims to:

- help develop in graduates, mature students and working professionals a thorough understanding of the theory and practice of new venture creation and the entrepreneurship process, their application in various organizational scenarios and the critical resolution of problems relating to such practice; and
- help students to develop a range of relevant skills, competencies and values together with the ability to create, codify, analyse and disseminate knowledge of the subject through a systematic application of learning techniques.

The main course objectives are to:

- help participants to develop critical analytical, problem-solving, creative and learning skills, and a critical awareness of the constituent elements of the study and practice of entrepreneurship;
- help students develop a critical awareness of the economic, social and technological contexts of entrepreneurship, small business development, social enterprise and self-employment;
- equip students with a thorough understanding of the value of entrepreneurship research and appropriate skills in research techniques for effective problem solving, in-depth investigation of key issues, and use of cutting-edge learning materials;
- prepare students for careers in higher education (as teachers and researchers in entrepreneurship),

as entrepreneurs, owner-managers, policy makers in support services, and in entrepreneurial management in different types of organizations;

- help students to manage their own learning and personal development;
- enable students to start developing business and personal plans with a view to starting their own business and/or projects in existing organizations;
- help students to become part of a learning, innovative and entrepreneurial community;
- enable students to be directly involved in 'enterprise laboratories' located at participating small firms over a period of three months.

*Course structure.* Divided into three stages – certificate, diploma and Masters – the programme will be modular in nature with (a) a block-release mode and (b) a full-time mode. Modules will combine the two modes where this is deemed profitable to students.

The block-release mode is aimed at home students, drawn mainly from the graduate student and support service market, from others contemplating a 'career' in self-employment or new business creation, from large firms (either as a result of downsizing or spin-off opportunities) and from academics in other disciplines who may be considering a change in career. The full-time mode is aimed at both home and international students, with possibly the greater share coming from the latter group.

*Rationale for sharing of the modules.* Entrepreneurship is a global phenomenon, and in an increasingly global economic environment, it is imperative that students acquire a broad international perspective to their studies. This is especially the case at the postgraduate level, when students bring to the programme different social and cultural experiences. The use and mix of such experiences through structured and informal means is key to the successful evolution of the programme. The sharing of part-time and full-time modules is therefore of advantage to the full-time students, many of whom will be from outside the UK, in enabling them to have day-to-day contact with practitioners and individuals involved in the local economy; and of advantage to the part-time students, most of whom will be from the local area, in enabling contact with individuals involved in overseas business and with the experience, context and practices that lend an international perspective to their studies.

In addition to improving the learning experience of students through peer association, the sharing of modules also improves the learning experience through flexibility. This flexibility enables more contact between full-time students and entrepreneurs, effective group work, research opportunities, specialization, personal development and innovation development. This dimension of the course will also help develop the 'self-reliance skills' associated with effective time management and employability issues.

Further details of the programme can be obtained from the author.

## Conclusion

This article sets out a holistic approach to entrepreneurship education. It offers a kind of non-prescriptive route map to the development of a specific programme, drawing as it does on a range of managerial and economic theories and evidence of recent practice to demonstrate the value of a fresh approach to entrepreneurship programmes. No definitive answers are necessarily to be found in this essay on new development initiatives. In essence, however, some critical steps should be taken to create new programmes, and these include:

(1) a consideration of underpinning economic, sociological and man-agement theories;
(2) a consideration of influences and practices that inform and mould individual behaviour and orga-nizational change management practice;
(3) a need to develop a clear, but not necessarily simple, mechanism or structure for drawing on a wide range of issues, experiences, the development of cognitive capabil-ity and reflective thinking;
(4) the need to inform the devel-opment through an active pro-gramme of research and related developmental activities;
(5) the need to churn programmes, products and services that reflect entrepreneurial practice;
(6) the need to involve different com-munities of learning as a part of a socially constructed environment for study and engagement with practice; and

(7) the location of the concept of entrepreneurship within different organizational and socio-economic contexts.

In addressing these issues, a revisit to the art gallery is well worth the effort – to contemplate Velasquez once more and learn from the depths of visual art, from ways of seeing people in organizations and organizations in their environment, all as part of an evolving frame of reference. To conceptualize before observation is to lose the opportunity to see entrepreneurship for what it is and what it has to offer – beyond simplistic ideas of the subject as refined and renamed versions of business studies or functional areas such as marketing, finance and human resources. The observation is in the seeing, as in the seeing of pictures. As John Berger (1980) so eloquently suggests:

> Seeing comes before words. . . .
> It is seeing which establishes our place in the surrounding world; we explain that world with words, but words can never undo the fact that we are surrounded by it. The relation between what we see and what we know is never settled.

The relationship between what we learn and what we think we know about entrepreneurship is never perfectly formed.

## References

Aldrich, H. (1999), *Organisations Evolving*, London, Sage.
Berger, J. (1980), *Ways of Seeing*, BBC and Penguin, London.

Birch (1979), 'The job generation process', in *MIT Program on Neighbourhood and Regional Change*, MIT Press, Cambridge, MA.

Christensen C. M. and Overdorf, M. (2000), 'Meeting the challenge of disruptive change', *Harvard Business Review*, Vol 78, No 2, pp 66–77.

Coehlo-Rodriguez, A. (2001), 'Euro Info Centre expands to EU candidate countries', Enterprise Europe, *Enterprise Policy News and Reviews*, Enterprise Directorate General, European Commission, January.

Dodgson, M. and Rothwell, R. (1989), 'Technology strategies in small and medium sized firms', in Dodgson. M., ed, *Technology Strategy and the Firm: Management and Public Policy*, Longman, London.

Easterby-Smith, M., Thorpe, R. and Lowe, A. (2002), *Management Research: An Introduction*, Sage, London.

ENSR (1997), *The European Observatory for SMEs – Fifth Annual Report*, EIM Small Business Research and Consultancy, Zoetermeer.

Gibb, A. (1996), 'Entrepreneurship and small business management: can we afford to neglect them in the twenty-first-century business school?', *British Journal of Management*, Vol 7, pp 309–321.

Gibb, A. (2001), in Mitra, J. and Haynes, P., eds, *The International Entrepreneurship Forum (IEF): Building New Vistas in Enterprise and Innovation*, Enterprise Research and Development Centre, Business School, University of Central England, Birmingham.

Handy, C. (1984), *The Future of Work*, Basil Blackwell, Oxford.

Hills, G. and Morris, M. H. (1998), 'Entrepreneurship education: a conceptual model and review', in Scott, M. G., Rosa, P. and Klandt, H., eds, *Educating Entrepreneurs for Wealth Creation*, Ashgate, Aldershot.

Ivancevich, J. M. (1991), 'A traditional faculty member's perspective on entrepreneurship', *Journal of Business Venturing*, Vol 6, pp 1–7.

Jones (2002), 'Velasquezfe [4] dwarf sitting on the floor (c1645)', in 'Portrait of the Week', No 103, *Guardian*, 13 April.

Lawrence, P. R. and Lorsch, J. W. (1969), *Developing Organisations: Diagnosis and Action*, Addison Wesley, New York.

Matlay, H. and Mitra, J. (2002), 'Entrepreneurship and learning: the double act in the triple helix', *International Journal of Entrepreneurship and Innovation*, Vol 3, No 1, pp 7–16.

Mitra, J. (2000), 'Making connections: innovation and collective learning in small businesses', *Education and Training*, Vol 42, No 4/5, pp 228–236.

Mitra, J. and Haynes, P., eds (2001), *The International Entrepreneurship Forum (IEF): Building New Vistas in Enterprise and Innovation*, Enterprise Research and Development Centre, Business School, University of Central England, Birmingham.

Nadler, D. A. and Tushman, M. L. (1983), 'A general diagnostic model for organisational behaviour: applying a congruence perspective', in Hackman, J. R., Lawler, E. E. and Porter, L. W., eds, *Perspectives on Behaviour in Organizations*, McGraw-Hill, New York, pp 112–128.

Noteboom, B. (2000), *Learning and Innovation in Organisations and Economies*, Oxford University Press, Oxford.

Pinchot, G. III (1985), *Intrapreneuring*, Harper and Row, New York.

Porter, L. W. and McKibbin, L. E. (1988), *Management Education and Development: Drift or Thrust into the 21st Century?*, McGraw-Hill, New York.

Pyke, F., Beccatini, G. and Sengenberger, W., eds (1990), *Industrial Districts and Inter-Firm Cooperation in Italy*, International Labour Organisation, Geneva, p 232.

Ronstadt, R. (1985), 'The educated entrepreneurs: a new era of entrepreneurial education is beginning', *American Journal of Small Business*, Vol 10, No 1, pp 7–23.

Schein, E. (1973), *Professional Education*, McGraw-Hill, New York.

Schon, D. A. (1999), *The Reflective Practitioner: How Professionals Think in Action*, Ashgate, Aldershot.

Stanworth, J. and Gray, C., eds (1991), *Bolton 20 Years On: The Small Firm in the 1990s*, Paul Chapman, London.

Stevenson, H., Roberts, M. J. and Grousebeck, H. (1985), *New Business Ventures and the Entrepreneur*, Richard D. Irwin, Homewood, IL.

Storey, D. (1998), *Understanding the Small Business Sector*, International Thompson Business Press, London.

TACIT (1997), *Enterprise Culture and Its Implications for Higher Education in Britain*, TACIT (Theory and Applications of Continuous Interaction Techniques), London.

Timmons, J.A. and Stevenson, H. (1985), 'Entrepreneurship education in the 1980s: what entrepreneurs say', in Kao, J. and Stevenson, H., eds, *Entrepreneurship: What It Is and How To Teach It*, Harvard Business School, Cambridge, MA, pp 115–134.

# Triple Helix systems

## An analytical framework for innovation policy and practice in the Knowledge Society

**Marina Ranga and Henry Etzkowitz**

**Abstract:** *This paper introduces the concept of Triple Helix systems as an analytical construct that synthesizes the key features of university–industry–government (Triple Helix) interactions into an 'innovation system' format, defined according to systems theory as a set of components, relationships and functions. Among the components of Triple Helix systems, a distinction is made between (a) R&D and non-R&D innovators; (b) 'single-sphere' and 'multi-sphere' (hybrid) institutions; and (c) individual and institutional innovators. The relationships between components are synthesized into five main types: technology transfer; collaboration and conflict moderation; collaborative leadership; substitution; and networking. The overall function of Triple Helix systems – knowledge and innovation generation, diffusion and use – is realized through a set of activities in the knowledge, innovation and consensus spaces. This perspective provides an explicit framework for the systemic interaction between Triple Helix actors that was previously lacking and a more fine-grained view of the circulation of knowledge flows and resources within and among the spaces, helping to identify existing blockages or gaps. From a Triple Helix systems perspective, the articulation and the non-linear interactions between the spaces can generate new combinations of knowledge and resources that can advance innovation theory and practice, especially at the regional level.*

**Keywords:** *Triple Helix systems; knowledge space; innovation space; consensus space; university–industry–government interaction; innovation systems; regional innovation policy*

*Marina Ranga (corresponding author) is with the Human Sciences and Technology Advanced Research Institute (H-STAR), 210 Panama Street, Cordura Hall, Stanford University, Stanford, CA 94305, USA. E-mail: marina. ranga@stanford.edu  Henry Etzkowitz is with the International Institute of Triple Helix, Palo Alto and Beijing (www.triplehelix.net). E-mail: henry.etzkowitz@ triplehelixassociation.org*

Recent decades have seen a shift from innovation sources confined to a single institutional sphere, whether new product development in industry, policy making in government or the creation and dissemination of knowledge in academia, to the interaction among these three institutional spheres as the source of new and innovative organizational designs and social interactions. This shift entails not only various mechanisms of restructuring of the sources and development path of innovation, but also a rethinking of our main models for conceptualizing innovation (for example, national, regional, sectoral, technological innovation systems, the Triple Helix, and so on) that may often fail to capture important innovation dynamics because of issues such as diffuseness and loose definition, methodological or performance measurement gaps.

The concept of the Triple Helix of university–industry–government relationships initiated in the 1990s by Etzkowitz (1993) and Etzkowitz and Leydesdorff (1995), encompassing elements of precursor works by Lowe (1982) and Sabato and Mackenzi (1982), interprets the shift from a dominating industry–government dyad in the Industrial Society to a growing triadic relationship between university, industry and government in the Knowledge Society. The Triple Helix thesis is that the potential for innovation and economic development in a Knowledge Society lies in a more prominent role for the university and in the hybridization of elements from university, industry and government to generate new institutional and social formats for the production, transfer and application of knowledge. This vision encompasses not only the creative destruction that appears as a natural innovation dynamic (Schumpeter, 1942), but also the creative renewal that arises within each of the three institutional spheres – university, industry and government – as well as at their intersections.

Through subsequent development, a significant body of Triple Helix theoretical and empirical research has grown over the last two decades that provides a general framework for exploring complex innovation dynamics and for informing national, regional and international innovation and development policy making.[1,2] This body of research has an implicit systemic dimension that arises primarily from the vision of Triple Helix interactions as manifestations of social systems, but does not provide an explicit analytical framework for conceptualizing Triple Helix interactions into an innovation system.

The novel analytical concept of Triple Helix systems introduced in this paper aims to fill this gap. Triple Helix interactions (heretofore loosely referred to as a 'metaphor' or a 'framework') are synthesized into an 'innovation system' format that encompasses structural and functional concepts of innovation systems theory (Carlsson and Stankiewicz, 1991; Carlsson *et al,* 2002; Carlsson, 2003; Edquist 2005; Bergek *et al,* 2008). Thus, Triple Helix systems are defined as a set of the following.

(1) *Components,* consisting of the institutional spheres of university, industry and government, each with a wide array of actors, among whom a distinction is made between: (a) individual and institutional innovators; (b) R&D and non-R&D innovators; and (c) 'single-sphere' and 'multi-sphere' (hybrid) institutions.
(2) *Relationships between components* (technology transfer, collaboration and conflict moderation, collaborative leadership, substitution, and networking).
(3) *Functions,* in the sense of competencies of the system components that determine the system's performance. The main function of a Triple Helix system is seen in a broader sense, that of generation, diffusion and utilization of knowledge and innovation. This function is realized not only with the techno-economic competencies described in innovation system theory, but also with entrepreneurial, societal, cultural and policy competencies that are embedded in what we call the 'Triple Helix spaces': the knowledge, innovation and consensus spaces.

Triple Helix systems provide a fine-grained view of innovation actors and the relationships between them, in a vision of a dynamic, boundary-spanning and diachronic transition of knowledge flows within the system. Triple Helix systems accommodate both institutional and individual roles in innovation and explain variations in innovative performance in relation to the development of and articulation between the knowledge, innovation and consensus spaces. Transcending sectoral or technology boundaries, Triple Helix systems emphasize boundary permeability among the institutional spheres as an important source of organizational creativity, allowing individuals to move within and between the spheres and engage in recombination of elements to create new types of organizations. Empirical guidelines for policy makers, university and business managers can be derived from this analytical framework, in order to strengthen collaboration among Triple Helix actors and enhance regional development.

The paper is organized as follows. The next section introduces the conceptual framework of Triple Helix systems and summarizes the literature upon which it relies. The subsequent three sections provide a detailed account of the structural elements of Triple Helix systems: components, relationships between components, and functions. The penultimate section describes the formation and functioning of Triple Helix spaces; and the final section provides a summary of the findings, a discussion of the policy relevance of Triple Helix systems for regional innovation policy, especially in developing countries, a set of policy recommendations and directions for further research.

## Triple Helix systems: conceptual framework

A substantial body of the Triple Helix literature has been developed over the last two decades that can be broadly viewed from two complementary perspectives.

First, there is the *(neo-) institutional perspective*, which examines the growing prominence of the university among innovation actors through national and regional case studies (for example, in Latin America: Mello and Rocha, 2004; Etzkowitz, Mello and Almeida, 2005; Saenz, 2008; Bianco and Viscardi, 2008; Luna and Tirtido, 2008; in Africa: Konde, 2004; Kruss, 2008; Booyens, 2011; in the USA: Campbell *et al,* 2004; Feldman and Desrochers, 2004; Boardman 2009; Wang and Shapira, 2012; in Europe: Klofsten *et al,* 1999, 2010; Inzelt, 2004; Geuna and Nesta, 2006; Lawton Smith and Bagchi-Sen, 2010; Geuna and Rossi, 2011; Svensson *et al,* 2012) and through comparative historical analyses (for example, Etzkowitz, 2002; Furman and MacGarvie, 2009). These studies look at various aspects of the university's 'third mission' of research commercialization and involvement in socio-economic development, such as forms, stakeholders, drivers, barriers, benefits and impact, university technology transfer and entrepreneurship, contribution to regional development, government policies aimed to strengthen university–industry links, and so on.

The (neo-) institutional perspective distinguishes between three main configurations in the positioning of the university, industry and government institutional spheres relative to each other (see Figure 1):

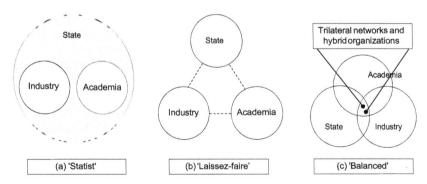

**Figure 1.** Triple Helix configurations.
*Source:* Etzkowitz and Leydesdorff (2000).

(1) A *statist* configuration, in which government plays the lead role, driving academia and industry, but also limiting their capacity to initiate and develop innovative transformations (as, for example, in Russia, China, and some Latin American and Eastern European countries);

(2) A *laissez-faire* configuration, characterized by limited state intervention in the economy (such as in the USA and some Western European countries), with industry as the driving force and the other two spheres acting as ancillary support structures with limited roles in innovation – universities acting mainly as providers of skilled human capital and government mainly as a regulator of social and economic mechanisms; and

(3) A *balanced* configuration, specific to the transition to a Knowledge Society, in which university and other knowledge institutions act in partnership with industry and government and even take the lead in joint initiatives (Etzkowitz and Leydesdorff, 2000).

The balanced configuration offers the most important insights for innovation, because the most favourable environments for innovation are created at the intersections of the spheres. This is where creative synergies emerge and set in motion a process of 'innovation in innovation', create new venues for interaction and new organizational formats, as individual and organisational actors not only perform their own role, but also 'take the role of the other' when the other is weak or under-performing (Etzkowitz, 2003, 2008). Through this creative process, the relationships among the institutional spheres of university, industry and government are continuously reshaped in 'an endless transition' (Etzkowitz and Leydesdorff, 1998), in order to enhance innovation by bringing forth new technologies, new firms and new types of relationships.

The second of the two perspectives is the *(neo-) evolutionary perspective,* inspired by the theory of social systems of communication (Luhmann, 1975, 1984) and the mathematical theory of communication (Shannon, 1948). From this perspective, university, industry and government are co-evolving sub-sets of social systems that interact through an overlay of recursive networks and organizations that reshape their institutional arrangements through reflexive sub-dynamics, such as markets and technological innovations (see, for example, Leydesdorff, 1996, 1997, 2000, 2006, 2008; Leydesdorff and Meyer, 2006; Dolfsma and Leydesdorff, 2009). These interactions are part of two processes of communication and differentiation: a *functional* one, between science and markets, and an *institutional* one, between private and public control at the level of universities, industries and government, which allow various degrees of selective mutual adjustment (Leydesdorff and Etzkowitz, 1996, 1998). In addition, *internal differentiation* within each institutional sphere generates new types of links and structures between the spheres, such as industrial liaison offices in universities or strategic alliances among companies, creating new network integration mechanisms

(Leydesdorff and Etzkowitz, 1998). The institutional spheres are also seen as *selection environments*, and the institutional communications between them act as *selection mechanisms*, which may generate new innovation environments and thus ensure the 'regeneration' of the system (Etzkowitz and Leydesdorff, 2000; Leydesdorff, 2000). The interactions between the Triple Helix actors can be measured in terms of probabilistic entropy, which, when negative, suggests a self-organizing dynamic that may be temporarily stabilized in the overlay of communications among the carrying agencies (see, for example, Leydesdorff, 2003; Leydesdorff *et al,* 2006). The interaction is also captured by specific indicators (such as bibliometrics, patent indicators) that can provide insights into trends and patterns of public–private cooperation, its geographical concentrations and implications (for example, Kwon *et al,* 2012; Tijssen 2006, 2012; Azagra-Caro *et al,* 2010; Leydesdorff and Meyer, 2010).

Both these perspectives have an implicit, underlying systemic dimension of Triple Helix interactions originating from their vision of such interactions as manifestations of social systems characterized by action (Parsons, 1951; Parsons and Shils, 1951; Parsons and Smelser, 1956) and communication (Luhmann, 1975, 1984; Shannon, 1948). However, neither provides an explicit analytical framework for conceptualizing Triple Helix interactions as innovation systems. To fill this gap, we introduce the concept of Triple Helix systems as an analytical construct defined from the perspective of innovation systems

theory, discussed briefly below and highlighting some relevant elements for our study.

The 'innovation systems' concept was introduced in the late 1980s to examine the influence of knowledge and innovation on economic growth in evolutionary systems, in which institutions and learning processes are of central importance (Freeman, 1987; Freeman and Lundvall, 1988). The systems perspective was used to understand better how institutional arrangements could facilitate interactions among economic actors in market as well as non-market transfer of knowledge (Carlsson, 2003). The concept was refined as 'national innovation systems' (NIS), which includes a set of innovation actors (firms, universities, research institutes, financial institutions, government regulatory bodies, and so on), their activities and their inter-linkages at the aggregate level (Freeman, 1988; Dosi *et al*, 1988; Lundvall, 1988, 1992; Nelson, 1993; Edquist, 1997, 2005). The 'national' dimension of innovation systems favoured user–producer interactions through cultural and institutional proximity and localized learning (Lundvall, 1992).[3] Nevertheless, it became increasingly blurred as a result of business and technology internationalization extending technological capabilities beyond national borders, and the growing integration of innovation systems, driven by economic and political processes, such as European Union consolidation.

Because the NIS approach did not fully capture the interactions between innovation actors, more disaggregated levels of the innovation system were introduced, such as the following.

- *Regional Innovation Systems* (for example, Cooke, 1996; Maskell and Malmberg, 1997) emerged in the context of the increasing regionalisation of the early 1990s at technological, economic, political or cultural levels in many countries. The concept has a broad definition: it encompasses, for instance, a set of regional actors aiming to reinforce regional innovation capability and competitiveness through technological learning (Doloreux and Parto, 2005), regional 'technology coalitions' arising from geographical distribution of economic and technological effects over time (Storper, 1995), or dynamic, self-organizing business environments (Johannson *et al*, 2005), and so on.
- *Sectoral Innovation Systems* (Breschi and Malerba, 1997; Malerba, 2002) examine industry structure as a determinant the performance heterogeneity of a firm and explore coordination forms in supply chains (hierarchy, market and hybrid forms)
- *Technological Innovation Systems* (Carlsson and Stankiewicz, 1991; Carlsson, 1997; Bergek *et al*, 2007)

focus on the network of agents that interact in functions of a specific technology or set of technologies.

All these system frameworks are characterized by three elements (Carlsson and Stankiewicz, 1991; Carlsson, 1998, 2003; Carlsson *et al*, 2002; Hekkert *et al*, 2008), as follows.

(1) *Components (and boundaries) of the system.* The components include various actors that normally interact in the process of innovation (individuals and firms, higher education and research institutions, government agencies, financial and trade associations and other units making up the institutional infrastructure). The boundaries between components can be defined by geography or administrative units, as in the case of spatially bounded systems (regional, national innovation systems), or by economic sectors or technologies, as is the case with spatially open systems (such as technology innovation systems or sectoral innovation systems).

(2) *Relationships among system components*, which include new

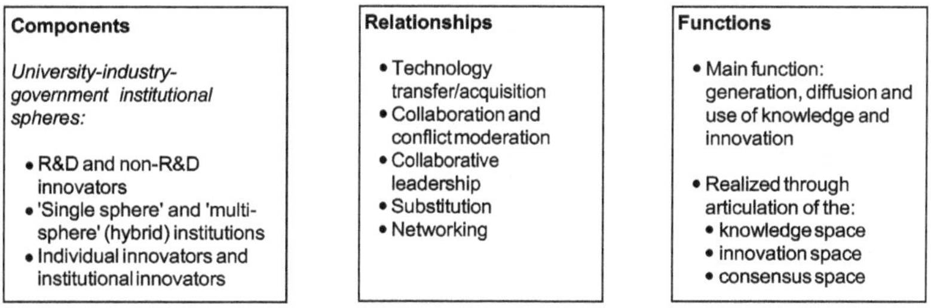

| Components | Relationships | Functions |
|---|---|---|
| *University-industry-government institutional spheres:* <br><br> • R&D and non-R&D innovators <br> • 'Single sphere' and 'multi-sphere' (hybrid) institutions <br> • Individual innovators and institutional innovators | • Technology transfer/acquisition <br> • Collaboration and conflict moderation <br> • Collaborative leadership <br> • Substitution <br> • Networking | • Main function: generation, diffusion and use of knowledge and innovation <br><br> • Realized through articulation of the: <br> • knowledge space <br> • innovation space <br> • consensus space |

**Figure 2.** A synthetic representation of Triple Helix systems.

knowledge combinations generated by the innovation actors, either through own efforts or by using technology transfer from other actors, provided they have sufficient absorptive capacity. Internal R&D capacity of the actors is essential in this process, but non-R&D (non-market) interactions are also important.

(3) *Functions of the system*, in the sense of competencies of the components that determine the system's performance. The main function of an innovation system is defined as the generation, diffusion and utilization of technology, while the competencies necessary to achieve this function are described in terms of four types of capabilities: (a) selective (strategic) capability; (b) organizational (integrative or coordinating) ability; (c) technical or functional ability; and (d) learning (adaptive) ability.[4]

Building on this structural characterization of innovation systems, combined with a structure/process approach of innovation systems (Bergek *et al,* 2008) that relates the structure of the system with the processes (dynamics and achievements) in which the system is involved, we define a Triple Helix system (Figure 2) as a set of the following.

(1) *Components (and boundaries):* the components are represented by the institutional spheres of university, industry and government, each with its own institutional and individual actors. Among these actors, a distinction is made between:

(a) individual and institutional innovators; (b) R&D and non-R&D innovators; and (c) 'single-sphere' and 'multi-sphere' (hybrid) institutions. The boundaries identified in other innovation systems take on a new meaning in Triple Helix systems because they are no longer separating elements between the university, industry and government spheres, but unifying ones. Geographical, sectoral and technology boundaries are superseded in Triple Helix systems by the boundary permeability among the university, industry and government spheres. This allows a better circulation of people, ideas, knowledge and capital within and across the institutional spheres, stimulates organizational creativity as well as the combination of regional and local resources for realizing joint objectives and new institutional formats.

(2) *Relationships among system components:* the market and non-market relationships between system components, emphasized in the innovation systems theory and manifested primarily through technology transfer or acquisition, are also important in Triple Helix systems. In addition, we include here other relationships derived from the triadic nature of the interaction, such as: collaboration and conflict moderation, collaborative leadership and substitution. Networking, which is not a manifestation specific to triadic systems, but rather of the increasingly collective nature of science, technology and innovation, is also relevant here and is included among the relationships. These relationships

are important because they reflect change-inducing, evolutionary social and economic mechanisms at work in Triple Helix interactions.

(3) *Functions of the system:* if innovation systems theory defines the main function of an innovation system as the generation, diffusion and utilization of technology (for example, Carlsson *et al*, 2002, p 235), we see the main function of a Triple Helix system in a broader sense, as that of generating, diffusing and utilizing knowledge and innovation. This goes beyond technology and involves a broader set of competencies that extend beyond the four types of competencies described by the innovation systems theory (selective, organizational, technical and learning abilities), to incorporate in addition entrepreneurial, societal, cultural and policy aspects. These competencies are manifested in what we call the 'Triple Helix Spaces': the Knowledge, Innovation and Consensus Spaces, which encompass these cumulated competencies and bring them to a next level as a result of multiple combinations that allow new opportunities for innovation.

## Components of Triple Helix systems

Much of the Triple Helix literature focuses on the institutional spheres of university, industry and government as holistic, 'block' entities, without going deeper to the level of sphere-specific actors. This obscures some specific institutional identities, missions, objectives and needs, and

the way they influence the interaction dynamics. On the one hand, this simplified perspective can sometimes be beneficial, especially in contexts where one or more of the spheres are still in the early development phases and the culture of collaboration is weak, as it may increase the applicability and suitability of the Triple Helix model to local policy and practice. The simplicity of the model is appealing to policy makers and may help mobilize local innovation agents, bring legitimacy to policy efforts and improve coherence between different policy strands involved in innovation (Rodrigues and Melo, 2010). On the other hand, in more advanced contexts, where innovation stakeholders are more mature and have attained more complex forms of interaction, that simplified perspective is no longer sufficient. A more differentiated approach to the Triple Helix actors is necessary to understand their behaviour and specific contributions to a complex division of labour in the production and use of knowledge for innovation. To substantiate this differentiated approach, we make three important distinctions between:

• Individual and institutional innovators;
• R&D and non-R&D innovators; and
• 'Single-sphere' and 'multi-sphere' (hybrid) institutions.

### *Individual and institutional innovators*

Innovation systems focus predominantly on institutions

(especially firms), which are seen as key explanatory factors in understanding why some innovation processes in certain regions, countries or sectors fare better than others (Edquist, 1997, 2005).

However, various definitions of 'institutions' in studies may be confusing about what institutions are, what role they play and what the mechanisms are through which they work (Carlsson, 2003). In addition, this strong reliance on institutions gives low visibility to the individual innovator.

Triple Helix systems acknowledge the importance of individual innovators (scientists, businesspeople, policy makers, students, entrepreneurs, venture capitalists, business angels, and so on) and their role in initiating and consolidating institutional processes. Individual roles in innovation are accommodated through concepts such as the 'innovation organizer' and the 'entrepreneurial scientist' that provide a phenomenology of behavioural types (Schutz, 1964) and highlight ways in which individual and institutional innovation initiate and reinforce each other.

- The *innovation organizer* is defined as a person who typically occupies a key institutional position, enunciates a vision for knowledge-based development and has sufficient respect and authority to exercise convening power to bring the leadership of the institutional spheres together (see examples in Box 1). Innovation organizers can come from any institutional sphere. They coordinate a mix of top-down and bottom-up processes and innovation

stakeholders from different organizational backgrounds and perspectives, who come together to build a platform for new ideas, promote economic and social development and ensure agreement and support for their realization. A process of 'cross-institutional entrepreneurship' spanning the Triple Helix spheres is thus initiated for improving the conditions for knowledge-based development.

- The *entrepreneurial scientist* concept combines academic and business elements. The entrepreneurial scientist simultaneously attends to advancing the frontiers of knowledge and mining its practical and commercial results for industrial and financial returns. The underlying foundation of this development is the polyvalent nature of knowledge, which is at the same time theoretical and practical, publishable and patentable. Different academic entrepreneurial styles and degrees of involvement can be distinguished, including: (a) a direct interest in the formation of a spin-off firm and in taking a leading role in this process; (b) handing over these results to a technology transfer office for disposition; (c) playing a supporting role, typically as member of a Scientific Advisory Board; and (d) having no interest in entrepreneurship, but rather in firm formation as a useful source for developing technology needed to advance basic research goals. Communities of complementary entrepreneurial individuals are particularly visible in high-tech entrepreneurship, which is nearly always a collective phenomenon.

A new high-tech firm typically takes off with the support of individuals with technical and business expertise backed by an experienced entrepreneur, constituting together the 'collective entrepreneur', because only rarely does a single individual embody all of these required elements. However, national cultural differences are important in this respect. In the USA, there is a strong ideology of individual entrepreneurship that usually suppresses the contributions of collaborators and pushes a single individual to the forefront (Freiberger and Swaine, 2000).[6] In contrast, in the Nordic countries – for example Finland – work is extremely collectively focused and it is unusual for the role of an individual in a workplace to be over-emphasized. In Sweden, individuals are culturally inhibited from attempting an entrepreneurial act unless backed up by a group, so that collective entrepreneurship is rather the norm.

---

**Box 1.   Innovation organizers.**

In 1930s New England, MIT's President Compton was the innovation organizer who played a key role in getting support for a new model of knowledge-based economic development that relied heavily on university-originated technologies and that included the invention of the venture capital firm (Etzkowitz, 2002). In mid-1990s New York, the head of the New York Federal Reserve Bank took the lead in calling for high-tech development to be seen as the engine of New York's economy, as an alternative to finance. Later, in 2011, New York's Mayor Bloomberg took on the innovation organizer role with an initiative to attract to the city leading technological universities, like Cornell, to fill the gap in the region's innovation environment (Saul *et al,* 2011).

A relevant example in Europe is the general manager of Belgium's Catholic University of Leuven (K. U. Leuven), Koenraad Debackere, who has had a central role in organizing and promoting technology transfer and entrepreneurship at the university and in the region. He brought together ideas, people and resources from all the Triple Helix strands – the university, local government and the business community – as a K. U. Leuven professor, managing director of the university's technology transfer office, chairman of the university's venture fund, co-founder and chairman of Leuven Inc, the innovation network of Leuven high-tech entrepreneurs, as well as a board member of IWT-Vlaanderen, the Flemish government agency that supports science and technology development in Flemish industry.

The innovation organizer role can also be extended from an individual to an institution, or indeed a consortium of institutions, as in the case of Birmingham University's consortium of Triple Helix actors who projected the post-Rover, post-automotive future of the UK's West Midlands region. The consortium envisaged the development of the region as a future technology corridor including a biomedical complex based on area research, steered by boundary-spanning collaborative leadership that was capable of transcending entrenched local interests (Gibney, Copeland and Murie, 2009).

*R&D and non-R&D innovators*

This distinction is based on whether or not there is in-house (intramural) R&D. It emerges from the recognition that R&D is not the only driver of innovation. Other factors can also drive organizational innovative capacity, such as firm/business unit size and industry effects (Cohen *et al,* 1987), intangible resources (Galende and Suarez, 1999), internal factors (Galende and de la Fuente, 2003), informal processes of learning and experience-based know-how (Jensen *et al,* 2007), technology adoption, incremental changes, imitation and new combinations of existing knowledge (Arundel *et al,* 2008). In low- and medium-high-technology industries which are characterized by weak internal innovation capabilities, there are strong dependencies on the external provision of machines, equipment, software and suppliers, as well as on process, organizational and marketing innovations (Heidenreich, 2009).

- *R&D innovators* can be found in each of the university, industry and government institutional spheres and, beyond that, in the non-profit sector (for example, charities, foundations, professional/trade associations, service organizations, non-profit corporations and trusts). In universities, key R&D performers are academic research groups and interdisciplinary research centres; in the business sector, company R&D divisions or departments; in the government sector, public research organizations, mission-oriented research laboratories, and so on. One can also mention here a functional equivalent of R&D activities in arts and design fields, or more broadly in the creative industries, which generates artistic and cultural activities in a similar fashion to scientific R&D but with their own distinct discovery, methodologies, validation and dissemination procedures.[7]

- *Non-R&D innovators* are most often associated with company units involved in non-R&D activities, such as design, production, marketing, sales, acquisition of technology or machinery produced elsewhere, customization or modification of products and processes obtained from elsewhere, personnel training and competence building, interaction with users, acquisition of patents and licences, consultancy services and so on. On a broader scale, non-R&D innovation is also present in technology transfer, incubation activities, financing, negotiation, creation and change of organizations and so on. These activities are not confined to industry borders and can also be found in various forms in government and academia as well as in the non-profit sector.

*'Single-sphere' and 'multi-sphere' (hybrid) institutions*

This distinction arises from the transition from the Industrial to the Knowledge Society which is characterized by increasing knowledge-intensive activities, communication and interconnectivity between people and institutions, mobility of people and financial capital, delocalization and globalization of production sites, labour and social relationships and so on.

Elements such as generation and internalization of new skills and abilities required for integration into dynamic work environments, uneven development of scientific and technological (including organizational) knowledge across different sectors of activity, approach to intellectual property rights and the privatisation of knowledge, as well as the approach of trust, memory and the fragmentation of knowledge (David and Foray, 2003) make an important difference between the single- and multi-sphere (hybrid) institutions.

- *Single-sphere institutions*, delineated within the boundaries of a single institutional sphere, whether university or industry or government, are characterized by rigid institutional boundaries, low levels of interaction with another institutional sphere, a high degree of specialization and work centralization, limited mobility of workers and so on. Their functioning is specific to the *laissez-faire* configuration described in Figure 1.
- *Multi-sphere (hybrid) institutions* operate at the intersection of the university, industry and government institutional spheres and synthesize elements of each sphere in their institutional design. They are representative of the *balanced* Triple Helix configuration

described in Figure 1. Technology transfer offices in universities and government research laboratories, industrial liaison offices, business support institutions (science parks, business and technology incubators, start-up accelerators), financial support institutions (public and private venture capital firms, angel networks, seed capital funds and so on) can be included in this category. They have smaller-scale hierarchies, with fewer layers and less centralized decision making, in order to increase flexibility and responsiveness to changing market demands. In addition, institutional boundaries are more permeable (Etzkowitz, 2012) because the single institutional spheres of university, industry and government become more laterally diversified and increase collaboration in order to improve work effectiveness. Subsequently, boundaries between the job categories involved in these hybrid structures become looser and jobs require greater sharing of tasks and knowledge.

## Relationships among components of Triple Helix systems

### Technology transfer

Technology transfer via markets or non-market interactions is recognized as the core activity in an innovation system (Carlsson *et al*, 2002, p 234). It is also important in Triple Helix systems because universities increasingly generate and transfer technology, especially in areas such as biotechnology, nanotechnology, ICT or medical technologies (for example, Cooke, 2004; Meyer, 2006; Van Looy *et al*, 2007; Wong, 2007; Lawton Smith and Bagchi-Sen, 2010). Due to their greater capacity to generate and transfer technology, universities are no longer just a traditional source of human resources and knowledge, but are also key innovation stakeholders, with ever-increasing internal organizational mechanisms and resources allocated to this purpose rather than placing reliance solely on informal ties. Technology transfer offices, science parks, business incubators, start-up accelerators and venture capital capacities have been created as intermediary elements within university administrative structures in order to facilitate the capitalization of knowledge and ensure the interface with the external world.

Greater university involvement in technology transfer has also brought about greater university involvement in the protection of intellectual property in order to manage ethically the uses of university inventions in the public interest that also had significant implications for regional economic development and self-generation of resources for university development – see Baldini (2006) for a review of literature on university patenting and licensing. The harmonization of the individual inventor and the university's interests regarding the development of an invention and the allocation of financial rewards became a key issue that took different forms in different countries – for example, the professors' privilege in Scandinavian countries (see, for example, Iversen *et al,* 2007; Mets, 2010).

The involvement of universities in technology transfer has also increased their capacity to provide graduates with entrepreneurial education and talent, who can contribute to economic growth through firm formation and job creation. Various forms of entrepreneurship education are now being delivered in universities around the world in order to develop entrepreneurial skills, theoretical and practical experience in developing a business, to stimulate new ways of learning and to achieve an entrepreneurial mindset as an additional asset in approaching careers. Academic entrepreneurship also has benefits for faculty, who can secure more research funding for academic projects and ensure the stability of their research laboratories and continuous engagement of the students employed by the laboratory, develop a greater responsiveness to the needs of local business and entrepreneurs and have the possibility of testing their expertise outside the university boundaries, often making an impact on the regional and national economy. Important gains have also been noted at the community level, where economic benefits such as job creation and tax revenues from university start-ups are combined with social and cultural benefits such as positive social perception of entrepreneurs, stronger bonds between the university and the community and increased attractiveness of the university and the region to national and international talent and investors. Gaining the status of 'university city' is very important for many cities around the world and offers them the possibility of access to highly skilled employees, high-growth entrepreneurs and venture capital investment, often leading to the transformation of the region into a world-class entrepreneurial ecosystem (Ranga *et al*, 2013). Universities are also extending their capabilities from educating individuals to educating organizations, through entrepreneurship and incubation programmes and new training modules (Almeida *et al*, 2012).

*Collaboration and conflict moderation*

Collaboration and conflict moderation is a specific form of interaction in triadic entities, which have a higher potential for turning tension and conflict of interest into convergence and confluence of interest, compared to dyadic relationships, which are more subject to collapse into oppositional modes (Simmel, [1922] 1955). This capacity to transform tension and conflict of interest into converging interests relating to common objectives and 'win-win' situations is all the more important given that the very nature of conflicts and tensions is changing in the Knowledge Society, in line with the changing nature of work, the workplace and organizations (Heerwagen *et al*, 2010). Useful analytical tools for exploring conflict moderation in Triple Helix systems can be taken from the organizational innovation and cross-functional collaboration literature (see De Clercq *et al*, 2009, for a detailed review), which identifies two key conflict dimensions: (a) *task conflict (functional, cognitive or constructive conflict),* which is content driven and

is generated by differences of opinions of an organization's functional departments about particular tasks (Amason and Sapienza, 1997); and (b) *relationship conflict (dysfunctional, affective or destructive conflict),* which is person driven and is generated by incompatibilities or clashes between different personalities in different departments, leading to negative feelings such as tension and frustration (Jehn and Mannix, 2001; Finkelstein and Mooney, 2003).

Task conflict has been shown to play a positive role in innovation by leading to a reconsideration of dominant perspectives and beliefs in an organization and stimulation of original and divergent viewpoints (Van Dyne and Saavedra, 1996), while relationship conflict has a negative effect on the high-quality knowledge exchanges and decision making (Jehn, 1995; Amason, 1996; Jehn and Mannix, 2001; Pelled *et al*, 1999).

In Triple Helix systems, task conflicts can sometimes arise within the university sphere, where 'third mission' activities clash with long-established academic norms, procedures and reward systems. Many academics fear a loss of their research freedom or a weaker academic performance caused by the entrepreneurial engagement. Relationship conflict is sometimes found at the university–business interface because of cultural differences and diverging interests between firms and universities that may impede knowledge exchange and bring challenges on collaborative projects if not properly addressed. Potential sources of conflict can also be found both at the micro level of interacting individuals and at the meso level of institutional frameworks, rules and regulations (or lack thereof) that can create obstacles for the collaboration (for example, a weak culture of collaboration and organizational silos, a lack of incentives for the entrepreneurial behaviour of academics, the obligation in some universities for faculty to take a leave of absence to develop a spin-off, bias in the reporting of results, scarcity of data to evaluate technology transfer activities and so on).

Conflict resolution implies not only addressing institutional gaps and diverging institutional logics, better monitoring of university–industry relationships and the dissemination of best entrepreneurial practices, but also using social skills and dialogue to manage expectations, addressing individual fears and creating shared cultural spaces for knowledge exchange (Campbell *et al,* 2004; Mets *et al,* 2008; Goldstein, 2010; Bjerregaard, 2010). These conflict-moderating measures can be initiated and developed from both the university and industry sides, while the government helix can exert an additional moderating effect by promoting supportive policies and programmes (see, for example, Brazil's 2004 Innovation Law, which establishes the legal framework for public–private partnerships and provides incentives for building and strengthening collaboration between universities, research institutes and private companies; incentives to encourage the participation of universities and research institutes in the innovation process; and

incentives for promoting innovation within private companies).[8]

*Collaborative leadership*

Collaborative leadership is an integral part of the collaboration and conflict-moderation capacity. 'Innovation organizers' as individual or institutional leaders play a key role in this type of relationship. They can connect people from different sectors to bridge gaps, bring together differing views, generate consensus and balance conflicts of interest. They can integrate skills and enable people to develop their own competence according to specific challenges, foster change in thinking and practical implementation through vision and reflection and create new opportunities for knowledge exchange (for example, Chrislip, 2002; Archer and Cameron, 2009). They can develop clear project charters, conduct joint problem-solving tasks and ensure a high level of project satisfaction by the individual members of the partnership (Ruuska and Teigland, 2009).

*Substitution*

This type of interaction arises when institutional spheres fill gaps that emerge when another sphere is weak. Substitution between spheres is exemplified by government agencies taking up, in addition to their traditional function of regulation and control, that of investment and provision of public venture capital – a traditional task for the industry sphere (see, for example, Huggins, 2008; Gebhardt, 2012). Similarly, universities, in addition to their teaching and research activities, often engage in technology transfer and firm formation, providing support and even funding to encourage entrepreneurial ventures, thus enacting some of the traditional role of industry. Industry can also take the role of the university in developing proprietary education and training solutions, often at the same high level as universities (see, for example, Pixar University, Intel Educator Academy, Cisco Networking Academy, Apple University).[9,10,11,12] Substitution between spheres can also be observed at a higher level, in countries with no or weak regional governments, where there may not be a governmental actor available to take the lead in promoting innovation developments, but other actors – such as universities, firms or regional development agencies – may come forward to set a future achievable objective (playing an Innovation Organizer role, as described above). *Substitution within spheres* is also possible, especially in ecosystems with small, low-tech firms with little or no R&D potential that find collaboration with vocational training institutions more attractive and suited to their needs than collaboration with the university (Ranga *et al*, 2008).

### Networking

Networking in formal and informal structures at national, regional and international level is not a phenomenon unique to Triple Helix interactions, but is widely found in this case too, as a manifestation of the collective nature of science, technology and innovation. The aggregation may be stronger or weaker, depending on the network's age, scope, membership,

activities and visibility in the public domain (the Association of University Technology Managers [AUTM], the European Technology Platforms and the Joint Technology Initiatives are just three examples).[13] Networks have been described over the last decades under diverse labels, such as 'techno-economic networks' (Callon, 1992) and 'networks of innovators' (Cusumano and Elenkov, 1994; DeBresson and Amesse, 1991; Freeman, 1991) and have emerged as an organizational form better suited to the limitations of hierarchies and markets – 'neither market nor hierarchy' (for example, Powell, 1990). More flexible than hierarchies, more invested in the public good than markets and more effective in responding to changing conditions than either hierarchies or markets, networks have been seen as 'the middle way' between the loose coupling of markets and the tight relationships of hierarchies.

Research networks in academia have been compared to a 'joint venture', whose stability appears to be of critical importance socially, politically and economically, in order to generate a particular division of labour among the participants (David *et al,* 1999). Networking reflects the growing non-linearity and interactivity of innovation processes (Kaufmann and Tödtling, 2001) and provides several benefits (Steinmueller, 1994).[14]

## Functions of Triple Helix systems

The main function of Triple Helix systems to generate, diffuse and utilize knowledge and innovation goes beyond the technology function and four types of competencies (selective, organizational, technical and learning) described in the innovation systems theory. It incorporates a broader set of knowledge, learning, entrepreneurial, societal, cultural and policy competencies that are achieved in what we label the 'Triple Helix spaces': the knowledge, innovation and consensus spaces.

## The knowledge space

The knowledge space encompasses the competencies of knowledge generation, diffusion and use of the Triple Helix components. The construction of this space is an essential step in the transition to a Knowledge Society and has the purpose of creating and developing knowledge resources in order to strengthen the local, regional and national knowledge base, to avoid fragmentation and to reduce the duplication of research efforts. To this end, knowledge resources can be aggregated locally within a region, nationally or internationally across regions (for example, the European Commission's initiatives to consolidate the European Research Area) through a wide range of mechanisms, from dispersal or relocation of existing resources, to creation of new ones through institution formation, to physical and virtual networking. All these mechanisms also have social, cultural and policy dimensions, as exemplified in Box 2.

## The innovation space

The innovation space consists in particular of the competencies of the 'multi-sphere' (hybrid) organizations and entrepreneurial individuals and institutions discussed earlier. Its ultimate purpose is the development of local innovative firms, in parallel with the attraction of talent and innovative firms from elsewhere, the creation and development of intellectual and entrepreneurial potential, and competitive advantage for the region and the country. These joint institutional and individual innovation efforts that come together in a form of 'public' entrepreneurship go well beyond formation of firms and provide the energy and focus for a variety of institution-formation projects (Schumpeter, 1951; Etzkowitz and Schaflander, 1969). The new institutional formats that thus emerge depend on the strengths and weaknesses of the actors involved, their motivations, aptitudes, location, entrepreneurial capacities, institutional support for new firm formation and level of local economic and technological performance (Mason and Harrison, 1992; Thwaites and Wynarczyk, 1996; Lee and Peterson, 2000). The new institutional formats need to be integrated into a broader, national or region-wide innovative and entrepreneurial environment that provides a broader range of services and support structures (for example, to market intellectual property, create spin-off firms, identify market opportunities and partners) and partner with local city and regional governments to secure resources in order to achieve their objectives.

The creation of an innovation space can take place through various mechanisms, including, for example, the creation of a university in regions without higher education capacity, building an integrated environment for university technology transfer and entrepreneurship or relocation of artists to declining urban districts to stimulate arts-/technology-based economic renewal. As in the case of the knowledge space, all these mechanisms go beyond the single function of technology generation, diffusion and use and encompass entrepreneurial, social, cultural and policy competences, as exemplified in Box 3.

*The consensus space*

The consensus space is the set of competences that bring together the Triple Helix system components to engage in 'blue-sky' thinking, discuss and evaluate proposals for advancement towards a knowledge-based regime. Even when the initiative comes from a particular strand of the Triple Helix, it needs to draw actors from other spheres into a collaborative process, where the collaborative leadership and conflict moderation relationships between system components are most prominent. Through cross-fertilizing diverse perspectives, ideas may be generated and results may be achieved that actors are not likely to have accomplished individually. The consensus space reflects various aspects of the governance concept, in a broader sense, including government and non-government actors who interact continuously to exchange resources and negotiate shared purposes. Although government does not occupy a privileged position, it can participate and take an initiating role, like others. That contributes to shifting the state boundaries towards more transparent delineations between public, private and voluntary sectors:

---

**Box 2. Mechanisms for the creation of a knowledge space.**

1. *Dispersal of some national public research resources from more research-intensive regions to less research-intensive ones.* Some government research labs were moved from Mexico City to other regions of Mexico after the mid-1980s earthquake, with a double rationale: to protect them from a new earthquake and to provide research capacity to regions where it had hitherto been lacking and so address the problems of the locality. This policy was eventually broadened to an explicit knowledge-based regional development strategy, with more research institutes being transferred from the capital to other regions to strengthen their knowledge base (Casas *et al,* 2000).

2. *Relocation and aggregation of existing research resources.* The North Carolina state used its political clout to induce the relocation of federal government labs from outside the state to North Carolina's Research Triangle Park, where they were used as an attractor of corporate labs, within what became an initial framework for high-tech development strategy (Hamilton, 1966).

*(Continued)*

3. *Attraction of leading researchers through the foundation of a science-based university.* The San Diego branch of the University of California, gestated in the 1950s, became the basis for a leading high-tech complex and contributed to the transformation of San Diego from a naval base and military retirement community to a knowledge-based conurbation. The coalition of academic, business and political leaders that called for the founding of this campus recognized the attraction of leading researchers in fields with commercial potential, like molecular biology, as an economic development strategy. The strategy of the San Diego campus was replicated by the Merced campus, recently established as an 'entrepreneurial university' to promote high-tech development in an agricultural region and create location-specific knowledge assets to induce new investment and create new value.

4. *Creation of new university resources to support the development of new industries or raise existing ones to a higher level.* The State University of Rio de Janeiro in Friburgo created a new campus providing an IT-oriented PhD programme to supply knowledge inputs to a neighbouring declining industrial region, rather than simply training support personnel for existing firms as might have happened on an undergraduate campus. In Norkopping, Sweden, in the wake of deindustrialization, a Council representing the city region's business and political leadership was established. It decided to create a university campus with advanced academic research groups to revive the paper industry, one of the local traditional industries (Svensson *et al,* 2011). The New York Inter-University Seminar on Innovation, bringing together innovation scholars and practitioners across the metropolitan region in the mid-1990s, through Triple Helix leadership, hypothesized the lack of an MIT-like academic institution as the missing link to catalyse the city's strong academic research base for economic development. This analysis eventually percolated to the city's leadership. Mayor Bloomberg's recent competition to fill the gap resulted in the creation of the Cornell-Technion Technology Graduate School and the upgrading of NYU and Columbia innovation initiatives. Amsterdam's mayor, working with the Amsterdam Economic Board, is currently engaged in organizing a similar initiative (according to Rik Bleeker, Amsterdam Economic Board, interview with the 2nd author, 17 May 2013).

5. *Virtual congregation of geographically dispersed groups from university and industry around common research themes, with government support.* The Canadian Networks of Centres of Excellence (NCE) brought together widely dispersed academic and firm research units, motivated to work together by large government sponsorship, typically dividing up the funds to extend existing local projects, with a suitable overlay of collaborative rhetoric. The interaction and discussion necessary to prepare a proposal generated new research ideas and genuine intellectual collaborations spanning geographical and organizational boundaries.

6. *Networking of existing knowledge-based organisations and creation of new ones through collaboration among existing players, in order to become internationally competitive.* The Stockholm School of Entrepreneurship was created as a joint initiative of Stockholm University, Royal Institute of Technology (KTH) and more recently included the Royal Art College.

The Oresund project, linking southern Sweden (Skane) and Copenhagen, included the creation of Oresund University, which encourages collaboration between universities on both sides of the strait that previously divided this cross-border region. The Karolinska Institute initiated a university-building strategy of incorporating several small schools in the biological sciences, nursing and other loosely related fields scattered across Sweden and even across the Norwegian border, in order to create a greater 'critical mass' of research, training and commercialization activities.

---

**Box 3.   Mechanisms for the creation of an innovation space.**

1. *Creation of a university in a region without higher education capacity, as a means of raising the technological level of existing clusters or as a source of new ones.* MIT is the classic instance of a university founded to raise the technological level of existing clusters. It was founded in 1862 to support the Boston textile, leather and mechanical industries by infusing them with new ideas from science-based technology. Limited resources at the time precluded much effort in this direction apart from providing industry with trained engineers. By the time MIT had developed research capabilities in the early 20th century, the industries it was intended to support had largely moved from the region to be close to raw materials, lines of distribution and access to inexpensive labour. In this context, MIT moved to the next stage of regional development, from supporting existing industries to contributing to the creation of new industries through firm formation from its research programmes and by playing a collaborative role with business and government in creating a venture capital industry to support new firm formation and growth (Etzkowitz, 2002). In the 1950s, the regional leadership of San Diego deployed this explicit model of a science-based entrepreneurial university as a strategy for the creation of a new science-based industry in a region that was heretofore known as a naval base and retirement community. A new campus of the University of California was created as part of a long-term strategy to foster industrial development and recruited leading scientists in areas with both theoretical and practical potential, such as biotechnology. A few decades later, by assiduously pursuing the strategy of developing a critical mass of research groups and institutes in biotechnology-related fields, the foundations were laid for significant firms to emerge from this base. San Diego has since grown to be one of the three major centres of industrial biotechnology in the USA, along with Boston and Northern California. Indeed, the regional biotechnology industry is larger than the entire UK industry in this field (Caspar, 2007).

2. *Building an integrated environment for university technology transfer and entrepreneurship.* Over the last two decades, the Flemish Catholic University of Leuven (K. U. Leuven) and its technology transfer office Leuven

(*Continued*)

R&D have become the core of a thriving regional innovation network including incubators, science parks, business centres, venture capitalists, spin-off companies and international R&D intensive companies, several networking initiatives and technology clusters (Debackere, 2000; Debackere and Veugelers, 2005).

3. *Relocation of artists to declining urban districts to stimulate arts-/ technology-based economic renewal.* The creative use of New York City zoning authority, allowing professional artists to move into abandoned industrial buildings and organize themselves as a Foundation for the Community of Artists, preserved Soho for a time as a low-cost space for qualified artists and regulated the transition of a declining manufacturing district into Soho as the arts equivalent of a Science City based on advanced academic research (Etzkowitz and Raiken, 1980). Barcelona's @22 urban science park project, aimed to recycle an old industrial district into a platform for knowledge-based enterprises, has been very successful in attracting national and multinational firms to locate in Barcelona. However, its top-down design failed to take account of and incorporate spontaneous bottom-up developments, like the influx of artists that could have made it an even greater success as a hybrid technology/arts district, with greater potential to spawn creative industries at the interface. Recently the @22 leadership realized the earlier error to remove the artists and developed a scheme to attract them back.

'The processes of consensus-building, decision-making or even implementation of decisions are not merely determined by state actors or formal governments. Rather, due to growing complexity and segmentation of modern societies and issue areas, it is the interaction of societal and state actors that defines problems, builds up the necessary degree of consensus on problems and solutions, consolidates conflicting interests, and (pre-) determines political decisions.' (Kuhlmann, 2001, p 957)

This interaction is rooted in trust and is regulated by rules of the game negotiated and agreed by the participants. Organizations in the consensus space are interdependent: rather than seeing themselves as isolated entities, firms, universities and local government actors begin to see themselves as part of a larger whole or, in some cases, of newly created identities such as Oresund (linking Copenhagen in Denmark and Skane in Southern Sweden) or the Leuven-Aachen-Eindhoven Triangle; and, at other times, of a reviving traditional locality such as Norrköping, Sweden (Svensson *et al*, 2012). Achieving consensus may make the difference between an environment with untapped resources and one that has put them to use to achieve economic and social development. Several mechanisms for creating a consensus space are possible, from the creation or transformation of an organization to analyse problems and formulate solutions, to the provision of access to the resources required to implement a project, or provision of solutions to conflict or crisis situations (see Box 4 for details).

## Formation and functioning of the Triple Helix spaces

The formation of the knowledge, consensus and innovation spaces is conceptualized as the result of the interaction between the university, industry and government spheres, which gradually get closer together and start to overlap. Figure 3 presents the formation of a space in a 3D adaptation of the Cassini ovals.[15] It shows four configurations of the transition from independent to overlapping spheres that are equivalent to the transition from the *laissez-faire* to the *balanced* configuration represented in Figure 1. This is a simplified representation of the interaction among the university, industry and government institutional spheres, profiling relatively equal contributions to the formation of a 'space'. In real life, there are different degrees of involvement of the spheres (asymmetrical contributions) to the 'space'. In fact, this different degree of involvement of the spheres is the main factor that induces the substitution mechanisms discussed above, whereby the stronger sphere 'takes the role' of the weaker one or enhances its development.

The 'space' thus created is considered as the functional equivalent of a 'stem cell space', which will further differentiate to become a knowledge, an innovation or a consensus space through the mobilization of specific components,

relationships and resources and creation of new institutional formats, under the influence of specific environment factors, like local or regional needs, geographical location, local and regional resources and assets, and so on. We see this process as similar to the stem cell differentiation determined by the interaction of a cell's genes with the physical and chemical conditions outside the cell, usually through signalling proteins embedded in the cell surface. The mechanisms for the formation of the knowledge, innovation and consensus spaces presented above illustrate this differentiation.

Once the spaces have been formed, they interact with each other in a continuous and diachronic transition that occurs in different directions as a non-linear process.

For example, the consensus space is a key factor in catalysing the interaction between the knowledge and innovation spaces when these are present, or for speeding up their development when they are weak or absent. Also, when a knowledge space or an innovation space exists without a consensus space, full advantage is unlikely to be taken of their potential due to the lack of a convening and organizing process to create the intermediary and transfer organizations and networks – the innovation space – that are the breeding ground of new knowledge-based clusters.

The directions of transition depend on different regional circumstances and different stages of regional development that were defined elsewhere in a four-stage model of regional growth and renewal (Etzkowitz and Klofsten, 2005), as follows.

(1) *Genesis*: creating the idea for a new regional development model.
(2) *Implementation:* starting new activities and developing infrastructure to realize the idea.
(3) *Consolidation and adjustment:* integration of activities to improve the efficiency of the new activities and infrastructure.
(4) *Self-sustaining growth and renewal of the system,* by identifying new areas of growth.

Three examples of interactions between spaces are discussed below, in connection with these different regional development stages.

*New England Council, USA, 1920–1950*

The New England Council case (Figure 4) exemplifies the importance of the knowledge and consensus spaces at the 'genesis' stage for initiating the innovation space. A transition from the consensus space to the knowledge space and further to the innovation space is identified in this case. The formation of the consensus space is exemplified by the creation of the Council by the Governors of the six New England states, by putting together resources to develop a renewal strategy for a region that had been in economic decline from the early 20th century due to the departure of industries and firms to regions with raw materials and cheap labour. After initial attempts to attract branch plants and renew SMEs in dying industries, the Council turned to the region's unique resource and comparative advantage – its high concentration of academic resources, including MIT, Harvard and a wide range of other academic institutions, which represented an already strong knowledge space. The Council focused on enhancing the start-up phenomenon of firms emanating from the turn of the century from MIT and Harvard, involved with scientific instruments and the newly emerging radio industry in the 1920s, and invented the venture capital firm to expand and intensify the creation of the innovation space.

---

**Box 4.    Mechanisms for the creation of a consensus space.**

1.  *Creation or transformation of an organization to provide a home for brainstorming, analysis of problems and formulation of plans.* Examples include the Pittsburgh High-Tech Council, the Petropolis Technopole in Rio de Janeiro State (Mello and Rocha, 2004), or the Board of the Recife Brazil Science Park, explicitly representing key local innovation actors playing a 'quasi-political' role for enhancing local innovation capacity. Similarly, the Knowledge Circle of Amsterdam meets regularly

*(Continued)*

to formulate and propose ideas for enhancing knowledge-based development. After-hours clubs in New York City can also be considered as a consensus space, providing venues for artists, fashion designers and other creative individuals to develop new projects across arts and fashion disciplines (Currid, 2007).

2. *Provision of access to the resources required to implement a project.* This can be achieved through the very process of including actors from different backgrounds in the strategy review and formulation process. An example is the 1930s New England Council representing university, industry and government leadership in the region, which invented the contemporary format for the venture capital firm, building on family investment firms with a professional staff. They worked out a political strategy to make the venture capital firm a viable entity by lobbying to change laws that prevented large financial institutions from investing in risky ventures (Etzkowitz, 2002).

3. *Providing solutions to conflict or crisis situations, such as socio-economic crises caused by loss of manufacturing industries and failure to create alternative industries, financial and social crises, etc* (Etzkowitz et al, 2008). This was the case of the US when it faced the first wave of loss of manufacturing industries to foreign competitors in the 1970s, which triggered a compromise between opponents and proponents of direct government support for industry, a controversial concept in a national system in which industry was expected to be the prime mover and source of innovation, while the firm, led by 'heroic entrepreneurs', was the protagonist.

Japan faced economic and social stasis in the 1990s, when the production capacities of national manufacturing industries were increasingly outsourced abroad, leaving a gap that could not be filled by a real estate bubble that eventually burst, or by emerging companies that proved to be too weak to restart the economy. A shift to a knowledge-based economy was sought, in which universities would play a greater role, moving on from the position of R&D labs for industry they had played earlier.

Sweden's movement of leading corporations and entrepreneurs abroad in the early 1990s or mergers with foreign firms that also outsourced economic activities abroad caused a financial crisis and a policy dilemma of whether to continue to support a relatively small group of older, large corporations, several of which, like Volvo and Saab, had become branches of multinational corporations, or to shift focus to firm formation as a strategy for discontinuous innovation in emerging technologies. The dilemma was solved by adopting a start-up culture to revive the national industrial base with large national participation. Brazil's strategy to address persisting extremes of wealth and poverty included various government policy measures encouraging innovation as a renewal and growth strategy, made possible by the introduction of the Innovation Law in 2004 (*ibid*).

*Silicon Valley, California, in the mid-1990s*

Silicon Valley in the mid-1990s exemplifies a transition from a knowledge space to a consensus space and then to an innovation space in the self-sustaining growth and renewal' phase (Figure 5). In the innovation space, many successful firms had either outgrown their university links or were spin-offs of an earlier generation of firms and had never developed extensive academic links. Indeed, by this time many of the Valley's high-tech firms tended to view themselves as a self-generated phenomenon, a cluster of inter-related firms, rather than as part of a broader university–industry–government complex. However, in the economic downturn of the mid-1990s, such firms felt the need to connect or reconnect to academic institutions and local government in order to move the region forward. A new organization, Joint Venture Silicon Valley, was established for this purpose and a public process, in the form of a series of open meetings focused on generating ideas for the future technological candidates, was initiated. A venture capital approach was adopted, with a few promising ideas, such as computer networking, winnowed from a larger collection (Miller, 1997).

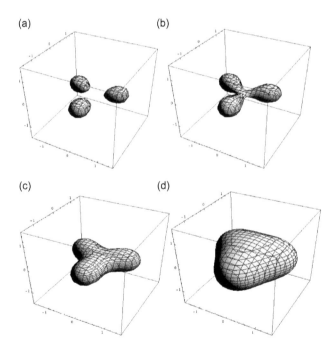

**Figure 3.** Interaction between the Triple Helix institutional spheres in the formation of a space: (a) institutional spheres apart – a *laissez-faire* regime; (b) institutional spheres getting closer together and starting to interact; (c) institutional spheres increasingly overlapping; and (d) institutional spheres overlapping in a balanced regime – formation of a 'stem cell space'.

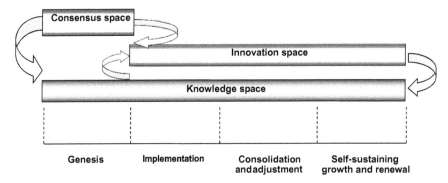

**Figure 4.** New England Council, 1920–1950.

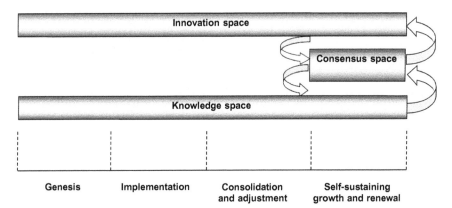

**Figure 5.** Silicon Valley in the mid-1990s.

*Stockholm's Kista Science City, Sweden*

The development of Stockholm's Kista Science City exemplifies how a successful consensus space further enhanced a knowledge-intensive and business-intensive platform created through the interplay between the knowledge and the innovation spaces (Figure 6). The history of Kista starts in the early 1970s when an Ericsson unit moved there, soon to be followed by IBM.[16] In the early 1980s, Stockholm's mayor envisaged the creation of an electronics centre which, once completed a few years later, attracted a significant number of electronics, engineering and computer science research institutes, academic research units and business firms and became an established ICT centre of national and international prestige – known also in the late 1980s as Sweden's Silicon Valley. In 2000, Stockholm's business community, academia and municipality saw the centre as the cornerstone for the foundation of Kista Science City. To implement this vision, Kista Science City AB was created and was soon ranked second by *Wired* magazine alongside similar developments in Boston and Israel. In 2002, the IT university was opened as a joint venture between the Royal Institute of Technology KTH and the University of Stockholm, and this fuelled the formation of new business networks in Kista Science City's growth areas, especially ICT. Ericsson and many other businesses moved their offices to Kista and activities expanded to the entire region. In 2010, Kista Science City hosted more than 1,000 ICT companies and more than 5,000 ICT students and scientists – a high concentration of expertise, innovation and business opportunities within ICT that is unique in Sweden.

## Policy relevance and implications and further research

This paper introduces the concept of Triple Helix systems as an analytical construct that organizes the key features of university–industry–government (Triple Helix) interactions into an 'innovation system' format defined according to systems theory as a set of components, relationships and functions. This perspective provides an explicit framework for the systemic interaction between Triple Helix institutional actors that was hitherto lacking. In defining the components of Triple Helix systems, three important distinctions are made: between R&D and non-R&D innovators; between 'single-sphere' and 'multi-sphere' (hybrid) institutions; and between individuals and institutions. The relationships between components are synthesized into five main types: technology transfer, collaboration and conflict moderation, collaborative leadership, substitution and networking. The functions of Triple Helix systems are defined as a set of competencies that are achieved in what we call the 'knowledge, innovation and consensus spaces' and are designed to realize the Triple Helix systems' overall function of knowledge and innovation generation, diffusion and use. The formation of

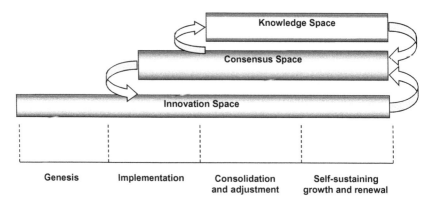

**Figure 6.** Stockholm's Kista Science City.

the spaces is envisioned as a two-step process: interaction of the Triple Helix institutional spheres and formation of a 'stem cell space', followed by the differentiation of the 'stem cell space' into a knowledge, innovation or a consensus space through the mobilization of actors, relations and resources and the creation of new institutional formats. The differentiation is triggered by specific environmental factors (such as local or regional needs), similar to stem cell differentiation induced by signalling proteins embedded in the cell surface.

The functioning of Triple Helix systems relies on the non-linear, diachronic transition from one space to another in varying directions, with one space catalysing the interaction between the others when they are present, or speeding up their development when they are weak or absent. The direction of transitions is related to different regional circumstances and development stages, which highlights the relevance of the Triple Helix systems to regional innovation strategies.

*Policy relevance and policy implications*

The Triple Helix systems approach offers a broad perspective for understanding the sources and development paths of innovation in different contexts. By introducing the Triple Helix model into a systems framework, a clearer, more fine-grained view can be achieved of:

- Key contributors to innovation and their interactions in correlation with their specific roles;

- Circulation of knowledge flows and resources within and among the knowledge, innovation and consensus spaces and identification of existing blockages or gaps; and
- New combinations of knowledge and resources that can be generated through the articulation between the spaces, generating a conceptual machinery for the advancement of innovation theory and practice.

An innovation strategy centred on the Triple Helix systems can be an attractive, novel perspective for policy makers, especially in regions that aim to pursue a knowledge-intensive development model and thus enhance their knowledge base and build 'steeples of excellence' from research themes with commercial potential and innovative firms that can realize that potential. Such regions can be found in both developed and developing countries, as shown by the recent 2011 categorisation of OECD regions using innovation-related variables that distinguishes between knowledge hubs, innovation production zones and non-S&T-driven regions (Ajmone Marsan and Maguire, 2011).

Various innovation policy approaches have been adopted at the regional level. Some European regions view innovation activities and the business innovation process as a network process, in which business and interactions with other partners play a significant part (Sternberg, 2000), while other European regions have focused on SME policy, on how SMEs innovate and to what extent they rely on other firms and organizations in their innovation activities (Asheim *et al,* 2003; Tödtling and Kaufmann,

2001). Several Nordic regions have adopted a cluster policy to explore similarities and differences between regional clusters of SMEs in different countries and develop social networking arrangements to boost and secure social capital and trust (Asheim *et al*, 2003). Several Canadian regions have also followed a cluster policy based on two main types of 'emerging' models of clusters:

(1) Regionally embedded and anchored regions where the local knowledge/science base represents a major generator of new, unique knowledge assets; and
(2) 'Entrepot' regions where much of the knowledge base required for innovation and production is acquired through straightforward market transactions, often from non-local sources (Holbrook and Wolfe, 2002; Wolfe, 2003) (see details in Doloreux and Parto, 2004).

Some developing countries, where regional innovation policy is in its infancy, have only started to build their first regional innovation strategies under the coordination of the local regional innovation agencies or regional development agencies – for example, Izmir, the first region in Turkey to develop its own Regional Innovation Strategy (see Izmir Development Agency, 2012).

A Triple Helix systems-centred regional innovation strategy can be particularly relevant in the context of developing countries, because these countries, while seeking inspiration from the experience of developed countries, are also looking for novel models and solutions that could be better adapted to the realities and challenges of their own environment. A multitude of labels has emerged for these new innovation models, from 'pro-poor innovation' and 'grassroots innovation', to 'frugal innovation' and 'inclusive innovation' and so on. Irrespective of the name, common objectives of these models are the creation of new markets for innovative goods and services among those at the base of the pyramid, introduction of new technologies – particularly information and communication technologies – and creation of new contexts and new locations for innovation (UNIDO, 2003).

Developing countries committed to the transition to a knowledge-based development model also aim to develop a better research infrastructure, a highly qualified workforce and greater innovative potential of domestic enterprises, with a stronger competitive advantage. A shift from an exogenous regional development approach, based on relocation/attraction of firms from elsewhere, often subsidiaries or R&D centres of large multinationals, to an endogenous regional development approach, based on local factors – such as strong knowledge base, skilled labour services, proximity to knowledge sources, and regional technology strategies and plans – is in progress in many developing countries that want to increase their innovation potential.

New ways of achieving all of these objectives can be found from adopting a Triple Helix systems perspective, through consolidation of and articulation between the knowledge, innovation and consensus spaces. As we have shown earlier, when one space is weak or missing, the other spaces can accelerate its formation and development, creating new innovation opportunities. At the same time, the non-linear interactions and communications between the spaces also need to take into account the correlation of regional R&D and innovation policies with other policies (education, employment, trade, exports, fiscal). Going beyond a single region to the level of multi-regional collaboration is also key to creating a 'critical mass' of human and financial resources for broad-scope projects that involve higher risks and raise higher coordination challenges. These objectives resonate to a large extent with the European Union's new focus on 'research and innovation strategies for smart specialization'. The new policy requires national and regional authorities across Europe to identify unique characteristics and assets of each country and region, highlighting each region's competitive advantages, and rallying regional stakeholders and resources around an excellence-driven vision of their future, in order to use the EU's Structural Funds more efficiently and create synergies between different EU, national and regional policies, as well as between public and private investments (European Commission, 2013).

The policy implications arising from the adoption of a Triple Helix systems approach to innovation focus in particular on the measures that support the formation and consolidation of the Knowledge, Innovation and Consensus spaces.

We have shown earlier that an important condition for creating and strengthening a Knowledge Space is the achievement of a 'critical mass' of R&D and non-R&D actors, academic research and education resources in a local area. Policies to develop this 'critical mass' could concentrate on mapping regional/national innovation actors and analysing their evolution and future trends; understanding their priority setting; the scope of operations (regional, national, international); and regional impact. Policy initiatives might also be directed at improving human resources for R&D in sciences and arts at national or regional level, improving the labour market for researchers, promoting better policies for employment, education and training, and immigration to attract world-class researchers, thus making research careers more available and attractive, especially for women and minorities, reducing 'brain drain' and improving 'brain gain'.

Similar policy actions are important in developing the innovation space: mapping of 'single-sphere' and 'multi-sphere' (hybrid) institutions and promoting policies that support their formation and activity; creation of seed funds; increased participation of industry and other private stakeholders in university and public research institutes' priority setting; stimulation of the commercialization of university-generated technologies; fiscal measures to encourage the creation of innovative, high-tech start-ups; implementation of national and regional programmes to promote risk and venture capital funds; improved access to equity financing for research and innovation activities; and so on.

The formation and development of the consensus space can be accelerated by strengthening the dialogue and collaboration between national and regional innovation stakeholders and creating new platforms for communication, promoting collaborative governance measures, such as public consultation and feedback and collaborative leadership models and practices.

*Further research*

The analytical construct of Triple Helix systems we propose here still needs a better understanding of several issues, including the following.

*The development of the knowledge, innovation and consensus spaces.* First, the formation and differentiation of the spaces depend essentially on the motivation of the Triple Helix actors to engage in joint projects and set common goals. This is not an easy process, because setting joint agendas often involves changes of vision, crossing organizational silos, thinking beyond the boundaries of a single institutional sphere, harmonizing institutional and individual objectives, resources, cultures and so on. Such outcomes can be accelerated by top-down or bottom-up initiatives that not only need a favourable environment to reach fruition but also require policy measures that integrate innovation and entrepreneurship better within the larger socio-economic context and especially research, education, labour market and development policies. Individual and collective Innovation Organizers,

whether in Ontario, Brainport Research Triangle (Leuven-Aachen-Eindhoven) or the Lagos Innovation Council – among others – are key to overcoming institutional inertia.

Second, we also need to understand more about the growth of the spaces over time, especially in relation to the regional development stages, and about the functional requirements that are necessary for supporting each development stage. For example, we know that economic downturn and political crises are major catalysts in the creation of the consensus space, but how do consensus spaces get created in times of economic upturn? Or how can cross-institutional leadership arise in them where, to date, it has been conspicuously absent? A comparative analysis of the creation of consensus spaces under various regional conditions in different historical periods and stages of regional development will be most useful to clarify what impetuses lead Triple Helix actors to come together to create a consensus space. We also need to refine our analysis of good practice in creating innovation spaces: what are the conditions under which importation of organizational innovations is successful, and when do these innovations impede development? What methodology should be developed for such an analysis? What gaps need to be filled with what type of organizational innovation, and what elements need to be brought together to create organizational innovation? In the past, the venture capital model was created from such an analysis (Etzkowitz, 2002); what form should such analysis and solutions take in our present context? An initial step might be a synthesis of models that highlight the importance of creative leadership and counter-cyclical funding, targeted at innovation gaps and 'valleys of death' that emerge as a consequence of economic crises (Benner, 2012; Ranga and Etzkowitz, 2012).

*Assessing the performance of Triple Helix systems by means of hybrid indicators* that capture dynamic processes at the intersection of the university, industry and government institutional spheres rather than within single spheres. Such indicators are currently rare.[17] Also, the design of indicators that characterize the specific dynamics of each space may be a challenging process, especially for the innovation and consensus spaces. For example, the number of spin-offs that have graduated from university incubators, monitored in some universities, could be a relevant indicator for the innovation space, while the number of collaborative projects involving Triple Helix actors, also often monitored in entrepreneurial universities, could become a good proxy for the consensus space.

## Conclusions

To conclude, it is interesting to note that while Schumpeter's theory of creative destruction shows how outmoded economic regimes disappeared, the Triple Helix systems delineate how new regimes appear through creative reconstruction. By revealing the 'workings of the engine', they provide new insights into the process of knowledge-based development that is often considered opaque and hidden, such insights

encouraging initiatives and practices that carry the seeds of innovative developments.

Moreover, by providing a clearer view of innovation actors, knowledge and resources flows within and among the spaces and of existing blockages and gaps between them, the Triple Helix systems can help accelerate the transition from the low-risk, low-gain development model that is currently in place in many regions and countries and is conducive to slow, incremental innovation patterns with low economic returns, to a higher-risk, higher-gain development model that could favour more radical innovations and the accelerated creation of new markets, new growth opportunities, new jobs and new skills.

## Notes

[1] An important part of this research has been published in special issues of refereed journals introducing papers presented at the Triple Helix conferences held since 1996 until present – see Appendix 1. Other examples of Triple Helix research can be found, for example, in Rothaermel *et al's* (2007) literature review that identified 173 academic articles published in peer-reviewed scholarly journals between 1981–2005.

[2] See, for example, the VINN Excellence Centres and the VINNVL7XT Programme of the Swedish Governmental Agency for Innovation Systems VINNOVA, or Brazil's 2004 Innovation Law that incentivizes the interaction between firms, public universities and research centres or the European Union's Europe 2020 Strategy and its Innovation Union flagship initiative.

[3] In the sense of specific national factors, like history and culture, institutions, laws and policies that shaped technological capabilities of a country.

[4] These capabilities ensure the capacity of a system to make innovative choices of markets, products, technologies and organizational structure; to engage in entrepreneurial activity; to select key personnel

and acquire key resources, including new competence; to organize and coordinate the resources and economic activities within the organization; to implement technologies and utilize them effectively in the market; to learn from success as well as failure, to read and interpret market signals and take appropriate actions, and to diffuse technology throughout the system (Carlsson *et al*, 2002, p 235).

[5] Carlsson (2003) refers to views of institutions as networks or organizations supporting technical innovation (Freeman, 1987; Nelson and Rosenberg, 1993), as rules or regimes that determine behaviour (Lundvall, 1992) and as institutional arrangements defining both regimes and organizations (Carlsson and Stankiewicz, 1991).

[6] For example, in the creation of the Apple origin myth, Steve Jobs moved to the foreground, while Steve Wozniak, the technical collaborator, and Mark Makula, the experienced semiconductor executive, who gave the original duo credibility with suppliers and financers, were elided (Freiberger and Swaine, 2000).

[7] For example, The Kitchen in New York City's Soho District invents new forms of conceptual art, new artistic formats and modes of performance that inspire other artists and are disseminated through international performance tours. Although The Kitchen members do not explicitly view themselves from an innovation perspective, they instigate an innovation process in their domain. The fashion department of the Antwerp Academy in Belgium encourages students to create and explore innovative forms, original treatments of materials, stimulate experimentation and improvisation, in a way similar to the teaching laboratory. The Costume Institute at the Metropolitan Museum of Art in New York is the cultural memory of the industry that is regularly utilized as a source of ideas in the form of historical styles that may be reinterpreted in new ways with new materials or hybridized into new formats.

[8] See details on Brazil's 2004 Innovation Law at http://www.scidev.net/en/editorials/brazils-innovation-law-lessons-for-latin-america.html.

[9] See http://www.sfgate.com/news/article/Pixar-University-Thinking-Outside-The-Mouse-2611923.php.

[10] See http://www.eucys2012.eu/index.php?option=comcontent&view=article&id=49&Itemid=36.

[11] See http://www.cisco.com/web/learning/netacad/academy/index.html.

[12] See http~/appleinsider.com/ articles/11/10/06/apple_university_revealed_as_plan_to_teach_executives_to_think_like_steve_jobs.

[13] The European Technology Platforms (ETPs) are industry-led multinational networks (36 ETPs in 2011) of various stakeholders who define a common vision and implement a medium- to long-term Strategic Research Agenda in key industrial areas for Europe's competitiveness and economic growth (http://cordis.europa.eu/technology-platforms/). The ETPs have provided major input to European research programmes such as FP7, and some have been involved in the establishment of the Joint Technology Initiatives (JTIs), a form of long-term public–private partnerships that combine private-sector investment and/or national and European public funding (five JTIs in 2011) (http://cordis.europa.eu/fp7/jtis/).

[14] For example, increasing network value with higher numbers of participants, reduction of research projects overlapping through network centralisation, complementary investments for information dissemination that may lead to economic benefits and easier access to information flows within the network by governments and firms, increasing their choices about specialisation, co-operation and competition (Steinmueller, 1994).

[15] The Cassini ovals (ellipses) are a family of curves identified by the astronomer Giovanni Cassini in 1860, which he believed defined the path the Earth takes around the Sun. A Cassini oval is a plane curve defined as the set (locus) of points in the plane where the product of the distances from the point to two fixed points situated at a distance 2a apart is a constant called b2. The Cartesian equation of a Cassini oval is $((x–a)2 +y2)((x+a)2 +y2) = b4$, where the x and y are two points in the plane. The general appearance of the oval is dictated by the relative values of a and b. If a < b, the curve forms a single loop. This loop becomes increasingly pinched as a approaches b. When a > b, the curve is made up of two loops, while at a = b it is the same as the 'Bernoulli's lemniscate' that was documented about 14 years later (see further details at http://mathworld.wolfram.com/CassiniOvals.html). Here we present an adaptation of the Cassini ovals from two to three spheres, to accommodate our three institutional spheres, the principle remaining the same.

[16] Selected from 'A History of Kista Science City' at: http://blog.naver.com/PostView.

nhn?blogId=beyondui&logNo=13008951563
2&parentCategoryNo=96&viewDate=&cur-
rentPage=1&listtype=0.
[17]For example, among the 25 indicators of
the 2011 Innovation Union Scoreboard only
one, public–private publications, captures
the effect of collaboration between the
university and industry spheres, while most
of the others describe single-sphere effects
(for example, the indicators under the 'Firm
activities' and 'Output' categories reflect
firm-specific processes, and some of the
indicators under 'Enablers' reflect some
academic processes). The OECD Science,
Technology and Industry Scoreboard 2011
has two such indicators: Government-fi-
nanced R&D in business (government–
industry interface), and Patents citing
non-patent literature and average citations
received per patent cited (industry–university interface).

# References

Ajmone Marsan, G., and Maguire, K.
(2011), 'Categorisation of OECD
regions using innovation-related
variables', *OECD Regional Development Working Papers,* 2011/03,
OECD Publishing, http://dx.doi.
Org/10.1787/5kg8bf42qv7k-en.

Almeida, M., Mello, J.M.C., and Etzkowitz,
H. (2012), 'Social innovation in a devel-
oping country: invention and diffusion
of the Brazilian cooperative incubator',
*International Journal of Technology and
Globalisation,* Vol 6, No 3, pp 206–224.

Amason, A.C. (1996), 'Distinguishing the
effect of functional and dysfunctional
conflict on strategic decision making:
resolving a paradox for top management
teams', *Academy of Management Journal,* Vol 39, pp 123–148.

Amason, A.C., and Sapienza, H.J. (1997),
'The effects of top management team
size and interaction norms on cognitive
and affective conflict', *Journal of Management,* Vol 23, pp 495–516.

Archer, D., and Cameron, A. (2009),
*Collaborative Leadership – How to
Succeed in an Interconnected World,*
Butterworth-Heinemann, Oxford.

Arundel, A., Bordoy, C., and Kanerva, M.
(2008), 'Neglected innovators: how do
innovative firms that do not perform
R&D innovate? – results of an analysis
of the Innobarometer 2007 survey, No
215', *INNO-Metrics Thematic Paper,*
European Commission, DG Enterprise,
Brussels.

Asheim, B., Coenen, L., and
Svensson-Henning, M. (2003), *Nordic
SMEs and Regional Innovation Sys-
tems,* Nordisk Industrifond, Oslo.

Azagra-Caro, J.M., Carat, G., and Pontika-
kis, D. (2010), 'Geographical implications of the TH: inclining the columns
to make the temple look straight, a
first glance at monetary indicators
on university–industry cooperation',
*Research Evaluation,* Vol 19, No 2,
pp 119–128.

Baldini, N. (2006), 'University patenting
and licensing activity: a review of the
literature', *Research Evaluation,* Vol 15,
No 3, pp 197–207.

Benner, M. (2012), 'Innovation policy in
hard times: lessons from the Nordic
countries', *European Planning Studies,*
Vol 20, No 9, pp 1455–1468.

Bergek, A., Jacobsson S., and Hekkert,
M. (2007), 'Attributes in innovation
systems: a framework for analysing
energy system dynamics and identifying goals for system-building activities
by entrepreneurs and policy makers',
in Foxon, T., Kohler, J., and Oughton,
C., eds, *Innovations for a Low Carbon
Economy: Economic, Institutional and
Management Approaches,* Edward
Elgar, Cheltenham.

Bergek, A., Jacobsson, S., Carlsson, B.,
Lindmark, S., and Rickne, A. (2008),
'Analyzing the functional dynamics of
technological innovation systems: a
scheme of analysis', *Research Policy,*
Vol 37, No 3, pp 407–429.

Bianco, M., and Viscardi, N. (2008),
'Research organization in the university:
the case of a leading Uruguayan group
in basic science', *International Journal of
Technology Management and Sustainable
Development,* Vol 7, No 3, pp 237–249.

Bjerregaard, T. (2010), 'Industry
and academia in convergence:
micro-institutional dimensions of R&D
collaboration', *Technovation,* Vol 30,
No 2, pp 100–108.

Boardman, P.C. (2009), 'Government
centrality to university–industry interactions: university research centers and
the industry involvement of academic
researchers', *Research Policy,* Vol 38,
No 10, pp 1505–1516.

Booyens, I. (2011), 'Are small, medium-
and micro-sized enterprises engines of
innovation? – the reality in South Africa',
*Science and Public Policy,* Vol 38, No 1,
pp 67–78.

Breschi, S., and Malerba, F. (1997), 'Sectoral innovation systems: technological

regimes, Schumpeterian dynamics and spatial boundaries', in Edquist, C., ed, *Systems of Innovation: Technologies, Institutions and Organizations,* Pinter/Cassell Academic, London and Washington.

Callon, M. (1992), 'The dynamics of techno-economic networks', in Coombs, R., Saviotti, P., and Walsh, V., eds, *Technological Change and Company Strategies: Economic and Sociological Perspectives,* Academic Press, London.

Campbell, E. G., Powers, J. B., Blumenthal, D., and Biles, B. (2004), 'Inside the Triple Helix: technology transfer and commercialization in the life sciences', *Health Affairs,* Vol 23, No 1, pp 64–76.

Carlsson, B., ed (1997), *Technological Systems and Industrial Dynamics,* Kluwer Academic Publishers, Boston/Dordrecht/London.

Carlsson, B. (1998), 'Innovation and knowledge spillovers: a systems cum evolutionary perspective', in Eliasson, G., and Green, C., eds, *Microfoundations of Economic Growth: A Schumpeterian Perspective,* University of Michigan Press, Ann Arbor, MI, pp 156–168.

Carlsson, B. (2003), 'Innovation systems: a survey of the literature from a Schumpeterian perspective', *paper for The Elgar Companion to Neo-Schumpeterian Economics,* downloaded 09 April 2012 from: http://faculty.weatherhead.case.edu/carlsson/documents/InnovationSystemsSurveypaper6.pdf.

Carlsson, B., Jacobsson, S., Holmén, M., and Rickne, A. (2002), 'Innovation systems: analytical and methodological issues', *Research Policy,* Vol 31, No 2, pp 233–245.

Carlsson, B., and Stankiewicz, R. (1991), 'On the nature, function, and composition of technological systems', *Journal of Evolutionary Economics,* No 1, pp 93–118.

Casas, R., de Gortari, R., and Santos, M. J. (2000), 'The building of knowledge spaces in Mexico: a regional approach to networking', *Research Policy,* Vol 29, No 2, pp 229–241.

Chrislip, D. (2002), *The Collaborative Leadership Fieldbook: A Guide for Citizens and Civic Leaders,* Jossey-Bass, San Francisco, CA.

Cohen, W. M., Levin, R. C., and Mowery, D. C. (1987), 'Firm size and R&D intensity: a re-examination', *Journal of Industrial Economics,* Vol 35, pp 543–563.

Cooke, P. (1996), *Regional Innovation Systems,* UCL Press, London.

Cooke, P. (2004), 'The molecular biology revolution and the rise of bioscience megacentres in North America and Europe', *Environment and Planning C: Government and Policy,* Vol 22, No 2, pp 161–177.

Currid, E. (2007), *The Warhol Economy,* Princeton University Press, Princeton, NJ.

Cusumano, M.A., and Elenkov, D. (1994), 'Linking international technology transfer with strategy and management: a literary commentary', *Research Policy,* Vol 23, No 2, pp 195–215.

David, P.A., and Foray, D. (2003), 'Economic fundamentals of the Knowledge Society', *Policy Futures in Education,* Vol 1, pp 20–49.

David, P.A., Foray, D., and Steinmueller, W. E. (1999), 'The research network and the new economics of science: from metaphors to organizational behaviours', in Gambardella, A., and Malerba, F., eds, *The Organisation of Innovative Activities in Europe,* Cambridge University Press, Cambridge.

De Clercq, D., Thongpapanl N., and Dimov, D. (2009), 'When good conflict gets better and bad conflict becomes worse: the role of social capital in the conflict–innovation relationship', *Journal of the Academy of Marketing Science,* Vol 37, pp 283–297.

Debackere, K. (2000), 'Managing academic R&D as a business at KU Leuven: context, structure and process', *R&D Management,* Vol 30, pp 323–328.

Debackere, K., and Veugelers, R. (2005), 'Improving industry science links through university technology transfer units: an analysis and a case', *Research Policy,* Vol 34, No 3, pp 321–342.

DeBresson, C., and Amesse, F. (1991), 'Networks of innovators: a review and introduction to the issue', *Research Policy,* Vol 20, No 5, pp 363–379.

Dolfsma, W., and Leydesdorff, L. (2009), 'Lock-in and break-out from technological trajectories: modelling and policy implications', *Technological Forecasting and Social Change,* Vol 76, pp 932–941.

Doloreux, D., and Parto, S. (2004), 'Regional innovation systems: a critical review', *ERSA Conference Papers,* ersa04p56, see: http://www.ulb.ac.be/soco/asrdlf/documents/RIS_Doloreux-Parto_000.pdf

Doloreux, D., and Parto, S. (2005), 'Regional innovation systems: current discourse and unresolved issues', *Technology in Society,* Vol 27, pp 133–153.

Dosi, G., Freeman, C., Nelson, R. R., Silverberg, G., and Soete, L., eds (1998), *Technology and Economic Theory,* Pinter, London.

Edquist, C. (1997), 'Systems of innovation approaches: their emergence and characteristics', in Edquist, C., ed, *Systems of Innovation: Technologies, Institutions and Organizations,* Pinter, London.

Edquist, C. (2005), 'Systems of innovation: perspectives and challenges', in Fagerberg, J., Mowery, D. C., and Nelson, R. R., eds, *The Oxford Handbook of Innovation,* Oxford University Press, New York, pp 181–208.

Etzkowitz, H. (1993), 'Technology transfer: the second academic revolution', *Technology Access Report,* No 6, pp 7–9.

Etzkowitz, H. (2002J, *MIT and the Rise of Entrepreneurial Science*, Routledge, London.

Etzkowitz, H. (2003), Innovation in innovation: the Triple Helix of university–industry–government relations', *Social Science Information,* Vol 42, pp 293–338.

Etzkowitz, H. (2008), *The Triple Helix: University–Industry–Government Innovation in Action*, Routledge, London.

Etzkowitz, H. (2012), 'Triple Helix clusters: boundary permeability at university–industry–government interfaces as a regional innovation strategy', *Environment and Planning C: Government and Policy,* Vol 30, No 5, pp 766–779.

Etzkowitz, H., and Klofsten, M. (2005), 'The innovating region: towards a theory of knowledge-based regional development', *R&D Management*, Vol 35, pp 243–255.

Etzkowitz, H., and Leydesdorff, L. (1995), 'The Triple Helix: university–industry–government relations: a laboratory for knowledge-based economic development', *EASST Review,* Vol 14, pp 14–19.

Etzkowitz, H., and Leydesdorff, L. (1998), 'The endless transition: a "triple helix" of university–industry–government relations', *Minerva,* Vol 36, pp 203–208.

Etzkowitz, H., and Leydesdorff, L. (2000), 'The dynamics of innovation: from national systems and "Mode 2" to a Triple Helix of university–industry–government relations', *Research Policy,* Vol 29, No 2, pp 109–123.

Etzkowitz, H., and Raiken, L. (1980), 'Artists' social movements of the 1960's and 70's: from protest to institution-formation', *paper presented at Eastern Sociological Society Thematic Session,* Boston, MA, distributed by ERIC Clearinghouse, ERIC No ED186326, see: http://www.eric.ed.gov/.

Etzkowitz, H., and Schaflander, G. (1969), *Ghetto Crisis,* Little Brown, Boston, MA.

Etzkowitz, H., Mello, J.M.C., and Almeida, M. (2005), 'Towards "meta-innovation" in Brazil: the evolution of the incubator and the emergence of a Triple Helix', *Research Policy,* Vol 34, No 4, pp 411–424.

Etzkowitz, H., Ranga, M., Benner, M., Guaranys, L., Maculan, A. M., and Kneller, R. (2008), 'Pathways to the entrepreneurial university: towards a global convergence', *Science and Public Policy,* Vol 35, pp 1–15.

European Commission (2013), 'Research and innovation strategies for smart specialisation', see: http://ec.europa.eu/regionalpolicy/sources/docgener/informat/2014/smart specialisation en.pdf.

Feldman, M. P., and Desrochers, P. (2004), 'Truth for its own sake: academic culture and technology transfer at Johns Hopkins University', *Minerva,* Vol 42, No 2, pp 105–126.

Finkelstein, S., and Mooney, A. C. (2003), 'Not the usual suspects: how to use board process to make boards better', *Academy of Management Executive*, Vol 17, No 2, pp 101–113.

Freeman, C. (1987), *Technology Policy and Economic Performance: Lessons from Japan,* Pinter, London.

Freeman, C. (1988), 'Japan: a new national innovation system?', in Dosi, G., Freeman, C., Nelson, R. R., Silverberg, G., and Soete, L., eds, *Technical Change and Economic Theory,* Pinter, London.

Freeman, C. (1991), 'Networks of innovators: a synthesis of research issues', *Research Policy,* Vol 20, No 5, pp 499–514.

Freeman, C., and Lundvall, B.-A., eds (1988), *Small Countries Facing the Technological Revolution,* Pinter, London.

Freiberger, P., and Swaine, M. (2000), *Fire in the Valley: The Making of the Personal Computer,* McGraw-Hill, New York.

Furman, J. L., and MacGarvie, M. (2009), 'Academic collaboration and organizational innovation: the development of research capabilities in the US pharmaceutical industry, 1927–1946', *Industrial and Corporate Change,* Vol 18, No 5, pp 929–961.

Galende, J., and de la Fuente, J.M. (2003), 'Internal factors determining a firm's innovative behaviour', *Research Policy,* Vol 32, No 5, pp 715–736.

Galende, J., and Suarez Gonzales, I. (1999), 'A resource-based analysis of the factors determining a firm's R&D activities', *Research Policy,* Vol 28, No 8, pp 891–905.

Gebhardt, C. (2012), 'The entrepreneurial state: the German entrepreneurial regions program as an attenuator for the financial crisis', *European Planning Studies,* Vol 20, No 9, pp 1469–1482.

Geuna, A., and Nesta, L.J.J. (2006), 'University patenting and its effects on academic research: the emerging European evidence', *Research Policy,* Vol 35, No 6, pp 790–807.

Geuna, A., and Rossi, F. (2011), 'Changes to university IPR regulations in Europe and the impact on academic patenting', *Research Policy,* Vol 40, No 8, pp 1068–1076.

Gibney, J., Copeland, S., and Murie, A. (2009), 'Towards a "new" strategic leadership of place for the knowledge-based economy', *Leadership,* Vol 5, pp 5–23.

Goldstein, H.A. (2010), 'The "entrepreneurial turn" and regional economic development mission of universities', *Annals of Regional Science,* Vol 44, No 1, pp 83–109.

Hamilton, W.B. (1966), 'The research triangle of North Carolina: a study in leadership for the common weal', *South Atlantic Quarterly,* Vol 65, pp 254–278.

Heerwagen, J., Kelly, K., and Kampschroer, K. (2010), 'The changing nature of organizations, work and workplace', downloaded on 08 April 2013 from: http://www.wbdg.org/resources/chngorgwork.php.

Heidenreich, M. (2009), 'Innovation patterns and location of European low- and medium-technology industries', *Research Policy,* Vol 38, No 3, pp 483–494.

Hekkert, M., Suurs, R.A.A., Negro, S., Kuhlmann, S., and Smits, R. (2008), 'Attributes of innovation systems: a new approach for analysing technological change', *Technological Forecasting and Social Change,* Vol 74, pp 413–432.

Holbrook, A., and Wolfe, D. (2002), *Knowledge, Clusters and Regional Innovation: Economic Development in Canada,* Queen's School of Policy Studies, Kingston, Ontario.

Huggins, R. (2008), 'Universities and knowledge-based venturing: finance, management and networks in London', *Entrepreneurship and Regional Development,* Vol 20, No 2, pp 185–206.

Inzelt, A. (2004), 'The evolution of university–industry–government relationships during transition', *Research Policy,* Vol 33, No 6–7, pp 975–995.

Iversen, E.J., Gulbrandsen, M., and Klitkou, A. (2007), 'A baseline for the impact of academic patenting legislation in Norway', *Scientometrics,* Vol 70, No 2, pp 393–414.

Izmir Development Agency (2012), *Izmir Regional Innovation Strategy,* see: http://www.izka.org.tr/en/izmirde-yatirim/izmirde-yatirim-ortami/izmir-kalkinma-ajansi/.

Jehn, K.A. (1995), 'A multi-method examination of the benefits and detriments of intra-group conflict', *Administrative Science Quarterly,* Vol 40, pp 256–282.

Jehn, K.A., and Mannix, E.A. (2001), 'The dynamic nature of conflict: a longitudinal study of intra-group conflict and group performance', *Academy of Management Journal,* Vol 44, No 238–251.

Jensen, M.B., Johnson, B., Lorenz, E., and Lundvall B.A. (2007), 'Forms of knowledge and modes of innovation', *Research Policy,* Vol 36, No 5, pp 680–693.

Kaufmann, A., and Tödtling, F. (2001), 'Science–industry interaction in the process of innovation: the importance of boundary-crossing between systems', *Research Policy,* Vol 30, No 5, pp 791–804.

Klofsten, M., Jones-Evans, D., and Schärberg, C. (1999), 'Growing the Linköping Technopole: longitudinal study of the Triple Helix development in Sweden', *Journal of Technology Transfer,* Vol 24, No 2–3, pp 125–138.

Konde, V. (2004), 'Internet development in Zambia: a Triple Helix of government–university–partners', *International Journal of Technology Management,* Vol 27, No 5, pp 440–451.

Kruss, G. (2008), 'Balancing old and new organisational forms: changing dynamics of government, industry and university interaction in South Africa', *Technology Analysis and Strategic Management* Vol 20, No 6, pp 667–682.

Kuhlmann, S. (2001), 'Future governance of innovation policy in Europe: three scenarios', *Research Policy,* Vol 30, No 6, pp 953–976.

Kwon, K.S., Park, H.W., So, M., and Leydesdorff, L. (2012), 'Has globalization strengthened South Korea's national research system? – national and inter-national dynamics of the Triple Helix of scientific co-authorship relationships in South Korea', *Scientometrics,* Vol 90, No 1, pp 163–176.

Lawton Smith, H., and Bagchi-Sen Sharmistha, S. (2010), 'Triple Helix and regional development: a perspective from Oxfordshire in the UK', *Technology Analysis and Strategic Management,* Vol 22, pp 805–818.

Lee, M. S., and Peterson, S. J. (2000), 'Culture, entrepreneurial orientation and global competitiveness', *Journal of World Business,* Vol 35, pp 401–416.

Leydesdorff, L. (1996), 'Luhmann's socio-logical theory: its operationalisation and future perspectives', *Social Science Information,* Vol 35, pp 283–306.

Leydesdorff, L. (1997), 'The new communi-cation regime of university–industry–gov-ernment relations', in Etzkowitz, H., and Leydesdorff, L., eds, *Universities and the Global Knowledge Economy: A Triple Helix of University–Industry–Government Relations,* Cassell Academic, London.

Leydesdorff, L. (2000), 'The Triple Helix: an evolutionary model of innovations', *Research Policy,* Vol 29, No 2, pp 243–255.

Leydesdorff, L. (2003), 'The mutual informa-tion of university–industry–government relations: an indicator of the Triple Helix dynamics', *Scientometrics,* Vol 58, pp 445–467.

Leydesdorff, L. (2006), *The Knowledge-Based Economy: Modeled, Measured, Simulated,* Universal Publishers, Boca Raton, FL.

Leydesdorff, L. (2008), 'Configurational information as potentially negative entropy: the Triple Helix model', *Entropy,* Vol 10, pp 391–410.

Leydesdorff, L., and Etzkowitz, H. (1996), 'Emergence of a Triple Helix of university–industry–government rela-tions', *Science and Public Policy,* Vol 23, pp 279–86.

Leydesdorff, L., and Etzkowitz, H. (1998), 'The Triple Helix as a model for innova-tion studies', *Science and Public Policy,* Vol 25, pp 195–203.

Leydesdorff, L., and Meyer, M. (2006), 'Tri-ple Helix indicators of knowledge-based innovation systems: introduction to the Special Issue', *Research Policy,* Vol 35, No 10, pp 1441–1449.

Leydesdorff, L., and Meyer, M. (2010), 'The decline of university patenting and the end of the Bayh-Dole effect', *Sciento-metrics,* Vol 83, No 2, pp 355–362.

Leydesdorff, L., Dolfsma, W., and Van der Panne, G. (2006), 'Measuring the knowl-edge base of an economy in terms of Triple Helix relations among technology, organization and territory', *Research Policy,* Vol 35, No 2, pp 181–199.

Lowe, C. U. (1982), 'The Triple Helix – NIH, industry, and the academic World', *Yale Journal of Biology and Medicine,* Vol 55, pp 239–246.

Luhmann, N. (1975), 'Systemtheorie, Evolutionstheorie und Kommunikations-theorie', *Soziologische Gids,* Vol 22, No 3, pp 154–168.

Luhmann, N. (1984), *Soziale Systeme: Grundriß einer allgemeinen Theorie,* Suhrkamp, Frankfurt, published in English (1995), as *Social Systems,* Stanford University Press, Stanford, CA.

Luna, M., and Tirtido, R. (2008), 'Business associations and their contribution to knowledge networks in Mexico', *Interna-tional Journal of Technology Manage-ment and Sustainable Development,* Vol 7, No 3, pp 251–264.

Lundvall, B.-A. (1988), 'Innovation as an interactive process: from user–producer interaction to national systems of innovation', in Dosi, G., ed, *Technology and Economic Theory,* Pinter, London.

Lundvall, B.-A., ed. (1992), *National Sys-tems of Innovation,* Pinter, London.

Malerba, F. (2002), 'Sectoral systems of innovation and production', *Research Policy,* Vol 31, No 2, pp 247–264.

Maskell, P., and Malmberg, A. (1997), 'Towards an explanation of regional specialization and industry agglomera-tion', *European Planning Studies,* Vol 5, pp 25–41.

Mason, C., and Harrison, R. (1992), 'Strategy for closing the small firms finance gap', in Caley, D., Leigh, R., and Smallbone, D., eds, *Small Enterprise Development,* Paul Chapman, London.

Mello, J.M.C., and Alves Rocha, F. C. (2004), 'Networking for regional innova-tion and economic growth: the Brazilian Petropolis technopole', *International Journal of Technology Management,* Vol 27, No 5, pp 488–497.

Mets, T. (2010), 'Entrepreneurial business model for classical research university', *Inzinerine Ekonomika – Engineering Economics,* Vol 21, No 1, pp 80–89.

Mets, T., Andrijevskaja, J., and Varblane, U. (2008), 'The role of the University of Tartu in the development of entre-preneurship in the region of South Estonia', *International Journal of*

*Entrepreneurship and Innovation Management, Vol 8, No 6, pp 648–664.*

Meyer, M. (2006), 'Are patenting scientists the better scholars? – an exploratory comparison of inventor-authors with their non-inventing peers in nano-science and technology', *Research Policy,* Vol 35, No 10, pp 1646–1662.

Miller, W. (1997), 'Stanford University Business School and Joint Venture Silicon Valley', verbal interview with Henry Etzkowitz.

Nelson, R. R., ed. (1993), *National Innovation Systems,* Oxford University Press, New York.

Nelson, R. R., and Rosenberg, N. (1993), 'Technical innovation and national systems', in Nelson, R. R., ed, *National Innovation Systems,* Oxford University Press, Oxford, pp 321.

Parsons, T. (1951), *The Social System,* The Free Press, New York.

Parsons, T., and Shils, E., eds (1951), *Toward a General Theory of Action,* Harvard University Press, Cambridge, MA.

Parsons, T., and Smelser N. J. (1956), *Economy and Society,* Routledge and Kegan Paul, London.

Pelled, L. H., Eisenhardt, K. M., and Xin, K. R. (1999), 'Exploring the black box: an analysis of work group diversity, conflict and performance', *Administrative Science Quarterly,* Vol 44, pp 1–28.

Powell, W. W. (1990), 'Neither market nor hierarchy: network forms of organization', *Research in Organizational Behavior,* Vol 12, pp 295–336.

Ranga, L. M., Miedema, J. L., and Jorna, R. J. (2008), 'Enhancing the innovative capacity of small firms through Triple Helix interactions: challenges and opportunities', *Technology Analysis and Strategic Management,* Vol 20, pp 697–716.

Ranga, M., and Etzkowitz, H. (2012), 'Great expectations: an innovation solution to the contemporary economic crisis', *European Planning Studies,* Vol 20, No 9, pp 1429–1438.

Ranga, M., Perälampi, J., and Kansikas, J. (2013), 'University brainpower unchained: a comparative analysis of university–business cooperation in the US and Finland', *Entrepreneurship Theory and Practice* (forthcoming).

Rodrigues, C., and Melo, A. (2010), 'The Triple Helix Model as inspiration for local development policies: an experience-based perspective', *Working Paper SACSJP,* University of Aveiro, Aveiro.

Rothaermel, F. T., Agung, S. D., and Jiang, L. (2007), 'University entrepreneurship: a taxonomy of the literature', *Industrial and Corporate Change,* Vol 16, No 4, pp 691–791.

Ruuska, I., and Teigland, R. (2009), 'Ensuring project success through collective competence and creative conflict in public–private partnerships: a case study of Bygga Villa, a Swedish Triple Helix e-government initiative', *International Journal of Project Management,* Vol 27, No 4, pp 323–334.

Sabato, J., and Mackenzi, M. (1982), *La Produccion de Technologia: Autonoma o Transnacional,* Nueva Imagen, Mexico.

Saenz, T. W. (2008), 'The path to innovation: the Cuban experience', *International Journal of Technology Management and Sustainable Development,* Vol 7, No 3, pp 205–221.

Saul, M. H., Gershman, J., and Grossman, A. (2011), 'Cornell wins contest for city tech campus', *The Wall Street Journal,* 19 December 2011, see: http://online.wsi.com/article/SB100001424052970204879004577107190097493490.html.

Schumpeter, J. A. (1942), *Capitalism, Socialism and Democracy,* George Allen and Unwin, New York.

Schumpeter, J. (1951), *Essays on Economic Topics,* Kennikat Press, Port Washington, New York.

Schutz, A. (1964), *Collected Papers II: Studies in Social Theory,* Brodersen, A., ed, Martinus Nijhoff, Dordrecht.

Shannon, C. E. (1948), 'A mathematical theory of communication', *Bell System Technical Journal,* Vol 27, pp 379–423 and pp 623–656.

Simmel, G. (1922 [1955]), *Conflict and the Web of Group Affiliations,* Wolff. K, translator and ed, Free Press, Glencoe, IL.

Steinmueller, W. E. (1994), 'Basic research and industrial innovation', in Dodgson, M., and Rothwell, R., eds, *The Handbook of Industrial Innovation,* Edward Elgar, Cheltenham, pp 54–66.

Sternberg, R. (2000), 'Innovation networks and regional development: evidence from the European Regional Innovation Survey (FRIS)', *European Planning Studies,* Vol 8, No 4, pp 389–407.

Storper, M. (1997), *The Regional World,* The Guilford Press, New York.

Svensson, P., Klofsten, M., and Etzkowitz, H. (2012), 'The Norrkoping way: a knowledge-based strategy for renewing a declining industrial city', *European Planning Studies,* Vol 20, No 4, pp 505–525.

Thwaites, A., and Wynarczyk, P. (1996), 'The economic performance of innovative small firms in the South East region and elsewhere in the UK', *Regional Studies,* Vol 30, pp 135–149.

Tijssen, R.J.W. (2006), 'Universities and industrially relevant science: towards measurement models and indicators of entrepreneurial orientation', *Research Policy,* Vol 35, No 10, pp 1569–1585.

Tijssen, R.J.W. (2012), 'Co-authored research publications and strategic analysis of public–private collaboration', *Research Evaluation,* Vol 21, No 3, pp 204–215.

Tödtling, F., and Kaufmann, A. (2001), 'The role of the region for innovation activities of SMEs', *European Urban and Regional Studies,* Vol 8, No 3, pp 203–215.

UNIDO (2003), 'Strategies for regional innovation systems: learning transfer and applications', *Policy Paper,* see http://www.unido.org/fileadmin/usermedia/Publications/Pub_free/Strategies_for_regional_innovation_systems.pdf.

Van Dyne, L., and Saavedra, R. (1996), 'A naturalistic minority influence experiment: effects on divergent thinking, conflict and originality in work-groups', *British Journal of Social Psychology,* Vol 35, No 1, pp 151–168.

Van Looy, B., Magerman, T., and Debackere, K. (2007), 'Developing technology in the vicinity of science: an examination of the relationship between science intensity (of patents) and technological productivity within the field of biotechnology', *Scientometrics,* Vol 70, No 2, pp 441–458.

Wang, J., and Shapira, P. (2012), 'Partnering with universities: a good choice for nanotechnology start-up firms?', *Small Business Economics,* Vol 38, No 2, pp 197–215.

Wolfe, D. (2003), *Clusters Old and New: The Transition to a Knowledge Economy in Canada's Regions,* Queen's School of Policy Studies, Kingston, Ontario.

Wong, P.K. (2007), 'Commercializing biomedical science in a rapidly changing "Triple Helix" nexus: the experience of the National University of Singapore', *Journal of Technology Transfer,* Vol 32, No 4, pp 367–395.

# Appendix 1

**Journal special issues based on papers presented at Triple Helix conferences (1996–2011)**

| Journal reference | Special Issue name and guest editors |
| --- | --- |
| *Science and Public Policy* Vol 24, No 1 (1997). | 'Science policy dimensions of the Triple Helix of university–industry–government relations' (Henry Etzkowitz and Loet Leydesdorff). |
| *Minerva* Vol 36, No 3 (1998) | 'The endless transition' (Henry Etzkowitz and Loet Leydesdorff). |
| *Industry and Higher Education* Vol 12, No 4 (1998). | 'A Triple Helix of university–industry–government relations' (Henry Etzkowitz and Loet Leydesdorff). |
| *Science and Public Policy* Vol 25, No 6 (1998). | 'The Triple Helix of innovation' (Henry Etzkowitz and Loet Leydesdorff). |
| *Journal of Technology Transfer* Vol 24, No 2–3 (1999). | 'University–industry–government relations: a Triple Helix' (Henry Etzkowitz and Loet Leydesdorff). |
| *Research Policy* Vol 29, No 2 (2000). | 'Triple Helix' (Henry Etzkowitz and Loet Leydesdorff). |
| *Science and Public Policy* Vol 27, No 4 (2000). | 'The Eastern European transition' (Henry Etzkowitz and Karel Muller). |

*(Continued)*

## Appendix 1 (Continued)

| Journal reference | Special Issue name and guest editors |
|---|---|
| *Science, Technology & Human Values* Vol 28, No 1 (2003). | |
| *International Journal of Technology Management & Sustainable Development* Vol 7, No 3 (2008). | 'Knowledge for innovation in Latin America' (Jose Manoel Carvalho de Mello). |
| *Scientometrics* Vol 58, No 2 (2003). | 'The Triple Helix of university–industry–government relations, (Loet Leydesdorff and Martin Meyer). |
| *Science and Public Policy* Vol 30, No 4 (2003). | 'Boundary organisations in science: from discourse to construction' (Tomas Hellström and Merle Jacob). |
| *International Journal of Technology Management* Vol 27, No 5 (2004). | |
| *Technology Analysis and Strategic Management* Vol 17, No 1 (2005). | 'The management of innovation revisited: strategy, control and culture' (Markus Pohlman, Christiane Gebhardt and Henry Etzkowitz). |
| *Research Policy* Vol 35, No 10 (2006). | 'Triple Helix indicators of knowledge-based innovation systems' (Loet Leydesdorff and M. Meyer). |
| *Scientometrics* Vol 70, No 2 (2007). | 'The scientometrics of a Triple Helix of university–industry– government relations' (Loet Leydesdorff and Martin Meyer). |
| *Science and Public Policy* Vol 35, No 9 (2008). | 'Building the entrepreneurial university: a global perspective' (Henry Etzkowitz and Chunyan Zhou). |
| *Industry and Higher Education* Vol 24, No 3 (2010). | 'Knowledge exchange and the Third Mission of universities' (Girma Zawdie and John Edmondson). |
| *Journal of Technology Management and Innovation* Vol 5, No 1 (2010). | 'Gender dimension in technology, innovation and entrepreneurship' (Marina Ranga and Henry Etzkowitz). |
| *Technology Analysis and Strategic Management* Vol 22, No 7 (2010). | 'The Triple Helix and innovation systems (Girma Zawdie and Loet Leydesdorff). |
| *Science and Public Policy* Vol 38, No 1 (2011). | 'Triple Helix in the context of developing countries' (Mohammed Saad and Girma Zawdie). |
| *Industry and Higher Education* Vol 27, No 4 (2013) | 'Innovation policy as a concept for developing economies: renewed perspectives on the Triple Helix system' (Dessy Irawati and Christiane Gebhardt). |
| *Social Science Information* Vol 52, No 4 (2013) | 'Silicon Valley: global model or unique anomaly?' (Henry Etzkowitz). |

# Individual and institutional drivers of technology transfer in open innovation

**Giancarlo Lauto, Massimo Bau'**
**and Cristiana Compagno**

**Abstract:** *The open innovation perspective offers a powerful framework which can be used in developing an understanding of the relationships that are established between academia and industry in the process of technology transfer. This paper develops a fourfold classification of technology transfer activities based on consultancy and the protection of intellectual property rights and identifies the factors characterizing each activity. An empirical study was conducted with a sample of 249 researchers affiliated to Italian universities, and the results indicate that specific forms of technology transfer are associated with particular configurations of regional systems of innovation, academic organizations and the motivations of researchers. The authors find that exchanges of tacit knowledge benefit from social interaction, while those based on codified knowledge are less context dependent. In addition, more complex forms of technology transfer – those combining tacit and codified knowledge – require a broader endowment of resources, at both individual and contextual levels.*

**Keywords:** *technology transfer; consultancy; open innovation; regional innovation systems; research incentives; intellectual property rights*

*Giancarlo Lauto (corresponding author) and Cristiana Compagno are with the Department of Economics and Statistics, University of Udine, via Tomadini 30a, I-33100 Udine, Italy. E-mail: giancarlo.lauto@uniud.it; cristiana.compagno@uniud.it. Massimo Bau' is with CeFEO and ESOL, Jönköping International Business School, PO Box 1026, SE-55111, Jönköping, Sweden. E-mail: massimo.bau@jibs.hj.se*

As a consequence of the increased demand for social accountability of academic activities (Gibbons *et al*, 1994), universities are emphasizing their role in society as active participants in socio-economic development at regional and local levels. The transformation of the role of the university in society has taken many forms. Initially, universities extended their mission from knowledge production (research) and dissemination (teaching) to the exploitation of the outcomes of applied research, in the process of innovation. To this end, they promoted relationships concerning technology transfer (TT) with the industrial sector. In addition, science itself, as represented by academia, has moved closer to industry, with recently emerged fields such as the biosciences, nano-sciences and computer sciences starting to give rise to technology streams that can be directly exploited by commercial enterprises (Stokes, 1997). On the industrial side, firms have increasingly activated strategies designed to achieve the systematic incorporation of external inputs into their internal R&D activities (Chesbrough, 2005, 2006). As a result, management of activities at the interface between universities and industry has come to be regarded as of particular relevance with regard to the development of innovation processes (Woollard *et al*, 2007; Fraser, 2010).

In order to perform the task of TT, universities introduced new organizational units and incentive mechanisms (Etzkowitz and Kemelgor, 1998; Etzkowitz, 2002). The literature emphasizes the role of institutional factors – such as the responsiveness of the innovation system – in enabling the effectiveness of the process of TT. The Triple Helix model (Leydesdorff and Etzkowitz, 1998) epitomizes this relationship. But to what extent do the features of a local system of innovation affect scientists' propensity to engage in TT? Or, rather, is TT driven by individual cognitive and social resources and by scientists' willingness to break free from the 'ivory tower'? Are different forms of TT enabled by specific configurations of individual, organizational and institutional factors?

This paper examines how the contextual setting and individual factors affect the activation of three distinct forms of TT defined by the provision of consultancy services and the protection of intellectual property rights (IPR). The paper is structured as follows. After discussing the concept of TT in an open innovation framework, we identify the individual and contextual factors affecting TT and, based on this literature, we derive a series of hypotheses. This is followed by a description of the methodology used for the empirical study. After discussing the results, we offer concluding remarks, in the final section.

## Technology transfer in an open innovation framework

The open innovation perspective (Chesbrough, 2005) offers a powerful framework for the analysis of university–industry linkages. According to the open innovation paradigm, firms generate technological innovation by recombining internal and external knowledge flows

(Chesbrough *et al*, 2006). The prominent role of external sources in this process highlights the fact that innovation is generated within inter-organizational networks, rather than by firms isolated from the environment in which they operate (Coombs *et al*, 2003). This perspective emphasizes the network as a mechanism of coordination of innovation activities, distinct from market transactions (Perkmann and Walsh, 2007). The importance of networks as a source of innovation increases with the complexity and the novelty of the technology developed (Powell *et al*, 1996): innovation in science-based industries and discontinuous technological innovation are heavily dependent on the activation of knowledge flows with institutional producers of knowledge, such as universities and research centres (Audretsch *et al,* 2002; Lynskey, 2010). Although collaborative networks are defined by several kinds of relationships between actors in the system of innovation, formal collaboration represents one of the 'strong' mechanisms for knowledge exchange within an open system of interconnected firms and organizations with related interests (Dodgson and Hinze, 2001). Mechanisms of TT include a wide array of tools, such as spin-off companies, protection and licensing of patents and other IPR, collaborative projects including academic and industrial scientists, and provision of consultancy and advice services (Bozeman, 2000).

The literature has pointed out that collaboration between academia and industry is impeded by a divergence in goals and incentives. While the scientific system seeks to achieve advancement of the frontiers of knowledge and the diffusion of discoveries, commercial enterprises are motivated by economic demands and tend to maintain secrecy with regard to the results of research activities (Dasgupta and David, 1994). The establishment of university–industry collaborative activities requires scientists to overcome these institutional differences – which expose scholars to a trade-off between the activities of scientific production and TT (Sandelin, 2010). The trade-off between the active promotion of entrepreneurial activities by science policy (De Pablo *et al*, 2011) and the complementary aspects of research and commercialization at contextual and individual levels (Buenstorf, 2009; Larsen, 2011) still strongly affects scientists' professional choices in terms of research strategy and commitment to non-academic activities, despite recent changes in the incentive structure of academia.

Most of the open innovation literature adopts the perspective of firms in the university–industry relationship (De Wit *et al*, 2007; Gassmann and Enkel, 2004). Perkmann and Walsh (2007) move out of the mainstream, however, analyzing the processes of TT from the point of view of the university. These authors discuss seven types of TT (summarized in Table 1) which identify specific linkages between universities and industry in an open innovation environment.

As firms increasingly innovate by using external resources and knowledge, universities seek to identify new opportunities for the application and commercialization of the outcomes of scientific research in order to generate additional research funding and to accomplish their mission in society. In order to understand better the insights offered by the open innovation theory, it is important to consider the systemic dimension in which the knowledge flows take place. Regional systems of innovation – paving the way for knowledge transfer between multiple actors located in the same territory (Asheim and Isaksen, 2002; Cassia *et al*, 2008; Cooke and Uranga, 1997) – offer a platform for the activation of networks in an open innovation perspective (Komninos, 2004; Torkkeli *et al*, 2007).

This present study sets out to provide an empirical answer to two issues raised by Perkmann and Walsh's (2007) research agenda about the university–industry relationships in an open innovation framework. It is suggested that there is a need to develop a deeper understanding of (a) the search and match processes preceding university–industry interactions and (b) the organization and management of collaboration arrangements. The first issue considers the influence of network mechanisms on the type of innovation outcomes. The second issue focuses, *inter alia*, on the role of individual-level incentives and motivations. We address these issues by investigating how forms of TT are associated with different levels of networking capability at the contextual level – that is, regional innovation systems and academia – and with specific resources and incentives at the individual level.

We conceptualize four profiles of researchers based on involvement in two of the aforementioned mechanisms of university–industry collaboration: IPR protection and

**Table 1. Typologies of university–industry linkages.**

| | |
|---|---|
| **Research partnerships** | Inter-organizational arrangements for pursuing collaborative R&D |
| **Research services** | Activities commissioned by industrial clients including contract research and consulting. |
| **Academic entrepreneurship** | Development and commercial exploitation of technologies pursued by academic inventors through a company they (partly) own. |
| **Human resource transfer** | Multi-context learning mechanisms such as training of industry employees, postgraduate training in industry, graduate trainees and secondments to industry, adjunct faculty. |
| **Informal interaction** | Formation of social relationships and networks at conferences, etc. |
| **Commercialization of property rights** | Transfer of university-generated IP (such as patents) to firms – for example, via licensing. |
| **Scientific publications** | Use of codified scientific knowledge in industry |

*Source:* Perkmann and Walsh, 2007, p 262.

|  |  | No IPR protection | IPR protection |
|---|---|---|---|
| **Propensity to consultancy** | **High** | Consultant | Complex |
|  | **low** | No TT activity | Technological |

**Figure 1.** The four profiles of technology transfer conceptualized in the theoretical model.

consultancy. The four profiles, summarized in Figure 1, are as follows:

- 'complex', which characterizes scientists who both protect IPR arising from their research and provide consultancy services;
- 'technological', which characterizes scientists who protect IPR but do not provide consultancy services;
- 'consultant', which characterizes scientists who provide consultancy services but do not protect IPR; and
- 'not engaged in TT', which characterizes scientists who are not involved in any of the aforementioned TT activities.

## Individual and contextual factors affecting technology transfer

Regarding the first issue identified by Perkmann and Walsh (2007) – the role of networks in search and matching processes – we assume that university–industry relationships facilitate the recognition of opportunities for the exploitation of research (Braczyk *et al*, 1998; Landry *et al*, 2003; Torkkeli *et al*, 2007); that

is, networks comprising different actors involved in innovation-related activities that are co-located in a given region can offer a favourable platform for collaboration (Feldman and Kogler 2010). To exploit fully the benefits of collaboration with universities, firms need to set up adequate organizational and cognitive mechanisms that provide for absorption of knowledge produced in the scientific system (Cohen and Levinthal, 1990). By performing formalized research and development (R&D) activities internally, firms develop the competencies needed to interact effectively with other actors in the system of innovation and to benefit from external cognitive inputs; moreover, formal R&D signals the involvement of firms in exploration projects that are more likely to benefit from the contribution of academic research. The literature on the geography of innovation emphasizes that the absorptive capability of a territory is particularly important for activating transfer of tacit knowledge, while it plays a lesser role in the transfer of codified knowledge (Feldman and Kogler 2010; Asheim *et al*, 2011). We therefore propose the following hypothesis.

Hypothesis 1. *The engagement of a researcher in TT activities involving a tacit component – identified here by the 'consultancy' and 'complex' profiles – is positively related to the level of business R&D of the region in which the researcher is based.*

University–industry relationships are often mediated by organizations such as university TT offices (TTOs) whose primary purpose is to support researchers willing to engage with industry and publicize the scientific competencies of a university. Moreover, TTOs influence researchers' decisions to undertake TT activities, promoting the culture of academic entrepreneurship and commercialization of research within the academic community (O'Shea *et al*, 2005). While many universities have established TTOs, the efficacy of such offices in brokerage and cultural processes varies greatly. We suggest that by considering the volume of activity of a TTO in terms of IPR protection – the most frequent TT activity – both the level of experience of TTO professionals and the diffusion of a culture favourable to TT can be identified. Indeed, scientists intensely involved in TT may activate imitation dynamics in their immediate social environment.

Hypothesis 2. *The engagement of a researcher in TT is positively related to the quantity of patent applications and award of the university with which the researcher is affiliated.*

Referring to Perkmann and Walsh (2007) on the need to establish better organization and management of collaboration arrangements, through understanding of the individual and contextual level of university–industry relationships, we suggest that the decision to engage in TT and the type of TT activities performed are affected by individual variations in incentives and the resources mobilized in the process.

Previous studies (see, for example, Landry *et al*, 2007) presented analyses of how the endowment of financial and social resources and human capital affects scientists' propensity to TT. We suggest an extension of the analytical framework, introducing the dimension of the rewards offered by the incentive structure of science.

Considering the financial dimension, the nature of the funding institution influences the orientation and the goals of a scientist's research. While organizations that are part of the academic system tend to grant research funds on the grounds of the scientific relevance of a project, non-academic organizations tend to favour the industrial or societal impact of a project. Scientists having obtained finance from private companies, the European Union or through public–private schemes benefit from additional resources that allow them to pursue larger-scale projects that, arguably, are aimed at achieving marke table – that is, commercially attractive and viable – results (Carayol and Matt, 2004; O'Shea *et al*, 2005).

Hypothesis 3. *The engagement of a researcher in TT is positively related to the availability of funding granted by non-academic organizations.*

Relations with non-academic actors (such as firms, business associations, technology brokers and public agencies) are beneficial to TT not only in terms of financing but also to generate opportunities for knowledge exchange (Landry *et al*, 2003). By interacting with firms, scientists can access new information or develop a more business-oriented approach (Haeussler and Colyvas, 2011). Poyago-Theotoky *et al,* (2002) stress the importance of collaboration between universities and enterprises as a source of opportunities regarding the complementary aspects of resources and expertise.

> Hypothesis 4. *The engagement of a researcher in TT is positively related to the breadth of the researcher's social capital.*

Finally, we consider the dimension of the incentives set by the academic community and the individual motivations that affect a scientist's decision to engage, or not, in TT.

Academic science is characterized by an incentive structure that rewards the disclosure of research results and relies on the publication system for the circulation of these outcomes. In contrast, industrial research prefers secrecy, as a mechanism for appropriating the economic value of knowledge (Dasgupta and David, 1994). Thus, the reputation – and career progression – of academic scientists are associated with contributions to the advancement of science through publication in prestigious journals. The introduction of TT as one of the missions of academic science may generate a conflict with the goals and strategies of researchers, particularly so when TT is seen as potentially harmful for a researcher's reputation in the scientific community or for their career. It should be noted that engagement in TT may absorb intellectual resources, distracting the researcher from 'traditional' activities – which are the most important criteria for assessment of researchers' performance.

It can reasonably be anticipated that academic ranking influences the propensity of a researcher to engage in TT. Numerous studies show that the productivity of scientists peaks in the period immediately subsequent to achievement of a doctorate, when the incentives to focus on research to obtain a tenured position are most powerful, and then decreases slowly (Levin and Stephan, 1991; Bonaccorsi and Daraio, 2007). In addition, TT – unlike research – generally ensures a financial return in the shorter term, although with a greater degree of uncertainty, something that might be of interest for researchers in later stages of their careers (Carayol, 2007). Finally, academic ranking is an indicator of a researcher's human capital and thus a higher ranking indicates a greater knowledge and expertise that can be transferred.

> Hypothesis 5. *The engagement of a researcher in TT is positively related to their academic ranking.*

Independent of the pressure to publish, to achieve career advancements, the propensity towards TT depends on the extent to which a researcher conceives the goals of commercialization as being compatible with the mission to produce knowledge and disseminate it to the public domain. It is reasonable to expect that all academic scientists share the norms of universalism, communalism, disinterestedness, originality and organized scepticism (Merton, 1973; Ziman, 2000). Nonetheless, the commitment of individuals to these values may vary, and it is equally reasonable to expect that scientists who express a 'radical' adherence to the values of open science are less inclined to engage in TT.

> Hypothesis 6. *The engagement of a researcher in TT activities is negatively related to their commitment to the values of open science.*

## Sample description and methodology

The empirical study described here seeks to develop an understanding of the drivers of the four 'profiles of TT' outlined in the theory section. The study is based on a survey of researchers working in Italian universities, integrated with data obtained from publicly available sources.

In order to produce a comprehensive picture of the dynamics of TT in the scientific community, we included assistant professors, associate professors, full professors and doctoral students and research assistants in the survey. We gathered information from these individuals using a questionnaire sent by e-mail in the period September–October 2007; and 249 valid responses were received from scholars affiliated to 27 universities.

The study considers the TT activities undertaken by the researchers in the five years preceding the survey, the period regarded as that in which the onset of the diffusion of the entrepreneurial culture in Italian academia occurred (Piccaluga and Balderi, 2007). The distribution of the respondents according to their academic status and gender mirrors that of the Italian academic population as of 31 December 2006. The distribution of respondents according to field of study shows the dominance of engineering, computer science and chemistry, accounting for some 37% of the sample, probably the result of greater interest in TT in these disciplines.

We characterized each researcher according to the infrastructural and organizational features of their university and of the regional innovation system in which the institution is located. Data were gathered from public sources such as the Eurostat Database, the EPO (European Patent Office Database) and MIUR (Italian Ministry of Education, University and Research). We considered data with a one-year time-lag in order to account for the delayed effect of infrastructural variables on individual performance.

Two dependent variables were considered: 'engagement', a binary variable that takes the value of 1 if the researcher concerned has undertaken activities of IPR protection and/or consultancy and 0 (zero) otherwise; and 'profile', which captures the four TT profiles defined in the theory section: consultancy, technological, complex and not engaged in TT.

In addition, the following explanatory variables were also considered. At the level of the individual, we account for the reliance of scientists on non-academic sources of funding; and their social capital. 'External funding' and 'social capital' are additive indexes based respectively on the following components: the importance for the scientist of finance from private companies, from public–private schemes and from the European Union; and the frequency of relations with private companies, government agencies, business associations, centres of TT, and the media. The importance and frequency of each item are reported on Likert scales from 1 to 5. We are aware that 'external funding' and 'social capital' could be endogenous, given that they may be regarded as an expression of underlying attributes of the researcher; that is, the 'ability' of the researcher. This ability of scientists affects both their propensity towards TT and the likelihood of their accessing external funding and building social capital. In order to correct for this potential omission of a variable, we include 'scientific productivity' in the model as a proxy for researcher 'ability', in accordance with the work of Wooldridge (2008). This variable is a self-reported count of research outputs – articles, books and book chapters – with international publications being weighted by a factor of 5. We consider a dummy variable, to capture researchers' 'devotion to science', which takes the value of 1 for scientists who attribute a score of 5 out of 5 to their desire to contribute

to scientific progress and to the prestige of the scientific profession as motivations for following an academic career path. By using a dummy rather than a continuous variable, we are able to capture the effect of an 'extreme' adherence to the values of open science.

It should be noted that for a scientist, the importance of external finance, social capital, scientific productivity and adherence to the values of open science may increase as a consequence of involvement in TT. Since scientists active in TT may report higher levels of these variables, our analyses may overestimate their effect on TT. However, our empirical study provides results that are useful in attempting to understand the nature of the association among forms of TT and explanatory variables.

Four categories of academic ranking are considered: PhD student and research assistant, assistant professor, associate professor and full professor – with associate professor serving as a benchmark in the regression analysis. We control for gender and academic discipline, distinguishing between agriculture and veterinary, medicine and biology, social sciences and humanities, computer science and (the group of) engineering, chemistry, physics and earth sciences that serves as the benchmark in the regression analysis.

At the contextual level, we considered the 'intensity of business R&D', which expresses the extent of investment in R&D as a proportion of GDP by firms located in the same region as the university of the scientist concerned. The variable 'intensity of patenting' captures the number of patents per 1,000 science and technology researchers obtained by the university in which the scientist is located, thus expressing the commitment of the university to TT. To control for the possible effect of a larger resource endowment on the level of TT performance, a dummy expressing the 'size of university' was introduced, which takes the value of 1 if the university employed, as of 31 December 2006, a number of researchers higher than the median (731) and the value of 0 (zero) otherwise.

We present the empirical study in three steps. First, we provide a descriptive analysis of the distribution of the respondents across the profiles of TT and along the explanatory variables. Second, we assess the factors associated with engagement in *any* TT activity using a logistic regression; and, finally, we consider and discriminate between the different profiles of TT, identifying the drivers of each by means of a multinomial logistic regression.

We exclude consideration that the estimates of the regression models are biased by multicollinearity, because the maximum level of the variance inflation factor is well below the threshold value of 10 and only in one case is the pairwise coefficient of correlation (Table 2) above 0.500 (between 'size of university' and 'intensity of patenting').

## Discussion

The descriptive statistics (Table 2) indicate that almost one third of the respondents are engaged in TT. The 'consultancy' and 'technological'

profiles account for a similar number of cases, while the more demanding 'complex' profile is sensitively less frequent. In Table 3 we report the results of a series of tests comparing the mean of the independent continuous variables and the distribution of the discrete variables between the groups of scientists engaged in TT and not engaged in TT, and the four profiles of TT.

The tests show that, on average, scientists engaging in TT have a richer social capital and are more reliant on non-academic sources of funding. The distribution of these variables is also significantly different across profiles of TT. Furthermore, we find that the distribution of scientists by ranking, discipline and localization in a R&D-intensive local system differs across profiles.

In order to find more robust support for this preliminary evidence, and to control for possible spurious relationships between variables, we employed a logistic regression to identify what factors are associated with the participation of scientists in any TT activity (Table 4). In Model 1 we consider only the controls, while in Model 2 we introduce all the explanatory variables. Model 2 confirms that scientists financed by non-academic institutions and interacting frequently with actors outside academia (rows a, b) are positively associated with engagement in TT. Furthermore, the model reveals that untenured researchers are less likely to initiate TT than associate professors (row e) and researchers with any other academic ranking – as Wald tests (not presented here) showed. Surprisingly, Model 2 does not indicate any effect of the characteristics of the innovation system and the university in which a researcher operates (rows i, j).

However, these results tell only part of the story since they do not indicate how the three profiles of TT differ in their driving factors. To this end, we used a multinomial logistic regression because the four TT profiles correspond to the outcomes of a categorical variable expressing the types of involvement in TT. The estimates indicate what factors are associated with undertaking a specific TT activity, as compared to the baseline case of absence of involvement in TT. In Table 5, following presentation of the controls-only Model 3, we introduce the contextual-level variables relative to the system of innovation and to the university, in Model 4; and, finally, in Model 5 we include all the explanatory variables.

The results reveal that each profile is characterized by specific drivers, suggesting that TT, rather than being a uniform phenomenon, can be better understood if separated into its multiple aspects. Hypothesis 1 predicted a positive association between systems of innovation characterized by a strong orientation of firms towards R&D and the activation of forms of TT characterized by the transfer of tacit knowledge. Model 5 provides support for Hypothesis 1, showing that the level of business R&D of the region in which a scientist operates is significantly higher for scientists in the complex and consultancy profiles (rows 'consultant' h and 'complex' h) than in the baseline, while it does not

differ between scientists generating patents and those not active in TT (row 'technological' h).

These results suggest that the presence of a community of R&D-oriented firms in proximity to a knowledge producer is a prerequisite for the transfer of tacit knowledge. In contrast, patenting and licensing can effectively link researchers and firms located in different territories, given the codified and impersonal nature of those TT mechanisms. This result reaffirms the consolidated literature about the localized nature of tacit knowledge transfer (Asheim *et al*, 2011). With regard to the university-level factors, we find that the control expressing the size of the university is always irrelevant; rather, scientists belonging to the complex profile (row 'complex' i) tend to work in universities characterized by a higher intensity of patent activity. This result provides partial support for Hypothesis 2, which predicted a positive effect for all the forms of TT. It can be argued that more sophisticated forms of TT benefit from a culture open to academic entrepreneurship and from experience of support units, while these factors do not make a difference in the case of simpler forms of TT. Comparing Model 5 with Model 4 shows that the effect of contextual factors on the 'complex' profile is statistically significant only when individual-level variables are included – suggesting that the individual- and contextual-level factors are somehow interrelated.

Moving to the individual-level variables, we find a general tendency for more senior scientists to be

# Table 2. Descriptive statistics and correlation matrix.

| Dependent variables | Number (%) | Min; Max | 1 | 2 | 3 | 4 | 5 | 6 | 7 | 8 | 9 | 10 | 11 | 12 | 13 | 14 | 15 | 16 | 17 | 18 | 19 | 20 | 21 | 22 |
|---|---|---|---|---|---|---|---|---|---|---|---|---|---|---|---|---|---|---|---|---|---|---|---|---|
| 1. Complex profile | 16 (6.43%) | 0; 1 | 1 | | | | | | | | | | | | | | | | | | | | | |
| 2. Technological profile | 30 (12.05%) | 0; 1 | -0.569 | 1 | | | | | | | | | | | | | | | | | | | | |
| 3. Consultant profile | 32 (12.85%) | 0; 1 | -0.548 | -0.142 | 1 | | | | | | | | | | | | | | | | | | | |
| 4. No technology transfer | 171 (68.67%) | 0; 1 | -0.388 | -0.101 | -0.097 | 1 | | | | | | | | | | | | | | | | | | |
| 5. Engagement | 78 (31.33%) | 0; 1 | -1 | 0.569 | 0.548 | 0.388 | 1 | | | | | | | | | | | | | | | | | |
| **Dependent variables — Continuous** (Mean (SD)) | | | | | | | | | | | | | | | | | | | | | | | | |
| 6. Intensity of business R&D | 0.573 (0.230) | 0.035; 1.37 | -0.086 | -0.037 | 0.067 | -0.046 | 0.132 | 1 | | | | | | | | | | | | | | | | |
| 7. Intensity of patenting | 45.986 (25.503) | 0; 234 | -0.037 | 0.062 | -0.105 | 0.123 | 0.037 | 0.154 | 1 | | | | | | | | | | | | | | | |
| 8. External funding | 7.108 (3.096) | 1; 15 | -0.209 | 0.099 | 0.087 | 0.145 | 0.209 | 0.058 | 0.031 | 1 | | | | | | | | | | | | | | |
| 9. Social capital | 12.020 (4.468) | 5; 25 | -0.362 | 0.302 | 0.029 | 0.234 | 0.362 | 0.011 | 0.073 | 0.240 | 1 | | | | | | | | | | | | | |
| 10. Scientific productivity | 45.932 (54.078) | 0; 361 | -0.104 | -0.087 | 0.166 | 0.094 | 0.104 | -0.085 | -0.145 | 0.001 | 0.081 | 1 | | | | | | | | | | | | |
| **Discrete** (n (%)) | | | | | | | | | | | | | | | | | | | | | | | | |
| 11. Size of university | 102 (40.96%) | 0; 1 | -0.071 | -0.076 | 0.118 | 0.082 | 0.071 | 0.359 | -0.525 | 0.121 | -0.081 | 0.058 | 1 | | | | | | | | | | | |
| 12. Devotion to science | 126 (50.60%) | 0; 1 | 0.026 | -0.029 | 0.020 | -0.036 | -0.026 | -0.044 | -0.057 | -0.002 | 0.051 | 0.167 | 0.072 | 1 | | | | | | | | | | |
| 13. Untenured | 101 (40.56%) | 0; 1 | 0.135 | 0.049 | -0.155 | -0.116 | -0.135 | 0.191 | 0.181 | 0.228 | -0.088 | -0.476 | -0.006 | -0.214 | 1 | | | | | | | | | |
| 14. Assistant professor | 60 (24.10%) | 0; 1 | -0.004 | -0.048 | 0.080 | -0.033 | 0.004 | -0.006 | -0.169 | -0.190 | -0.110 | 0.067 | 0.123 | -0.006 | -0.466 | 1 | | | | | | | | |
| 15. Associate professor | 44 (17.67%) | 0; 1 | -0.050 | 0.074 | 0.023 | -0.036 | 0.050 | -0.109 | -0.034 | 0.008 | 0.005 | 0.165 | -0.065 | 0.121 | -0.383 | -0.261 | 1 | | | | | | | |
| 16. Full professor | 44 (17.67%) | 0; 1 | -0.118 | -0.084 | 0.087 | 0.222 | 0.118 | -0.131 | -0.010 | -0.088 | 0.232 | 0.372 | -0.065 | 0.100 | -0.383 | -0.261 | -0.215 | 1 | | | | | | |
| 17. Engineering, Chemistry | 111 (44.58%) | 0; 1 | -0.178 | 0.042 | 0.115 | 0.127 | 0.178 | 0.083 | -0.152 | 0.214 | -0.053 | 0.184 | 0.305 | 0.046 | -0.066 | 0.024 | 0.051 | 0.008 | 1 | | | | | |
| 18. Biomedicine | 16 (6.43%) | 0; 1 | 0.106 | -0.101 | 0.004 | -0.069 | -0.106 | -0.018 | -0.057 | -0.189 | -0.170 | 0.190 | 0.048 | 0.095 | -0.183 | 0.006 | 0.136 | 0.093 | -0.235 | 1 | | | | |
| 19. Social Sciences, Humanities | 66 (26.51%) | 0; 1 | 0.053 | 0.123 | -0.138 | -0.083 | -0.053 | -0.085 | 0.064 | -0.221 | 0.052 | -0.290 | -0.204 | -0.062 | 0.078 | 0.066 | -0.111 | -0.064 | -0.539 | -0.157 | 1 | | | |
| 20. Computer Science | 24 (9.64%) | 0; 1 | 0.133 | -0.125 | -0.037 | -0.030 | -0.133 | -0.039 | 0.117 | 0.226 | 0.087 | 0.021 | -0.106 | -0.004 | 0.091 | -0.120 | 0.027 | -0.009 | -0.293 | -0.086 | -0.196 | 1 | | |
| 21. Agriculture, Veterinary | 32 (12.85%) | 0; 1 | 0.001 | -0.040 | 0.042 | -0.003 | -0.001 | 0.037 | 0.081 | -0.087 | 0.058 | -0.049 | -0.125 | -0.053 | 0.049 | -0.020 | -0.052 | 0.011 | -0.344 | -0.101 | -0.231 | -0.125 | 1 | |
| 22. Gender (female) | 81 (32.53%) | 0; 1 | 0.044 | 0.015 | -0.099 | 0.028 | -0.044 | 0.095 | 0.033 | -0.077 | -0.111 | -0.151 | 0.084 | -0.017 | 0.142 | 0.050 | -0.142 | -0.097 | -0.071 | -0.042 | 0.224 | -0.198 | 0.015 | 1 |

**Table 3. Comparison of relevant independent variables between the profiles of technology transfer.**

| Profile | No TT | Consultancy | Technological | Complex | Chi-squared test with ties[a] |
|---|---|---|---|---|---|
| External funding | 6.673 | 7.906 | 7.833 | 8.813 | 14.553*** (3 df) |
| Social capital | 10.930 | 15.531 | 12.367 | 16 | 38.582*** (3 df) |
| Scientific productivity | 42.140 | 33.781 | 70.133 | 65.375 | 9.447** (3 df) |
| Intensity of business R&D | 0.560 | 0.614 | 0.545 | 0.689 | 9.137** (3 df) |
| | | | | | Chi-squared test |
| Devotion to science | 51.5% | 46.9% | 53.3% | 43.8% | 0.619 (3 df) |
| Ranking | | | | | 22.246*** (9 df) |
| Untenured | 30.9% | 6.0% | 2.4% | 1.2% | |
| Assistant Professor | 16.5% | 2.4% | 4.0% | 1.2% | |
| Associate Professor | 11.2% | 3.2% | 2.4% | 0.8% | |
| Full Professor | 10.0% | 1.2% | 3.2% | 3.2% | |
| Discipline | | | | | 21.457** (12 df) |
| Engineering and chemistry | 26.5% | 6.4% | 7.2% | 4.4% | |
| Biomedical | 5.6% | 0.0% | 0.8% | 0.0% | |
| Social science and humanities | 19.3% | 5.2% | 1.2% | 0.8% | |
| Computer science | 8.4% | 0.0% | 0.8% | 0.4% | |
| Agriculture and veterinary | 8.8% | 1.2% | 2.0% | 0.8% | |

Note: ***,** Significant at the 1% and 5% levels, respectively. [a] Kruskal-Wallis test for equality of populations.

**Table 4. Drivers of technology transfer: results of logistic regression.**

| | | Model 1 | | Model 2 | |
|---|---|---|---|---|---|
| a | External funding | | | 0.157*** | (0.060) |
| b | Social capital | | | 0.189*** | (0.038) |
| c | Scientific productivity | | | 0.001 | (0.003) |
| d | Devotion to science | | | −0.552 | (0.349) |
| | Ranking (base=Associate professor) | | | | |
| e | Untenured | | | −0.919* | (0.537) |
| f | Assistant Professor | | | −0.026 | (0.507) |
| g | Full Professor | | | 0.051 | (0.532) |
| h | Intensity of business R&D | | | 0.524 | (0.856) |
| i | Intensity of university patenting | | | 0.009 | (0.008) |
| j | Size of university | | | 0.407 | (0.458) |
| | Discipline (base=engineering and chemistry) | | | | |
| k | Biomedical | −1.577** | (0.776) | −1.098 | (0.765) |
| l | Social science and humanities | −0.540 | (0.344) | −0.419 | (0.444) |
| m | Computer science | −1.632** | (0.650) | −2.199*** | (0.775) |
| n | Agriculture and veterinary | −0.391 | (0.434) | −0.413 | (0.517) |
| o | Gender | −0.286 | (0.309) | −0.097 | (0.366) |
| | Constant | −0.302 | (0.212) | −4.275*** | (0.829) |
| Number of observations | | 249 | | 249 | |
| Log pseudo-likelihood | | −148.127 | (5) | −122.559 | (15) |
| Wald test Chi2 (df) | | 11.71 *** | | 51.85*** | |
| Pseudo $R^2$ | | 0.039 | | | 0.208 |

Note: Robust standard errors are in parentheses

***,**,* Significant at the 1% and 5% and 10% levels, respectively.

associated with more advanced forms of TT. This suggests that sophisticated forms of TT demand a greater amount of human capital in order to be effective. In fact, ranking reflects the visibility and the experience of, and the scientific knowledge accumulated by, a researcher. In particular, we find that full professorship is negatively related to consultancy activities (row 'consultant' g), as compared to all the other academic rankings. In contrast, it supports – better than any other ranking – 'complex' forms of TT (row 'complex' g). With regard to untenured scientists, we find that they are negatively related to the 'technological' and 'complex' profiles (rows 'technological' e and 'complex' e) but not to the – arguably less demanding – 'consultancy' profile (row 'consultant' e). Using calculations on the coefficients (not presented here) we found that untenured scientists have less propensity to pursue patent and 'complex' TT activities than scientists with any other ranking, but are similar in terms of propensity to consultancy. Finally, we do not find statistically significant differences between assistant professors and associate professors.

The picture that emerges from this analysis provides support for Hypothesis 5, which predicted that the more advanced forms of TT are pursued by scientists with higher human capital and less pressure to publish, such as full professors. This finding is in agreement with the literature, indicating that researchers with higher status tend to undertake extramural activities, being more

'free' from the pressures of career progression. The combination of these results suggests that the entry barriers to consulting activities are significantly lower than those of more complex activities: consultancy does not distract younger scholars from career goals; rather, it may represent a source of additional income. It is worth noting that Model 5 provides a much more nuanced picture than Model 2 (which latter indicates a penalty in being untenured faculty in starting TT).

It is interesting to analyse the motivational dimension in greater depth. Model 5 reveals that a high level of commitment to the values of open science is negatively related to the 'complex' profile (row 'complex' d), while such a linkage is not found with the others (rows 'consultant' d and 'technological' d). This suggests that scientists who feel a strong sense of belonging to the scientific community are less likely to engage in more advanced forms of TT: this provides partial support for Hypothesis 6. It can be argued that complex forms of TT are significantly more demanding than the (two) others and it seems that these activities tend to be substitutes for, rather than complementary to, the traditional activities of teaching and research, so that scientists deeply committed to the values of open science tend not to engage in more demanding forms of TT.

We also find that the roles of financial resources from non-academic providers and social capital are different across the profiles of TT. The availability of both is related to the 'complex' profile (rows 'complex' a, b). External funding is positively associated with the 'technological' and 'consultancy' profiles (rows 'technological' a, 'consultant' a), while the opposite is the case for social capital (rows 'consultant' b, 'technological' b). The drivers of the 'technological' profile seem to indicate that the involvement of non-academic partners – firms and the European Union – increases the pool of resources available to a research project and orients the study towards more applied objectives. These projects seem more likely to generate ground-breaking scientific results and technologies, characterized by the level of novelty necessary to receive patent protection. While the drivers of the 'technological' profile suggest that patents incorporate frontier knowledge, the 'consultancy' profile is associated neither with higher ranking nor with access to complementary financial resources. This suggests that consultancy appears to be a mechanism suitable for the transfer of more mature knowledge. In line with this perspective, we find a positive association between consultancy and social capital: it seems that opportunities for consultancy arise from personal connections, rather than formal financing agreements, with managers of firms and public agencies. Furthermore, we interpret the positive association of social capital with consultancy, and not patent activity, as a consequence of the higher levels of tacit knowledge transferred with the former mechanisms of TT. Because the 'complex' profile combines

consultancy and IPR protection, we find that both access to external funds and social capital are positively related to engagement of a scientist in this form of TT.

To summarize, there is full support for Hypotheses 3 and 4, dealing with non-academic sources of finance and social capital, with regard to the 'complex' profile, and only partial support for the other two. Finally, with regard to the controls, we find that the kind of mechanism activated to transfer knowledge to the industrial sector differs according to academic discipline and that the level of scientific production does not vary between researchers engaged and not engaged in TT.

## Concluding remarks

This paper contributes to a better interpretation of the literature on the university–industry relationship, highlighting how scientists activate distinct mechanisms of TT – or do not engage in TT – in the presence of specific configurations of resources at individual and contextual levels. We make a distinction in the mechanisms of TT between those particularly suitable for the transfer of tacit or codified knowledge; that is, consultancy and IPR. Based on those two mechanisms, we have produced a fourfold classification of TT profiles, defined by the activation of none, one, or both of the primary tools of TT.

Our results, summarized in Figure 2, indicate that the activation of more sophisticated forms of TT is supported by the mobilization of an

Table 5. Drivers of the profiles of technology transfer: results of multinomial logistic regression.

| Profile Consultant | | Model 3 | | Model 4 | | Model 5 | |
|---|---|---|---|---|---|---|---|
| a | External funding | | | | | 0.091 | (0.102) |
| b | Social capital | | | | | 0.326*** | (0.064) |
| c | Scientific productivity | | | | | -0.003 | (0.005) |
| d | Devotion to science | | | | | -0.427 | (0.521) |
| | *Ranking* (base = Associate professor) | | | | | | |
| e | Untenured | | | | | -0.469 | (0.720) |
| f | Assistant Professor | | | | | -0.407 | (0.758) |
| g | Full Professor | | | | | -1.478* | (0.896) |
| h | Intensity of business R&D | | | 1.564* | (0.893) | 1.636* | (0.968) |
| i | Intensity of university patenting | | | .002 | (0.010) | 0.007 | (0.010) |
| j | Size of University | | | -.723 | (0.626) | -0.785 | (0.709) |
| | *Discipline* (base = engineering and chemistry) | | | | | | |
| k | Biomedical | -33.646*** | (0.387) | -32.634*** | (0.421) | -36.451*** | (0.678) |
| l | Social science and humanities | 0.161 | (0.431) | 0.013 | (0.450) | -0.470 | (0.561) |
| m | Computer science | -33.669*** | (0.369) | -32.822*** | (0.419) | -38.813*** | (0.648) |
| n | Agriculture and veterinary | -0.561 | (0.678) | -.797 | (0.722) | -1.243 | (0.821) |
| o | Gender | -0.250 | (0.429) | -.271 | (0.442) | -0.111 | (0.557) |
| | Constant | -1.345*** | (0.303) | -2.050*** | (0.744) | -6.309*** | (1.632) |
| | | | | | | -6.777 | (1.682) |
| | **Technological** | | | | | | |
| a | External funding | | | | | 0.160** | (0.084) |
| b | Social capital | | | | | 0.064 | (0.049) |

| | (1) | | (2) | | (3) | |
|---|---|---|---|---|---|---|
| c | Scientific productivity | | | | 0.002 | (0.004) |
| d | Devotion to science | | | | −0.486 | (0.473) |
| | *Ranking* (base = Associate Professor) | | | | | |
| e | Untenured | | | | −1.143* | (0.722) |
| f | Assistant Professor | | | | 0.347 | (0.639) |
| g | Full Professor | | | | 0.383 | (0.677) |
| h | Intensity of business R&D | | −0.912 | (1.266) | −0.784 | (1.722) |
| i | Intensity of university patenting | | 0.002 | (0.010) | 0.008 | (0.013) |
| j | Size of university | | 0.849 | (0.568) | 0.981 | (0.629) |
| | *Discipline* (base = engineering and chemistry) | | | | | |
| k | Biomedical | −0.672 (0.796) | −0.640 | (0.748) | −0.654 | (0.693) |
| l | Social science and humanities | −1.348*** (0.658) | −1.123 | (0.687) | −0.824 | (0.724) |
| m | Computer science | −1.192 (0.792) | −0.990 | (0.820) | −1.291 | (0.827) |
| n | Agriculture and veterinary | −0.149 (0.572) | 0.163 | (0.625) | 0.249 | (0.651) |
| o | Gender | −0.654 (0.493) | −.735 | (0.489) | −0.562 | (0.562) |
| | Constant | −1.137*** (0.289) | −1.241*** | (0.717) | −3.342*** | (0.983) |
| | **Complex** | | | | | |
| a | External funding | | | | 0.346*** | (0.113) |
| b | Social capital | | | | 0.224** | (0.089) |
| c | Scientific productivity | | | | 0.000 | (0.004) |
| d | Devotion to science | | | | −1.391** | (0.675) |
| | *Status* (base = Associate Professor) | | | | | |
| e | Untenured | | | | −2.619* | (1.348) |
| f | Assistant Professor | | | | −0.174 | (1.155) |
| g | Full Professor | | | | 1.564* | (1.051) |
| h | Intensity of business R&D | | 0.910 | (1.123) | 3.172** | (1.507) |

(Continued)

**Table 5.** (continued)

| Profile Consultant | | Model 3 | | Model 4 | | Model 5 | |
|---|---|---|---|---|---|---|---|
| i | Intensity of university patenting | | | 0.024 | (0.015) | 0.025* | (0.015) |
| j | Size of university | | | 0.697 | (0.807) | 0.520 | (0.893) |
| | *Discipline* (base=engineering and chemistry) | | | | | | |
| k | Biomedical | −33.936*** | (0.424) | −32.442*** | (0.513) | −35.015*** | (0.653) |
| l | Social science and humanities | −1.433* | (0.809) | −1.051 | (0.827) | −1.329 | (1.096) |
| m | Computer science | −1.188 | (1.085) | −1.081 | (1.192) | −2.017 | (1.583) |
| n | Agriculture and veterinary | −0.619 | (0.806) | −0.380 | (0.856) | −1.061 | (1.242) |
| o | Gender | 0.223 | (0.566) | −0.042 | (0.574) | 0.966 | (0.740) |
| | Constant | −1.866*** | (0.381) | −4.025*** | (1.193) | 10.314*** | (2.026) |
| | Number of observations | 249 | | 249 | | 249 | |
| | Log pseudo-likelihood | −222.087 | | −214.388 | | −173.436 | |
| | Wald test Chi² (df) | 22033.53*** | (15) | 18756.08*** | (24) | 14053.320*** | (45) |
| | Pseudo $R^2$ | 0.064 | | 0.097 | | 0.262 | |

*Note:* Robust standard errors are in parentheses. \*\*\*, \*\*, \* Significant at the 1% and 5% and 10% levels, respectively

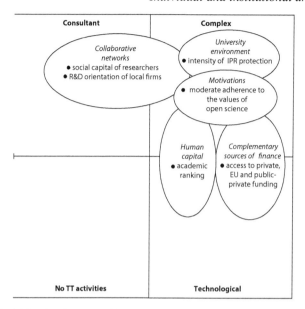

**Figure 2.** Variables having a positive association with the profiles of technology transfer.

increasing endowment of individual and contextual resources. With regard to the level of the innovation system, we find that the establishment of exchanges of tacit knowledge – in both the profiles based on consultancy – is enabled by the existence of an appropriate level of absorptive capacity and orientation towards innovation in the firms located in proximity to the university in which the scientists operate. This is not a prerequisite for patenting: knowledge codified in patents can be transferred at longer distances, and thus IPR protection is less dependent on the condition of the system of innovation in which a scientist is located.

At the level of the institution, we find that universities characterized by an inclination to obtaining patents are more likely to favour undertaking more complex TT activities. However, one limitation of our empirical study lies in the fact that the extent and the intensity of the patent activities is only a partial measure of effectiveness and efficiency of a TTO and of the diffusion of a culture of academic entrepreneurship. Further studies should use variables more expressive of those drivers of technology transfer.

These considerations suggest that the university senior management should assign to TTOs the mission of acting as brokers with the industrial system and specify this mission at two levels. The first task for TTOs is to elicit the demand – often unexpressed – for innovation from firms located in proximity to the university, in order to find possible matches with firms that would benefit from access to the existing knowledge base of the university, through low-value-added services such as consultancy. At the same time, they should actively search at global level for sponsors of large-scale projects that may generate discontinuous innovations and for potential users of technologies emerging from projects that are more leading edge.

The study contributes to the literature on how the academic community functions, suggesting the ability to undertake activities in addition to research is the result of a complex interaction of factors related to the nature of the discipline and the resource endowment of researchers. We find that social capital is positively related to tacit knowledge transfer, while access to external funding is positively related to codified knowledge transfer. We also find an additive effect of these two factors: complex knowledge transfers, which combine tacit and codified knowledge, require both types of resource. Moreover, the study reveals that a weaker commitment to the values of science is positively related to engagement in the most demanding, complex TT activities: this hints at the existence of a possible trade-off between 'traditional' and 'novel' missions of science.

Another limitation of the study lies in the fact that the unit of analysis – the individual researcher – does not allow consideration of factors such as team dynamics, which are particularly relevant for larger and more sophisticated research projects.

More studies remain necessary to address the other questions posed by Perkmann and Walsh (2007) on TT relationships in an open innovation perspective, such as the variation of organizational models and innovation-relevant outputs, the strategies used by firms for exploiting academic knowledge or the impact of institutions on the shape, extent and effects of university–industry relationships.

# References

Asheim, B., Boschma, R., and Cooke, P. (2011), 'Constructing regional advantage: platform policies based on related variety and differentiated knowledge bases', *Regional Studies*, Vol 45, No 7, pp 893–904.

Asheim, B., and Isaksen, A. (2002), 'Regional innovation systems: the integration of local "sticky" and global "ubiquitous" knowledge', *Journal of Technology Transfer*, Vol 27, No 1, pp 77–86.

Audretsch, D. B., Bozeman, B., Combs, K. L., Feldman, M. P., Link, A. N., Siegel, D. S., Stephan, P. E., Tassey, G., and Wessner, C. (2002), 'The economics of science and technology', *Journal of Technology Transfer*, Vol 27, No 2, pp 155–203.

Bonaccorsi, A., and Daraio, C. (2007), *Universities and Strategic Knowledge Creation: Specialization and Performance in Europe*, Edward Elgar, Cheltenham.

Bozeman, B. (2000), 'Technology transfer and public policy: a review of research and theory', *Research Policy*, Vol 29, No 4–5, pp 627–656.

Braczyk, H., Cooke, P., and Heidenreich, M. (1998), *Regional Innovation Systems: The Role of Governances in a Globalized World*, University College of London Press, London.

Buenstorf, G. (2009), 'Is commercialization good or bad for science? Individual-level evidence from the Max Planck Society', *Research Policy*, Vol 38, No 2, pp 281–292.

Carayol, N. (2007), 'Academic incentives, research organization and patenting at a large French university', *Economics of Innovation and New Technology*, Vol 16, No 2, pp 119–138.

Carayol, N., and Matt, M. (2004), 'Does research organization influence academic production? Laboratory level evidence from a large European university', *Research Policy*, Vol 33, No 8, pp 1081–1102.

Cassia, L., Colombelli, A., and Paleari, S. (2008), 'Regional transformation processes through the universities–institutions–industry relationship', *Industry and Higher Education*, Vol 22, No 2, pp 105–118.

Chesbrough, H. (2005), *Open Innovation: The New Imperative for Creating and Profiting from Technology*, Harvard Business School Press, Cambridge, MA.

Chesbrough, H., Vanhaverbeke, W., and West, J. (2006), *Open Innovation: Researching a New Paradigm*, Oxford University Press, Oxford.

Cohen, W., and Levinthal, D. (1990), 'Absorptive capacity: a new perspective on learning and innovation', *Administrative Science Quarterly*, Vol 35, No 1, pp 128–152.

Cooke, P., and Uranga, G. (1997), 'Regional innovation systems: institutional and organisational dimensions', *Research Policy*, Vol 26, No 4–5, pp 475–491.

Coombs, R., Harvey, M., and Tether, B. (2003), 'Analysing distributed processes of provision and innovation', *Industrial and Corporate Change*, Vol 12, No 6, pp 1125–1155.

Dasgupta, P., and David, P.A. (1994), 'Toward a new economics of science', *Research Policy*, Vol 23, pp 487–521.

De Pablo, I., Alfaro F., Rodriguez, M., and Valdés, E. (2011), 'Promoting entrepreneurial culture in the university: the institutional collaborative model at the Universidad Autonoma de Madrid', *Industry and Higher Education*, Vol 25, No 5, pp 375–382.

De Wit, J., Dankbaar, B., and Vissers, G. (2007), 'Open innovation: the new way of knowledge transfer?', *Journal of Business Chemistry*, Vol 4, No 1, pp 11–19.

Dodgson, M., and Hinze, S. (2001), 'Measuring Innovation', in *International Conference on Measuring and Evaluating Industrial R&D and Innovation in the Knowledge-based Economy*, 23–24 August, Taipei.

Etzkowitz, H. (2002), *The Triple Helix: MIT and the Rise of Entrepreneurial Science*, Gordon and Breach, London.

Etzkowitz, H., and Kemelgor, C. (1998), 'The role of research centres in the collectivisation of academic science', *Minerva*, Vol 36, No 3, pp 271–288.

Feldman, M. P., and Kogler, D. F. (2010), 'Stylized facts in the geography of innovation', in Hall, B. H., and Rosenberg, N., eds, *Handbook of The Economics of Innovation, Volume 1*, Elsevier, Amsterdam, pp 381–410.

Fraser, J. (2010), 'Academic technology transfer: tracking, measuring and enhancing its impact', *Industry and Higher Education*, Vol 24, No 5, pp 311–317.

Gassmann, O., and Enkel, E. (2004), 'Towards a theory of open innovation: three core process archetypes', *Proceedings of the R&D Management Conference*, 6–9 July, Lisbon.

Gibbons, M., Limoges, C., Nowotny, H., Schwartzman, S., Scott, S., and Trow, P. (1994), *The New Production of Knowledge: The Dynamics of Science and Research in Contemporary Societies*, Sage, London.

Haeussler, C., and Colyvas, J.A. (2011), 'Breaking the ivory tower: academic entrepreneurship in the life sciences in UK and Germany', *Research Policy*, Vol 40, No 1, pp 41–54.

Komninos, N. (2004), 'Regional intelligence: distributed localised information systems for innovation and development', *International Journal of Technology Management*, Vol 28, No 3, pp 483–506.

Landry, R., Amara, N., and Ouimet, M. (2007), 'Determinants of knowledge transfer: evidence from Canadian university researchers in natural sciences and engineering', *Journal of Technology Transfer*, Vol 32, No 6, pp 561–592.

Landry, R., Lamari, M., and Amara, N. (2003), 'Extent and determinants of utilization of university research in public administration', *Public Administration Review*, Vol 63, No 2, pp 191–204.

Larsen, M.T. (2011), 'The implications of academic enterprise for public science: an overview of the empirical evidence', *Research Policy*, Vol 40, No 1, pp 6–19.

Levin, S., and Stephan, P. (1991), 'Research productivity over the life cycle: evidence for academic scientists', *American Economic Review*, Vol 81, No 1, pp 114–132.

Leydesdorff, L., and Etzkowitz, H. (1998), 'The Triple Helix as a model for innovation studies', *Science and Public Policy*, Vol 25, No 3, pp 195–203.

Lynskey, M. J. (2010), 'Capitalizing on knowledge from public research institutions: indications from new technology-based firms in Japan',

*Industry and Higher Education*, Vol 24, No 1, pp 29–45.

Merton, R. K. (1973), 'The normative structure of science', in Merton, R. K., ed, *The Sociology of Science: Theoretical and Empirical Investigations*, University of Chicago Press, Chicago, IL.

O'Shea, R., Allen, T., Chevalier, A., and Roche, F. (2005), 'Entrepreneurial orientation, technology transfer and spinoff performance of US universities', *Research Policy*, Vol 34, No 7, pp 994–1009.

Perkmann, M., and Walsh, K. (2007), 'University–industry relationships and open innovation: towards a research agenda', *International Journal of Management Reviews*, Vol 9, No 4, pp 259–80.

Piccaluga, A., and Balderi, C. (2007), *Consistenza ed evoluzione delle imprese spin-off della ricerca pubblica in Italia*, available at http://web1.sssup.it/pubblicazioni/ugovfiles/2675 2007 2675.pdf.

Powell, W. W., Koput, K. W., and Smith-Doerr, L. (1996), 'Interorganizational collaboration and the locus of innovation: networks of learning in biotechnology', *Administrative Science Quarterly*, Vol 41, No 1, pp 116–145.

Poyago-Theotoky, J., Beath, J., and Siegel, D. (2002), 'Universities and fundamental research: reflections on the growth of university–industry partnerships', *Oxford Review of Economic Policy*, Vol 18, No 1, p 10.

Sandelin, J. (2010), 'University–industry relationships: benefits and risks', *Industry and Higher Education*, Vol 24 No 1, pp 55–62.

Stokes, D. (1997), *Pasteur's Quadrant: Basic Science and Technological Innovation*, Brookings Institution Press, Washington DC.

Torkkeli, M., Kotonen, T., and Ahonen, P. (2007), 'Regional open innovation system as a platform for SMEs: a survey', *International Journal of Foresight and Innovation Policy*, Vol 3, No 4, pp 336–350.

Wooldridge, J. (2008), *Introductory Econometrics: A Modern Approach*, South-Western College Publishing, Cincinnati, OH.

Woollard, D., Zhang, M., and Jones, O. (2007), 'Academic enterprise and regional economic growth: towards an enterprising university', *Industry and Higher Education*, Vol 21, No 6, pp 387–404.

Ziman, J. (2000), *Real Science: What It Is and What It Means*, Cambridge University Press, Cambridge.

## Acknowledgements

The authors would like to thank Daniel Pittino and Francesca Visintin for their valuable support and Paola Mazzurana and Elena Fornasier for help in data collection. They are also grateful to two anonymous reviewers for their constructive comments. Any errors are the authors' own.

# PART II: CREATING THE CULTURE: EDUCATING ENTREPRENEURIALLY

# Creating conducive environments for learning and entrepreneurship

## Living with, dealing with, creating and enjoying uncertainty and complexity

**Allan Gibb**

*Abstract: The paper argues that there is a need to move away from the conventional focus of entrepreneurship education on new venture management, business plans and growth and innovation, to a broader concept based on an understanding of the way entrepreneurs live and learn. Seven challenges are proposed in this respect: (1) that of creating the 'way of life' of the entrepreneur; (2) the sharing of culture and values; (3) supporting the development of behaviours, attributes and skills; (4) designing the entrepreneurial organization; (5) developing the learning-to-learn capacity; (6) being sensitive to the demands of different contexts; and (7) adding value to existing ways of learning. The paper concludes that meeting these challenges cannot easily be achieved within the existing structure, values and beliefs of business schools and that new organizations are needed within a university context.*

*Keywords: learning; small business; training design*

*The author is Professor Emeritus, University of Durham, UK.*
*E-mail: allan_gibb@hotmail.com*

The aim of this paper is to look beyond the issue of *what* should be taught in entrepreneurial learning to *how* the environment for 'teaching' it should be organized and *how* the knowledge frameworks themselves might be more appropriately presented. These seem to be issues that, while not wholly neglected in academic debates, are frequently dealt with superficially (Gibb, 2001). The issue of creating a 'conducive learning environment' for entrepreneurship can be approached from several different perspectives. The first concerns the very rationale for entrepreneurial behaviour – namely, the ability to cope with uncertainty and complexity. The second focuses on the design of environments and organizations to facilitate and promote 'effective' entrepreneurial behaviour. The aim is to enhance the capacity of individuals to practise such behaviour in a way that will, hopefully, enrich their lives and help their organizations to perform better. The third concerns the opportunity for individuals to create and enjoy their own entrepreneurial environment of uncertainty and complexity.

The emphasis in this paper is on the development of entrepreneurial (or enterprising) behaviour. A basic assumption is that entrepreneurial behaviour should not be exclusively located in a business or even a market economy context. Societies of very different ideologies can embrace a culture that values such behaviour, and organizations of all kinds can be designed to facilitate effective entrepreneurial behaviour. The word 'effective' is used (and has been discussed in more detail elsewhere – Gibb, 1999) in recognition of the point that entrepreneurial behaviours in society and organizations can be deviant or even criminal and certainly either immoral or amoral. Effective entrepreneurial behaviour is posited as that which is morally and ethically acceptable within the conventions of

society and which enables individuals and organizations to fulfil their objectives more wholesomely.

There will be no debate in this paper as to why the issue of entrepreneurial behaviour in all kinds of organizations and contexts is becoming more important. This has also been discussed extensively elsewhere (Gibb, 1999). It should be sufficient to note that governments, almost throughout the world, have been increasingly extolling the virtues of the 'enterprise culture' over the past decade as a means of meeting the demands for flexibility and dynamism created by the globalization phenomenon (Blair, 1998; European Commission, 1998). Almost universally, the boundaries between the state and the individual have been redrawn. Public expenditure has been reduced and individuals and local communities have been urged to develop a stronger capacity for 'self-help'. Large organizations have downsized and restructured themselves, creating the so-called 'flexible labour market' both inside and outside the firm (Rajan *et al*, 1997) – and there has been an associated growth of small enterprises. The market paradigm has been introduced into all kinds of public services. Individuals as consumers, workers and as members of families therefore face greater levels of uncertainty and complexity in their lives. Mobility, geographical, occupational and even relational (in the personal sense), is a key contributing component.

The environment in which individuals are living their lives is one of greater uncertainty and complexity.

The challenge to education and training organizations is to equip individuals and organizations to deal with this. This paper argues that acceptance of this challenge creates an imperative to redesign approaches to learning and the organization of knowledge in a manner that builds confidence and capacity to deal with uncertainty and complexity. It will be argued that to achieve this, there is a need to move away from the current narrow paradigm of entrepreneurship to a wider notion of entrepreneurial behaviour. Acceptance of this has implications for the way we seek to 'bring forward' the environment in which entrepreneurial people operate, as part of the learning process.

There is an implicit recognition in the above argument that entrepreneurship can be taught in a non-entrepreneurial manner or that lip service can be paid to enterprising approaches to teaching without subjecting them to the same rigorous scrutiny that is awarded to knowledge. In the university context, for example, in designing new degree programmes, it is the author's experience that the focus is almost entirely on the knowledge content and its structure. A possible explanation for this is that the 'contract' with the student is for the delivery and acceptance of knowledge rather than the development of the person. It is, therefore, no accident that notions of enterprise and entrepreneurship appear to be more acceptable in primary schools than they do at universities (Ma, 2000).

Against this background the notion of a 'conducive environment' for learning and entrepreneurship can be taken to mean the bringing forward of the environment in which knowledge will be used, and therefore in which true learning takes place as part of the 'doing' process. This has implications not only for the way that the classroom is organized, but also for the ways institutions organize knowledge, the contexts for knowledge that are applied and the values and beliefs that underpin learning approaches.

The paper begins with a brief review of the current narrow paradigm under which entrepreneurship seems to be taught. It argues that this model is inappropriate because of its traditional emphasis on business. It then focuses on a number of challenges relating to an entrepreneurial approach to learning:

(1) the creation of a learning environment in which individuals can experience key aspects of the 'way of life' of the 'entrepreneur';
(2) appreciation of the values that underpin the approach to learning and influence the capacity for use of the learning;
(3) the kinds of behaviours, skills and attributes that need to be enhanced and the associated pedagogical challenge;
(4) the way in which organizations might be developed in order to provide an environment that is conducive to entrepreneurial learning;
(5) creation of the capacity of students to learn to learn from their environment and particularly from key stakeholders;
(6) to understand the importance of embracing a variety of contexts in teaching; and

(7) to develop an overall approach that focuses on adding value to the 'experience' that individuals already have.

The paper concludes with reflections on whether the environment in business schools and universities is truly conducive to such approaches.

## The current narrow paradigm

Recent reviews of what is being taught in the field of entrepreneurship in Europe and North America (Brown, 1999; European Commission, 2000; Gartner and Vesper, 1999; Hayward, 2000; Hills, 1998; Levie, 1999; Mason, 2000) indicate that the emphasis is substantially on the process of new venture creation using the business plan as the framework for organizing knowledge. This is complemented by a focus on emerging, growing and innovative businesses. This in turn is supplemented by 'appropriate' functional inputs, often provided by the core faculty. To this menu may be added a number of options, such as family business, IT, franchising, etc. The pedagogical process frequently makes use of projects, of entrepreneurs as role models (and occasionally as teachers) and engages stakeholders such as banks, accountants and solicitors in presentations. Overall there is a strong cognitive and business focus with knowledge organized in such a way that it can be easily tested.

Most entrepreneurship teaching is delivered by business schools or economics faculties, and there is only minor outreach into science and arts faculties. Programme brochures and 'models' frequently embody statements about the development of entrepreneurial behaviours, but there are few precise statements as to how these are to be 'achieved' or indeed assessed (Bates, 1998). In many student programmes, assessment is by projects, although essays and examinations still predominate. It is argued below that the emphasis on knowledge *per se* as a basis for delivery and assessment may lead to neglect of a number of key challenges related to the development of the capacity of students to 'feel' entrepreneurship and learn in entrepreneurial ways.

## Challenge 1 – creating the way of life

When individuals move from employment or a position of relative security into self-employment, a number of changes take place in their 'life world'. These changes challenge their capacity to cope with and indeed enjoy the entrepreneurial experience. Key characteristics of their new 'life world' include:

- greater freedom and ownership;
- greater control over what goes on;
- greater responsibility – more of the 'buck stops with you';
- more autonomy to make things happen;
- doing everything – coping with wider range of management tasks;
- rewards linked more directly/ immediately to the customer;
- personal assets and security more at risk;
- the ego more widely exposed;
- living day to day with greater uncertainty;

- greater vulnerability to the environment;
- wider interdependence on a range of stakeholders;
- 'know-who' becomes much more important – to build trust;
- working longer and more variable hours;
- social, family and business life more highly integrated;
- social status tied more to business status;
- more learning by doing, under pressure (more tacit than explicit); and
- loneliness.

The individual enters into a position of greater freedom and greater ownership and control, but greater responsibility. Personal assets are usually at risk, and rewards (the ability to make a living) are linked closely to the customer. There is greater autonomy to make things happen, but a wide range of tasks have to be undertaken. Interdependence on a diverse group of people has to be managed and networks of trust have to be built as a basis for this. New entrepreneurs are likely to work longer and more variable hours, at least in the beginning. Their friendship patterns are likely to change, as are their relationship patterns within the family. Their ego is probably more substantially at risk and ultimately their social status is likely to be considerably influenced by the success or otherwise of the business. Much of the new learning will be by doing and responsibility for learning and self-development rests with themselves.

It is possible to help individuals to create business plans, provide all relevant knowledge, and indeed assist in obtaining finance and setting up the business without providing any of the above experience. Yet much of this way of life can be rehearsed by use of appropriate pedagogy. Some key notions in this respect are set out in Appendix 1. Overall, the aim should be to familiarize participants with the environment of 'living day to day with uncertainty' and managing this in a confident manner. This necessitates abandonment of the notion that all teaching has to be 'instructional' and controlled and that all learning takes place in the classroom. Thus instead of a taught session on marketing, students might be sent out to explore the validity of a business idea by finding and interviewing five potential customers. The 'material' collected, with all its probable ambiguity and inadequacy, becomes the basis for the next 'teaching' session.

Although the above life world is drawn from a self-employment analogy, it can be argued that many individuals employed in public and private organizations increasingly share this life world (Gibb, 2000a). Managers in downsized, decentralized large corporations, employees in education, health and other public services in which a 'market' paradigm has been introduced increasingly share some life world features with the conventional 'entrepreneur' (Quinn, 1985; Worrell *et al*, 2000). The ability to cope with and enjoy this way of life is therefore an asset that goes beyond a business context.

## Challenge 2 – sharing cultures and values

What we teach, and the way we feel we need to teach it, reflect our underlying values and beliefs not only concerning methods of education, but also the kind of knowledge that is selected for delivery. What we teach and how we teach it are also reflective of the kinds of institutions within which we work. The business school model, for example, can be characterized as one focused on valuing objectivity and a 'rational/analytical' stance. It emphasizes the cognitive aspects of learning with a neglect of affective (enjoyment) and connative (motivational) aspects (Ruohotie and Karanen, 2000). Moreover, while case studies are used to facilitate practice at problem solving (usually within the rational model), the emphasis is on teaching 'about' rather than 'for'. This emphasis is underpinned by the notion that teaching 'about' is more academically respectable than teaching for, with its emphasis on practice (Levie, 1999). Associated with this stance is the rather loose intellectual notion that concepts and theory cannot be explored via a process of practice, a notion that natural scientists and philosophers might find strange (Shusterman, 1999).

It can be argued that underpinning the conventions of business school teaching are a number of beliefs derived from, and associated substantially with, a bureaucratic/corporate model as set out in the left-hand column of Table 1. The emphasis in this 'implicit' model is upon the 'value' of information, accountability, systems, planning, demarcation, transparency, formal planning, formal methods of appraisal, and so on. The aim is seemingly to reduce the world in order to organize and make sense of it. This approach is underpinned by the division of schools into departments of marketing, finance, production, etc. Seeking to fit these together into a 'holistic' model, arguably necessary to support the pursuit of entrepreneurship, can be described as akin to the creation of Frankenstein's monster. All the pieces are there ('scientifically' underpinned), but the creature that emerges does not seem to move (or be moulded together) very well in the necessary organic fashion!

The world of enterprise – the right-hand column of Table 1 – is arguably characterized by ambiguity, imprecision and constant judgements as to how best to make sense of things. A core value underpinning these ways of doing and looking at things is the notion of trust achieved through the building of personal relationships and 'dealings'. It can be argued that trust is the very basis of an entrepreneurial society and organization (Fukuyama, 1995). It is the absence of trust that leads to the demand for more and more accountability, more and more information, more and more transparency, more and more systems, and more and more 'objective' forms of personal and organizational appraisal.

In summary, the left-hand side of the table can be seen as being 'business-like' in the professional sense of the word. It carries with it associated professional values and beliefs.

While the table is deliberately dichotomous, it is nevertheless useful. It has been used, for example, by the author to contrast the values of the banker with the small entrepreneur

**Table 1. The cultural divide? The bureaucratic–corporate–entrepreneurial dilemma.**

| Government/corporate (looking for) | Entrepreneurial (small business) (as being) |
|---|---|
| Order | Untidy |
| Formality | Informal |
| Accountability | Trusting |
| Information | Personally observing |
| Clear demarcation | Overlapping |
| Planning | Intuitive |
| Corporate strategy | Tactically strategic |
| Control measures | Personally led |
| Formal standards | Personally observed |
| Transparency | Ambiguous |
| Functional expertise | Holistic |
| Systems | Reliant on 'feel' |
| Positional authority | Owner-managed |
| Formal performance appraisal | Customer/network exposed |

as a basis for exploring difficulties in their relationship. It has also been used to examine problems that arise in the operation of donor assistance in developing and transitional economies (Gibb, 2000b). In this context, the end client group is frequently the informal sector arguably characterized by the right-hand column of the table. On the left is the donor organization with its imperative to spend taxpayers' money soundly and accountably. In the middle (not shown) is the NGO recipient of donor funds that can easily see the customer as the donor rather than the informal micro-enterprise. There is a power asymmetry that pulls the NGO, its behaviour and its systems to the left, leading to numerous potential problems.

Overall, therefore, recognition of the values and beliefs underpinning what is taught, and questioning these, is arguably an essential part of creating a conducive environment for entrepreneurial learning. This might, for example, lead us to a rethinking of the concept and value of the business plan as a focal point for the organization of teaching. It is almost certain that business plans were not invented by entrepreneurs, but by people within corporate organizations such as banks that need personal risk-reduction documents in order to justify to the hierarchy their release of resources.

## Challenge 3 – pedagogy to develop behaviours, skills and attributes

As noted above, many institutions engaged in entrepreneurship programmes pay lip service to the need to develop and practise entrepreneurial behaviours (European Commission FIT, 2000). There are many examples of lists of such behaviours but no universal agreement as to the core. Such lists often combine *behaviours* that can be observed, *attributes* that are deemed to be part of the personality but are arguably open to influence from the environment and *skills* that can be developed. There would seem to be some measure of agreement as to key behaviours, which include: finding opportunities; grasping opportunities; bringing networks together effectively; taking initiatives; being able to take risks under conditions of uncertainty and through judgement; persevering to achieve a goal; and strategic thinking (thinking on one's feet, not just tactically). Related to these are a number of supporting attributes around which there is a considerable 'trait' literature. These include: motivation to achieve; self-confidence and self-belief; creativity; autonomy and high locus of control; hard work; commitment; and determination. In turn, related to these are skills that include negotiation, persuasion, selling, proposing, project management, time management, formulating strategy, and creative problem solving. While there may be disputes about the above list and absences from it (for example, planning), what is most important is that the stance taken can be clearly defended from the literature.

Once this has been achieved, the pedagogical challenge is to create the learning environment that provides opportunities for practising and developing these behaviours, reinforces the attributes, and develops the skills. This requires careful appraisal and use of the wide range of available pedagogical approaches that might enhance and develop specific behaviours, attributes or skills. While much more research is needed in this area, it is possible to make a determined effort in this respect. This will, however, entail

a full analysis of what each of the behaviours might mean (Harris, 1996). For example, opportunity-finding behaviours may embrace creative problem solving; harvesting ideas from competitors and peer businesses; undertaking detailed ongoing customer analysis and communication; internal brainstorming; research and development; use of the Web; attendance at exhibitions; and travel abroad. Such an analysis provides an agenda as to the kinds of 'how-tos' that should be brought into the education programme. It also, however, provides the basis for an exploration of appropriate pedagogies. For example, in Appendix 2 a list of pedagogies is provided, linked indicatively with the potential to help develop certain behaviours. Searching, brainstorming, audits, competitions, panels and projects can all support opportunity finding.

A major problem in systematically developing such approaches in a higher education context is that they are not generally deemed to have academic value. For example, the use of drama to encourage creativity and insight into the needs of different stakeholders would not rank well along side a series of knowledge-intensive seminars. Students themselves, having been fed knowledge at school and university, may have problems in accepting a different kind of learning contract related to their personal development and the practice of internalizing knowledge into behaviour This presents an intellectual as well as a personal challenge to the 'teacher'. The final barrier to creating this environment conducive to development of entrepreneurial behaviour is that it cannot easily be assessed, and almost certainly not in a way that is conventionally academically acceptable (Ma, 2000).

## Challenge 4 – designing the entrepreneurial organization

A key aspect of creating environments conducive to entrepreneurial learning is recognition that the way we regulate and govern our society and design our organizations can facilitate or hinder the practice of entrepreneurial behaviour. It is, for example, clearly evident to those who have worked in transitional economies that the structure of state companies could lead only to deviant or ineffective entrepreneurial behaviour (Gibb and Lyapunov, 1995). It is also evident that some organizations (for example, small businesses and political parties) can be run by people who are perceived by the external environment to be highly entrepreneurial. Yet, as in the case of the classical autocratic entrepreneur, they may run their own organizations in a manner that excludes the opportunity for individuals to enjoy the kinds of freedom and control necessary for the pursuit of entrepreneurial behaviour.

Recognition of this aspect of creating the conducive environment is arguably becoming increasingly important as corporate business methods are moved into schools and health and welfare services. It has also been argued elsewhere (Gibb, 2000a) that large corporations, in downsizing, may have failed to redesign their core organization to enable those retained in the business to cope more comfortably with greater uncertainty and complexity. As a result, there are much greater levels of anxiety and stress

(Grimshaw *et al*, 2000). Moreover, inappropriate design may encourage pursuit of 'ineffective' entrepreneurial behaviour in order to ensure that new benchmarked standards and targets are met. For example, in a police force a new category of offence entitled 'car interference' may be developed in order to improve 'clear-up rates' relating to car theft. This means that failed attempts at car theft are removed from the relevant statistics in order to meet targets. Similarly, radar trap mechanisms on motorways can be adjusted for speeds in order to ensure that targets are met precisely.

It is important in organizational design to recognize that entrepreneurial behaviour is contingent on the needs of the task environment. There are certainly many environments in which entrepreneurial behaviours are not required – for example, flying an aircraft! It has been argued elsewhere that the entrepreneurial organization will be designed to facilitate enjoyment of the 'internal life world' set out earlier and support effective behaviour (Gibb 1999) – see Table 2.

The teacher will therefore need to develop and discuss concepts of organizational design related to flattening hierarchies; achieving customer focus; linking appraisal to stakeholder and customer feedback; broadening task structures to achieve 'holism'; allowing 'effective' mistake making for learning purposes; supporting action learning; finding ways of decentralizing and giving ownership in businesses; and indeed creating a stronger feeling of 'independence'. There are many different models in large and small companies that can be used in this respect.

**Table 2. Design criteria for the entrepreneurial organization.**

Creating and reinforcing a strong sense of ownership
Reinforcing feelings of freedom and autonomy
Maximizing opportunities for holistic management
Tolerating ambiguity
Developing responsibility to see things through
Seeking to build commitment over time
Encouraging building of relevant personal stakeholder networks
Tying rewards to customer and stakeholder credibility
Allowing mistakes with support for learning
Supporting learning from stakeholders
Facilitating enterprising learning methods
Avoiding strict demarcation and hierarchical control systems
Allowing management overlap as a basis for learning and trust Encouraging strategic thinking
Encouraging personal contact as basis for building trust

## Challenge 5 – the learning to learn capacity

A conducive environment is one in which there is recognition that learning does not take place solely in an 'instructional' context. The bulk of lifelong learning takes place in an uncontrolled pedagogical environment. The key challenge is therefore to create an environment in which participants can learn to learn in the way that will be demanded of them in entrepreneurial circumstances. This means recognition of the fact that most of the learning that will take place will be through relationships with the relevant stakeholder environment. The entrepreneur will learn from customers, suppliers, intermediary organizations, banks, accountants and solicitors, their peers, competitors from local government and from their own staff and family and even from regulators and government officials (Gibb, 1997). The doctor in his or her practice will learn from patients, health authorities, local government, medical councils, other doctors and hospital consultants.

Effective learning from stakeholders will reduce transaction costs and will lead, arguably, to greater organizational efficiency and effectiveness. This will also be enhanced when the entrepreneur and doctor seek to understand the learning needs of each of their stakeholders and systematically set out to educate them and, indeed, 'bring forward the future for them'.

To create an environment conducive to learning from stakeholders will make several major demands on the teaching organization. The first of these is recognition of the importance of tacit as well as explicit learning and the need to encourage students to make sense of things from their experience and feed this into the explicit learning process. It will also demand an understanding of how learning needs arise from the development processes of the business, so that needs can be met at an appropriate time. Perhaps too often the would-be business start up is fed a teaching diet of conventional functional management, including marketing, finance, production, information systems and human resource development, to name but a few. The onus is then left on the individual to apply this mass of knowledge to the start-up process. Little attempt is made, except through the odd case, to relate precisely the knowledge to the development process of the venture.

Appendix 3 provides an example of how, in the new venture development process, learning needs can be related to the tasks at each stage of the business growth. Such an approach is arguably important, even though it can be recognized that new ventures do not proceed smoothly from one stage to another but engage in a process of iteration in order to find the right balance. Nevertheless, at each stage of the process problems can be identified and opportunities recognized in advance and met by appropriate learning. A key aspect of this approach is therefore that knowledge is organized not only around the development process – whether it be start-up, survival and growth, exporting or new product development, for example – but around the notion of the problems and opportunities that might be confronted. Here the challenge to entrepreneurship education is to use the medical school approach of moving out from a particular problem (like a painful knee), working out all possible causes, examining what is known about these causes and how they interact, how they relate to the workings of other parts of the anatomy (aspects of the business), what research and scholarship there is to help, and what theories there are that might help in the process of diagnosis. While thus meeting 'academic standards', the emphasis is continuously on solving the problem as effectively as possible in the light of available knowledge.

It can be argued therefore that entrepreneurship knowledge agendas should be derived from a problem/opportunity focus. Figure 1 provides an example of this. It sets out many of the problems that are known to arise in the early years of the business (well documented in research). Each of these needs to be explored and explained. Each has related concepts associated with it that can be reviewed: but ultimately there is a need to know how to recognize, solve or avoid the problem. Thus a 'need to know' is matched by 'know-how'.

One further critical aspect of this approach of learning to learn is 'know-who' – in recognition of the fact that empathy with key stakeholders, personal relationships and trust and networking are key aspects of entrepreneurial behaviour. 'Know-who' is not something that is conventionally taught at business schools, or indeed valued academically, but it is a critical element in all aspects of business development. It can be linked strongly with theory (Boissevain and Mitchell, 1973) but there is a need to encourage practice.

Overall, creating the conducive environment for entrepreneurial 'learning to learn' has a major positioning challenge for the educational institution. The teaching institution as a learning organization needs to position itself as the interface organization between the relevant stakeholder environment and the student. As such, it must understand

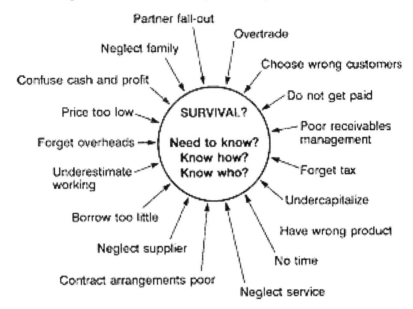

**Figure 1.** Survival problems.

precisely how the sets of relationships between the student and stakeholders work in order to enhance possibilities for learning both ways. Here there will be a clear demand for the reorganization of knowledge and more research will be needed to underpin it (DUBS, 1999). Do we, for example, know enough about how the banks develop and build relationships with small businesses at various stages of their development, what they need to learn from them and how they need to educate them – and vice versa from the small business perspective? Without such knowledge, it is impossible to teach 'relationship learning'.

## Challenge 6 – sensitivity to context

A major challenge in creating 'conducive environments' for entrepreneurial learning is that of adapting to the very different contexts into which entrepreneurial learning can be introduced. A starting point is re-examination of the customer base for entrepreneurship. The research in Europe and in North America indicates that the major focus within higher education is on business school students (Menzies, 1998; NCOE, 2001). There is, however, a recognized need to extend the offer into science and arts departments. This may mean taking the 'offer' directly out of the business context, which has (in the light of the earlier discussion) some advantages and some disadvantages. It presents an opportunity to explore wider notions of enterprise and organizational design, as argued above. Yet even the new venture approach can be applied to a variety of different contexts not necessarily relating to business – for example, the setting up of a new medical practice.

Another advantage of exploring entrepreneurial behaviour outside the business context is that it can be removed from its ideologically and politically charged link with notions of market liberalization. Entrepreneurial behaviour in health and education services is not conditional upon the introduction of market reforms, or for that matter private business practice (Gibb and Li, 2002). Indeed, it has been argued above that much of this practice may be anti-entrepreneurial. Exploring concepts of entrepreneurial organizational design and the encouragement of effective entrepreneurial behaviour in all kinds of organizational contexts will also help to relieve us of the burden of the 'heroic' ideology (Ogbor, 2000) embodied in the 'creative destruction' metaphor (Schumpeter, 1934). This 'ideology' associates entrepreneurship with major innovations and company growth and is dysfunctional in the exploration of the concept in a wider range of contexts. It is clear, for example, that many self-employed individuals operate in task environments that are highly complex and uncertain and that demand a great deal of entrepreneurial behaviour. On the other hand, some growth companies operate in more certain and even simple environments that demand sound management rather than entrepreneurship. Moreover, the association of growth with uncertainty, complexity and indeed rapid change itself may be misleading. Research at the University of Durham 17 years ago indicated that firms facing declining markets and fighting to retain turnover, and indeed survive, faced major changes and might be extremely

dynamic in their responses (Gibb and Scott, 1985). Associating growth with entrepreneurship may therefore be loose thinking. Growth in turnover is not a proxy for entrepreneurial change.

Overall, work in the field of entrepreneurship needs to address the question of why the entrepreneurial paradigm is currently widely embraced by politicians and modern gurus. It has been demonstrated elsewhere (Gibb, 1999) that there is a major challenge in linking the development of the entrepreneurial paradigm with the uncertainties and complexities resulting from global change (as noted in the introduction to this paper). Focusing on the global issues that are creating more uncertainty and complexity in a wide variety of contexts can provide a strong and rich content base for entrepreneurship programmes much wider than those that can be drawn from the new venture process.

## Challenge 7 – adding value appropriately

Most of the above arguments constitute a major challenge to our approach to learning. They move it away from a focus on instruction within a narrow institutional context (the classroom and university) to the creation of learning opportunities from a variety of sources. They underpin the notion that true learning environments need to provide opportunities for the application of knowledge, for supporting behaviours and for using knowledge to think more effectively. Thus knowledge adds to experience but also helps to give wider meaning to that experience. An environment conducive to entrepreneurial learning is one that recognizes the importance of reinforcing positive attitudes to the enjoyment of learning and of influencing the individual's view of the desirability of this learning. Such an approach directly challenges the association of 'academic' with learning 'about' as opposed to pursuing 'for'. There is substantial intellectual support for this view. In the UK, 19th-century notions of the concept of a university placed emphasis on the use of knowledge rather than its acquisition and the creative use of imagination based on knowledge (Macauley 1828; Newman, 1852; and Whitehead quoted in Chia, 1996). There is more recent acceptance of a view of universities as being equally concerned with the scholarship of relevance and the integration of knowledge as with the scholarship of discovery (research) and teaching (Carnegie 1990; Gibb, 1996). Thus the added value in the learning environment that is conducive to entrepreneurship is achieved by moving from 'what you have remembered' and 'what you have learned' to 'what you think' and 'what you can do'.

## Conclusion

This paper has argued that there is a need to move away from the narrow conventions of entrepreneurship education, with its focus on new venture management and business, to the notion of enterprising or entrepreneurial behaviour. Such a notion can be applied to the design of

learning for individuals in a variety of different contexts and related to the design of a variety of different organizations. The common aim is to help both individual and organization to cope better with uncertainty and complexity in the task environment, and indeed to remove barriers to the creation of such uncertainty and complexity when the opportunity presents itself. The argument has been that this position cannot be achieved by a pure focus on knowledge delivered within the conventional paradigms of business school education, but demands a holistic and pluralistic approach that is essentially post-modern (Kyro, 2000). It means moving away from rational-, objective- and positivist-dominated philosophies to those that are more sensitive to the essential ambiguities of the 'way of life' of the entrepreneur, his or her culture, and the difficulty in this world of using other reductionist and functionalist approaches.

If accepted, this approach to development of appropriate learning environments for the pursuit of entrepreneurial behaviour will demand that, ultimately, students are empathetic to sets of values and beliefs that underpin the entrepreneurial: ways of doing; ways of seeing; ways of feeling; ways of communicating; ways of organizing; and ways of learning.

There is an element of revolution in this philosophy. It therefore begs questions as to whether such a revolution can be carried out within a conventional business school context. The author, from his experience, would doubt this very much. There is too much vested interest in the corporate business models, in functionalism, in beliefs about the value of an objective/rationalist approach underpinned by journals and research publications that provide an ever-narrowing focus. It has been argued elsewhere that to embrace the conducive learning environment of entrepreneurship requires of organizations that they are heavily networked with the stakeholder environment and positioned in such a way that they can learn from the demands of this environment and evaluate their own excellence via the multiple perceptions of stakeholders. This appears to be beyond the capacity of schools which are dominated by heavy supply-side provision and delivery of conventional MBA certification. Yet many of the approaches needed to underpin the conducive entrepreneurial learning field can be embraced within the philosophy of university practice. Perhaps, therefore, the time has come to design new institutions under the university umbrella that will help to lead it, without losing its purity, to respond more effectively to the demands of the enterprise society.

# References

Bates, J. (1998), 'The evaluation of entrepreneurial management', paper presented at the ISBA Conference, Durham, November.

Blair, A., 'The Third Way', speech by the UK Prime Minister to the French National Assembly, 24 March, Paris.

Brown, C. (1999), 'Teaching new dogs new tricks: the rise of entrepreneurship education in graduate schools of business', Kaufmann Center for Entrepreneurial Leadership, *Kansas Digest*, No 99–2, December.

Boissevain, J. and Mitchell, J. C. (1973), *Network Analysis: Studies in Human Interaction*, Mouton, The Hague.

Carnegie Foundation for the Advancement of Teaching (1990), *Scholarship Reconsidered: Priorities of the Professoriate*, Washington, DC.

Chia, R. (1996), 'Teaching paradigm shifts in management education: university business schools and the entrepreneurial imagination', *Journal of Management Studies*, Vol 33, No 4, pp 409–428.

DUBS (1999), *Building SME Stakeholder Learning Relationships*, Report to the UK Department for Education and Employment, Durham University Business School, Durham.

European Commission (1998), *Promoting Entrepreneurship and Competitiveness*, Brussels, September.

European Commission, Enterprise Directorate General, FIT Project (2000), *The Development and Implementation of European Entrepreneurship Training Curricula*, European Union, Brussels.

European Training Foundation (1996), *Training for Enterprise. Conference of Ministers from the Member States of the European Union and the Countries of Central and Eastern Europe and Central Asia*, Italian Presidency of the European Union Council of Ministers, pp 3–79.

Fukuyama, F. (1995), *Trust: the Social Virtues and the Creation of Prosperity*, Hamish Hamilton, London.

Gartner, W. B., and Vesper, K. H. (1999), Entrepreneurship Education 1998, *Lloyd Grief Center for Entrepreneurial Studies, The Anderson School, University of California, Los Angeles, CA*.

Gibb, A.A. (1996), 'Entrepreneurship and small business management: can we afford to neglect them in the twenty-first century business school?', *British Journal of Management*, Vol 7, pp 309–321.

Gibb, A.A. (1997), 'Small firms' training and competitiveness: building upon the small business as a learning organisation', *International Small Business Journal*, Vol 15, pp 13–29.

Gibb, A.A. (1999), 'Can we build 'effective' entrepreneurship through management development?', *Journal of General*

*Management*, Vol 24, No 4, summer, pp 1–2.

Gibb, A.A. (2000a), 'Corporate restructuring and entrepreneurship: what can large organisations learn from small?', *Enterprise and Innovation Management Studies*, Vol 1, No 1, pp 19–35.

Gibb, A.A. (2000b), 'Creating an entrepreneurial culture in support of SmEs', *Small Enterprise Development*, Vol 10, No 4, pp 27–38.

Gibb, A.A. (2001), 'Creative destruction, new values, new ways of doing things and new combinations of knowledge', Guest Speaker Address to the Annual Conference of the Administrative Sciences Association of Canada, London, Ontario, May.

Gibb, A.A., and Li, J. (2002), 'Organizing for enterprise in China', *Futures*, forthcoming.

Gibb, A.A. and Lyapunov, S. (1995), 'Creating small businesses out of large in Central and Eastern Europe', *Small Enterprise Development*, Vol 6, No 3, pp 5–17.

Gibb, A.A., and Scott, M. (1985), 'Strategic awareness, personal commitment and the process of planning in the small firm', *Journal of Management Studies*, Vol 22, No 6, pp 597–631.

Grimshaw, D., Ward, K.G., Rubery, J., and Beynon, H. (2000), 'Organisations and the transformation of the internal labour market', *Work, Employment and Society*, Vol 14, March, pp 25–54.

Harris, A. (1996), 'Teaching approaches in enterprise education: a classroom study', *British Journal of Education and Work*, Vol 8, No 1, pp 49–58.

Hayward, G. (2000), *Evaluating Entrepreneurship in Scottish Universities*, University of Oxford Education Department, Oxford.

Hills, G.E. (1998), 'Variations in university entrepreneurial education: an empirical study in an evolving field', *Journal of Business Venturing*, No 3, pp 109–122.

Kyro, P. (2000), 'Is there a pedagogical basis for entrepreneurship education?', *Academy of Entrepreneurship Journal*, European edition, Jönköping International Business School.

Levie, J. (1999), *Enterprising Education in Higher Education in England*, Department for Education and Employment, London.

Ma, R. (2000), *Enterprise Education and its Relationship to Enterprising Behaviours: A Methodological and Conceptual Investigation*, PhD thesis, Durham University, Durham.

Macauley, T.R. (1828), 'History', in Alden, R.M., ed (1917), *Readings in English Prose of the 19th Century*, The Riverside Press, Cambridge, MA, pp 268–275.

Mason, C. (2000), *Teaching Entrepreneurship to Undergraduates: Lessons from Leading Centres of Entrepreneurship Education*, University of Southampton, Southampton.

Menzies, T.V. (1998), *Entrepreneurship in Canadian Universities*: Report of a National Study, Brock University, St Catherines, Ontario.

National Commission on Entrepreneurship (2001), 'Report on NCOE-Kennedy School Conference on Entrepreneurship and Public Policy: New Growth Strategies for the 21st Century', *NCoEUpdate*, No 28, April.

Newman, J.H. (1852), 'Knowledge, learning and professional skill', in Alden, R.M., ed (1917), *Readings in English Prose of the 19th Century*, Riverside Press, Cambridge, MA, pp 418–439.

Ogbor, J.O. (2000), 'Mythicising and reification in entrepreneurial discourse: ideology – critique or entrepreneurial studies', *Journal of Management Studies*, Vol 37, No 5, July, pp 605–637.

Quinn, J.B. (1985), 'Managing innovation: controlled chaos', *Harvard Business Review*, Vol 63, pp 73–84.

Rajan, A., van Eupen, P., and Jaspers, A. (1997), 'Britain's flexible labour market: what next?', *Create UK*.

Ruohotie, P. and Karanen, N. (2000), *Building Connative Constructs into Entrepreneurship Education*, University of Tampere, Tampere.

Schumpeter, J. (1934), *Theory of Economic Development*, Harvard University Press, Cambridge, MA.

Shusterman, R., ed (1999), *Bourdieu: A Critical Reader*, Blackwell, Oxford.

Worrell, L., Kempbell, F.K. and Cooper, G.C. (2000), 'The new reality for UK managers: perpetual change and employment instability', *Work, Employment and Society*, Vol 14, No 2, pp 647–669.

**Appendix 1. Simulating the entrepreneurial way of life – the pedagogical challenge.**

1. Developing *commitment* by:
   focusing the programme on the participant's own project;
   setting up peer review/counselling procedures to monitor progress;
   individual counselling on project progress;
   formal presentations of project to other participants;
   setting up independent panels for review;
   building sound links with resources.

2. Developing a *strong sense of responsibility* by:
   exercises to develop parts of the proposal (finding customers, suppliers, negotiating with resource providers, etc);
   encouraging development of action plan;
   setting times for completion of certain activities.

3. Developing a strong sense of *ownership* by:
   a strong focus on the participants project;
   exercises in defending the project in class.

4. Developing capacity to cope with *risk, money and social status* by:
   developing a plan;
   developing 'what if' scenarios for key assumptions in the plan;
   exploring ways to reduce the financial outlay (by subcontracting, etc);
   exercises to get participants to see stakeholder perceptions;
   discussions with existing businesses as to their position in local society.

5. Developing capacity to cope with *long and flexible hours* by:
   time management exercises;
   developing organizational systems;
   presentations on managing time by other entrepreneurs;
   setting systems for customer delivery schedules;
   setting aside contingency time.

6. Developing a sense of *freedom and independence* by:
   exercises on what it will be like to 'be on your own';
   exploration of what responsibilities freedom will bring;
   interviews with existing entrepreneurs on what it means to them;
   review of participant personal goals and the business.

*(Continued)*

## Appendix 1. (Continued)

7. Developing capacity to make *decisions under uncertainty* with *limited data* by:
    - exercises on making decisions with no or little hard data;
    - reviewing situations where there is 'paralysis by analysis';
    - asking participants to use 'tacit' knowledge to make decisions.

8. Developing ability to manage *interdependency* on key *stakeholders* by:
    - identification of key stakeholders;
    - exercises on what stakeholders are looking for and why;
    - exercises on the way stakeholders learn and ways of educating them.

9. Developing capacity to take *initiatives* and be *proactive* by:
    - exercises on who they know and how well they know them;
    - exercises on the strategic development of 'know-who'.

10. Developing ability to cope with *income fluctuations and customer dependency* for *rewards* by:
    - setting a clear view of what levels of personal income are targeted;
    - review of what levels of turnover and margin these are based upon;
    - examination of how income might vary and how they will cope;
    - examination of ways of smoothing out income;
    - consideration of other ways of making income in an emergency;
    - consideration of the role of savings.

11. Developing ability to manage changes in *social and family* relations by:
    - exercises in considering all family issues (divorce, succession, tax, etc);
    - 'what if' scenarios on family affairs;
    - exploring how other entrepreneurs plan for family issues.

12. Developing capacity to manage/control *holistic task structure* by:
    - exercises in clarifying exactly what participants will have to do;
    - developing training focused on these needs – simulations.

13. Developing capability to *learn to learn* as entrepreneurs by:
    - a focus on learning by doing, mistake making, copying, problem solving, experiment, peer review, feedback from stakeholders, etc.

14. Developing capacity to cope with *loneliness* by:
    - encouraging membership of clubs and associations;
    - time management exercises;
    - building links with peers and using counsellors.

**Appendix 2.** Linking entrepreneurial behaviours and skills to 'teaching' methods.

| | Seeking opportunities | Taking initiatives/ acting independently | Solving problems creatively | Persuading/ influencing others | Making things happen | Dealing with uncertainty | Flexibly responding | Negotiating a deal successfully | Taking decisions | Presenting confidently | Managing interdependence successfully |
|---|---|---|---|---|---|---|---|---|---|---|---|
| Lectures | | | | | | | | | | | |
| Seminars | | | * | | | | | * | | * | * |
| Workshops on problems/ opportunities | ** | | *** | * | | | | ** | | | |
| Critiques | | | * | * | | | | | * | * | |
| Cases | | * | | | | | * | | | | |
| Searches | * | | | | * | * | | | | | * |
| Critical incidents | | | * | | * | * | | | * | | |
| Discussion groups | | | * | * | | | | * | | | * |
| Projects | * | * | * | | * | * | | * | * | * | * |
| Presentations | | | | ** | | | | | | ** | |
| Debates | | | | ** | | | | | | ** | |
| Interviews | | | * | * | | * | * | * | | | |
| Goldfish bowl | | | | * | | | * | * | | | * |
| Simulations | | | * | * | | | * | * | * | * | * |
| Evaluations | ** | | | | | | | | | | |
| Mentoring each other | | | * | * | | * | * | * | | | * |
| Interactive video | | | | | | | * | | * | | |
| Internet | | | | | | | | | | | |
| Games | * | * | * | * | * | * | * | * | * | * | * |

(*Continued*)

**Appendix 2. (Continued)**

| | Seeking opportunities | Taking initiatives/ acting independently | Solving problems creatively | Persuading/ influencing others | Making things happen | Dealing with uncertainty | Flexibly responding | Negotiating a deal successfully | Taking decisions confidently | Presenting confidently | Managing interdependence successfully |
|---|---|---|---|---|---|---|---|---|---|---|---|
| Organizing events | ** | ** | * | ** | ** | ** | | ** | ** | | * |
| Competitions | | | | | | | | | | | |
| Audit (self-instruments) | | | | | | | | | | | |
| Audit (business instruments) | | | | | | | | | | | |
| Drawings | | | * | * | | | | | | | |
| Drama | | | * | * | | * | | | | * | |
| Investigations | | | | | * | | | | * | | |
| Role models | | | | | | | | | | | * |
| Panel observation | | | | * | | | | * | * | | * |
| Topic discussion | | * | | * | | | * | | | * | * |
| Debate | | * | | * | | | | | | | |
| Adventure training | * | * | * | | | * | * | | * | | * |
| Teaching others | | | * | * | | * | * | * | | * | * |
| Counselling | | | * | * | | | * | * | | | |

**Appendix 3. Linking personal learning to business development: a new venture process example.**

| | Stage | Key tasks | Key learning and development needs |
|---|---|---|---|
| 1. | From idea and motivation acquisition to raw idea. | • To find an idea.<br>• To generate an idea.<br>• To explore personal capability and motivation for self-employment. | • The process of idea generation and evaluation.<br>• Knowledge of sources of ideas.<br>• Understanding of the ways in which existing personal skills/knowledge might be used in self-employment.<br>• Understanding of what self-employment means.<br>• Personal insight into self-employment.<br>• Positive role image/ exploration/feedback.<br>• Self-evaluation. |
| 2. | From raw idea to valid idea. | • Clarify idea.<br>• Clarify what needs it meets.<br>• Make it.<br>• See it works.<br>• See it works in operating conditions<br>• Ensure can do it or make it to satisfactory quality.<br>• Explore customer acceptability – enough customers at the price?<br>• Explore legality.<br>• Ensure can get into business (no insurmountable barriers).<br>• Identify and learn from competition. | • What constitutes valid idea?<br>• Understanding the process of making/doing it.<br>• Technical skill to make/do it.<br>• Customer needs analysis.<br>• Customer identification.<br>• Who else does it/makes it?<br>• Idea protection.<br>• Pricing and rough costing.<br>• Ways of getting into a market.<br>• Quality standards.<br>• Competition analysis. |

(Continued)

**Appendix 3. (Continued)**

| | Stage | Key tasks | Key learning and development needs |
|---|---|---|---|
| 3. | From valid idea to scale of operation and resource identification. | • Identify market as number, location, type of customers.<br>• Clarify how will reach the market (promotional).<br>• Identify minimum desirable scale to 'make a living'.<br>• Identify physical resource requirements at that scale.<br>• Estimate additional physical resource requirements.<br>• Estimate financial requirements.<br>• Identify any additional financial requirements needed. | • Market research.<br>• Marketing mix (promotion, etc) (ways of reaching the customer).<br>• Pricing.<br>• Production forecasting and process planning to set standards for utilization, efficiency, etc.<br>• Distribution systems.<br>• Materials estimating and wastage.<br>• Estimating labour, material, capital requirements.<br>• Profit/loss and cash flow forecasting. |
| 4. | From 'scale' to business plan and negotiation. | • Develop business plan and proposal.<br>• Negotiate with customers, labour, suppliers of materials, premises, capital suppliers, land, etc, to ensure orders and physical supply capability.<br>• Negotiate with banks, financiers for resources. | • Business plan development.<br>• Negotiation and presentation skills.<br>• Knowledge of suppliers of land, etc.<br>• Contracts and forms of agreement.<br>• Knowledge of different ways of paying.<br>• Understanding of bankers, and other sources of finance.<br>• Understand forms of assistance available. |
| 5. | From negotiation to birth. | • Complete all legal requirements for business incorporation.<br>• Meet all statutory requirements<br>• Set up basic business systems. | • Business incorporation.<br>• Statutory obligations (tax, legal).<br>• Business production, marketing, financial systems and control.<br>• What advisers can do.<br>• Understand how to manage people (if have labour force). |

6. From birth to survival.

- Consolidate business systems for processing.
- Ensure adequate financial control (debtors, creditors, bank, etc).
- Develop market, attract and retain customers.
- Meet all legal obligations.
- Monitor and anticipate change.
- Maintain good relations with banks, customers, suppliers and all environment contacts.
- Provide effective leadership development for staff.

- Management control systems.
- Cash planning.
- Debtor/creditor control.
- Marketing.
- Selling skills.
- Environmental scanning and market research.
- Leadership skills.
- Delegation, time planning.

# Experiential internships

## Understanding the process of student learning in small business internships

**Mary E. Varghese, Loran Carleton Parker, Omolola Adedokun, Monica Shively, Wilella Burgess, Amy Childress and Ann Bessenbacher**

**Abstract:** *This qualitative study examines the process of student learning in a small-business experiential internship programme that pairs highly qualified undergraduates with local small or start-up companies. The Cognitive Apprenticeship model developed by Collins et al (1991) was used to conceptualize students' reported experiences. The results revealed that the internship structure allowed students to acquire knowledge successfully from experts in the field, situate their learning in the environment of practice, and learn valuable professional and entrepreneurial skills not found in traditional classroom settings. Students reported an increase in self-efficacy and indicated that their interests in working in a small business were solidified or further enhanced. It is argued that these findings have important implications for researchers, small business owners and entrepreneurial and small business support initiatives in higher education.*

**Keywords**: *small business; internship; experiential learning; cognitive apprenticeship*

*The authors are with the Discovery Learning Research Center, Purdue University, 207 S Martin Jischke Drive, Suite 203, West Lafayette, IN 47907, USA. Mary E. Varghese is the corresponding author, e-mail: mvarghes@purdue.edu*

Career and technical education programmes have long been interested in providing students a learning environment with opportunities to gain professional experience and develop career skills in practical contexts. Higher education has traditionally formed partnerships with prominent, established businesses to provide students with such opportunities. However, these opportunities may not serve as the best models for the future work environments students will experience after graduation. Many graduates will end up either working in small, start-up firms or launching businesses of their own. Additionally, many valuable learning opportunities may be found in small/start-up company internships to a greater extent than in large corporate internships, such as gaining practical experience in a diverse array of disciplines, holding more responsibility and facing more challenges, and creating novel ideas and solutions (Chigunta, 2002; Heriot and Lahm, 2009). Internship opportunities in the small or start-up business sector can benefit students by providing a rich learning experience that models future work environments and allows them to develop valuable skills that will prove beneficial in a variety of professional endeavours.

Small businesses are a pivotal driving force in the global economy. In a 2006 US report, small businesses (defined as companies having fewer than 500 employees) comprised 99.7% of all employers in the USA, employed half of all American non-government employees, produced half of the country's non-farm output and generated 13 to 14 times more patents per employee than large firms (Leebaert, 2006). Additionally, the US Small Business Administration reported in 2008 that businesses with fewer than 500 employees created 74% of the net new jobs in the nation, while firms with fewer than 20 employees created 22% of new jobs (Small Business Administration, 2008). In the European Union, small and medium-sized enterprises (SMEs) provided more than two thirds of private-sector employment opportunities and, in 2010, 92% of all EU businesses were micro-firms with less than 10 employees (Wymenga *et al*, 2011). Entrepreneurship has also proved to be an important source of economic growth and job creation in developing countries and transitional economies (Ahmed *et al*, 2010; Iakovleva *et al*, 2011; Roxas *et al*, 2008). Innovative, hardworking and determined small business owners and entrepreneurs create jobs in the community, decentralize economic power, stimulate the economy and allow employees to share in the success of their pursuits (Barreto, 2006). Given the importance of small businesses to the global economy, initiatives to stimulate and nurture small business growth and entrepreneurial interest in the community are vital. Previous research highlights the successful outcomes of various entrepreneurship support programmes that enhance perceptions of entrepreneurship in college students (Peterman and Kennedy, 2003; Roxas *et al*, 2008). Today, providing entrepreneurial education and enhancing interest in and understanding of small businesses are of increasing interest in higher education.

Previous studies have examined factors influencing entrepreneurial intent, including intrinsic personality traits, perceived barriers and support, and the socio-political-economical context (Boyd and Vozikis, 1994; Luthje and Franke, 2003). Research has also shown that the opportunity to acquire skills and experience achievement through applied internships reinforces self-efficacy, which in turn influences entrepreneurial intent (Boyd and Vozikis, 1994; Chen *et al*, 1998; Herron and Sapienza, 1992; Zhao *et al*, 2005). These findings imply that experiential internship programmes can have an effect on student understanding, attitudes, perceptions and intentions with regard to entrepreneurship and small businesses.

However, the current literature focuses predominantly on outcomes of experiential entrepreneurial programmes with little attention given to the process of student learning and development within programmes. Nonetheless, understanding both process and outcomes is important for educators, administrators and funding agencies who aim to design effective programmes (Adedokun *et al*, 2011). This present study aims to fill this gap in the literature and examine the process of student learning in an entrepreneurial internship programme.

## Theoretical framework: Cognitive Apprenticeship

Cognitive Apprenticeship, CA, (Collins *et al*, 1991) is a well-recognized conceptual framework that has been employed to design learning environments in which experts transfer knowledge to students and students gain knowledge that is situated in the authentic activities of a particular discipline or profession.

In the CA model, students work closely with professionals to complete and reflect upon meaningful tasks (Lave, 1997). The CA model has been used to explain student learning in internships in science fields (for example, undergraduate research; Kardash, 2000) and health fields (for example, nursing residencies; Taylor and Care, 1999). Although the principles and goals of CA seem to fit appropriately with internships in entrepreneurial education, we are not aware of any published empirical study or observation of Cognitive Apprenticeship in this setting. The purpose of this paper is to apply CA to describe the process of student learning during undergraduate internships at small or start-up companies.

The CA framework comprises four broad dimensions: content, method, sequence and sociology. Additionally, these dimensions feature several different elements that characterize optimal learning environments. The components of CA are further depicted in Figure 1. Content refers to the strategic knowledge that experts use in solving problems and accomplishing tasks. In CA, the content dimension includes four components: domain knowledge, heuristic strategies, control strategies and learning strategies.

Domain knowledge includes 'concepts, facts, and procedures explicitly identified with a particular subject matter' (Collins *et al*, 1991, p 13). Heuristic strategies are generally regarded as the 'tricks of the trade' that experts use in carrying out tasks within their specific disciplines. Control strategies are techniques for

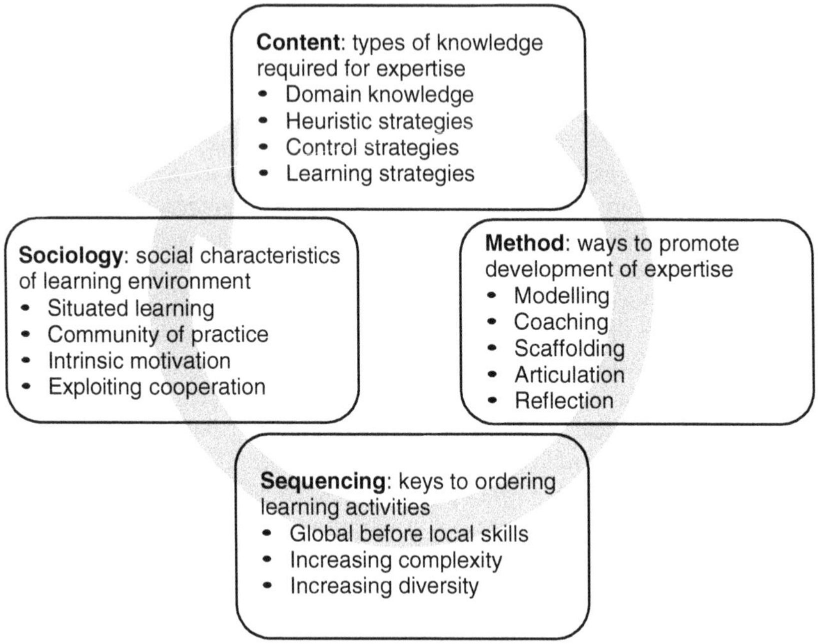

**Figure 1.** Components of cognitive apprenticeship.

managing the process of carrying out a task, including assessing a problem and identifying the most effective problem-solving strategy. Learning strategies refer to strategies for learning content that aids in carrying out complex tasks and exploring new domains.

In describing the method dimension, Collins *et al*, (1991) argue that teaching methods within a CA framework should 'give students the opportunity to observe, engage in, and invent or discover expert strategies in context' (*ibid*, p 13). The researchers further outline six components of teaching methods: modelling, coaching, scaffolding, articulation, reflection and exploration. Modelling occurs when students are able to observe experts performing a task and develop a conceptual model. Coaching entails experts observing students carrying out tasks and offering guidance through various means of scaffolding. Scaffolding refers to the types of support students receive from experts to help them, the students, carry out tasks. Articulation consists of experiences allowing students to describe their knowledge base and how they apply their knowledge in problem solving. In reflection, students are able to compare their practice with their own previous practice or with the practice of experts or other students. Collins *et al*, (1991) describe exploration as the 'natural culmination of the fading of supports' *(ibid*, p 14). Exploration involves creating opportunities for students to solve problems on their own.

The third dimension of CA is known as sequencing and has three main components: global before local skills, increasing complexity and increasing diversity. Collins *et al*, (1991) argue that appropriate sequencing of learning activities for students provides structure and meaning to their learning. In the 'global before local skills' component of sequencing, Collins *et al*, (1991) explain that building a conceptual model of a target skill or process before learning the specific details for carrying out the process allows students to make sense of their tasks, monitor their progress and develop self-correction skills. Increasing complexity refers to sequencing tasks so that the integration of more and more skills is required for expert performance. Increasing diversity refers to sequencing tasks so that a wider variety of strategies and skills are required.

The sociology dimension refers to four elements that allow for the integration of students into the actual practice environment of their profession: situated learning, community of practice, intrinsic motivation and exploiting cooperation. Situated learning is a critical element of learning that allows students to apply their knowledge in an environment that 'reflects the multiple uses to which their knowledge will be put in the future' (Collins *et al*, 1991, p 16). A community of practice refers to

a learning environment in which students can actively participate and engage with other experts in the community. Intrinsic motivation refers to the importance of fostering a learning environment in which students eventually perform tasks out of an internal motivation and interest rather than a solely external motivation. Exploiting cooperation refers to having students learn through collaborative problem solving.

Using the CA model as a guiding framework for this study offers several advantages. First, the descriptive, dimensional nature of the model is appropriate for describing the components that explain the process of student learning. Second, CA can serve as an effective construct for understanding experiential entrepreneurial learning specifically because of the emphasis on transferring knowledge from experts and situating learning in a practical environment. Third, the concept of apprenticeship is universal and one that has been practised for centuries in several different cultures. Thus, the findings from this study are cross-culturally relevant and can be applied in many different contexts. However, a major limitation to the CA model is that it does not appear to be ideal for evaluating programme outcomes or cause-and-effect relationships.

## Internship programme

Interns for Indiana (IfI) is an internship programme created by a large, midwestern research university in the USA as part of a novel initiative to enhance undergraduate students' entrepreneurial skills and motivation to work in small companies or start their own businesses. The programme also promotes regional economic development by supporting early-stage start-up companies. If I is uniquely distinct from other internship programmes in that it provides experiential opportunities for students to work in fast-paced entrepreneurial environments. Students are paired with local high-tech start-up companies in which they are typically given more autonomy and responsibility than in corporate internship programmes. Since the inception of the programme in 2004, 477 students and 160 companies have participated. Highly qualified, self-selected undergraduate juniors and seniors from a wide range of colleges and majors are accepted into the programme; qualified companies from a variety of high-tech industries (including biomedical, software development, and aerospace) also apply for participation in the programme. Students are interviewed by selected companies and matches are created based on both student and company rankings, needs of the company and student skills. Students then complete an internship for the full academic year or summer semester. On average, interns work 150 hours during each academic-year semester (300 hours total) or 400 hours in the summer and receive credit and a scholarship (academic year) or a stipend (summer) for their participation. Academic-year interns work with their supervisors to develop a flexible schedule so as not to interfere with their academic obligations.

The If I programme is also unique in that it offers a classroom component that allows students to integrate their internship experience with their academic experience. If I students participate in a seminar course which includes small-group discussions of internship experiences, a poster session in which students present the outcomes of their specific projects to their peers and other interested members in the community and a guided reflective writing assignment in which students compare their expectations and preconceptions prior to starting the internship with their actual experiences as interns. Additionally, students participate in individual interviews mid-semester and focus-group discussions at the end of the semester. During these activities, students have the opportunity to articulate and identify their gains, challenges, perspectives and growth throughout the internship experience. These supplemental activities are included in order to allow students to reflect on their internship and construct meaning from their experience. In the following sections, we will demonstrate how the Cognitive Apprenticeship framework can be used to conceptualize the learning process of students in If I.

## Methods

*Participants and data collection*

Sixty-six students from a large midwestern university participated in Interns for Indiana over the course of five academic terms between fall (autumn) 2009 and spring 2011. Academic terms at the university are distinct grading periods that are approximately three months long.

Of the participants, 18 (27%) were women and 48 (73%) were men. The gender distribution of the participants in the study reflects the overall gender distribution in business and STEM (science, technology, engineering and mathematics) majors at the university in which the population is 26% female and 74% male. Additionally, 18 (26%) were juniors and 48 (73%) were seniors; 25 (38%) were engineering majors, 21 (32%) were business majors, 6 (9%) were natural science majors, 8 (12%) were computer sciences majors and 6 (9%) students were from various other majors.

Data for this analysis come from three key sources. First, a programme representative conducted mid-semester one-on-one interviews with interns at their internship site. The representative asked interns questions concerning lessons learned, challenges and successes and perceptions of start-up companies. Interviews, typically lasting 10–15 minutes, were recorded and later transcribed. Second, students completed prompted reflective writing assignments, at mid-semester, on topics including expectations, personal lessons learned, challenges and rewards, and attitude towards working in small/start-up companies.

Third, an assessment specialist conducted focus-group sessions with all interns after the completion of their internship. Participants were encouraged to engage in open dialogue about their views on the programme, internship influence on their career plans and suggestions for programme enhancement. Sessions typically lasted 45 minutes to an hour and were recorded and later transcribed.

*Data analysis*

A directed content analysis was used to conceptualize and analyse the qualitative data according to the Cognitive Apprenticeship framework. Directed content analysis allows researchers to use a structured deductive approach to data analysis in order to 'validate or extend conceptually a theoretical framework or theory' (Hsieh and Shannon, 2005, p 1281). Directed content analysis involves securing units of analyses, identifying textual passages representing a particular phenomenon, developing a categorization matrix based on the key concepts of a theory and coding selected passages into the matrix. In order to increase trustworthiness, researchers can include an additional step which involves assigning new codes to text not categorized in the initial coding scheme (interested readers should see Hsieh and Shannon, 2005, for a detailed description of directed content analysis).

In the current study, students' reflective writings and verbatim transcriptions from the focus groups and interviews served as units of analyses. Prior to coding, the researchers read through and reviewed the data thoroughly several times. During this review, textual examples illustrating the phenomenon of student learning were identified. The categories and subcategories of the CA framework (shown in Figure 1) provided a predetermined categorization matrix that guided the coding of the data (Elo and Kyngas, 2007). The identified text was then coded into categories using this categorization matrix. The frequency count for each category was determined by the number of students who mentioned the category at least once. The categories were then grouped into the four distinct dimensions of CA. During analysis, additional themes emerged that fell outside the CA coding scheme. These themes were assigned codes and are briefly discussed but were not relevant to the explanation of the phenomenon of student learning. NVivo 8.0, the qualitative analysis software, was used to record and organize textual data.

## Results

We integrated findings from all data sources to illustrate the different components of the four CA dimensions found in the internship programme.[1]

*Content dimension*

Students reported that their internship experiences allowed them to gain important knowledge not taught in traditional classrooms, such as learning the different components of running a business or how to work with real-life clients and customers.

*1. Domain knowledge.* Students reported entering the internship programme with domain knowledge from classes in various subjects such as engineering, business, computer science, etc. Most students had internships related to their academic major and thus were familiar with the technical background of concepts they were exposed to in the workplace. One student commented,

'I'm [a] biology major and I went to a biomedical firm; the stuff I was dealing with was building off of what I had already learned.'

However, students soon realized that domain knowledge alone was insufficient for surviving in the workforce. One student commented on his initial struggle with the discrepancy between school and work:

'Majoring in economics with minors in mathematics and statistics, I used to think that I have very strong analytical and quantitative skills. However, when I started my internship, the problem occurred to me was how I can use these skills I learned. Work is different from study, as no one will give us problem sets to solve during work.'

From their early internship experiences, students learned they would need to acquire a new skill set in order to successfully translate their academic knowledge into practical work behaviour.

*2. Heuristic strategies.* In their internships, students reported learning specific heuristic strategies from their bosses and co-workers about work issues such as dealing with difficult customers, managing stress effectively and maximizing output from experiments. These strategies are distinct from domain knowledge and were learned through direct experiences on the job. One student described learning tricks of the trade from company founders:

'The founders watched over us and gave us tips as our direct supervisor, a former Intern for Indiana participant, had gone through many of the same things I was experiencing.'

Students mentioned that the heuristic strategies they learned in the workplace were vital to success but could not be properly learned from traditional methods of learning such as reading a textbook or listening to a lecture.

*3. Control strategies.* Collins *et al,* (1991) reported that as students expand their bank of heuristic strategies, they often encounter new control problems. This phenomenon was also apparent in students' internship experiences. Many students reported initially facing a challenge in balancing the increasing demands of their internship. Students were often given multiple tasks at once or asked to work on different projects simultaneously. Students found the internship structure (modelled on the structure of a real small business working environment) very different from the more linear, sequential structure of traditional classes. Thus, many students reported having to adopt new strategies for prioritizing tasks and effectively managing their time. One student's journal response illustrates examples of new control strategies he learned during his internship:

'I have learned to prioritize my goals and tasks and look at the overall picture to realize the value of each task. This has in turn lead to better overall time management efficient use of my day. Before my internship, I would do general tasks around the house or schoolwork in random order. This took away from my day as I was not efficient. Through my time in the internship, I realized the economic value of aligning tasks in the best way possible.'

Accordingly, many students reported that the control strategies they learned from their internships were skills which would be useful in their future career and professional development.

*4. Learning strategies.* After learning effective control strategies, students described having to learn to choose or modify strategies most appropriate for specific tasks:

'However, it's never too late to learn. Having realized this problem, I am planning to spend more of my spare time on readings and other subjects. To make this change happen, I will have to speed up a little bit in order to leap from the learning stage to the production stage.'

Students also mentioned that the structures of their small companies were fluid and dynamic and thus they were continuously adapting to changing environments and structures. Although some students noted this as an initial challenge, students reported flexibility and adaptability would be lifelong career skills. Additional learning strategies students mentioned were conducting background research, learning to ask for help, and brainstorming with a group.

*Method*

In the practical component of the internship programme, supervisors and co-workers at the internship sites served as informal instructors, while activities in the classroom component provided more traditional instructional methods related to students' informal learning.

*1. Modelling.* Students reported that interning in a small business allowed them to hold important responsibilities and work closely with their supervisors and other company employees:

> 'From being in the same office almost every time I worked with people like [my supervisors] I was able to gain some understanding of what the industry is all about.'

Thus students were exposed to a plethora of modelling opportunities. Students observed hard work, dedication and other necessary components for starting a business:

> 'I think that knowing how busy [my boss] is and being able to observe that first hand doesn't compare to [my entrepreneurial classes] . . . Actually getting to work with [my boss] has really opened my eyes to how much it actually takes to start and run your own business.'

Students also reported learning important entrepreneurial lessons from observing their bosses such as professional etiquette, how to work with a team and work independently, how to communicate with different professionals, and how to raise money from investors.

*2. Coaching.* Students' reports of experiences of coaching varied, according to their internship sites. A few students mentioned being initially paired with an employee in the company who served as an instructor for using technical equipment and software. Other students mentioned having regularly scheduled meetings at which they brought questions and concerns and received feedback and guidance. Many students described having 'open-door policies' in which they were able to seek help and advice from supervisors as needed. Thus it appeared that most companies had structures in place to coach interns. However, six students reported not receiving as much coaching as they expected, due to limited resources and lack of expertise in specific areas within their companies. For example, one student reported:

> '. . . there's not a lot of direction necessarily. I'll be given a task and [my supervisor] doesn't really have a good idea of what needs to be done to accomplish the task so putting the brain power in to figure out what I have to do exactly has been a bit of a challenge.'

*3. Scaffolding.* Students reported that the open environment of their small companies allowed them to communicate easily with supervisors and other employees and thus gave them access to ample scaffolding.

According to student reports, scaffolding generally took the form of specific technical advice, tips for conceptualizing and writing business plans, clarification of questions, guidance in constructing long-term goals and constructive feedback.

*4. Articulation.* Students were given an opportunity to articulate their knowledge and experience in the classroom component of the internship programme. Students engaged in group discussions with other interns in the programme and presented a poster at the end of the semester detailing their work projects. Students mentioned that these experiences helped them improve their presentation and communication skills. In addition, one student mentioned that the opportunity to train a new intern at her internship site allowed her to understand and internalize better the knowledge she had acquired.

*5. Reflection.* Students were given opportunities for reflection during the classroom component in which they engaged in group discussion and completed reflective writing activities. Students reported using their reflective writing to identify positive changes they had made throughout the semester as well as identifying areas for improvement. Students also realized the benefit of reflection in future career pursuits.

*6. Exploration.* Several students reported that working in a small company allowed them to hold many important responsibilities and make meaningful contributions to the company, to an extent not typical in other types of internships. Students also reported that they eventually had to make important decisions and solve complicated problems with little or no guidance. Many students initially found this to be a challenge and were unsure of their capabilities, but they learned to integrate their skills along with heuristic, learning and control strategies to carry out their tasks. For example, one intern stated:

> 'I was then expecting to be told how I was to go about solving this problem. However, I was instead told to design an experiment myself. At first, this was a very overwhelming task for me. I believe this challenge ended up being one of the most rewarding experiences of my internship. I had to step outside of my comfort zone and do what I didn't think I was capable of.'

Students stated that they learned many other important entrepreneurial skills such as taking initiative, working independently, problem solving and learning how and where to ask for help.

### Sequencing

Student reports indicate that the learning experiences provided by their internships embodied the three principles of sequencing.

*1. Global before local skills.* Students reported that their supervisors asked them to spend the beginning stages of their internship researching their area and learning broad theories and basics about topics such as market competition and programming. Although some students said that they did not enjoy researching, they were able to appreciate the value and importance of having a strong conceptual understanding of their field. For example, one student described his experience:

> 'I feel like I have only been researching during the internship so far. I understand that I need to understand the entire market and all of the companies in it . . . I think it was good for me to do this on my own so I could get my own idea of the market so when I talk with [my bosses] I will not be influenced by the ideas they already have. I could have asked for a couple of smaller jobs that were not research oriented but overall I feel like I have learned a lot so I am happy with my experience so far.'

*2. Increasing complexity.* Students reported that their tasks progressively increased in complexity and they simultaneously received less coaching and scaffolding. For example, one student reported:

> 'Initially . . . I was paired with a specific employee within the company, and for the first couple of weeks, he showed me how some of the equipment was used and how to perform some experiments. However, for the next couple of weeks, my responsibilities were not at all what I expected. I was given a specific project and a question to answer.'

Students stated that after mastering the initial learning curve, they were able to accomplish increasingly complex tasks, using the broad knowledge base they had acquired.

*3. Increasing diversity.* Several students reported that working in a small group of professional staff, where they were in constant contact with many different departments, allowed them to gain exposure to different disciplines in the workplace and develop a diverse skill set. For example, one student commented:

> 'All of the interns gained some quality sales experience, but we were all given the chance to work on different projects or even lead projects in different fields. I was able to focus on lead generation through marketing. I have many projects that gave me marketing experience and knowledge which will help in future jobs.'

Students also mentioned that they learned how to adapt their acquired skills for different environments.

*Sociology*

Students described feeling fully integrated into their companies and being immersed in the small business/entrepreneurial culture.

*1. Situated learning.* Students reported that their internship gave them valuable opportunities to apply their knowledge in a real work setting and thus learned many practical lessons and acquired skills that are not taught in traditional classrooms. For example, one student commented:

> 'A lot of things I've learned here is about marketing products that you don't really learn a lot about in engineering classes but it's nice to get the aspect of being able to design something to be marketable; I'm used to designing things to make it function the best.'

Other students commented that they gained a new appreciation for different work tasks (for example, laboratory work, research) after witnessing the functional purposes of such tasks.

2. *Community of practice.* Student reports revealed that students felt fully integrated in their internship communities and found the small business culture to be significantly different from what they perceived to be corporate culture. Several students compared the relationship dynamics within their companies to that of a family. Students also appreciated being able to develop personal relationships with their bosses and other employees, feeling valued and being able to make meaningful contributions to the company. Students contrasted these favorable characteristics of their small business sites with their perception of working in a large corporation as 'being stuck in a cubicle', 'making coffee runs' and being told 'here's your paycheck. Go home.'

3. *Intrinsic motivation.* Through their internship experiences, students discovered aspects of working that

they found exciting and truly enjoyed. Some students were even surprised when they realized how much they enjoyed their work:

> 'One thing that I learned about myself is that I enjoy research work. I am always eager to conduct experiments, look at the resulting data, and analyse it. My excitement would especially peak right before the data becomes visible. It is fascinating to examine data for trends and using robust statistical tests to prove or disprove their significance.'

For many of the interns, being able to witness the practical impact of their work provided a strong intrinsic motivation for them to produce results. Students described their motivation to produce results at work as stronger than motivation to get good grades in school:

> 'I seem more motivated to work for a company than for grades. The motivation seems to stem from my fascination that something I am researching and working on can actually be used by people and can make [the] company money. '

4. *Exploiting cooperation.* Throughout their internship, many students reported realizing the integral role of teamwork in the operation of small/ start-up companies:

> 'I believe in order for a start-up business to be successful everyone needs to be willing to brainstorm

new ideas and communicate with each other.'

Accordingly, many interns worked closely in teams or with other employees in their companies. Through these teamwork experiences, students reported being able to improve their communication skills and learn how to use co-workers as resources for brainstorming and problem-solving. Students also mentioned learning the importance of responsibility and accountability when working in a team.

## Implications and recommendations

This paper provides a conceptual extension of the Cognitive Apprenticeship framework to the process of student learning in an experiential entrepreneurial internship. Our analyses revealed that student experiences in the Interns for Indiana programme match the dimensions of CA theory and that using the CA framework to interpret evidence of student learning yields significant insight into the process of student learning. The results from this study raise important implications for researchers, educators, administrators and small businesses. We would argue that integrative internship programmes with small/start-up companies can effectively teach students critical entrepreneurial skills not taught in traditional classrooms or large corporate internships. Administrators and funding agencies interested in developing educational endeavours aimed at providing entrepreneurial education and promoting entrepreneurial intent can be successful by designing similar programmes that embody the principles of CA. The findings from this study are also likely to be beneficial and informative for small/start-up businesses wishing to promote interest and education in small businesses and entrepreneurship among undergraduates in their community. Companies wishing to provide experiential internships can use the CA framework to design their internship programmes and create a conducive learning environment.

Exposure to the different components of CA during the internship allowed students to successfully acquire knowledge from experts in the field and situate their learning in the environment of practice. As a result of these critical CA learning experiences, students were able to learn crucial entrepreneurial skills that are beneficial to a variety of professional endeavours.

### Content dimension

Students found that they could not rely on their pre-existing domain knowledge alone to perform successfully in their internship. Heuristic, control and learning strategies specific to the industry proved crucial in helping students bridge the gap between academic knowledge and practical work behaviour. Students further mentioned that these important lessons were acquired informally on the job. These findings regarding the content dimension hold important implications for meaningful entrepreneurial internships. For example, employers may need to place special emphasis on informal contact with interns in order to pass down heuristic knowledge and valuable entrepreneurial skills such as how to work with real-life clients, how to efficiently manage time and the different components of running a business. In line with our findings, earlier studies (for example, Roxas *et al*, 2008) have suggested that acquisition of such entrepreneurial knowledge positively influences entrepreneurial self-efficacy and perceived desirability of entrepreneurship which, in turn, influences entrepreneurial intent.

*Method dimension*

The simultaneous classroom component of IfI complemented and supplemented students' internship experiences and provided students with a unique integrated learning environment in which they were able to acquire skills through observation and guided practice and experience autonomy in applying their skills. We recommend that programme creators devise effective strategies (such as classroom experiences) for fostering a community of support for interns and include a reflective component that allows students to reflect consciously on their growth and articulate their experiences. Additionally, one challenge some students reported facing was the perception of not receiving adequate support or coaching on the job. This finding reflects a central challenge for many small and start-up companies that may struggle with allocating already limited resources to intern

development. Indeed, earlier studies (for example, Rohde *et al*, 2005) have noted that the establishment of a cohesive community of practice between student interns and start-up company practitioners can be hindered by limited resources of company time and personnel. In this study, however, interns who reported having knowledge of systems in place, in which they had a place or set time to seek additional resources or ask questions, perceived more support and coaching being available from their employers. Establishing a precedent of clear communication and actively creating explicit support structures to allow for coaching opportunities may, therefore, be some of the ways in which companies can compensate for having only limited resources. When assessing potential companies for inclusion, internship programme administrators can also take into account the stability of the company as well as its capacity to provide resources for intern development.

Also, students who reported having several opportunities to learn by modelling in their internships reported learning several important entrepreneurial lessons and techniques for performing their jobs. Modelling therefore appears to be an effective method for informal teaching that does not necessarily require many company resources. Once these coaching systems are set in place, employers can gradually 'fade' them in order to facilitate intern exploration. Students who reported having several exploration opportunities also reported that they felt a strong sense of accomplishment and an increase in self-efficacy after successfully completing tasks on their own.

### Sequence dimension

Sequencing appeared to be a crucial component in students' acquisition and integration of valuable entrepreneurial skills. Students who acquired global before local skills gained an in-depth understanding of their respective fields, identified how smaller tasks contributed to the overall big picture and were able to think critically about current strategies and new ideas. Students further described this global understanding as being a critical component of entrepreneurship. In addition, students stated that after mastering the initial learning curve, they were able to accomplish increasingly complex tasks, using the broad knowledge base they had acquired. Because of this sequencing dimension, students were able to grasp a holistic understanding of business processes and product development, something they deemed crucial to entrepreneurship. Students also mentioned that they learned how to adapt their acquired skills to accommodate the needs of different environments. They concluded that gaining a cohesive understanding of how different disciplines collaborate in developing a finished product is important in entrepreneurship. Our finding is in line with previous studies that show having a wide diversity of educational experiences, rather than a highly specialized education, positively predicts successful entrepreneurial ventures (Dutta *et al*, 2011). We therefore recommend that employers keep track of students'

development, decrease coaching and scaffolding as appropriate and, incrementally, add more challenging and diverse tasks in order to optimize students' learning and understanding.

### Sociology dimension

A benefit of working in a small company environment that emerged from students' data was the opportunity to work closely with employers and experience integration. Students who reported being able to develop personal relationships with their supervisors and other employees were able to feel immersed in the company culture and also identified many benefits of working in a small/start-up company. Furthermore, students who were immersed in their company environment were also able to apply their knowledge directly to their tasks and situate their learning effectively. Students also reported that being able to work as a member of a team helped them learn many important professional skills such as communication, problem solving and accountability. Another benefit that many students attributed to the small business environment was that they were able to perform meaningful tasks and directly see their contributions to the company. Students described finding their work personally rewarding and feeling a sense of personal achievement. Many mentioned gaining more self-confidence and self-efficacy and experiencing personal growth. These students also reported gaining a holistic understanding of their work and were more likely to start their own business as a result of their increased insight. Our finding is supported by earlier research which showed that the opportunity to acquire skills and experience achievement reinforces self-efficacy, which, in turn, influences entrepreneurial intent (Boyd and Vozikis, 1994; Chen *et al*, 1998; Herron and Sapienza, 1992; Zhao *et al*, 2005). Based on these findings, we recommend that employers should cultivate a close community of practice in their companies by creating opportunities for interns to work collaboratively as members of teams or with other employees, apply their knowledge in the industry of the company and understand the impact of their work on the overall company goals.

## Limitations and future work

One limitation to be noted is that because of the use of a self-selected sample, the results cannot be definitively generalized beyond the scope and context of the study. Furthermore, it is likely that students' internship experiences varied according to the characteristics of the companies with which they were placed, whether they were enrolled during the summer or academic term and other environmental and economic conditions specific to the time frame in which they completed their internship. It is possible, therefore, that not every student in the study experienced separately each element of Cognitive Apprenticeship in the same way. For example, some students mentioned receiving plenty of coaching and scaffolding from their supervisors, while others in significantly smaller companies

reported receiving relatively little. However, our results indicate that the programme as a whole provided students with opportunities to learn through Cognitive Apprenticeship and provided examples of how elements of CA can be incorporated into internship programmes.

Furthermore, we observed CA themes mentioned across cohorts, suggesting that in general, small business internships do provide the elements of CA. Future studies can further control for outside variables and examine how variations in experiences within a CA framework affect students' learning. Another limitation of the study is that it was based solely on the experiences of companies and students in the midwest USA. Future studies can expand our findings by applying the model presented here to entrepreneurial internships in other regions and countries.

Although the focus of our study was to explain the process of student learning, additional themes related to student outcomes emerged from the students' responses. The internship experience seemed to enhance students' attitudes about small and start-up businesses, and they further reported increased interest, confidence and motivation in starting their own company or working in a small business. These preliminary findings serve as a rationale for a follow-up study examining the impact of Interns for Indiana on students' attitudes towards small businesses and the subsequent likelihood of starting their own business or working in a small business. Furthermore, we make a strong argument that the

Cognitive Apprenticeship theory is an appropriate descriptive theory for the process of experiential entrepreneurial learning. Future studies can expand upon our findings by testing a model of entrepreneurial learning or entrepreneurial intent using the principles of CA.

## Notes

[1] Additional information about collected data is available upon request.

## References

Adedokun, O.A., Childress, A.L., and Burgess, W.D. (2011), 'Testing conceptual frameworks of non-experimental programme evaluation designs using structural equation modeling', *American Journal of Evaluation*, Vol 32, pp 480–493.

Ahmed, I., Nawaz, M.M., Ahmad, Z., Shaukat, M.Z., Usman, A., Rehman, W., and Ahmed, N. (2010), 'Determinants of students' entrepreneurial career intentions: evidence from business graduates', *European Journal of Social Sciences*, Vol 15, No 2, pp 14–22.

Baretto, H.W. (2006), 'Introduction: entrepreneurship and small business', *Economic Perspectives*, Vol 11, No 1, pp 2–26, last retrieved 11 July 2011 from: http://usinfo.state.gov/journals/journals.htm.

Boyd, N.G., and Vozikis, G.S. (1994), 'The influence of self-efficacy on the development of entrepreneurial intentions and actions', *Entrepreneurship: Theory and Practice*, Vol 18, No 4, pp 63–77.

Chen, C.C., Greene, P.G., and Crick, A. (1998), 'Does entrepreneurial self-efficacy distinguish entrepreneurs from managers?', Journal of Business Venturing, Vol 13, pp 295–316.

Chigunta, F. (2002), 'Youth entrepreneurship: meeting the key policy challenges', retrieved from: www.yesweb.org/gkr/res/bg.entrep.ta.doc.

Collins, A., Brown, S.B., and Holum, A., (1991), 'Cognitive apprenticeship: making thinking visible', *American Educator*, Vol 15, No 3, pp 4–46.

Dutta, D.K., Li, J., and Merenda, M. (2011), 'Fostering entrepreneurship: impact of specialization and diversity in education', *International Entrepreneurship and Management Journal*, Vol 7, pp 163–179.

Elo, S., and Kyngäs, H. (2007), 'The qualitative content analysis process', Journal of Advanced Nursing, Vol 62, No 1, pp 107–115.

Heriot, K., and Lahm, B. (2009), 'Entrepreneurship internships differ from traditional business and management internships: a framework for implementation', *Small Business Institute National Proceedings*, Vol 33, pp 124–139.

Herron, L., and Sapienza, H.J. (1992), 'The entrepreneur and the initiation of new venture launch activities', *Entrepreneurship Theory and Practice*, Vol 17, No 1, pp 49–55.

Hsieh, H.-F., and Shannon, S.E. (2005), 'Three approaches to qualitative content analysis', Qualitative Health Research, Vol 15, No 9, pp 1277–1288.

Iakovleva, T., Kolvereid, L., and Stephan, U. (2011), 'Entrepreneurial intentions in developing and developed countries', *Education + Training*, Vol 53, pp 353–370.

Kardash, C.M. (2000), 'Evaluation of undergraduate research experience: perceptions of undergraduate interns and their faculty mentors', *Journal of Educational Psychology*, Vol 92, No 1, 191–201.

Lave, J. (1997), 'The culture of acquisition and the practice of understanding', in Kirshner, D., and Whitson, J.A., eds, *Situated Cognition: Social, Semiotic and Psychological Perspectives*, Lawrence Erlbaum Associates, Mahwah, NJ, pp 17–36.

Leebaert, D. (2006), 'How small businesses contribute to US economic expansion', *Economic Perspectives*, Vol 11, No 1, pp 2–26, last retrieved 11 July 2011 from: http://usinfo.state.gov/journals/journals.htm.

Luthje, C., and Franke, N. (2003), 'The "making" of an entrepreneur: testing a model of entrepreneurial intent among engineering students at MIT', R&D Management, Vol 33, pp 135–147.

Peterman, N.E., and Kennedy, J. (2003), 'Enterprise education: influencing students' perceptions of entrepreneurship', Entrepreneurship: Theory and Practice, Vol 28, No 2, pp 129–144.

Rohde, M., Klamma, R., and Wulf, V. (2005), 'Establishing communities of practice among students and start-up companies', in *Proceedings of the 2005*

*Conference on Computer Support for Collaborative Learning*, Taipei, Taiwan, pp 514–519.

Roxas, B. G., Cayoca-Panizales, R., and Mae de Jesus, R. (2008), 'Entrepreneurial knowledge and its effects on entrepreneurial intentions: development of a conceptual framework', *Asia-Pacific Social Science Review*, Vol 8, No 2, pp 61–77.

Small Business Administration (2008), 'The small business economy: a report to the president', SBA Office of Advocacy, last retrieved 11 July 2011 from: http://www.sba.gov/advocacy/.

Taylor, K. L. and Care, W. D. (1999), 'Nursing education as cognitive apprenticeship: a framework for clinical education', *Nurse Educator*, Vol 24, No 4, pp 31–36.

Wymenga, P., Spanikova, V., Derbyshire, J., and Barker, A. (2011), 'Are EU SME's recovering from the crisis?' *Annual Report on EU Small and Medium Sized Enterprises*, pp 1–59.

Zhao, H., Seibert, S. E., and Hills, G. E. (2005), 'The mediating role of self-efficacy in the development of entrepreneurial intentions', Journal of Applied *Psychology*, Vol 90, No 6, pp 1265–1272.

# The Purdue University Experience

## Nurturing an entrepreneurial ecosystem in the Midwest of the United States

**Nathalie Duval-Couetil and Scott Hutcheson**

## Introduction

Universities have long played a role in entrepreneurship, from educating and graduating captains of industry to studying economic trends and optimal business models to incubating research that leads to valuable new products and services. While this may have been done somewhat haphazardly in the past, in recent years, many universities have begun to be more deliberate about integrating the components of entrepreneurship, including education, technology commercialization, and community engagement, to develop and articulate a construct for entrepreneurship as a system. This paper focuses on key policies and programs that Purdue University, a large university in the Midwest of the United States, has initiated over the past 10 years to (1) create a culture of entrepreneurship across its campus, (2) enhance its pipeline to deliver faculty-generated innovation to market and (3) to become a primary driver of economic development in its community and the nation.

## Background of university involvement in economic development

The role that research universities play in economic development and entrepreneurship in the United States and elsewhere has been well documented (Phan & Siegel, 2006). Historically, technology innovation resulting from funded university research labs has been at the core of the successful launching of start-up companies. From high-strength materials developed at universities in the 1930s and the recombinant DNA breakthrough of the 1970s to the creation of the first digital computer, Internet search engines, medical imaging devices and fluoride toothpaste, universities have been integral to US innovation and global competitiveness ('University Inventions', 2010). The National

Council of Entrepreneurial Tech Transfer (2010) illustrates the compelling impact of university-based research:

- *Federal funding is a key ingredient in start-up creation*. More than 400 university start-ups are created in the United States each year based on federally funded research and development. Among the most prolific funders are the National Institutes of Health, National Sciences Foundation, and the US Department of Defense. Examples of start-ups resulting from federal funding are Google, Netscape, Genentech, Lycos, Sun Microsystems, Silicon Graphics and Cisco Systems.
- *Universities are fertile grounds for nurturing successful start-ups*. About 8% of all university start-ups go public, in comparison to 0.07% for other US enterprises – a 114-times difference.
- *University start-ups have greater staying power*. Sixty-eight per cent (68%) of university start-ups created between 1980 and 2000 remained in business in 2001, while regular start-ups experienced a 90% failure rate during that same period.

The entrepreneurial reach of universities has expanded over the years. Universities have stepped up their technology transfer, business development and business incubation activities to maximize the value of their intellectual property portfolios. There has been a proliferation of entrepreneurship education programs driven by a need to teach students how to create value and jobs

(Finkle & Deeds, 2001; Kuratko, 2005) and a movement to extend entrepreneurship education beyond colleges of management or business to other academic disciplines such as engineering, science and the arts (Streeter, Jacquette & Hovis, 2002). A number of factors have contributed to the increased emphasis universities placed on entrepreneurship. In the area of innovation, the Bayh Dole Act pushed universities to become more proactive in their technology transfer activities and policies (Graff, Heiman & Zilberman, 2002; Phan & Siegel, 2006). More attention to commercialization has also been driven by an increased emphasis on applied research leading to commercially viable technologies and products by major US funding agencies such as the National Science Foundation (NSF) and National Institutes of Health (NIH). In the area of education and workforce preparation, economic trends mean that students who traditionally sought stable jobs in large companies must also be prepared for jobs in smaller companies that require entrepreneurial skills. The Kauffman Foundation, a catalyst for embedding entrepreneurship on college campuses, has provided millions of dollars in funding to a wide variety of institutions to develop programs that will accomplish this ('Entrepreneurship Education Without Boundaries', 2010). Local, state and federal government agencies have also realized that economic development strategies focused exclusively on industrial attraction are not an effective way to grow a regional economy. Successfully landing the next big manufacturing plant employing hundreds of workers is an infrequent occurrence for most communities, and investing in launching start-ups, particularly technology start-ups, is proving to be an effective economic-growth strategy.

MIT, Stanford and other universities in regions of the country that are densely populated and with access to capital and talent have traditionally had a significant competitive advantage over universities that lack proximity to these resources. Social norms and tacit approval of entrepreneurship were also found to be critical factors in successful entrepreneurial activity at MIT even two decades ago (Roberts, 1991). A recent study by the Kauffman Foundation examined the economic impact of MIT and reinforced the importance of universities in driving entrepreneurial growth (Roberts & Eesley, 2009). The survey of alumni found 6,900 MIT alumni-founded companies in Massachusetts were responsible for creating an estimated one million jobs. These companies accounted for worldwide sales of approximately $164 billion and represented 26% of the sales of all Massachusetts companies. The study reported that without MIT, most of these companies never would have been located in Massachusetts because fewer than 10% of MIT undergraduates were natives of the state. These firms were primarily knowledge-based companies in software, biotech, manufacturing (electronics, instruments, machinery) or consulting (architects, business consultants, engineers). The authors stated that these companies had a

disproportionate importance to their local economies because they typically represented advanced technologies and usually sold to out-of-state and world markets, their global revenues per employee were far greater than the revenues produced by the average company, they employed higher-skilled as well as higher-paid employees and they tended to have far lower pollution impact on their local environments.

Most research universities in the United States, however, lack proximity to the capital markets and the large pool of entrepreneurial talent that can be found in places like Boston and Silicon Valley. Furthermore, while research has long been a focal point of universities, entrepreneurship and company formation have not. Fortunately, this trend is beginning to change, although significant challenges in getting university innovation to the marketplace remain, including:

- *Faculty training*. Although faculty can be quite entrepreneurial in their role as researchers and are innovative in their technical specialties, few have education or experience in business. Until they have an active interest in starting a company, faculty usually give little thought to acquiring the skill and knowledge base required for entrepreneurship.
- *Marketplace relevance*. Great ideas formulated in a lab or academic environment aren't always relevant to commercial marketplaces. This is due, in part, to a lack of knowledge faculty have about the market for their research, competitors, regulations and other factors that

can make or break a new product or service. Such information can be critical in making adjustments, small or large, to a technology and thereby improving its chances of commercial success.

• *Early-stage funding.* While funds exist for basic research, the money required to transform a great idea to commercially viable technology is lacking. Typically, investors and corporations who could benefit most from university-generated ideas are reluctant to invest in very early-stage intellectual property.

The subsequent sections of this chapter will outline key policies and programs that Purdue University, a large university in the Midwest of the United States, has initiated over the past decade to overcome these barriers and cultivate an entrepreneurial ecosystem both within and extending beyond the walls of the university. These policies include supporting programs that foster a culture of entrepreneurship among students and faculty across disciplines, mechanisms to enhance its product and service pipeline of innovations making their way into the marketplace and assisting local and regional communities in becoming places where new ventures can launch and grow.

## Purdue's strategic framework for an entrepreneurship ecosystem

Purdue University is a large, public research university in a mostly rural region of the Midwest United States. The university encompasses three campuses within the state and

10 academic colleges at its main campus, including agriculture, health and human sciences, education, engineering, liberal arts, management, pharmacy, science, technology and veterinary medicine. Many of Purdue's colleges are top ranked nationally within their disciplines (Purdue University, 2010). During the 2008–09 academic year, the university received $327M in research funding, with 68% of the total coming from the colleges of engineering ($109M), science ($62M) and agriculture ($50M). On the main campus, there are 400 research labs, 40,000 students and more than 2,000 faculty and 15,000 staff members.

Although Purdue University has been very successful in attracting sponsored research funding, it is not located in a geographic area known for being suited for high-tech, start-up companies. For many decades, the primary drivers of Indiana's economy were agriculture and manufacturing – with much of the state's workforce and investment being focused on these areas. The state did not have a reputation for being well suited to support entrepreneurs; those seeking careers in more entrepreneurial or technology-driven businesses often left the state to find opportunities. A decade ago, a study found that only one third of students graduating from top Indiana universities in the fields of engineering and the sciences stayed in the state after graduation ('Graduate Migration from Indiana's Postsecondary Institutions', 1999).

Founded in 1869 as the land-grant institution for the State of Indiana, Purdue has a long history of commitment to economic development. Land-grant universities were created to focus on the teaching of agriculture, science and engineering as a response to the industrial revolution and in contrast to higher education's traditional focus on classical studies (Rasmussen, 1989). The purpose of these institutions was to connect university resources and research to the surrounding communities in a more applied fashion. Today, as states have begun to include a focus on technology and innovation-based economic development, land-grant institutions are taking on an even more prominent role in economic development in many regions of the United States.

In recent years, many of Indiana's state and local government leaders recognized that the restructuring of the manufacturing sector created the need for a more diversified economy, in particular one that supports innovative, high-growth companies and small businesses. As a result, they invested in initiatives designed to become more attractive to high-tech entrepreneurs and small businesses. To a great extent, the drivers and beneficiaries of these programs have been the state's public universities and the technologies that emerge from them. These government initiatives include competitive loans/ grants to 'seed' the development of promising early-stage technologies, investments in business incubators and technology parks, support of entrepreneurial workshops and professional organizations, a network of small business advisors throughout the state and attractive tax credits for investing in local start-up companies.

Over the past several years, a major emphasis of Purdue University's

strategic plan has been 'Discovery with Delivery', a statement that reflects the university's desire to encourage research and innovation that translates to real-world applications. This more proactive approach to innovation, commercialization and entrepreneurship has a number of potential benefits to the university. The university continues to be competitive for research funding, some of which increasingly requires a 'bench-to-business' or translational emphasis. There are also significant financial returns in the form of royalties from the licensing of technology and holding equity positions in start-up companies. Benefiting society through the development of innovative technologies also translates into returns such as improved university stature, rankings, successful faculty and student recruitment and increased regional and economic development.

Entrepreneurship activities are integrated into many parts of the university's strategic direction, and although there is much interaction and overlap, entrepreneurship activities that occur at Purdue University are divided primarily across three entities:

- *The academic campus*: The University itself supports entrepreneurship through faculty research, academic courses at the undergraduate and graduate levels and experiential learning programs for students. It also supports a number of research centers and facilities that directly impact the university's commercialization and entrepreneurship activities.
- *Purdue Research Foundation*: A non-profit entity created in 1930,

the foundation manages donations to the university, makes funding available to aid in research or education, operates four technology parks across the state of Indiana and manages intellectual property and business-development activities for the university through its Office of Technology Commercialization.

- *Engagement and extension*: Purdue's Office of Engagement oversees the university's outreach activities, including the Purdue Center for Regional Development (PCRD), which provides research tools and innovation-based strategies for regional economic development. Another vital engagement entity is the university Cooperative Extension Service, which fulfils the university's land-grant mission by providing research-based information to the public in various areas, including entrepreneurship.

Prior to the year 2000, much of the entrepreneurship activity occurring at the university could be found at the Purdue Research Foundation and its Office of Technology Commercialization, which assists faculty with intellectual property protection and licensing opportunities. A greater emphasis on entrepreneurship across Purdue's campus began in 2004 with the establishment of Purdue's Burton D. Morgan Center for Entrepreneurship. The center was part of the development of Purdue's Discovery Park, an interdisciplinary research park composed of several entities focused on the 'grand challenges' of the future, including

energy, the environment, oncology, nanotechnology, biosciences and science, technology, engineering and math (STEM) education. Discovery Park gained initial momentum with a $50 million grant from the Lilly Endowment, an Indiana-based private philanthropic foundation created by the Lilly Family (Eli Lilly and Company), and it has since attracted an additional $175 million in investment for facilities and equipment. Burton D. Morgan was a Purdue graduate and successful entrepreneur who donated the funding for the entrepreneurship center.

At the time, locating the Burton D. Morgan Center for Entrepreneurship within the interdisciplinary research park was a novel approach, as most US university-based entrepreneurship centers were typically housed within or alongside a business college. Although the center has a strong connection to Purdue's Krannert School of Management, policy makers foresaw benefits to expanding entrepreneurship education and resources to other disciplines. The new physical space of the entrepreneurship center catalysed the development of several new programs designed to serve faculty and students in all of Purdue's colleges as well as the community. Experienced staff and streamlined policies and programs were able to create a bridges among the campus, the Purdue Research Foundation, and the community.

Over the past 10 years, Purdue's uniqueness in terms of policy lies in the institution's commitment to entrepreneurship, the scope of its business-development initiatives and the speed at which they were implemented. This paper will describe several key programs in which the authors of this paper were involved that are part of this cross-campus, multi-disciplinary entrepreneurship effort.

## Educating students and faculty

As discussed earlier in this chapter, a key component in developing an entrepreneurship ecosystem is providing individuals with the skills and knowledge they need to identify opportunities, evaluate their technical and market feasibility and assemble the resources necessary to start new ventures. Prior to 2005, a few courses related to entrepreneurship were offered around campus; however, these were only available to students in specific disciplines, primarily management and technology, and provided no formal academic credential. Today, Purdue's portfolio of entrepreneurship training includes programs for high school students, tenured university faculty and nearly everyone in between. The following is an overview of several programs that help equip emerging entrepreneurs.

*Student programs*

*Entrepreneurship education for undergraduate students*: Purdue policy makers understood that to create an entrepreneurial culture, a good place to start was with the 30,000 undergraduate students enrolled at Purdue's main campus. In 2005, the Certificate in Entrepreneurship and Innovation Program was launched as a way to offer entrepreneurship education to students in all undergraduate disciplines. Similar to a minor or concentration, the program was designed to complement a student's major area of study. Its primary objective is to make entrepreneurship an accessible career option for students and to help them to (1) learn how to research prospective products, services or technologies and present critical analyses of their potential, (2) develop the leadership and communication skills necessary to advocate for prospective ventures and (3) enhance student performance and marketability within their disciplines. The requirements of the program are the completion of a series of five courses or experiential learning programs. These include (1) two 'core' entrepreneurship courses that cover basic knowledge and skills, (2) two 'option' courses that provide depth in an industry or discipline related to entrepreneurship and (3) one 'capstone' course or experience, which requires students to engage in entrepreneurial activity, either through writing business plans for new ventures or doing internships in start-up companies.

*Technology commercialization education for graduate students*: Since many graduate students are involved in research, the Technology Realization Program was created to teach the principles for moving ideas and technologies emerging from the lab bench out to the marketplace as a viable business opportunity. The program is open to graduate students in all disciplines, and it provides them with an understanding of the challenges of managing the development and introduction of new ideas/technologies, along with starting and managing new business ventures both within existing businesses and as independent start-ups. A seminar, offered every fall semester, presents topics related to technology commercialization and entrepreneurship through readings, class discussion and presentations by invited speakers. A workshop, offered every spring semester, introduces specific methodologies and techniques that students apply through case studies and hands-on class projects.

*Biomedical entrepreneurship training for graduate students:* Biomedship is an innovative joint venture among Purdue's Weldon School of Biomedical Engineering, Purdue's Krannert School of Management and the Indiana University School of Medicine. It is designed to develop leaders in the biomedical technology and the medical device industry by providing formal training in innovation and entrepreneurship. The program targets graduate students in engineering and MBA programs and provides them with the knowledge and skills that are essential for the early development and management of new biomedical technologies. Through a two-course sequence, it enhances students' abilities to identify new opportunities for innovation, assess clinical and market potential and take the critical first steps in invention, patenting, early prototyping, development of new concepts and movement toward commercialization.

*Internships in entrepreneurial companies:* The Interns for Indiana Program was developed in response to the challenge of 'brain drain'

facing the state, that is, the loss of talented Purdue graduates to large metropolitan and/or coastal regions with ample high-paying, high-tech jobs. The program matches thoroughly screened students from all disciplines with internships in a variety of roles within technology-based companies. The program has three goals: (1) to offer students professional training through experiential learning, (2) to introduce students to the wide variety of occupational opportunities within smaller companies across the state and (3) to foster economic growth of local businesses by offering them increased access to talent at a reasonable cost. Internships are done part time during the academic year or full time in the summer. The program also includes an academic component that requires attendance at professional development seminars and written analyses of individual student experiences throughout their internship.

*Entrepreneurial competitions:* Throughout the year, Purdue hosts a number of entrepreneurship-related competitions, the main one being the Burton D. Morgan Business Plan Competition, created in 1987, the third-oldest business plan competition in the country. This competition awards $100,000 to undergraduate and graduate students at Purdue who compete in two separate divisions. An Elevator Pitch Competition was launched in 2007 as part of the Certificate in Entrepreneurship and Innovation program as a means of increasing awareness of the importance of effective communication in the practice of entrepreneurship. It involves undergraduate and graduate students as well as entrepreneurs from Purdue's technology parks. Purdue also hosts industry-sector business plan competitions in the life sciences and nanotechnology, and product development and innovation competitions are in held in several colleges, such as engineering and agriculture, throughout the year.

*Entrepreneurship summer camp for high school students:* As part of its outreach and engagement activities, the Purdue Research Foundation organizes a week-long summer entrepreneurship camp for high school. The program focuses on introducing entrepreneurship to students who are high achievers in the STEM disciplines. The academy connects these students with high-tech entrepreneurs and introduces them to the concept that they can 'make a job' as well as 'take a job' in highly technical fields. Students who complete the program and choose to enrol at Purdue after their graduation from high school are eligible to have one requirement of the Certificate in Entrepreneurship and Innovation Program waived.

## Faculty programs

Historically, the primary drivers of 'Discovery with Delivery' have been faculty researchers conducting research primarily in engineering and the sciences. In most cases, few of these faculty innovators have knowledge or experience with entrepreneurship, and most do not have the background to take on roles as CEOs, marketers, manufacturing supervisors, human resource managers or stockholders. A number of programs were developed to increase faculty awareness of and collaboration and involvement in entrepreneurship.

*Entrepreneurial leadership academy:* Each year, a group of 10 entrepreneurially minded faculty from all disciplines are selected from a pool of applicants to participate in a year-long program designed to expose them to entrepreneurship and leadership opportunities on campus through monthly meetings which feature Purdue administrators, entrepreneurship program leaders and university-affiliated entrepreneurs. These gatherings are intended to foster relationships and networking that will lead to outcomes such as increased participation in technology commercialization, business development activities or the design of entrepreneurial curriculum. Academy participants are given modest grants to support related curriculum development, seminars or travel. Each year, one faculty member is selected to be the Entrepreneurship Academy Scholar and receives additional funding to pursue and/or expand his/her entrepreneurial activities.

*Entrepreneurship Boot Camp:* This annual event educates Purdue faculty and graduate students about company formation and funding. Key topics include intellectual property protection, company formation, selecting a CEO, packaging and selling ideas, sources of capital and company valuation. The boot camp also includes follow-on sessions focused on developing investment presentations, which teach attendees how to tailor presentations to their audience and how to exploit their 'face time' with potential investors. Emerging companies can be assigned company coaches, who provide further assistance with refining 15-minute investment pitches. As an incentive, a panel of experts selects the best companies for an annual, all-expense-paid trip to Silicon Valley to network and present to venture capitalists. This full-day event is held during the university's fall break, when faculty and graduate students do not have teaching or other commitments.

*Entrepreneurship seminars and workshops:* A number of seminars and workshops are offered throughout the year on a host of topics such as intellectual property protection, licensing and patent procedures and what venture capital firms are looking for when making investments. Other seminars have covered topics such as how to navigate the US Food and Drug Administration (FDA) Approval Process, legal issues related to company formation and how to analyze and negotiate term sheets with investors.

## Enhancing the technology commercialization pipeline

More than 90% of Purdue's research output is unrestricted, meaning that the university is free to commercialize most of the innovation being developed in its labs. Typically this is done by engaging external partners such as companies willing to license technologies, entrepreneurs willing to start new companies and/ or investors. The pipeline from innovation to business creation involves a number of components that must come together at a critical time and that are addressed to very different degrees across universities. These include (1) technology and market evaluations, (2) funding for early-stage commercial development and (3) access to talent and networks. Because Purdue is not located in a dense metropolitan area, programs were developed to proactively package Purdue innovation and expertise and connect to the networks and resources necessary for business development.

*Technology evaluations*: Among the most important services Purdue University provides to its faculty innovators are technology evaluations. Conducted by the Office of Technology Commercialization, these provide faculty with a comprehensive, highly productive early-stage due diligence process that concentrates on three key areas: (1) an objective review of select technologies and their strengths, weaknesses and opportunities, (2) a thorough analysis of the market landscape to include customers, competitors, markets and industry and (3) financial models. The objective of this early-stage feasibility analysis is to generate important insight into a new product or service's true commercial potential that will assist faculty entrepreneurs with refining their technology, strengthening their overall business plan and identifying paths for commercialization. The evaluations are useful in stimulating discussion, guiding innovation and maintaining faculty engagement. The analytical, fact-based approach makes communication with the faculty regarding the commercial potential of their invention much more productive.

*Business incubation:* The Purdue Portals business incubation program is offered to entrepreneurs via the Purdue Research Foundation's network of four technology parks across the state. The program is intended to function as a hands-on strategic advisor throughout the business-development process and help entrepreneurs save time, effort and money during the process of commercializing new technologies and starting new business ventures. Primary areas of assistance include business plan development, seasoned counsel, human resources, test marketing, financial and technical input, networking opportunities and direction from market-specific mentors. Purdue's satellite technology parks were created in recent years so that private business and industry throughout the state of Indiana could interact with and leverage university resources for mutual benefit.

*Funding for early-stage business development:* Given the uncertainty of the returns they can provide, emerging technologies developed in university labs usually aren't mature enough to attract the interest of angel investors or venture capitalists. To bridge this gap, Purdue created funding options to help make early-stage technologies 'investor ready' and thereby more attractive for investment. These infusions of capital, some delivered in stages and others in more sizeable amounts, are designed to move ideas from the lab to the marketplace in an ongoing and preferably uninterrupted fashion. These options include:

- *The Trask Innovation Fund:* Established in 1974, the Trask Innovation Fund is used to assist faculty in the development, protection and exploitation of inventive ideas assigned to the Purdue Research Foundation. The fund is competitive; faculty submit proposals to an award committee that evaluates the commercial value proposition, scientific merit and experimental design. Proposals go through a peer-review process to assure the quality of the science/technology. Annual funding ranges from $10,000 to $100,000 and is intended to strengthen the intellectual property position, validate proof of technical or clinical merit, increase marketability and leverage licensing negotiations. While awards can be used toward salaries for research assistants and graduate students, faculty salaries are not eligible. Any royalty income derived from a subsequent license deal must repay investments granted under the fund, which serves to sustain it.

- *The Emerging Innovations Fund:* Introduced in January 2009, the Emerging Innovations Fund is a partnership initiative of the Purdue Research Foundation and the university. It is a donor-based, philanthropic fund designed to provide financial support for early-stage companies. Small, finite, milestone-based investments in the range of $20,000 to $200,000, with a standard funding term of 12 to 18 months, are available on a competitive basis to

Purdue faculty, graduate students or companies in Purdue Research Park to advance technologies from the lab to the marketplace. The funds can be used for intellectual property enhancement, prototype development and testing, market research and commercial assessment, development of preliminary business plans, management or technical expertise and graduate or postdoctoral support. The intent is that this early-stage funding will improve the probability of attracting additional investment and market assistance as the technology develops. Initial capitalization of the fund is $1.5M, with the intent of creating a $5M evergreen fund (a fund in which the returns generated by its investments are automatically channelled back into the fund rather than being distributed back to investors).

*Connections to investor and talent networks:* In 2009, the Purdue Research Foundation created the P3 (Purdue, People, Performance) angel investor network in order to facilitate the introduction of pre-screened angel investors to new ventures founded on Purdue-owned intellectual property and to engage experienced investors in Purdue's business-development activities. For an annual fee, members receive an online subscription to the network's website and receive invitations to three or four annual events featuring company presentations, access to documentation from firms seeking angel-level investments and the ability to interact online with network participants and management.

# Developing entrepreneurship-friendly communities

The mission of Purdue's Office of Engagement is to use the university's resources to address issues affecting the state's prosperity and quality of life. Its areas of focus include economic development, K–12 education, community service and lifelong learning for individuals who may or may not have a formal affiliation with Purdue. Through the Office of Engagement and Cooperative Extension Service, Purdue houses a number of entities, programs and resources that encourage and support economic development and entrepreneurship throughout the state.

*Purdue Center for Regional Development (PCRD)*: PCRD plays a key role in supporting initiatives and obtaining grants to assist economic regions in Indiana to adopt development policies based on their unique assets. PCRD has created a variety of policy tools that provide local officials and economic developers information and analysis about industry clusters, occupational clusters, innovation capacity and other factors that can help guide regional entrepreneurship and innovation-based economic growth.

- *Workforce Innovation in Regional Economic Development (WIRED)*: In 2006, PCRD received a $15M grant from the US Department of Labor known as WIRED to develop new and innovative ways to merge workforce development and economic development in North Central Indiana. The project had four key strategic areas of focus, one of which was making the region one of the best in the Midwest to start and grow a business. This involved fostering an entrepreneurial culture in the region through an awareness campaign and funding educational programs targeted at a number of different populations, including early-stage entrepreneurs, existing businesses, dislocated workers and even elementary school students.

- *Economic gardening*: The concept of economic gardening was first developed in Littleton, Colorado, as a non-traditional approach to growing the local economy by focusing on growing existing businesses rather than relying on industrial recruitment. Over the last several years, this model has been replicated across the USA, and an increasing number of universities are serving as hubs for economic gardening activities. A core component of the approach is focused on providing strategic data to businesses to help them expand. Much of this information is available only through expensive subscription services that most local economic development organizations cannot afford. Many universities, including Purdue, have access to these data sources and are beginning to partner with economic development communities to pilot economic gardening programs.
- *Hometown Competitiveness*: Hometown Competitiveness, developed by the University of Nebraska, is a community development approach for rural communities that looks at economic growth and quality of life in a way that emphasizes entrepreneurship as well as a handful of other factors. Purdue partners with the state of Indiana to work with several communities each year to adopt the Hometown Competitiveness model. Community 'coaches' work with local communities to help them adopt entrepreneurship-friendly policies and programs.
- *Innovation Index*: The Innovation Index is an analytical tool developed for the US Economic Development Administration to assist policy makers and economic development practitioners to identify the innovation potential of their regional economies. These decision-making tools are available free of charge and can assist state, regional and local economies in developing policies and programs to support innovation-based economic development strategies.

*Small Business Development Center (SBDC)*: The SBDC is a state- and federally funded national network of 1,000 centers that provide support to small business through one-on-one business counselling, training, workshops and market intelligence data. The SBDC provides assistance to entrepreneurs at every stage of business development and is available to the public at no charge. Its mission is to have a positive and measurable impact on the formation, growth and sustainability of small businesses in Indiana and to develop a strong entrepreneurial community. Clients range from individuals who need assistance in deciding if self-employment is right for them to business owners looking to expand overseas. PCRD hosts two regional offices of the SBDC. One is located on Purdue's main campus in the Burton Morgan Center for Entrepreneurship and the other in one of Purdue's technology parks.

*Purdue Cooperative Extension Service*: With offices in each of Indiana's 92 counties, Purdue Extension provides educational programs and research-based information in several areas including economic and community development. Purdue Extension's entrepreneurship-related work includes working with local policy makers to help them develop and implement policies and programs that can make their communities more supportive of entrepreneurial-based economic development. One example of a local policy issue is the zoning related to home-based businesses. In 2009, Purdue Extension conducted a workshop delivered via distance learning in which local officials learned about how to balance the potential growth of home-based business, in an economy in which many newly displaced workers might be interested in starting a business out of their home, with the safety and quality of life needed in residential neighbourhoods.

*Agriculture Innovation & Commercial Center (AICC):* Housed within Purdue's Department of Agricultural Economics and linked to Purdue Cooperative Extension, the AICC was created in 2003 with support from the US Department of Agriculture to disseminate information and create tools to help individuals, primarily in the area of agriculture, to assess their venture ideas and achieve

their goal of starting a business. The AICC offers a wide range of how-to publications and workshops to assist start-ups on topics ranging from creating mission statements to protecting intellectual property and conducting market analysis. Two of the centrepiece programs of AICC include the New Ventures Team and the INVenture business-planning tool. The New Ventures Team is a collaborative effort of Purdue Extension educators and campus specialists that provide consulting to individuals interested in starting a food- or agriculture-related business. INVenture is an online business-planning tool that can help new entrepreneurs in any industry by guiding the development of a business plan through questioning users about their business idea.

## Results and insights from Purdue's experiences

Purdue University's policies and the initiatives described in this chapter have resulted in increased awareness of and involvement in entrepreneurship by students and faculty. One of the unique features of Purdue's efforts is that entrepreneurial activity is encouraged, accepted and promoted among students and faculty in all disciplines and not restricted to those in management or engineering. Based on its commitment to multi-disciplinary and cross-campus entrepreneurship, the university received a $1.5M grant in 2005 from the Kauffman Foundation as part of its Campus Initiatives Program. The following are outcomes related to the university-driven entrepreneurial ecosystem that Purdue has fostered in recent years.

*Increased student involvement
in entrepreneurship*

Since the launch of the Certificate
in Entrepreneurship and Innovation
Program in 2005, more than 2,500
undergraduate students from all
disciplines have enrolled in the
introductory course offered through
the program. By the end of 2010, more
than 500 students will have completed
the program, and approximately 1,000
students are enrolled in the program at
all times. Initially, strongest demand
was from students in academic
areas with curriculum most closely
aligned with entrepreneurship, such
as the colleges of management
and technology. However, demand
has grown among majors in other
programs such as engineering and the
sciences as more entrepreneurship
program curriculum has become
aligned with major and elective
requirements in their disciplines
(Table 1).

The Certificate Program attracts
motivated students from across
the University. In survey data
collected from students at the start
of the program, 58% described their
entrepreneurial ability as above
average or excellent. Reasons they
stated that they are interested in the
program were because they had a
general interest in entrepreneurship
(M = 4.5 on a 5-point Likert scale
'strongly disagree' to 'strongly
agree'); to broaden their career
choices (M = 4.4); to become an
entrepreneur (M = 4.2); and to find
out if they have what it takes to be
an entrepreneur (M = 4.1). Data
collected from students who have
completed the program showed that
they have made significant gains in
the program's learning objectives
and that most plan to put their
entrepreneurship education into
practice in their future careers. Exit
survey data showed that 85% or more
agreed that the program improved

**Table 1. Cumulative Enrolment in Introductory Entrepreneurship Course (Fall 2005 through Fall 2010).**

| Enrolment By College | Cumulative since launch (Fall 2005 thru Fall 2010) | | Fall Semester 2010 | |
| --- | --- | --- | --- | --- |
| | Number | Percent | Number | Percent |
| Technology | 558 | 22% | 59 | 20% |
| Management | 507 | 20% | 46 | 16% |
| Liberal Arts | 349 | 14% | 45 | 15% |
| Engineering | 320 | 13% | 52 | 18% |
| CFS | 227 | 9% | 22 | 7% |
| Undecided | 183 | 7% | 7 | 2% |
| Agriculture | 193 | 8% | 36 | 12% |
| Science | 124 | 5% | 18 | 6% |
| Pre-Pharmacy | 48 | 2% | 10 | 3% |
| Other | 31 | 1% | 2 | 1% |
| TOTAL | 2539 | 100% | 296 | 100% |

their analytical, communication and presentation skills; 92% agreed that the program improved their ability to evaluate ideas; and 88% agreed that the program improved their confidence that they can be entrepreneurs. In terms of their careers, 95% felt that the program will be useful to their future careers; 25% reported that they were currently involved in a start-up venture of some kind when they completed the program and 86% reported that they were likely to be involved in an entrepreneurial venture in the future.

Although undergraduate students do not play a significant role in bringing university-based research to market, the Certificate in Entrepreneurship and Innovation Program has been successful in raising awareness of entrepreneurship across the university by encouraging faculty to consider developing coursework to meet student demand and by involving faculty in students' entrepreneurial activities. The program has been successful in creating awareness among students of the university's involvement in technology commercialization and many entrepreneurship resources (e.g. incubator space, technology parks) which may be of benefit to Purdue graduates in their future careers. This academic program also serves as a pipeline to other entrepreneurship-related programs at the university, including competitions in which approximately 200 students participate per year. Through its outreach and engagement activities, the program has also connected students to entrepreneurs, venture capitalists and others involved in essential business development

networks throughout the state and country.

Purdue's involvement in stemming 'brain drain' through the Interns for Indiana Program appears to be successful in achieving its goal of encouraging more highly qualified Purdue students to seek in-state employment after graduation. Since its launch in 2004, the program has placed 414 students with 145 partner companies for more than 169,500 hours of labor. Nearly one in six companies has hired its intern for full-time employment, and 58% of the interns have remained in the state after graduation. More than 80% of the interns reported that the program increased their interest in working for a start-up company, while 62% expressed interest in starting their own companies. Of the companies offering internships through the program, 96% reported that the interns assisted in company growth.

Involving students from all disciplines in entrepreneurship education has proved to be very valuable in bridging the interface of technology and business and preparing them for technological business environment. These benefits have been described at length by Thursby (Thursby, Fuller & Thursby, 2009) in a description of a multidisciplinary technology commercialization program at Georgia Tech. Teaming PhD students in the sciences with MBA students has helped PhD students advance their research while learning about early-stage market research, feasibility analysis, venture financing and team building. This better prepares them for positions in industry and even for faculty positions at institutions where entrepreneurial activity is valued and rewarded. MBA students gain valuable experience working with researchers and gain experience in commercialization, market assessment and communication, which are essential for entrepreneurial careers and skills very marketable to employers. These collaborations have also led to increased participation by Purdue graduate students in entrepreneurial competitions across the country.

## Increased faculty involvement in entrepreneurship

Main indicators of faculty involvement in technology commercialization and entrepreneurship are the numbers of invention disclosures, patents filed and start-up companies created each year. In 2009, Purdue's Office of Technology Commercialization reported the filing of 227 invention disclosures, 187 provisional patent applications and 70 regular patents. During the year, university technologies were the foundation for the start-up of 10 companies and 79 licensing arrangements ('Purdue University', 2010). Analysis based on the Association of University Technology Managers preliminary 2009 data examined the university's performance relative to a group of universities it considers its 'peer' institutions, which include Georgia Tech, University of Illinois, University of Wisconsin, University of Michigan, Michigan State, Texas A&M, University of Texas and Penn State University. This analysis showed that Purdue ranked number one in patent filings and number two in both

innovation disclosures and licensing agreements. Purdue also ranks very highly among all US universities when one takes into consideration the relatively lower amount of sponsored research dollars it takes to generate a start-up, patent or disclosure at Purdue than at other universities.

## Increased involvement in entrepreneurship in the region and the state

There are many indicators of Purdue's success at developing entrepreneurship-friendly communities and being a resource to the public. One example is the Purdue Center for Regional Development's WIRED initiative, which over a four-year period had a significant impact on the entrepreneurship culture in North Central

**Table 2. Purdue Invention Disclosures, Patents and Start-Ups.**

| Measure | Number or $ | Purdue Rank |
|---|---|---|
| Number of start-up companies created | 11 | 10 |
| Number of patents filed | 175 | 11 |
| Number of disclosures | 227 | 26 |
| Sponsored research dollars per start-up | $45M | 2 |
| Sponsored research dollars per patent filed | $2.8M | 8 |
| Sponsored research dollars per disclosure | $2.2M | 8 |

*Source:* The Association of University Technology Managers (FY 2008 preliminary data)

Indiana through the funding of programs to train and support existing and emerging entrepreneurs. In a 2010 final report on the project (Hutcheson, 2010), the following impacts were provided.

Housing a regional office of the federal- and state-funded Small Business Development Center on the Purdue campus has also been a valuable resource for the campus and surrounding community. In 2009, the SBDC regional office offered 74 formal workshops to the public, which attracted 1,028

participants. Its business advisors provided nearly 400 hours of customized business planning and counselling to 435 clients. This led to the start-up of 58 new businesses that were able to secure $6,740,100 in financing.

As a result of Purdue University's emphasis on business incubation and economic development, the Purdue Technology Parks have become one of the largest university-affiliated business incubation complexes in the United States, employing more than 3,000 people. It was ranked the best business incubation facility in the USA in 2004 by the Association of University Research Parks and received the Excellence in Technology Transfer Award in 2005 from the Association of University Research Parks.

---

**Table 3. Entrepreneurship & Innovation Indicators for the 2004–2009 WIRED Initiative.**

| | |
|---|---|
| Existing and Emerging Adult Entrepreneurs Trained | 1,851 |
| K–12 Teachers Trained to Teach Entrepreneurship | 227 |
| New K–12 School Entrepreneurship Programs Started | 34 |
| K–12 Students Enrolled in Entrepreneurship Programs | 1,536 |
| New Products, Services and Top-Line Growth Ideas Created | 654 |
| Business Plans Developed | 102 |
| New Start-Up Businesses Launched | 10 |
| Jobs Created or Retained | 353 |
| Industry Cost Savings Realized | $3.5 million |
| Industry Anticipated Sales Growth | $1.6 million |
| Industry Anticipated Sales Retained | $4 million |

*Source:* Transforming the North Central Indiana Economy: Final Report to Shareholders, January 21, 2010, Kokomo, Indiana.

## Implications for community/industry

Purdue's experience shows that in a relatively short amount of time, universities can create a policy, a culture and a set of programs that are supportive of entrepreneurship and result in the development of resources that help faculty and students become involved in business development. Keys to success include:

- *Leadership*: The university administrators must believe strongly that the university should play an important role in driving economic development. This includes the vision to see the value of cross-entity, cross-discipline and cross-program collaboration in order to leverage the university's strengths and create high-impact programs. It also involves rewarding and recognizing faculty, administrators and staff for entrepreneurship-related efforts and accomplishments.

- *Financial support:* The university leadership must make resource allocation decisions that support university entities, people and programs that foster technology commercialization and business-development activities. Alumni, companies, foundations and government entities are all potential sources of financial support for the diverse range of university entrepreneurship activities that exist.
- *Experienced staff:* The university must recruit individuals who bring real-world business-development experience to the institution. These include technology commercialization professionals, seasoned entrepreneurs, experienced faculty, data analysts, grant writers and economic development specialists. It is important that individuals who speak the language of business and economic development are credible within essential entrepreneurial networks.
- *Faculty support:* A tenure and promotion process that rewards rather than penalizes faculty involvement in business-development activities can be key to attracting entrepreneurial faculty and in changing the culture to one in which research and business development are not mutually exclusive. Clear

intellectual property policies and practices can enhance faculty involvement in technology commercialization.

- *Community engagement:* The university must proactively involve key players outside of the university in the entrepreneurial ecosystem. This includes activities such as inviting venture capitalists to visit research labs and researchers, cultivating relationships with key politicians and government agencies, involving successful alumni and being a valuable resource to communities. In many cases, these individuals are willing to donate time to help the university, whether it be speaking, teaching or providing connections to networks of individuals in other parts of the state or world.
- *Information and communication:* Creating an ecosystem requires a communication strategy that tells the campus, region, entrepreneurs and investors that the university is a place to start and build businesses. An important piece of the success of Purdue's success has been a communications strategy which has been critical to (1) build awareness among students and faculty of the programs and resources that exist, (2) promote student and faculty successes, or in other words, 'what is possible' and (3) help spark the interest of investors and the entrepreneurial community in the business and technology that is being generated at Purdue.

For Purdue faculty, staff and students with a passion for research and innovation and for community leaders and entrepreneurs throughout Indiana, it has been an exciting time to be associated with Purdue. Over the past decade, the university has demonstrated an unprecedented commitment to recruiting, building, supporting and sustaining robust research, development and engagement activities in support of entrepreneurship and innovation. The entrepreneurial culture will continue to grow as more discoveries are delivered to the marketplace, as more students are equipped with entrepreneurial skills and as more Indiana communities become entrepreneurship friendly. All of these factors work together, forming vibrant entrepreneurial networks that are transforming Indiana's economy and providing a best-in-class example of how universities can nurture an entrepreneurial ecosystem.

## Bibliography

Entrepreneurship Education Without Boundaries: Kauffman Campuses Seek to Make Entrepreneurship Education a College-Wide Experience. (2010), from www.kauffman.org/entrepreneurship/kauffman-campuses.aspx

Finkle, T., & Deeds, D. (2001), Trends in the market for entrepreneurship faculty, 1989–1998. *Journal of Business Venturing*, 613–630.

Graduate Migration from Indiana's Post-secondary Institutions. (1999), *Indiana's Human Capital Retention Project* (p. 8). Indianapolis: Indiana Fiscal Policy Institute.

Graff, G., Heiman, A., & Zilberman, D. (2002), University Research and Offices of Technology Transfer. *California Management Review, 45*(1), 26.

Hutcheson, S. (2010), Transforming the North Central Indiana Economy: Final Report to Shareholders. In P.C.F.R. Development (Ed.), *Final Report*. West Lafayette: Purdue University.

Kuratko, D. (2005), The Emergence of Entrepreneurship Education: Development, Trends, and Challenges. *Entrepreneurship Theory & Practice, 29*(5), 20.

Phan, P., & Siegel, D. (2006), The Effectiveness of University Technology Transfer. *Foundations and Trends in Entrepreneurship, 2*(2), 69.

Purdue University Data Digest. (2010), Retrieved 2010 from www.purdue.edu/newsroom/rankings/ranking.html

Rasmussen, W. (1989), *Taking the university to the people: seventy-five years of cooperative extension*. Ames: Iowa State University Press.

Roberts, E. (1991), *Entrepreneurs in High Technology: Lessons from MIT and Beyond*. New York: Oxford University Press.

Roberts, E., & Eesley, C. (2009), Entrepreneurial Impact: The Role of MIT. In E.M.K. Foundation (Ed.), (p. 76). Kansas City: Ewing Marion Kauffman Foundation.

Streeter, D., Jacquette, J., & Hovis, K. (2002), *University-Wide Entrepreneurship Education: Alternative Models and Current Trends*. Working Paper. Working Paper. Department of Applied Economics and Management. Ithaca, NY: Cornell University.

Thursby, M., Fuller, A., & Thursby, J. (2009), An Integrated Approach to Educating Professionals for Careers in Innovation. *Academy of Management Learning and Education 8*(9), 399–405.

University Inventions that Changed the World. (2010), Retrieved September 2010 from uvapf.org/live_data/documents/FamousUniversityInventions.doc

# The end of entrepreneurship

## A holistic paradigm for teaching and learning about, for and through enterprise

Eugene Luczkiw

**Abstract:** *This paper builds a case that broadens the purpose of entrepreneurship education beyond the walls of the business school to include diverse fields of study at the tertiary level. Entrepreneurship, as a discipline, transcends traditional business school programmes that constrict its holistic nature. It has long been recognized that entrepreneurs are much more than small business owners/managers or self-employed people. They are more aptly described as agents of change and disruption and, more importantly, entrepreneurs can be found in every sector of society. The emerging science of complexity holds a great deal of promise as a theoretical framework for the entrepreneurial journey. The field of entrepreneurship is holistic and interdisciplinary in nature. Entrepreneurship requires a much broader sweep than what the business school curriculum alone can offer. The 'end' of entrepreneurship calls for a whole new field of study to unfold and emerge.*

**Keywords:** *entrepreneurship education; entrepreneurship curriculum; complexity sciences; creativity process; disruptive innovation; Enterprise Diamond*

*Eugene Luczkiw is Founding Director of the Institute for Enterprise Education and Adjunct Professor of Education, Brock University, 5230 South Service Road, Burlington, Ontario L7 L 5K2, Canada. Tel: +1 905 637 6600. Fax: +1 905 637 6603. E-mail: gene.luczkiw@entreplexity.ca*

This article's title, 'The end of entrepreneurship', honours the work of author Neil Postman (1995), whose seminal work *The End of Education* challenged leaders to change the existing state of education by arguing that the existing paradigm of education, without purpose, would cease to exist.

This paper uses the word 'end' in two distinct ways: first, as a means of challenging existing methods of delivering entrepreneurship education at the tertiary level and, second, as a 'vision' for the future of entrepreneurship education. The time has come to embrace each learner in society as a distinct contributor to its future success and to enable her or him to discover her or his niche in today's rapidly changing global environment.

It is this second 'end' that holds the greatest promise. By inculcating the entrepreneurial spirit into every person in every sector of society, we will begin to create the requisite conditions and cultures that nurture each person's distinct commitment and creativity. For this second 'end' to emerge, the purpose of entrepreneurship education must embrace the new rules of the 21st century.

Gibb (2006) argues that the dominant traditional paradigm of entrepreneurship education as it is taught in European and North American business schools is standing in the way of a new paradigm that would meet the needs of a much larger membership of societies who find themselves at different stages of development and within distinct cultures. According to Gibb, entreprencurship education transcends culture, and thus can serve to create an effective ecosystem that, like the Internet, connects everyone, everywhere, with everything.

We are living in a post-modern age, which Vaclav Havel, the former president of the Czech Republic, described as a post-modern era where everything is possible and nothing is certain. We are witnessing the emergence of a new global paradigm within what appears to be chaos and disruption. When the game changes, so do the rules. Facilitators of enterprise need to consider how to succeed within the emerging chaos and disruption.

To succeed in today's global environment, we must internalize a new set of rules. Those rules and regulations that served Western democratic societies well in the industrial era no longer serve us well today. The machine metaphor has been replaced by an organic network. The scientific method, the dominant science in the modern age, is being challenged by the new science of complexity as the emerging scientific paradigm.

The practice of entrepreneurship holds a great deal of promise for navigating in chaos, complexity and disruption. But the discipline of entrepreneurship reflects the science of complexity, while the university culture continues to be the repository of the scientific method. This clash of cultures must remain a critical consideration as to what, who, how, why, when and where entrepreneurship should be taught. From our extensive research of entrepreneurs around the globe, we have been able to identify patterns of navigation that increase the choices for entrepreneurial success, but even more importantly, we have discovered that the entrepreneur's network, and how it is nurtured, holds even greater promise in the birth and growth of successful enterprises.

In a number of Western democracies, entrepreneurship and small business are responsible for over 50% of employment. When we include the indirect benefits of these start-ups, the numbers escalate to more than 60%.

The purpose of this paper is to respond to the question, '*What should be the purpose of entrepreneurship education?*' In responding to this question, I propose to explore a series of questions that will guide the journey of the paper. These include the following:

• Why entrepreneurship education?
• What should be the basis of the content and methodologies that make up the entrepreneurship curriculum?
• At what levels of education should these programmes be delivered?
• What should be the nature of the external environment for teaching and learning about, for and through enterprise?

# Why entrepreneurship education?

My thesis is that we begin with an inherent understanding of why there should be entrepreneurship education. This first question provides the context for the other three by developing four critical themes, which are the essential prerequisites in developing effective strategies for teaching and learning

about, for and through enterprise. These foundational themes are:

• an understanding of emerging global forces and trends and their impact on local and national communities;
• a need for a new science to provide a theoretical framework for interacting in today's global environment;
• a shared understanding of the meaning of entrepreneurship; and
• identification of conditions and cultures that nurture the creation, development and growth of entrepreneurship and the sustainability of the enterprise.

By journeying across these four critical themes and examining case studies of entrepreneurship education in Europe and North America, we will be better able to address the who, what, how, why, where and when of teaching and learning about enterprise and through enterprise.

*Understanding global forces and trends and their impacts*

*The global context.* We live in an era of complexity, chaos and discontinuous change. Major demographic, economic, social, environmental and technological forces are creating disruptions and instability as new engines of economic growth begin to emerge. An interdependent culture is rapidly emerging as a new global paradigm takes shape, a paradigm that is transforming the culture of any one nation state. Whether we look at environmental, economic or social issues, this emerging global paradigm is beginning to exhibit more shared values between nation states than ever before.

This major paradigm shift is the result of the interplay of three critical forces: the movement of talent, capital and knowledge across borders. Thanks to the power of the Internet, anyone, anywhere, with strong commitment and perseverance, can disrupt most existing industry groups. Witness the role of mini mills in the transformation of the steel industry, on the one hand, and the consolidating of this industry by Lakshmi Mittal, who has grown his family's steel business in India into the world's largest.

This emerging external environment has its own complex and divergent structures, systems and behaviours. Traditional rules and regulations that governed boundaries in space and time during the industrial age have all but disappeared, as discontinuities – rapid structural and systemic changes, brought about by the information age – have stretched the rules to their limits. Geographical boundaries have been stripped of their significance as bits of information are transported by electronic means across borders. The challenge is to understand how this new world context will impact on the beliefs, behaviours and systems we develop for the future.

Globalization is first and foremost an economic force that derives from the creation of worldwide strategies by organizations seeking expansion on a global level. To understand the meaning of globalization, we need to look at it from an evolutionary perspective. Friedman (2005) notes that there have been three stages

of globalization. The first occurred between the 15th and 19th centuries – this was a process of globalization for the purposes of resource acquisition and the conquest of countries. Europe was at the centre of the universe and its states vied with each other to possess the greatest number of colonies, with their rich resources. The second stage took place in the 19th and 20th centuries, when there was a globalization of markets as large corporations began to leave the safety of home and compete in foreign markets around the globe. In this period, the power of the state was replaced by the power of the global conglomerate. Now, as we enter the third stage of globalization, we see the world shrinking further, with new economies from Asia emerging as a third force to compete with Europe and North America. Bangalore in India has now become the global centre for software development and tax preparation, while China is rapidly becoming a global manufacturing centre. What is most interesting in this third era, however, is that it is driven by a much more diverse form of macro-capitalism that is non-Western in content and form. We have reached a stage at which we no longer know where the next new disruptive technology will come from.

Wal-Mart, alone, imports over $18 billion worth of goods from more than 5,000 Chinese suppliers – they make up about 80% of Wal-Mart's supply chain. These cheap imports from China have saved US consumers more than $600 billion. In return, China and India have become market niches and opportunities for Western-based products and services by sharing their consumers with the world economy.

How, then, do Western democracies prosper and grow in the 21st century? Perhaps one of the most effective ways is to move up the value chain. This requires specialized knowledge and skills in order to create the superior products and services which can carry higher prices. United Parcel Service (UPS), for example, is more than just a delivery company: it also can set up an effective supply chain for its customers, and, in addition, it can repair computers for clients in house.

The emergence of 'work flow platforms', software that makes all kinds of computer applications and networking capabilities possible, will enable everyone to collaborate with anyone, anywhere. These platforms represent a sustainable breakthrough that has brought the world closer together. By compressing the global network in time and space, we see the emergence of millions of new niche opportunities to compete with mainstream products and services. The consumer, at times, becomes the producer, as in the case of the Dell Computers laptop that was created on the Web.

Furthermore, the costs of reaching the consumer are decreasing rapidly. Thanks to the Internet's capabilities, we see our orders fulfilled and downloaded to our own computers in seconds at the touch of a button. Such products as CDs and DVDs are only part of what can be delivered by powerful search engines and a critical mass of broadband.

While we have seen consumers work with producers to create their products online, we are now witnessing a home-based manufacturing revolution. For less than US$30,000, you can purchase a 3D printer for your home. This printer becomes a home-based factory that is capable of manufacturing anything in lot sizes of one. One day, these 3D printers will be as common as inkjets and will sell at the same price. Today, this 3D printer, using a laser, can turn liquid polymer or powder into hard plastic in any shape your programme desires. This ultimate manufacturing

| Stage One | Stage Two | Stage Three | Stage Four |
|---|---|---|---|
| 15th to 19th century | 19th to late 20th century | Late 20th to early 21st century | Early 21st century |
| Conquest for resources | Globalization of markets | Expansion of non-Western capitalism | Globalization of talent |
| Europe centred | North American centred | Eastern centred | Global centred |
| Colonization | Multi-nationalism branch plants | Development & growth of new global economies & markets | Birth of global entrepreneur |

**Figure 1.** Evolution of globalization: the four stages.

technology can work with liquid metals and synthetics to produce automotive parts, toys or machines directly in the consumer's home.

What impact will this have on existing manufacturing facilities? What new ventures will emerge as a result of this disruptive form of innovation? These disruptive innovations have led to what Florida (2005) calls the 'fourth era' of globalization, which, says Florida, is characterized by the new global competition for talent. The mobility of people is perhaps the single most significant factor in today's global economy – it is even more powerful than the emergence of new technologies or the mobility of capital. Within this type of environment, many places will gain specific advantages based on the diversity of their particular ecology. The global economy becomes more complex as a rich mosaic of participants, each with her or his own special brand of distinct capabilities, seeks out specialized niches for ideas. Florida describes these participants as the 'creative class'. This mobile group of diverse talent provides the substance from which new sources of value emerge to meet the ever-changing needs of the marketplace. Roughly, this creative class now accounts for 30% of the US workforce.

Figure 1 illustrates the four stages in the evolution of globalization.

Immigrants have played a significant role in US economic growth. According to Florida (2005), foreign-born CEOs ran 72 of America's top 500 entrepreneurial firms in the late 1990s. In addition, immigrant entrepreneurs were responsible for 30% of all Silicon Valley start-ups during the 1990s, accounting for nearly $20 billion in sales and more than 70,000 jobs. The USA also imports scientists from around the globe: nearly one in five of its scientists and engineers are immigrants, and 51% of doctorates in engineering are earned by foreigners.

According to the European Commission's 2003 Green Paper *Entrepreneurship in Europe*, 'Europe needs to foster entrepreneurial drive more effectively. It needs more new and thriving firms willing to reap the benefits of market openings and to embark on creative and innovative ventures for commercial exploitation on a larger scale.' The EC sets out an ambitious agenda, aiming to make Europe 'the most competitive and dynamic knowledge-based economy in the world, capable of sustainable economic growth with more and better jobs and greater social cohesion'. While the EC is aware of the need for a radical transformation of the European economy, it does not include the need for the transformation of the European society as a whole.

The impact of economic globalization leads to an acceleration of the commoditization of products and services, increasing price wars, cost reductions and job losses and shrinking profit margins. Another trend relates to consumers discovering similarities between brand-name products, making price the determinant of their buying decisions.

The reality is that anyone with intelligence, access to Google and a cheap, wireless laptop can now join the entrepreneurship game.

There are, however, negative effects from globalization that challenge our environment's capacity to renew and regenerate itself for our survival in the midst of threats such as disease and terrorism. With seamless boundaries among nation states, it is next to impossible to insulate oneself from destructive forces.

The common denominator in the economic sphere is the emergence of the entrepreneur as the heir apparent to the large corporation. In most cases, the entrepreneur is emerging in places other than Western democracies. Already, the necessary technologies and tools exist to create the future, and the entrepreneur will be the executor of these innovations. Unless countries take a proactive stance, therefore, to create the right conditions and programmes to nurture the growth of entrepreneurs, they will fall off the ledge of future economic and social growth.

Besides creating the right conditions and cultures for entrepreneurship, we need to view the world as a giant ecosystem made up of diverse living entities competing and collaborating at the same time. Entrepreneurs have embraced this paradigm instinctively, seeing themselves as independent agents who are part of a larger network of potential stakeholders. Within this primordial soup, they see external networks of customers, suppliers, distributors, financiers, professionals and even competitors who complement their internal network.

We need, then, to look at ourselves and the world in which we live with a new set of eyes. We require a new set of rules and regulations that will help us to navigate the turbulent waters of change. We need a new science that will shift our existing paradigms and offer a new formula for success. This science is the science of complexity.

### The need for a new science

If leaders are to build and nurture successful enterprises in the 21st century, they will need to understand the underlying principles that support their strategic thinking. The science of the industrial age relied on the scientific method to establish objective truth. This method of questioning viewed systems in isolation from one another and their environment. Two factors became critical in conducting research:

- One needed to separate the observer from what was being observed.
- There was a need to reduce every physical element to its lowest common denominator and use the parts to predict future behaviour.

The Newtonian mechanistic and reductionist system became the basis of scientific thought. The key components of this system were determinism, linearity, predictability and simplicity. By embodying these principles, Fredrick Taylor (Kelly & Allison, 1998) was able to create the Scientific Management Model, and this continues to influence individuals, leaders and organizations as they attempt to adapt to the realities of globalization.

However, we now face a major economic and social paradigm shift, with the exponential growth of information technologies and knowledge creating an ever-widening gap in our understanding of the impact and nature of this change. Paradigms are fundamental beliefs about the world (Kuhn, 1962). They provide the rules and regulations, establish boundaries and indicate the behaviours needed to succeed. Paradigms also suggest metaphors that are helpful in framing problems and which lead to their ultimate solution. On the other hand, paradigms can blind people to facts, data and challenges that are not consistent with the conventional thinking. Conflicts between exponents of different paradigms can also lead to irrational debate. This debate is currently taking place at all levels of the scientific, political, economic and social spectrums, as the traditional Newtonian mechanistic paradigm is being replaced by the emerging complexity sciences and the entrepreneurial metaphor.

A study by the Washington Centre for Complexity and Public Policy (2003), carried out on behalf of the US Department of Education, concludes that the current conventional policy planning methods used by decision makers in business, education and government are both inappropriate and ineffective. The study's findings point to a rise in the integration of knowledge across disciplines. The interdisciplinary nature of complexity science and its adoption of a systems view mean that questions which are too big for one discipline to answer are resolved by connecting knowledge across physical, biological and social boundaries.

The classical model of economics, based on scarcity of resources, no longer serves as a complete source of explanation, let alone as a tool for predicting future direction. Instead of looking at a *fixed pie* approach, we need to focus on an *expanding pie* as integral to the new network economy. The model of the expanding pie has three critical determinants – the law of increasing returns, lock-in and the power of networks.

Economist Brian Arthur (Kurtzman,1998) indicates that when we deal with scarce natural resources such as ore, after a certain point each additional ton of new ore extracted increases in cost (the law of diminishing returns). In the case of knowledge products, such as software, the cost of the first unit will be very high, reflecting the high cost of research and development, but each additional unit will be produced at a fraction of the cost (the law of increasing returns). Thus a software company like Microsoft can offer its Windows format at a low enough price to capture the market, 'locking in' customers to its network. It is this network of Microsoft users, as well as independent software developers, who gain the benefit of increased interaction with potential stakeholders, leading to increased possibilities and opportunities in their differentiated roles.

Kelly (1997) describes the power of this network. As networks have permeated our activities, the economy has come to resemble an ecology of organisms, interlinked and co-evolving, constantly in flux, deeply tangled and ever expanding at its edges. As we know from recent ecological studies, there is no balance in nature – rather, as evolution proceeds, there is perpetual disruption as new species displace old, as natural biomes shift in their make-up and as organisms and environments transform each other.

The emergence of these new rules in economics is part of a larger system that helps explain today's dynamic and highly disruptive environment.

*The science of complexity.* The science of complexity is the study of complex adaptive systems with the ability to process and integrate new information into their existing repertoire. Complexity is the bridge between chaos and order. A brief description of this theory follows.

The world is a complex system, like the human body, which consists of a series of organizational structures (economic, political, social) that interact with one another nationally and internationally. The science of complexity was conceived with this in mind to provide us with an understanding of the similarities between physical, biological and human systems and so to enable us to acquire a better appreciation of our relationship to the global environment.

A major tenet of complexity theory is the system itself. It consists of a set of units and elements so interconnected that a change in one unit produces changes in other parts. As an example, the body is a system of interconnected parts, which are useful only when they are part of the body as a whole. The same is true for individuals in society who recognize the need to work together to achieve a particular goal.

The science of complexity was developed by leading scientists from diverse fields of study and involves 'complex adaptive systems' (see Figure 2), which include cells, embryos, brains, ecologies, economies and political and social systems. These complex adaptive systems consist of diverse parts organically related to one another. Complexity is also a central principle of evolution, which effectively demonstrates how, through a process of differentiation and integration, humans can transcend their evolutionary path. It helps explain how organisms with a more integrated physiology or behavioural

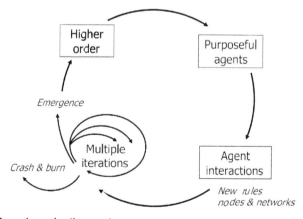

**Figure 2.** Complex adaptive systems.

repertoire tend to gain competitive advantage over others.

A complex adaptive system is generally defined as a system of independent agents acting in parallel to create new possibilities in the environment. Our immune system is defined as a complex adaptive system. And so is an enterprise. Like all living systems, complex adaptive systems work best in cultures of diversity, in which each person seeks to achieve a distinct mission (differentiation) within a network of stakeholders (integration). What emerges from these interactions for the individual participant could become a new market success or failure, as experienced by millions of sellers on the Web. It is only by means of determination, learning and persistence within this network that order emerges, in the form of acceptance of the individual's concept, product or service. There is a journey of many iterations and destinations before the trophy is won.

In order to understand the workings of these complex adaptive systems, we need to understand their constituent parts and how they interact with one another. Let us begin with the components:

- Agents are known as decision-making units and include individuals that make up an ecosystem for an enterprise.
- Rules determine how agents make choices. Each individual agent has her or his own rules of behaviour. People are distinct beings based on their genes, culture and gender. It is this diversity within

specific networks that enables new possibilities to emerge.
- Emergent properties are the result of individual agents, interacting with one another, following their own set of behavioural rules, creating a whole that is greater than the sum of their individual interactions.

By understanding how these agents interact with one another, we begin to internalize a process that leads us towards a higher order. This higher order is achieved by means of self-organization.

*The meaning of self-organization.* 'Self-organization' relates to how a system of agents organizes itself into a higher order:

- Complex behaviours result from individual units (agents).
- From these diverse individual inputs, interactions and interrelationships, a possible solution emerges.
- The robustness of the system, as a whole, is greater than the sum of its individual inputs.

The Internet provides an example of this. It integrates a wide breadth of knowledge, captures and displays vast quantities of information, processes information correctly, organizes information into a knowledge base and expands the reach across the globe. When millions of people are connected, the creative process of each individual is enhanced by a power of thousands.

A complex adaptive system is therefore a network of many individual agents (individuals) all acting in parallel and interacting with one another. The critical variable, which makes the system both complex and adaptive, is the idea that agents (cells, ants, neurons or individuals) in the system accumulate experience by interacting with other agents and then change themselves to adapt to the changing environment. If a complex adaptive system is continuously adapting, it is impossible for any such system, including the consumer market, ever to reach a state of perfect equilibrium. The complexity view is that a market is not rational, that it is organic, not mechanistic, and that it is imperfectly inefficient.

Whether we look at economic, political or social systems, they are complex (a large number of individual units) and adaptive (individual units adapting their behaviours on the basis of interaction with other units as well as with the systems as a whole). These systems have 'self-organizing properties' and, once organized, they generate emergent behaviours. Finally, these systems are constantly unstable and periodically reach a crisis.

There are two powerful tools for successful navigation within today's global environment – networks and symbiotic relationships. These are practical applications of complexity theory, and they are the critical determinants of those conditions and cultures that nurture innovation and entrepreneurship.

A network consists of individuals or groups each working to achieve their goals within a community of common interest. The purpose of a network is twofold:

- to enable individuals to pursue their mission; and

- to share their accomplishments with others.

A network consists of people who are so closely and directly affected by each other's actions that all parties ought to consider these actions before taking the initiative. For instance, in a business environment these include customers, suppliers, financiers and competitors. The most effective networks are those in which each person seeks to assist other members without any expectation that she or he will ever be served. However, the more you help others, the greater dependence you create on yourself. When you or your enterprise face a crisis, members of your network are obliged to assist you. This was clearly demonstrated in research carried out by the Canadian Institute for Enterprise Education into the growth of over 2,700 entrepreneurial ventures (IEE, 1995).

Apple Computer is a good business case that demonstrates the power of networks. Apple Computer continues to exist because of its network of stakeholders – customers, distributors, suppliers, financiers and competitors. These stakeholders have, on a number of occasions, ensured the company's continuance despite a number of critical strategic blunders. Recently, Apple's successful reinvention and regeneration has been the result of its successful launch of the iPod MP3 player with a library of downloadable music. Its recent market capitalization has rivalled that of the Sony Corporation.

'Symbiosis' is a biological term that describes how different organisms, living in intimate and interdependent associations, seek to co-create new possibilities that are mutually beneficial to all involved. It is about both competition and collaboration (co-opetition) in building strategic alliances.

The two main reasons for building strategic alliances are the need to accelerate the growth trajectory and to gain access to external core capabilities. As the number of nodes in the network increases incrementally, the value of the network increases exponentially. For instance, if you have three friends, you have three distinct one-to-one friendships, and if you have four friends, you have six distinct one-to-one friendships among them. Add a fifth friend and the friendships increase to ten; add a sixth and there are now fifteen relationships. As the number of friends increases, the total amount of relationships also escalates.

The power of a network, however, is not gauged only by the number of members. It also requires a diversity of members' talents, contributions and creativity. This collective wisdom provides the critical mass required to support the successful growth of both new and existing enterprises.

Two essential elements separate humans from non-humans in the study of complex adaptive systems. First, human beings have the capacity to become conscious of their actions and interactions and, secondly, they are able to reflect on their actions and interactions. As conscious beings, they have the opportunity to determine their purpose in life. In effect, they have the capacity not only to create their future by consciously pursuing their vision but also to reflect on their actions and interactions and adopt a strategy appropriate to the changing global environment. Thus we call human beings complex interactive systems in order to differentiate them from other complex adaptive systems.

### A shared understanding of the meaning of entrepreneurship

Entrepreneurs, as agents of change and disruption, demonstrate the principles of complex adaptive systems. Not only are they capable of adapting to their respective environments by identifying needs or opportunities, but they can also create novel solutions to meet those needs and take advantage of those opportunities. At first, their behaviour may seem simply chaotic and disruptive to outsiders, but once opportunity has been exploited, most bystanders see the merits and embrace it.

Two critical factors influence the current exponential growth of new enterprises: an increased need for entrepreneurial talent to deal with emerging global realities and people's consciousness of the need to find a coherent role in a world of rapidly increasing discontinuities. For the foreseeable future, we will see a growing need for entrepreneurs to develop structures, systems, processes and strategies that can deal with emerging complexities. This has significant implications not only for those seeking to begin and grow an enterprise but also for large monolithic organizations stuck in their existing paradigms and unable to take advantage of global opportunities.

The European Commission's 2003 Green Paper *Entrepreneurship in Europe* points out that entrepreneurship is first and foremost a mindset. 'Entrepreneurship,' it argues, is about people, their choices and actions in starting, taking over or running a business or their involvement in a firm's strategic decision making. It covers an individual's motivation and capacity, independently or within an organization, to identify an opportunity and to pursue it, in order to produce new value or economic success.'

The successful growth of an enterprise is dependent on an individual's ability to exploit emerging opportunities creatively, while constantly adapting and implementing the new products and/or services. The overall success of any enterprise is not based on the completion of a successful business plan but on the interrelationships between the intrinsic motivation of the entrepreneurs, their teams and the supportive extrinsic motivation in the community that enables them to grow their enterprises.

Before embarking on a more detailed analysis of entrepreneurs, it is important to differentiate the terms 'entrepreneur', 'small business owner' and 'self-employed person' – the differences were set out in a study by Carland *et al* (1984), and their definitions are supported by the research results of the Canadian Institute for Enterprise Education (1995). In summary:

- Entrepreneurs practise disruptive forms of innovation, as in the case of Michael Dell of Dell Computers and Richard Branson of Virgin.
- Small business owners practise management skills as the principle

activity of their enterprise. Examples include retail store owners and franchises, such as McDonald's.
- Self-employed individuals practise their skills or trades as part of their enterprise. Examples include artists, carpenters and electricians.

At best, small business owners and the self-employed practise incremental forms of innovation, while the entrepreneur practises disruptive forms. Based on these terminologies, a very small sector of the economy is made up of entrepreneurs. The needs of each of these three categories are distinct. The key is to ensure that governments, educational institutions and society as a whole understand the nature and quality of these distinct activities.

Entrepreneurs, as practitioners of disruptive innovation, do, however, serve as a model for every member of society, because they are effective in engaging their distinct creativity and turning it into action through innovation. While entrepreneurs themselves are a rare commodity, their practice holds promise for all. According to Miller (1999), creativity is an expression of who we are and not of what we do. Miller also points out that it is not the strongest species that survive, nor the most intelligent, but the ones that are most responsive to change.

A study of entrepreneurial behaviour by the Organisation of Economic Co-operation and Development (OECD, 1989) provides lessons as to how individuals can become 'enterprising' by connecting their distinct talents, meaning and motivation to create new opportunities and possibilities for themselves:

> 'In short, people will need to be creative, rather than passive; capable of self-initiated action, rather than dependent; they will need to know how to learn, rather than expect to be taught; they will need to be enterprising in their outlook, not think and act like an employee or client. The organizations in which they work, communities in which they live and societies in which they belong, will in turn, also need to possess all these qualities.'

A journey into the mind of the entrepreneur produces insights into the kind of conditions and culture that enable enterprise to thrive. Csikszentmihalyi (1990) proposes that extremely high levels of intrinsic motivation are marked by such strong interest and involvement in the work, and by such a perfect match of task difficulty with skill level, that people experience a kind of psychological 'flow', a sense of merging with the activity in which they are engaged. Amabile (1997) concludes that intrinsic motivation is conducive to an individual's creativity. Entrepreneurs generate and implement novel ideas in order to establish new ventures: they initiate the creative process and thereby demonstrate how other people can do the same.

The next question is: how is the influence of the external environment represented in the entrepreneur's experience? As Mitton (1989) puts it, 'Entrepreneurs see ways to put resources and information together in new combinations. They not only see the system (environment) as it is, but as it might be. They have a knack for looking at the usual and seeing the unusual; at the ordinary and seeing the extraordinary.' The key, according to Shaver (1991), is to concentrate on the person in his or her situational context. Situational variables can determine the degree of motivational synergy that we will experience. If external incentives and supports are presented in a manner that enhances the entrepreneur's vision, it is likely to support motivation and creativity. For instance, an onerous venture capital process may weaken entrepreneurial creativity, as may stringent controls and available government programmes, regulations and taxation.

There is a growing body of evidence that entrepreneurs, as agents of change, create what has not been created before and thus initiate the needed transformation. By focusing on the mindset of the entrepreneur, we begin to see how entrepreneurs break from their culture and genetic determinants to create the new.

*Conditions and cultures that nurture entrepreneurship and enterprise sustainability*

How can the conditions and culture be created that will each person's distinct contribution? And how do we enable people to engage their distinct talents in such a way as to align them with activities that lead to commitment and involvement in the workplace?

The development of an effective analytical framework for a local entrepreneurial culture requires the synthesis of various critical factors. A recent *Local Entrepreneur Review* (LEED, 2003) points to entrepreneurship as the principal source of economic development in local economies. Enabling people to create their own work and to have a degree of control over the nature of the work itself leads to an unleashing of the energy needed to meet the challenges and overcome the obstacles that are generally in the way of opportunity. While the challenges are the responsibility of the entrepreneur, the obstacles tend to be bureaucratic and structural and under the control of governments.

According to the Oxford English Dictionary (1997), 'culture' may be defined as 'the customs, civilization and achievement of a particular time or people, including the improvement by mental or physical training'. A culture involves group-wide practices that are passed on from generation to generation. Historically, culture evolved from a convergence of individual beliefs and values communicated by language. Communication became the critical element in passing on vital information. This enabled our ancestors to create societies that included the division of labour, entering into long-term obligations and extending cooperation beyond the bonds of kinship, while accumulating systemic knowledge, expertise and historical record (Quartz and Sejnowski, 2002).

The creation of an entrepreneurial culture begins with an understanding of how people can align their distinct contribution (talents) and creativity with the expressed needs of the community. It is, first and foremost, an obligation of society to ensure that its individual members can become all they are capable of becoming. To this end, we need to differentiate 'entrepreneurship' from 'enterprise'. 'Enterprise' is defined as the taking of an initiative to achieve a self-determined goal which will enable the individual to pursue his or her purpose in life, while at the same time contributing to the community. It is also becoming clear that entrepreneurship transcends culture and requires an ecological support system to ensure its growth and development.

*A tale of three communities.* A 2002 study by Institute for Enterprise Education identified three global communities that had a highly developed ecological infrastructure which had led to the successful development of small and medium-sized enterprises. While each of these communities had a distinct culture and history, their ecology was consistent. In all cases, there was clear evidence of the power of the network in bringing together diverse players to create the needed synergies, leading to win-win situations for entrepreneurs, stakeholders and the community. The three communities were Silicon Valley in California, USA; Oulu in Finland; and the Golden Technology Triangle in Ontario, Canada. The similarities observed included the following:

- The university in the region was a leader in achieving world-class status for its activities (differentiation).
- The university recognized a need to create a community technology centre that would draw in members

of the business community to make use of its research and innovation (ecosystem). Most importantly, the university saw itself as only one among a number of equals. It distanced the centre from the traditional university infrastructure.

- Many of the university's graduates became entrepreneurs and started their own enterprises (innovation and entrepreneurship).
- Existing businesses sought employees with technical skills to join their firms (knowledge workers).
- The early successes attracted the interest of professionals (accountants, lawyers, consultants, venture capitalists) in providing support to spin out new enterprises (networks).
- Early successes led to more successes, so that today many of the graduates are no longer going outside their respective communities. These regions are also importing knowledge workers from other communities (community interdependence).
- Most of the start-ups are globally focused, as they recognize the benefits of serving global markets (global vision).

The ecological process undergone by these communities holds promise, no matter what the economic driver. The key question is: what can we become the best in the world at? To answer it, we need to confront our existing realities and, as a community, commit to the pursuit of becoming the best.

If we are to be effective in facilitating the growth of entrepreneurs and enterprising people in light of the changing global reality, what should be the nature of the content and methodology that make up the entrepreneurship curriculum? The entrepreneurship curriculum needs to be multidisciplinary, and it needs to reflect the rules of the science of complexity.

Csikszentmihalyi (1990) points out that an individual's drive and determination emerge from a strong sense of intrinsic motivation. Intrinsic motivation focuses on internal needs for achieving competence, meaning and self-determination. It enables people to energize their behaviour to satisfy their desires as they seek out personal challenges. As these challenges require a leap into the unknown, they stretch abilities and interests. Enjoyment is derived from participating in those activities that lead to increased creativity and spontaneity. By pursuing self-determined goals, people achieve what Csikszentmihalyi calls 'flow'.

Csikszentmihalyi further argues that self-determined people are motivated by the activity rather than driven by their ego. Timmons (1989) noted that a common finding in research on successful entrepreneurs is that the key motivator is the journey rather than the destination. While entrepreneurs clearly demonstrate a passion for their distinct journeys, everyone has the same opportunity to become self-determining by discovering those activities that engage their particular talents and motivations. By making this connection with external opportunities, people have the potential to become intrinsically motivated.

After extensive research in the fields of human dynamics and enterprising behaviour, we share the conclusion of Shaver (1991). Economic circumstances are important; social networks are important; finance is important; even public agency assistance is important. But none of these alone creates a venture. For that, we need a person in whose mind all of the possibilities come together, who believes that innovation is possible, and who has the motivation to persist until the job is done.

New enterprises, according to Shaver, emerge and take the form they do because of deliberate choices made by individuals; thus the focus is on choice. From the perspective of an entrepreneur, two questions are critical: 'Can I make a difference?' and 'Do I want to make a difference?' The first question focuses on the perception of control and the second on the needed motivation. The answer to the first can be affirmative only if the person considers that the choice is theirs to make, has some initial success attributed to them and maintains an intrinsic interest in the project.

## The entrepreneurship curriculum

Gibb (2006) correctly points out that most entrepreneurship programmes in business faculties use the business management focus as the dominant theme of teaching and learning about entrepreneurship. However, research conducted by Saraswathy in 2001 and 2005 (Gibb, 2006) suggests that the essence of entrepreneurship lies in opportunism and timeliness, as demonstrated by the ability to get into a market space and to adjust and readjust what one discovers in accordance with customers' articulated or unarticulated needs.

Much of entrepreneurial learning should consist of trial-and-error education, but there is very little of that going on in educational practice. How much emphasis is given to discovering one's strengths and talents and turning these into entrepreneurial initiatives? How much importance do we give to discovering our striving instincts and emotions? How many studies will it take before academics are convinced that it is the entrepreneur's intrinsic motivation that provides the necessary energy to overcome challenges?

Any introductory course in entrepreneurship at the tertiary level should embody an understanding of emerging global forces and trends and their impact on the local, national and global communities. Once the environmental context has been developed, learners, by means of self-directed learning, need to identify the nature and structures of the emerging economic ecosystem and the rules by which they will have to navigate the turbulent waters of change. The science of complexity provides a theoretical framework in shaping these rules, while the practice of entrepreneurship executes them. The study of entrepreneurs enables learners to compare their findings with one another to discern emerging patterns and establish strategies for the successful identification of niches and opportunities. More importantly, however, learners must begin to discover the importance of self-knowledge and self-determination as precursors to intrinsic motivation. The mind of the entrepreneur becomes the critical factor in her or his determination and perseverance with regard to market opportunities.

An effective teaching and learning strategy about, for and through entrepreneurship needs to consider four critical determinants – the person, the idea, the opportunity and the resources – and their interdependence on one another (see Figure 3). It is the entrepreneur's strategic ability to connect these four elements of the 'Enterprise Diamond' that will determines her or his success in exploiting niches in the market or inside an organization (intrapreneurship). It may take an entrepreneur several iterations before success is achieved – and the constant reflection on and refining of these critical elements require the needed determination, intrinsic motivation and perseverance that have been highlighted in this paper. A brief outline of these four determinants and their use in the classroom follows.

The *person* is the most critical factor in determining the ultimate success or failure of a venture. It is the mind of the entrepreneur that offers the most promise for future research. From our research in fields of biology, neurosciences and psychology, we have been able to discover how the mind of the entrepreneur works in formulating strategies that deal with chaotic, complex and highly disruptive environments. Entrepreneurs are able to engage their distinct creativity by consciously and unconsciously connecting their strengths, talents, meaning, motivation and values to determine their commitment and creativity. As has been noted, various studies (Csikszentmihalyi 1990) point to the entrepreneur's intrinsic motivation or what Csikszentmihalyi calls 'autotelic personality', as the source of determination and perseverance. It is this internal drive

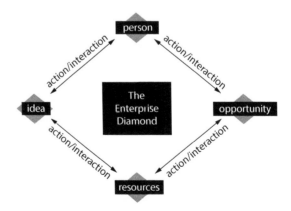

**Figure 3.** The Enterprise Diamond.

that becomes the critical fuel for journeying into the uncertain and unknown.

Students in an introductory undergraduate course in entrepreneurship should be provided with a number of practical assignments, including an interview with an entrepreneur and the completion of a number of assessment instruments focused on MacLean's Triune Brain to determine their distinct potential contribution and creativity (Herrmann, 1994). Based on the findings from these exercises, students could then be placed in teams to explore the nature of the entrepreneur's journey.

The *idea* emerges from the entrepreneur's distinct creativity and pursuit of many mental combinations. The process is non-linear and requires much iteration. In my own 'Creativity and the Entrepreneur' class, students were required to use trial-and-error and idea-generation techniques in order to search for potential ideas. The resulting ideas would then be presented in class and evaluated by classmates and visiting entrepreneurs. An evaluation report would be made available to every student. The final idea selection had to match the opportunity in the marketplace.

Ideas should be aligned with the relationship between the entrepreneur and his or her distinct creativity. It is the identified *opportunity*, however, that determines the suitability of the idea. Most entrepreneurs demonstrate a strong degree of proclivity to an opportunity focus. They may already have the idea in their mind and be seeking a niche – or they may sense an opportunity and attempt to generate an idea to meet the opportunity.

The classroom becomes a community as students seek out opportunities for their ideas or ideas for identified opportunities. A great deal of fieldwork is required to achieve these objectives. It is the connection between the person, the idea and the opportunity that will determine the ultimate concept, product or service. But it is the fourth element, *resources*, that will ensure its viability.

Throughout, students have been developing strategies to identify the nature of resources required to bring their venture to life. They have discovered their network of stakeholders (potential customers, competitors, distributors, professionals, industry associations, friends and relatives) critical to their successful exploitation of opportunities. As they will discover, the character, complexity and quality of their network will play a critical role in determining how successful they will be in their initial venture into the marketplace (IEE, 1995).

This series of non-linear iterations involving entrepreneur, idea, opportunity and resources creates the necessary dynamic to generate synergies that will ultimately lead to the birth of new products and services.

Teaching and learning about entrepreneurship requires a new set of strategies. The classroom must become a highly interactive environment, in which regular forums enable each learner to become an active participant. The ultimate objective is not simply to learn *about* enterprise but also, and most importantly, *for* and *through* enterprise (see Figure 4).

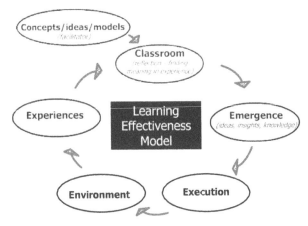

**Figure 4.** The Learning Effectiveness Model.

## At what levels of education should the programmes be delivered?

In addition to programmes delivered at the tertiary level, in Kajaani, Finland, Intotalo has developed a community-based entrepreneurship programme which provides a context for learning about, for and through enterprise.

Intotalo is a community-based learning environment that enhances the entrepreneurial skills of both secondary school and university students. Intotalo resembles an innovative working environment rather than a school. The basis of learning is by doing. The main foundation of Intotalo is communality. Its aim is to make entrepreneurship fun by creating opportunities to network with practising entrepreneurs and professionals.

Teaching and learning involve coaches as facilitators of team entrepreneurial activities. The role of Intotalo's coaches is distinct from that of coaches in traditional teaching methods. Learning becomes highly interactive in nature as everyone learns together.

The philosophy of the programme is that entrepreneurship arises from within the person and not from the business idea. The development of an entrepreneurial personality requires a personal approach. It is essential that people discover the nature of their entrepreneurship activity – be it innovation, self-employment or small business ownership. Intotalo also recognizes that networks are critical in the life of an entrepreneur. New entrepreneurs need to help other similar individuals. The network helps to ensure the success of the company.

The learning method in this programme is experientially based (see Figure 5). The teaching–learning interactions are led in team sessions by facilitators who demonstrate proficiency in the field of practice. Learners are led through a highly interactive and experiential process in an effort to construct new knowledge. During these sessions, there is a free flow of ideas, and then learners reflect on what they have learned in the dialogue and discuss issues arising out of the interaction.

Observing this model of teaching and learning at first hand, I noted that a high degree of community involvement was generated – and this community of 35,000 people has created a global network of partners to identify potential opportunities for its local entrepreneurs.

## The external environment

### *The case of the BCE*

One of the most interdependent models of community enterprise and economic development I have had an opportunity to observe was that in operation at the Burgoyne Centre for Entrepreneurship (BCE) of Canada's Brock University. The Centre was founded in 1988 as a partnership between the university and the city of St Catharines, Ontario.

It was formed to enable communities to become effective players in the global environment by nurturing and supporting innovation and entrepreneurship. The education system needed to be a partner in this enterprise.

In January 1989, Brock University entered into a partnership with the Burgoyne family, proprietors of the *St Catharines Standard*, a community newspaper, and together they established the BCE, a unique and innovative centre for entrepreneurship supported exclusively by business and university funding. The Centre's Advisory Committee, made up of prominent business people in the Niagara community, was chaired by Henry Burgoyne, CEO of the *St Catharines Standard*. The subsequent appointment as director of Dr Kenneth E. Loucks, an internationally recognized leader in entrepreneurship and business education, ensured sustained leadership and growth for the Centre.

To achieve its mission, the BCE recognized that it needed a

**Figure 5.** An entrepreneurship learning method.

broad-based community network of partnerships throughout the Niagara Peninsula of Ontario. Within three years, it had established strategic partnerships with the Lincoln County Board of Education and the Niagara Regional Development Corporation. These partnerships yielded important community collaborative innovations – a broad community-based network of entrepreneurs and professional advisers, the New Enterprise Store and the Niagara Enterprise Agency.

With these core partnerships firmly established, the BCE became a focal point for academic, private and governmental activities relating to entrepreneurial development in the Niagara Peninsula community. It is worth noting that it had achieved this status without duplicating or competing with the services offered by existing agencies and enterprises.

The synergy generated by these broadening community partnerships gained recognition for the BCE and its partners. It was named the National Centre for Entrepreneurship Education by the National Entrepreneurship Development Institute, a joint business–governmental organization dedicated to leadership in entrepreneurship education, and it was a finalist in the Conference Board of Canada National Excellence in Business–Education Partnerships Award. The strategies of the BCE were:

- to provide a focal point in the Niagara region for academic, private and public-sector interests in the development of existing business, new entrepreneurs and the facilitation of new venture creation;

- to maintain a physical location within the university itself, with recognized expertise on staff, and to be guided by an advisory council of academic and private-sector representatives (with demonstrated accomplishments either as entrepreneurs or as facilitators of the entrepreneurial process) which would provide continuous feedback on the effectiveness of its activities;

- to focus on the promotion of entrepreneurship teaching in secondary and post-secondary education as well as to professionals, business advisers and entrepreneurs beyond the campus;

- to develop and implement high-calibre entrepreneurship curricula at secondary and post-secondary institutions in the region; and

- in order to advance knowledge about and practice of entrepreneurship, to develop a research agenda with the assistance of visiting entrepreneurs, academics and facilitators (the research results were disseminated by means of seminars, conferences and publications).

*Innovativeness of the partnerships.* The BCE itself was, in its organization, operation and culture, entrepreneurial. It was designed to operate as a community-based partner rather than an institution unto itself. As an entrepreneurial institution, it operated by adapting to the community environment, networking and linking with a growing number of established or new community organizations rather than building competitive institutions, to promote its goals. In spite of its scope, the BCE deliberately avoided developing burdensome administrative organizations.

The BCE assumed an active consulting role with its partners to add value to their missions with the injection of 'intellectual capital'. This consultation process led the community's key economic development agency, the Niagara Regional Development Corporation, to propose and develop the Niagara Enterprise Agency. This agency, created by the Niagara Regional Development Corporation and the Burgoyne Centre, embodied a new concept in community-based economic development: it sought to intervene in large employer restructuring and recessionary job displacements by facilitating the development of new enterprises which would create new jobs in the region.

In addition, the creation of the New Enterprise Store, housed in an actual retail store, provided a community laboratory for curriculum research, development and teacher training. It became a community-accessible incubator where individuals could test the viability of a new idea or enterprise in the marketplace before financially launching a new enterprise.

With respect to entrepreneurial education and training, the BCE placed its educational emphasis on self-assessment, personal development and creativity rather than simply on teaching participants how to develop a business plan. The same educational model was used to train teachers to instruct entrepreneurial subjects. This overall approach was supplemented by the pooling of the educational and entrepreneurship resources of community partners.

Within the context of the community, successful entrepreneurs willingly and actively served on advisory committees of the BCE and the New Enterprise Store and frequently made guest presentations to students. In addition, many local lawyers, accountants and management consultants pledged their professional time at no charge to provide advice and counsel to students who were evaluating new venture concepts and business plans.

The BCE and the partnerships it fostered had a profoundly positive effect on individual development and on the cultural and strategic fabric of the community.

*Reflections on the partnerships.* The innovativeness of these developments cannot be stressed enough. The ecology that emerged from the partnerships developed its own dynamics in the community. The initiatives undertaken by the BCE meant that its leadership had to make instantaneous decisions. The Centre, however, was made accountable by means of the mechanistic bureaucratic and hierarchical structures that underlie the university's infrastructure. As one member of the university pointed out, 'For the university, entrepreneurship means anything faster than glacial speed.'

The entrepreneurial world view at BCE created a chasm between it and the university. Eventually, the ecology succumbed to the machine – leading towards its eventual breakdown in 1992. The university in its wisdom chose to focus on academic research and its undergraduate course. The community partners were left to do as they wished with the rest of the programmes.

In the end, two initiatives remained. The Enterprise Education Unit became the Institute for Enterprise Education, an independent centre for research and programme design in entrepreneurship, entrepreneurial leadership and enterprise education. This centre became a partner with the university's Faculty of Education in the design, development and delivery of a Bachelor of Education, Enterprise Education programme for pre-service secondary teachers in all subject fields. The Institute for Enterprise Education works closely with young people in delivering entrepreneurship programmes and with leaders of large organizations seeking to create entrepreneurial cultures. It also advises agencies worldwide that seek to instil the entrepreneurial spirit in their communities.

The other survivor, the Niagara Enterprise Agency, continues its efforts to intervene in employer restructuring and new venture creation. In recent years, its network of advisers and stakeholders has served as a source of angel investment and venture capital to high-growth SMEs.

These two smaller ecologies (the Institute for Enterprise Education and the Niagara Enterprise Agency) continue to develop relationships within and outside their regions. They are themselves largely entrepreneurially driven enterprises, relying mostly on private-sector funding to ensure their viability. The dream of a long-term community-based partnership, however, was disrupted by the dominance of a worldview that is no longer appropriate in today's chaotic, complex and disruptive environment, in which speed and adaptability are of the essence.

We are becoming well aware that the whole is greater than the sum of the parts. The rules of ecology trump the rules of the machine. This case study reflects the reality for most university and entrepreneurship partnerships that aspire to be engines of entrepreneurial community development: the machine can still dominate the ecology. This is becoming our greatest challenge as educators and facilitators of enterprise seek to inculcate the entrepreneurial spirit into every sector of society.

## Conclusion

The end of entrepreneurship is a comprehensive strategy for creating the conditions and culture that nurture and sustain the entrepreneurial spirit. If we are truly committed to developing the entrepreneurial spirit, then facilitators need at the very least to be agents of change who are committed to engaging, enabling and empowering students to become enterprising in whatever is their chosen career.

The aim of this paper has been to build a case for the teaching of and learning about entrepreneurship by aligning its principles and practices with similar organic teaching and learning methodologies. In order to deliver effective programmes in entrepreneurship, educators and community partners must recognize the changing dynamics of the global landscape and their major impact on teaching and learning – which must be directed towards the construction of communities that nurture innovation and entrepreneurship.

Any effective programme in entrepreneurship will need to begin with an understanding of each person's distinct gifts, talents, contribution and creativity. By connecting each individual with the emerging global reality, the opportunities for new enterprises will increase, and new enterprises themselves will precipitate further opportunities. These potential opportunities can be realized only if the community itself is structured as an ecology of partners dedicated to nurturing and supporting a culture of entrepreneurship. It is only under such conditions that the ecology of entrepreneurship will prosper and grow.

As has been argued throughout this paper, educational leaders need to envisage a compelling future that energizes us all to become more enterprising as we journey along the path of the entrepreneur or as we work to enable entrepreneurship.

# References

Amabile, T. M. (1997), 'Entrepreneurial creativity through motivational synergy', *Journal of Creative Behaviour – Creative Education Foundation*, Vol 31, No 1, pp 18–26.

Carland, J. W., Hoy, F., and Bolton, W. R. (1984), 'Differentiating entrepreneurs from small business owners: a conceptualization', *Academy of Management Review*, Vol 9, pp 335–339.

Csikszentmihalyi, M. (1990), *Flow: the Psychology of Optimal Experience*, Harper and Row, New York.

EC (2003), *Entrepreneurship in Europe*, Green Paper, Commission of the European Communities, Brussels.

Florida, R. (2005), *The Flight of the Creative Class: The New Global Competition for Talent*, Harper Business, New York.

Friedman, T. L. (2005), 'It's a flat world, after all', *The New York Times Magazine*, 3 April, www.nytimes.com/2005/04/03/magazine/03dominance.html.

Gibb, A. (2006), 'Entrepreneurship: unique solutions for unique environments: is it possible to achieve this with the existing paradigm?', paper presented at World Conference of the International Council for Small Business World Conference, Melbourne, 18–21 June.

Herrmann, N. (1994), *The Creative Brain*, 5th edition, Quebecor, Kingsport, Tn.

IEE (1995), *Profit 100 Study*, Institute for Enterprise Education, St Catharines, Ontario.

IEE (2002), *Finding Your Niche in Niagara: Bridging the Gap Between Youth and the Workplace*, Institute for Enterprise Education, St Catharines, Ontario.

Kelly, K. (1997), 'The new rules of the new economy', *Wired Magazine*, September, p 194.

Kelly, S., and Allison, M.A. (1998), *The Complexity Advantage*, McGraw Hill, New York.

Kuhn, T. S. (1962), *The Structure of Scientific Revolutions*, 2nd edition, University of Chicago Press, Chicago, IL, and London.

Kurtzman, J. (1998), 'An interview with W. Brian Arthur', *Strategy + Business*, Vol 11, 2nd Quarter, p 95.

LEED (2003), *Trentino Local Entrepreneurship Review*, Local Economic and Employment Development Programme of the Organization for Economic Co-operation and Development in collaboration with the Trentino Chamber of Commerce, Trentino.

Miller, W. C. (1999), *Flash of Brilliance: Inspiring Creativity Where You Work*, Perseus, New York.

Mitton, D. G. (1989), 'The compleat entrepreneur', *Entrepreneurship – Theory and Practice*, Vol 13, No 3, pp 9–19.

OECD (1989), 'Towards an enterprising culture: a challenge for education and training', CERI Monograph No 4, Organization for Economic Co-operation and Development, Paris.

Postman, N. (1995), *The End of Education: Redefining the Value of School*, Alfred A. Knopf, New York.

Quartz, S. R., and Sejnowski, T. J. (2002), *Liars, Lovers and Heroes*, Harper Collins, New York.

Shaver, K., and Scott, L. R. (1991), 'Person, process, choice: the psychology of new venture creation', *Entrepreneurship – Theory and Practice*, Vol 16, No 2, pp 23–45.

Timmons, J. (1989), *The Entrepreneurial Mind*, Prima, Boston, MA.

Washington Centre for Complexity and Public Policy (2003), *The Use of Complexity Science: A Survey of Federal Departments and Agencies, Private Foundations, Universities, and Independent Education and Research Centres*, Washington Centre for Complexity and Public Policy, Washington, DC.

# Changing struggles for relevance in eight fields of natural science

## Laurens K. Hessels, Harro van Lente, John Grin and Ruud E.H.M. Smits

**Abstract:** This paper investigates the consequences of institutional changes on academic research practices in eight fields of natural science in the Netherlands. The authors analyse the similarities and differences among the dynamics of these different fields and reflect on possible explanations for the changes observed. The study shows that the increasing pressure for productivity, as measured in bibliometric terms, can counteract the pressure for practical utility. Moreover, the work indicates that the dynamics of science varies much more across scientific fields than most of the literature suggests is the case.

**Keywords:** Mode 2; research funding; performance evaluation; credibility cycle

Laurens K. Hessels (corresponding author) is with the Department of Science System Assessment, Rathenau Instituut, Anna van Saksenlaan 51, 2593 HW The Hague, The Netherlands. E-mail: l.hessels@rathenau.nl. Harro van Lente and Ruud E.H.M. Smits are with the Copernicus Institute of Sustainable Development at Utrecht University, The Netherlands. John Grin is with the School of Social Science Research at the University of Amsterdam, The Netherlands.

This paper sets out to contribute to the understanding of transformations in the knowledge infrastructure, as discussed in a large and expanding literature (see, for example, Etzkowitz and Leydesdorff, 2000; Gibbons et al, 1994; Ziman, 2000). One of the central claims in this literature is that research practices are changing as research agendas are increasingly being oriented towards producing societal benefits; or, in other words, that the relevance of science is increasingly defined in terms of specific products or policy solutions. The changing role of universities is also a prominent topic in the Triple Helix discourse. Although the Triple Helix can also be regarded, from a neo-evolutionary perspective, as three selection environments operating upon one another (Leydesdorff and Zawdie, 2010), it is often interpreted as an institutional model of increasingly networked relationships between universities, industries and governments (Etzkowitz *et al*, 2000). Universities claim to engage increasingly in a 'third mission', alongside teaching and fundamental research (Etzkowitz *et al*, 2000) and to be directing their activities more towards 'Mode 2 knowledge production' (Gibbons *et al*, 1994).

However, the understanding of these dynamics is still limited, due to two problems: first, the empirical evidence supporting these claims is not fully convincing; and, second, one of the most influential concepts used in this debate ('Mode 2 knowledge production') suffers from conceptual weaknesses that inhibit proper implementation (Hessels and van Lente, 2008). Preliminary evidence suggests that changes in the academic research system may involve conflicting forces: shifts in funding stimulate scientists to make direct contributions to economic growth or other societal goals, but the rise of systematic performance evaluation increases the pressure to achieve scientific excellence as measured in bibliometric terms (Steele *et al*, 2006; Hessels and van Lente, 2011; Hessels *et al*, forthcoming).

What are the consequences of these institutional changes for the nature of academic research activities? Will such activities be more strongly oriented towards the third mission? Do university researchers in all fields of science interact increasingly with their stakeholders in society? In this paper, we address these questions based on an analysis of changing *struggles for relevance* in eight fields of natural science. Special attention is given to explaining the differences that occur across these fields.

## Theoretical framework

The opening assumption of this paper is that academic researchers struggle for relevance. Researchers will always encounter a certain pressure to position their work in a broader framework: to a greater or lesser extent, they need to make sure that their work is valuable to society, either directly or indirectly (Rip, 1988).[1] The struggle to achieve relevance can involve aligning one's research agenda to the needs of societal stakeholders. Another form of this struggle is the active transfer of knowledge to potential users. But, in principle, basic research that does not directly address external knowledge needs may also be relevant, depending on what counts as 'relevance'. In general, relevance refers to the possible (societal) benefits of science, but these benefits can come in many different forms, ranging from broad cultural values to the development of specific products or the creation of spin-off companies (Hessels *et al*, 2009).

Why would scientists strive for relevance? First, positioning one's activities in a broader context can deliver personal satisfaction[2] – for example, making a contribution to a larger goal can enhance one's work ethic. Second, considerations of potential societal benefits can also help to legitimize one's work to the outside world (van Lente, 1993). The third possible motivation is strongly related to the second: research of high relevance (in all its different forms) can provide access to funding and other valuable resources. Expected societal benefits have played a role in research funding since the emergence of modern science (Martin, 2003; Rip, 1997). Strong alignment of one's research agenda with the needs of external parties can help to secure funding, either directly or indirectly. Moreover, in some fields stakeholder interactions provide access to valuable knowledge, datasets or other research materials.

If relevance is so attractive, one may wonder why it would be an object of struggles. We would suggest that there are at least two reasons why striving for relevance is not a straightforward exercise. First, research issues that are considered highly 'relevant' by others do not always appear to be the most promising in terms of deriving personal satisfaction, producing high-impact scientific publications and obtaining peer recognition. This potential tension is particularly important because it appears that academic researchers are subject to increasing pressure to produce first-class performance, in terms of scientific productivity, as a result of the increasing number of performance evaluations over the past few decades (Steele *et al*, 2006). Second, struggles for relevance appear when the meaning of relevance is not clearly defined. The potential benefits of science are subject to speculation simply because there can be no certainty in advance

about any beneficial outcomes. There is also an ongoing dispute about the degree to which research activities should be directed towards (short-term) societal objectives (Gibbons, 1999; Ziman, 2003). In peer-review panels responsible for evaluating research proposals there are often disputes about the relative importance of 'social significance' as a selection criterion (Lamont, 2009).

Based on these considerations we propose the following tentative definition: the *struggle for relevance* is the combination of the efforts of scientists to make their work correspond with ruling standards of relevance and their efforts to influence these standards. Depending on the dominant standards of relevance, the possibilities for scientists to optimize the relevance of their work may include aligning their research agenda with the needs of societal stakeholders and transferring the knowledge to potential users. However, they can also employ rhetorical strategies to present their research in such a way that, it can be argued, it will comply with dominant standards of relevance (van Lente and van Til, 2008).

To study struggles for relevance in the daily work of university researchers, we used the 'credibility cycle' model (Latour and Woolgar, 1986), which explains how the need for reputation influences the behaviour of individual scientists. Its starting assumption is that a major motivation for a scientist's actions is the quest for credibility. On this basis, the research process can be depicted as a repetitive cycle in which conversions take place between money, staff, data, arguments, articles, recognition and so on – see also Hessels *et al* (2009).

But: scientists do not work independently. Their activities take place in the context of a 'research system'. In accordance with Rip and Van der Meulen (1996), we regard a research system as consisting of 'research performers (individuals, groups, institutions), other organizations and institutions, interactions, processes and procedures' (*ibid*). Such a system contains not only universities, related research institutes and funding agencies but also governmental organizations, commercial businesses and intermediary organizations, to the extent that they are part of the institutional environment. This institutional environment provides research organizations with incentives and constraints to conduct (particular kinds of) research.

Adopting a structuration perspective (Giddens, 1984), the research system can be seen as the structure influencing the agency of individual researchers. Existing structures are the product of practices and of dominant visions on the potential value of research outcomes. The institutions within this system give rise to certain conversions of credibility – for example, the possibility to convert recognition into money (Packer and Webster, 1996, Hessels and van Lente, 2011).

Simultaneously, funding bodies – it is presumed – take into account the outcomes of research practices when formulating their future priorities. In this way, research practices can strengthen these institutions, but they can also neglect them and put them under pressure. So, the research system can be seen as a structure that shapes research practices but is, at the same time, (re)produced by these practices.

## Methods

A case study approach (Yin, 2003) was used, focussing on eight scientific fields in the Netherlands selected to represent the variety of possible societal stakeholders of natural science (see Table 1). In each case, the discipline was studied for the period between 1975 and 2005. We chose 1975 as the starting point because this marks the beginning of a national government science policy in the Netherlands (Blume, 1985) that is generally considered to be a key event in the changing relationship of academic science with its societal context.

Data for the case studies have been drawn from in-depth interviews and

---

**Table 1. Fields selected in each case study and their stakeholders in society.**

| Discipline | Fields | Main stakeholders |
|---|---|---|
| Chemistry | Catalysis | Chemical industry |
| | Biochemistry | Biotech industry/Medicine |
| | Environmental chemistry | Environmental policy |
| Biology | Paleo-ecology | Oil industry |
| | Toxicology | Environmental policy |
| Agricultural science | Animal breeding and genetics (ABG) | Animal breeding firms |
| | Animal production systems (APS) | Farmers, agricultural policy |
| | Cell biology | (Veterinary) medicine |

analysis of the relevant literature. For the credibility cycle analysis of changing struggles for relevance, semi-structured in-depth interviews with 47 academic researchers were carried out. The respondents' academic status ranged from PhD student to full professor, and they were employed at five different universities in the Netherlands (see Table 2). They were asked questions about their current and past research activities, their personal motivation and their experiences and strategies concerning funding acquisition, publishing, scientific reputation and performance evaluations. Using NVivo (qualitative analysis software), we coded the interview transcripts in accordance with the different steps of the credibility cycle.[3]

Our analysis of the changing structural conditions of academic research is based on documents[4] combined with interviews with scholarly experts and representatives of firms, professional organizations, research councils and the government. The documents were selected on the basis of the prior knowledge of the authors, suggestions from interviewees, and the 'snowball method' (in which referrals from initial subjects generate additional subjects, and so on). The selection includes governmental policy documents, reports and strategic plans of research councils, foresight studies, evaluations and other important publications about the disciplines concerned. The findings from these documents were triangulated in interviews with the experts and stakeholders mentioned above.

**Table 2. Distribution of 47 respondents by field, university and academic rank.**

**Field**
Catalysis (9)
Paleo-ecology (8)
Toxicology (7)
Biochemistry (6)
Environmental chemistry (5)
Animal breeding and genetics (4)
Animal production systems (4)
Cell biology (4)

**University**
Utrecht University (18)
Wageningen University (12)
University of Amsterdam (11)
VU University Amsterdam (3)
Radboud University Nijmegen (1)
Eindhoven University of Technology (1)
Leiden University (1)

**Academic rank**
Retired full professor (6)
Full professor (13)
Associate professor (10)
Assistant professor (6)
Postdoctoral researcher (5)
PhD student (7)

# Results

In the period studied, we observed two major structural changes: shifts in the available funding and the increasing use of performance evaluations.

## Diversification of funding

The first general structural change is a trend of funding diversification. In all the fields studied, the relative share of public funding for basic research has decreased. Moreover, over the years, the relative share of unconditional funding (first money stream) has decreased. With the general expansion of public science systems (as opposed to those in the private sector), budgets have come under pressure and the need to account for public investments in academic research has grown (Ziman, 1994). In line with the ideologies of Neo-liberalism and 'New Public Management', the Dutch government has relaxed state control and introduced market mechanisms to enhance efficiency and effectiveness (de Boer *et al,* 2007). Since 1975, the starting point of our analysis, the government has transferred an increasing share of public funding to competitive arrangements, organized by research councils or other intermediary organizations. Between 1975 and 2005, the total amount of block grant support for universities has grown almost twofold in real terms (Versleijen, 2007), but its relative share in relation to more competitive funding sources has decreased (Jongbloed and Salerno, 2003). Around 1975, this funding stream was still sufficient for research groups to purchase necessary equipment and hire some temporary staff: now, however, some of the permanent academic staff need to be paid from project funding – and even that funding which has remained in this category has become less secure, as it has become subject to university policy and it is often required to 'match' externally acquired funds (Jongbloed and Salerno, 2003; AWT, 2004).

The 'second money stream' has also changed dramatically. Research councils were initially organized in sub-disciplinary Working Committees, but they have since been merged and reorganized into a general matrix organization supplying most funding in the form of multidisciplinary research programmes. While originally Dutch research councils exclusively funded basic research, they have expanded their territories to include application-oriented activities.

Moreover, the Dutch Organization for Scientific Research (NWO, the new umbrella organization encompassing all research councils) has developed a variety of hybrid funding configurations in collaboration with ministries, firms or other knowledge users.

In addition, the third money stream (all contract funding except that from NWO), which is more strongly oriented to practical applications, shows a spectacular increase in the 1980s and 1990s in all Dutch universities (see Figure 1). Between 1983 and 2000 the total size of this stream has increased from about V125M to about V638M. This represents an increase by a factor of 3.85 in real terms (Jongbloed and Salerno, 2003).

Simultaneous with this major shift towards application-oriented funding, however, a less pronounced trend occurred in the opposite direction. Over the last decade, the research council's policy to nurture and stimulate first-class researchers has created a small but significant subset of funding arrangements lacking any consideration of practical utility. In 2000, NWO introduced the highly competitive 'Vernieuwingsimpuls' grants as a policy instrument for supporting talented researchers. In the selection of proposals for these grants, the most important deciding factor is the quality of the individual applicant, assessed mainly using bibliometric criteria. With its emphasis on bibliometric quality indicators, this type of funding has probably contributed to the decreasing value of practical applications as a source of recognition. At present, the grants under this scheme consume about 20% of NWO's total budget.[5] However, the relative impact of this

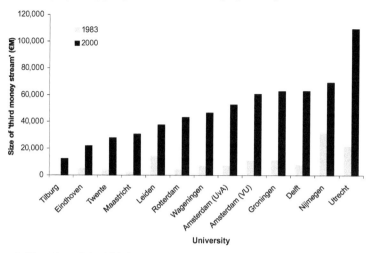

**Figure 1.** The size of the 'third money stream' in 1983 and 2000 (in current prices) at Dutch universities.
*Source:* Jongbloed and Salerno, 2003.

funding instrument is probably larger than its financial contribution because of its prestige and popularity.[6]

### Rise of performance evaluations

The second structural change is the rise of performance evaluations. After a number of pilot evaluations and foresight studies in the 1980s, a more or less standard approach has been developed for systematic evaluation of academic research groups (van der Meulen, 2008). Currently, every research group in the Netherlands is subject to regular evaluations. Research quality assessments officially use a variety of criteria, but in practice they tend to be dominated by bibliometric quality indicators: even if other dimensions such as viability or relevance are also measured, in the interpretation of the evaluation scores, it is numbers of publications and citation rates that dominate.[8]

The availability of digital bibliometric databases and the relative generic validity and cross-comparability of these indicators has resulted in their achieving recognition and success that is not equalled – yet – by any other indicators (Gläser and Laudel, 2007). Although the results of Dutch research evaluations do not have direct financial consequences, their outcomes do influence strategic decisions by deans and university boards; and high scores can also contribute to successful acquisition of external funding.

### Common trends in the credibility cycle

What has been the effect of these institutional changes on the credibility cycle of individual academic researchers? We have observed common trends at three steps in the credibility cycle: at the acquisition of data, recognition and money (see Figure 2).

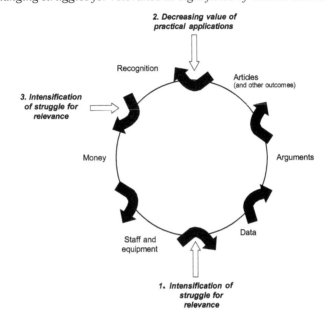

**Figure 2.** The three common trends in the struggles for relevance of eight fields of natural science, depicted in the credibility cycle.
*Source:* Adapted from Latour and Woolar (1986).

First, in most fields the struggle for relevance during the collection of data (the actual research process) has intensified. Over the past few decades, the role of societal stakeholders in this process has increased. Some researchers now collaborate to such an extent with knowledge users that they regard them as 'partners':

> 'We are free and they are free to go where they want. But you simply feel that they care about a long-lasting relationship. So we don't have a collaboration that is project-oriented. Then you would talk about customers. We talk about partners, [when we talk about] the firms.' (Researcher A7)

In agreement with the claims about the rise of 'Mode 2 knowledge production',

an increasing proportion of all Dutch academic research is conducted in 'the context of application'. In several fields, interactions with possible users of research outcomes were already common practice, but in general their frequency and level of importance have grown. In fields such as catalysis, animal breeding genetics (ABG) and toxicology, most projects are supervised by an industrial sponsor or by a 'users committee'. These receive regular updates about progress and provide feedback for future directions. In other fields, such as animal production systems (APS) and environmental chemistry, it has become common practice to conduct academic research projects in collaboration with applied researchers employed by public research institutes or private R&D laboratories. These types of interactions with stakeholders have increased the awareness of scientists of potential applications of their work and – to some extent – this awareness influences their choices in the laboratory. It should also be noted that there are fields in which researchers still hardly interact directly with societal stakeholders – in particular, biochemistry and cell biology.

The second major development that was visible in all fields we have studied relates to the way scientists earn recognition: on average, the value of practical applications as a source of academic recognition has decreased. Asked whether practical applications can help to achieve peer recognition, a biologist replied:

> 'Maybe it would count a bit, but also here the scientific content comes first and if it is applicable by accident, then that is so much to the good. I mean, it is like the cream on the pudding [sic], but . . . It makes it more fun, yes. But it is not . . . '
> (Researcher B20)

Since the 1970s recognition has become more and more linked to the production of scientific papers. Scientists are increasingly under pressure to be productive, both in quantitative and qualitative terms. In the credibility cycle, recognition has become so strongly based on numerical indicators of scientific productivity that academic researchers face the simple choice: 'publish or perish'. A strong publication list has become a crucial condition in order to qualify for particular types of funding, in particular grants from national research councils and from EU Framework Programmes. Moreover, scientific productivity is the main topic discussed during individual performance interviews, and it is also the main criterion for selecting candidates for academic positions.

Our interview data show that scientists are aware of the importance of scientific publications during the whole credibility cycle. Data collection is organized in such a way as to optimize the prospects for publication. Some scientists choose particular strategies because they either need to publish in a high-impact journal (Researcher B20) or because they perceive the need for a larger number of papers (Researcher A10), depending on the current status of their publication list. In addition, several strategies which might be regarded as 'cheating' are pursued, such as the formation of writing 'task-forces' whose members grant each other co-authorships without any actual collaboration (Researcher C5); submitting several papers each highlighting different aspects of the same research project; or dividing a particular contribution into its 'smallest publishable units' (Researcher A10).

Over the years, publication achievements have displaced – further – social or economic impact as a source of academic recognition. As we will specify below, practical applications are not always in competition with scientific papers: but in most fields they are. In the selection of material for publication in scientific journals, the societal relevance of the reported research does not play a significant role. Editors and peers largely decide whether or not to publish papers based on purely scientific considerations such as consistency, novelty value and methodological quality. In many fields, there is even a trade-off between research projects that are of high societal relevance and projects that are likely to result in (many) high-impact scientific papers.

The third generic trend visible in the period 1975–2005 concerns the intensification of the struggle for relevance in the context of funding acquisition. Earning sufficient income for continuing one's research activities has now become the outcome of active acquisition efforts. Our interview data give the impression that it has become common for senior researchers to spend between 10 and 20% of their time on networking, exploring funding options, writing proposals and negotiating contracts. Promises about practical applications often play a central role in the selection of project proposals. In all fields, the scientists we have interviewed report that aligning their work with the knowledge needs of societal stakeholders has become increasingly important for securing sufficient funding. In the credibility cycle, expected societal benefits strongly catalyse the conversion of recognition into money. Based on a certain amount of recognition (for example, expressed in one's publication list), the same researcher will more readily acquire funding if they manage to specify convincingly the societal value of a proposed research project:

'Yes. It is much easier to get money, there are much more possible sources to get money, if you have something that is relevant to society.' (Researcher C12)

There are possibilities for obtaining funding for research in the Netherlands without having to commit to producing societal benefits, mostly occurring at the national research council (NWO). However, such funds provided a substantial share of their budget for only a few of the 47 researchers interviewed.

*Changing struggles in different scientific fields*

To a certain extent the three common trends presented above were visible in all eight fields (in the Netherlands). However, a closer look also reveals significant differences across scientific fields in the manifestation of these changes. In our findings, four types of differences can be discerned among the eight fields studied, regarding the changes in their struggles for relevance (see Tables 3 and 4). The first three are directly linked to the general trends just described: the fourth concerns the tension that has arisen in some fields due to the combination of these trends.

First, although the role of stakeholders in the academic research process has generally grown, the *extent* to which stakeholders have become involved in data collection varies significantly across fields. Second, there is variation in the (limited) *degree* to which practical relevance is rewarded in terms of academic recognition. Third, in all fields, promising societal benefits can help to acquire funding, but the *degree* of involvement of societal stakeholders in the actual agenda setting differs. The fourth dimension that deserves to be addressed here is the relationship between practical applications and scientific publications: in some fields there is synergy between scientific productivity and practical relevance; in other fields there is conflict. Table 4 presents a classification of the eight fields in our sample based on this dimension. In the following, some the characteristics of the three categories of fields will be explored in terms of the other three 'dimensions' of the struggle for relevance.

In the two fields with the least intensive stakeholder interactions, biochemistry and cell biology, we observed a trade-off between scientific productivity and practical relevance. In these fields, scientists complained

**Table 3. Overview of differences among struggles for relevance in eight scientific fields.**

| Credibility conversion | Variable | Observed range |
|---|---|---|
| Acquiring data | Intensity of stakeholder interactions | Low-High |
| Acquiring recognition | Value of practical applications | Negligible-Considerable |
| Acquiring money | Influence of stakeholders on research agenda | Weak-Strong |
| (Generic) | Relationship practical applications – scientific productivity | Strong tension-Synergy |

**Table 4. Classification of the eight fields based on relationship between practical applications and scientific productivity.**

| Relationship practical applications and scientific productivity | Field | Intensity of stakeholder interactions during data collection | Value of practical applications for acquiring recognition | Influence of stakeholders on research agenda |
|---|---|---|---|---|
| Strong tension | Cell Biology | Slight increase | Negligible | Remains weak |
| | Biochemistry | Still low | Negligible | Remains weak |
| Weak tension | Environmental Chemistry | High but stable | Considerable | Strong but stable |
| | Animal Production Systems | High and growing | Considerable | Strong and increasing |
| | Toxicology | High but stable | Low | Strong, slight increase |
| Synergy | Catalysis | High and growing | Negligible | Strong and increasing |
| | Animal Breeding & Genetics | High and growing | Low | Strong and increasing |
| | Paleo-ecology | Slight increase | Low | Increasing |

that engaging in application-oriented research projects and interacting with societal stakeholders 'distracts' them from the main focus of their field. Efforts or achievements of this kind do not significantly yield peer recognition here. In biochemistry and cell biology, contributions to high-impact journals are usually based on projects paid by research councils affording considerable autonomy to the researchers to formulate their own research priorities and approaches. Enhancing the industrial, medical or agricultural relevance of one's work implies a move away from the central debates of these fields. To this end, one would have to move to other model systems (for example, using chickens rather than mice for research projects), or address other research questions (for example, relating to specific treatments rather than general understanding) which are less suitable for publishing in prestigious journals.

In a second class of fields, containing APS, environmental chemistry and toxicology, such a tension also exists, but it is weaker in nature. In this set of fields, interactions with stakeholders are quite common, both during the acquisition of funding and during data collection. Here, under certain conditions, application-oriented research can lead to impressive publications. The most important requirements for successfully combining practical applications with scientific productivity seem to be substantial project size and consistency across projects. If these conditions are met, the results of application-oriented projects can lead to improved understanding on a fundamental

level. In this way, the outcomes of (one or more) relatively practical projects can lead to scientific papers. For researchers involved in relatively short and diverse application-oriented projects, it is difficult to develop fundamental insights that can be published in prestigious scientific journals.

The situation is different in catalysis, paleo-ecology and ABG. In this class of fields, in which stakeholder interactions have grown significantly, we observed a synergy rather than a trade-off between scientific productivity and societal relevance. Interactions with stakeholders not only help to acquire funding but are also helpful in other credibility conversions. We identified three mechanisms that are responsible for this synergy. First, applied research projects for stakeholders can provide access to data that are also useful for more fundamental investigations. Second, the interactions with stakeholders often provide inspiration for challenging research questions. Third, some stakeholders simply sponsor fundamental research activities from which they expect benefits to be derived in the long term.

As Table 4 indicates, the relative value of applications – as compared to publications – as a source of recognition does not show a clear trend across the three sets of fields: that is, it does not correlate with the degree of synergy between practical applications and scientific productivity. It is lowest in biochemistry and cell biology, the fields with the least intensive stakeholder interactions. In these fields, recognition is almost exclusively based on academic achievements, in terms of scientific publications and citations. In the two other classes of fields the relative value of applications ranges from negligible to considerable. Practical applications are most rewarding in terms of recognition in APS and environmental chemistry, which occupy a middle position in Table 4. In these two fields, a scientific reputation is based not only on contributions to scientific debate but also on contributions to environmental policy or to the development of more sustainable agriculture. This may be related to the fact that in these two fields, scientists seem most strongly motivated to 'change the world'. More than in the other fields studied, they draw inspiration for their work from personal ambitions to contribute to external goals such as sustainable development.[9] In the same vein, they also value their colleagues' practical contributions to such goals, more so than do scientists in fields such as catalysis or toxicology.

## Discussion: explaining field differences

To recapitulate our empirical findings, we have observed three general changes in the struggles for relevance of Dutch chemistry, biology and agricultural science in the period 1975–2005.

(1) The struggle for relevance during data collection has intensified.
(2) The value of practical applications as a source of academic recognition has decreased.
(3) The struggle for relevance in the context of funding acquisition has intensified.

Moreover we have identified significant differences in the way these changes became manifest in different scientific fields and in the interplay between them. In some fields, a tension has developed between scientific productivity and practical applications, in others there was synergy. How can we explain the differences in the changing struggles for relevance of scientific fields? The remainder of this paper will present a possible explanation based on socio-organizational, cognitive and cultural field characteristics, combined with the characteristics of societal stakeholders.

*Variation in stakeholder interactions*

Our empirical analysis has shown that the degree to which stakeholder interactions have increased (both during data collection and during funding acquisition) varies strongly across fields. This can be partly explained by cognitive and socio-organizational characteristics of scientific fields, in particular their search pattern (Bonaccorsi, 2008) and strategic task uncertainty (Whitley, 2000). We have found that some fields with 'convergent' search patterns, namely biochemistry and cell biology, have developed relatively few interactions with societal stakeholders (see Tables 4 and 5). This is understandable, because convergent fields have a relatively sharp focus in terms of research problems and approaches. In these fields, the strategic task uncertainty is low. This implies that there is a strong overall consensus about the intellectual priorities, and scientists cannot easily develop a new, application-oriented research direction.

**Table 5. Classification of fields based on degree of convergence of their search pattern.**

| Search pattern | Chemistry | Biology | Agricultural science |
|---|---|---|---|
| Convergent | Biochemistry | Toxicology | Cell biology |
| | Catalysis | | Animal breeding and genetics |
| Divergent | Environmental | Paleo-ecology | Animal production systems |

In divergent fields, such as APS and environmental chemistry, it may be more likely that niches develop which meet the knowledge needs of societal stakeholders. Divergent fields typically have a high strategic task uncertainty: this means that a wide diversity of concurrent research directions is accepted because there is no overall consensus about the intellectual priorities. Researchers and employers are able to pursue distinct strategies and orientations without being penalized for theoretical deviation. In such fields, it is easier to develop new research directions that fit the needs of societal stakeholders.

*Variation in the value of practical applications*

The extent to which practical applications are valued as a source of credibility can be understood when taking into account the traditional communication culture of a scientific field. Fields with a divergent search pattern generally have a 'rural' communication style (Becher and Trowler, 2001) because they are not highly competitive and have a low people-to-problems ratio. In 'rural' fields, such as APS and environmental chemistry, relatively few researchers

work on a large number of dispersed problems, and mutual competition is limited. Because there is no broad consensus about overall quality standards, it is also difficult to formulate general evaluation criteria. Because of the theoretical diversity, knowledge accumulation is less efficient than in 'urban' fields, and there is usually a lower citation density. We can assume that in these fields, fewer high-impact journals are available, which makes it more difficult to achieve high scores in bibliometric evaluations. This implies that bibliometric quality indicators have limited validity, so that it is less likely that recognition will be based on publications alone and more likely that practical outcomes such as policy advice, patents or spin-off firms are also valued. In urban fields, with a high citation density, bibliometric quality indicators will be used more abundantly, not only in formal evaluations and management decisions but also in informal processes of exchanging recognition.

*Variation in relationship between practical applications and scientific productivity*

The variation in the relationship between practical applications and scientific productivity, which seems crucial for the fate of scientific fields, can be explained by taking into account characteristics of other participants in the research system, in particular the end users of academic research. Depending on its cognitive content, each field has different potential users outside academia. Of particular importance are 'upstream end users', stakeholders with formal channels to influence the strategies and programmes of a scientific field through research funding, regulation or policy (Lyall *et al,* 2004). In our case studies, the fields that were most successful in combining stakeholder interactions with academic performance were those with wealthy and powerful upstream end users having a long-term vision of the utility of scientific research (see Table 6). The chemical industry (in the case of catalysis) and the animal breeding industry (ABG) both invest substantial sums in academic research, in the expectation that there will be payback in the long term. Such companies support academic researchers in fundamental research activities, which in turn provide good opportunities for high-impact publications. In this way, the companies support scientists through the complete cycle of credibility. The same is true for environmental policy makers and oil companies, in the case of paleo-ecology.

Biochemistry and cell biology, in contrast, have hardly any upstream end users, although stakeholders – such as patient groups, farmers or veterinary surgeons – can of course be identified that may eventually benefit from these research activities. These stakeholders, however, function rather more as 'downstream' users, because they are not active players in the academic research system; they do not directly commission research or influence its directions. The only participants providing generous (that is, substantial) support for these fields and directly influencing their directions are research councils (at

**Table 6. The upstream end users of different scientific fields (fields ranked according to degree of synergy between practical applications and scientific productivity).**

| Relationship between practical applications and scientific productivity | Field | Upstream end users |
|---|---|---|
| | *Catalysis* | *Industry* |
| Synergy | ABG | Animal breeding firms |
| ↑ | Paleo-ecology | Policy makers Oil companies |
| | Environmental chemistry | Policy makers Industry NGOs |
| | APS | Farmers Policy makers |
| | Toxicology | Policy makers Industry NGOs |
| | Cell biology | – (some agro-food companies) |
| ↓ Tension | Biochemistry | – |

both national and European level); but they function more as intermediaries, providing channels to transfer knowledge to and from downstream end users.

In the third class of fields, including environmental chemistry, toxicology and APS, upstream end users can be identified as part of the research system, but these mainly support application-oriented research. These stakeholders definitely care about the research in these areas, but they cannot afford investments with a long time horizon. For instance, support from a governmental body for academic research in the area of toxicology or environmental chemistry is usually connected to a knowledge need related to a specific problem. This explains why researchers in these fields often experience a tension between end-user relevance and scientific productivity. The short time horizon of the projects commissioned by upstream end users is incompatible with the fundamental nature of dominant debates in scientific literature. In such cases, interactions with stakeholders catalyze some conversions of credibility (funding acquisition) but inhibit others (publishing).

Another significant variable is the homogeneity of the upstream end users in a particular field. In the cases of catalysis and ABG, the set of upstream end users is quite homogeneous; but in environmental chemistry, toxicology and APS it is heterogeneous. It seems that a homogeneous set of end users makes it easier to build a consistent project portfolio, which will help to identify and develop synergy between practical applications and scientific productivity.

## Changing science systems?

Our findings have two major implications for the debate about changing science systems. First, this study shows that the increasing pressure for productivity, as measured in bibliometric terms, can counteract the pressure for practical utility. In other words, there is a potential tension between the second and the third university missions. In some fields, such as catalysis and ABG, we have observed a synergistic relationship between societal impacts and scientific excellence. In other fields, however, such as biochemistry and toxicology, the pressure for academic productivity is at odds with the pressure of practical applications. In these fields, scientists have increased their efforts to produce papers in high-impact journals at the expense of the practical implications and implementation of their work. In these areas, research activities addressing the knowledge needs of societal stakeholders are not easily published in scientific journals. The increased publication pressure here inhibits the shift towards application-oriented research modes.

Second, our work indicates that a further differentiation is needed, because the dynamics of science varies much more across scientific fields than most literature suggests. This study adds to a number of other recent investigations that have reported varying reactions to institutional changes across scientific disciplines (Gläser *et al*, 2010; Reale and Seeber, forthcoming; Albert, 2003). This study confirms their call for disciplinary differentiation in science policy studies. Moreover, it reinforces it with a call for an even more fine-grained perspective that discriminates not only within complete disciplines but also within specific fields. Some of the diagnoses of changing science systems differentiate across scientific fields or disciplines – in particular, literature about post-normal science, finalization in science, Triple Helix and innovation systems. However, none contains a satisfactory framework for understanding the varying dynamics of scientific fields. Our study has indicated some possible building blocks for such a framework, in particular the concepts of search pattern regimes (Bonaccorsi, 2008), strategic task uncertainty (Whitley, 2000), communication culture (Becher and Trowler, 2001) and upstream end users (Lyall *et al*, 2004).

## Notes

1 The idea of 'struggles for relevance' was coined by Rip (Rip, 1988) in an analysis of changing science systems. He observed that with the emergence of '. . . a new layer of institutions, explicitly oriented to "missions", to programming, to strategic mobilization' in the 1970s and 1980s a shared repertoire for judging relevance had also emerged. This development gave rise to struggles for relevance, '. . . on top of struggles for fundability' (Rip 1988, p 70). In this paper we adopt the idea of 'struggles for relevance' in a generalized sense: we consider these struggles for relevance as a universal aspect of academic research with different manifestations over time and place.
2 Personal preference is known to be a very important criterion in scientific problem choice (Cooper, 2009).
3 NVivo is proprietary software used for data classification and analysis. See also: http://www.qsrinternational.com/products_nvivo.aspx, last accessed 24 August 2011.
4 A list of documents is available on request.
5 NWO (2010), 'Begroting 2010 en meerjarencijfers 2011 tot en met 2014', nWo, Den Haag.
6 Between 2000 and 2006, the success rate of this funding instrument was only 20% (Technopolis and Dialogic, 2007), while the overall average success rate at NWO was about 50% (see NWO (2005), *Jaarboek2004*, NWO, Den Haag).
7 VSNU, nWo & KNAW (2003), *Standard Evaluation Protocol 2003–2009 for Public Research Organisations.*
8 The newest protocol for Dutch research evaluations demands more explicitly the assessment of 'societal relevance' (VSNU, KNAW & NWO (2009), *Standard Evaluation Protocol 2009–2015: Protocol for Research Assessment in the Netherlands*); and a recent set of pilot studies has shown the potential of indicators for this criterion (ERiC 2010, *Handreiking Evaluatie van maatschappelijke relevantie van wetenschappelijk onderzoek*, ERiC publicatie 1001), but the effects of this development on academic research practices were not yet visible in our case studies.
9 For example: 'Yes, in the time that I started I had a strong passion. That there was a large problem which already received attention, but which was not known yet in its full proportions' (interview, Researcher C15).

## References

Albert, M. (2003), 'Universities and the market economy: the differential impact on knowledge production in sociology and economics', *Higher Education*, Vol 45, No 2, pp 147–182.

AWT (2004), *De prijs van succes – over matching van onderzoekssubsidies in kennisinstellingen*, AWT advies 58, April 2004, Den Haag.

Becher, T., and Trowler, P. R. (2001), *Academic Tribes and Territories*, SRHE and Open University Press, Maidenhead.

Blume, S. S. (1985), *The Development of Dutch Science Policy in International Perspective, 1965–1985*, Raad van

Advies voor het Wetenschapsbeleid, Zoetermeer.

Bonaccorsi, A. (2008), 'Search regimes and the industrial dynamics of science', *Minerva,* Vol 46, No pp 285–315.

de Boer, H., Enders, J., and Leisyte, L. (2007), 'Public sector reform in Dutch higher education: the organizational transformation of the university', *Public Administration,* Vol 85, No 1, pp 27–46.

Etzkowitz, H., and Leydesdorff, L. (2000), 'The dynamics of innovation: from National Systems and "Mode 2" to a Triple Helix of university–industry–government relations', *Research Policy,* Vol 29, No 2, pp 109–123.

Etzkowitz, H., Webster, A., Gebhardt, C., and Terra, B.R.C. (2000), 'The future of the university and the university of the future: evolution of ivory tower to entrepreneurial paradigm', *Research Policy,* Vol 29, No 2, pp 313–330.

Gibbons, M. (1999), 'Science's new social contract with society', *Nature,* Vol 402, pp c81–c84.

Gibbons, M., Limoges, C., Nowotny, H., Schwartzman, S., Scott, P., and Trow, M. (1994), *The New Production of Knowledge: The Dynamics of Science and Research in Contemporary Societies,* Sage, London.

Giddens, A. (1984), *The Constitution of Society: Outline of the Theory of Structuration,* Polity Press, Cambridge.

Gläser, J., Lange, S., Laudel, G., and Schimank, U. (2010), 'The limits of universality: how field-specific epistemic conditions affect authority relations and their consequences', in Whitley, R., Gläser, J., and Engwall, L., eds, *Reconfiguring Knowledge Production: Changing Authority Relationships in the Sciences and their Consequences for Intellectual Innovation,* Oxford University Press, Oxford.

Gläser, J., and Laudel, G. (2007), 'The social construction of bibliometric evaluations', in Whitley, R., and Gläser, J., eds, *The Changing Governance of the Sciences,* Springer, Dordrecht.

Hessels, L. K., Grin, J., and Smits, R.E.H.M. (2011), 'The effects of a changing institutional environment on academic research practices: three cases from agricultural science', *Science and Public Policy,* Vol 38, No 7, pp 555–568.

Hessels, L. K., and van Lente, H. (2008), 'Re-thinking new knowledge production: a literature review and a research agenda', *Research Policy,* Vol 37, No pp 740–760.

Hessels, L. K., and van Lente, H. (2011), 'Practical applications as a source of credibility: a comparison of three fields of Dutch academic chemistry', *Minerva,* Vol 49, No 2.

Hessels, L. K., van Lente, H., and Smits, R.E.H.M. (2009), 'In search of relevance: the changing contract between science and society', *Science and Public Policy,* Vol 36, No 5, pp 387–401.

Jongbloed, B., and Salerno, C. (2003), *De Bekostiging van het Universitaire Onderwijs en Onderzoek in Nederland: Modellen, Thema's en Trends,* Enschede, Center for Higher Education Policy Studies, Universiteit Twente.

Lamont, M. (2009), *How Professors Think: Inside the Curious World of Academic Judgment,* Harvard University Press, Cambridge, MA.

Latour, B., and Woolgar, S. (1986), *Laboratory Life: The Construction of Scientific Facts,* Sage, London.

Leydesdorff, L., and Zawdie, G. (2010), 'The Triple Helix perspective of innovation systems', *Technology Analysis and Strategic Management,* Vol 22, No 7, pp 789–804.

Lyall, C., Bruce, A., Firn, J., Firn, M., and Tait, J. (2004), 'Assessing end-use relevance of public sector research organisations', *Research Policy,* Vol 33, No 1, pp 73–87.

Martin, B. R. (2003), 'The changing social contract for science and the evolution of the university', in Geuna, A., Salter, A., and Steinmueller, W. E., eds, *Science and Innovation: Rethinking the Rationales for Funding and Governance,* Edward Elgar, Cheltenham.

Packer, K., and Webster, A. (1996), 'Patenting culture in science: reinventing the scientific wheel of credibility', *Science, Technology and Human Values,* Vol 21, No 4, pp 427–453.

Reale, E., and Seeber, M. (forthcoming), 'Organisation response to institutional pressures in Higher Education: the important role of the disciplines', submitted to *Higher Education.*

Rip, A. (1988), 'Contextual transformations in contemporary science', in Jamison, A., ed, *Keeping Science Straight: A Critical Look at the Assessment of Science and Technology,* Department of Theory of

Science, University of Gothenburg, Gothenburg.

Rip, A. (1997), 'A cognitive approach to relevance of science', *Social Science Information,* Vol 36, No 4, pp 615–640.

Rip, A., and van der Meulen, B.J.R. (1996), 'The post-modern research system', *Science and Public Policy,* Vol 23, No 6, pp 343–352.

Steele, C., Butler, L., and Kingsley, D. (2006), 'The publishing imperative: the pervasive influence of publication metrics', *Learned Publishing,* Vol 19, No 4, pp 277–290.

Technopolis and Dialogic (2007), *Evaluatie Vernieuwingsimpuls 2000–2006,* Dialogic, Utrecht.

van der Meulen, B.J.R. (2008), 'Interfering governance and emerging centres of control', in Whitley, R., and Gläser, J., eds, *The Changing Governance of the Sciences: The Advent of Research Evaluation Systems,* Springer, Dordrecht.

van Lente, H. (1993), *Promising Technology: The Dynamics of Expectations in Technological Developments,* Eburon, Delft.

van Lente, H., and van Til, J. I. (2008), 'Articulation of sustainability in the emerging field of nanocoatings', *Journal of Cleaner Production,* Vol 16, No 8–9, pp 967–976.

Versleijen, A., ed, (2007), *Dertig jaarpublieke onderzoeksfinanciering in Nederland 1975–2005: Historische trends, actuele discussies,* Rathenau Instituut, Den Haag.

Whitley, R. (2000), *The Intellectual and Social Organization of the Sciences,* Oxford University Press, Oxford.

Yin, R. K. (2003), *Case Study Research: Design and Methods,* Sage, Thousand Oaks, CA.

Ziman, J. (1994), *Prometheus Bound: Science in a Dynamic Steady State,* Cambridge University Press, Cambridge.

Ziman, J. (2000), *Real Science: What It Is, and What It Means,* Cambridge University Press, Cambridge.

Ziman, J. (2003), 'Non-instrumental roles of science', *Science and Engineering Ethics,* Vol 9, No 1, pp 17–27.

# Acknowledgements

The authors gratefully acknowledge the help of all interviewees and thank them for their cooperation. We further thank Stefan de Jong and Floor van de Wind for their contribution to the data collection and Daan Schuurbiers and Arend Zomer for their valuable comments on an earlier draft.

# PART III: GEARING COOPERATION AND ENTREPRENEURSHIP FOR REGIONAL GROWTH

# Entrepreneurship teaching and graduate start-up support in universities
## Assessment and good practice

**Jonathan Potter**

Centre for Entrepreneurship, SMEs and Local Development, Organisation for Economic Co-operation and Development, France[1]

## Introduction

Entrepreneurship engagement is a core component of the emerging 'third mission' of universities, involving the delivery of community and economic development activities that generate social and economic benefits alongside the traditional university missions of research and teaching. This chapter focuses on how universities promote entrepreneurship through the provision of entrepreneurship teaching and start-up support to students. This support has an important social purpose as a driver of economic growth and job creation. It also offers important rewards to both students and universities.

From the welfare perspective, there are a number of benefits from university support to graduate entrepreneurship, which explain why policy makers seek to overcome market and institutional barriers in this area. Graduate entrepreneurship support helps to develop the supply of more entrepreneurial workforces that business requires in the knowledge-based economy. The support, of course, is also aimed directly at facilitating venture starts, which contribute to economic growth by driving productivity improvements through Schumpeter's 'creative destruction' and by creating jobs in slack labour markets. Start-ups by graduates can also play an important role in commercialising knowledge that may otherwise remain unexploited in universities. While it is usually the academic entrepreneur who is seen to be the 'knowledge filter' in economic growth (Acs *et al*, 2004), students can also play a role since they are exposed to researcher ideas and may take them with them into business operation. They may indeed benefit from the collaboration of the academic professors and researchers in their commercialisation of the ideas. In the longer run, graduate entrepreneurship support can encourage more entrepreneurial societies and cultures by fostering entrepreneurial mindsets and positive attitudes to entrepreneurship in the population.

While the economic welfare benefits are clear, there is also strong demand for entrepreneurship courses and support from students as individuals. This reflects the attraction of many students to the idea of starting their own enterprises rather than working as employees. The university can contribute by helping the graduate to bridge the gap to obtain certain elements they lack for start-up (e.g. ideas, a loan, an office) and helping them obtain the skills needed to identify entrepreneurial opportunities and to turn their entrepreneurial ideas into successful ventures. While it is widely recognised that entrepreneurs will often require support with the start-up itself, the importance of skills to successful entrepreneurship is generally under-recognised in current entrepreneurship policy frameworks. Entrepreneurship teaching and start-up support offer graduates skills and confidence to start and run businesses and help with some of the first steps they will take. Even where student participants do not immediately start a business, they are likely to benefit from more entrepreneurial careers as employees or as business creators later in life.

The major advantage to universities of offering graduate entrepreneurship programmes is the ability to obtain financial and other resources in return. In many countries, university entrepreneurship engagement is encouraged by specific public financial support. Universities can also expect to benefit from an enhanced ability to attract fee-paying students who are interested in entrepreneurship. In certain cases, they may gain financially by taking stakes in the enterprises created or selling on intellectual property. Engagement with entrepreneurship can also bring other benefits, such as ideas for teaching and alumni networks ready to support the university.

In recognition of these benefits, many universities have established structures to manage and promote graduate entrepreneurship activities in recent years, such as entrepreneurship chairs, centres and departments, entrepreneurship courses and modules and a range of incubation, networking, financing, mentoring and other start-up support services. The state of development of graduate entrepreneurship support is nonetheless highly uneven across universities, and there are clearly leaders, followers and universities that have yet to engage. The new and uneven state of the field implies strong scope for bench learning, expanding successful approaches and adopting good practices more widely.

Furthermore, there are barriers to overcome in securing effective entrepreneurship teaching and start-up support in universities, and exchange of information on how to overcome them can be very useful. Whilst entrepreneurship is likely to be at the heart of the 21st-century economy, training of entrepreneurship skills is not a standard part of the formal higher education curriculum. Where it is included, the extent of provision, course content and methods of teaching and assessment could often be improved. Rather than just business school or engineering students, students from all disciplines can benefit from entrepreneurship teaching. Entrepreneurial behaviours need to be imparted as well as small business management techniques, and traditional classroom teaching and assessment methods are less well suited than practical experience and interaction with entrepreneurs to entrepreneurship skills development. For graduates to start businesses successfully, they also often need support with obtaining resources and consultancy, but these have not been a traditional part of university activities either. At the bottom of the difficulties is a mismatch among traditional academic cultures, conventions and governance arrangements that have not been designed for the entrepreneurial economy. Thus, as well as implying the need for new teaching programmes and start-up support, a more fundamental change in the institutional environment that surrounds university entrepreneurship support is also on the agenda.

This chapter examines the nature of the improvements that are required. The following sections cover the nature of entrepreneurship skills for graduates and how they may be taught, trends and current practices in entrepreneurship teaching and start-up support, good practices and learning models, a case study assessment in Berlin and recommendations and conclusions.

## What are entrepreneurship skills?

The OECD defines entrepreneurs as business owners who seek to generate value through the creation or expansion of economic activity by identifying and exploiting new products, processes or markets (OECD, 2009a). They will require certain skills to do this successfully, such as creativity, innovation, teamwork, understanding of the external environment and networking.

The literature on entrepreneurship skills is relatively new, however, and there is not yet a clear consensus on the precise nature of the skills involved or on how they should be taught. Indeed, a concern among certain training professionals and policy makers is that many current entrepreneurship teaching initiatives do not address the real skill needs of entrepreneurs, instead focusing too much on areas such as business planning and accounting skills that have been over-estimated in terms of their real importance to entrepreneurship (OECD, 2010a; Potter, 2008).

At the outset of consideration of these issues, a key distinction should be made between entrepreneurship skills and traits. It is sometimes argued that entrepreneurship cannot be taught because entrepreneurship stems from the innate character of the entrepreneur – that is, people are either inherently motivated, opportunity aware and so forth or not. This refers to entrepreneurship traits rather than skills. According to Oosterbeek *et al* (2009), they encompass: (i) need for achievement (e.g. striving for performance and appreciation of competition); (ii) need for autonomy (e.g. independent decision-making, problem-solving skills, etc.); (iii) need for power (i.e. to influence other people's behaviours and decisions to achieve one's own goals); (iv) social orientation (i.e. understanding of the importance of relationships to achieve objectives); (v) self-efficacy (i.e. self-confidence); (vi) endurance (i.e. ability to move on after setbacks and failures); and (vii) risk taking (i.e. willingness to take risks in front of uncertainties). At the same time, however, these traits may be influenced by training and brought out more strongly in people interested in entrepreneurship.

By contrast, Oosterbeek *et al* (2010) consider the following to be entrepreneurship skills: (i) market awareness (i.e. understanding customer needs and market trends, including competitors' behaviour); (ii) creativity (i.e. adopting views from different perspectives and trying new possibilities based on observations); and (iii) flexibility (i.e. turning problems into opportunities). These are seen to be the main focus of entrepreneurship teaching approaches.

More work is nonetheless needed to refine the list of entrepreneurship skills. A number of issues are important, such as risk assessment and warranting, strategic thinking, self-confidence, the ability to make the best of personal networks, motivating others to achieve a common goal, co-operation for success and the ability to deal with other challenges and requirements met by entrepreneurs (OECD, 2010b, p. 166). The ongoing OECD Skills for Entrepreneurship project seeks to develop this thinking further. It uses a three-fold classification that separates small business management from strategic skills and introduces in addition the category of entrepreneurial

traits, which while they may be a complex function of people's pasts may nonetheless be influenced by entrepreneurship training:

- *Small business management skills*: These skills are those that every small enterprise, including self-employment, needs to become a viable business. They involve the skills needed for start-ups and everyday business operations and include, *inter alia*, business planning, accounting, logistics, inventory keeping, etc.

- *Strategic skills*: These are more typically skills that an entrepreneur needs to grow his or her business. There is a broad class of 'conceptual skills', which encompass decision-making, risk-taking, innovative and information-processing skills. But in addition, these skills include opportunity recognition, resource organisation, market awareness (e.g. of customers, competitors and potential new markets) and product management.

- *Entrepreneurial traits*: These refer to aspects of the character of the entrepreneur and are more difficult to transmit through formal training but may nevertheless be encouraged where they are present. They include need for achievement and autonomy, leadership and relationship competencies, self-confidence, commitment, creativity and flexibility.

It is this broad set of skills and traits that university entrepreneurship teaching and associated graduate start-up support seeks to develop.

## Current practice in university entrepreneurship teaching and start-up support

*Extent of university entrepreneurship teaching and start-up support*

The extent of entrepreneurship teaching and start-up support in universities varies widely across universities. Systematic, comparative estimates are difficult to come by, but there are a number of studies that provide a partial assessment. The most fundamental issue concerns the proportion of students that accesses or is able to access entrepreneurship education. A recent survey of some 700 higher education institutions undertaken for the European Commission estimated that in 2008, some 5 million out of 21 million European university students were engaged in entrepreneurship education, or nearly one quarter (NIRAS *et al*, 2008). Some 86% of institutions in Europe were found to provide entrepreneurship education, but of these, only one half offered courses in which the entrepreneurship component accounted for more than one quarter of the curriculum, implying that the entrepreneurship teaching is often part of other courses rather than representing a course in itself. We may refer to these universities as those offering entrepreneurship-specific courses, at least in as far as the entrepreneurship content passes a threshold of 25% of total course content. A key point made by the study is that some 11 million students in Europe did not have any access to entrepreneurship-specific courses since they were not offered in their institution.

Hoffman *et al* (2008) offer some of the rare evidence comparing Europe and North America. Their study surveyed a selection of 27 universities in Denmark, Canada and the USA and found significant differences in student participation rates in entrepreneurship teaching. For example, at Stanford University and Cornell University in the United States, student participation in entrepreneurship programmes was 15% and 20%, respectively. In comparison, the participation rate at the Canadian universities surveyed was between 5% and 7%, while none of the Danish universities reported participation rates above 2.5%. While caution is needed in interpreting the results from a selective survey such as this, the clear observation that can be made is that the proportion of students accessing entrepreneurship teaching varies and can be very small.

It appears that the extent of entrepreneurship teaching may be of the same order in central, east and south-east Europe as in Europe as a whole. A survey undertaken for the OECD of some 800 institutions in central, east and south-east Europe in 2007 found that 47% offered entrepreneurship teaching through at least one entrepreneurship course (Varblane *et al*, 2008). This is lower than the 86% found by NIRAS *et al* (2008) for EU members and selected non-members, but the difficulty is that this is not comparing like with like, in that only one half of the 86% provided courses in which entrepreneurship represented at least one quarter of the content, while the Varblane *et al* courses are entrepreneurship specific. Furthermore, in terms of curricula, Varblane *et al* found that 8% of central, east and south-east European institutions provided bachelor-level curricula, 6% provided master's curricula and 3% provided doctoral curricula in entrepreneurship, proportions that are similar to those found in an earlier survey of entrepreneurship education in Europe (Wilson, 2004).

Another issue raised by the literature is that entrepreneurship teaching tends to be skewed towards certain university departments and is not well spread across faculty as a whole, although students from any discipline have the potential to start businesses. Entrepreneurship education tends to be concentrated in business schools, economics faculties and certain applied science faculties such as engineering. For example, a survey by the National Council for Graduate Entrepreneurship found that more than 60% of entrepreneurship teaching in the UK was provided in business schools (NCGE, 2007). In the USA, 31% of entrepreneurship courses were housed in business schools, while 23% were housed in departments of small business and entrepreneurship, although individual subject departments ran the majority of the remaining programmes (Solomon, 2008).

There appears to be only limited systematic evidence on the extent of complementary start-up support provision in universities, although this can be important in the process of instilling entrepreneurial skills. Case studies nonetheless indicate that support typically includes physical facilities such as business incubators, advice from advisors, mentors and coaches and start-up grants. The NIRAS *et al* (2008) survey indicates that more than one half of the group of European universities offering entrepreneurship-specific courses provided students with incubator facilities in which they could start up a business. In the UK, many universities have incubators and 'hatcheries', and there are a few examples of universities offering bursaries to recent graduates to facilitate the setting up of a new business (Botham and Mason, 2007). In recognition of the importance of this type of facility, the Irish government has introduced the Enterprise Platform Programme, a one-year rapid incubation programme open to graduates from any discipline in the country's Institutes of Technology. It aims to provide an appropriate balance of formal education, training, personal development, counselling, business mentoring and business guidance to support students to launch a growth business or strengthen the market position of their existing firm (Cooney and Murray, 2008).

The main message that can be drawn from this evidence is that there is a very uneven spread of entrepreneurship teaching across universities and that the majority of students are not exposed to entrepreneurship teaching. Even where entrepreneurship teaching is offered, it may be a small proportion of the total content of the course in which it is embedded. The principal challenge, then, is to increase the reach of entrepreneurship education and start-up support. Some governments have sought to increase the extent of entrepreneurship teaching and start-up support in their countries by introducing nation-wide programmes, requirements or guidance to universities. Examples of such national programmes include Belgium, Denmark and Poland (European Commission, 2008).

*Nature of entrepreneurship teaching and start-up support*

Entrepreneurship teaching in universities tends to be characterised by certain types of courses and methods. In the USA, Solomon (2008) shows that the most common courses in the broad field of entrepreneurship were in entrepreneurship (offered by 53% of surveyed universities), small business management (offered by 36%) and new venture creation (offered by 30%). The main other course areas were in technology and innovation, venture capital, small business consulting, small business strategy, franchising, new product development, entrepreneurial marketing, small business finance and creativity. Some authors argue, however, that the range of courses provided generally falls short with respect to entrepreneurs' skill needs, particularly because of an almost exclusive focus on business management skills (Cooney, 2009; Gibb, 2007) and therefore a lack of attention to more behaviour-oriented skills such as creativity, innovation and problem solving (Henry, Hill and Leitch, 2005).

Apart from classroom lectures, Solomon shows that the most frequent methods of teaching entrepreneurship in the USA were business plans (57% of courses used them frequently or very frequently), class discussions (60%), guest speakers (52%), case studies (50%) and lectures by business owners (48%). Other less frequent but still significant approaches were computer simulations, research projects, feasibility studies, internships, on-site visits and in-class exercises. In Europe, the most common teaching method is lecturing, but most institutions offering entrepreneurship-specific courses often use case studies too (NIRAS *et al*, 2008). Other widespread teaching methods were project teamwork and the use of guest lecturers. Both curricular and extra-curricular activities are important, such as seminars and workshops, business plan competitions, company visits and matchmaking events. However, these were not widespread across the system. For example, in the UK, some 36% of entrepreneurship activity was within the curriculum, while 64% was extra-curricular (European Commission, 2008).

Much of the start-up support available to accompany entrepreneurship teaching is offered in university business incubators or entrepreneurship centres. The main types of support appear to be with start-up premises, mentoring, finance, intellectual property advice and linking to alumni networks. Botham and Mason (2007) cite an interesting experience in the University of Staffordshire in the UK, which launched in 2005 the Year-Out Student Placement, in which bursary students live in university 'enterprise villages', attend enterprise master classes and meanwhile set up a business. In addition, many universities provide business plan competitions to match funds to the most promising student businesses. Hoffman *et al* (2008) point out that a key distinction between Danish universities and North American ones in this respect is the greater emphasis on business plan competitions and the much less frequent use of alumni networks in Denmark compared with Canadian and US counterparts.

What is most striking about the nature of entrepreneurship support provided is that while entrepreneurship skills development is essentially practical and built on experience, teaching remains dominated by classroom lectures. Project teams, business simulations and other interactive methods are used but are far from common. Introducing innovations in learning methods is one of the major challenges for entrepreneurship skills development. It could be argued that the problem of introducing innovative learning techniques is a similar one to that of introducing entrepreneurship teaching at all, in that both involve a risk to the teacher, who will be going outside of established conventions and incentive tracks, while teachers, as opposed to entrepreneurs, might be characterised as risk averse (Kuratko, 2005).

*Organisation of entrepreneurship teaching and start-up support*

The institutional setting of entrepreneurship teaching and start-up support is also important to success, such as in terms of co-ordination, the provision of financial and teaching resources, facilities, networking activities and so on.

Structures are often in place to co-ordinate and lead entrepreneurship support. For example, entrepreneurship centres often serve the function of co-ordinating and promoting entrepreneurship support across departments within a university, raising visibility and acting as a focal point for support. Solomon's survey in the USA found that approximately one third of universities had an entrepreneurship centre and the same proportion had an entrepreneurship professor or chair. In Europe, the NIRAS *et al* (2008) work indicates that 58% of higher education institutions (HEIs) with entrepreneurship-specific courses had a dedicated entrepreneurship centre and approximately two thirds had a chair in entrepreneurship. On the other hand, Varblane *et al* (2008) found that only 11% of central, east and south-east European universities had an entrepreneurship centre and only 7% had a chair or department in entrepreneurship. It is more in the lack of such frameworks than in the proportion of universities offering courses that there appears to be a lag with the rest of Europe and America.

In terms of teaching materials, some 60% of instructors in the USA developed their own sets of course materials rather than importing material from other institutions (Solomon, 2008), while almost all courses in Europe developed their own materials. This points up a wider challenge, which is to increase the degree of networking in university entrepreneurship support, for example to share the work load and learning curves of course material development among institutions and departments. This would provide for better quality and facilitate efforts to spread teaching to a larger set of students. There are also opportunities for increased networking in start-up support, for example with certain universities specialising in certain kinds of entrepreneurship support and cross-signposting to specialist support available from other universities or indeed external economic development agencies in the same city.

Another challenge is to strengthen the human resourcing of university entrepreneurship programmes. A common problem is that entrepreneurship teachers are rarely entrepreneurs. This often reflects regulations and cultures that limit who can teach. While entrepreneurs cannot be expected simply to teach without support and training, it is also critical that people with experience of entrepreneurship provide a significant part of the entrepreneurship teaching. In addition, more training for the trainers would help to bring in innovative teaching approaches. While in the USA, most universities provide education training for teacher-entrepreneurs, Hoffman et al (2008) found that entrepreneur training was non-existent in the surveyed Danish universities. Inter-university networks could have an important role to play in this respect in human resource development initiatives for entrepreneurship teachers.

Funding is also a key issue. In Europe, a significant proportion of university entrepreneurship support is financed from special public budgets. Thus, the NIRAS *et al* (2008) survey found that two thirds of the institutions with entrepreneurship-specific courses support their entrepreneurial goals with dedicated funding. On average, 56% was internal funding and 44% raised from external sources, largely from the public sector. The problem that arises is the consequent vulnerability of entrepreneurship support to changes in short-term funding streams. This issue is less important in North America, where universities are able to raise more resources from private sources, including venture capital firms, student fees and alumni networks.

Finally, as with other third-mission activities, entrepreneurship support will thrive only when it is an established part of the university strategy and promoted by top management. According to NIRAS *et al* (2008), some 71% of the European institutions with entrepreneurship-specific courses had entrepreneurship embedded within their written mission statement. But in only 59% of cases was the primary responsibility for entrepreneurship education held by the principal, pro-vice chancellor or dean. Many of the leading universities appear to be leaving the responsibility for entrepreneurship education to individual professors and lecturers, and this may be even more the case in those in which entrepreneurship is less established. The danger is that when entrepreneurship support is more the result of individual commitment than the result of a university-wide approach, it will be difficult to promote the entrepreneurship agenda, reach out to a wider group of students, obtain the necessary resources and institutionalise the entrepreneurship approach, enabling its expansion beyond the original pioneers.

# Good practice criteria

In order to analyse what could be improved in university entrepreneurship teaching and graduate start-up support in specific universities, it is useful to systematically examine universities against a number of criteria of good practice. This provides a benchmark against which each university can be assessed and recommendations can be made. The OECD is currently undertaking such an exercise in its Skills for Entrepreneurship reviews, which seek to identify the strengths and weaknesses of graduate entrepreneurship support in selected universities and make recommendations for improvements in each case based on an understanding of good practice internationally.

The framework proposes a set of six dimensions against which university entrepreneurship support can be assessed, with each of the dimensions containing a set of core principles or benchmarks concerning good practice policy. These dimensions and principles have been developed from a review of the entrepreneurship literature and case study work with a number of universities. As well as a forming the basic framework used by the OECD reviews, the good practice criteria are offered as a tool that universities can use to self-assess and re-orient their current strategies, structures and practices.

The six dimensions of good practice are set out below, with a brief discussion of the issues associated with each dimension:

- **Strategy**: University entrepreneurship support will struggle to achieve its potential if it is not underpinned by a clear university strategy. Support and encouragement are needed for those university staff and students willing to engage, who need to be rewarded. Governments may have a role to play in helping introduce entrepreneurship into university strategies by adding entrepreneurship support to the set of performance criteria they use to link funding to university outputs.

- **Resources**: Both human and financial resources need to be applied to deliver teaching and start-up support. In many OECD countries, the public sector is providing financial support. Yet this is often in the form of short-term funding, which prevents longer-term investment. Public funders and universities themselves need to seek longer-term and sustainable funding, including through exploring fully the opportunities for private-sector financial involvement, such as in the financing of entrepreneurship chairs and incubation facilities.

- **Support infrastructure**: A certain set of structures and facilities is required for successful entrepreneurship support, including incubation facilities to nurture start-ups and entrepreneurship departments and centres to co-ordinate and promote entrepreneurship engagement across universities. Networking with outside organisations and incentives for clear referral systems can be useful to increase the effectiveness and efficiency of start-up support and to reduce duplication, confusion and waste of resources.

- *Entrepreneurship education*: Entrepreneurship teaching needs to spread across the university to ensure that all students have access. It is useful to have a varied offer of courses, to use interactive teaching methods, and to reach out to appropriate teaching resources, including entrepreneurs and other alumni. Development of the teaching offer will benefit from exchange and networking across universities on teaching materials and methods.

- *Start-up support*: Universities can create a protected environment for nascent entrepreneurship. This can be an important stimulus for students and researchers to make a first step towards the creation of a venture. Yet, in order to avoid over-protection, early exposure to market conditions is advisable. A key success factor for university entrepreneurship support lies in private-sector collaboration, which provides finance, expertise and role models.

- *Evaluation*: There is a lack of evaluation evidence to indicate what works and does not work in university entrepreneurship support. As well as monitoring of teaching and start-up support and the outcomes associated with them, counterfactual analysis is required that will demonstrate the impact of university entrepreneurship support over and above what would have been achieved otherwise.

The principles of good practice within each dimension are presented in Box 1.

---

**Box 1.  Entrepreneurship support in universities: criteria for good practice**

**Strategy**

1. A broad understanding of entrepreneurship is a strategic objective of the university, and there is top-down support for it.
2. Objectives of entrepreneurship education and start-up support include generating entrepreneurial attitudes, behaviour and skills, as well as enhancing growth entrepreneurship (both high tech and low tech).
3. There are clear incentives and rewards for entrepreneurship educators, professors and researchers, who actively support graduate entrepreneurship (mentoring, sharing of research results, etc.).
4. Recruitment and career development of academic staff take into account entrepreneurial attitudes, behaviour and experience as well as entrepreneurship support activities.

**Resources**

1. A minimum long-term financing of staff costs and overheads for graduate entrepreneurship is agreed as part of the university's budget.
2. Self-sufficiency of university internal entrepreneurship support is a goal.

3. Human resource development for entrepreneurship educators and staff involved in entrepreneurship start-up support is in place.

## Support infrastructure

1. An entrepreneurship-dedicated structure within the university (chair, department, support centre) is in place, which closely collaborates, co-ordinates and integrates faculty–internal entrepreneurship support and ensures viable cross-faculty collaboration.
2. Either facilities for business incubation exist on the campus or assistance is offered to gain access to external facilities.
3. There is close co-operation and referral between university–internal and external business start-up and entrepreneurship support organisations; roles are clearly defined.

## Entrepreneurship education

1. Entrepreneurship education is progressively integrated in curricula, and the use of entrepreneurial pedagogies is advocated across faculties.
2. The entrepreneurship education offer is widely communicated, and measures are undertaken to increase the rate and capacity of take-up.
3. A suite of courses exists, which uses creative teaching methods and is tailored to the needs of undergraduate, graduate and post-graduate students.
4. The suite of courses has a differentiated offer that covers the pre-start-up phase, the start-up phase and the growth phase. For certain courses, active recruitment is practiced.
5. Outreach to alumni, business support organisations and firms is a key component of entrepreneurship education.
6. Results of entrepreneurship research are integrated into entrepreneurship education messages.

## Start-up support

1. Entrepreneurship education activities and start-up support are closely integrated.
2. Team building is actively facilitated by university staff.
3. Access to private financing is facilitated through networking and dedicated events.
4. Mentoring by professors and entrepreneurs is offered.
5. Entrepreneurship support in universities is closely integrated into external business support partnerships and networks and maintains close relationships with firms and alumni.

## Evaluation

1. Regular stock taking and performance checking of entrepreneurship activities is undertaken.
2. Evaluation of entrepreneurship activities is formalised and includes immediate (post-course), mid-term (graduation) and long-term (alumni and post-start-up) monitoring of the impact.

*Source:* OECD (2009)

# Good practice examples

Two examples of good practice are offered next from participants in recent OECD good practice exchanges (see OECD, 2010b, 2010c). They illustrate approaches that universities may take to deliver effective entrepreneurship support. The case of the Cambridge Centre for Entrepreneurial Learning is helpful in showing how to build the underlying skills and behaviours required for successful entrepreneurship. The case of the Chalmers School of Entrepreneurship is useful in showing how incubation and entrepreneurship education can be profitably linked.

## *Cambridge Centre for Entrepreneurial Learning, UK*

The focus of Cambridge Centre for Entrepreneurial Learning (CfEL) is on planning and implementing entrepreneurship courses for the whole university using a specific philosophy and a well-thought-out learning approach. The delivery of the entrepreneurship courses is largely taken care of by some 200 entrepreneurs and practitioners (entrepreneurs, venture capitalists, business angels, bankers, etc.).

All activities aim at developing self-confidence and self-efficacy amongst students. This reflects the underpinning view of entrepreneurship as a set of skills, attitudes and behaviours rather than just venture creation. Teaching methods range from lecturing, video and online assignments to problem-based learning, project work on real technologies and entrepreneurs in the classroom. A broad recruitment package includes a website, brochures, posters and a series of information events. Close collaboration with the various university departments allows circulation of information to student mailing lists and the organisation of tailored information events.

In addition to the teaching for university students, the centre co-operates with the Institute of Continuing Education to offer an Advanced Diploma in Entrepreneurship, which provides a highly practical programme designed specifically for people who either are considering embarking on an entrepreneurial career pathway or have taken the first steps in starting up a business. This is organised as a part-time programme over 27 months.

A key strength of the approach is its focus on soft skills (developing student self-confidence and self-efficacy, helping students to understand the why and the when of becoming an entrepreneur, learning to deal with uncertainty, learning by trying, trial and error, learning from mistakes and failures) instead of a how-to approach that emphasises business administration skills and tools to develop a business plan.

## *Chalmers School of Entrepreneurship, Sweden*

Chalmers School of Entrepreneurship at the University of Chalmers is an example of success in matching technology-based ideas from the university with teams of students who are supported in turning them into viable ventures. The benefits combine commercialisation of university intellectual assets with practical hands-on entrepreneurship education for students. Thus Chalmers

School of Entrepreneurship (CSE) is both an educational platform where entrepreneurship skills can be acquired and a pre-incubator to developed early-stage business ideas and to starting up a company. Core to the success is a network bringing students and university staff together with innovative individuals and firms from outside the university interested in developing and commercialising early-stage technology-based ideas with high market potential.

CSE practices an 'E-cubation' process, that is, it offers a master's degree combined with business incubation through an incubator organisation called an 'Encubator'. Most students start a company during the project year of their master's degree. The ideas for these businesses are provided by university researchers, who can follow their idea and grow in partnership with the student team and an international network of experienced business people, venture capitalists and others, supported with coaching and advice from CSE. If a limited company is founded, the idea provider will have a share in the new venture.

Venture finance may be provided by ChalmersInvest, a wholly owned company of Chalmers University that invests in university spin-off companies. ChalmersInvest currently owns equity in some 40 companies. ChalmersInvest also helps CSE ventures to link with external investors.

## A case study assessment

Among other work, the OECD has recently undertaken an assessment of entrepreneurship support in the State of Berlin in Germany, as set out in OECD (2010b). Major conclusions on the strengths and weaknesses of the approach are discussed next with the aim of identifying models to follow and areas of improvement that may be more widely relevant.

### Context

Three of Berlin's 34 university institutions and academies were the principal subject of the analysis: the Free University Berlin, the Technical University of Berlin and the Beuth Technical University of Applied Sciences (Beuth Hochschule). The case study work included the preparation of background reports, gathering of information from questionnaires involving a broad group of local stakeholders and meetings and interviews with key actors in the respective university entrepreneurship support systems. For the latter, international review panels were formed and a study visit undertaken in 2009.

Entrepreneurship education at the reviewed universities, as well as at Berlin city level, is in an early phase of development, reflected in a small breadth of entrepreneurship education activities and a small proportion of students benefiting from them (currently 5–7% of the total student population). Nonetheless, Berlin has a good track record in graduate entrepreneurship, a rich support framework, a strong science base and a top-level student body.

### Structures

In order to encourage entrepreneurship, Centres for Entrepreneurship have been established at all three universities to group together start-up support activities and to promote entrepreneurship education activities. They provide information, facilitate access to finance and manage the utilisation of university premises and laboratories by firm founders. Their directors report to the university boards (rector or vice-rector), symbolising their importance to the overall university entrepreneurship strategy. One of their strengths is their wide networks of contacts and collaborations with alumni founders, business consultants and business support organisations, business angels and venture capitalists that bring a practical input to start-up activities and entrepreneurship education. The centres have also established networks with external support organisations to which students and graduates are referred. For example, a key partner is the Investitionsbank Berlin (IBB), Berlin's development bank, which runs coaching facilities and organises the annual Berlin-Brandenburg Business Plan competition.

*Entrepreneurship education activities*

Each of the universities offers entrepreneurship teaching. Whereas the Free University centralises entrepreneurship education in an entrepreneurship foundation attached to the faculty of education science and psychology in the Technical University, in Beuth Hochschule, entrepreneurship education is spread across individual academic departments, albeit with co-ordination and additional activities provided by

their Centres for Entrepreneurship. A large proportion of the entrepreneurship teaching activities across the three universities are extra-curricular seminars, workshops, and so on.

Each of the universities has some interesting initiatives:

1. *Free University Berlin.* Entrepreneurship education in the university has been pioneered by Professor Faltin, who has developed his own teaching materials based on the notion of the business model. There is a strong use of videos for teaching. Other professors within the Educational Science and Psychology faculty are also involved in developing teaching material, particularly in the field of social entrepreneurship, in which videos offering critical voices on the topic have been produced and used.

2. *Technical University Berlin.* The Venture Campus seminar programme is an innovative way to organise inter-disciplinary business plan courses, based on collaboration among five University chairs and external experts. It is a five-month programme offered twice a year to the students, alumni and university staff from all faculties. So far, more than 300 participants have followed this start-up seminar, more than 100 business plans have been written and 14 new or existing ventures have been developed. The participants are requested to combine their already-acquired technological

knowledge and know-how with managerial expertise and operational business methods by working on the elaboration process of a real company, successfully develop a promising and realistic business model, which could serve as the initial point for a true start-up venture and write a business plan, which is the final deliverable. The contents of the seminar include five compulsory modules (business concept generation, market analysis and marketing, financing and financial planning, trademarks, patents and registered designs and tax), two optional modules (presentation skills and project management for start-ups) and mentoring sessions and guest speeches.

3. *Beuth Hochschule.* Entrepreneurship courses are delivered as part of a small number of academic programmes in Ophthalmics, Print and Media Technology and International Technology Transfer Management. In addition, a range of entrepreneurship courses are offered as non-mandatory options across all faculties: 'Business Start-ups', 'Practice-oriented Business Start-ups', 'Successful Start-ups as Freelancers', 'Prerequisites for Successful Business Start-up', and the like. These courses are very practice oriented and focus generally on the business plan elaboration and the start-up phases. For example, the core 'Practice-oriented Business start-ups' course uses an experiential learning pedagogy and covers entrepreneurial and

managerial topics such as business idea formation, market research and marketing, legal requirements and taxes, business planning, financing and funding. Regular surveys of students are undertaken to understand their profiles and the impact of the teaching activities.

### Start-up support activities

The start-up support framework across the three universities is well endowed with programmes and initiatives to assist students and graduates in starting up a business. Key features of the start-up support arrangements include:

1. *Business planning.* The Berlin-Brandenburg Business Plan Competition and several other smaller university internal business plan events are key instruments in 'marketing' entrepreneurship. The strong emphasis on a business plan approach means that many of the support mechanisms are tailored to the very early stages of entrepreneurship.
2. *Coaching and mentoring.* Subsidised coaching and mentoring for start-up teams are key components of the support framework.
3. *Access to finance.* The Centres for Entrepreneurship provide information on the various financing possibilities for graduate enterprises in Berlin, which include subsidised grant and loan schemes, business angels, venture capital and bank loans.
4. *Premises.* All three universities offer premises for selected

founders, either on or off campus, and free access to laboratories. Assistance with business planning, help in raising finance, networking and training in accounting and marketing are available to tenants.

*Areas for improvement*

The OECD assessment revealed a number of potential areas for improvement of the graduate entrepreneurship support framework in the three Berlin universities. The first main area involves a lack of strategy at the state and university levels. So far, public policy has been the main driver for entrepreneurship promotion by Berlin universities, led by programmes offered by the Berlin Senate, the federal government and the European Union. However, at the senate level, there appears to be a lack of a clear vision, strategy and evaluation framework to guide the entrepreneurship support programmes. At the level of individual universities, the current entrepreneurship support structure is more the result of a bottom-up process brought forward by a few key professors and staff rather than a real university policy. Thus activities are strongly dependent upon the individual commitment of few staff, entrepreneurship is not seen as a major priority by university top management and departments and structures are delivering their own activities without a common framework.

A second area for improvement involves scaling up and institutionalising entrepreneurship education. Entrepreneurship education is not sufficiently integrated into curricula. Courses, seminars and lectures are offered as electives, bearing few or no credits, which reduces the take-up rate and means that students who take entrepreneurship courses are often overloaded. In addition, there were caps on enrolment, and activities were not widely known amongst students. The selection of entrepreneurship courses is also limited, with a strong focus on business plan development and the how-to approach. Going back to our earlier categorisation of entrepreneurship skills, the focus can be characterised as being more about small business management than strategic skills and traits. Furthermore, there are limited number of qualified entrepreneurship teachers, a lack of teaching resource management and development through training and practice/experience exchange. At the same time, there are few incentives for faculty members to be more active in teaching entrepreneurship.

The third area for improvement concerns the manner in which start-up support is provided. While there is a wide set of public programmes available, interviews with graduates showed that they are often not aware of parts of the support and could not identify what was relevant to them. There are some 50 programmes in Berlin, but not all were considered productive or active. Student entrepreneurs also reported frustrations with the bureaucracy involved in certain programmes, such as the federal government's EXIST programme providing subsidies for technology-based start-ups. Funding rules did not allow for certain relevant types of spending. Furthermore, much of the start-up support is restricted by time-limited public funding from the European Social Fund, the federal government and the Berlin Senate. This leaves the entrepreneurship support vulnerable to the withdrawal of funds and constrains the development of the system.

## Conclusions and recommendations

This final section of the chapter presents some main conclusions and recommendations for universities more widely from OECD work in this area. The major argument of the chapter is that a range of new approaches to university entrepreneurship teaching and start-up support is emerging, despite a university institutional context that was not originally designed to promote entrepreneurship. However, there is a challenge now to extend these approaches across institutions and faculties and to increase the proportions of students involved. In strengthening university entrepreneurship support further, universities should pay attention to the good practice criteria presented in Box 1. In addition, the following major recommendations are offered (OECD, 2010a):

- Scale up, smartly. Increase the number of entrepreneurship courses and participating students where there is evidence of success. Make sure that the entrepreneurship teaching fulfils high quality standards and is extended across subjects to reach a wide range of potential entrepreneurs. Provide training, encouragement and support for staff embarking on entrepreneurship teaching activities. Facilitate teaching activities for existing and former entrepreneurs.

- Encourage growth-oriented entrepreneurship. Shift emphasis from business management to enterprise growth challenges, including finance and internationalisation. Teach the skills required for growth, including opportunity identification, risk taking, strategy making, leadership, negotiation, networking, building strategic alliances and intellectual property protection.

- Introduce interactive teaching methods that incorporate practical experience. Encourage learning by doing in contrast to more traditional forms of academic learning. Introduce cross-functional problem-solving approaches that replicate the bundle of activities and functions that need to be applied in entrepreneurship situations rather than breaking up teaching into separate business functions as in traditional management courses. Involve entrepreneurs in the design and teaching of entrepreneurship courses. Expose students to entrepreneur role models, for example by using entrepreneurs as mentors, speakers and interview subjects. Provide students with opportunities to work in existing small and medium-sized enterprised (SMEs) and to add value to these firms through placements and consulting projects. Develop case studies tailored to the environment that students will face.

- Link into wider networks. Tap into the resources of alumni networks to help fund and support entrepreneurship programmes, for example by asking alumni to get involved in teaching, using them to support links to companies for placements, using them as mentors and so on. Monitor alumni and build relationships with them to this end. Facilitate access to common materials and sharing of good practice by favouring networking among institutions and teachers and providing support for the inter-institution mobility of entrepreneurship teachers.

To assist in assessing conditions in specific case study regions and universities and in putting specific recommendations into action, the OECD Centre for Entrepreneurship, SMEs and Local Development is pursuing a series of Skills for Entrepreneurship reviews. These reviews aim to support national, regional and governments, development agencies, universities and other training providers (including from vocational education) to strengthen their approaches to entrepreneurship training using information gained from field research, student questionnaires, international review panels, action-oriented workshops and international comparisons. Among the core questions addressed for each place are: Is the scale of entrepreneurship training right, do training programmes have the right content, is the right set of teaching methods employed, and are programmes accessible? Universities,

governments and development agencies are encouraged to take part so that our body of knowledge on entrepreneurship approaches can grow and practice can improve on the ground.

## Note

[1] The author acknowledges valuable input and material for this chapter from Andrea-Rosalinde Hofer and Marco Marchese and research assistance from Barbara Barone, all of the OECD LEED Division Secretariat. The chapter also draws on material prepared by consultants for the review of university entrepreneurship support in Berlin, namely Alain Fayolle, Magnus Gulbrandsen, Paul Hannon, Rebecca Harding, Asa Lindholm Dahlstrand and Phillip Phan.

## References

Acs, Z., Audretsch, D., Braunerhjelm, P. and Carlsson, B. (2004) The Missing Link: The Knowledge Filter and Entrepreneurship in Economic Growth, Centre for Economic Policy Performance Working Paper 4538, Centre for Economic Policy Research, London.

Botham, R. and Mason, C. (2007) *Good Practice in Enterprise Development in UK Higher Education*, National Council for Graduate Entrepreneurship Research Report 004/2007: Birmingham.

Cooney, T. (2009) What Entrepreneurship Skills Are Important to Innovation in SMEs and How Should They Be Promoted Through Policy? Paper prepared for the OECD conference on SMEs, Entrepreneurship and Innovation in Udine, Italy, October 2009, OECD LEED Programme, Paris.

Cooney, T. and Murray, T. (2008) *Entrepreneurship Education in the Third-Level Sector in Ireland*, National Council of Graduate Entrepreneurship: Birmingham.

European Commission. (2008) Entrepreneurship in Higher Education, Especially in Non-Business Studies, final report of the Expert Group,

European Commission Enterprise and Industry Directorate-General, Brussels.

Gibb, A. (2007) *Towards the Entrepreneurial University: Entrepreneurship Education as a Lever for Change*, National Council for Graduate Entrepreneurship (NCGE): Birmingham.

Henry, C., Hill, F. and Leitch, C. (2005) Entrepreneurship Education Training: Can Entrepreneurship Be Taught? Part I, *Entrepreneurship Education and Training*, 47.2, 98–111.

Hoffman, A., Vibholt, N. M., Larsen, M. and Moffet, M. (2008) Benchmarking Entrepreneurship Education across US, Canadian and Danish Universities, ch. 6, 139–164, in J. Potter (ed.) *Entrepreneurship and Higher Education*, OECD: Paris.

Kuratko, D. (2005) The Emergence of Entrepreneurship Education: Development, Trends, and Challenges, *Entrepreneurship Theory and Practice*, 29.5, 577–598.

NGCE. (2007) *Enterprise and Entrepreneurship in Higher Education*, National Council for Graduate Entrepreneurship: Birmingham, UK.

NIRAS Consultants, FORA and ECON Pöyry. (2008) *Survey of Entrepreneurship Education in Higher Education in Europe*, European Commission, Directorate-General for Enterprise and Industry: Brussels.

OECD. (2009a) *Measuring Entrepreneurship: A Collection of Indicators 2009 Edition*, OECD-Eurostat Entrepreneurship Indicators Programme, OECD: Paris.

OECD. (2009b) Universities, Innovation and Entrepreneurship: Criteria and Examples of Good Practice, report prepared by the OECD Local Economic and Employment Development Division, OECD: Paris.

OECD. (2010a) *SMEs, Entrepreneurship and Innovation*, OECD: Paris.

OECD. (2010b) From Strategy to Practice in University Entrepreneurship Support, final report on Strengthening Entrepreneurship and Economic Development in Eastern Germany: Youth, Entrepreneurship and Innovation prepared by the OECD Local Economic and Employment Development Division, OECD: Paris.

OECD. (2010c) Shooting for the Moon: Good Practices in Local Youth Entrepreneurship Support, report prepared by the OECD Local Economic and Employment Development Division, OECD: Paris.

Oosterbeek, H., van Praag, M., and Ijsselstein, A. (2010) The Impact of Entrepreneurship Education on Entrepreneurship Skills and Motivation. *European Economic Review*, 54, 442–454.

Potter, J. (2008) *Entrepreneurship and Higher Education*, OECD: Paris.

Solomon, G. (2008) Entrepreneurship Education in the United States, ch. 4, 95–118, in J. Potter (ed.) *Entrepreneurship and Higher Education*, OECD: Paris.

Varblane, U., Mets, T. and Formica, P. (2008) Developments in the Teaching of Entrepreneurship in European Transition Economies, ch. 8, 193–212, in J. Potter (ed.) *Entrepreneurship and Higher Education*, OECD: Paris.

Wilson, K. (2004) Entrepreneurship Education at European Universities. Results of a Joint Pilot Survey, European Foundation of Entrepreneurial Research, Hilversum, Netherlands.

# Common trajectories of regional competitiveness in the knowledge economy
## A European investigation

Maria Sole Brioschi and Lucio Cassia

**Abstract:** *This paper analyses a number of European regions which, in the last two decades, have exhibited a significant shift towards knowledge-intensive industrial sectors coupled with a considerable increase in competitiveness and growth. The analysis identifies the main factors of territorial development behind each regional renewal process and captures a number of common trajectories of regional competitiveness. Interestingly, all the regional 'success stories' are strongly dependent on the presence of a tri-polar regional innovation system that glues together firms, government institutions and academia.*

**Keywords:** *regional innovation system; regional development; regional competitiveness; actors in regional development; Europe*

*The authors are with the Department of Management and Information Technology, Faculty of Engineering, University of Bergamo, Viale Marconi 5, 24044 Dalmine (BG), Italy. E-mail: brioschi@unibg.it lucio.cassia@unibg.it*

There has recently been a growing interest on the part of both regional economists and geographers in the phenomenon of the geographical agglomeration of economic activity. One reason for this may lie in the so-called 'location paradox', also known in the literature as the 'puzzle of sticky places in a slippery space' (Markusen, 1996) – in other words, the fact that in a more and more globalized world, where distance should not be an obstacle and capital and knowledge should travel freely and at high speed, we observe a tendency towards the spatial concentration of economic activities.

In this research context, the aim of this paper is to identify the main success factors behind the development of a number of European regions into knowledge economies (that is, economies directly based on the production, distribution and use of knowledge and information). The emergence of the knowledge economy concept, based on the recognition of knowledge creation and technical progress as important determinants of economic growth and competitive advantage at both national and local levels, was fuelled, especially during 1990–2000, by rapid technical progress in computing, biotechnology, telecommunications and transportation. This profoundly changed the way economies, organizations and governments work. Moreover, the marked growth in knowledge-intensive services, coupled with the profound shift in workplaces towards high-skilled labour, signified the transition from the industrial to the post-industrial era. Within this framework, regional economies (as seats of value-added activities, institutions and organizations) benefit from synergies and interdependencies among territorial actors and need to maintain a high level of competitiveness and attention to local processes of change in order to support firms in their renewal processes.

In this paper, we consider seven European regions which, in the last two decades, have exhibited a significant shift towards knowledge-intensive industrial sectors coupled with a remarkable increase in competitiveness and growth. We analyse these regions'

development processes with the twofold aim of capturing the main determinants behind each regional success story and identifying a number of common trajectories of regional competitiveness.

The paper is organized as follows. The next section reviews the key features of the literature on regional economic development. The subsequent section identifies the main factors of development for each of the seven regions under inquiry. We then give a tentative generalization of the results, suggesting a taxonomy of trajectories of regional competitiveness, each of which encompasses a number of development factors and is relevant to various regions. Finally, we present our conclusions.

# Review of the literature on regional economic development

The importance of regions and the location of firms was recognized in the economic literature more than a century ago. In fact, Marshall developed the notion of the industrial district in the *Principles of Economics* (1890) and in *Industry and Trade* (1919), studying the industrial configuration of the English region of Lancashire and establishing that the economic development of the area was driven by a network of small and very small producers operating on an optimal scale thanks to the division of labour. Marshall introduced the notion of agglomeration economies to take account of the locally bounded competitiveness he observed, suggesting a threefold classification of centripetal forces: labour market pooling, access to a great variety of specialized intermediate goods and services, and knowledge spillovers. In his view, firms in clusters benefited from better access to workers, had easier and more efficient relations with suppliers and customers and absorbed knowledge accumulated by other firms, suppliers, customers and workers via market and non-market channels.

The debate on Marshallian externalities found new impetus in the 1970s and 1980s when, in addition to the perceived importance of mutual trust and cooperation among rival firms and the recognized supporting role of local institutions, his notions were employed by a variety of scholars to detail the industrial organization and economic structure of industrial districts (see, among others, Becattini, 1979; Brusco, 1982; Piore and Sabel, 1984; Pyke *et al,* 1990). Furthermore, the concepts developed by Marshall were adopted in the 1990s by the literature on local economic development to account for the success of a number of high-tech regions, such as Silicon Valley, Route 128 and Cambridge. The theoretical contributions in this area can essentially be grouped along two research streams according to which territorial actor is considered to be the fundamental engine of regional dynamics.

The first stream of research may be identified as starting from the ideas of the *Groupe de Recherche Européen sur les Milieux Innovateurs* (GREMI), whose pioneering work dates back to Aydalot (1986), Aydalot and Keeble (1988) and

Camagni (1991). According to this school, local development must be interpreted in the light of the notions of *untraded interdependencies* among firms (Perroux, 1950a, 1950b; Leontief, 1953; Richardson, 1973; Dosi, 1988), *innovative milieux* and regional *processes of collective learning* (Camagni, 1991; Lorenz, 1992; Lawson, 1997; Lawson and Lorenz, 1997; Keeble *et al,* 1999). In particular, the notion of collective learning developed by this group refers to the ability of an innovative milieu to generate and circulate innovative behaviour by the firms that belong to it. The local milieu may be defined as 'a set of territorial relationships encompassing in a coherent way a production system, different economic and social actors, a specific culture and a representation system, and generating a dynamic collective learning process' (Keeble *et al,* 1999). The formation of untraded interdependencies refers to a community of shared conventions, informal rules and habits that coordinate economic actors under conditions of uncertainty. The main argument of this school of thought is that interaction among local firms fosters local development by reducing the degree of uncertainty the firms face in a rapidly changing technological environment.

The second line of research is associated with the work of Asheim (1996), Morgan (1997a) and Simmie (1997), who developed the concept of the *learning region,* and with that of Cooke (1992), Cooke *et al* (1997, 1998, 2004) and Braczyk *et al* (1998), who studied regional dynamics based on the concept of the *regional innovation system* (RIS). Innovation may be defined as the commercialization of original knowledge – that is, the transformation of knowledge into novel wealth-creating technologies, products and services (Cooke *et al*, 2003). The region is viewed as the key jurisdiction for innovation, given the social and often tacit nature of innovation, 'animated as it is by the agglomeration of specialized and localized skills, knowledge, learning, public and private institutions and other resources that make up the region' (Cooke *et al*, 2003). In particular, the focus of the RIS approach is on determining a certain institutional configuration capable of promoting innovation within a region. The link of this second school of thought with the traditional literature on industrial districts may be identified in the common importance given to the 'institutional foundations' of regional competitive advantage.

We could then conclude that the main difference between the two contemporary strands of research on regional economic development is that the collective learning literature posits that local development is powered mainly by local firms' networking activities, whereas the regional innovation system approach focuses on the key role played by local (private-sector and governmental) institutions. In sum, since Marshall, the model of local economic development has been bi-polar, built on the two variables *firms* and *local institutions*, and the various theories developed in the literature have differed from one another essentially in terms of the relative importance given to each of the two basic components of development.

More recently, and in parallel with the increase in empirical investigations into European high-tech clusters, Etzkowitz and Leydesdorff (1997, 2000) have highlighted the active presence of an additional variable – the (technical and scientific) *university* – and have developed the Triple Helix model. This conceptual model endeavours to account for the existence of a new configuration of institutional forces (university, firms and local institutions) within the innovation system. Within this model, the university, defined as an institution focused on the production and diffusion of knowledge (Etzkowitz and Leydesdorff, 2000), represents a key element in the innovativeness of the local system. In this sense, universities are referred to as 'entrepreneurial' institutions, involved in a 'spiral' of relations with the other two institutional spheres (public and private) along the paths of industrial innovation and policy making. Now, the fact that universities are important sources of new knowledge and that their presence nurtures the local labour market with people who have technical and managerial skills has been well known in the literature for a long time (see, for example, OECD, 1981). However, that the university represents one of the chief components of local economic development by fostering innovation (through research collaborations with firms and institutions) and by stimulating the local entrepreneurial spirit (through spin-off activities) is, as has been stated, the outcome of relatively recent theoretical and empirical studies (for the latter see, for example, Athreye, 2001; Gerszewski and Krieger, 2002; Paci and Usai, 2003).

The case study analysis presented in this paper is focused on the regional innovation system literature. With regard to this approach, Edquist (2005, p 186) points out that 'it is certainly not a formal theory, in the sense of providing specific propositions regarding causal relations among variables. [. . .] Because of the relative absence of well-established empirical regularities, "systems of innovations" should be labelled an approach or a conceptual framework rather than a theory'. In the same vein, we adopt the RIS concept as a framework to analyse the regions we consider to be virtuous models of regional development.

## Main factors of regional competitiveness

In this paper, we consider seven European regions that have recently exhibited significant growth and increased competitiveness: Finland, Sweden, Ireland, Scotland, Wales, Cambridge (UK) and Grenoble (France) (see Table 1). The choice of these regions was motivated by the fact that, after experiencing a period of recession (or at least of economic slowdown) or a financial crisis during the 1980s and 1990s, they now show significant signs of renewal. The crises seem to have given these regions the opportunity to implement a strategic change in their economies, leading to a rapid increase in the levels of output and employment and resulting in structural transformation and a resurge in competitiveness. We analyse their transformation through

the lens of the Triple Helix regional innovation system approach with the aims of identifying the main competitive factors behind each regional success story and capturing common trajectories of regional competitiveness.[1]

We chose a comparative case study methodology because, by highlighting generalities and specificities of the regions selected, it provides important insights into the drivers of regional development. As advocated by Edquist (2005, p 201), 'comparative case studies have a great potential, comparing innovation systems of various kinds as well as the determinants of innovation processes within them'. Similarly, Cooke et al (1998, p 12) argue that 'conducting such comparable studies can lead to identification of some functional equivalents for specific as well as generic problems within the innovation process'. Nevertheless, we are aware that comparative case study methods cannot provide conclusive outcomes, as the description of the unique features of the regional development processes under investigation can raise questions about the repeatability of the same phenomenon in a different context (Doloreux, 2002).

*Finland*

Finland occupies the extreme north-eastern part of Europe and has about 5·2 million inhabitants. More than 65% of its surface is covered by forests, while only 8% is devoted to agricultural land and human settlements. Its geographical position has traditionally allowed the country to act as a base for international trade

Table 1. Summary statistics of the regions under investigation.

| | Population, 2003 (thousands) | GDP per capita, 2002 (PPS) | GDP per capita, 2002 (% EU 25) | Real GDP growth rate, 2004–05 (%) | Unemployment rate, 2004 (%) | Total students, 2003 (% population) | GERD, 2004 (%GDP) |
|---|---|---|---|---|---|---|---|
| Sweden | 8,940.8 | 24,304.3 | 114.8 | 2.7 | 6.5 | 27.3 | 3.74 |
| Finland | 5,206.3 | 24,089.6 | 113.8 | 1.5 | 8.8 | 25.6 | 3.51 |
| Ireland | 3,963.7 | 28,088.7 | 132.7 | 4.7 | 4.5 | 25.3 | 1.20 |
| Scotland | 5,054.8 | 23,776.1 | 112.3 | na | 5.7 | 27.6 | na |
| Wales | 2,918.7 | 19,102.7 | 90.2 | na | 4.5 | 30.3 | na |
| Cambridgeshire | 2,190.9[a] | 26,429.6 | 124.8 | na | 3.5 | na | na |
| Isère | 5,835.5[b] | 23,529.9 | 111.1 | na | 8.4 | 24.8[b] | na |
| EU 25 | 454,930.9 | 21,170.1 | 100.0 | 1.6 | 9.2 | na | 1.90 |
| EU 15 | 383,047.4 | 23,161.5 | 109.4 | 1.5 | 8.2 | na | 1.95 |

[a]East Anglia region; [b]Rhône–Alpes region.

Source: Eurostat.

among EU, Nordic European countries and Russia. After a very severe depression in the early 1990s, largely caused by a domestic financial crisis and the collapse of the USSR, since the mid-1990s, Finland has emerged as one of the most flourishing, dynamic and competitive OECD countries. The average annual GDP growth rate increased from an average of –3.5% in 1991–93 to an average of 4.7% in 1994–2000. Unemployment dropped from 20% in 1993 to about 9% in 2000 (Blomström *et al*, 2002).

Traditionally dominated by raw material–based industries – paper, wood and metal products – the Finnish economy recovered by rapidly concentrating on high-technology products, particularly telecommunications equipment. Within a decade, Finland had converted itself from one of the largest net importers of ICT products in Europe to one of the largest net exporters of high-tech goods and the largest exporter of telecommunications equipment (Berggren and Laestadius, 2003). The increase of export specialization in telecoms equipment (Table 2) occurred in spite of the very high export specialization in forest-based products (the highest among the OECD countries), which also represent a very significant share of Finland's exports (Table 3).

Nokia may be regarded as the chief engine and symbol of Finland's transformative process, having itself moved its core business from pulp and paper products to communications in the early 1990s.[2] This shift was triggered by a peculiarity of the Finnish market – the telephone network, as a legacy of Russian rule,[3] had never been

**Table 2. Export specialization indices for telecommunications equipment (Standard International Trade Classification, Revision 3, Div 76), OECD=1·00.**

|         | 1988 | 1990 | 1993 | 1996 | 1998 | 2000 |
|---------|------|------|------|------|------|------|
| Finland | 1.02 | 1.40 | 1.66 | 2.25 | 3.79 | 4.35 |
| Sweden  | 1.36 | 1.51 | 1.85 | 2.31 | 3.31 | 3.24 |

*Source:* Berggren and Laestadius (2003).

**Table 3. Shares of output and exports of the main Finnish industrial clusters, 1980–2000 (as % of total output and total exports).**

|          |         | 1980 | 1990 | 2000 |
|----------|---------|------|------|------|
| ICT      | Output  | 4.6  | 7.6  | 29.4 |
|          | Exports | 4    | 12   | 30   |
| Forest   | Output  | 25.3 | 23.8 | 21   |
| products | Exports | 45   | 39   | 29   |
| Metal    | Output  | 8.5  | 10.6 | 10.1 |
| products | Exports | 25   | 31   | 24   |

*Source:* IMF (2001), Table 2.

under the government monopoly. The presence of several telephone operators had two main effects on the development of domestic telecommunications. First, it tightened competition for customers and contributed to fast technological change in the industry. The pioneering first-generation Nordic cellular network, NMT, was launched in the early 1980s, and its successor, the European digital mobile network GSM, was introduced in 1991 by Nokia. Trained with the Nordic network experience, Finland exhibited an extraordinarily high penetration ratio for mobile phones. Nokia recognized that cellular phones 'were entering mass markets' (Berggren and Laestadius, 2003, p 103) and strategically began to develop customer-oriented phones, focusing on style, colour and user friendliness. Today, Finland has the highest mobile phone density in the world, with 65·0 mobile subscribers per 100 inhabitants compared to an OECD average of 32·4 (OECD, 2001).

Secondly, Nokia took advantage of the presence of the multi-operator telecommunications industry by setting up a number of joint ventures (mostly R&D) with the public operator and with foreign ICT companies operating domestically. This strategy allowed the Finnish company to integrate its technological know-how and to finance the investment projects needed for the development of the new digital networks.

However, Nokia's competitiveness is due not only to the company's ability to seize the opportunities of a rapidly growing market coupled with a marked international orientation, but also to its renowned strategy, aimed at improving the quality of human capital and managerial skills. From the late 1970s, Nokia invested heavily in both specialized in-house training programmes to raise the educational level of existing staff and financial aid to Finnish technical and scientific universities to spread knowledge among the younger generation. Nokia University was founded in 1980. Today, Nokia is one of the world's largest corporations, with sales of V34–2 billion (of which almost 99% is exported, mainly to the USA, the UK, Germany and China) and a market capitalization of V7T6 billion, equal to 35·2% of the Helsinki stock exchange's total market capitalization.

Nokia's development drove the growth of hundreds of local suppliers, giving rise to a remarkable increase in the Finnish ICT sector: as shown in Table 3, between 1990 and 2000, the share of production of the ITC cluster in the Finnish economy surged from 7·6% to 29·4%, and the corresponding share of exports rose from 12% to 30%.

In addition to the key role played by Nokia and the ICT cluster, Finland's rapid increase in growth and competitiveness since the early 1990s may also be explained by government efforts to raise research intensity in the economy. The government's first area of intervention was that of science and technology, with policies aimed at rising R&D investments. In particular, research collaborations between universities and industry were promoted; in 1983, the National Agency for Technology, TEKES, was founded with the objective of supporting industrial and applied research; in 1987 the national Scientific Council was rethought and renamed the Science and Technology Policy Council (STPC), whose function was to act as a think tank for the main actors of Finland's economic, business and scientific communities. In those years, the government also took steps in the direction of liberalizing the financial sector, which in turn offered new financing opportunities to the most innovative high-technology firms.

Both Nokia's mounting role within the ICT sector and the effects of research-enhancing public policies can be appreciated if one considers the extraordinary increase in R&D investments in Finland since 1985. Taking into account both public and private investments, R&D expenses as a percentage of GDP rose from

1·55% in 1985 to 2·17% in 1993 and up to 3·40% in 2001. Nokia itself accounts for almost 30% of R&D investments: more than one third of its 58,000 employees work in a research division in one of its 55 centres and labs located in 15 different countries. However, even excluding Nokia, Finland's R&D investments in the year 2000 would have topped 2·4% of GDP – a higher share than the OECD average (Blomström *et al,* 2002).

*Sweden*

With 8·9 million inhabitants and more than 60% of its land covered by forests, Sweden's success story is in many respects similar to that of Finland, although there are a few noteworthy differences. Sweden was severely hit by a domestic real estate and financial crisis that spread to all sectors of the economy during 1991–93, but it rapidly regained productivity and competitiveness: exports rose from 30% of GDP in the early 1990s to almost 50% in 2000 (Blomström *et al,* 2002). As for Finland, the development of Sweden was led by the ICT sector, in turn headed by Nokia's Swedish competitor Ericsson (Table 2).

Unlike Nokia, Ericsson already had deep roots in the telecommunications business when the modern mobile phone technology emerged in the 1970s, as the company was founded in 1876 to manufacture telephones and switchboards. In the development of the Swedish telecommunications industry, Ericsson had a key partner, the state-owned Televerket, which had started to invest and work on mobile systems (regarding them as a 'public good') since the 1950s.

The relationship between Ericsson and Televerket fits the concept of the public–private 'development pair' suggested by Fridlund (1999), as several technologies (from the digital switches of fixed telephones to the advanced mobile technology–related equipment) were developed together. Cooperation with Televerket allowed Ericsson to comply with the high technological standards set by the public operator and to share the long-term financing of R&D costs of mobile technologies in their early development stage, when the business was very risky and its outcomes uncertain. In particular, Ericsson and Televerket (together with researchers from four Swedish technical universities) set up a research group in 1977 to develop the specifications for the GSM network. Interestingly, this research group, which would have later made Ericsson a world player, was not recognized by its top management until the early 1990s when, with the breakthrough of the GSM technology, the company finally appreciated the group's work and recognized the importance of mobile handset production.

As in the case of Nokia, the key to Ericsson's success was the management's international orientation. By adapting its production to the different standards of various countries, it started to expand abroad. Ericsson succeeded in entering the US market very early, and by the late 1990s, it had become one of the world-leading cellular infrastructure suppliers, with 30% of the US market and competitive positions in the UK, Germany, Italy and Japan (Blomström and Kokko, 2002). Paradoxically, Ericsson's international perspective and success in the export business stem from the strong market share held historically in the home country by the public operator and system manufacturer Televerket (Berggren and Laestadius, 2003). Today, Ericsson has sales of 151·8 billion Krona (V16–3 billion, of which 95% is exported), more than 56,000 employees and a market capitalization of 469.3 billion Krona (V50–4 billion), equal to a share of 11·2% of the Stockholm total market capitalization.

Again as in the case of Nokia, Ericsson's performance and the rapid growth of the ICT sector in Sweden must be considered within a wider framework so as to include the role of government institutions and public policies in supporting knowledge diffusion and contributing to the improvement of the business climate. First, public policies were put in place to encourage Swedish firms' R&D investments. For instance, tax deductions were introduced for R&D spending, and in 1968, the National Board of Technical Development (STU) was funded to support private projects of applied technical research and to plan incentives for firms' research spending. As a result, Sweden has been one of the world's leading countries for research intensity from as far back as the 1960s. In 1993, Sweden became the first country in the world to have a share of R&D investments over GDP of 3·27% and it has maintained the top position ever since, reaching a share of 4·28% in 2001.

Investments in higher education were another important factor in Sweden's development. Relative to other OECD countries, in fact,

at the beginning of the 1990s, the Swedish manufacturing industry exhibited a low ratio of professionals with third-level education to total employment, particularly in technical and scientific disciplines. This was undoubtedly partly due to the high and progressive income tax burden, but it was also attributable to the limited supply of most university programmes. In response to this lack, measures were taken by the government to expand academic courses and programmes, and various adult education schemes were put in place by firms with governmental aid.

## Ireland

Ireland has some four million inhabitants, over a third of whom live in the Dublin area. Its demography differs from that of most EU countries in that it is characterized by a younger population (38% are under 25) and a higher birth rate (see Table 4). This demographic structure has been a factor in Ireland's economic development and recent growth.

Over the last 15 years, Ireland has undergone a structural transformation, moving from a slow-paced, low-skills and low-pay economy to a dynamic, high-skills and high-pay economy based on knowledge-intensive industries. As shown in Table 4, between 1988 and 1998, the Irish economy grew at a much greater pace than the EU (with differentials even rising in the second half of the 1990s), exhibiting an annual average growth rate in GDP of 6·5%, against a 2·0% growth rate in the EU 15.[4] By 1997 the Irish per capita GDP had exceeded the EU average, meaning that high growth rates had produced a remarkable

**Table 4. GDP and population growth in Ireland.**

|  | Period | Ireland | EU 15 |
|---|---|---|---|
| Annual average % change in GDP | 1988–98 | 6.5 | 2.0 |
|  | 1988–93 | 4.4 | 1.7 |
|  | 1993–98 | 8.7 | 2.5 |
| Annual average % change in population | 1988–98 | 0.5 | 0.4 |
|  | 1988–93 | 0.2 | 0.5 |
|  | 1993–98 | 0.7 | 0.3 |
| Per-capita GDP (PPS), EU 15 = 100 | 1989 | 66.3 | 100.0 |
|  | 1991 | 74.7 | 100.0 |
|  | 1993 | 82.5 | 100.0 |
|  | 1995 | 93.3 | 100.0 |
|  | 1997 | 103.7 | 100.0 |
|  | 1999 | 112.2 | 100.0 |
|  | 2001 | 117.9 | 100.0 |

*Source:* Farrell (2004).

degree of convergence in income levels during the 1990s (Table 4).

There were several determinants in Ireland's conversion into a modern and competitive country. The key factor in what is often referred to in the literature as the 'Irish miracle' was the ability of the region to attract substantial foreign direct investments (FDIs) through attractive packages of public grants, concessions and tax incentives in favour of foreign investors (including a 12% corporate tax rate compared to a European average of around 32%) and, through the establishment of a regional development agency, the Industrial Development Agency (IDA). The policy orientation towards the attraction of FDIs began in the late 1950s after the failure of the protectionist policy that had characterized the indigenous industry since the declaration of Ireland's independence. This policy of FDI support has been systematically cultivated by the various governments that have ruled the country in the last 15 years, generating a climate of

certainty and trust which is crucial for the location choices of multinational enterprises (MNEs). As a result, by the late 1990s, multinational corporations were employing over 40% of the total workforce and accounted for almost 90% of exports (Farrell, 2004). With regard to software, for instance, today Ireland is the world's fifth-largest producer and second-largest exporter, with about 90% of the output and exports originating from overseas MNEs located in the country (O'Gorman and Kautonen, 2004).

The Industrial Development Agency was founded with the specific aim of pursuing policies of industrial development and policies designed to attract FDIs. From the 1970s, the agency identified industries such as electronics, pharmaceuticals and chemicals as its key targets and focused on the strongest companies in these industries as potential sources of FDI projects. The USA was also chosen as the preferred country for incoming foreign investments. As a consequence of the proactive role of the IDA, several multinational enterprises, such as Apple, Verbatim, Intel, Microsoft, IBM, HP and Kodak, set up operations in Ireland. This organization has been a major force for Irish industrial development, and it is considered to be among the world's best agencies for attracting foreign investment (O'Connor, 2001).

Another key factor in Ireland's transformation was EU membership, obtained in 1973. Access to the European Single Market boosted international trade and made Ireland more attractive for MNEs looking for a strategic (low-cost) position from which to penetrate the growing European market. As a matter of fact, Ireland was a magnet for FDIs in the years immediately following its access to the EU. Moreover, it made good use of the European Structural Funds (ERDF, ESF) received since its entry into the EU, heavily investing in physical infrastructure such as telecommunications, roads, seaports and airports (36·3% of total funds received), human resource development (28·4%) and private-sector development, especially investment and innovation activities (ESRI, 1997).[5] An important aspect of the endowment of European Funds is that it forced the Irish government into medium-term and long-term policy planning, bringing short-sighted and intermittent investment policies to a halt.

Central to the identification of Ireland as location choice for FDIs is the high educational level of the workforce. More than 40% of the people who make up the Irish workforce have been educated to tertiary level (against the EU average of 20%), and more than 80% have a secondary school diploma, ranking Ireland among the top OECD countries for educational level. Since the 1990s, the Irish government has pursued a strategy of investment in science, technology and innovation, devoting substantial funds to these sectors. In particular, between 1989 and 1991, nine Programmes in Advanced Technology (PATs)[6] were established between the tertiary education sector and the industrial development arm of the state and its agencies with the aim of channelling expertise and funds in a coherent way towards key technological industries. Both investments in education and the presence of MNEs supplied the Irish workforce and managers with high skills and competences. Furthermore, many highly educated Irish emigrants returned to Ireland with experience and skills acquired abroad.

*Wales and Scotland*

The British regions of Wales and Scotland, with populations of 2·9 and 5 million, respectively (4·9% and 8·5% of the UK's total population), have also experienced a profound transformation of their industrial structure in the last 15 years, moving from economies dominated by declining sectors such as coal mining and steel to higher growth and more profitable high-tech and service sectors.

In the early 1980s the UK faced an economic slowdown: sea trade was less and less dependent on British seaports, heavy industry was subject to an unprecedented process of rescaling and coal mining was disappearing. The UK government's response to this situation was to promote the country strongly to foreign entrepreneurs, and in a few years this policy brought substantial investment inflows from Europe, the USA and Japan. In this context, the regional development of Wales and Scotland may be associated with that of Ireland, for their industrial renewal was driven largely by inward investment. Looking at the regional shares of new jobs attributable to FDIs in the UK since the 1980s, it can be seen that Scotland and Wales were the foremost destinations for overseas projects. Scotland has the longest tradition in foreign enterprise, ranking first almost invariably throughout the 1980s and the 1990s, whereas Wales gradually achieved competitiveness – so that in the 1990s, it was able to attract up to 20% of total UK inward investment projects (Tewdwr-Jones and Phelps, 2000). In Wales, following the 100,000 job losses during the 1970s and 1980s due to the crisis in the coal mining sector, new overseas investments generated 160,000 jobs, and the unemployment rate dropped from 7·3% in 1989 to 5·3% in 2001. Scotland also exhibits a declining unemployment rate since the 1980s by virtue of FDI attraction, even if the unemployment rate in 2001 was still somewhat higher than the UK average (6·6% against 5·1%).

The recent economic development in Scotland and Wales crucially depended on the proactive role of the two regional development agencies – Scottish Enterprise (SE) and the Welsh Development Agency (WDA) – in attracting and supporting foreign investors. As Morgan (1997b, p 70) notes, 'in less favoured regions, where private institutions are often thin on the ground, public sector agencies invariably have to assume the leading role in animating economic development'. In the years following their inception, these agencies were essentially engaged in ensuring that the basic conditions were in place for the location of foreign enterprises in their regions – assisting, for example, in the search for building sites and providing administrative and financial advice. In the later years, the agencies' role became more significant, as the needs of foreign investors were continuously developing and they required more and more social infrastructure, skilled labour and networking opportunities with other firms. As a result, the two agencies began to participate in the formulation of regional development strategies in cooperation with the other key actors in the regional system – local authorities, other institutions, universities and the business community – thus contributing to the process of regional 'institutional thickening' and the formation of interdependencies among territorial actors in Scotland and Wales. In this regard, the Welsh Development Agency and Scottish Enterprise promoted a number of *ad hoc* institutions. In Wales among the most significant initiatives were Team Wales, a programme bringing together local actors from the private and the public sectors with the purpose of establishing strategies to make Wales an attractive business location, and Eurolink and Global Link, which aimed to promote the internationalization of indigenous firms via the foundation of partnerships with foreign enterprises. Similar initiatives promoted in Scotland by Scottish Enterprise were

Global Connection, to help local firms to access international markets, and Small Business Gateway, a vehicle to assist the development of new start-ups.

The strong presence of MNEs is concentrated in electronics and IT, which represent a substantial component of the two regions' industry and exports. In Scotland, for example, foreign manufacturing firms employ about one quarter of total manufacturing employment – some estimates indicate that this figure doubles if one includes the indirect effects of employment in related supplier and service sectors (Collinson, 2000). The key role played by these institutions was soon recognized by the central government, and in 1999, regional development agencies were founded in the other UK regions.

Beyond 'institutional capacity', other important factors explaining the ability of Wales and Scotland to attract inward investment are the light regulation of the labour market, the presence of skilled work and, last but not least, the English language.

### Cambridge

The term 'Cambridge Phenomenon' was coined by Segal, Quince and Wicksteed in 1985 to describe the mushrooming of over 300 high-tech firms in the Cambridge region, roughly defined as encompassing the area around the university town of Cambridge up to a distance of 25 km. This number of firms has grown steadily over the years, and today the region hosts almost 1,000, employing over 52,000 people and operating in various technology-based sectors (R&D, computer hardware, computer services, electrical and electronic, chemicals, instrument engineering, biomedical). The literature on the Cambridge Phenomenon (see, for example, Castells and Hall, 1994; Druilhe and Garnsey, 2000) associates the origins of the cluster with the creation of the Cambridge Science Park, which occurred in 1970.

What caused a high-technology cluster of firms to locate in a rural area, poorly served in terms of infrastructural services and communications links and historically far from the country's primary centres of industrial development? In other words, and directly to the point of our study, what are the key factors that allowed the Cambridge region to become so competitive that it came to be seen as Europe's Silicon Valley?

First, there is little doubt that the active role of the University of Cambridge was central to the emergence of the phenomenon. In addition to the university's reputation for excellence and prestige (certainly important in attracting high-quality workers), the key factor in the transformation process of Cambridge has been the liberal policy of the university towards faculty members, who are free to engage in outside work and to exploit their know-how and skills commercially (Segal, Quince and Wicksteed, 1985, 2000; Keeble *et al,* 1999; Druilhe and Garnsey, 2000; Athreye, 2001). This policy encouraged academics to start up businesses or become technical and scientific consultants to the high-tech firms of the region: as a result, 30% of the firms in the cluster have their direct origin in the university – even if the university may be considered, directly or indirectly, to be the source of all the cluster's firms (Segal, Quince and Wicksteed, 1985).

The cooperative climate between university and industry may also be assessed by the extent of the research collaboration that has taken place since the 1990s: giant corporations such as Microsoft, Oracle, Unilever, British Petroleum and Hutchinson Whompoa substantially financed the setting up of research laboratories and centres to be operated by Cambridge University researchers and scientists.

A second important factor adding to the phenomenon was the availability of private financing and business support services. In the late 1970s, Barclays Bank took a strategic decision to open an office in Cambridge to finance first-time high-tech entrepreneurs and help them develop and implement a business plan. Since then, a large number of banks and venture capital firms, along with a wide array of other business support facilities (among which is the British Patent Office), have settled in Cambridge and helped local high-tech businesses to start up and prosper (Segal, 1992). In addition to the Cambridge Science Park, which today accounts for 71 companies with some 5,000 employees, in 1987, another key business support initiative was launched: the St John's Innovation Centre. This centre was established to provide incubation facilities, finance and management programmes for high-technology firms located in the region.

A third important reason for the Cambridge Phenomenon lies in the marked entrepreneurial motivation and talent in evidence. This was triggered by the excellence of the people attracted to the region and the liberal policy of the university, as noted above, but also by an additional factor – the absence of an industrial past. The fact that in the Cambridge area, there has never been heavy industry or a unionized labour force 'has helped create a labour market and a general attitude in which flexibility and individualism have never been suppressed' (Segal, 1992).

Last but not least, networking activities among local firms played an important role in developing a cooperative and supportive business environment within the emerging cluster. For instance, the Cambridge Network was established in 1997 among Cambridge IT firms and it set up a Website, Cambridge Connect, with the aim of increasing member firms' external visibility and promoting business support facilities available in the region (Athreye, 2001). The Greater Cambridge Partnership was founded a year later by local firms, local institutions and the university to develop a consensus on local development strategies.

*Grenoble*

The economic development of Grenoble exhibits striking similarities to that of Cambridge. Both cities are well-known examples of high-technology poles, characterized by a high birth rate of new technology-based firms and clustered around a major science park. Among the first science parks to be created in France, the Zone pour l'Innovation et les Réalisations Scientifiques et Techniques (ZIRST) was founded in Grenoble in 1972 as the result of a project carried out by local entrepreneurs, academics and civil servants. The cluster initially developed with a number of spin-offs from computing firms and expanded through the formation of academic firms, thanks to a favourable climate and technology transfer policies in universities and research centres. By the mid-1980s, there were 130 firms on the ZIRST science park (Bernardy de Sigoyer and Boisgontier, 1988). Today, the park hosts 270 enterprises accounting for some 8,500 employees, mainly operating in the computing, electronics and communications industries (Table 5).

Historically speaking, there are no common factors that would have led to the expectation that Grenoble and Cambridge would have become high-technology centres. As discussed above, for centuries Cambridge was a sleepy university town built in a rural area with virtually no industry. In contrast, the alpine city of Grenoble became involved in manufacturing activities as early as the end of the 19th century, with the development of hydroelectricity for the paper industry. Hydroelectricity fostered the region's economic expansion, favouring the development of other sectors, and encouraged the formation of academic expertise.

The key element to the emergence of a high-technology pole in Grenoble was the local innovative culture, which was based on strong relationships between the university, research and industry. In particular, the scientific community had historically developed as a result of industrial needs. For example, going back to the origins of Grenoble's industrialization, local entrepreneurs from the hydroelectric sector pushed the formation of applied research institutes, and in the 1950s, the nuclear industry developed thanks to the work of Professor Louis Néel, the Nobel laureate, who was a professor at Grenoble University.

Through the accumulation of scientific resources by virtue of a continuous interchange between industry and science, Grenoble is now the second university and research pole in France (after Paris) with about 55,000 students and 13,000 research staff in four universities, 10 engineering schools (such as the Institut National Polytechnique de Grenoble, INPG), five public research institutes (such as the Centre d'Études Nucléaires de Grenoble, CENG), a number of supranational research centres (such as the European Synchrotron Radiation Facility) and several corporate research institutes. The main areas of specialization are electronics, engineering, computing, physics, biotechnology and medical science.

On the basis of such a massive presence, the technology transfer policies of academic and research

**Table 5. Distribution of Grenoble ZIRST high-technology firms by sector of activity (2004).**

| Sector | Grenoble ZIRST (%) |
|---|---|
| Software and hardware | 31 |
| Electronics | 16 |
| Communication | 11 |
| Biomedical | 8 |
| Automation | 8 |
| CAO/DAD | 7 |
| Mechanics | 7 |
| Constructions | 6 |
| Telecom | 6 |
| *Base (270 firms)* | *100* |

*Source:* ZIRST (2005).

centres nurtured the cluster with high-technology activities. Particularly in the 1980s, many new technology-based firms were founded by academics and researchers via spin-offs from an academic institution or a research centre. For instance, several enterprises spun out from the CENG or one of its applied research centres. Also, the INPG encouraged its graduates to create enterprises (even establishing an incubator) to the extent that in 1988, it was estimated that 40 of the 138 firms on the ZIRST had been founded by INPG graduates (Druilhe and Garnsey, 2000). The multitude of inter-firm relations and networking activities in the region is often a reflection of the fact that entrepreneurs come from the same university or the same research centre.

The high reputation of Grenoble's high-technology pole and the opportunity to take advantage of agglomeration externalities and technology spillovers attracted many R&D corporate centres to the region: Bull, Ranx-Xerox, the Maxwell Institute and Sun Microsystems are a few examples of MNEs located in the Grenoble area.

As in Cambridge, a distinctive feature of the Grenoble high-technology cluster, which today accounts for about 30,000 employees, is the absence of direct state funding.[7] The cluster firms have traditionally been founded through private channels and local initiatives. A peculiarity in this regard is that the small average size of the Grenoble cluster firm encouraged a wave of external acquisitions that, on the one hand, provided additional funding for development but, on the other hand, caused a gradual loss of control by local entrepreneurs over local businesses. Table 6 shows the size of the cluster firms on the ZIRST science park.

## Common trajectories of regional competitiveness

Based on the above investigation, we identified various factors that are driving regional competitiveness. We then divided them into three groups, according to the three territorial actors encompassing a Triple Helix regional innovation system: firms, universities and institutions.

Among the factors relevant to firms, we included entrepreneurial motivation and talent,[8] networking activities among firms (that is, firms belonging to associations, organizations and formal or informal networks), managerial skills and

---

**Table 6. Distribution of high-technology firms by number of employees – Grenoble ZIRST and Cambridgeshire (1997 and 2004).**

| Size | Grenoble ZIRST 2004 (%) | Grenoble ZIRST 1997 (%) | Cambridgeshire 1997 (%) |
|------|--------------------------|--------------------------|--------------------------|
| 1–10 | 53 | 60 | 57 |
| 11–49 | 34 | 30 | 30 |
| 50–99 | 6 | 4 | 6 |
| 100+ | 7 | 6 | 7 |
| Base | 100 (270) | 100 (243) | 100 (1,158) |

*Note:* The number of firms is shown in parentheses.

*Sources:* Druilhe and Garnsey (2000); ZIRST (2005).

international openness/export orientation.

As regards the determinants of regional competitiveness relating to universities, our case studies established the importance of the presence of a local university for the qualification of the local labour market. The analysis also highlighted the relevance of industry–university links, which took up a variety of forms in the regions studied, including research collaboration, the setting up of research centres and laboratories, and the promotion of academic and business committees aimed at fostering regional visibility. University spin-offs were found to be another extremely relevant factor, representing a direct measure of a university's contribution to new firm formation and, hence, to regional economic development.

Finally, we identified a set of regional development factors related to local 'institutional thickness' (Amin and Thrift, 1995). Within this set, we first divided private-sector from public-sector institutions and then split financial from non-financial support schemes, thereby obtaining four main factors of regional development: access to private financing (such as banks and venture capital), other private business support services (such as science parks and consulting firms), the availability of public financing/fiscal incentives (so important in the policies of FDI attraction and support) and other public business support services (such as development agencies and chambers of commerce).

The regional development factors are summarized in Table 7.

By reviewing the main factors driving the transformation paths of the seven European regions studied, we were able to identify three trajectories of regional competitiveness:

- the *Nokia economies* trajectory;
- the *knowledge creation on invitation* trajectory;
- and the *Cambridge way* trajectory.

These trajectories, along with the factors of regional development on which they depend, are shown in Figure 1. In particular, the factors of regional competitiveness (depicted in the figure as squares) are grouped by category of territorial actor – firms, institutions, universities – following the regional innovation system approach to local development. The trajectories of regional competitiveness are represented by the

**Table 7. Main factors of regional competitiveness by territorial actor.**

| Actor | Factors of regional competitiveness |
|---|---|
| Firms | Entrepreneurial motivation/ talent |
| | Networking activities among local firms |
| | Managerial skills |
| | International openness/ export orientation |
| Universities | Presence |
| | Industry–university linkages |
| | University spin-off activities |
| Institutions | Access to private financing (such as banks, venture capital) |
| | Other private business support services (such as consulting firms) |
| | Availability of public financing/tax incentives |
| | Other public business support services (such as development agencies) |

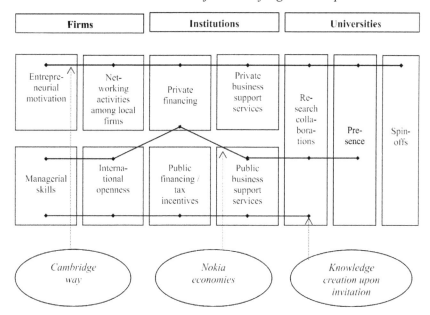

**Figure 1.** Trajectories of regional competitiveness.

solid lines that 'cross' the territorial poles: each trajectory is characterized by a specific combination of factors of competitiveness, and all trajectories are characterized by the simultaneous presence of factors related to all three poles of the model, providing evidence of the systemic character of regional competitiveness.

The *Nokia economies* trajectory includes the Nordic countries of Finland and Sweden, recently boosted around two giant companies, Nokia and Ericsson, capable of gaining a world-leading position in ICT and driving the growth of hundreds of satellite suppliers. The leading development factors of these regions boil down to the successful development strategies of Ericsson and Nokia, in turn based on excellent managerial and organizational skills and a strong international orientation. Crucially, these countries have

also benefited from a supportive system of government bodies and policies aimed at increasing domestic research intensity and innovativeness. A key aspect of the Finnish-Swedish trajectory has been the strong relationship between Nokia and Ericsson and their PTT counterparts, the publicly owned telecommunications operators. Furthermore, we have highlighted the vital role played by the university system in both countries and specifically in the technical research collaborations with Nokia and Ericsson.

The second trajectory of regional competitiveness refers to Ireland, Scotland and Wales, characterized by an 'industrialization upon invitation' type of development based on foreign direct investments. The policies of FDI attraction were supported by public incentives in the form of grants, concessions and/or tax incentives for foreign investors and owe their success to the leading role taken by regional development agencies in improving regional visibility and defining regional industrial and development policies in cooperation with the other territorial actors. Key issues in attracting multinational enterprises to the regions considered within this trajectory were the English language and EU membership.

The last trajectory of regional competitiveness, the *Cambridge way,* relates to the development around a major science park of high-technology clusters in the regions of Cambridge and Grenoble. Both owe their growth into high-tech poles essentially to the presence of higher education and research institutions. The Cambridge Phenomenon emerged and developed thanks basically to the active role of Cambridge University in nurturing the cluster with people who were excellent in their field and in allowing faculty members to exploit their skills and technical know-how commercially. Grenoble flourished thanks to a favourable local culture based on strong university–research–industry linkages. Central to the development of both clusters were the access to private financing and the availability of other private business support services.

The development path of the Cambridge high-tech cluster is often associated with that of Silicon Valley: in fact, the literature highlights a number of similarities between the two local economies, such as the active role of the university and the absence of any state intervention, but also a number of differences, essentially relating to the absence of large firms

in the Cambridge region and its smaller scale (Athreye, 2001).

The literature agrees on the importance of the systemic and regional nature of economic development processes. The very concept of regional innovation systems integrates two different aspects: the systemic character of innovation and the regional dimension of innovation processes. The first aspect – the systemic and interrelated nature of innovation – is rooted in the national innovation system literature (Freeman, 1987; Lundvall, 1992; Nelson, 1993). Freeman (1987) defines a national innovation system as 'the network of institutions in the public and private sectors whose activities and interactions initiate, import, modify and diffuse new technologies'. In other words, the system approach stems from the specific characterization of innovation as the result of social interaction between different actors in producing, diffusing and applying new and economically useful knowledge (Lundvall, 1992). Moreover, in a recent study which aimed to identify possible scenarios of economic development for a number of Italian highly industrialized regions based on a benchmark of European regional innovation systems, Brioschi *et al* (2005) corroborate the centrality of the systemic component of regional development processes.

However, taking a 'provocative' position, we may wish to disentangle the systemic organization and maintain that each trajectory identified in this paper has a pivotal territorial actor driving regional competitiveness. In this framework, we would associate the *Nokia economies* trajectory with firms (Nokia and Ericsson in particular) which were able to push the Finnish and Swedish ICT clusters up to top position at national level in terms of both output and export shares. The *knowledge creation upon invitation* trajectory might be linked to institutions, given the central role played by regional development agencies in promoting FDIs and fostering regional competitiveness in Ireland, Scotland and Wales. Finally, the *Cambridge way* trajectory would be related to universities and, more generally, to the local presence of a strong scientific community. Interestingly, while in Cambridge the impulse behind the cluster formation was its highly prestigious university (thus fitting the concept of 'entrepreneurial university' described above), in Grenoble, the concentration of higher education and research historically arose as an outcome of industrial needs.

## Concluding summary

We analysed selected European regions which in the 1980s and 1990s went through a process of industrial, organizational and institutional renewal, leading to significant improvements in their competitiveness. Our aim was to highlight the key development factors behind their progress. Our analysis focused on the transformation process of three small North European countries (Finland, Sweden and Ireland), two UK regions (Scotland and Wales) and two regions that have grown around the university cities of Cambridge (UK) and Grenoble (France). Based on our analysis, various factors driving regional development were identified

and three trajectories of regional competitiveness, each characterized by a subset of those factors, were detected: the *Nokia economies* trajectory, the *knowledge creation upon invitation* trajectory and the *Cambridge way* trajectory. The *Nokia economies* trajectory explains the development model of Finland and Sweden, which recently emerged as two of the most flourishing, dynamic and competitive OECD countries by virtue of globally competitive ICT sectors. The *knowledge creation upon invitation* trajectory fits the development path of Ireland, Scotland and Wales, able to attract substantial overseas investments in knowledge-intensive industrial sectors thanks to the key role played by regional development agencies in formulating policies of FDI promotion and regional competitiveness. Finally, the *Cambridge way* trajectory fits the regional development model of two clusters of relatively small high-technology firms which have mushroomed since the 1980s around the British university town of Cambridge and the French alpine city of Grenoble.

## Notes

[1] Our aim here is to identify the pivotal factors boosting regional development and not to give a full account of the presence of a system of innovation in the regions under inquiry.
[2] Also due to Finland's severe financial crisis and the Soviet Union's collapse, between 1989 and 1992, Nokia literally struggled for survival and sold its paper, rubber and consumer electronics divisions to focus on mobile phones (Blomström *et al*, 2002).
[3] Under the control of the Russian army (Finland was a Grand Duchy within the Russian Empire), in the middle of the 19th century, government authorities concentrated on telegraphy, leaving the

telephone industry to private companies and cooperatives (Turpeinen, 1997; Blomström *et al,* 2002).
[4]In the period 1987–2000, the Irish GNP grew by 140%, compared to 40% in the USA and 35% in the EU 15 (Farrell, 2004).
[5]EU Structural Funds are allocated according to three 'Objectives'. Objective 1 is aimed at regions lagging behind, where these regions are defined as having a per-capita GDP that is less than 75% of the EU average. Objective 2 is aimed at the economic and social restructuring of regions dependent on industries in decline, agriculture or fisheries or areas suffering from urbanization-related problems. Objective 3 is aimed at modernizing education and increasing employment. Any region can qualify for Objective 3 funding, provided it does not receive Objective 1 funding. Historically, the largest proportion of Structural Funds has been allocated to Objective 1 regions: throughout the 1990s, they represented an increase to national GDP of around 35% for Portugal, around 3% for Spain, 25–3% for Greece, and 2.6% for Ireland (Farrell, 2004).
[6]The PATS were founded in the following areas: bio-research, advanced manufacturing technology, opto-electronics, software, materials, power electronics, microelectronics and telecommunications.
[7]In this regard, as reported by Druilhe and Garnsey (2000), the development of the Grenoble RIS differs sharply from that of other French *technopoles.* Sophia-Antinopolis, although lacking endogenous factors, became a high-technology pole due to substantial public funding. Toulouse's high-technology activities boosted in response to focused public policies. In Nancy, the *technopole* arose as a result of a plan of local industrial regeneration.
[8]In the literature, entrepreneurial motivation is regarded as comprising a number of individual characteristics of the entrepreneur, such as personality, skills, values, background and training (see, for example, Herron and Robinson, 1993).

# References

Amin A., and Thrift, N. (1995), 'Globalization, institutional "thickness" and the local economy', in Healey P., Cameron, S., Davoudi, S., Graham, S., and Madani-Pour, A., eds, *Managing Cities: the New Urban Context,* John Wiley, Chichester.

Asheim B. (1996), 'Industrial districts as "learning regions": a condition for prosperity?', *European Planning Studies,* Vol 4, pp 379–400.

Athreye, S. (2001), 'Agglomeration and growth: a study of the Cambridge hi-tech cluster', SIEPR Discussion Paper 00–42, Stanford Institute for Economic Policy Research, Stanford, CA.

Aydalot P., ed (1986), *Milieux Innovateurs en Europe,* GREMI, Paris.

Aydalot P., and Keeble, D., eds (1988), *High-Technology Industry and Innovative Environments: the European Experience,* Routledge, London.

Becattini G. (1979), 'Dal "settore" industriale al "distretto" industriale: alcune considerazioni sull'unita di indagine dell'economia industriale', *Rivista di Economia e Politica Industriale,* Vol 5, No 1, pp 7–21.

Berggren C., and Laestadius, S. (2003), 'Co-development and composite clusters? The secular strength of Nordic telecommunications', Industrial and Corporate Change, Vol 12, No 1, pp 91–114.

Bernardy de Sigoyer, M., and Boisgontier, P. (1988), *Grains de Technopole,* PUG, Grenoble.

Blomström M., and Kokko, A. (2002), 'From natural resources to high-tech production: the evolution of industrial competitiveness in Sweden and Finland', Working Paper, Stockholm School of Economics, Stockholm.

Blomström, M., Kokko, A., and Sjöholm, F. (2002), 'Growth and innovation policies for a knowledge economy: experiences from Finland, Sweden and Singapore', Working Paper 156, Stockholm School of Economics, Stockholm.

Braczyk, H. J., Cooke, P., and Heidenreich, M. (1998), *Regional Innovation Systems,* UCL Press, London.

Brioschi, M. S., Cassia, L., and Colombelli, A. (2005), 'Common frameworks for regional competitiveness: insights from a number of local knowledge economies', paper presented at the 45th Annual Conference of the European Regional Science Association (ERSA), Amsterdam, 23–27 August.

Brusco, S. (1982), 'The Emilian model: production decentralization and social integration', Cambridge Journal of Economics, Vol 2, pp 167–184.

Camagni, R. (1991), 'Local "milieux", uncertainty and innovation networks: towards a new dynamic theory of economic space', in Camagni, R., ed, *Innovation Networks: Spatial Perspectives*, Belhaven, London, pp 121–142.

Castells, M., and Hall, P. (1994), *Technopoles of the World: the Making of the Twenty-First Century Industrial Complex*, Routledge, London.

Collinson, S. (2000), 'Knowledge networks for innovation in small Scottish software firms', Entrepreneurship and Regional Development, Vol 12, pp 217–244.

Cooke, P. (1992), 'Regional innovation systems, competitive regulation in the new Europe', Geoforum, Vol 23, pp 365–382.

Cooke, P., Uranga, M., and Extebarria, G. (1997), 'Regional innovation systems: institutional and organizational dimensions', Research Policy, Vol 26, pp 475–491.

Cooke, P., Boekholt, P., and Tödling, F. (1998), *Regional Innovation Systems: Designing for the Future*, Final Report to DG12 of the REGIS TSER Project, Centre for Advanced Studies in the Social Sciences, University of Wales, Cardiff.

Cooke P., Roper, S., and Wylie, P. (2003), 'The golden thread of innovation and Northern Ireland's evolving regional innovation system', Regional Studies, Vol 37, No 4, pp 365–379.

Cooke, P., Heidenreich, M., and Braczyk, H.-J. (2004), *Regional Innovation Systems*, 2nd edition, Routledge, London.

Doloreux, D. (2002), 'What we should know about regional systems of innovation', Technology in Society, Vol 24, pp 243–263.

Dosi, G. (1988), 'Sources, procedures and microeconomic effects of innovation', *Journal of Economic Literature*, Vol 26, pp 1120–1171.

Druilhe, C., and Garnsey, E. (2000), 'Emergence and growth of high-tech activity in Cambridge and Grenoble', Entrepreneurship & Regional Development, Vol 12, pp 163–177.

Edquist, C. (2005), 'Systems of innovation: perspectives and challenges', in Fagerberg, J., Mowery, D., and Nelson, R., eds, *The Oxford Handbook of Innovation*, Oxford University Press, Oxford.

ESRI (1997), *Medium-Term Reviews 1997–2003*, Economic and Social Research Institute, Dublin.

Etzkowitz, H., and Leydesdorff, L. (1997), *Universities in the Global Economy: a Triple Helix of University–Industry–Government Relations*, Cassell, London.

Etzkowitz, H., and Leydesdorff, L. (2000), 'The dynamics of innovation: from "National Systems" and "Mode 2" to a Triple Helix of university–industry–government relations, Research Policy, Vol 29, pp 109–123.

Farrell, M. (2004), 'Regional integration and cohesion – lessons from Spain and Ireland in the EU', *Journal of Asian Economics*, Vol 14, pp 927–946.

Freeman, C. (1987), *Technology, Policy, and Economic Performance – Lessons from Japan*, Frances Pinter, London.

Fridlund, M. (1999), *Den gemensamma utvecklingen – Staten, storföretaget och samarbetet kring den svenska elkrafttekniken*, Brutus Östlings Bokförlag Symposion, Stockholm.

Gerszewski, S., and Krieger, F. (2002), 'The city and University of Dortmund: from coexistence to partnership', Industry and Higher Education, Vol 16, No 2, pp 105–112.

Herron, L., and Robinson, R. (1993), 'A structural model of the effects of entrepreneurial characteristics on venture performance', *Journal of Business Venturing*, Vol 8, pp 281–294.

Keeble, D., Lawson, C., Moore, B., and Wilkinson, F. (1999), 'Collective learning processes, networking and "institutional thickness" in the Cambridge region', Regional Studies, Vol 33, No 4, pp 319–332.

IMF (2001), *Finland: Selected Issues*, IMF Country Report No 01/215, International Monetary Fund, Washington, DC.

Lawson C. (1997), 'Territorial clustering and high technology innovation: from industrial districts to innovative milieux', Working Paper 54, ESRC Centre for Business Research, University of Cambridge, Cambridge.

Lawson, C., and Lorenz, E. (1997), 'Collective learning, tacit knowledge and regional innovative capacity', Regional Studies, Vol 33, No 4, pp 305–317.

Leontief, W. (1953), *Studies in the Structure of the American Economy*, Oxford University Press, New York.

Lorenz, E. (1992), 'Trust, community and co-operation: towards a theory of industrial districts', in Storper, M., and Scott, A., eds, *Pathways to Industrialization and Regional Development*, Routledge, London, pp 195–204.

Lundvall, B. (1992), *National Systems of Innovation: Towards a Theory of Innovation and Interactive Learning*, Frances Pinter, London.

Markusen, A. (1996), 'Sticky places in a slippery space: a typology of industrial districts', Economic Geography, Vol 72, pp 293–313.

Marshall, A. (1890), *Principles of Economics,* Macmillan, London.

Marshall, A. (1919), *Industry and Trade,* Macmillan, London.

Morgan, K. (1997a), 'The learning region: institutions, innovation and regional renewal', Regional Studies, Vol 31, No 5, pp 491–503.

Morgan, K. (1997b), 'The regional animateur: taking stock of the Welsh Development Agency', *Regional & Federal Sudies,* Vol 7, No 2, pp 70–94.

Nelson, R., ed (1993), *National Innovation Systems: a Comparative Analysis,* Oxford University Press, Oxford.

O'Connor, T. P. (2001), 'Foreign direct investment and indigenous industry in Ireland: review of evidence', Working Paper 22/01, ESRC, London.

OECD (1981), *The Future of University Research,* Organization for Economic Cooperation and Development, Paris.

OECD (2001), *Communications Outlook,* Organization for Economic Cooperation and Development, Paris.

O' Gorman, C., and Kautonen, M. (2004), 'Policies to promote new knowledge-intensive industrial agglomerations', Entrepreneurship and Regional Development, Vol 16, pp 459–479.

Paci, R., and Usai, S. (2003), 'Spatial externalities and local employment dynamics', paper presented at conference on 'Reinventing Space: the Geography of Globalization', Bergamo, 19–20 December.

Perroux, F. (1950a), 'Economic space: theory and applications', Quarterly Journal of Economics, Vol 64, pp 89–104.

Perroux, F. (1950b), 'Les espaces économiques', *Économie Appliquée,* Vol 1, pp 302–320.

Piore, M., and Sabel, C. (1984), *The Second Industrial Divide – Possibilities for Prosperity,* Basic Books, New York.

Pulkkinen, M. (1997), *The Breakthrough of Nokia Mobile Phones,* Series A:122, Helsinki School of Economics and Business Administration, Helsinki.

Pyke F., Becattini, G., and Sengenberger, W., eds (1990), *Industrial Districts and Inter-Firm Co-operation in Italy,* International Labour Office (ILO), Geneva.

Richardson, H. (1973), *Regional Growth Theory,* Macmillan, London.

Segal, N. S. (1992), 'The Cambridge Phenomenon', Regional Studies. Vol 19, No 6, pp 563–578.

Segal, Quince and Wicksteed (1985), *The Cambridge Phenomenon: the Growth of High Technology Industry in a University Town,* Segal, Quince and Wicksteed, Cambridge.

Segal, Quince and Wicksteed (2000), *The Cambridge Phenomenon Revisited,* Segal, Quince and Wicksteed, Cambridge.

Simmie J., ed (1997), *Innovation, Networks and Learning Regions,* Jessica Kingsley, London.

Sweeney P. (1998), *The Celtic Tiger: Ireland's Economic Miracle Explained,* Oak Tree Press, Dublin.

Tewdwr-Jones, M., and Phelps, N. (2000), 'Levelling the uneven playing field: inward investments, interregional rivalry and the planning system', Regional Studies. Vol 34, No 5, pp 429–440.

Turpeinen, O. (1997), *Telecommunications Since 1796,* Telecom Finland, Helsinki.

ZIRST (2005), *Annual Report,* www.zirst.com.

# Building regional innovation capacity
## The San Diego experience

**Mary L. Walshok, Edward Furtek,
Carolyn W. B. Lee and Patrick H. Windham**

**Abstract:** *San Diego, California is now one of the most innovative regions in the USA. In the past 15 years it has transformed itself from an economy dominated by defence contracts, tourism and real estate into a major centre for academic research and high-tech industry. This article examines the various means by which this transformation has been achieved and suggests that the experience of San Diego offers guiding principles for developing innovative capacity in regions elsewhere in the USA and in other countries. The paper concentrates on the three major 'hooks' that the authors identify as critical to successful, regional development: (a) the store of intellectual capital in the region; (b) the character and extent of catalytic business and financial networks; and (c) the breadth and depth of the advanced skills and knowledge of the human capital. With specific reference to San Diego's biotechnology and telecommunications clusters, the authors demonstrate how non-profit research institutions have created powerful research clusters in the region and how these clusters, in partnership with technology-focused networks of business and professional leadership, have provided those three essential ingredients. While certain elements of the San Diego story are attributable to the specific history and assets of the region, the key factors that have shaped its growth suggest principles of economic transformation that are applicable throughout the world.*

**Keywords:** *regional innovation; R&D capacity; San Diego*

*Mary L. Walshok is Associate Vice Chancellor for Public Programs and Dean of University Extension, University of California at San Diego (UCSD), 9500 Gilman Drive, La Jolla, CA 92093–0176, USA. E-mail: mwalshok@ucsd.edu. Edward Furtek is Associate Vice Chancellor for Science and Technology Policy and Projects, UCSD. E-mail: efurtek@ucsd.edu Carolyn W. B. Lee is Director of Research for Public Programs, UCSD. E-mail: cwlee@ucsd.edu. Patrick H. Windham is a Research Analyst in the Office of Science Technology Policy and Projects, UCSD. E-mail: patwindham@aol.com*

In the past two decades, the San Diego, California, region has transformed itself into one of the most innovative regions in the USA. The University of California, San Diego (UCSD) together with the Salk Institute, the Scripps Research Institute, the Neurosciences Institute, the Burnham Cancer Research Institute and the Sidney Kimmel Cancer Center, garner close to two billion dollars in basic research annually. In addition, more than 1,500 high-technology companies have sprung up in the area surrounding these world-class research institutions. San Diego is now a major centre for academic research and high-tech industry in fields such as biotechnology, wireless telecommunications and genomics. Little more than 15 years ago, the region was still dominated by defence contractors, tourism and real estate development.

How has San Diego engineered such a transformation? A variety of state and regional economic crises from the late 1970s to the mid-1980s necessitated a regional shift in direction. Regional leadership, in collaboration with UCSD, mobilized to help grow knowledge-based industries at an accelerated rate.

This article documents the interconnections between the research and development (R&D) and educational capacities of UCSD and related research institutions on a hillside near the Pacific Ocean (known as the Torrey Pines Mesa) with the growth of the region's new industrial clusters. We focus on only two of San Diego's robust technology clusters, biotechnology and telecommunications, especially wireless telecommunications. Drawing on regional renderings of national data on federal funding, the article describes existing 'new economy' clusters as well as documenting current R&D activities as a way to begin to anticipate what technologies will emerge in the future to shape the regional economy. These numbers are quite stunning and document a robust R&D capacity which should spawn continued regional innovation. The original research that made the development of these databases possible was funded by the University of California's Office of the President, the California Commission for Science and Technology and the State of California's Trade and Commerce Agency.

In addition, we report on San Diego survey results and in-depth interviews with technology leaders from a project led by Furtek and Windham funded by UC's Office of the President building on a relationship developed by the San Diego Science and Technology Council, whose CEO is Furtek. This work enabled the US Council on Competitiveness to secure access to valuable information and insights from more than 40 regional leaders. The Council on Competitiveness, a private group of business, labour and educational leaders based in Washington, DC, is surveying business leaders from five regions (Atlanta, Pittsburgh, Raleigh/Durham, San Diego and Wichita). Its surveys ask business leaders about the role that R&D and research universities play in the creation and growth of their companies and how research universities contribute to innovation in their region.

To help tell the story of how academic research grew in San Diego and how that research in turn played an important role in the region's high-technology industries, this article summarizes such factors as federal and state R&D awards, SBIR grants[1] and numbers of PhD students and post-docs in the region, as well as support programmes at UCSD such as CONNECT, a social networking and business support organization, and University Extension. The sources of these data include UCSD's Office of Technology Transfer, the Office of Graduate Studies and Research at UCSD, UCSD CONNECT and University Extension. The Contracts and Grants Offices of UCSD, Salk, Scripps and other institutions also provided information, as did the San Diego Regional Technology Alliance on regional labour force characteristics. We discovered that it is very difficult to collect data of the type needed to describe innovation capacity and possible 'emergent' technology clusters because no one office (or organization in the San Diego region) keeps track of it all. This article represents an effort to begin offering some metrics drawing upon work in which each of the four authors is engaged.

Nonetheless, the available data do help tell a story of a growing academic research community and the contributions that it has made to the regional economy.

Our results indicate that UCSD, Scripps, Salk and the other non-profit research institutions have created strong and dynamic research clusters in San Diego and that these research clusters, in partnership with technology-focused networks of business and professional leadership, have contributed to the region's telecommunications and biotechnology industries in three important ways. We describe these three contributors as 'building intellectual capital', 'creating catalytic social networks' (of financial and management know-how) and 'developing human capital':

- *Research institutions with world-class scientists and engineers prime a region for innovation.* Interviewees repeatedly told us that the founding of UCSD 40 years ago had been the key turning point in San Diego's high-tech history. The 'hard' data substantiate this perception. Even though the initial scientists and engineers attracted to this area did not have entrepreneurship in mind, their presence created a critical mass of world-class scientific and research talent in San Diego that had not been there before, resulting in one of the highest R&D funded regions in the USA today. This represents the region's primary intellectual capital.
- *Social networks and business services to help move research from the laboratory into industry.* Interviewees also pointed out another necessary ingredient of San Diego's success – deliberate regional initiatives such as UCSD CONNECT brought entrepreneurs, researchers and the business community together to form new social networks. This process set up mutually beneficial learning communities and networks of

competency and resources that significantly accelerated the growth of the telecommunications and biotechnology sectors. Quantitative data affirm the extent to which new sources of capital and expertise made possible by these relationships resulted in the founding of new companies and thousands of new, high-wage jobs. This is what we mean by catalytic social networks.

• *The continuing role played by UCSD and other research institutions in assisting cluster growth.* Interviewees also reported on the continuing importance of UCSD and other research institutions in the area. Educational programmes at both undergraduate and graduate levels, as well as specialized training programmes through UCSD Extension, help to assure a workforce with the knowledge and skills needed by science-based companies. UCSD and the other research institutions also continue to conduct the cutting-edge research that is critical to the biotechnology industry and is of increasing value to the telecommunications sector. Our data reveal the extent to which entrepreneurs continue to base start-up ventures on university inventions and licences, use doctoral and post-doctoral talent in their labs and partner with UCSD's continuing education programmes to design professional-development courses for their employees. This is what we mean by developing human capital. Our data analysis identifies and highlights (a) the research capabilities of UCSD in particular, as well as other research institutions in the region, and (b) the catalytic role played by UCSD CONNECT, with its superior network of financial and management know-how critical to the formation and growth of San Diego's telecommunications and biotechnology clusters. Our findings suggest some general principles for other regions with research capabilities interested in using high-tech industry clusters to jump-start their regional economy.

• *Build up world-class capacity in basic research.* Business leaders from innovative companies told us that they liked to locate their companies near world-class research institutions. While all regions across the USA may not be able to achieve this, work by Tornatzky (2002) and Saxenian (1994) suggests that research is as critical to the renewal of existing industries as to the building of new ones. In addition, industry likes the continual access to recent graduates and continuing education offered by research universities.

• *Foster regional initiatives to accelerate technology commercialization efforts.* Business leaders identified UCSD CONNECT as critical, not only to their own company's success but also to the success of the entire San Diego region. CONNECT met a critical need for social networking relevant to the new economy that had been lacking in the region. CONNECT has become a model for other regions to build on and has been replicated in two other sites in California, in Hawaii and in

New York as well as in seven other countries.

- *Sustaining regional innovation clusters requires continual interaction between research centres, universities and local business leaders in order to sustain cluster growth and the development of new science-based industries.* As industry clusters emerge in a region, the role of research institutions will deepen and broaden to encompass workforce development and training as well as technology transfer and technology commercialization.

It is useful to focus on each of these three factors individually as a way of elucidating both their distinct characteristics and, ultimately, how they interact to contribute to the capacity of a region to sustain innovation and prosperity in a globally linked, knowledge-based economy.

## Building intellectual capital: role of research institutions

San Diego has undergone a substantial economic renewal over the past two decades. Despite the severe defence cutbacks of the 1990s, San Diego actually has more high-technology employment today than it did a decade ago; 110,285 jobs in 1999 compared to 102,994 in 1991 (Greater San Diego Chamber of Commerce, 1999). The economy has prospered because it has diversified and grown new industries. In particular, it has grown new industries based on advanced R&D. The industrial clusters include telecommunications, biotechnology, computing, other electronics, software and the Internet and energy and environmental technologies. Defence activities remain very important to San Diego, but the region is no longer primarily dependent on defence for its prosperity. Our work is focused on a key component of the San Diego story – the role that the region's research institutions have played in creating research clusters and, in turn, the role of these research clusters in supporting the emergence and growth of new industries. To illustrate this story, we focus on two of San Diego's most important new R&D-based sectors: advanced telecommunications and biotechnology.

'Research clusters' are geographically concentrated groups of non-profit research institutions or groups within research institutions that have expertise in specific fields of science and technology. San Diego has a very dense cluster of biomedical research institutions on and near the Torrey Pines Mesa. This density is unrivalled, even when compared to other areas of the state. All of the institutions listed below are located less than 2.5 miles from each other. The majority were established in the 1960s and 1970s, and each has been extremely successful in attracting world-class scientific talent to the San Diego region, which is now reputed to have one of the highest percentages in the USA of PhDs and MDs in its population.

- UCSD (noted for its School of Engineering, School of Medicine, Department of Biology, Center for Wireless Communications, and other research centres)
- The Scripps Research Institute
- The Salk Institute for Biological Studies
- The Burnham Institute

- The Sidney Kimmel Cancer Center
- The Neurosciences Institute
- The La Jolla Institute for Allergies and Immunology

Collectively, these world-class research institutions attracted approximately $1.26 billion in non-classified research funding to the San Diego region in FY1999.[2]

California as a whole received $14.4 billion (Fossum *et al*, 2000).[3] San Diego's success in obtaining R&D funding, relative to other regions of California, is not fully appreciated. A county-by-county comparison illustrates San Diego's density of R&D activity relative to both the San Francisco Bay Area and Greater Los Angeles regions, both multi-county metropolitan statistical areas (MSAs), whereas San Diego is a single-county MSA. In terms of federal R&D funding, San Diego County ranks second in California; only Los Angeles County receives a higher total.[4] See Figures 1 and 2 for a breakdown of R&D funding to California and San Diego.

Of the approximately $1.26 billion in non-classified R&D funding to San Diego, over $627 million (or 49.7%) comes from the Department of Health and Human Services (HHS). Over 75% of HHS funding[5] is distributed to UCSD and other non-profit research institutions such as Scripps, Salk and the Burnham Institute, all located, as noted above, within an area of five square miles on Torrey Pines Mesa.

While the total amount of R&D funding is important, the ability to transfer and commercialize the R&D results is no less important for industry cluster growth. The ability of a region to attract SBIR award funding which supports more 'applied' work is one measure of the effectiveness of technology-transfer efforts in the USA. SBIR funds represent a significant source of federal matching funds for research initiatives with great commercialization potential. In FY1999, the state of California received $91.79 million in SBIR funding. Of this, $17.32 million was awarded to initiatives in San Diego County. Figure 3

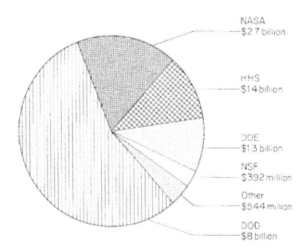

**Figure 1.** R&D funding to the State of California in FY 1999 (total $14.4 billion).

*Source:* RaDiUS

illustrates the agency breakdown for non-classified SBIR funding given to California as a whole. Figure 4 reveals the agency breakdown for San Diego County's share of SBIR funding. Nearly 60% of San Diego's SBIR funding comes from HHS. This represents another measure of San Diego's research and commercialization strengths in the life sciences. Even though SBIR funding is less than 5% of what venture capital put into companies (as reported in Table 1), it represents funding for 'translational' research.

In addition to the government-sponsored venture funding (SBIR awards), San Diego received $1.215 billion in private venture funding for 2000 (PriceWaterhouse Coopers, MoneyTree™ Report, 2000). The major industry clusters funded are listed in Table 1.

San Diego's success in basic research investments is paralleled

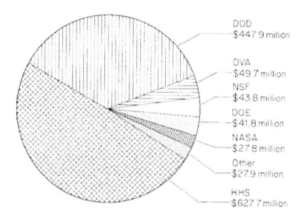

**Figure 2.** Non-classified R&D funding to San Diego County in FY 1999 (total $1.26 billion).

*Source*: RaDiUS

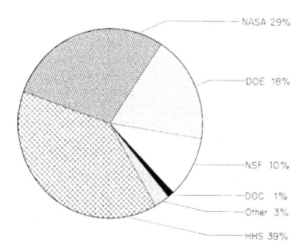

**Figure 3.** SBIR funding to the State of California in FY 1999 (total $91.79 million).

**Table 1. Private venture capital to San Diego County in 2000.**

| Industry | Funding |
|---|---|
| Telecommunications | $314 million |
| Biotechnology | $255 million |
| Software | $155 million |
| Medical devices | $106 million |
| Other | $385 million |
| *Total* | *$1,215 billion* |

*Source:* PricewaterhouseCoopers, MoneyTree™ Report, 2000.

**Table 2. High-tech industry employment in San Diego County.**

| Industry cluster | 1990 | 1998 |
|---|---|---|
| Biotechnology/ biomedical products[a] | 18,630 | 28,773 |
| Telecommunications | 6,890 | 20,619 |
| Defence[b] and transportation manufacturing | 39,114 | 19,109 |
| Other industry clusters | 251,148 | 307,284 |
| *Total* | *315,782* | *375,785* |

*Source:* San Diego Association of Governments (2001).
[a]The definition of 'biotechnology' used by the San Diego Association of Governments is a broad one in order to capture the entire value chain. These companies span the range from emerging biotech start-up companies being incubated on Torrey Pines Mesa to conventional laboratory and chemical suppliers.
[b]'Defence' excludes uniformed military personnel.

by its success in funding initiatives that support the growth of high-tech companies which have contributed to an increasing number of high-paying jobs for the regional economy, as Table 2 illustrates. The new industry clusters have more than offset job losses from the decline of the defence sector.

*Regional 'value added' of research institutions*

To build and sustain competitive R&D-based industries, a region needs top researchers doing cutting-edge work in science and technology. These are the people who have advanced knowledge, produce the most recent research and understand the most promising new ideas. We emphasize general research activity rather than just universities because in fields such as IT, most of the companies have come out of federal contracts to and R&D within commercial enterprises. PhD-level researchers may reside in universities or corporate research laboratories or other institutions, but a region without at least one institution, private or public, engaged in significant R&D is at a major disadvantage when competing in knowledge-based industries. Our later discussion describing the distinct histories of IT

and biotechnology in the San Diego region drive home this point. A strong pool of intellectual capital, regardless of research setting, drives knowledge development and makes possible innovation and entrepreneurship.

Before the 1960s, San Diego had no research university. It had an economy led by tourism, the military and defence contractors and certainly was not a centre of civilian high-technology industry. But the region did have three important research centres that attracted talented scientists, and with them federal and foundation funding to the region which stimulated technology development.

*The Scripps Institution of Oceanography (SIO).* SIO was a University of California research station established in 1903. During

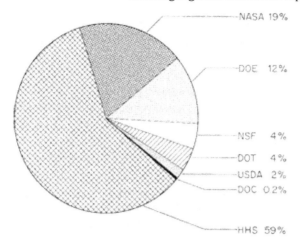

**Figure 4.** SBIR funding to San Diego County in FY 1999 (total $20.45 million).

*Source:* RaDiUS (non-classified funding only)

the Second World War and the Cold War, SIO became a major centre for federally funded research in anti-submarine work and other areas of oceanography relevant to naval operations and communications. Leadership at SIO was pivotal to the establishment of the UC San Diego Campus in La Jolla in the 1960s.

*General Atomics.* General Atomics (GA) started in 1953 as a division of General Dynamics, a leading US aerospace company at that time. GA attracted top physicists and other scientists to San Diego to work on nuclear research for the government. While the original GA did not create a culture that encouraged commercial entrepreneurship, it did bring skilled people to San Diego and helped to create a new image of San Diego as a place where serious, world-class researchers could live and work. On a modest scale, General Atomics created the equivalent of a national laboratory in San Diego. It attracted a number of bright people, some of whom went on

to start other companies, such as SAIC and Maxwell Technologies, which today are major drivers in San Diego's high-tech economy.

*The Scripps Research Institute.* In 1955, the Scripps Clinic (a healthcare provider) established a Scripps Clinic and Research Foundation to conduct biomedical research. In 1961, the Foundation recruited a world-class biomedical research team from the University of Pittsburgh. In time, it became the Scripps Research Institute (TSRI). Scripps helped pioneer what later became a San Diego pattern of doing research – recruit world-class people by offering them not only a beautiful climate and top colleagues but also the freedom to work on topics of interest to them, to work in new or interdisciplinary fields and to work closely with company researchers. Today the research budget of Scripps exceeds $200 million annually.

In the 1960s, San Diego's business leaders worked vigorously to convince two additional institutions with significant research and teaching missions to locate on the undeveloped mesa north of the downtown area which in the Second World War had been used primarily as a Marine Corps training facility, Camp Matthews. These two institutions were the Salk Institute for Biological Studies and the University of California. The decisions by the federal government to 'deed' Camp Matthews over to the University of California and by the city to zone its Torrey Pines Mesa holdings for research and industrial purposes opened the door to creating a major R&D capability in San Diego. An impressive array of additional institutions was established in the 1960s and 1970s subsequent to Salk and UCSD locating on the mesa.

*The Salk Institute*. Jonas Salk, who pioneered the polio vaccine, wanted to build a world-class research centre. He was captivated by a site on Torrey Pines Mesa, north of La Jolla, overlooking the ocean. The City of San Diego agreed to donate this land for the new Institute. In the 1970s, the city zoned a great deal of Torrey Pines Mesa for biomedical research – a decision that has generated enormous benefits for both research and the growth of San Diego's biotechnology industry. The Salk Institute soon benefited from the earlier research capabilities of the region, as GA's Frederic de Hoffman, a respected scientist and research administrator, became its president.

*UCSD*. In 1964 the University of California, San Diego enrolled its first class of undergraduates. Local companies had pressed hard for a campus to help provide the engineers needed by the defence industry. SIO's Roger Revelle took the lead role in working for the campus, whose establishment was by no means a certainty. However, UCSD did not become the engineering training centre local companies had originally envisaged. Instead, UCSD's founders focused on creating a world-class scientific research institution, an 'MIT of the West'. In fact, UCSD began in 1960 by recruiting full professors who brought significant research grants and PhD students to the campus, prior to launching any undergraduate programmes. The emphasis was on physics and medicine and securing federally funded basic research. The objective was to recruit the world's best researchers to run an academic institution. Ties to local industry were not even a consideration in the early days of the campus. UC established this new campus on the Torrey Pines Mesa, near the Salk Institute and the Scripps Clinic & Research Foundation, thus setting the stage for the creation of a critical mass of biomedical researchers in close proximity (Anderson, 1993). In the space of 40 short years, UCSD has risen to rank fifth among all universities in the nation in the amount of federal funding received for R&D and related activities.[6] In terms of prestige, UCSD currently has more than 60 members of the National Academy of Sciences, more than a dozen members of the National Academy of Engineering, and 16 members of the Institute of Medicine, comparing favourably with more well-established and much older institutions in the USA.

*Later biomedical institutions*. In recent decades, several other non-profit biomedical research institutions also arose in the region. They include the Burnham Institute, the Sidney Kimmel Cancer Center, the Neurosciences Institute and the La Jolla Institute for Allergies and Immunology. These research centres enhanced the geographical density of an already concentrated biomedical research cluster. They represent hundreds of additional PhD researchers and millions of dollars of additional research funding to the region.

The quality of faculty members, technicians and full-time researchers recruited to these new research institutions was and remains high. But in addition to quality, our interviews revealed some interesting characteristics about the types of people who agreed to come to San Diego. One interviewee told us that San Diego attracted 'pioneers'. Faculty members who left places such as Harvard, Penn State and NIH were attracted to UCSD because they were scientific entrepreneurs. Others told us in informal conversations that people came to UCSD, Scripps and Salk not just because of the research

money offered but also because of the freedom to work on what interested them, including interdisciplinary projects or research in fields outside their original disciplines. We also heard that some of the longest-serving faculty members came because they were experiencing life transitions and were looking for new beginnings.

There is also a consensus that San Diego's receptivity to interdisciplinary research is important not only as a feature of the local research culture but also as a key to the region's economic success. One of our interviewees, a biotech CEO, told us that one of the key reasons for San Diego's superior innovation capacity was its understanding that interdisciplinary research was the key to making discoveries. The combination of high-quality research institutions, active recruiting and plentiful federal funding built up San Diego's unique research capabilities. This was particularly true in two areas we examined – biomedicine and certain aspects of defence electronics. Federal funding was vital. One San Diego leader whom we interviewed

**Table 3. Number of post-doctoral researchers at selected San Diego research institutes.**

| Research institute | 1997 | 1998 | 1999 | 2000 | 2001 |
|---|---|---|---|---|---|
| Scripps Research Institute | 550 | 607 | 705 | 790 | 763 |
| Salk Institute for Biological Studies | 242 | 250 | 242 | 252 | 263 |
| Burnham Institute | 101 | 99 | 113 | 130 | 127 |
| Sidney Kimmel Cancer Center | 14 | 11 | 17 | 17 | 23 |
| Neurosciences Institute | 2 | 10 | NA | 9 | 14 |
| *Total* | *893* | *956* | *1,060* | *1,172* | *1,153* |

*Note:* The significance of the data shown in this table is discussed in the section 'Post-doctoral training'.

said, 'I see that we are what we are today because we focused on scientific endeavours that were priorities of the government'.

In time, the biomedical research institutions on Torrey Pines Mesa became a dense research cluster. Most scholarly theories of clusters focus on industry groupings and emphasize the value of having a local concentration of similar companies that compete with each other while also sharing information and suppliers and otherwise getting the benefits of working in the same region. But along with industry clusters, San Diego developed something else – a major biomedical *research* cluster. These institutions compete for federal (and now private) funding and offer different models of how to organize research while also fostering high levels of informal collaboration among researchers. They also feed off one another, so that the Salk Institute with only 50 senior researchers imports large numbers of post-docs from UCSD to enrich its capacity (post-doc data are reported in Table 3). By the late 1990s, San Diego received more NIH funding than any other region of the country. Two biomedical leaders we interviewed emphasized this combination of competition and cooperation among these geographically close institutions as a great strength for the region.

Defence funding for electronics research also was high in the 1960s and 1970s. Most of that funding went to companies and was relevant to military objectives. Because UCSD initially lacked an engineering school, San Diego was not a large centre for federally funded academic research in electronics during this period.

Nonetheless, the prominence of military-related R&D in the region throughout the 1950s, 1960s and 1970s created a foundation for this R&D cluster. Additionally, the UCSD campus did work hard to recruit independent-minded, high-quality researchers in physics and related areas. The government contracting to electronics and engineering companies had a similar 'R&D cluster' development effect to that created by the government funding for basic research in the biosciences. The growth of scientific talent at UCSD solidified with a School of Engineering which today is ranked in the top 20 in the USA, with annual research revenues of approximately $40 million. UCSD is also home to a major new centre of research on applied telecommunications funded at $300 million over the next five years and it is the location of one of the nation's leading supercomputer centres.

The world-class scientists and engineers recruited by these institutions and the research they do have contributed to San Diego's new high-tech economy in significant ways. Some of the early professors became pioneering entrepreneurs. In 1968, UCSD professor Irwin Jacobs and UCLA professor Andrew Viterbi started Linkabit, San Diego's pioneering advanced telecommunications company. Primarily a defence and government contracting enterprise, it nonetheless pioneered wireless communications technologies which today have myriad civic and commercial applications. Jacobs and Viterbi went on to found Qualcomm, which after 15 years became a Fortune 500 company. Jacobs and Viterbi's initiative represented the first step in establishing the region's wireless digital communications industry. In 1978, UCSD Medical School researchers Ivor Royston and Howard Birndorf created Hybritech, San Diego's first biotechnology firm based on the need for a steady supply of monoclonal antibodies for laboratory work in the new field of molecular biology. Sold to Eli Lilly in 1985 for $500 million, Hybritech has spawned dozens of spin-off bioscience R&D companies. It was partly serendipity that Dr Jacobs and Dr Royston came to San Diego to work at UCSD and that their first companies proved successful. While university officials and top research administrators did not actively encourage entrepreneurship among academics in the early days of UCSD, they created a critical mass of researchers from which a few entrepreneurs emerged.

After the sale of Hybritech and Linkabit to large, established companies, the founders of these firms and many of the technical managers they had hired moved on to create new companies. Hybritech and Linkabit managers became San Diego's analogues to Silicon Valley's 'Fairchild Eight' – the semiconductor pioneers from Fairchild who went on to create Intel, AMD, National Semiconductor and the venture firm Kleiner Perkins. In San Diego, Linkabit alumni went on to create QUALCOMM and over 30 other telecommunications companies. Hybritech alumni went on to establish over 50 biotechnology companies and related ventures. Today, San Diego ranks 1st in the USA for the number of wireless companies and 3rd for the number of bioscience companies.

## Catalytic social networks for new-economy companies

Over the last two decades it has become abundantly clear that the presence of world-class research institutions in a region is a necessary but not a sufficient basis for building science-based companies that create new high-wage jobs and wealth for the region. It is also essential to develop resources and social networks that can effectively assess promising applications and commercialization potential, provide access to angel, venture and corporate funding and assure the availability of management and professional know-how *vis-à-vis* global entrepreneurial science-based companies. These forms of expertise used to be concentrated within a few major urban areas or inside a few hundred global corporations. Today, regions need these capacities, or at least ready access to resources and expertise, if they are to develop their innovation capacity in order to build 'new-economy' clusters. San Diego is a remarkable example of a community that built not only a research capacity but also a regional support network of sophisticated, entrepreneurial business and professional service providers. It could be argued that the existence of this business network and culture is as important as a world-class research network and culture.

In a previous report (Walshok *et al*, 2001), the authors have summed up the unique 'character transformation' in San Diego in terms of four dominant factors:

- First, the 'amenities of place' – the quality of life a particular location provides – is a crucial factor in attracting the intellectual capital that is the basis of innovation and entrepreneurship in knowledge-based companies. People like to live in places they enjoy, and San Diego appeals to a wide variety of tastes. However, other places with good weather and a high quality of life have not succeeded in growing high-tech industry clusters, so 'amenities of place' alone are insufficient to jump-start innovation.

- The development of a core group of innovators and entrepreneurs is key. In the case of San Diego, one of the critical factors was Jonas Salk's decision to site his research centre here – even before there was a UCSD campus. Salk's decision was driven by San Diego's beauty and the availability of land. However, once he had taken that decision, it brought a number of highly skilled bioscientists to San Diego and gave the region increased visibility as a centre of research.

- The effort led by SIO's Director Roger Revelle to establish a UC campus in San Diego was another critical step in starting a 'snowball effect' of attracting intellectual capital to the region. The promise of newness, the chance to do interdisciplinary work and independence proved to be powerful. San Diego's research institutions (including General Atomics) attracted the best scientists in their fields, and those scientists later became the people who started or helped to start many new firms.

- The culture in San Diego, influenced by a frontier mentality, a tradition of entrepreneurship and the absence of a traditional business and ' old

family' establishment, supported the development of new social networks within the business community that stimulated innovation. Organizations can be initially successful thanks to the insight or innovation of a 'superstar'. However, organizations and regions achieve lasting success through the creation of continuously innovating 'super teams'. San Diego has formed such teams of researchers, investors, attorneys, accountants, managers and marketers. They are informed about technology, expert in their fields and adept at putting together deals and supporting growing science-based enterprises. This 'churn' is what sustains regional innovation.

How did San Diego go about developing these networks where little existed before? Given its previous government contracting, defence industry–based economy, San Diego's local networks were less important to business development than were government relations, well into the 1980s. Local capital did not fuel General Dynamics, General Atomics, Rohr or National Steel and Shipbuilding. These enterprises were based on federal government contracts. As a consequence, for early non-defence high-tech entrepreneurs in San Diego, getting access to capital and other resources was a problem. In the 1970s, San Diego had no major banks or venture capital firms of its own. Nor did it have any professional or business services to support science-based, commercially focused innovation. Early entrepreneurs had to rely on personal contacts to obtain introductions to the resources they needed, usually located outside the region. At the same time, local business service providers with contacts in the wider venture capital and management consulting community knew little about high-tech start-ups and did not know how to service the needs of these clients.

Starting a company then was a hit-or-miss process. For example, Hybritech's founders, Ivor Royston and Howard Birndorf, received venture funding from Kleiner, Perkins, Caufield & Byers, one of Silicon Valley's top venture firms, through personal contacts. Kleiner Perkins approved the proposal that the company should stay in San Diego, because Royston's research at UCSD provided the underlying technology. The venture firm not only provided financing; it also helped Hybritech to hire the experienced technical managers it needed from large pharmaceutical firms outside San Diego. If Royston had not had these personal contacts in Silicon Valley, it is unclear whether his new firm would have received the funding and other help it needed.

Local service providers in San Diego were not aware of Hybritech or its needs. One leading service provider in San Diego told us that he heard about Hybritech while he was working for his firm on another assignment in Brussels. On returning to San Diego, this individual realized that young entrepreneurial companies like Hybritech needed assistance to break into European markets and that servicing these San Diego start-ups might become a major growth area for his firm. He then devoted time and energy to learning more about these new companies, as did a few other pioneering business service providers in San Diego. However, there was no *formal mechanism* for facilitating this process in a deliberate and high-impact way across the region.

## UCSD CONNECT

San Diego business and education leaders founded CONNECT in 1985 in a deliberate attempt to jump-start the process of developing contacts, social networks and business services of the type that had not been readily available to early entrepreneurs like Jacobs in IT and Royston in the biosciences. Its origins – and the strong commitment people made to it – derive from the economic turmoil San Diego experienced in the early and mid-1980s.

Even before the reduction in defence spending in the 1990s, San Diego faced a series of serious economic disruptions, culminating in the US savings and loan industry crisis of the late 1980s. These crises led to a rethinking of economic development strategies in the region. By the early 1980s, it had become clear that traditional business development strategies were not working. Regional leaders realized that they needed to envisage San Diego's future beyond an economy based solely on banking, real estate, defence and tourism. San Diego then attempted to attract two major research consortia, the Microelectronics and Computer Technology Corporation (MCC) and SEMATECH, and lost both in the final rounds. In reaction to this time of turmoil, the San Diego community began looking for new ways to 'grow' the regional economy.

Richard C. Atkinson, then chancellor at UCSD, asked some of his key staff to explore a proper route for the university to assist in reinvigorating the regional economy. One-on-one interviews and round tables yielded a number of creative ideas about how the university and the community could collaborate on this issue. UCSD CONNECT was created out of this process. Its purpose was to link academic researchers with entrepreneurs and to link both of these parties to venture capitalists and business service providers in order to grow new companies that would create high-wage jobs and regional prosperity at a time when a number of regional economic 'drivers' such as real estate, banking and defence contracting were in disarray.

CONNECT was developed after extensive consultation with university researchers, private-sector executives and professional business service providers. Programme components over the years have included:

• *Meet the Entrepreneur and Meet the Researcher events*. San Diego had academic scientists with promising ideas as well as non–research-oriented business entrepreneurs looking for new and promising technologies. It became clear that these entrepreneurs and researchers had very little understanding about the issues that each faced or their respective modes of working. There was almost no connection between the two groups. These initial events attracted hundreds of participants, demonstrating that there was a perceived need for these two groups to learn more about each other.

• *Financial forums*. In response to input from entrepreneurial researchers and regional business leaders about the absence of angel and venture funding in the region, one of CONNECT's major initiatives was to help to attract leading capital providers to the region to learn more about San Diego companies. The resulting forums also began connecting entrepreneurs with business support services (law, accounting, marketing and other service providers) to help them write business proposals that would be attractive to capital providers. CONNECT, in partnership with business and financial leaders, developed two annual financial forums: the San Diego Technology Financial Forum, in which pre-screened companies from all fields of high technology present their proposals to venture capitalists from across the nation, and the San Diego Biotechnology/Biomedical Corporate Partnership Forum, in which biotechnology entrepreneurs present their plans to global firms interested in innovative start-ups.

• *Springboard Program*. The Springboard Program provides early feedback and coaching on promising technology business plans for about 50 start-up companies annually. CONNECT staff work with entrepreneurs to review their technology and business plans and coach them on effective presentation techniques. After appropriate preparation, the entrepreneurs present a business plan to a group of 10 to 15 selected investors/service providers/corporate executives, who provide further feedback. This has helped entrepreneurs develop more effective strategies for success as well as building a very large community of diverse professionals who interact on a *pro bono* basis and get to know one another while they learn about what new ideas and technologies are emerging.

- *The Most Innovative New Products Award*. This programme serves two vital functions. First, it gives public recognition to local firms creating innovative new products. Second, it celebrates regional success in nurturing high-tech companies and industry clusters. Committees of volunteers review nominations (100 plus annually), and awards are given at an annual luncheon attended by 1,000 plus: a veritable 'Who's Who' in the regional high-tech economy.
- *Educating service providers and others*. UCSD CONNECT plays a vital role in cross-educating the various constituent groups regarding their distinct needs and challenges. It fosters cross-industry and cross-discipline seminars, courses and discussions and so helps to build the competency of local business service providers.

CONNECT is fully funded by annual members (over 1,000 companies and firms), underwriting and fees for services. It sponsors more than 80 events annually and continues to grow after 15 years of activity in the region.

Today, San Diego has a critical mass of business service providers and local venture capitalists who are experienced in helping technology entrepreneurs. They provide not only technical assistance but also are themselves sources of valuable contacts and advice. They constitute a regional resource that can help new entrepreneurs in new and emerging fields of technology. They have become an important part of San Diego's regional innovation capacity. Simultaneous with the growth of CONNECT, a variety of related regional organizations – the local association of governments SANDAG, the federally funded Defense Industries Consortium, the state-funded Regional Technology Alliance and the research community–based Science and Technology Council – began to focus on what it takes to grow regional companies. In addition, a proliferation of support organizations for high-tech companies has evolved since the founding of CONNECT. Among the organizations in the complex network that exists today are:

- *BIOCOM*, the region's industry council for biotechnology. Affiliated with BIO, the nationwide Biotechnology Industry Organization, BIOCOM serves a number of roles: networking opportunities, an opportunity for executives to learn from each other, a means to develop positions on public policy issues and a mechanism for providing selected services (such as group insurance policies).
- *San Diego Telecommunications Council*. This relatively new organization plays a similar role to BIOCOM in the communications sector.
- *The Software Industry Council*. Also relatively new, this organization

has been a voice for the needs and concerns of software companies.

- *San Diego Regional Economic Development Corporation.* Originally a downtown- and city-focused Economic Development Council, this organization has become a regional 'umbrella' organization, with members from all San Diego industries. It tracks key economic trends and works with local, state and federal agencies on issues of concern to the business community. Twenty-five years old, it is only in the last few years that this organization has become a strong voice for 'high tech'.

- *Private, informal networks.* As San Diego's high-tech industries grow, individuals have built dense networks of contacts. Two of the most notable are those among the 'alumni' of Linkabit and Hybritech. Today, leading business service providers are themselves at the centre of other important social networks. There is also now a local network of over one hundred 'Angel Investors', who meet monthly.

Local circumstances also helped to shape the role and impact of San Diego's social networks. A San Diego leader told us that one feature of the region, not always understood by people from elsewhere, is that the relative geographical isolation of San Diego has helped to build a community and a sense of partnership. In addition, the defence downturn of the early 1990s also encouraged cooperation: one interviewee commented that 'the immediate loss of an industry led to the need to focus on being more competitive and to seek out new industries'. Other interviewees referred to the relatively compact geographical setting of San Diego businesses, which also facilitated cooperation. Yet another referred to a precious commodity – trust. There is, he said, a strong culture of mutual support in San Diego. There seems to be much more trust in the region than in Silicon Valley. 'We do not walk around with non-disclosure agreements like in the Valley,' he added.

Another interviewee, from the biotechnology industry, called the region's business service providers 'venture catalysts' – people who can help to put ventures together quickly and reliably. He said that San Diego now had a critical mass of service providers, such as intellectual property attorneys and business planners, but that these people were not in the region when the first biotechnology firms began. He gives CONNECT much of the credit for helping to build that mass of service providers and for institutionalizing the 'socialization of innovation'. Another interviewee reinforced this remark by noting that in recent years, there had been a major expansion of venture capital funding. This individual indicated that CONNECT had played a role in convincing the venture capitalists to come down from the Bay Area. Since that initial beginning, San Diego has grown local venture capital and angel funding to supplement the outside venture capital.

San Diego today is a very different place from what it was 40 years ago. This is certainly true in terms of research capacity, as we have pointed out in the previous section. However, it is also a very different place from what it was a mere 20 years ago in terms of entrepreneurial *business* capacity. Local firms have transformed or expanded their expertise. Equally important, however, has been the influx of new investors, law firms, global marketing firms and sophisticated management know-how into the region because of the opportunity-rich context and the well-networked 'new economy' community.

## Developing human capital: research institutions and sustaining cluster growth

As San Diego entrepreneurs have formed additional telecommunications and biotechnology companies, UCSD and the other non-profit research institutions in the region have helped to support that growth. This section focuses on three of their contributions:

- continued support for researchers and research;
- educating the new-economy workforce; and
- CONNECT's role, with others, in working with local business and government to create a favourable business climate and to address specific public policy challenges facing the region.

The first two categories reflect the importance of intellectual capital in sustaining the region's research clusters – and thus sustaining the industrial clusters that draw upon those research clusters. They provide people with know-how, the cutting-edge, advanced knowledge needed to sustain clusters and not just

Table 4. Five-year trend in UCSD research funding ($million, 1996–2000), by school or division.

|  | FY1996 | FY1997 | FY1998 | FY1999 | FY2000 |
|---|---|---|---|---|---|
| **School of Medicine** | | | | | |
| Federal | 107.73 | 109.96 | 131.42 | 127.86 | 135.76 |
| Industrial | 22.89 | 21.37 | 28.63 | 31.86 | 26.27 |
| State of California/UCOP | 7.75 | 5.98 | 10.30 | 9.24 | 12.77 |
| *Subtotal* | *138.37* | *137.31* | *170.35* | *168.96* | *174.80* |
| **School of Engineering** | | | | | |
| Federal | 17.58 | 17.48 | 26.34 | 22.23 | 22.81 |
| Industrial | 2.89 | 4.06 | 4.87 | 5.10 | 3.05 |
| State of California/UCOP | 1.67 | 16.28 | 4.11 | 3.72 | 7.83 |
| *Subtotal* | *22.14* | *37.82* | *35.32* | *31.05* | *33.69* |
| **Division of Biology** | | | | | |
| Federal | 15.87 | 14.67 | 18.13 | 20.79 | 20.49 |
| Industrial | | 0.54 | 0.92 | 0.68 | 0.81 |
| State of California/UCOP | 0.22 | 0.23 | 0.49 | 0.32 | 0.82 |
| *Subtotal* | *16.09* | *15.44* | *19.54* | *21.79* | *22.12* |
| **Division of Physical Sciences** | | | | | |
| Federal | 14.46 | 17.81 | 18.72 | 16.42 | 18.97 |
| Industrial | 0.59 | 1.06 | 1.10 | 0.62 | 0.75 |
| State of California/UCOP | 0.39 | 0.99 | 0.88 | 0.77 | 0.96 |
| *Subtotal* | *15.44* | *19.86* | *20.70* | *17.81* | *20.68* |
| ***Total*** | ***324.57*** | ***351.43*** | ***412.38*** | ***446.12*** | ***461.71*** |

*Source:* UCSD Office of Contracts and Grants Administration.
UCOP – University of California's Office of the President.

maintain current operations. The third category shows the value of finding ways for emerging industries to work with the overall business community and with government ('know-who').

## Continued support for research

R&D-based industrial clusters must stay constantly innovative in order to remain competitive. One part of being innovative is to maintain ready access to world-class researchers who are continually carrying out cutting-edge research. A wide variety of research institutes in San Diego are playing that role; the talent pool and research funding are increasing region-wide. However, UCSD is the largest centre, and a closer look at its growth can provide some insight into this process. For example, Table 4 summarizes key amounts of outside funding won recently by major divisions of UCSD – the School of Medicine, the School of Engineering, Biology and the Physical Sciences.

One significant step at UCSD has been the growth of the School of Engineering. Established only in 1992, it has grown steadily. After a mere decade, it has 130 faculty members and was ranked 16th among engineering schools in the nation in the 2002 edition of *US News & World Report*'s annual survey of America's 'Best Graduate Schools' (*US News & World Report*, 2001). Equally important for San Diego's telecommunications industry, the school has established a Center for Wireless Communication. UCSD is now well on the way to becoming the centre of a San Diego research cluster in wireless telecommunications.

The School of Medicine has also experienced significant growth in recent years, increasing by nearly $40 million in FY1998. Cancer research, Alzheimer's disease, cardiology and molecular medicine represent the areas of most significant growth and continue to be fields which attract multiyear/multimillion-dollar research grants.

## Educating the workforce

In the case of emerging science-based fields such as information technology, molecular medicine and biotechnology, UCSD and the region's other non-profit research institutions are educating the knowledge workers of the future as well as hiring the world-class researchers of today. Educating skilled workers is an important contribution that these institutions make to the region's growing high-tech clusters. In addition to educating undergraduates, UCSD makes three other types of contributions: graduate degrees, post-doctoral training and continuing education for a post-baccalaureate workforce.

*Graduate education*. UCSD is the major provider of PhD-level training in the San Diego region. While there are other institutions of higher education in the region, the size of their PhD training programmes runs from small to non-existent in comparison to that of UCSD. The two California State universities, San Diego State University and CSU San Marcos, have extensive graduate programmes at the Masters level but partner with UCSD to offer small

**Table 5. Five-year trend in UCSD's graduate student enrolments (1999–2000).**

|  | 1995 | 1996 | 1997 | 1998 | 1999 | 2000 |
|---|---|---|---|---|---|---|
| **All subjects** | | | | | | |
| Masters | 488 | 537 | 594 | 601 | 706 | 696 |
| PhD | 1,917 | 1,888 | 1,876 | 1,856 | 1,869 | 1,883 |
| *Total* | *2,405* | *2,425* | *2,470* | *2,457* | *2,575* | *2,579* |
| S&E, SIO & Health Sciences only[a] | 1,451 | 1,462 | 1,513 | 1,518 | 1,639 | 1,644 |
| *% of total* | *60%* | *60%* | *61%* | *62%* | *64%* | *64%* |
| Life Sciences only[b] | 388 | 401 | 419 | 407 | 420 | 404 |
| *% of total* | *16%* | *17%* | *17%* | *17%* | *16%* | *16%* |

*Source:* UCSD Office of Graduate Studies and Research. These numbers also include all students enrolled in the Joint Programs with San Diego State University.

[a]S&E – Science and Engineering; SIO – The Scripps Institution of Oceanography; Health Sciences – Biomedical Sciences, Molecular Pathology, and Neurosciences. Does not include MD, RN or Pharmacy students.
[b]Life Sciences – Biological Sciences and Health Sciences only.

**Table 6. Five-year trend in PhD student enrolments at the Scripps Research Institute (Fall 1997–2001).[a]**

| Year | Fall enrolments |
|---|---|
| 1997 | 120 |
| 1998 | 132 |
| 1999 | 141 |
| 2000 | 145 |
| 2001 | 158 |

[a]The Scripps Research Institute PhD programmes are all in the life sciences.

joint PhD programmes in the sciences. Likewise, the University of San Diego, a private institution, offers Masters-level programmes but not PhD-level training. The only other institution that offers PhD-level training is the Scripps Research Institute; all of its students are enrolled in the life sciences. These enrolment figures are detailed in Tables 5 and 6.

*Post-doctoral training.* In addition to graduate students, the San Diego region provides a rich training ground for post-doctoral fellows in a variety of fields, especially the life sciences. These individuals may be key to the region's biotechnology human capital. Although PhD graduates and post-doctoral fellows constitute a highly mobile workforce, these workers are eagerly seeking permanent employment after their training. Post-docs are even more motivated to find permanent job opportunities than newly minted PhDs. While a certain percentage of these highly trained individuals will go on to academic careers, in San Diego or elsewhere, a larger percentage can be tapped to become a part of the industrial R&D infrastructure of the region.

UCSD is the largest employer of post-doctoral fellows and researchers, but it is not the sole training ground for these skilled workers (see Table 7). See Table 3 (p 33) for a partial survey of post-doctoral fellows in the San Diego

**Table 7. UCSD's population of post-doctoral researchers (1996–2000).**

| Schools and divisions | 1996 | 1997 | 1998 | 1999 | 2000 |
|---|---|---|---|---|---|
| Arts & Humanities | 1 | 5 | 9 | 10 | 7 |
| Biology | 137 | 130 | 133 | 163 | 157 |
| Engineering | 56 | 67 | 59 | 64 | 60 |
| International Relations & Pacific Studies | 1 | 1 | 0 | 0 | 0 |
| Medicine | 422 | 422 | 405 | 467 | 422 |
| Sciences | 114 | 104 | 124 | 144 | 147 |
| Scripps Institution of Oceanography | 82 | 72 | 58 | 61 | 73 |
| Social Sciences | 22 | 22 | 23 | 28 | 22 |
| Other | 0 | 0 | 0 | 0 | 1 |
| *Total* | *835* | *823* | *811* | *937* | *889* |
| *Subtotal (Science, Engineering, SIO & Health)* | *811* | *795* | *779* | *899* | *859* |
| *% (Science, Engineering, SIO & Health)* | *97%* | *97%* | *96%* | *96%* | *97%* |
| *Subtotal (Life Sciences only)* | *559* | *552* | *538* | *630* | *579* |
| *% Life Sciences* | *67%* | *67%* | *66%* | *67%* | *65%* |

area's life sciences research institutes. Combined, these research institutes train a larger number of post-doctoral fellows than UCSD alone.

Anecdotal evidence suggests that companies are choosing to relocate or site R&D establishments in San Diego to take advantage of the specialized human capital that is developing in this region. As job opportunities increase, these highly skilled workers can be lured from company to company, forming and retaining informal technical and business networks (that is, the formation of 'churn'), a process that is vital to creating a region's competitive advantage.

*Continuing education for post-baccalaureate professionals.* In addition to regular degree programmes, San Diego's area universities provide specialized educational programmes for working professionals. For example, UCSD has a large and growing Extension programme which provides post-baccalaureate continuing education in fields especially relevant to science-based companies, ranging from specialized courses in technical areas such as CDMA engineering to introductory courses in new emerging areas such as drug development and clinical trials management to intensive managerial workshops for bench scientists making the transition to managerial duties.

Regional enrolments in continuing education can be substantial. In a recent study, Lee and Walshok (2001) show that continuing education enrolments in California are significant and can dwarf regular full-time undergraduate and graduate enrolments combined. Furthermore, on a per-capita basis, regions with thriving high-tech industry clusters

**Table 8. Comparison of full-time and Extension enrolments for high-tech v low-tech regions of Southern California.[a]**

| | Full-time enrolments[b] | Extension/continuing education enrolments |
|---|---|---|
| UC San Diego | 18,054 | 39,282 |
| San Diego State | 31,040 | 70,810 |
| CSU San Marcos | 5,758 | 10,833 |
| *Total (San Diego)* | *54,852* | *120,925* |
| UC Riverside | 11,224 | 25,019 |
| CSU San Bernardino | 14,168 | 8,136 |
| *Total (Inland Empire)* | *25,392* | *33,155* |
| Per capita enrolments: [c] San Diego County | 0.019 | 0.043 |
| Inland Empire | 0.008 | 0.010 |

[a]The 'Inland Empire' consists of Riverside–San Bernardino Counties combined. The regions of San Diego and Inland Empire were chosen for comparison because they have similar populations and are located close to each other.
[b]Based on academic year 1999–2000 full-time head counts for both graduate and undergraduate students.
[c]Based on US Census populations (est 7/99).

(like San Diego) have higher Extension enrolments in science and technology programmes than regions that do not (such as Riverside–San Bernardino). See Table 8.

Taken together, the 60,000 plus employees in technology companies, the close to 3,000 active graduate students, and the 2,000 plus post-doctoral fellows represent an enormous source of talent for creative innovation. Add to this the large number of post-baccalaureate Extension students and it is easy to see how an innovative region like San Diego is continuously growing and adapting its talent pool to the innovative challenges of the moment.

# Conclusion

What we suspect from our preliminary findings from Southern California research that is now in progress throughout the state and the work of colleagues such as Doug Henton at Collaborative Economics and Lou Tornatsky from the Southern Regional Technology Alliance is that the research-technology commercialization-job creation nexus is increasingly complex. Advances in science and technology are requiring a much more varied set of conditions and relationships to assure the establishment and development of companies at the regional level that create high-wage jobs and new forms of wealth. We have asserted throughout this article that the three major 'hooks' to think about are:

(1) the store of intellectual capital in a region;
(2) the character and extent of catalytic business and financial networks; and

(3) the breadth and depth of the advanced skills and knowledge of the human capital resident in the region.

When we examine the phenomenal transformation of a region such as San Diego over the last two decades, the data are quite compelling. The research capacity has grown, the managerial and business competency of the region has increased, the pool of investment capital has grown and the expansion of education and training programmes in advanced skills has been significant. Most of these activities are externally funded. They are not subsidized by the State of California. Competitively won research grants are coming from national foundations and federal sources; the regional networks are funded by local companies and business service providers, and the advanced education and training programmes are supported largely by employer reimbursements. Parallel to the growth in research capacity, the community appears to be making an investment in its own development. That investment appears to be paying off in terms of new companies formed and jobs created.

Many might be inclined to argue that one cannot extrapolate from the unique experience of a single region such as San Diego, a new research institution such as UCSD or a specialized programme such as UCSD CONNECT. Our response would be that clearly the San Diego experience, in terms of both the growth of its research institutions and the development of the CONNECT programme, may be unique to the history and circumstances of a particular place. Nonetheless, our ideas about the three guiding principles for thinking about regional innovation capacity grow out of our knowledge of developments in San Diego, the Silicon Valley, North Carolina, Austin and a number of other regions that have experienced similar transformations over the past couple of years. Each of these, as evidenced by Doug Henton's and Louis Tomatzky's papers in this issue of *Industry and Higher Education*, has made substantial investments in building capacity along the three dimensions we have discussed. Regional authorities and civic leaders have made significant efforts to build a regionally anchored research capacity in science and technology, initiatives have been taken to create networked communities of competence and expertise supportive of technology commercialization, and educational institutions have mobilized to provide skills and knowledge in areas relevant to emerging technology clusters.

Our work continues, and we are using these metrics in other regions across the State of California and across the USA as a way of further elucidating dimensions of regional innovation capacity that are not typically discussed among economic development specialists and civic leaders. We suspect that these metrics will help regions better to understand their assets as well as their gaps. They also can help communities to benchmark where they stand *vis-à-vis* other regions with similar aspirations. What is so promising about the new economy and the expansion of knowledge in fields such as engineering, biochemistry, computer science and the life sciences is the wealth of new products, processes and interventions that promise to benefit humankind. Whether it be in communications, materials science, pharmaceuticals, agricultural bio-tech or in new and emerging fields such as bio-inframatics, the opportunities are expanding in terms of research questions as well the useful applications of technologies. This means that many regions with narrower capacity still can pursue the development of industrial clusters that generate high-wage jobs and new wealth for their regions. A region such as San Diego is blessed with multiple capabilities in science and technology because of its unique history. Therefore, it may not represent a 'model' for other regions. However, as we have argued throughout this article, some of the key factors that have shaped the growth of the San Diego region – the intellectual, human and networking capacities that have developed over the last two decades – may represent principles of transformation useful to the analysis of other regions around the globe.

## Notes

1SBIR is the Small Business Innovation Research Program of the US National Science Foundation.
2*Source:* RaDiUS, a RAND–developed database encompassing all R&D funded by various US federal agencies. Public access to the classified section of RaDiUS is prohibited. Therefore, the numbers quoted in this report consist of non-classified R&D only (including non-classified funding from the Department of Defense), unless otherwise noted. Total R&D funding, including classified R&D funding, would be substantially higher.

3This figure includes classified and non-classified research funding.
4If one were to break funding out by loosely defined metropolitan areas such as the 'Bay Area', 'Greater LA', and 'San Diego', San Diego would always come in a distant third. We would argue that this breakdown leaves much to be desired: for example, the Bay Area is an area from four to nine counties in size, depending on the definition chosen. A similar situation exists for the Greater Los Angeles area.
5HHS is a proxy for NIH (the National Institutes of Health).
6*Source:* National Science Foundation. The FY 1998 figure was $297,340,000 in federal obligations for science and engineering.

## References

Anderson, Nancy Scott (1993), *An Improbable Venture: A History of the University of California, San Diego*, The UCSD Press, La Jolla, CA.

Castells, Manuel, and Hall, Peter (1994), *Technopoles of the World: The Making of 21st Century Industrial Complexes*, Routledge, London and New York.

Collaborative Economics (1999), *Innovative Regions: the Importance of Place and Networks in the Innovative Society*, report sponsored by the Heinz Endowments, Innovation Works, Inc, and the Pittsburgh Regional Alliance, Collaborative Economics, Mountain View, CA.

Cox, Marney, and Eary, Matthew (undated), *Industrial Cluster Based Regional Economic Development Information System*, report submitted to San Diego Regional Technology Alliance, San Diego, CA.

DeBresson, Chris, and Amesse, Fernand (1991), 'Networks of innovators: a review and introduction to the issue', *Research Policy*, Vol 20, pp 363–379.

Fossum, Donna, Painter, Lawrence S., Williams, Valerie, Yezril, Allison, Newton, Elaine, and Trinkle, David (2000), *Discovery and Innovation: Federal Research and Development Activities in the Fifty States, District of Columbia, and Puerto Rico (2000)*, RAND, Santa Monica, CA.

Greater San Diego Chamber of Commerce (1999), *Economic Bulletin: Technology 1999*, Vol 47, No 8.

Horvath, Michael T. K., *California Venture Capital Infrastructure Study*, report to the California Council on Science and Technology, 8 April 1999.

Lee, C.W.B., and Walshok, M. (2001), *Critical Path Analysis of California's S&T Education System: Alternative Paths to Competency Through Continuing Education and Lifelong Learning*, report for the California Council on Science and Technology, April.

Lee, Carolyn, and Walshok, Mary (2000), *Making Connections: The Evolution of Links Between UCSD Researchers and San Diego's Biotech Industry*, UCSD CONNECT, San Diego, CA.

Palmintera, Diane, *et al* (2000), *Developing High-Technology Communities: San Diego*, report produced by Innovation Associates, Inc, under contract to the Office of Advocacy, US Small Business Administration.

Porter, Michael E. (1998), *On Competition*, Harvard Business School Press, Cambridge, MA.

PriceWaterhouse Coopers (2000), *MoneyTreeTM Survey Report*, PwC.

San Diego Association of Governments (2001), *San Diego Regional Employment Clusters: Engines of the Modern Economy*, SANDAG, San Diego, CA, August.

Saxenian, AnnaLee (1991), 'The origins and dynamics of production networks in Silicon Valley', *Research Policy*, Vol 20, pp 423–437.

Saxenian, AnnaLee (1994), *Regional Advantage: Culture and Competition in Silicon Valley and Route 128*, Harvard University Press, Cambridge, MA.

Scott, Allen J. (1991), 'The aerospace-electronics industrial complex of Southern California: the formative years, 1940–1960', *Research Policy*, Vol 20, pp 439–456.

Stephan, Paula E. (1999), 'Using human resource data to illuminate innovation and research utilization', an issues paper prepared for the Workshop on Using Human Resources to Assess Research Utilization and Innovation, Board on Science, Technology and Economic Policy, National Research Council, Washington, DC, 23 November.

Swann, Peter, and Prevezer, Martha (1996), 'A comparison of the dynamics of industrial clustering in computing and biotechnology', *Research Policy*, Vol 25, pp 1139–1157.

Tornatzky, Louis G. (2002), 'Technology-based economic development in Atlanta and Georgia: the role of university partnerships', *Industry and Higher Education*, Vol 16, No 1, pp 19–26.

US News & World Report (2001), *Best Graduate Schools*, 2002 edition, Washington, DC.

Walshok, Mary Lindenstein (1995), *Knowledge Without Boundaries: What America's Research Universities Can Do for the Economy, the Workplace, and the Community*, Jossey-Bass Publishers, San Francisco, CA.

Walshok, M., Lee, C., Furtek, E., and Windham, P. (2001), *Networks of Innovation: Contributions to San Diego's Telecommunications and Biotechnology Clusters*, report for the Industry and Cooperative Research Program of the University of California, May.

Zucker, Lynne G., and Darby, Michael R. (1996), 'Star scientists and institutional transformation: patterns of invention and innovation in the formation of the biotechnology industry', *Proceedings of the National Academy of Sciences USA*, Vol 93, pp 12709–12716.

# Universities and their local partners

## The case of the University of Joensuu, Finland

**Perttu Vartiainen and Arto Viiri**

**Abstract**: In the 1990s Finland began to emphasize a 'new', expertise-based regional policy driven by local initiatives and networking. An essential part of this approach is the intertwining of the universities and regional development processes, in which a major role is played by such facilities as science parks. At the heart of the regional impact of the University of Joensuu is the research and training carried out in its basic academic units. The greatest regional effect of the university is due to its internationally competitive research and education, as well as to the development of strategic priority areas. The strategic focal points and strengths of the University of Joensuu, the Joensuu Science Park and the North Karelia region of Finland complement one another well. In addition to the university's own departments, a key channel for transferring expertise is the Joensuu Science Park. The park is responsible for technology transfer, training, development measures and networking with other actors in their fields of expertise.

**Keywords:** regional development; university–science park cooperation; university–region cooperation; Joensuu; Finland

Perttu Vartiainen is Rector of the University of Joensuu, Administration, PO Box 111, 80101 Joensuu, Finland. Arto Viiri is Planning Officer at the University of Joensuu.

The Finnish system of higher education is divided into two parts: universities and polytechnics. Only the university sphere includes basic research and research training. There are 21 universities in Finland,

10 of which are multi-faculty. The universities are situated in 11 locations, but their activities extend elsewhere. Including project activities financed externally, university education is provided in at least 35 different places in Finland. Furthermore, the country has an extensive, regional, open university network that offers credit-bearing university courses. New features of the system include project-based university research centres established in smaller towns, and locally funded research professorships. In addition to the universities, there are 31 polytechnics operating in more than 80 locations.

The decentralization of the university system beyond the major cities of Helsinki and Turku occurred mainly in the late 1950s through to the 1970s. The University of Joensuu, established in 1969, is a middle-sized comprehensive university with 6,500 students pursuing degrees. From the perspective of the Finnish regional structure, its operational environment is the periphery. Both the North Karelia region, where the main Joensuu campus is located, and the area of Savonlinna in the South Savo region, the home of its second campus, are part of the Eastern Finland Objective 1 region for the period 2000–2006 for European Union regional and structural policies.

In the period from its inception until the early 1990s, the University of Joensuu gradually shed its image as a provincial university and teacher training college. The background to this was largely the internal logic of the university system: ambitious young scholars wanted to build a true university functioning in disciplines of its own choosing, and measuring up to international criteria. The goal was to become a research institution that could compete internationally. A regional focus appeared to run contrary to these desires. Thus some of the university's regional obligations were transferred to the Continuing Education Centre, established in the mid-1980s.

The aim of the University of Joensuu is to find a balance between diversity and specialization, achieving a sufficiently diversified whole, while at the same time permitting specialization in a few strong disciplines.

The university's strategic fields of excellence are:

- a multidisciplinary teacher education programme preparing teachers for all levels of the educational system;
- research and teaching pertaining to forests, other renewable resources and the environment;
- proficiency in the development and application of high technology; and
- research on the social and cultural development of European peripheral areas and border regions.

In the high-technology area, each of the university's natural sciences faculties specializes in one or two fields. In forestry, alongside the traditional expertise in forest management, there has been increasing specialization in wood technology. The humanities and education faculties, in turn, specialize in educational and language technology.

## Role of universities in old and new regional policy

The establishment of today's regional universities in Finland is considered to have been one of the prime achievements of the so-called 'old' (1960s–1980s) regional policy. First, the new universities have had significant immediate and indirect effects on the employment and income situation in the towns in which they are located – see, for example, the assessment of the economic influence of the University of Joensuu (Linnosmaa, 1998) compiled for a report on the regional impacts of universities in Eastern Finland (Dahllöf *et al,* 1998). Second, the presence of academic activity and the provision of services by universities have also created the conditions for success in other economic and cultural fields. Third, as a result of the trained labour force that they produce, the influence of the new universities has extended throughout a significant area beyond the university towns themselves (cf Antikainen & Jolkkonen, 1994).

Regional development in Finland from the mid-1970s until the early 1990s was relatively balanced. In the Joensuu travel-to-work area this was reflected in continued growth from the 1960s to the mid-1990s. The new universities, with growing numbers of students and staff, played a significant role. The main reason behind the regional decentralization of the university system was the need of the welfare state for expertise. The expansion of regional administration also supported the development of the towns housing the new universities.

More recently, knowledge and expertise (competence) have become central production factors in regional as well as national economic development. In the 1990s Finland started to emphasize a 'new', expertise-based regional policy driven by local initiatives and networking (Vartiainen, 1998). We may speak of a dual process of globalization and localization. With the reduced importance of the nation state, economic growth is determined primarily by global, or at least by transnational, integration and competition. On the other hand, local solutions and initiatives are increasingly critical competitive factors. The framework of the global information economy (Castells, 1996) is, in addition to expertise and internationalization, deepening local interaction.

The two-way course of development of globalization and localization is also substantially changing the operating conditions of universities and the challenges they face (in the international context see Chatterton and Goddard, 2000). Universities assume a completely new regional role. An essential part of this new challenge is the intertwining of the universities with regional development processes, in which a major role seems to be played by such facilities as science parks. Universities are now a part of a regionally constructed innovation system, comprising universities and polytechnics as well as other educational and research institutions, science parks and centres of expertise, knowledge-intensive enterprises and the like. The regional connection is no longer a less valued feature of provincial universities, and science parks and technology centres engaged in technology transfer and new innovative business activities in the vicinity of a university have been created alongside many of the world's leading universities.

Universities are expected to have effects that are strategically directed and based on local co-operation processes, and not simply to improve the general income and employment situation or raise the general level of education. Logically, to achieve this development universities today have to play an active role in regional development as one of a number of local actors.

## The university as engine of regional development

In the global information economy, the prime success stories in Finland are to be seen in Helsinki, Oulu and Tampere, and to a lesser extent in Turku and Jyväskylä – that is, in all the larger university cities. In this discussion the Joensuu region is at an institutional divide which separates university sites into winners and losers. The region's development image darkened in the mid-1990s. As a result, voices have been raised in Finland sceptical about the idea that the decentralization of the university system was a far-reaching blessing of Finnish regional policy. Only a few universities are seen to have succeeded in generating an increase of jobs in high-technology fields in their surrounding regions.

Seen from this perspective, universities are primarily innovation generators rather than traditional educational institutions. When we assess the development of Finland's regional differentiation in the 1990s, we must remember that it has been exceptionally IT and generally technologically centred. In the technology-centred approach to achieving the desired regional impact of universities, over-ambitious goals are set with unrealistic deadlines. The regional impact is often measured simply on the basis of how many graduates are placed in the university area or how many technological enterprises are established in the vicinity of the campus.

Consequently, we should not accept short-sighted interpretations of the development potential of different regions. Many regional universities have emphasized disciplines that should provide a workforce for a region larger than their immediate area. For example, teacher training at the University of Joensuu is such a discipline; by supporting its development, the university created a basic structure on which a high-quality education system for all of Eastern Finland could be built. Now, in the face of a current threatened shortage of teachers, the fundamental importance of this approach has again been recognized – hopefully not too late, since, from the standpoint of recruitment in the technology fields, the particular threat is to teacher training in the areas of mathematics and science.

It is specifically through the provision of labour that the effects of the new universities have significantly extended beyond the confines of their local communities. On the other hand, it is clear that the regional universities, originally established to serve the needs of the welfare state and the public sector, will also strengthen the new knowledge-based society and the growth areas of the private sector. There have been indications in recent years of expansion in informationintensive fields in smaller university towns, although they are well behind the more successful growth centres.

Among the university cities in Eastern Finland, population and employment development in the Joensuu region took a turn for the better in the late 1990s (Vartiainen, 2001). However, university regions have not been able to prevent a relative recession throughout the whole of the large regional periphery. We can only guess at how much worse the economic climate of Eastern Finland would have been following the depression of the 1990s without its three universities.

On the other hand, it seems that the fast-growing Oulu region has not been able to generate positive development in the entire region of Northern Finland, where development has been even more strongly polarized than in the Eastern region of the country.

## Interaction between the University of Joensuu and its region

From a broad perspective, the interaction between a university and its region can be examined in terms of three circles of influence (Figure 1). The technology-driven model functions in the smallest circle of the three, in which the prime motors are research and product development and the professional training required by high-tech enterprises. The motive power of the broader second circle is science and arts in the classical context of academic research and the learning based on it. The third and broadest circle concerns the general regional environment, in which the sought-after ideal is a creative and tolerant milieu.

We examine the regional role of the University of Joensuu on the basis of these three circles. In the group of medium-sized or small university towns in Finland, Joensuu has the only clearly liberal arts university. The strengths of the liberal arts university are presented in the second circle. At the heart of the regional impact of the University of Joensuu are the research and training carried out in its basic academic units. In addition, the university has three autonomous units – the Continuing Education Centre, the Savonlinna Centre for Continuing Education and Regional Development and the Karelian Institute – that play a key role in transferring expertise to points outside the university towns. University disciplines, however, require constant reinforcement and well-formulated profiles. At present the educational profiles of those academic disciplines that more directly support information-intensive economic knowledge and skills need to be strengthened. With this in mind, the University of Joensuu has recently concentrated on developing the fields of computer science, business studies and law. Activities at the university's Savonlinna campus have emphasized the development of such fields as tourism and translation technology.

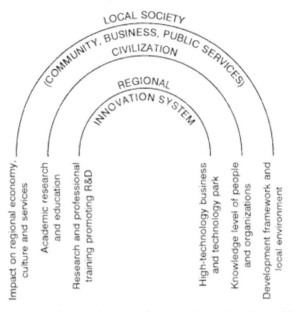

**Figure 1.** The three circles of interaction between the university and its region.

The Continuing Education Centre in Joensuu and the Savonlinna Centre for Continuing Education and Regional Development oversee the development of adult expertise. They are responsible for several projects supported by the European Social Fund (ESF) which assist community development and small business as well as employment policy. The projects also involve numerous enterprises, the North Karelia Chamber of Commerce and the North Karelia Business Association. Corresponding research to serve these areas has been initiated in conjunction with the Karelian Institute, which also receives support from European Structural Funds.

In the mid-1990s the administrative responsibility for regional development shifted from state regional organizations to municipal federation-like regional councils. The university actively participated in the 1990s in strategic activities in North Karelia and in the two towns in which it is situated. Correspondingly, the regions of North Karelia and South Savo have increasingly based their development work on university strengths, especially in technology-related fields.

In recent years, the university has emphasized the needs for active cooperation with the university towns and urban regions. Strong sectors in the Joensuu region and North Karelia include forestry and wood technology, the plastics and metals industry and a number of special areas of information technology. In addition, the university's demonstrated expertise in border areas and Russia has developed into a key focal area. Correspondingly, in Savonlinna the university has supported a concentration of expertise in tourism and translation technology, as part of information technology.

Furthermore, the university's excellence in environmental matters is significantly related to the study of natural sciences and the humanities. There is a strong concentration of forestry and environmental expertise in Joensuu: the Finnish Forestry Research Institute, the European Forest Institute, the Game and Fisheries Research Institute and the North Karelia Regional Environmental Centre are all located there.

On the other hand, in the future Finland will require not only interdisciplinary information technology applications, but completely new growth areas as well. Such expertise is to be found at the University of Joensuu, for example, in optics, materials research and plant biotechnology. In order to strengthen and expand this expertise, plans are now underway to establish jointly financed professorships in all the priority areas of the Joensuu Science Park. The first two of these, professorships in wood science and material chemistry, were inaugurated in 2001.

## Technology-driven partnership in practice

In addition to the university's own departments, key channels for the transfer of expertise are the Joensuu Science Park and the North Karelia Center of Expertise, which the park administers. The role of these facilities is emphasized in the second, technology-driven circle of Figure 1. It is characteristic of the Finnish innovation system that municipalities and municipal federations play a strong role as local intermediary organizations. In this way the regional innovation system relies on a tripartite interaction: universities and other educational institutions, public authorities (municipalities and state sector administrations) and business.

The flagship of the new Finnish regional policy is the Centre of Expertise Programme. This programme represents the Finnish model for directing regional and national resources towards the development of internationally competitive areas of competence. The programme has been functioning in Finland since early 1994. At present there are 14 regional centres of expertise and two national network centres. The main principle behind the implementation of the Centre of Expertise Programme is that of mutual competition. Acceptance into the programme is contingent on the existence of a concentration of high-level competence, a programme of innovative and influential activities and efficient organization. The centres of expertise also compete for annual basic funding provided by the state, which guarantees their continued development work.

In almost all centres of expertise, the actual coordinator and nucleus is the local science park or technology centre. The Joensuu Science Park Ltd was founded in April 1990, with the City of Joensuu as its main shareholder. Other shareholders are the University of Joensuu Foundation and the state, represented by the

University of Joensuu, the Regional Council of North Karelia, the North Karelia Polytechnic, and the North Karelia Educational Federation of Municipalities.

Apart from building services, the key activities of the Joensuu Science Park revolve around:

- the development of new innovative business activities;
- a focus on selected key technological areas; and
- the activities of the North Karelia Center of Expertise.

The park is a member of the Association of Finnish Technology Centres (TEKEL), the European Business and Innovation Centre Network (EBN) and the International Association of Science Parks (IASP).

The Joensuu Science Park and the University of Joensuu provide a concentration of high-level expertise just outside the centre of Joensuu. The main building of the park constitutes a convergence of information technology, media, optics and innovative planning enterprises, and also houses the teaching and research facilities of the university's Department of Computer Science, laboratories for plant biotechnology and natural materials research and training and research facilities in information technology and the media, as well as the project and service operations of the North Karelia Polytechnic.

The facilities of the science park comprise 13,800 square metres of business, laboratory and teaching space. Forty-five firms are currently on the site. The building extension now underway will provide an additional 12,700 square metres of floor space. The park will then become the home of 800 employees and 700 students. It will form an operational sphere in which business personnel and researchers, teachers and students can meet one another and develop ideas and possibilities.

The Joensuu Science Park Ltd oversees the operations of the North Karelia Centre of Expertise, which focuses on the two areas of plastics and metals technology and wood technology and forestry. The main activities in the field of wood technology and forestry are located in the Wood Technology Centre, while the plastics and metals technology expertise is concentrated in the Injection Moulding and Tooling Engineering Centre. The North Karelia Centre of Expertise is responsible for technology transfer, training, development measures and networking with other actors and academic experts.

The main goal of the centre is the creation and development of internationally successful enterprises by increasing capability and the introduction of new technology, as well as through the establishment of new cooperative models for businesses and research and educational institutions. Figure 2 shows how the strengths of the university, park and region complement each other. In the near future, the specialization of the University of Joensuu in the social and cultural development of peripheral and local areas, and its multidisciplinary expertise on Russia, could provide the basis for a third area of competence of the centre.

As a result of the rapid development of the science park and the centre of expertise, Joensuu has made great strides in recent years in the first (that is, the technology-driven) circle. The university, in close cooperation with the Joensuu Science Park and the North Karelia Center of Expertise, is today a strong element in the regional innovation system, which also includes other major actors, such as information-intensive enterprises like Abloy, Perlos, Novo; the North Karelia Polytechnic; the Forestry Research Institute, which has strengthened its activities in Joensuu; other educational and research institutions; and other public and quasi-public intermediary organizations (like the new Joensuu Region Development Company or the National Technology Agency under state regional administration).

The bottleneck in technology-driven development in an area like Joensuu is not necessarily due to a lack of sufficient high-level research potential or the lack of a technical faculty, but the scarcity of intensive business R&D. So the relative share of R&D expenditure of the region's universities is, in a sense, disproportionately large. In the regions surrounding two university towns in Eastern Finland, North Savo and North Karelia, the university share comprises about half of the region's R&D expenditure, while in the region surrounding Helsinki it is less than 20%.

## The university in local society

From the standpoint of the third circle of Figure 1, the evolution of an appropriate climate for development,

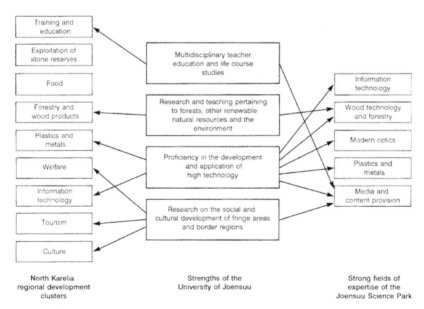

**Figure 2.** The strategic priority areas and strengths of the North Karelia region complement one another well.

the importance of the university is also decisive. In terms of the regional economy, taking into account only the direct effects on income and employment, in both the towns in which it is situated, the university is the most stable organization of all. The intellectual and non-partisan culture and the service provision of the university in its campus towns have been prerequisites in their own success in other economic and cultural areas. An innovative local environment is a major factor in competing for quality researchers and students and, from the standpoint of university funding, for the creation of important new partnerships.

There are several outstanding examples of such special partnerships in the Joensuu region. Cooperation with the City of Joensuu has resulted in the Carelia auditorium and concert hall and its congress services, the Botania botanical gardens and the library. The Joensuu campus and the science park are located near to the city's most attractive area for leisure activities. Furthermore, the company responsible for student apartments is City owned – and providing and developing quality student housing is one of the key objectives of housing policy in both Joensuu and Savonlinna.

## The academic and universal mission

In Finland, interaction between a university and its region is based largely on money from EU Structural Funds and municipal finance. Direct business funding plays a lesser part. In addition, the National Technology Agency (TEKES) has a significant role in funding product development and research projects. The university itself chiefly provides intellectual resources and infrastructure. The Ministry of Education emphasizes the third task of the universities, but this is not recognized in the budget for tertiary-level education which actually sets limits on direct financial investment. This prohibition on university funding activities is in conflict with the EU principle of 'additionality' and has hindered universities' participation in development work in their regions.

In the case of Joensuu, it has been possible to reduce these funding difficulties through the financial support of the University of Joensuu Foundation. In addition, businesses and municipal authorities in the region have supported the development of training and research in areas that respond to the needs of local business through endowment professorships.

European Union Structural Funds are used to support the community's regional and structural policy measures. The task of the European Regional Development Fund (ERDF) is to reduce disparities in regional development. Its measures are chiefly directed towards increasing investment in production and improving the level of infrastructure. The European Social Fund is the Community's most important instrument for developing the human resources of a region. Its measures are directed mainly towards training and increasing expertise and vocational skills. The University of Joensuu makes use of the financial opportunities offered by Structural Funds to enable it to direct its work

**Table 1. EU Structural Fund projects of the University of Joensuu in 2000–2001.**

| | Multidisciplinary teacher education and life course studies | Research and teaching pertaining to forests, other renewable natural resources and the environment | Proficiency in the development and application of high technology | Research on the social and cultural development of fringe areas and border regions | Other research topics | Total |
|---|---|---|---|---|---|---|
| ESF | 4 | 1 | 3 | 9 | 1 | 18 |
| ERDF | | 3 | 6 | | | 9 |
| Total | 4 | 4 | 9[a] | 9 | 1 | 27 |

[a] Specifc areas of these projects are: plant biotechnology; materials research; media culture; translation technology (3 projects); educational technology (2 projects); modern optics.

in such a way as to support the implementation of regional objectives.

In Finland, projects financed through Structural Funds are generally approved in the regional units of various administrative sectors. Prior to such decisions being made, the projects are assessed by the regional management committee which comprises the region's political groupings, state regional administration authorities and representatives of management and labour. The University of Joensuu is also represented in North Karelia's regional management committee. The key task of this committee is to ensure the compatibility of the projects with regional objectives. Structural Fund projects of the University of Joensuu have been strongly directed towards selected priority areas (Table 1).

In speaking of 'regionalism', it is tempting to regard it in narrow terms as constituting a separate 'third task' and a separate operational level of the university. This 'third task' of universities, however, should not be considered in isolation from the context of their two traditional functions, education and research. At the same time, regionalism and internationalism go hand in hand. The regional impact of the university is at its best when it is based on internationally competitive research and education and the development of strategic priority areas. Without a sufficiently strong and innovative academic core, the effects of the universities will be short term and dependent on narrow economic and political interests.

## References

Antikainen, A., and Jolkkonen, A. (1994), 'New universities, welfare state and markets: the case of Finland', in Dahllöf and Selander (1994).

Castells, M. (1996), *The Rise of the Network Society,* Blackwell, Oxford.

Chatterton, P., and Goddard, J. (2000), 'The response of higher education institutions to regional needs', *European Journal of Education,* Vol 35, pp 475–496.

Dahllöf, U., and Selander, S. (eds) (1994), 'New universities and regional context', *Acta Universitatis Upsaliensis [Uppsala Studies in Education],* Vol 56, pp 249–257.

Dahllöf, U., *et al* (1998), *Towards the Responsive University: the Regional Role of Eastern Finnish Universities,* Publication of Higher Education Evaluation Council No 8, Edita, Helsinki.

Linnosmaa, I. (1998), 'Economic effects of the University of Joensuu', in *University of Joensuu Self-Evaluation Report,* Appendix 9, University of Joensuu, Joensuu (mimeo).

Vartiainen, P. (1998), *Suomalaisen aluepolitiikan kehitysvaiheita,* SisäasiainministeriQ Aluekehitysosaston julkaisu, 6/1998.

Vartiainen, P. (2001), *Kasvukeskukset globaalin* informaatiotalouden solmukohtina, *Tietoyhteiskuntaja alueellinen keskittyminen, Kuntapuntari* 1/2001, pp 70–75.

# University enterprise
## The growth and impact of university-related companies in London

Dave Chapman, Helen Lawton Smith, Peter Wood, Timothy Barnes and Saverio Romeo

**Abstract:** *Over the last decade, policies framing the enterprise agenda for UK higher education institutions (HEIs) have consistently emphasized the potential impact of successful universities on both regional and national economies. Such policies have been backed by significant public funding to ensure that the UK HEI sector is able to compete globally in the creation and exploitation of cutting-edge science. Collectively, these initiatives have led to the development of a 'third mission' for universities – increasing the pace and impact of knowledge-exchange activities – while simultaneously maintaining and improving their more traditional research and teaching activities. Previous studies have demonstrated the contribution of universities to the growth of high-technology clusters as well as to knowledge-exchange activities more generally. However, the extent to which these activities, particularly the formation of new university-related companies, deliver benefits to particular regions and cities is imperfectly understood. As a consequence, the economic and social impact of companies originating in universities in the UK is generally under-reported by official surveys, which frequently fail to capture details of the trajectories of such companies after formation. These considerations form the context for this paper, which presents the results from a detailed study of the impact of science- and technology-based academic spin-offs from a cross-section of London's HEIs.*

**Keywords:** *academic entrepreneurship; university spin-offs; university enterprise; London*

Dave Chapman (corresponding author) is with the Department of Management Science and Innovation, University College London (UCL), Gower Street London WC1E 6BT, UK. E-mail: d.chapman@ucl.ac.uk. Helen Lawton Smith and Saverio Romeo are with the Department of Management, Birkbeck, University of London, London, UK. Peter Wood is with the Department of Geography at UCL, and Timothy Barnes is with UCL Advances.

Since 2001, data collection on UK university-related company formation has been formalized as part of an annual survey of higher education–business and community interaction (HE-BCI), for the Higher Education Funding Council for England. Whilst such surveys hint at the volume of academic entrepreneurship, they offer little insight into the lifecycle of such enterprises after formation; in particular they contain few details of the subsequent growth of university-related firms.

In the UK, recent longitudinal studies (Anyadike-Danes *et al*, 2009; Mason *et al*, 2009) showed that the wider UK economy possesses a small but significant minority of high-growth firms that have achieved annual growth rates of 20% or higher over a recent three-year period. Such firms can be found within a wide range of industries (financial and business services performing particularly well), with approximately one third located in London and the South East region of England.

This stock of high-growth, high-impact firms is critical with regard to the growth of regional economic activity. For example, in the UK between 2002 and 2008, the 6% of businesses with the highest growth rates generated half of all new jobs created by existing businesses (NESTA, 2009). Many authors have identified the importance of the creation of young 'gazelle' firms which are able to sustain above-average growth in employment or sales over a number of years (see OECD, 2008, for a formal definition) and have argued in favour of interventions that target firms with higher growth potential (Holzl and Friesenbichler, 2008; Anyadike-Danes, *op cit*).

Whilst these surveys present no evidence that high-tech or knowledge-based industries significantly outperform other sectors, one might anticipate that, given the resources available to young university-related firms, these might contribute disproportionately to the stock of such high-performing firms. However, to date there have been relatively few attempts to monitor UK university-related companies over time (Lawton Smith and Ho, 2006; PACEC, 2003; Library House, 2006).

Thus, through the analysis of a cross section of universities in London this article presents an initial attempt to address three questions: (1) what are the key characteristics of university-related companies in London?; (2) how have such activities developed over time? and (3) how do such companies perform in comparison with the general stock of UK companies?

# Universities and entrepreneurship

By 2011, the UK Government will have invested almost £1 billion in the support of enterprise-related activities to help shape how the higher education (HE) sector serves the wider aims of society (PACEC, 2009). Such policies have been underpinned by the belief that increasing entrepreneurial activity is central to the UK's drive for international competitiveness and that the UK's world-class HE sector has a vital role to play in the development of entrepreneurial talent and opportunities. This focus raises new challenges for universities that are required to consolidate and expand a new enterprise-oriented 'third mission' without compromising traditional teaching and research activities.

In striking an appropriate balance, 'entrepreneurial universities' (Gibb and Hannon, 2006) must weigh the perceived mission of their institution against the interests and aspirations of individual researchers (Meyer, 2003; Shane, 2006) within the context of the local and regional economic ecosystem (Porter and Ketels, 2003). Institutional support for technology transfer in the form of company creation continues to evolve in response to external funding stimuli and feedback from the increasingly professionalized technology transfer office (TTO) community (see, for example, recent training programmes, conferences and reports by PraxisUnico in the UK[1] and ASTP in Europe[2]). This has led to a range of incubation strategies with different objectives which may include: maximizing the number; the

potential returns to the university; or the overall financial gain at the point of exit (Clarysse *et al*, 2005).

The successful nurturing of university-related firms requires the establishment of supportive institutional arrangements that stimulate, support and promote new-venture creation. These may include formal modifications of internal procedures, such as the recognizing of enterprise activity in academic promotion criteria, and thus fall within an academic's normal expectations (O'Shea *et al*, 2008). Such measures operate alongside more intangible contributions to a culture of enterprise within the university, including, for instance, the recognition, celebration and consequent legitimization of enterprise achievement amongst academic peers. If this is not the case, then role model effects may be limited (Bercovitz and Feldman, 2004).

In addition to institutions and individual academics willing to participate, the university-related companies must also attract the managerial and financial resources, the absences of which are often perceived as significant barriers to growth (Wright *et al*, 2004). Warren *et al* (2008) found that where universities are isolated from supportive innovation systems, using the availability of venture capital as a proxy, their ability to transfer technology is reduced. They also suggested that in areas where there are weak entrepreneurship communities, new firms must rely more on the universities to provide early-stage financing, facilities and other resources.

# The London context

By many measures, London is the most innovative region of the UK economy. As well as being one of the world's leading business and financial centres it is the second-highest-ranked region in Europe in terms of per-capita venture capital investment. London is also home to more than 42 institutes of higher education and accounts for more than 20% of total UK spending on higher education[3] and 27% of UK research council grant funding. Employing more than 94,000 staff, these institutions educate more than 56,000 graduates per year who can choose from some 11,000 undergraduate and nearly 4,000 postgraduate courses. In technology-related disciplines, London has over 5,000 researchers working in top-ranked research departments. These present a huge array of overlapping and complementary spin-off opportunities, ranging from the physical, engineering, biological and medical sciences to architecture, media and industrial and product design.

On the basis of many innovation theories, this dense network of institutions and entrepreneurial individuals and enterprises should provide a rich ecosystem for innovation (see, for example, Porter and Ketels, 2003). However, the embedding of so many independent university cultures within the very diverse economic landscape of the capital city poses significant problems for the assessment of their impact on regional economic activity. Unlike in the university cities of Oxford and Cambridge, the size and diversity of London-based HE institutions has resulted in a rather piecemeal approach to the provision

of facilities to incubate and support new academic enterprises. Indeed, in analysing survey data from London HEIs, Huggins (2008) reports that '. . . it became highly apparent that the networks between the academic and finance communities in London lack either visibility or transparency', suggesting that this could be related '. . . to the sheer size and number of players and in its financial community, leading to networks between actors that are at best disjointed and at worst disconnected'.

This has led several authors to conclude that London's university-related innovation outputs underperform equivalent activities in other regions. For example, in his analysis of 2004 HE-BCI data, Huggins (2008) concludes that on many dimensions the London region performs poorly. Whilst such analyses often fail to reflect the diversity of institutional size, mission and specialization, even after controlling for institutional size,[4] London's average performance judged on the basis of the HE-BCI return may appear rather modest (see Appendix 1 for more details).

This article seeks to explore further an analysis of London's university-related companies in order to provide additional evidence that will help inform debates about the challenges and achievements of this group of companies.

# Building the database of university-related companies

London HEIs range from large world-class, multi-department institutions, such as University

College London (UCL) and Imperial College (recently ranked 4th and 5th, respectively, in the world[5]), the various other colleges of the University of London, eight other modern universities and many much smaller, specialist institutions. This diversity of institutions, missions and programmes thus represents a distinctive educational ecosystem which supports a wide variety of technological and non-technological entrepreneurial activities.

The results presented here are from a pilot study of 13 HEIs. Those institutions selected reflect the diversity of London HEIs and were initially chosen to represent potential entrepreneurial activity in the creative arts as well as in science and technology. The sample (see Table 1) includes: six University of London colleges (UCL, King's, Queen Mary, Royal Holloway, Birkbeck and Goldsmiths), two universities that received their charters in 1966 (City and Brunel) and three modern universities (London Metropolitan, South Bank and Westminster). Imperial College and the Courtauld Institute of Art are now self-governing institutes, having left London University in 2003. For the purposes of this analysis, the creative arts activities of the Courtauld Institute are omitted.

UK data collection on university-related companies has been formalized in recent years. The annual higher education-business and community interaction (HE-BCI) survey for HEFCE, the Higher Education Funding Council for England, was launched in 2001 and provides key data for measuring policy impact in terms of the counts of university-related companies (HEFCE, 2004). Unfortunately, these data do not list individual company details and provide no significant information regarding company trajectories beyond formation. Thus the starting point for this analysis was the identification of a list of university-related companies.

In order to augment the raw counts available through HE-BCI data, details of company names and, where possible, academic founders were determined from a range of sources, including institutional technology transfer managers and TTO websites. These

Table 1. London HEIs in pilot project.

| High research intensity[a] | Medium research intensity | Low research intensity | Arts and design |
|---|---|---|---|
| Imperial College | Brunel University | London Metropolitan University | Courtauld Institute |
| UCL | Birkbeck College | | |
| King's College | City University | | |
| Queen Mary, University of London | Goldsmiths College | | |
| Royal Holloway, University of London | London South Bank University | | |
| London School of Pharmacy | University of Westminster | | |

[a]HEI cluster as defined by PACEC (PACEC, 2009, Appendix E).

data were supplemented by interviews with academics and with information provided by the London Technology Network (LTN) Business Fellows associated with each institution.[6]

The study identified a total of 244 university-related companies (Table 2); of these, 176 were spin-offs, 53 were staff start-ups and 15 were graduate start-ups.[7] The two large, research-intensive colleges – Imperial College and University College London (UCL) – have the highest number of academic entrepreneurs producing the highest number of university-related companies (each producing more than 80 companies, 71% of the total). However, one of the post-1992 universities, South Bank, with 14 companies, outperformed many of the older universities in terms of the number of firms established.

The company data were enhanced through desk research to add attributes drawn from Companies House via the Bureau van Dijk FAME database system. This provided access to data relating to key dates in the lifecycle of individual companies (for example, date of incorporation) and the sectoral classification, financial and other performance data. It also provided access to information on company officers and shareholders, which revealed that they were more likely to be established by predominantly male (95% of 536 founders), mid-career (average age at founding of 46) academics.

When compared to the official 2006–2007 HE-BCI returns for the 13 institutions, we find that the institutional returns generally confirmed our estimates for university spin-offs (166 active companies *v* 176 estimated) but that they significantly under-report staff start-ups (10 *v* 53, active *v* estimated companies). Whilst the overall totals for graduate start-ups are similar (14 *v* 15) the HE-BCI figures derive from only three of the smaller institutions.

Thus it appears that large HEIs in our sample are unable to estimate reliably both staff and graduate start-ups in which the parent

**Table 2. University-related companies identified by the survey.**

| Institution | Spin-off | Staff start-up | Student start-up | Total |
|---|---|---|---|---|
| UCL | 53 | 28 | 4 | 85 |
| Imperial College | 72 | 9 | 3 | 84 |
| King's College | 14 | 6 | 1 | 21 |
| Brunel University | 10 | 4 | | 14 |
| South Bank University | 10 | | 4 | 14 |
| Queen Mary | 11 | 1 | | 12 |
| Royal Holloway | 3 | 2 | 1 | 6 |
| Goldsmiths | 1 | | 2 | 3 |
| University of Westminster | 1 | 1 | | 2 |
| London Metropolitan University | | 1 | | 1 |
| Birkbeck | 1 | | | 1 |
| London School of Pharmacy | | 1 | | 1 |
| Courtauld Institute | 0 | 0 | 0 | 0 |
| *Totals* | *176* | *53* | *15* | *244* |

institution holds no IP (intellectual property) position. Further evidence for this can be found in the subsequent 2007–2008 HE-BCI returns where anomalies in reporting would seem to contribute to a high proportion of zero returns in the graduate start-up category (32 out of 40 London HEIs). We believe that these could be interpreted more correctly as null returns, reflecting the lack of infrastructure to capture this activity systematically; further evidence for this comes from the dramatic year-on-year fluctuations (for example, University of Oxford, which returned 135 graduate start-ups in 2006–2007 and zero in 2007–2008).[8]

## Key characteristics of university-related companies in London

Unfortunately, the diversity of industry sectors in our sample is not reflected by their Companies House Standard Industry Classifications (SIC). We found that more than 20% were classed as 'Not specified' or fell into the category of 'Other business activities'. Thus, in order to segment spin-off and start-up companies into meaningful categories, we classified each company on the basis of the academic discipline of the founder and the classification of activities according to target sectors provided by the London Development Agency (Table 3). This enabled analysis of company formation and survival for different scientific or business groupings to be carried out, from which we could identify sector concentrations similar to those found in other studies (see, for example,

Shane, 2006; O'Shea, 2006; PACEC, 2003; Lenoir and Gianella, 2006) highlighting the relative importance of pharmaceuticals and biotechnology and software and computer services.

To standardize the spin-off data for the different sizes of institutions, Table 4 compares the spin-off totals between 1998 and 2005 with their numbers of Full Person Equivalent (FPE) academic staff in 2007–2008. The results indicate a wide range of spinout 'performances', with Imperial College, South Bank University and Brunel University showing above-average activity. As can be seen from Table 3, university-related companies are overwhelmingly found in STEM (science, technology, engineering and medical) fields. To allow for the varying mission of each institution, therefore, we also standardized for the number of academic staff in these disciplines. Standardizing spin-off activity against the number of research staff also allows comparison with the performance of European institutes which is captured on an annual basis by the ASTP (Arundel and Bordoy, 2006). This reports a Europe-wide average number of spin-offs per 1,000 research staff of 1.48 (for 2004) and 1.63 (for 2005) based upon responses from 49 institutions.

Our database also provided access to details of changes in ownership throughout the life of the companies. These data may offer some insights into the network of relationships that exist between the academic and finance communities in London, contributing to visibility and transparency that Huggins (2008) identifies as an issue. Figure 1 presents a two-mode graphical representation of the

**Table 3. Counts of HEI spin-off companies by commercial and academic discipline.[a]**

| Industry sector | Academic discipline of founder | | | | | | | Totals |
|---|---|---|---|---|---|---|---|---|
| | Engineering | Humanities | Medical | Other | Science | Technical | (blank) | |
| Chemicals | 5 | 1 | 4 | 1 | 11 | | | 22 |
| Consultancy | 3 | | | 1 | | | | 4 |
| Creative industries | 3 | | 1 | 1 | | | | 5 |
| Electricity | 5 | | | | 2 | | | 7 |
| Electronic and electrical equipment | 4 | | 2 | | 6 | | | 12 |
| Health care equipment and services | 6 | | 5 | | 3 | | | 14 |
| Industrial engineering | 6 | | 3 | | 3 | | | 12 |
| Pharmaceuticals and biotechnology | 4 | | 49 | 2 | 23 | 1 | 1 | 80 |
| Software and computer services | 8 | 1 | 4 | 2 | 4 | 16 | | 35 |
| Technology hardware and equipment | 1 | | | | | | | 1 |
| Telecommunications | 2 | | 1 | | 1 | 1 | | 4 |
| N/A | 1 | | 2 | | 1 | 2 | | 6 |
| *Totals* | 48 | 2 | 71 | 7 | 53 | 20 | 1 | 202 |

[a]Using classification in PACEC (PACEC, 2009, Appendix F).

**Table 4.** University spin-offs by size of institutions (full person equivalents, FPEs) for all academic staff and for those in STEM subjects.

| | Spin-offs, Jan 1998–Dec 2005 | Academic staff (FPE, 2007–2008) | STEM academic staff (FPE 2007–2008) | LQ (FPE) | Average spin-offs per 1,000 staff | Average spin-offs per 1,000 FPE (STEM) staff |
|---|---|---|---|---|---|---|
| Imperial College | 59 | 3,300 | 3,158 | 2.6 | 2.2 | 2.3 |
| South Bank University | 8 | 760 | 310 | 1.5 | 1.3 | 3.2 |
| Brunel University | 10 | 1,040 | 394 | 1.4 | 1.2 | 3.2 |
| UCL | 37 | 4,930 | 3,418 | 1.1 | 0.9 | 1.4 |
| Queen Mary | 9 | 1,780 | 1,104 | 0.7 | 0.6 | 1.0 |
| King's College | 12 | 3,050 | 1,995 | 0.6 | 0.5 | 0.8 |
| Royal Holloway | 2 | 1,085 | 298 | 0.3 | 0.2 | 0.8 |
| University of Westminster | 1 | 1,795 | 658 | 0.1 | 0.1 | 0.2 |
| Goldsmiths | 1 | 565 | 50 | 0.3 | 0.2 | 2.5 |
| Birkbeck College | 1 | 1,715 | 267 | 0.1 | 0.1 | 0.5 |
| *Totals* | *140* | *20020* | *12188* | *1.0* | *0.9* | *1.4* |

*Source:* Higher Education Database for Institutions, http://www.heidi.ac.uk/.

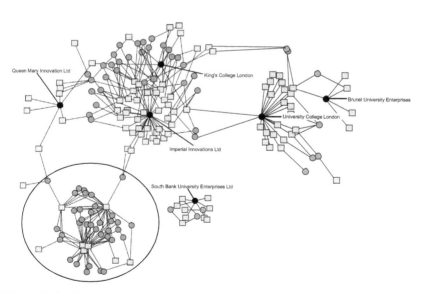

**Figure 1.** Social network of current ownership of university-related firms.

*Note:* Circles represent unique shareholders; squares represent university-related companies; universities are as identified. The encircled area is a group of pharmaceutical companies in which the various universities have cashed in their equity stake.

relationships between the *current* owners (represented by squares) and the university-related companies (represented by circles) in our portfolio. The network has been processed to remove pendants (that is, investors in single companies or companies with only a single owner), leaving a web of co-investors who have an equity stake in two or more university-related companies. The diagram suggests that the web of relationships may not be as tightly woven as one might expect, with relatively few investors having current holdings across the different university portfolios. The diagram also clearly identifies a group of pharmaceutical companies (circled) in which the various universities have cashed in their equity stake.

## Development timeline

Academic enterprise is not a new phenomenon in London (Figure 2). However, when compared to surveys such as those for Oxford University[9] (Lawton-Smith and Ho, 2006) or MIT (BankBoston, 1997), we were able to find only relatively few records relating to long-established companies. Despite our best efforts, we have been unable to identify a significant, equivalent cohort of university-related companies for our London-based HEIs. This may relate to the lack of a long-term 'institutional memory' pre-dating the creation of TTOs. It is therefore entirely possible that other long-established companies exist but have not been identified by the survey respondents.

The earliest identified surviving London spin-off was established in 1965, but both formation rates and survival rates remained low until 1997 with an average of only two surviving university-related companies being formed each year. Thus the vast majority of surviving London university-related companies were formed between 1998 and 2006, and

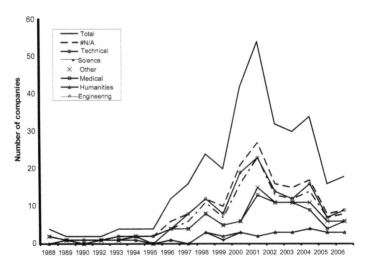

**Figure 2.** Counts of HEI spin-off companies by academic discipline of founder.

almost 70% of identified companies were established between 2000 and 2006. This suggests that even though TTOs have been established in UCL and Imperial since the 1980s, it was not until the mid-1990s that the rate of spin-off activity started to accelerate.

## Portfolio performance

It is relatively easy to record the survival rates of new companies. For companies founded since 2000 we found the average three- and five-year survival rates to be 93% and 83% respectively (Tables 5 and 6). However, survival rates provide a very poor measure of company success because many firms may close through a planned exit strategy – through a trade sale, for instance – or other orderly liquidation, whilst other 'lifestyle' firms can struggle on for years without returning significant value to founders or investors. As such we attempted to identify the financial and employment measures that provide some indication of the impact and growth of these companies. However, since many small companies in the UK are now only required to

file abbreviated accounts (that is, an abbreviated balance sheet, with no statutory obligation to produce, for public consumption, a profit-and-loss statement), financial data from Companies House were only available for 43% of university-related companies in our database.

Employment data for university-related companies were available for 40% (101 of 244) of the entire sample of university-related companies. Using the European Commission definition of SMEs, in 2005 the entire sample group

**Table 5. Counts and three-year and five-year survival rates (%) for HEI spin-out companies incorporated between 2000 and 2005.**

| Category | Count | 3-year survival | 5-year survival |
|---|---|---|---|
| Spin-off | 145 | 92% | 82% |
| Staff start-up | 43 | 98% | 91% |
| Student start-up | 9 | 89% | 67% |
| *Totals* | *197* | *93%* | *83%* |

**Table 6. Counts and three-year and five-year survival rates (%) for HEI spin-out companies incorporated between 2000 and 2005, by sector.**

| Sector | Count | 3-year survival | 5-year survival |
|---|---|---|---|
| Chemicals | 18 | 94% | 94% |
| Consultancy | 1 | 100% | 100% |
| Creative industries | 4 | 100% | 100% |
| Electricity | 5 | 100% | 100% |
| Electronic and electrical equipment | 11 | 91% | 73% |
| Healthcare equipment and services | 14 | 100% | 93% |
| Industrial engineering | 14 | 79% | 71% |
| Pharmaceuticals and biotechnology | 81 | 95% | 84% |
| Software and computer services | 34 | 88% | 76% |
| Technology hardware and equipment | 2 | 100% | 100% |
| Tele-communications | 4 | 100% | 100% |
| *Totals* | *188* | *93%* | *84%* |

of university-related companies was composed of 63 micro enterprises, 27 small enterprises, 10 medium enterprises and only 1 large enterprise.[10] Almost 90% of university-related companies are micro or small enterprises; however, as of 2008, the 10% of companies larger than 250 employees provided more than 50% of the total employment of 3,100 (Figure 3). Plotting company size against age (Figure 4), we found that it is only after year five that substantial growth in the number of medium size enterprises is recorded, which suggests that long-term monitoring of companies may be necessary in order to determine contributions to employment.

In general, Anyadike-Danes *et al* (2009) found that the UK economy possesses a small

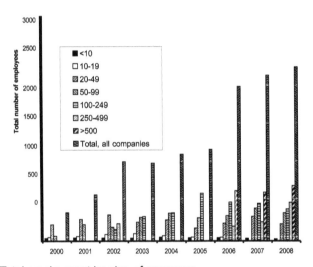

**Figure 3.** Total employment by size of company.

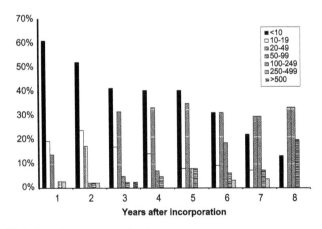

**Figure 4.** Variations in company size by age.

minority of high-growth firms that have achieved annual growth rates of 20% or higher in a recent three-year period. Using the OECD definition for high-growth firms,[11] for the period 2005–2008, the data from this survey showed that about 6% of all firms passed this threshold. In our data, we found that, overall, 31 of the 89 firms for which we had obtained financial returns met the criteria for at least one three-year period since incorporation (Table 7). For the 2005–2008 period corresponding to Anyadike-Danes' survey, we had financial and employment data for only 26 from a database of 180 surviving firms, of which 15 met the 'high growth' threshold – corresponding to a minimum of 8% of the total population (Table 8).

Table 7 shows how quickly companies in our sample reached their first period of high-growth, with 21 of the 31 in our sample achieving this within five years

of incorporation. These 'gazelle' firms are viewed as being particularly important in driving competitiveness, since such firms have become widely acknowledged as outstanding job creators (see, for example, Henrekson and Johansson, 2008).[12]

Given the importance of such firms in terms of growth and employment, it is interesting to compare the performance of the company portfolios from different institutions (Table 9). For those companies for which we obtained data, approximately one third of both spin-offs and staff start-ups demonstrated high growth. If we assume that those companies for which we had no data fail to meet our criteria for high growth, this translates to 15% of both the spin-offs and staff start-up portfolio.

**Table 7. Number of high-growth companies by age.**

| Years after incorporation | Companies achieving high growth |
|---|---|
| 3 | 6 |
| 4 | 7 |
| 5 | 8 |
| 6 | 1 |
| 7 | 1 |
| 8 | 2 |
| 11 | 2 |
| 12 | 2 |
| 14 | 1 |
| 15 | 1 |
| *Total* | *31* |

**Table 8. Number of high-growth companies, 2005–08.**

| Sector | Low-growth, 2005–2008 | High-growth, 2005–2008 |
|---|---|---|
| Pharmaceuticals and biotechnology | 6 | 9 |
| Software and computer services | 1 | 2 |
| Electronic and electrical equipment | 1 | 2 |
| Health care equipment and services | 1 | 1 |
| Electricity | | 1 |
| Telecommunications | 1 | |
| Creative industries | 1 | |
| *Totals* | *11* | *15* |

**Table 9. Counts of high-growth firms by institution.**

| Institution | Spin-off | | | Staff start-up | | |
|---|---|---|---|---|---|---|
| | High-growth | Low-growth/no-growth | N/A | High-growth | Low-growth/no-growth | N/A |
| Imperial College | 13 | 22 | 35 | 1 | 2 | 6 |
| UCL | 8 | 16 | 24 | 5 | 9 | 11 |
| King's College | 1 | 1 | 11 | 1 | | 3 |
| Brunel University | | 1 | 9 | | 2 | 1 |
| Queen Mary | 2 | | 7 | | 2 | |
| South Bank University | | | 7 | | | |
| Royal Holloway | | | 2 | | 1 | |
| University of Westminster | | 1 | | | | 1 |
| Goldsmiths | | | 1 | | | |
| Birkbeck College | | 1 | | | | |
| London School of Pharmacy | | | | | | 1 |
| *Totals* | *24* | *42* | *96* | *7* | *16* | *23* |

## Conclusions

As in other studies (see, for example, Shane, 2006), academic founders were predominately in the pharmaceuticals and biotechnology sectors, followed by software and computer services. However, by polling a wide range of contacts within and outside university TTOs, the study identified a significant number of companies (particularly staff start-ups) that were previously unreported. It also became clear that few institutions had robust strategies to identify and monitor graduate start-ups and that official HE-BCI returns in this category could not be reliably reproduced. Given the importance placed on such activities within the current policy context, it is clear that there is considerable scope for more robust monitoring of the whole portfolio of university-related companies.

The survey also confirms the difficulty of assessing portfolio performance, particularly when attempting to monitor companies in which the institution holds no equity position and may have very limited access to financial and employment data. Nevertheless, by tracking individual companies over an extended period of time, we were able to provide some insights beyond simple counts of survival rates.

Much further work is thus required to extend this analysis in order to develop a fuller picture of university-related start-up activities within the capital. This should include primary research (for example, an annual survey) of surviving companies and more systematic attempts to identify and monitor the start-up activities of both staff and graduate students. Until such systems are fully embedded, official returns such as the HE-BCI should be treated with some caution by regional and national policy makers.

# Notes

[1]http://www.praxisunico.org.uk/, last accessed 05 September 2011.

[2]The Association of European Science Technology Transfer Professionals, http://www.astp.net/, last accessed 05 September 2011.

[3]http://www.londonhigher.ac.uk/fileadmin/ documents/ HESAResourcesFinances2006 07.pdf, last accessed October 12, 2009.

[4]For example, by computing Location Quotients based upon number of academic staff.

[5]http://www.topuniversities.com/ university-rankings/world-university-rankings/2009/results, last accessed 12 October 2009.

[6]http://www.ltnetwork.org/bfora/systems/ xmlviewer/default.asp?arg=DS_LTN_ PARTART_24/_firsttitle.xsl/20, last accessed 09 October 2009.

[7]Based on HE-BCI definitions, see http:// www.hefce.ac.uk/pubs/ hefce/2009/09_23/, 'spin-offs' are defined as companies set up to exploit IP that has originated from within the HEI; 'staff start-ups' are defined as those companies set up by active (or recent) HEI staff but not based on IP from the institution; and 'graduate start-ups' are defined as those which include all new businesses started by recent graduates (within 2 years of graduation) regardless of where any IP resides.

[8]http://www.hefce.ac.uk/pubs/ hefce/2009/09 23/

[9]For example, in a recent survey relating to Oxford University, 35 firms (including consultancy companies not counted here) had roots that could be traced back to the university prior to 1987 with nearly 40% of the overall total being established by 1993 (Lawton Smith and Ho, 2006).

[10]A company is a micro enterprise if the number of employees is less than 10, small enterprise if the number of employees is between 11 and 50, medium enterprise if the number is between 51 and 250, and large enterprise if the number is more than 251; see http://ec.europa.eu/enterprise/ enterprise policy/sme definition/index en.htm.

[11]The recommended definition of 'high-growth enterprises' is as follows: 'All enterprises with average annualized growth greater than 20% per annum, over a three year period should be considered as high-growth enterprises. Growth can be measured by the number of employees or by turnover' (OECD, 2008).

[12]Gazelles are the subset of high-growth enterprises which are up to five years old. The definition is: 'All enterprises up to 5 years old with average annualized growth greater than 20% per annum, over a three year period, should be considered as gazelles' (OECD, 2008).

# References

Arundel, A., and Bordoy, C.(2006), 'Final report: the 2006 ASTP survey', Association of European Science and Technology Transfer Professionals, www.astp.net/Survey/Final%20 ASTP%20report%20June%2014%20 2006.pdf, last accessed 29 July 2010.

Anyadike-Danes, M., Bonner, K., Hart, M., and Mason, C. (2009), 'Measuring business growth: high-growth firms and their contribution to employment in the UK', NESTA, London, www.nesta.org.uk/library/documents/ Measuring-Business-Growth-v18.pdf, last accessed 29 July 2010.

BankBoston (1997), *MIT: The Impact of Innovation*, BankBoston Economics Department, Boston, MA.

Bercovitz, J., and Feldman, M. (2004), 'Academic entrepreneurs: social learning and participation in university technology transfer', http://www.hhh. umn.edu/img/assets/11469/BERCOVITZ academic entrepreneurs.pdf, downloaded 03 February 2009.

Clarysse, B., Wright, M., Lockett. A., Van de Velde, E., and Vohora, A. (2005), 'Spinning out new ventures: a typology of incubation strategies from European research institutions', *Journal of Business Venturing,* Vol 20, pp 183–216.

Gibb, A.A., and Hannon, P. (2006), 'Towards the entrepreneurial university', *International Journal of Entrepreneurship Education*, Vol 4, p 73.

HE-BCI (2007), *Higher Education-Business and Community Interaction Survey 2004–05 and 2005–06*, http://www. hefce.ac.uk/pubs/hefce/2007/07 17/, last accessed 31 August 2009.

HEFCE (2004), *Higher Education–Business Interaction Survey 2001–02*, http://www.hefce.ac.uk/pubs/ hefce/2004/04 07/, last accessed 31 August 2009.

Henrekson, M., and Johansson, D. (2008), 'Gazelles as job creators – a survey and interpretation of the evidence', 12 February 2008, *IFN Working Paper* Number 733 http://ssrn.com/abstract= 1092938, last accessed 29 July 2010.

Holzl, W., and Friesenbichler, K. (2008), *Final Sector Report: Gazelles*, Europe Innova, Vienna, WIFO. archive.europe-innova.eu/servlet/Doc?cid=10529&lg=EN, last accessed 29 July 2010.

Huggins, R. (2008), 'Universities and knowledge-based venturing: finance, management and networks in London', *Entrepreneurship and Regional Development*, Vol 20, No 2, pp 185–206.

Lawton Smith, H., and Ho, K. W. (2006), 'Measuring the performance of Oxfordshire's spin-off companies', *Research Policy,* Vol 35, pp 1554–1568.

Lenoir, T., and Gianella, E. (2006), 'Mapping the impact of federally funded extra-university research and development on the emergence of self-sustaining knowledge domains: the case of microarray technologies', paper presented at the *University Technology Transfer and Commercialisation of Research: Antecedents and Consequences Symposium*, Academy of Management Conference, Atlanta, GA.

Library House (2006), *The Impact of the University of* Cambridge on the UK Economy and Society, *Library House, Cambridge and East of England Development Agency, Histon, Cambridge.*

Mason, G., Bishop, K., and Robinson, C. (2009), 'Business Growth and Innovation: the wider impact of rapidly growing firms in UK city regions', National Endowment for Science, Technology and the Arts (NESTA), London, www.nesta.org.uk/library/documents/Measuring-Business-Growth-v18.pdf, last accessed 29 July 2010.

Meyer, M. (2003), 'Academic entrepreneurs or entrepreneurial academics? Research-based ventures and public support mechanisms', *R&D Management,* Vol 33, pp 107–115.

NESTA (2009), 'The vital 6 per cent: how high-growth innovative businesses generate prosperity and jobs', NESTA, London, www.nesta.org.uk/library/documents/Report-Summary-Vital-6-per-cent-v13.pdf, last accessed 29 July 2010.

OECD (2008), *Eurostat-OECD Manual on Business Demography Statistics*, OECD, Paris.

O'Shea, R., Chugh, H., and Allen, T. J. (2008), 'Determinants and consequences of university spinoff activity: a conceptual framework', *Journal of Technology Transfer*, Vol 33, No 6, pp 653–666.

PACEC (2003), *The Cambridge Phenomenon: Fulfilling the Potential*, PACEC, Cambridge.

PACEC (2009), 'Evaluation of the effectiveness and role of HEFCE/OSI third stream funding', http://www.hefce.ac.uk/ pubs/hefce/2009/09_15/, last accessed 09 October 2009.

Porter, M. E., and Ketels, H. M. (2003), 'UK Competitiveness: moving to the next stage', DTI, London, www.berr.gov.uk/files/file14771.pdf, last accessed 29 July 2010.

Shane, S. (2006), *Academic Entrepreneurship*, Edward Elgar, Cheltenham.

Warren, A., Hanke, R., and Trozer, D. (2008), 'Models for university technology transfer: resolving conflicts between mission and methods and the dependency on geographic location', *Cambridge Journal of Regions, Economy and Society*, Vol 1, No 2, pp 219–232.

Wright, M., Birley, S., and Mosey, S. (2004), 'Entrepreneurship and university technology transfer', *Journal of Technology Transfer.* Vol 29, No 3–4, pp 235–246.

# Appendix 1

## Performance of London's HEIs judged on the basis of the HE-BCI return

Table A1. Regional location quotients for key HE-BCI (2007–08) indicators.

| Area | Academic staff | Spin-offs with some HEI ownership | Formal spin-offs, not HEI owned | | Staff start-ups | | |
|---|---|---|---|---|---|---|---|
| | | 2007–2008 | 2006–2007 | 2007–2008 | 2006–2007 | 2007–2008 | 2006–2007 |
| North East | 6,550 | 1.7 | 0.4 | 0.0 | 0.0 | 0.0 | 0.0 |
| North West | 15,790 | 0.8 | 1.6 | 2.7 | 2.4 | 2.0 | 0.7 |
| Yorkshire and the Humber | 13,795 | 1.5 | 1.3 | 0.0 | 0.0 | 0.3 | 0.4 |
| East Midlands | 11,375 | 2.2 | 1.7 | 2.3 | 1.1 | 1.2 | 1.7 |
| West Midlands | 11,360 | 0.9 | 0.4 | 0.0 | 0.5 | 0.4 | 0.7 |
| East of England | 10,540 | 0.4 | 0.3 | 0.0 | 0.0 | 0.4 | 0.8 |
| London | 36,415 | 1.0 | 1.1 | 1.4 | 1.2 | 0.7 | 0.8 |
| South East | 21,500 | 0.5 | 1.0 | 0.4 | 0.9 | 0.0 | 0.8 |
| South West | 9,860 | 0.6 | 0.3 | 0.9 | 1.9 | 5.4 | 3.9 |
| England | 137,185 | 1.0 | 1.0 | 1.0 | 1.0 | 1.0 | 1.0 |

# PART IV: GEARING COOPERATION AND ENTREPRENEURSHIP FOR NATIONAL GROWTH

# Harnessing innovation potential?

## Institutional approaches to industry–higher education research partnerships in South Africa

**Glenda Kruss**

**Abstract:** *This article presents an overview of research partnership activity across the South African higher education system in three cutting-edge high-technology fields. An analytical matrix of partnership forms is developed, shaped by distinct responses to the tension between the new financial imperatives and the traditional intellectual project of higher education. Using the matrix, four groups of institutional response to partnership are identified. These may be distinguished in terms of their level of research capacity and the sets of strategic policies, institutional structures and interface mechanisms they have in place to promote partnerships with industry. The core argument of the paper is that more institutions need to develop the capacity to harness the potential for innovation rather than allow the unregulated proliferation of contract and consultancy forms of partnership with industry that can undermine their core long-term knowledge-generation function.*

**Keywords:** *higher education–industry partnerships; innovation; networks; South Africa*

Glenda Kruss is a Chief Research Specialist, Research Programme: Human Resources Development at the Human Sciences Research Council, Private Bag X9182, Cape Town 8000, South Africa. E-mail: gkruss@hsrc.ac.za

Universities and technikons in South Africa, like their global counterparts, are being challenged to rethink the nature of and the balance between their core functions of teaching, research and outreach. There is a call for institutions to become more responsive both to pressing social demands and to economic competitiveness in a national and global context shaped by the imperatives of a knowledge economy, held in tension with the call to address poverty and inequality. Since 1994, institutions in South Africa have been faced with potentially competing sets of demands, from state restructuring of their organizational forms to curriculum and programme change in line with new institutional missions. The research funding environment has shifted significantly, with a decrease in state subsidy, shifts in priorities of national research-funding agencies towards redress and capacity building and government calls to achieve greater responsiveness and accountability through strategic and applied research and partnerships with industry and community.

With a stronger orientation to global competitiveness, there have also been changes in the way industry funds and conducts research.

It was to begin to understand these complex shifts and challenges for institutions that the Human Sciences Research Council (HSRC) initiated a large-scale, multi-phase exploratory research project that focused on the state of higher education–industry research partnerships in three cutting-edge high-technology fields identified as critical in national foresight studies – information and communications technology (ICT), new materials development (NMD) and biotechnology. This article draws on an empirical study conducted across all 35 South African universities and technikons in 2003[1] to identify the scale and forms of research partnerships with industry, and the mechanisms that facilitate

or constrain them, in distinct higher education contexts and knowledge fields (see Kruss, forthcoming).[2]

## Understanding forms of industry partnership in the HE context

In this project, 'partnership' was initially defined in its broadest possible sense as any form of linkage of mutual benefit or mutual interest between higher education and industry. A mechanism was then required to discern what was included under the general rubric of partnership in the South African higher education sector. What are the ways in which researchers and academics describe their partnerships? Is there evidence of the new forms of networks and collaborations, or do partnerships take older, more traditional forms? As Smith and Katz (2000) remind us, terms like 'partnership', 'collaboration' and 'network' have multiple meanings, developed in complex environments at various levels – individual, group, department, institution, sector and country. Which forms of partnership are typically found in which forms of institution, given their historical legacy, uneven research capacity, institutional capacity and financial base?

A strong tension has been identified between the imperatives of the market and the traditional knowledge imperatives of the academy (see, for instance, Slaughter and Leslie, 1997; Jacob and Hellström, 2000; Muller, 2001; Ravjee, 2002). In a context of fiscal austerity and changes in the state funding of universities, there are pressures on South African institutions to become more financially self-sufficient. Again and again, the academic researchers and managers interviewed expressed a tension between an intellectual and a financial imperative shaping their research partnerships. Many academics prioritized research that could be seen to make an intellectual contribution to their field or future but felt compelled to pursue partnerships with industry in order to ensure the financial sustainability of their research programmes. There was a wide variety of ways in which academics in different research entities at different institutions responded to this tension. There was a similar tension in industry, whether it prioritized research with a strong knowledge element that could lead to innovation or research to solve short-term problems and ensure immediate competitiveness.

An analytical matrix was constructed to represent the responses to this tension in the intersecting relationship between higher education and industry, which shaped the forms of partnership that resulted, represented diagrammatically in Figure 1. In effect, the matrix represents two intersecting continua, with the poles defined by either the primarily financial or the primarily intellectual imperatives that shape the form a partnership will take. These are not either-or alternatives, because in reality both operate simultaneously. As Castells (2001) argues about the contradictory functions of higher education, these poles represent resolutions of contradictions more strongly in favour of a particular imperative.

## Ideal types of partnership

Ideal types of the partnerships evident in South African institutions were defined systematically and mapped onto this matrix, grounded in the empirical data on all forms of partnership (Kruss, forthcoming). They can be summarized only briefly here. Traditional forms of partnership continue in the present. Donation, one of the oldest forms of partnership, is conceptualized as benefaction or philanthropy on the part of industry, typically in the form of the endowment of a chair or building. Closely related to this is sponsorship, with post-graduate student research funding a core focus, given the imperative for industry to respond to socio-economic development needs in the 'new South Africa' and to strengthen its corporate social responsibility portfolios. In these forms of partnership, the relationship between higher education and industry is primarily limited to a financial one, and higher education is left free to continue with its intellectual projects, with few conditions imposed.

The dominant forms of partnership currently in evidence across the system are consultancies and contracts, strongly shaped by higher education's financial imperatives. In consultancies, typically an individual researcher in higher education acts in an advisory capacity to address the immediate knowledge problems of a firm, usually in exchange for individual financial benefit. Likewise, contracts may be linked to solving potentially interesting scientific problems or, more likely, to addressing a specific and immediate industrial problem but are primarily motivated by higher education's need to attract funding for research. Design solution is a related form that has emerged, in which technikons with appropriate technological expertise set up centres for prototyping and testing, offering design solutions to industry. These forms of partnership place potentially severe restrictions on the intellectual project of researchers in order to protect the financial interests of industry.

There is small but growing evidence of new entrepreneurial forms of partnership, such as commercialization, in which higher education researchers take on a strongly entrepreneurial role, attempting to commercialize prior intellectual work in the form of a spin-off company or in collaboration with an existing company willing to exploit intellectual property in the form of royalties, licences and patents or through venture capital. Here, the relationship is primarily shaped by financial imperatives for both industry and higher education.

New forms of partnership that have emerged include incentivized partnerships, with a weak form of intellectual collaboration, stimulated by government funding aimed at developing research and development (R&D) and innovative capacity in South Africa, by encouraging technology transfer between higher education and industry. Collaboration partnerships have a knowledge-based linkage in which all partners make an intellectual contribution. Finally,

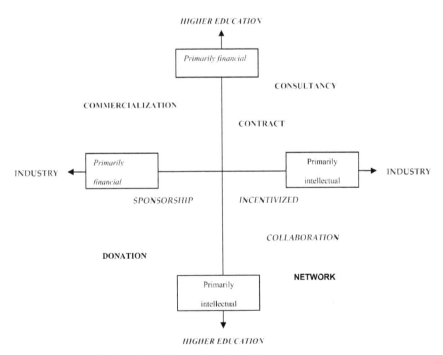

Figure 1. Analytical matrix of forms of partnership.

in a minority of institutions, there is evidence of complex network forms of partnership, in the sense of Castells's (1996) definition that they facilitate the acquisition of product design and production technology, enable joint production and process development and permit generic scientific knowledge and R&D to be shared between a number of industrial organizations and researchers from (several) higher education institutions. These are knowledge-intensive forms of partnership and are shaped primarily by the intellectual imperatives of both industry and higher education partners.

A single institution is likely to have a range of partnership forms co-existing in different faculties and departments, or even in a research centre, to meet distinct purposes. For instance, a research unit may have core funding from a science council, supplemented by sponsorship to fund postgraduate students and a range of small consultancies to meet specific financial requirements. However, each form of partnership has specific implications. So, for instance, consultancies are favoured as a means of staff incentive and retention, as well as a means of initially drawing in potential industry partners. On the downside, consultancies have a potentially negative impact on the research and teaching functions of academic centres and departments in that they draw away the focus and energies of academic staff into projects for their own private gain. Many institutions endeavour to put mechanisms in place to monitor and check potential excesses. However, to stay with this form of partnership for

the moment, if academics are pursuing consultancies, and institutions are focusing energies into managing them, this limits the possibilities for pursuing other forms of partnership and for directing energy towards promoting or managing these. In particular, consultancies may militate against the development of research expertise that can contribute to new scientific knowledge and innovation or strategic applications in terms of national social or economic developmental goals.

Similar tensions are inherent in the contract forms of partnership which, the data suggest, have become critical to institutional income. The potential restrictions on intellectual property imposed by industry partners, particularly with respect to peer-reviewed journal publication and postgraduate theses, can impact negatively on an institution's research productivity and reputation. Likewise, many institutions have been attracted to commercialization as a source of institutional income, but there were cases in which 'entrepreneurial novices' put in place unsustainable and even unprofitable schemes with potential financial dangers for the institution, as well as implications for the core task of knowledge production.

The network and some incentivized and collaboration forms of partnership seem best placed to make a contribution to enhancing the knowledge field of academics while still meeting the long-term technology needs of industry and hence contributing to innovation and national economic and social development.

This analytical matrix of forms of partnership can be a useful tool for exploring partnerships across the higher education sector in South Africa – or, indeed, within an institution or research unit – as the following section illustrates.

## Institutional responses to partnership with industry

The response of higher education institutions to the contemporary partnership challenge is shaped by their differential historical legacies. As Castells (2001) argues, the core tasks of universities are given different emphases according to countries, historical periods and specific institutions, but they all take place simultaneously within the same structure, which results in a complex and contradictory reality. Thus, as individual institutions grapple with contemporary challenges and myriad competing demands, they respond in complex, uneven and 'messy' ways. Some universities in South Africa were established in the late 19th century to serve colonial elites and continued to serve a primarily advantaged, racially defined constituency for many years, while others were established in remote rural areas as recently as the late 1970s to serve the *apartheid* 'homelands' policy. The technikons were formally established in the 1970s to serve the demand for career-oriented, technological education and training (Creamer, 2000), were granted degree-awarding status in 1993 and were designated 'universities of technology' in 2004. Consequently, there are considerable differences among institutions in the balance between teaching and research, in science and technology

research capacity and productivity and in the cultures and forms of research management that have evolved – all of which shape their response to the new financial and intellectual imperatives that drive partnership.

Thus, when the matrix of forms of partnership was used to analyse the empirical data on partnerships in the three high-technology fields detailed above, it became clear that only 18 of the 35 institutions had research capacity in the fields of focus. These form the initial focus of discussion in this section. More significantly, clusters of universities and technikons with a similar scale and pattern of old and new forms of partnership could be discerned. The question, then, was what could explain these distinct institutional responses to imperatives to forge research partnerships with industry? One key distinction between the clusters was the extent to which institutions had either a strong or an emergent research capacity in science and technology in general and in relation to the three high-technology fields in particular. A second key distinction was the extent to which institutions had a highly structured, regulated and proactive organizational response in an attempt to promote partnership with industry, or whether they had a largely unregulated organizational response. These two dimensions were assigned to two axes to create an empirically based classification of four ideal types of institutional response to partnership with industry (see Figure 2):

- harnessing innovation potential;
- emerging entrepreneurialism;

- *laissez-faire* aspirational; and
- *laissez-faire* traditional.

The core distinguishing features of each of these four categories will be outlined in the following sections, but they are summarized in Table 1 to provide an initial comparative overview.

*Harnessing innovation potential*

The first category of institutions that may be discerned is in many respects an ideal. This group of three universities has a small number of network, collaboration, incentivized and commercialized forms of partnerships among its total spread, alongside consultancies, contracts and donations, which are significant in scale relative to all the other institutions.

Their sound research capacity and structured institutional response help us to understand why these specific institutions are able to host such new forms of partnership. They are among the oldest and historically most advantaged universities in South Africa, serving a privileged community for many decades. They have extensive fiscal resources and long-standing links with business and industry, some with research roots and expertise strongly shaped by military R&D in the *apartheid* period. Significantly, they each have a sound science and technology research base[3] from which to respond to the challenges of the present and evidence of considerable capacity in each of the three high-technology fields. Research excellence is prioritized, and hence there is an attempt to create a balance in favour of fundamental research while strategically exploiting opportunities for applied and strategic research that can contribute to greater economic responsiveness.

These universities have well-articulated and well-integrated formal institutional strategic and research policies, accompanied by long-established structures and mechanisms to coordinate and support research activity in general at both central and faculty levels. Formal strategic policy explicitly

Figure 2. Responses of higher education institutions to partnership with industry.

supports innovation, encompassing a conception of partnership framed in terms of developing a 'strategic balance'. Policies encompass the aspiration to relate to industry in academically beneficial terms and are not explicitly driven solely by financial imperatives; they seek to develop forms of partnership that can contribute to innovation. Intellectual property rights policy typically reflects a concern that potential tensions be resolved, that partnerships should be structured and designed such that they are able to generate research from which the academic can derive a publications record which does not compromise the commercial interests of the industry partner.

Drawing on a study by Martin (2000) of the institutional practices typically established to manage university–industry relations in 12 developing countries, a distinction was drawn between internal and external interface structures. Internal interface structures refers to those dedicated forms of organizational development created within an institution to support relations with industry, such as specialized internal structures for technology transfer, dedicated managerial posts, offices for continuing education or technology innovation centres. External interface structures play a similar role, but they typically have a separate legal status from the institution to enhance flexibility and responsiveness and to create a professional, higher-status, market-related interface, such as university-owned companies, incubators, science parks and consultancy centres. These differ in the degree of decentralization involved in that they may be attached to central research management or to faculties or departments or even to research centres.

What stands out in the institutions in this category is the extent of centralized steering and supportive structures created by management to promote partnerships. Various high-level internal interface structures have been established by central research management, such as dedicated structures to manage and process all external contracts and to provide expertise to support the process of patent applications, royalties and protecting intellectual property. They have also created external interface structures to facilitate and manage the relationship with industry, such as university-owned companies and involvement in incubators established in response to national incentivization schemes in specific technology fields.

It must be borne in mind that, while an institution may formally have adopted policies and established institutional structures and mechanisms, the extent to which these had permeated through faculty and departmental structures and were reflected in the experience of individual academics varied considerably within and between institutions. The average researcher experiences pressures from all directions – from government, peers, institutional management and the new nature of important problems – which makes implementation of institutional plans extremely complex. Institutional research managers reported the strategies and structures described as if they were successful, whereas

**Table 1. Characteristics of four institutional responses to partnership with industry.**

**Harnessing innovation potential**

Partnerships happen because of two things: significant institutional steering and support and through individual champions based in faculties, academic departments or research units.

Partnerships are premised on a sound science and technology research base.

Regulation of research is a key feature.

Underpinned by a coherent institutional strategy for research.

Led from the centre and at faculty level by institutional leadership.

Internal and external interface structures and mechanisms planned to support partnership.

*Institutional examples:* Historically advantaged, well-established universities located near major economic centres.

**Emerging entrepreneurialism**

Partnerships happen because of two things: significant institutional steering and support and through individual champions who are based in faculties, academic departments or research units.

Partnerships are premised on an emergent science and technology research base.

Regulation of research is an emergent feature.

Underpinned by a coherent institutional strategy for research as 'third-stream' income.

Led from the centre by institutional leadership.

Internal and particularly external commercialization interface structures and mechanisms planned to support partnership.

*Institutional examples:* Historically advantaged Afrikaans universities and historically advantaged technikons located in urban areas, one near a major economic centre, the others near regional economic centres.

**_Laissez-faire_ traditional**

Partnerships happen in a decentralized manner because of individual champions, research professors who are based in academic departments or research units.

Partnerships are premised on a sound science and technology research base.

Research environment not regulated.

No overall coherent institutional strategy.

Central institutional leadership not proactive and little central steering.

Internal and external interface structures develop on an *ad hoc* basis.

*Institutional examples:* Historically advantaged, well-established universities located near major economic centres.

**_Laissez-faire_ aspirational**

Partnerships happen in a decentralized manner, because of individual champions based in academic departments and through research managers acting in an individual capacity.

Partnerships are premised on an emergent science and technology research base.

Research environment not regulated.

No overall coherent institutional strategy.

Individuals in central leadership proactive but minimal central steering by key individuals.

Internal and external interface structures develop on an *ad hoc* basis.

*Institutional examples:* A historically disadvantaged university, a historically advantaged university and technikons, mostly located near major economic centres but also near regional centres.

interviews with academic research staff at project level often revealed starkly contrasting perspectives. Nevertheless, these universities stand out in their attempt to harness the innovation potential of their research, in partnership with industry, in ways that can contribute to innovation and provide an indication of what is possible in the South African context.

### Emerging entrepreneurialism

Closely related to the above is a second set of institutions that display an emerging entrepreneurialism, including a number of younger Afrikaans-language universities with a specific ideological orientation that was shaped by and favoured under the *apartheid* system, as well as a number of historically advantaged technikons. The technikons have a specific mandate to concentrate on vocational and career-oriented education geared towards the promotion and transfer of technology in support of the developmental needs of the country, and this shapes their response. Over the next year, these institutions will all be subject to a process of institutional merger that will impact directly on the restructuring and research strategies they are attempting to put in place in both the short and medium terms.

The institutions in this category are more explicitly driven by the financial imperatives facing higher education and at the same time are trying to consolidate and develop their scientific research capacity. The growth of partnership is underpinned by a coherent institutional attempt to develop research expertise in potentially lucrative directions and to generate 'third-stream income' for the institution. They explicitly articulate the discourse of an entrepreneurial university or university of technology and foreground the concerted attempt to respond in a strategic manner to position the institution favourably in a new policy context. There is a conception that the institutions should allow for different modes of research, from basic research to research in application, addressing problems experienced by the public sector, the private sector and the community. However, priority tends to be given to applied and strategic research. The technikons specifically aim to become key players in the development and transfer of technology, to contribute to the process of technological innovation.

The scale of partnership with industry tends to be small. What stands out among the forms of partnership is the promotion of commercialization and forms of partnership that offer design solutions at technikons, as well as an extremely small number of fledgling incentivized networks. These exist alongside predominantly contract and consultancy forms of partnership.

These institutions are distinct from the previous category in that the imperatives of a new policy and funding emphasis stimulated these heretofore primarily teaching institutions to adopt a stronger focus on research than in the past. They currently have limited research expertise and capacity in science and technology and hence a more limited base for partnership in high-technology areas. Most have only very recently articulated a formal institutional research policy and development plan, which typically aims to develop and improve research capacity. The regulation of research is largely emergent or very new. They too have a highly regulated, structured, proactive institutional response, led strongly from the centre by institutional leadership. In the strategies and structures they are developing to realize their aspirations, these universities and technikons have adopted the 'textbook' features they have come to believe promote partnerships, drawn from international 'best practice' – particularly investment in external interface structures. Through the establishment of technology stations, a science and technology park, technology incubators that focus on small, medium-sized and micro-enterprises (SMMEs), or 'design solutions' centres such as prototype product development, they reveal ambitious plans, but the scale of operations is generally modest. Notably, they are driven by central management and are based largely in dedicated structures outside the mainstream structures of institutional power. In some cases, they were driven by an enterprising academic or research unit, separate from official initiatives but subsequently formalized.

Thus the extent to which these forms of partnership have taken root in institutions and permeated down to all levels of practice varies, but there is evidence to suggest that at this point new practices are still emergent or embryonic, outside of small pockets of expertise. It was evident that a research culture was still budding, with research capacity unevenly distributed. High teaching demands in the technikon sector in particular were frequently cited as a constraint. Typically, only a few active individual researchers manage to enter into and sustain industry partnerships. Again and again, researchers in these institutions bemoaned the fact that new systems did not always work effectively or were often too bureaucratic and that there was insufficient understanding of the implications of applied research and interaction with industry. Research leaders indicated that changing institutional culture was a slow process, with one professor wryly remarking that 'getting things done in the university environment is like mating elephants. It takes place at a very high level, with a lot of noise and takes two years to produce results.'

Their location in relation to major economic centres or 'hubs' is also significant in explaining the scale and pattern of partnerships in these institutions. A lack of industry interest is directly ascribed to the relatively isolated location of the institutions in some provinces or to the relatively poor state of the economy in a city or region, particularly those that rely primarily on agriculture and the services industry. No matter how good the policies, structures and mechanisms an institution puts in place, it may struggle to realize its potential if it is not situated in an economic environment in which industry is willing and able to enter into partnerships. External structural constraints often mean that their institutional plans are still largely aspirational.

*Laissez-faire aspirational*

A third group of younger, primarily historically advantaged universities and technikons contains the largest number of institutions. These institutions are distinguished by a generally positive attitude towards partnerships. Institutional policy tends to enshrine a view of partnership as an 'essential necessity' that can contribute to the funding base of the institution's research and to its commitment to responsiveness and community relevance. They do not have a significant scale of partnerships in the three fields, and it is notable that the universities do not have engineering faculties, with most partnerships concentrated in departments in a science faculty. The forms of partnership are primarily driven by the financial imperatives impacting on higher education – typically in the form of contracts or consultancies. These problem-related partnerships use applied-research techniques in which there is usually little space for graduate students to do original research towards a higher degree. Given the historical legacy of some institutions as historically black and hence disadvantaged, there are a few sponsorships that aim to build capacity, a very few incentivized partnerships at each institution, as well as a tiny number of commercialization partnerships, in the form of spin-off companies, at some of the universities. Collaborative partnerships with other universities are a significant feature of the technikons, at which the challenge of developing a research ethos was particularly evident. It was noted typically that some industry

relationships were built through the cooperative learning system that could form the basis of research partnerships in future.

We can explain why this group of institutions reflects such a pattern by examining a number of intersecting features. Like the institutions with an 'emerging entrepreneurial' approach, they are still developing research capacity, with a small emergent research base in niche areas. Unlike those institutions, however, they have a largely unregulated and unstructured approach to partnership. These institutions do not have clearly formulated and well-structured explicit institutional policies, structures or mechanisms to support partnerships specifically. The policy and vision is of course shaped by each institution's unique history, culture and traditions, but in general there tends to be a stronger commitment to economic and social development, and partnerships are envisioned in this light. In contrast to the institutions in the previous two categories, they do not have a substantive, detailed set of policy articulations to strategically drive partnership or the allocation of intellectual property rights. They tend to have policy documents that are largely symbolic and aspirational, providing frameworks for future institutional development. Similarly, these institutions tend to have or are developing internal interface structures that support and facilitate research rather than promoting partnerships specifically. There are few formally structured entities that are less inserted into institutional structures of power, to provide an easier external interface with industry in the three high-technology fields of focus (although there are instances in other fields of expertise).

Thus they may be said to have a *laissez-faire* approach to partnership, leaving much of the initiative to be driven by individual academic 'champions' on an *ad hoc* basis or facilitation in terms of the tacit knowledge and expertise lodged in an individual manager at central level. The *laissez-faire* approach is believed to allow academics the freedom to exploit their intellectual property on their own initiative. The typically small size of these institutions means that it is possible for managers to respond as the need arises. A key question is whether research partnerships have flourished in these institutions despite the *laissez-faire* approach or precisely because of the lack of centralized control mechanisms, which gives individual researchers leeway to pursue their interests with a degree of individualized support.

Given this *laissez-faire* management approach to partnership, in practice the financial imperatives driving partnerships tend to prevail in shaping the predominant forms of contract and consultancy, which do not contribute to innovation or long-term knowledge generation in a field and hence potentially undermine an institution's vision.

There are different reasons behind these patterns. For instance, one technikon has a *laissez-faire* approach because institutional energies are concentrated on merger processes. Once the merger has been more fully consolidated, the institution and its partnerships may develop in a different direction.

Another technikon prioritizes the development of a research culture and research management structures, and yet another has the added focus of devolving research leadership and structures to faculty level. This is very different from a relatively young university, which has a more stable history and research tradition but which tends to leave academics to follow their own interests – and will now have new directions arising from the merger process. A historically disadvantaged university has a *laissez-faire* approach in response to its attempt to enhance its legacy in changed conditions to contribute to social and economic responsiveness. And a historically advantaged university in an isolated location has the strongest research base and the most clearly articulated policies and embryonic support structures, but its smallness means that those with initiative can take innovative ideas to top management and receive institutional support on an *ad hoc, laissez-faire* basis.

It is conceivable that over the next few years, some of these institutions may develop in the direction of those institutions that 'harness innovation potential', but on a smaller scale. This is a key reminder that such categories are not fixed and that individual institutions are dynamic and changing and may develop significant new features in a short time.

## *Laissez-faire traditional*

The fourth category also evinces a *laissez-faire* approach to partnership in terms of institutional strategy, in that there are few dedicated strategies, structures or mechanisms to facilitate partnership. However, there is an ambivalent to negative attitude to partnerships. While individuals may engage in industry partnerships, the institutional policy and leadership in general tends to tolerate them as a 'necessary evil' that has to be controlled. Even more significantly, there is a concerted institutional lobby opposed to partnership as 'inimical to traditional academic practice'. This is in the context of historically advantaged universities which for the most part have strong, well-established research capacity in science and technology, like those universities in the 'harnessing innovation potential' category. Most partnerships take the form of contracts and consultancies that involve straight commercial relationships, with the presence of some incentivized and historical sponsorship forms of partnership, such as from the mining industry and in relation to student funding. There are very few commercialization or network forms of partnership at these institutions, particularly when considered relative to their counterparts with sound research capacity.

Unlike the other strong research universities, these institutions tend not to have a centralized formal research policy or strategy, nor do they have a coherent policy or strategy relating to partnerships. Central institutional leadership is not proactive, and there has been little central steering of partnership activity. These universities have begun, in a rather *ad hoc* and inexplicit way, to implement policies and practices in relation to partnership, specifically those related to intellectual policy and third-stream income. However, given the conception of partnerships as a 'necessary evil', there is an attempt to control the potential 'excesses' in the interests of protecting the traditional academic project of the institution. As a senior research manager stated, the policy is 'to stop us from being taken for a ride by industry'. For instance, at one university, consultancy-type partnerships were defined as 'contract work that is done under the table for private gain', and there were considerable efforts to limit these endeavours. Moreover, there was evidence of strong contestation in these institutions around the acceptance of proposed new policies – for instance, in relation to intellectual property rights and private remunerative work. This was seen by some as a setback for the development of partnerships with industry, leaving critical areas governed by older policies and a degree of ambivalence. Likewise, new internal interface structures primarily aimed at consolidating and enhancing the institution's traditional research base were being proposed at the time of the empirical research in 2003 but were in the early stages of implementation, and appeared to be subject to a great deal of contestation. Thus a *laissez-faire* approach prevails in practice.

These institutions had attempted to set up centralized external interface structures in the past, but decentralized structures appear to have had more success. The negative experience and poor returns of a science park at one university may have contributed to the current negative *laissez-faire* institutional thrust. Greater success was achieved from spin-off companies on a much smaller scale and founded on the basis of existing research and established technologies at the initiative of individual researchers. These provide a more organically rooted base of experience for the institution, which may be at the cutting edge of new developments from the bottom up. At another university, the institution's bureaucracy was seen to hamper rather than enable partnerships. The *laissez-faire* institutional approach was seen as a significant constraint by those researchers who desired to or did pursue partnerships with industry. Together, these dynamics resulted in academics or faculties establishing their own spin-off companies, which provided the financial and governance freedom required to work with industry, enabling them to retain all intellectual property rights. Such interface structures act in an *ad hoc* manner to fulfil the interests of specific departments or individual researchers. They tend to be more firmly driven by the short-term needs of industry and may be at odds with the central institutional strategic thrust. This represents a potential danger for the institution and for the long-term development of knowledge in a field. It helps to explain why the scale of partnership in the three fields of focus is smaller and why there are fewer 'network' forms of partnership that can contribute to innovation. Nevertheless, it is possible that these interface structures, based in the considerable research strengths of individual faculties and departments,

can provide a future base to shift the institutional approach in the direction of harnessing the potential for innovation in a more rooted manner.

## Emergent alternatives?

At the time of the study, 17 institutions did not display research capacity in the three high-technology fields of focus. They are primarily, but not entirely, historically black universities and technikons in isolated rural locations, with a focus on teaching, and for whom research was not part of the core mission. The focus at all of these institutions was on building research capacity – in science and technology, and in general – and an institutional research culture. Thus these institutions are under a financial imperative to pursue partnership with industry in order to fund research activities differently. In relation to research capacity building, there is public-sector support and a small degree of private-sector support in sponsorships initiated by large corporations, as well as a degree of donor support. Ironically, despite their historically unequal funding, the non-materialization of expected redress funding and their general financial pressures, many of these institutions are not driven to pursue contract and consultancy forms of partnership to support research *specifically*, to the same degree as those institutions with high-technology capacity.

There is evidence of recent concerted efforts to build research capacity, but the research in science and technology currently being carried out is still in a nascent stage at most of these universities and technikons. The dimensions of a research culture and structure are still at the developmental or 'infancy' stage, as one research manager phrased it.

Should these institutions succeed in developing greater research capacity over the next few years, they are likely to become similar to the institutions grouped in the four ideal typical categories. However, they vary in the way they would approach partnerships with industry, were they to have a more developed research base. One group of technikons focusing on developing capacity in high-technology areas displays features that make it logically akin to technikons in either the *laissez-faire* aspirational or the emerging entrepreneurialism categories.

A second group of universities that historically have focused their resources on the development and consolidation of their primary teaching effort (particularly distance institutions) constitutes in effect a set of extreme cases logically akin to those in the *laissez-faire* traditional category.

A third sizeable group of historically black universities and technikons has a distinct legacy. This arises from the fact that the institutions were established as part of the *apartheid* political strategy. Their founding mission was to train a bureaucracy to support the 'homelands' or separate states created by *apartheid* policy, which largely precluded the development of a strong academic research orientation, with little emphasis on the production of new knowledge in the form of research or postgraduate programmes

(Nkomo and Sehoole, 2004). This was exacerbated by unequal funding to black universities, inadequate to sustain a vibrant intellectual culture, and by their isolated rural location. However, as Reddy (2004) reminds us, some of these institutions became important sites of political resistance among both academics and students, developing a basis for the production and dissemination of democratic values, policy and practices. Thus there evolved a 'community development' model of outreach activities that involved academics in participatory processes drawing on their teaching and research to varying degrees.

In the current context, these institutions are logically most akin to the institutions that are harnessing the potential for innovation, albeit with an alternative development vision that is potentially significant in the South African context. They articulate a strong aspiration towards the use of technology in poverty reduction and sustainable development and focus on partnerships that facilitate community development and impact positively on the quality of life. Some of these universities have articulated a strategic research vision and identity that emphasize a commitment to regional and local socio-economic development more than to the development of high-technology capacity to enhance global competitiveness. There is an attempt to turn the disadvantage of their isolated rural location, far from economic activity, into a comparative advantage. In some cases, the specific features of the institution's location act as an incentive for research collaboration and the development of expertise. For instance, it was proposed that the biophysical characteristics of one region lent themselves ideally to research opportunities in natural resource management and the ecology of terrestrial and marine habitats with high levels of biodiversity.

Much of the small scale of partnership activity is related to the dissemination of knowledge in new contexts and to critical social applications of knowledge. There is also a small scale of knowledge generation in relation to harnessing indigenous knowledge structures in innovative ways, such as the biotechnological investigation of the potential of medicinal plants. At this stage, many strategic plans function primarily as statements of symbolic intent which capture the future vision and aspirations of the institution. They will need a great deal of support to be translated into substantive policy and concrete transformation at the institutional, faculty and sub-faculty levels, particularly given the constraints of the institutions' legacies. However, these forms of partnership represent an emergent alternative position, with potential opportunities to contribute to innovation in a social developmental manner, appropriate to and shaped specifically by the South African context.

## A stronger strategic approach

This article and the research on which it is based are an attempt to place conceptual order on the forms of partnerships with industry evident across an entire national higher education system, at a particular point in time, in cutting-edge high-technology fields only.

In the context of transition and the imperatives of transformation of the higher education system in South Africa, there has been an increasingly negative public perception of the higher education system (Cloete, 2002) and a perceived weakening and vulnerability of the sector that precludes it from determining its future trajectory (Ndebele, 2004). In contrast, the empirical evidence of the study is cause for optimism in the sector, as it reveals the wide range of ways in which institutions can and do contribute to social and economic development through their research (see also *Mail & Guardian*, 2004, and NSTF, 2003). Significant scientific advances have been made in partnership with industry which contribute both to global competitiveness and to the quality of life.

The research highlighted the significance of the external conditions that support or constrain partnerships, such as government incentivization funding, regional location and proximity to economic centres – conditions over which institutions have little control. Above all, the article illustrates the complex and diverse ways in which individual institutions respond to global and national imperatives to develop research partnership with industry.

Innovative capacity in high-technology cutting-edge fields currently exists in five or six universities, with pockets of innovative capacity in universities and technikons that have emergent science and technology capacity.

The ideal forms of the knowledge economy – knowledge-intensive collaboration and networks between higher education researchers and industry – are typically found in a small minority of partnerships in a small number of universities. Indeed, collaboration between institutions on a regional basis, or even between cognate departments in the same institution, does not seem to occur on a wide scale. In the industry–research partnerships that take the form of networks, collaboration and, to a lesser extent, incentivization, higher education's role is most likely to include open-ended intellectual inquiry in the form of fundamental or strategic research, motivated by the intrinsic demands of a discipline or field of knowledge. It will probably include multiple disciplinary partners within higher education and science councils, as well as multiple industry partners.

This concurs with Castells's (2001) claim that critical to developing institutions as centres of innovation is cross-fertilization between different disciplines, together with detachment from the immediate needs of the economy. Academics can and do derive significant traditional benefits from such industry partnerships, from yielding a high number of publications to successful postgraduate students to enriched undergraduate teaching to enhancing the reputation of a department or institution. In these network forms of partnership, higher education is most able to balance its intellectual imperatives with new financial imperatives in the long-term interest of higher education, of an industrial sector and of economic and social development needs for innovation that enhances the quality

of life. Biotechnology research that develops drought-resistant seeds suited to the Southern African climate is but one example of many described in the study.

However, such forms of partnership are not well entrenched. In most institutions, partnerships take the form of consultancies and contracts, particularly in those institutions with a *laissez-faire* approach, whether aspirational or traditional. The reaction to an increase in consultancies and contracts reflects the desire to protect fundamental research activity from a utilitarian, immediatist and economistic approach. The irony and danger are that a *laissez-faire* institutional approach may allow large numbers of consultancies and contracts to develop in practice in individual research units, departments and faculties. This creates negative precedents and may create future problems for sustaining an institution, its academic project and the research base in a knowledge field.

Thus the study suggests that a far stronger and more systematic strategic mindset is required on the part of higher education institutions in order to 'harness potential' more widely across the system in South Africa. This would allow higher education institutions to contribute to innovation, facing both the global economy and pressing demands for national development that will enhance the quality of life of all South Africans.

## Notes

1 A process of mergers between higher education institutions has already begun and will significantly alter the institutional landscape by 2005.

[2] A database of active researchers in the three fields and a profile of the research capacity and productivity of each institution were compiled prior to site visits. During the visits, interviews were conducted with senior research managers, faculty deans and senior academic research project leaders.
[3] This is in terms of the qualifications of academic research staff, their ratings as scientists on national measures, their research publications output, research funding and levels of postgraduate supervision.

# References

Castells, M. (1996), *The Rise of the Network Society: the Information Age: Economy, Society and Culture*, Blackwell, Oxford.

Castells, M. (2001), 'The new global economy', in Muller, J., Cloete, N., and Badat, S., eds, *Challenges of Globalization: South African Debates with Manuel Castells*, Maskew Miller Longman, Cape Town.

Cloete, N. (2002), 'South African higher education and social transformation', *CHET Policy/Change Dialogues*, www.chet.org.za/issues/socialts.pdf.

Creamer, K. (2000), 'Knowledge for development: positioning technikons to meet the challenge of employment creation and development in South Africa', paper prepared for the Institute for African Alternatives (IFAA), London. (See also www.ifaanet.org.)

Jacob, M., and Hellström, T. (2000), 'From networking researchers to the networked university', in Jacob, M., and Hellström, T., eds, *The Future of Knowledge Production in the Academy*, Open University Press, Buckingham.

Kruss, G. (forthcoming), *Financial or Intellectual Imperatives? Mapping Higher Education – Industry Research Partnerships in South Africa*, HSRC, Pretoria.

*Mail & Guardian* (2004), 'Innovations' special supplement, 10–16 September, Vol 20, No 37.

Martin, M. (2000), *Managing University–Industry Relations: a Study of Institutional Practices from Twelve Different Countries*, International Institute for Educational Planning, Paris.

Muller, J. (2001), 'Return to user: responsivity and innovation in higher education', unpublished paper prepared for the Centre for Higher Education Transformation (CHET), Pretoria.

NSTF (2003), *The Who's Who of Science, Engineering and Technology in South Africa 2003. Contributions and Profiles of the Top Scientists, Engineers and Technologists in South Africa*, National Science and Technology Forum, Pretoria.

Ndebele, N. (2004), 'Higher education and political transformation', *Izwi: Voice of HE Leadership*, Vol 2, Second Quarter.

Nkomo, M., and Sehoole, C.T. (2004), 'Rural-based universities in South Africa: albatrosses or potential nodes for sustainable development?', paper prepared for the Environmental Management for Sustainable Universities Conference, Monterey, 9–11 June.

Ravjee, N. (2002), 'Neither ivory towers nor corporate universities: moving public universities beyond the "mode 2" logic', South African Journal of Higher Education, Vol 16, No 3, pp 82–88.

Reddy, T. (2004), *Higher Education and Social Transformation: South Africa Case Study*, report produced for the Council on Higher Education, Pretoria, February.

Slaughter, S., and Leslie, L. L. (1997), *Academic Capitalism: Politics, Policies, and the Entrepreneurial University*, Johns Hopkins University Press, Baltimore, MD.

Smith, D., and Katz, J. S. (2000), *Collaborative Approaches to Research: HEFCE Fundamental Review of Research Policy and Funding – Final Report*, University of Leeds Higher Education Policy Unit and University of Sussex Science Policy Research Unit, Leeds and Brighton.

# Toward an ecosystem for innovation in a newly industrialized economy

## Singapore and the life sciences

**Poh-Kam Wong**

**Abstract:** *In the late 1990s the Singapore government embarked on a set of far-reaching strategies intended to develop the city-state into one of the major life science R&D and industrial clusters in Asia. Besides efforts to attract leading overseas life science companies to establish operations in Singapore, the government has developed new life science public research institutions to attract overseas research talents. Outside the government, the local university sector is also emerging as an important player. Adapting the 'Triple Helix' framework to the life sciences in a newly industrialized economy, this paper reviews the policies and programmes implemented by the Singapore government and the National University of Singapore and discusses the implications for universities in other latecomer countries seeking to catch up in the global biotech race.*

**Keywords:** *university technology commercialization; innovation policy; life sciences; biotechnology; Singapore*

*The author is Director of the NUS Entrepreneurship Centre, National University of Singapore, 10 Kent Ridge Crescent, E3A Level 6, Singapore 119260. Tel: +65 6516 6323. E-mail: pohkam@nus.edu.sg*

There is now a vast literature on the genesis and growth of biotechnology clusters throughout the world (see, for example, Cooke 2003, 2004). Notwithstanding some regional variations, there is a general consensus that universities and public research institutes (PRIs) play a critical role in the emergence, sustained growth and capacity for continuous innovation of every major biotechnology cluster (Feldman and Francis, 2003; Casper,

2003). This paper examines the national strategy to develop Singapore into a regional hub not simply for manufacturing but also for innovation in the life sciences industry. An integral part of this strategy is the changing role of Singapore's leading university, the National University of Singapore (NUS). While many countries are similarly promoting life science R&D, what makes Singapore of particular interest is the scale and intensity of the government's effort in targeting the life science industry as a major driver of economic development. Even more impressive is that Singapore's initial position is arguably farther away from the biomedical technology frontier than were those of many other advanced OECD countries pursuing similar goals. The experience of Singapore is thus of relevance in any study of how the mission and governance of local universities in newly industrialized economies can be reformed to enable a faster 'catch-up' in the global biotech race.

## Life science in a small, open, newly industrialized economy

As argued by Etzkowitz *et al* (2000), universities around the world increasingly operate within a 'Triple Helix' nexus, involving interaction with government institutions and private industries. In the context of life science the nexus is characterized by a number of special features, as summarized in Table 1.

As suggested by Cooke (2003), the science-driven nature of the biomedical industry suggests that a greater governmental role is required in the life sciences than in other industries. In the context of small, open economies, especially late industrializing economies like Singapore's, Finegold *et al* (2004) and Wong (2006) argue that *foreign* actors, particularly global pharmaceutical multinational corporations, are also expected to play an important role, especially in the early stages of industry development. Before examining the particular role of Singapore's National University, we need to understand the changing contexts of private-sector and government involvement in the country's biomedical industrial development.

As highlighted by Wong (2001, 2005), Singapore achieved rapid economic development between political independence in 1965 and the late 1990s through a strategy of attracting direct foreign investment by multinational corporations and leveraging them to exploit technologies and know-how developed elsewhere. It was not until the mid-1990s that Singapore started to develop its own technological innovation capabilities and to create its own intellectual property.

After significant success in using the foreign investment promotion strategy to build Singapore into a major ICT/electronics manufacturing hub in Asia, in the 1990s the government began to promote the country as a major pharmaceutical manufacturing hub. Again, the strategy proved successful: pharmaceutical manufacturing output (almost entirely by foreign multinationals) rose from just S$1 billion in 1990 to over S$15 billion in 2004 (Wong, 2006).

**Table 1. Key actors in the Triple Helix nexus of life science.**

**Private industry**
Large global pharmaceutical multinationals
Dedicated biotech firms
Venture capital firms

**Government**
Public research institutes
Public hospitals
Regulatory institutions (drug approval
  authority, healthcare policy agencies, etc.)

**Universities**
Teaching faculty/research laboratories
Technology licensing/commercialization arms

*Source:* Wong (2006)

# Emergence of a life science cluster strategy

Recognizing the need to go beyond manufacturing capability to the development of innovative capabilities, in 2000 the Singapore government announced that biomedical science and technology would become a leading sector in the city-state's 21st-century economy. The plan was to turn Singapore into Asia's premier hub for biomedical sciences, with world-class capabilities across the entire value chain, from scientific discovery to technology commercialization and production (Biomed-Singapore, 2003). Towards this end, an initial allocation of US$1 billion was approved. Since the announcement of the new initiative, the government has moved decisively in implementation on several fronts – see below and Finegold *et al*, 2004, Tsui-Auch, 2004, and Wong, 2006 for more details.

*Public R&D funding and establishment of PRIs.* A new Biomedical Research Council (BMRC) was established to allocate R&D funding to strategic biomedical research areas, and four new public research institutes (PRIs) were founded during 2000–02. Although most of these new PRIs maintain some affiliation with the existing university (NUS), they have been funded separately by the BMRC and are largely autonomous. These two moves have increased government-sponsored biomedical-related R&D expenditures from less than S$50 million in 2000 to almost S$400 million in 2004. In that same period, university biomedical R&D increased more moderately from S$62.5 million to S$124.9 million (Wong, 2006).

*Physical infrastructure development.* All four public research institutes are located in a new integrated life sciences complex named 'Biopolis', which is strategically located to foster a collaborative culture with the nearby National University of Singapore, National University Hospital (NUH) and Singapore's Science Parks at an estimated total cost of S$500 million. The Biopolis hub has already attracted significant demand from biotechnology and pharmaceutical companies, with over 90% occupancy in its Phase I structure.

*Attracting foreign talent.* Because of the ambitious scale and speed of development, attracting foreign talent has become an integral part of the government's life sciences strategy. Locally, there was a dearth of 'star' researchers with sufficient international reputation and stature to serve as magnets in attracting other younger researchers (Zucker and Darby, 1996). To remedy this, the government initially focused much attention on attracting several internationally renowned scientists to Singapore.

*Developing local talent.* At the same time, in order to encourage more local students to study life sciences, the government both provides funding for new life science programmes and courses at local universities and polytechnics and offers generous scholarships for Singaporean and foreign students alike to pursue doctoral programmes in biomedical fields at leading universities overseas. A new medical school with a strong focus on research is also being established, modelled on the US postgraduate medical schools.

The government's foreign investment promotion policy has expanded still further in recent years to include clinical research organization, clinical research trials and bioinformatics services. Some of these developments were facilitated through investment by venture capital funds managed outside Singapore (see below).

*Developing a venture capital industry.* The government has also taken a lead role in directly managing a number of life science–related funds totalling over S$1.2 billion, now centralized under one fund management umbrella called 'BioOne Capital'. To date, BioOne Capital has reported investments in 40 portfolio companies globally, 15 with operations in Singapore. BioOne has also invested funds in five other life science venture capital funds, perhaps as an inducement for these funds to operate in Singapore.

*Other public infrastructure and support services.* To encourage commercialization activities in public-sector organizations, various direct funding schemes, such as the Proof of Concept (POF) and the Medtech schemes, have been launched to help scientists at tertiary institutes, hospitals and PRIs to translate early research ideas into commercialized products in the market. In addition, the government has put in place a range of 'soft' infrastructural measures, including significant improvements in the regulatory and promotional landscape for life science industry development.

Among these are a policy framework for promoting and regulating stem cell research, bioethics guidelines, an accreditation scheme for Singapore-based testing services and an industry networking organization (BioSingapore). At the same time, the government has launched a programme to liberalize the national healthcare system and increase competition among hospitals.

As a result of all these efforts, Singapore's total R&D expenditure in biomedical fields rose sharply from less than 5% of total R&D in the 1990s to over 10% in the five-year period 2000–04. Of the S$760 million spent in 2004, 31% was private-sector spending. More to the point for the purposes of this paper, the cumulative number of biomedical patents granted by the United States Patent and Trademark Office (USPTO) to Singapore-based inventors more than doubled in the five years between 2000 and 2004 compared to the period before 2000 (see Wong, 2006, for further details).

In addition to the growth in R&D, there are now 20 dedicated biotechnology firms (DFB) in Singapore, most of them founded since 2000. Although still small compared to the leading biotech clusters in the world, given that there were almost none seven to eight years ago, this record is commendable. Complementing these firms are about a dozen global pharmaceutical companies and several independent contract research organizations now with R&D operations in Singapore. In 2005, GlaxoKlineSmith and Welch Allyn announced plans to expand their R&D activities in Singapore.

# The emerging role of NUS

Established in 1905, the National University of Singapore is the oldest and largest public university in Singapore. Having the country's only medical school and faculty of science, NUS had a practical monopoly on biomedical research and biomedical education until the establishment of the new PRIs (described above). With typically more than one-third of its annual R&D expenditure (about S$160 million in 2004) devoted to biomedical-related fields, NUS was the largest biomedical R&D organization in Singapore and it maintained very high standards, as reflected in international scientific publications. Indeed, in 2005 NUS was ranked 15th in the world in the field

of biomedicine by the *Times Higher Education Supplement* – up from 22nd in 2004. However, its research achievements notwithstanding, up to the end of the 1990s NUS did not have a track record in bringing major biomedical innovations to market, because of its traditional focus on education and basic research. This began to change in the late 1990s.

*Moulding an 'entrepreneurial' university*

In line with emerging trends among universities the world over (Etzkowitz *et al*, 2000), in the late 1990s NUS started to become more of an 'entrepreneurial' university, moving beyond its education and research missions to take on technology commercialization in the context of economic development. This shift was given particular impetus in 2000 with the appointment of a new university president, who is US trained and has both industrial and university research administration experience in the USA. Emphasizing the need to make the institution more entrepreneurial, he authored a new vision statement for NUS – *Towards a Global Knowledge Enterprise* – to drive home the new strategic focus of the university.

An integral part of this strategy is the establishment of a new division in the university called 'NUS Enterprise', which is intended to inject a more entrepreneurial dimension into the university's educational and research activities. Under NUS Enterprise, the technology licensing office has been reorganized to become more 'inventor friendly', with an overall focus on transferring a larger proportion of

NUS discoveries to the market, whether through licensing to existing firms or by spinning off new firms. A New Venture Support (NVS) unit has also been established to provide assistance to NUS professors who want to commercialize their inventions and/or their expertise. NVS provides incubator facilities, a seed fund for NUS spin-off companies and a student start-up fund. A university-level Entrepreneurship Centre completes the set, providing entrepreneurship education and putting in place a network of entrepreneurs, venture capitalists and angel investors to provide NUS spin-offs with mentoring by practitioners and access to external venture funding.

The new president is also seeking to 'globalize' the university by revising faculty compensation and thus making it possible for the university to attract top talent from around the world. Meanwhile, the tenure and promotion policy for locals has been aligned with the more stringent and performance-based criteria of leading universities in the USA. The intake of foreign students has also increased, while a larger share of local students are encouraged to go on exchange programmes abroad for at least a semester.

A new initiative, the NUS Overseas College programme (NOC), was also introduced, integrating a global perspective with entrepreneurship. Under the programme, NUS sends its brightest undergraduate students to five entrepreneurial hubs around the world to work as interns in high-tech start-up companies for one year, during which they also take entrepreneurship-related courses at partner universities in the region.

The first location was Silicon Valley in 2002, followed by Philadelphia in 2003, Shanghai in 2004, Stockholm in 2005 and Bangalore in 2006. The choice of Philadelphia is noteworthy, as it is a major hub for pharmaceutical companies and of especial value to students interested in entrepreneurial life sciences.

*Life sciences education*

Responding to the national focus on promoting life science as a leading industrial cluster, NUS has also undertaken specific policy and organizational changes in life science education and research. An Office of Life Sciences (OLS) was formally established in 2001 with the mission to make NUS a world-class hub for life sciences by coordinating, integrating and facilitating the various disciplines that make up the life sciences throughout the university and its affiliated institutions.

The OLS is also charged with launching new research initiatives and teaching programmes. One such initiative is an integrated Life Science Undergraduate Major programme, involving the participation of the five core faculties – Computing, Dentistry, Engineering, Medicine and Science. Another is the new bio-engineering division, which crosses traditional departmental boundaries in the Engineering School.

In terms of research, the OLS brings together researchers from the five core faculties to identify collectively 10 strategic areas of research, grouped under the two broad headings of 'Diseases' and 'Platform Technologies'.

Finally, the university recently obtained government approval to establish a second medical school, modelled on the US postgraduate, professional medical school, with students drawn from various disciplines and academics who emphasize research. The school was established in collaboration with a leading US medical school (at Duke University) and is located next to Singapore's largest public hospital (SGH) to facilitate close interaction, particularly in research and clinical trials.

*NUS life science commercialization*

As NUS has become more oriented towards technology commercialization, there has been a visible increase in patenting in the biomedical area. At the end of 2004, NUS became the single largest biomedical patent holder in Singapore, accounting for 25 out of 86 US patents granted to Singapore-based inventors in the field of biomedical technology during 1977–2004.

Biomedical-related spin-offs from NUS have also increased. Of the more than 40 companies that were spun off by NUS up to 2004, 11 (of which 7 were established after 2000) are in biomedical-related fields. However, it should be noted that virtually all those companies have concentrated on biomedical technology, bioinformatics and healthcare products rather than on therapeutic drug discovery (for which, because of the costly trials needed for FDA approval, venture funding requirements are much more daunting). The amount of external venture funding attracted by these spin-offs remains modest, with the majority being funded by the founders themselves and business angel investors rather than by formal venture capital firms, which are still fairly new on the scene.

In terms of technology licensing, the market reach of NUS has been more extensive. At the end of 2004, there were 31 active licensees of biomedical-related patents, ranging from NUS spin-offs to local dedicated biotech firms and global pharmaceutical companies. Although the cumulative amount of royalties generated to date has not been published, it is likely to be modest since the majority of the licensing deals were concluded only in the last two to three years.

Notwithstanding the modest progress to date, NUS Enterprise is expected to accelerate considerably the pace of innovation commercialization in the university's life science fields, especially as the life science educational programmes and R&D expand.

## Results

Table 2 summarizes the key changes described so far. At the risk of oversimplification, the early 2000s have seen the role of government increase dramatically, an embryonic dedicated biotech sector starting to emerge and an increased R&D presence on the part of subsidiaries of global pharmaceutical firms. At the same time the university itself, responding to the new government and industry agenda for the life sciences as well as to self-instituted reforms, has begun the transition from a

**Table 2. Changes to Singapore's innovation ecosystem for life sciences.**

| Sector | Up to late 1990s | From 2000 |
|---|---|---|
| Large pharmaceutical companies | Primarily manufacturing operations by foreign multinationals. | Continued expansion of foreign multinational manufacturing, but some R&D activities by foreign multinationals are emerging. |
| *Manpower recruitment role* | Primarily to staff operational needs of manufacturing. | Recruiting for both manufacturing and R&D. |
| *Research sponsorship role* | Relatively minor. | Increasing in importance. |
| Dedicated biotech firms | Negligible presence. | Emergence of a cluster, including both locals and foreign implants. |
| Government | | |
| *Public research institutes* | Relatively small presence (IMCB). | Significant growth: five major PRIs. |
| *Physical infrastructure* | General science park; no specific life science focus. | Ambitious Biopolis plan adjacent to NUS. |
| *Financial infrastructure* | General venture capital industry promotion; no life science focus. Public R&D funding not significantly dedicated to life sciences. | Sizable life science venture capital funds, but mainly government funded. Significant dedicated strategic public R&D funding allocated to life science via BMRC. |
| *Manpower development* | Scholarships not significantly targeted for students in life sciences. | Significant dedicated scholarship programme for life science studies. Foreign talent attraction programme. |
| *Policy infrastructure* | General IP framework, not specific to the life sciences. | Bioethics guidelines. |
| *Public healthcare institutions* | High regulatory control, limited competition. | Controlled competition. |
| University | | |
| *Mission* | Traditional university model: primarily manpower development, some basic research. | Entrepreneurial university model: manpower development, research and technology commercialization. |
| *Organization of research and teaching* | Compartmentalization by traditional disciplines. Ambiguous relationship with university hospital. | Emergence of cross-disciplinary integration (Office of Life Sciences). University hospital an integral part of the life sciences programme. New postgraduate medical school model introduced. |

*(Continued)*

Table 2. (Continued)

| Sector | Up to late 1990s | From 2000 |
|---|---|---|
| *Institutional support for technology commercialization* | Embryonic technology licensing office, limited support services (mainly patent filing). No spin-off support. No training programme. | Revamped technology licensing office, broader marketing role. Venture support programme, incubator facilities and seed funding. Training programme and seminars. |
| *Technology commercialization governance policy* | Technology commercialization policy in flux, royalty revenue oriented. | Clear policy favourable to inventor and spin-off founders, equity in lieu of royalty. |

*Source:* Wong (2006).

traditional public university model to an 'entrepreneurial' university.

# Conclusion

Singapore's efforts to develop the island state into a leading biomedical innovation hub have involved separate but related developments among private, government and university sectors. As a newly industrialized economy comparatively late in entering the global biotech race (compared to the USA, the UK and Japan), Singapore has placed strong emphasis on attracting *both* overseas scientific talent and overseas life science firms to locate their R&D activities on the island, as a means of jump-starting the innovation catch-up process. While reliance on foreign talent and firms carries the longer-term risk of indigenization failure (Tsui-Auch, 2004), Singapore had, arguably, little choice given the long gestation period that would have been required to nurture local talents and firms. A key challenge now is to ensure that a sufficient quantity of

foreign talent settles permanently in Singapore.

As in Japan and Germany (Lehrer and Asakawa, 2004), while the national strategy also emphasizes the development of indigenous innovative capabilities in the local universities, to date this has been accorded a lower level of priority, partly because of the limitations on how quickly and to what extent the local universities can be adapted to the needs of the national agenda.

NUS has actually responded rather rapidly by putting in place new life science education and research initiatives and achieving a tangible increase in the pace of biomedical innovations, as measured by the numbers of patents, spin-offs and technology licensing.

The lessons from the Singapore experience are threefold. First, universities in developing economies need to make a transition from the traditional to the entrepreneurial model lest they become marginalized as, in their haste to catch up in the global biotech race, government development agencies give preference to autonomous public research institutes. Second, drug discovery commercialization is unlikely to result from policy changes at the university level *alone*; more fundamental changes in the overall innovation eco-system are needed.

And last but not least, the experience of Singapore suggests that policy makers need to weigh long-term against short-term policies. While there is a temptation for government developmental agencies to favour autonomous public research institutes to spearhead R&D in the short run, without a synergistic integration of the public research institutes with the local universities this may be a counterproductive strategy in the long run (Lehrer and Asakawa, 2004).

## References

Biomed-Singapore (2003), http://www. biomed-singapore. com/bms/gi_mc.jsp.

Casper, S. (2003), 'Commercializing science in Europe: the Cambridge biotechnology cluster', *European Planning Studies*, Vol 11, pp 825–823.

Cooke, P. (2003), 'The evolution of biotechnology in three continents: Schumpeterian or Penrosian?', *European Planning Studies*, Vol 11, pp 757–763.

Cooke, P. (2004), 'The accelerating evolution of biotechnology clusters', *European Planning Studies*, Vol 12, pp 915–920.

Etzkowitz, H., Webster, A., Gebhardt, C., and Terra, B.R.C. (2000), 'The future of the university and the university of the future: evolution of ivory tower to entrepreneurial paradigm', *Research Policy*, Vol 29, pp 313–330.

Feldman, M.P., and Francis, J.L. (2003), 'Fortune favours the prepared region:

the case of entrepreneurship and the Capitol Region biotechnology cluster', *European Planning Studies*, Vol 11, pp 765–787.

Finegold, D., Wong, P.K., and Cheah, T.C. (2004), 'Adapting a foreign direct investment strategy to the knowledge economy: the case of Singapore's emerging biotechnology cluster', *European Planning Studies*, Vol 12, No 7, pp 921–941.

Lehrer, M., and Asakawa, K. (2004), 'Rethinking the public sector: idiosyncrasies of biotechnology commercialization as motors of national R&D reform in Germany and Japan', *Research Policy*, Vol 33, pp 921–938.

Tsui-Auch, L.S. (2004), 'Bureaucratic rationality and nodal agency in a developmental state: the case of state-led biotechnology development in Singapore', *International Sociology*, Vol 19, No 4, pp 451–477.

Wong, P.K. (2001), 'Leveraging multinational corporations, fostering technopreneurship: the changing role of S&T policy in Singapore', *International Journal of Technology Management*, Vol 22, No 5/6, pp 539–567.

Wong, P.K. (2005), 'From technology adopter to innovator: the dynamics of change in the national system of innovation in Singapore', in Edquist, C., and Hommen, L., eds, *Small Economy Innovation Systems: Comparing Globalization, Change and Policy in Asia and Europe*, Edward Elgar, Cheltenham.

Wong, P.K. (2006), 'Commercializing biomedical science in a rapidly changing 'Triple Helix' nexus: the experience of the National University of Singapore', *Journal of Technology Transfer.*

Zucker, L., and Darby, M. (1996), 'Star scientists and institutional transformation: patterns of invention and innovation in the formation of the biotechnology industry', *Proceedings of the National Academy of Sciences*, Vol 93, pp 12709–12716.

Portions of this paper draw substantially on a previous work by the author (Wong, 2006), which provides more detailed data on Singapore's life sciences R&D and industry, as well as more in-depth case studies of selected life science commercialization from NUS.

# Fuelling a national innovation system in Colombia

## Diana Lucio-Arias

**Abstract:** *This presentation of the innovation-driven environment in Colombia derives from important national efforts to gather and store pertinent information. Two large surveys have tested the 'innovative behaviour' of Colombian manufacturing firms – the more recent of these was in 2005. Another information source is the Scienti platform, an online effort to collect and store information about research and researchers nationwide. Finally there is the SNIES, the national higher education information system which inventories curricula, admission criteria, study costs, physical resources, research activities, teachers and students of all institutions of higher education in the country. Although all of these instruments have their problems and are still in their consolidation phases, they constitute an invaluable asset for the country's scientific policy making.*

**Keywords:** *innovation; national innovation system; university–industry relations; Colombia*

Diana Lucio-Arias is with the Observatorio colombiano de ciencia y tecnologia (the Colombian Observatory of Science and Technology), Carrera 15 No 37–59, Bogota, DC, Colombia. She is currently on leave and is working at the Amsterdam School of Communication Research, Kloveniersburgwal 48, 1012 CX Amsterdam, The Netherlands. E-mail: dlucioarias@fmg.uva.nl; dlucio@ocyt.org.co

It has been widely acknowledged by business leaders, economists and social scientists alike that knowledge production and dissemination are becoming more important for sustainable economic growth than either capital or the accumulation of industrial/manufacturing plants (or both). It is also generally accepted that, if knowledge-based innovation is to flourish, a network of ties is essential, providing multiple and reciprocal linkages among the various actors in the innovation process (Etzkowitz and Leydesdorff, 1997). According to Arocena and Sutz (2000), 'innovation is hardly any more the outcome of isolated entrepreneurial genius: it is a systemic and complex social process involving people in different [economic, social, cultural, and political] roles'. As is noted elsewhere in this special issue of *Industry and Higher Education*, knowledge becomes relevant when it is put to fruitful use in the economic system.

This paper focuses on the social linkages that either already exist or can be created between institutions destined to play a role in innovation. Historically, these systems have been studied as social domains demonstrating the interaction of ideas; now, innovation is perceived as an engine of national competitiveness. Consequently, various policy actions have been taken in different countries in an effort to encourage innovation-oriented environments and to strengthen innovation systems. Particularly in the case of Colombia, the effort to foster innovation has been coupled with the strengthening of a system in which science interacts with the different economic sectors in the country. Innovation has been recognized as systemic – as the result of a coalition that brings science to society and to the economy.

---

*A national system of innovation can be defined as a network of institutions in which activities and relations start, import, modify and diffuse new knowledge and technology. It is a set of elements and their relations that participate in the production, diffusion and use of new and economically useful knowledge (Freeman, 1987; Lundvall, 1992).*

---

These principles are set forth in the 'Bogota Manual' (RICyT *et al*, 2001).[1] The Manual highlights the importance of considering the innovation agent as embedded in a network in which ideal interactions (networking) among the components provide the means for its development. Efficient exchanges of knowledge depend primarily on functioning communications networks that bring together disparate elements of the system. A single individual or firm involved in the innovation process does not operate simply within the structure of his or her own firm, but together with all other institutions of the innovation system.

## Towards a national system of innovation

National support for science and technology has been on the Colombian political agenda since 1968, the year Colciencias was created as a public fund for financing and promoting scientific activities. For 22 years Colciencias fulfilled its task of supporting and strengthening national scientific capacities through research funding programmes.

In the early 1990s, Colombia made important changes following the constitutional reform of 1991 and the opening of the national market to foreign goods and services.[2] For the industrial sector, however, this constituted a perceived threat to its domestic market, which led in turn to a search for alternative competitive advantages and new ways to support national industries.

The success of the work of Colciencias and science-related institutions, as well as the challenges posed by the new competitive environment, defined a new role for science in society. In 1990 the National Science and Technology System (NSTS) was established[3] to strengthen Colombia's scientific and technological capacities and to articulate them with other sectors of society. Colciencias[4] plays an important role as an organizer of the system and is responsible for the country's scientific policy. Academic, productive and regulatory bodies take part in the NSTS and are represented on the National Science and Technology Board,[5] which acts as the system's control and coordination hub.

The NSTS is defined as a 'system of activities', meaning that all scientific and technological activities and all national efforts in the form of programmes and mechanisms to promote their development are part of the system, regardless of the institution in which they are housed.

Despite the introduction of the NSTS, communication between industry and the scientific community remained weak in the 1990s. Although the NSTS was designed to bring science to industry, the relationship between the scientific and technological and the business/industrial communities remained distant and, as a result, there was an inadequate demand from Colombian firms for science and technology. At the same time, data collection was insufficient to permit an understanding of the dynamics of innovation in the country.

In light of this situation, finding a way to consolidate innovation became a stronger priority in the mid-1990s and the National System of Innovation (NSI) was legally established[6] in June 1995. The NSI is a *component* of the NSTS, with the specific purpose of stimulating national competitiveness through the development of exportable goods and services. An appropriate interaction between the scientific, technological, productive and financial communities was the major objective of this initiative.

Since this new system, the NSI, was created under the umbrella of the NSTS, it is not defined in itself as a system of activities, but rather in terms of its specific objective – the promotion of a desirable environment for the transfer of knowledge with business and industry at the helm. Specifically, NSI was designed to achieve an increase in the number and quality of innovative firms in Colombia.

The NSTS and NSI should have provided the right framework for the development of an institutional infrastructure for innovation. However, it was still rare for a firm to introduce a national scientific development into its operations or to engage in an alliance with a university or scientific institution. Although there was clear intent on the part of the government to provide an environment conducive to interaction and, thus, innovation, it was apparent that there was a further need for a network of agents that could interact with the various sectors and build relationships among them.

A national network of technological development centres (CDTs) was therefore introduced as a component of NSI. The main purpose of these CDTs is to intermediate between industries and universities and assist the process of knowledge transfer. The network was supported by government and significant public resources were invested in the development of each centre. The CDTs are mainly non-profit private institutions, specializing in industry-oriented disciplines that can contribute significantly to economic development. Thus there are centres that focus on applying biotechnological developments to the agricultural sector, centres that support the research and application of new technologies,[7] and so on. By 2004 there were 84 institutions in the network.

## Effect of the new organizations

In Colombia, as elsewhere, there is a growing demand for better-organized and-structured information so that trends can be properly tracked. In the field of scientific research, the *Scienti* platform includes an updated database of researchers' CVs and the activities of research groups. Additional data sets are planned, but for the moment the very fact that a large volume of information about the country's researchers and research activities can be retrieved from a single source is a major achievement. There is motivation too for researchers to keep their CVs and research interests up to date, since this is a condition of most government funding – and, besides, the database provides a means for researchers to increase their visibility. In a country with the characteristics of Colombia,[8] much research never finds its way into international journals or databases. Hence the *Scienti* platform is becoming an important source of information about research activities being carried out in Colombia.

The recently reported results of the second innovation survey in Colombia[9] constitute another important source of information. The survey was administered to the entire directory of industrial entrepreneurs, and achieved a response rate of almost 93%. The basic aim was to gather information for 2003 and 2004 on three fronts: the dynamics of the activities leading to innovation as defined in the Bogota Manual, the degree of use of the tools and mechanisms designed by the government to support innovation and the educational background of employers. Although all the information is not yet fully available, the first results have already been published.

The last source of data is Colombia's higher education

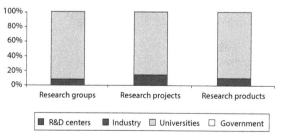

**Figure 1.** Research activities in Colombia.
*Source: Scienti.*

information system, which holds, among other things, information about students and graduates from technical, technological, Bachelor's, Master's and PhD programmes.

## Data on research and innovative behaviour

In Colombia, research activities are conducted mainly in universities (see Figure 1). Universities have the most research groups, of which 54% are in public and 46% are in private universities. Eighty-four per cent of research projects are carried out with the participation of universities, and 88% of scientific results[10] are attributable to them. If innovation in Colombia were strongly linked with research, one could make the argument that there would be room for more and better linkages between universities and industry. In fact, innovation in Colombia is *not* strongly linked with research activities; only 6.2% of the firms responding to the innovation survey reported that they had supported any R&D activities at all in 2004 (see Table 1).[11]

This lack of interest in research, and the perceived low rate of return from innovation generated through research, accounts for the poor relationship between Colombia's universities and private enterprises. Less than 1% of all the research projects conducted in the country involve business enterprises, and of these just two are done in collaboration with non-business agencies.

Considering that most of the centres in Figure 2 are CDTs, it seems that government initiatives and programmes to promote links between universities and industry and to bring firms closer to national scientific developments have yet to bear fruit.

## Education and employment

It is in the nature of global capitalism to accelerate the process of obsolescence, not only of products but of knowledge itself and expertise (Pineda, 2003). Thus to sustain an innovative ecosystem, the education of young people has to be brought into the equation and with it stronger

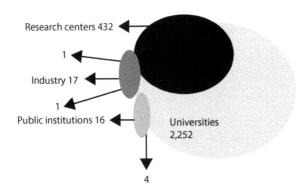

**Figure 2.** Research-related linkages.
*Source: Scienti.*

Table 1. Number of Colombian firms investing in innovation-seeking activities.

| Innovation activity (as defined in Bogota Manual) | 2003 | 2004 |
|---|---|---|
| Technologies embodied in capital equipment | 2,732 | 3,354 |
| Management technologies | 2,237 | 2,649 |
| Transversal technologies | 2,791 | 3,287 |
| R&D | 301 | 382 |
| Technological training | 2,334 | 3,109 |
| *Number of firms surveyed* | *6,172* | *6,172* |

*Source:* DANE, DNP, Colciencias.

links with workforce demand and enhancement.

The higher education system in Colombia comprises a variety of heterogeneous institutions – public and private universities and higher technical, technological and higher education institutions. In what follows, these distinctions will be ignored.

For the most part, higher education studies in Colombia are pursued to the level of the Bachelor's degree. In fact, in 2002 there were only 315 Master's programmes and 45 PhD programmes (see Figure 3).

A change in the subject preferences among tertiary education students may be associated with a stronger desire to pursue a career in the private industrial sector. In 1995 the field in which most Bachelor's and Master's students graduated was associated with teacher training (23% and 37% respectively), but by 2002 there was a clear preference for degrees in preparation for careers in engineering and administration (engineering disciplines accounted for 19% of Bachelor's and 18% of Master's graduates, and administration-related degrees accounted for 23% of Bachelor's and 16% of Master's graduates). Programmes offering a PhD degree

also expanded their enrolments, and, by 2002, there were graduate students working for PhDs in physics, agronomy, education, engineering, biology, mathematics, geography and medicine.

There is a tendency to believe that professionals and highly qualified workers in science and technology will bring continuous innovative products and processes to the market, generating increased employment opportunities and prosperity. But the innovation surveys suggest otherwise. Fifty-two per cent of the 555,975 people employed in the firms surveyed had nothing more than a high school diploma. Just 14% had completed professional training.

What is more worrying is that some highly qualified professionals are choosing to leave the country once they have finished their studies, which represents a lost investment for their homeland.

## Conclusion

In the case of Colombia, there has been a sustained national effort to increase innovation through the strengthening of communication between universities and industry. The goal is to channel new knowledge

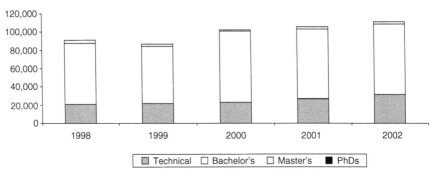

**Figure 3.** Graduating students, by type of degree.
*Source:* Daza and Lucio (2004).

fruitfully into the economy and to ensure that the universities are aware of the new knowledge requirements. Legislation and government programmes have been put in place to implement the National System of Science and Technology and the National Innovation System. Nevertheless, and despite these efforts, linkages between research and innovation remain inadequate. The technological centres that have been sponsored have not fully developed as intermediaries between research activities in universities and the demand for new knowledge at the level of the firm or the industrial sector.

The weak communication links between Colombia's universities and industry betray the absence of a feedback mechanism to communicate the needs of business and the educational and research activities of universities. There is no obvious way to channel the needs of industry into the desired characteristics of the ideal employee. Nor is there a strong presence of university graduates in the workforces of the firms surveyed.

As the university student population increases without an equivalent demand for workers with degree-level qualifications, another brain drain of young skilled professionals could result.

In Colombia normative and legal mechanisms have been designed and adopted to provide an adequate environment for the innovation process. Especially since 1990, a very complex normative infrastructure has been put in place, in accordance with the needs of the country. Nevertheless, for this infrastructure to achieve its purpose, there must be consolidation of national capacities at the institutional level, and this remains a missing link. Normative efforts to create a system have to be accompanied by the real capacity to create a network of interactions.

This is not an easy task. Colombia's outlook is not very positive: a long-standing situation of delayed development, significant poverty rates, inequality in wealth distribution, low levels of health and education, institutional weaknesses, underdevelopment of the productive sector, and decades of armed conflict are all structural factors that have impeded the proper allocation of attention and resources that is essential if the goals that have been set are to be accomplished.

## Notes

[1] The Bogota Manual is the result of the revision and adjustment of the Oslo Manual (OECD, 1997) for the study of innovation in relation to the special characteristics of Latin American countries.

[2] Colombia reduced its barriers to external products and services through a drastic process, beginning in 1990, of reducing custom duties and internal industrial subsidies.

[3] Through the 'Ley 29, 1990'.

[4] Until 1990, Colciencias had depended on the Ministry of Education and its annual budget was part of the overall ministerial budget. From 1990 Colciencias became an independent public body and a participant in the National *Fuelling innovation in Colombia* General Budget that is calculated annually and shared among the public institutions.

[5] Comprising the Director of DNP, the Ministry of Education, the Ministry of Economy, the Ministry of Agriculture, one rector of a public university, one rector of a private university, a member of the scientific community, a member of the industrial sector and the director of Colciencias.

[6] As a decision of the National Science and Technology Board.

[7] A complete list of the centres can be found at www.colciencias.gov.co.

[8] There is general recognition that some publications could not be represented in the ISI indexes due to linguistic, thematic and geographical factors (see, for example, Vessuri, 2002).

[9] The first innovation survey in Colombia was held in 1996 and contains information about a sample of 885 industrial firms.

[10] Books, book chapters, scientific articles, short reviews, industrial design, multimedia, norms, pilots, protopilots, and PhD and Master's theses are recognized as scientific results in Colombia.

[11] A 1997 study of 3,117 firms concluded that 24% had carried out R&D activities in the past *(Plan Estrategico del Programa*

*Nacional de Desarrollo Tecnologico Industrial y Calidad, 2000 –2010).*

## References

Arocena, Rodrigo, and Sutz, Judith (2000), 'Looking at national systems of innovation from the South', *Industry and Innovation*, Vol 7, No 1, pp 55–75.

Consejo Nacional de Ciencia y Tecnologia (1995), *Politica Nacional de Innovacion y Desarrollo Tecnologico*, Bogota.

DANE, DNP and Colciencias (2005), *Innovacion y Desarrollo Tecnologico en la Industria Manufacturer Colombia 2003–2004*, www.dane.gov.co/files/investigaciones/industria/innovacion_tecnol_ind_manufacturera.pdf.

Daza, S., and Lucio, D., eds (2004), *Indicadores de Ciencia y Tecnologia, Colombia, 2004*, Observatorio Colombiano de Ciencia y Tecnologia, Bogota, www.ocyt.org.co.

Etzkowitz, H., and Leydesdorff, L., eds (1997), *Universities and the Global Knowledge Economy: a Triple Helix of University–Industry–Government Relations*, Cassell, London.

Freeman, C. (1987), *Technology Policy and Economic Performance: Lessons from Japan*, Pinter, London.

Lundvall, B.-A., ed (1992), *National Systems of Innovation: Towards a Theory of Innovation and Interactive Learning*, Pinter, London.

Ministerio de Desarrollo Economico, Ministerio de Comercio Exterior, Departamento Nacional de Planeacion, SENA, Colciencias (2000), *Plan Estrategico del Programa Nacional de Desarrollo Tecnologico Industrial y Calidad, 2000–2010*, Bogota.

Pineda, L. (2003), *Memorias de la primera reunion de expertos de los paises del Convenio Andrés Bello en Innovacion y Gestion Cientifico y Tecnologica para el Desarrollo*, Documentos de Ciencia, Tecnologia e Innovacion de los paises del CAB, Covenio Andrés Bello, Bogota.

Republica de Colombia (1990), Ley 29 de 1990, available at: www.ocyt.org.co.

Republica de Colombia (1991), Decreto 585, available at: www.ocyt.org.co.

RICyT, OEA, CYTED, Colciencias and OCyT (2001), Normalizacion de Indicadores de Innovacion Tecnologica en América Latina y el Caribe, *Manual de Bogota, available at www.ocyt.org.co.*

Sutz, Judith (2000), 'University–industry–government relations in Latin America', *Research Policy*, Vol 29, pp 279–290.

Vessuri, H. (2002), 'El ejercicio de la observation sociotécnica: a proposito de los observatorios de ciencia y tecnologia', *Cuadernos del Cendes*, Vol 19, No 51, pp 1–17.

# Knowledge transfer between SMEs and higher education institutions

## Differences between universities and colleges of higher education in the Netherlands

**Heike Delfmann and Sierdjan Koster**

**Abstract:** *Knowledge transfer (KT) between higher education institutions (HEIs) and businesses is seen as a key element of innovation in knowledge-driven economies: HEIs generate knowledge that can be adopted in the regional economy. This process of valorization has been studied extensively, mainly with a focus on universities. In the Netherlands, there is a binary system of higher education comprising universities and the more practice-oriented colleges of higher education. From 2001 these colleges have played an increasingly important role in KT, which gives rise to the question of whether there are differences in the frequency and structure of KT involving universities and KT involving colleges. Colleges appear easier to access for SMEs because of their focus on business practices. The interactions between universities and SMEs are more localized, suggesting the need for face-to-face interactions in those contacts. Furthermore, the results reiterate the importance of the absorptive capacity of firms and previously established contacts of entrepreneurs in explaining firm–HEI interaction.*

**Keywords:** *knowledge transfer; colleges of higher education; HEI–SME interaction; SMEs; Netherlands*

*Heike Delfmann (corresponding author) and Sierdjan Koster are with the Urban and Regional Studies Institute, Faculty of Spatial Science, University of Groningen, PO Box 800, 9700AV Groningen, The Netherlands. E-mail: h.s.delfmann@rug.nl*

Innovation is now considered by many to be the most important driving factor for sustainable economic development (Cornett, 2009; De Bruijn and Lagendijk, 2005); and knowledge transfer (KT) is widely recognized as a key element in the innovation process in knowledge-driven economies. Furthermore, the creation, integration and transfer of knowledge form the basis for competitive advantage and organizational capability (Argote and Ingram, 2000; Boschma, 2005; Grant, 1996). Collaboration between the public and private sectors is of particular importance in areas dominated by small businesses (Cornett, 2009). Higher education institutes (HEIs) are considered to be essential for KT because they generate knowledge, and most enterprises cannot operate without external knowledge (Muizer, 2003). A smooth transfer of knowledge is crucial for ensuring that the available knowledge reaches (smaller) organizations.

In the Netherlands, higher education is offered at two types of institutes: research universities and colleges of higher education (referred to respectively as the 'university' and the 'college' in this article). Colleges constitute a significant part of the higher education system, with approximately 400,000 students enrolled (HBO-raad, 2010). Universities have some 230,000 students (VSNU, 2010). There are differences between the two types of institutes. First, the level of education, the access requirements and the final graduate qualifications are all slightly lower at colleges. College graduates attain a Bachelor's degree in four years, whereas at the university a Bachelor's degree is achieved in three. Students with a college Bachelor's degree can enrol at a university to obtain a Master's degree (Jonge and Berger, 2006). Another relevant difference is that universities are traditionally geared more towards research than colleges. This may partly explain why colleges have been largely neglected in research on knowledge spill-overs and valorization. In contrast, university–industry linkages and their impact on innovation are an established subject of analysis (Agrawal, 2001; Cornett, 2009; Perkmann and Walsh, 2007). Recently, however, Dutch colleges have expanded their research programmes. In order to promote knowledge transfer between colleges and small and medium-sized enterprises (SMEs), so-called 'lectors' and 'knowledge circles' were introduced in 2001. A lector is expected to facilitate and initiate knowledge transfer between colleges and firms, in particular SMEs, and society in general (Jonge and Berger, 2006). Lectors have four principal tasks: knowledge development (research), professionalization of lecturers at their college, renewing education curricula, and knowledge circulation from and to society (OECD, 2009). Each lector is expected to form a knowledge circle consisting of college lecturers and professionals from the work field. Knowledge circles are also expected to strengthen the interaction between educational institutes and firms (Jonge and Berger, 2006).

Given that colleges now have a more pronounced role in the creation of knowledge (research) and its dissemination, this study assesses the extent to which the function of colleges in the process of knowledge circulation differs from that of universities. In particular, the fact that colleges adopt a practical approach to education – including, for instance, compulsory internships for students – may make colleges attractive partners for local businesses. Given the different focus of the educational programme, the types of linkages with SMEs may also be different and, as a result, their evaluation by the firms. We approached the issue from two perspectives. Firstly, the study addresses the interaction between education institutes and firms. The main research question we aim to answer from this perspective is: How many firms interact with institutes of higher education and what are the characteristics of those interactions? Second, we focus on the characteristics of the firms that interact with the institutes. Which firms interact and do SMEs differ depending on the institute they interact with? In other words, do colleges and universities serve different markets?

Understanding the possible differences between KT involving universities and colleges is important both from a policy point of view and from a more research-oriented view. Clark *et al* (2008) state that the failure of knowledge transfer for any of the parties involved (educational institutes and firms) may jeopardize the sustainable future of the KT process. This underlines the importance of research that addresses different modes and methods of knowledge transfer. Goldstein and Drucker (2006) stress that distinguishing the different ways in which colleges and

universities operate and appeal to organizations in the context of KT is fundamental for assessing their economic impact.

This present study adds to existing literature by simultaneously assessing several sources of knowledge (colleges and universities) so that the interaction patterns with local businesses can be compared. Because the study takes all sectors into account, it also provides an overall picture of the types of firms that interact with local knowledge institutes and the intensity of the interactions between HEIs and SMEs in a given region.

The remainder of this paper is organized as follows. The next section describes the context of KT in the Netherlands by first discussing the differences between colleges and universities as providers of knowledge. Next, we introduce firm-level characteristics that influence the interaction. The data and methodology are then discussed, followed by a presentation of the key findings in which differences in organizational and entrepreneurial characteristics for organizations that seek information at universities and colleges are addressed. The final section summarizes the arguments of the paper.

## Background

'Cooperation is good, more cooperation is better'. Although this quote by Freel (2006, p 104) may be somewhat of a simplification, it does illustrate well the ascribed importance of innovation based on cooperation and mutual knowledge transfer in knowledge-based economies (Cooke and Leydesdorff, 2006). The diffusion of knowledge is considered to be equally as important as its creation (Zheng and Harris, 2007). Argote and Ingram (2000) describe knowledge transfer as the process through which one unit (a group, department or division) is affected by the experience of another. Even though Argote and Ingram focus on knowledge transfer within organizations, the definition applies equally to interactions between different organizations. Recent studies addressing the role of cooperation and KT in innovation systems are strongly influenced by the Triple Helix theory (see, for example, Etzkowitz and Leydesdorff, 2000). The theory proposes that HEIs, sovereign states (governments) and firms together make up the innovation system. Rather than a directional approach to knowledge diffusion and consequent innovation, in which HEIs produce knowledge that can be used for innovation in firms, the theory propagates a dynamic system in which knowledge production and innovation is the result of a cooperative process. The actors involved take on different roles, and knowledge is mutually exchanged rather than dispensed unidirectionally. The common goal is to achieve 'an innovative environment consisting of university spin-off firms, tri-lateral initiatives for knowledge-based economic development and strategic alliances among firms, government laboratories, and academic research groups' (Etzkowitz and Leydesdorff, 2000, p 112).

The Triple Helix theory thus suggests that analysing such a complex innovation system involves a comprehensive approach that assesses in depth the roles of the different actors. However, analysing the system indicates that it can be regarded as a collection of network connections between the different actors. Network theory can then be used to describe why actors would engage in mutual interaction. Such an approach precludes any inferences pertaining to the whole innovation system. It does inform us, however, about why certain relationships between actors will be established. By studying the directed link between HEIs and SMEs, we thus focus on part of the more complex Triple Helix innovation system.

Ebers (1997) conceptualizes the motivation for interaction between actors in terms of flows. He distinguishes between resource and information flows between the actors on the one hand and the expectations about the interaction on the other hand. Interactions are sustainable if the resources or information exchanged are complementary and if the expectations of both parties involved in the interaction match. The first aspect, resource and information transfer, is influenced by the content of the flows themselves. In the current case: can a university or college provide SMEs with relevant information for their businesses? In addition, the absorptive capacity of the receiving firms is important (Cohen and Levinthal, 1990). The firms need to be able to integrate the information meaningfully into their production processes in order to secure competitive advantage (Grant, 1996). If this is not the case, a sustainable relationship is unlikely to develop because it provides too few benefits for the receiving firm. In addition to organizational features, Brass *et al* (2004) stress the importance of the characteristics of the people involved in the interaction. They contend that interactions tend to be path dependent: individuals are likely to interact with familiar people or organizations. Knowledge of the source organization facilitates accessing the information sought. In addition, familiarity often translates into trust, which influences positively the expectations concerning the interaction. It is thus anticipated that the second aspect, expectations, is improved if the entrepreneur involved is familiar with the HEI.

In the following, we will develop these ideas further in the context of KT between colleges and universities and SMEs. First, we will address the type and availability of information in universities and colleges; and then the absorptive capacity of SMEs and the previously established links of the entrepreneurs will be discussed.

## Colleges as sources of knowledge

Knowledge transfer between HEIs and SMEs can be expected to vary as the characteristics of the institutes differ. There are two main differences in the Dutch context: the number of colleges and the different focus of colleges.

Colleges outnumber universities in the Netherlands. Not only are there twice as many students in colleges, there are also considerably more colleges than there are universities. The university sector consists of 14 government-funded universities: in contrast, there are 41 colleges that receive government funding (OECD,

2009).[1] Equally, the geographic location of the institutes varies: on average, the physical distance between SMEs and colleges is small compared to that between SMEs and universities. This can have a positive effect on cooperation between colleges and small businesses (EIM, 2007), for two reasons. A purely mathematical reason is that firms, when looking for an institute to cooperate with, have a greater inclination to select a college as the nearest option. The second reason is that proximity plays an important role in the interaction itself. Transaction costs are generally lower when the distance between actors is shorter. Shorter distances allow for easier face-to-face contact, which not only improves information transfer but also enhances monitoring of the effectiveness of the interaction. The 'distance-decay' effect can be very strong, and interactions are maintained best at the local level (Agrawal, 2001; Brass *et al*, 2004). As the average distance between SMEs and colleges is shorter than that between universities and SMEs, colleges may on average be more attractive to contact. When assessing the intrinsic value of the colleges versus the university, the effect of distance should be accounted for in order to avoid spurious relationships (see also 'Methodology and data').

The second difference between the two types of institute is the more practical educational approach of colleges, which may make the information they provide particularly relevant for SMEs. Colleges prepare their students for specific jobs: universities, in principle, prepare their students for conducting scientific research. A telling illustration of the practice-oriented education is the fact that all college students need to carry out an internship or work placement as part of their curriculum. Colleges thus have a vested interest in interacting with businesses in the local areas, which should be reflected in enhanced accessibility and more relevant information being available to transfer between the actors. This could result in lower barriers for small organizations seeking to approach colleges when looking for information. The importance of internships may also influence the characteristics and channels for knowledge transfer. Existing studies generally consider some subset of publications, patents, consulting, informal meetings, recruiting, licensing, joint ventures, research contracts and personal exchange as the most important channels for interaction (Agrawal, 2001; Cohen *et al*, 2002; Schartinger *et al*, 2002). However, they rarely include the one thing that colleges have the most of: students. In particular, small firms are expected to benefit from the influx of students, who bring new knowledge from the institute (Bekkers and Bodas Freitas, 2008). Schartinger *et al* (2002) did consider students as a type of interaction between university and firms; they included joint supervision of PhDs and Master's theses. Their relative importance was in the upper quarter, lower than consulting and collaborative research but higher than joint publications, training and guest lectures. Students and graduates from colleges can contribute substantially to renewal in SMEs. This may not be high-tech innovation, but it can still be

of great relevance for SMEs wishing to strengthen their position in a competitive market (MKB Nederland and VNO-NCW, 2006). Interaction through students may be a defining characteristic of the relationship between colleges and local firms. We expect that college students can also have significant value for smaller organizations because of the organizations' preference for less formal contacts (Cohen and Levinthal, 1990; De Jong and Hulsink, 2010; Malecki, 2008).

The practice-oriented approach of colleges may also influence the spatial dimension of interactions with SMEs. Universities often produce specialist knowledge, whereas colleges of higher education possess relatively high-quality knowledge that is less directly relevant at regional level (Vermeulen, 1996). For that reason, colleges can be more suitable for small businesses in the process of KT and so the colleges may therefore be particularly important in the regional context.

## Characteristics of firms

The relationship between educational institutes and SMEs is dependent not only on the characteristics of the HEI but also on the characteristics of the other actor involved, the SME. The most important notion that describes to what extent firms are effective receptors of knowledge (or any other resource, for that matter) and to what extent they interact with research institutes is *absorptive capacity*. Cohen and Levinthal (1990) define absorptive capacity as the ability of an organization to recognize the value of new, external information, assimilate it and apply it to commercial ends. Firms with higher levels of absorptive capacity are therefore better able to engage in collaborations (De Jong and Hulsink, 2010). There are important characteristics of firms that relate to absorptive capacity.

## Absorptive capacity

The most important characteristic of firms for determining absorptive capacity is *firm size*. Firm size is positively related to the propensity for collaboration (Freel, 2006) and to the level of absorptive capacity (Bekkers and Bodas Freitas, 2008; De Jong and Hulsink, 2010; Veugelers and Cassiman, 2005). Larger firms are typically better structured and professionalized; and, as an organization grows, it becomes better equipped for using particular channels of university–industry knowledge transfer (De Jong and Hulsink, 2010). Results from the Eurostat Community Innovation Survey (2009), for instance, show that more than half (54%) of all large enterprises actively engaged in innovation were involved in innovation partnerships, compared to 22% of small enterprises. For the majority of SMEs, it may be more realistic to connect with colleges of higher education (WRR, 2008).

Absorptive capacity can also be influenced by *employee skills*, which can be particularly relevant in the case of small firms not involved in high-tech activities (De Jong and Freel, 2010; Schmidt, 2009). In addition, the *company's age* can also influence absorptive capacity. As an organization ages, it develops

learning skills which may enhance the absorptive capacity. As a result, the current level of absorptive capacity depends on past knowledge (Zahra and George, 2002).

The firm's *industry type* can determine interaction between firms and knowledge institutes as well. Various studies find that university–industry interaction is more important in science-based technologies (see, for example, Bekkers and Bodas Freitas, 2008; Schartinger *et al*, 2002). A difference between service sectors and manufacturing sectors is also observed (Cowan *et al*, 2001; Eurostat CIS, 2009). Traditionally, knowledge transfer mechanisms focus on the manufacturing sector. The service industry sector is known to engage in less formal R&D. Analysis of transfer channels reveals that service firms do use the same channels as manufacturing firms, though the appropriateness and intensity of use differs between the two sectors (Cowan *et al*, 2001). Given the relative importance of human capital in the service sector compared to manufacturing, we expect that interactions involving student placements (for example, internships) are particularly important for the service sector.

## Path dependence of personal contacts

Finally, in addition to organizational characteristics, the personal characteristics of the entrepreneur play a role in explaining interactions between education institutes and SMEs (Brass *et al*, 2004). Especially so in SMEs, the management of the firm can be heavily influenced by one person, generally the owner (Risseeuw and Thurik, 2003). It is to be anticipated that there is a certain path dependence in the contacts between entrepreneurs and HEIs in the sense that the individuals concerned may be inclined to contact institutes that are familiar to them because they, for example, studied there. By taking the existing paths, cognitive proximity is maximized and risks are minimized (Boschma, 2005). In their research, Knoben and Oerlemans (2006) stated that in order for organizations to communicate and transfer knowledge effectively and efficiently, participants need to have similar frames of reference. In other words, closer cognitive proximity of the participants is beneficial for collaboration (Boschma, 2005). In terms of the network framework proposed by Ebers (1997), the familiarity with norms and procedures helps in aligning mutual expectations about the interaction. There can also be more practical reasons: entrepreneurs may still know people to contact in the organization. This leads to two expectations. The first is that the propensity for interacting with an HEI declines with the years elapsed since graduation. Immediately after graduation, the social network in the organization is still well developed, whereas later on, due to changes in the HEI and the development of different networks by the entrepreneur, the network may be less suitable for interaction. The second expectation is that entrepreneurs with a college education are more inclined to contact colleges, whereas entrepreneurs with a university degree prefer to contact universities.

In summary, using a framework adopted from network theory, we anticipated that the interactions between HEIs and SMEs would depend on the type of information that is available in the colleges, the absorptive capacity of the SMEs involved and also the personal history of the entrepreneurs involved. Given the different foci of universities and colleges, we can thus expect differences in the patterns of interaction between the two institutes. Again, a personal connection with the institutes is expected to be an important variable in this respect.

## Methodology and data

Although industry–university linkages have been widely studied, few studies have offered a comparison of two institutes using a survey approach. Most studies adopt a case-study approach that, for example, describes in detail the linkages on one research park: such an approach fits well with a Triple Helix approach to innovation. However, this present study attempts to present a more general picture, and data therefore needed to be collected from a wider population of SMEs. In order to achieve this, a questionnaire was sent to a sample of all SMEs in the Groningen region,[2] as shown in Figure 1. The firms were asked questions regarding the entrepreneurs' interactions with Hanze University Groningen (Hanze, the college[3]) and University of Groningen (RUG, the university) in the preceding year.

The questionnaire survey was conducted in November 2009; thus the data collected about the interactions relate to the period of November 2008 to November 2009. 'Interaction' was

**Figure 1.** Location of research area.

defined as the entrepreneur having contacted one of the institutes with a business objective: the question asked was, *'How often did your firm interact with knowledge institutes in the preceding year?'* The questionnaire consisted primarily of closed questions mainly with 5-point Likert scale answer options, complemented with a 'not applicable' option. Questions were asked in Dutch.

The questionnaire was sent to 2,000 companies that were randomly selected in a stratified process; 1,500 companies had 2 to 50 employees and 500 firms had only 1 employee. This resulted in a distribution of organization size with a mode of 2 and a mean of 7. Retail and catering firms were excluded from the survey. Addresses were obtained from the business register kept by the local Chamber of Commerce. In total, 197 completed questionnaires were returned that were suitable for analysis, a response rate of almost 10% – a reasonable result for a postal survey. Due to missing values in some of the returned questionnaires, the number of observations used in the analyses varies.

The Groningen region was chosen as the study area because it offers a 'near natural experimental' research setting for studying the research topic. The region houses one university (the University of Groningen) and one college (Hanze University Groningen). Both HEIs are medium-sized institutes and offer broad educational programmes. In addition, both institutes operate in relative isolation to other HEIs, which are located at least one hour's travel away. Groningen is the most important concentration of population, employment and education in the north of the Netherlands. As a result, the findings are not influenced by possible competition with HEIs in other cities and the results are not biased as they might have been if colleges had outnumbered universities (or *vice versa*): firms have a choice of just one college or one university. A drawback of this research setting is that idiosyncratic organizational characteristics in either one of the institutes may influence results, making it more difficult to generalize the outcomes, although a comparison of different cities carried out by Delfmann *et al* (2010) showed little regional variation in the percentage of firms that interact with colleges and universities.

## Results

Using the dataset described in the previous section, the research questions can now be addressed. First, descriptive results about the interactions between HEIs and SMEs in the Groningen region are presented. We focus on the characteristics of the interactions and the differences between universities and colleges. Second, logit/probit models are presented in which the likelihood of SMEs to interact with (one of) the HEIs is considered.

*SME–HEI interactions*

The SMEs in the sample can be divided into four groups: firms that did not have any interaction with either HEI in the previous year, firms that interacted with the college (Hanze) only, firms that interacted only with the university

**Table 1. Interactions between HEIs and SMEs.**

|  | N | % |
|---|---|---|
| No interaction | 104 | 55.9 |
| Hanze only | 37 | 19.9 |
| RUG only | 14 | 7.5 |
| Both HEIs | 31 | 16.7 |
| Total | 186 | 100.0 |

(RUG) and firms that interacted with both institutes. Table 1 shows the breakdown of these groups.

Almost half of all respondents (44.1%) indicated that they had interacted with an HEI in the 12 months covered by the study. It is difficult to interpret this proportion because, to the best of our knowledge, there are no similar studies that provide a broad overview of the number and characteristics of interactions. Research that has been done focuses on specific subgroups of firms and specific types of interactions, resulting in much lower values. The Eurostat Community Innovation Survey, for instance, shows that in 2000 less than 10% of innovative firms had cooperative agreements with universities (Veugelers and Cassiman, 2005). Compared to the EC study, the share of interaction reported here seems rather high. However, it must be said that most interactions appear incidental. Nearly 75% of all firms contacted the Hanze only a few times per year. For the university, interactions seemed somewhat more intensive, on average. Some 60% of all firms interacted with the university only a few times per with HEIs in other cities, and the results are not biased as they might have been if colleges had outnumbered universities (or *vice versa*): firms have a choice of just one college or one university. A drawback of this research setting is that idiosyncratic organizational characteristics in either one of the institutes may influence results, making it more difficult to generalize year. A small number of the firms developed intensive interactions: 7.5% of all firms had intensive contact with the college or the university. This means that they interacted on at least a weekly basis. This is the same order of magnitude as the 10% of firms that were found to have cooperative agreements (Veugelers and Cassiman, 2005), which presumably also involved intensive interactions.

Not only does the intensity of interactions differ between the university and the college; the number of interactions also varies. In total, 36.7% of the firms interacted with the Hanze and 24.2% interacted with the university. Of these firms, nearly 17% interacted with both HEIs. This confirms the expectation that colleges are more easily accessible for SMEs than are universities. It shows the relevance of colleges for SMEs, and it offers an argument to include these types of interaction in further analyses. When considering the types of interactions, student-related contacts are the most important for colleges. Most interactions consist of internships or research activities by students. It might be expected that the types of interactions are different for universities, although information on this was not included in the survey. This precludes a direct comparison; but Schartinger *et al* (2002) did find that contacts with universities consisted mainly of consultancy work

and collaborative research. Joint supervision of PhD and Master's theses is the third most common channel through which firms interact with universities.

In contrast to the number of interactions, the perceived benefits gained from interacting are greater for universities (Figure 2). The left bars in Figure 2 show the share of firms that interacted with the respective organization (these shares are the same as in Table 1), and the right bars represent the evaluation of the interactions in the previous year. The bars show the share of firms that classified the interaction with the HEI as either important or very important on a five-point Likert scale. Overall, the evaluation of interacting is quite positive. For the whole sample, more than 60% of the SMEs are satisfied with the interactions with one of the institutes in the 12-month period that was covered by the study.

The results from the simple descriptive analysis on the intensity and the perceived quality of the interactions suggest that there is a trade-off between the accessibility of the organization and the quality of the relationship. SMEs are more inclined to interact with colleges, which is understandable given the more practice-oriented approach of the organization: SMEs find it easier to interact with colleges. However, problem-solving capabilities seem to be better for universities, and in that regard SMEs are generally more satisfied with the benefits gained from interacting with a university.

In addition to the characteristics and the intensity of the interactions, the geographical dimension of the interaction was assessed. Interactions

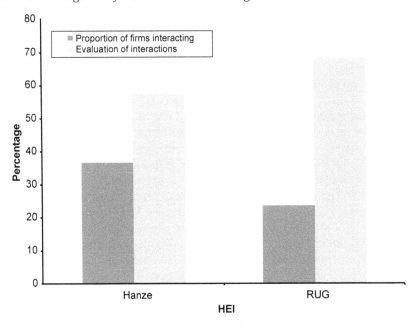

**Figure 2.** Share and value of contacting HEIs (*N* = 185).

between SMEs and the HEIs considered are very local. Some 10% of all respondents contacted an HEI geographically located outside the Groningen region (9.9% university and 10.7% college). Only 2.7% of all SMEs interacted solely with an HEI not located in the city of Groningen.

This means that 'outside' contacts are generally made in addition to the contacts already established in the Groningen region. Although this is quite a special region, in the sense that there are no alternative HEIs in the vicinity, the results do reiterate those from existing research – that there is a rapid rate of 'distance decay' in the establishment and monitoring of these types of interactions (Agrawal, 2001). This argument is strengthened when the frequency and evaluation of the interactions are considered. Comparing firms

in the city of Groningen to firms in the surrounding municipalities, we found that SMEs from the city had interactions more frequently as well as recording higher-quality evaluations of the interactions. Thus the perceived quality of the interactions also benefits from spatial proximity, possibly because monitoring of the interactions and managing the expectations is facilitated by geographical nearness. The effect is stronger for the university than it is for the college, which implies that the geographical reach of colleges (in terms of interactions) is greater than that of the universities.

This is somewhat counterintuitive, because the knowledge of universities is expected to reach further as a result of its more specialized nature (see Vermeulen, 1996). Given the scale of the study, this result needs to be carefully interpreted, however. The study only considers municipalities geographically contiguous to Groningen, whereas other contacts of the universities may be more widely dispersed. There may be a degree of variability in the geographical distribution of interactions. For instance, if the whole of the Netherlands were considered, it is possible that more distant interactions would be found for universities. Also, the interactions between universities and firms may require more face-to-face contacts, putting a premium on being close. At the scale of this present study, firms interacting with universities may therefore tend to reside in the city rather than in the surrounding municipalities. Finally, it could be that firms that use knowledge from a university are located in cities and less often in the hinterland (geographical sorting): different types of organizations exist in cities compared to those in the periphery.

*Interacting versus not interacting firms*

The second part of the analysis considers the question of which types of SME are most likely to interact with HEIs. The analysis was done in two steps, as shown in Figure 3. First, a logit model was estimated that explained whether SMEs interacted with one of the HEIs. In the second step, possible differences in the firms, depending on the type of HEI with which they interacted, were considered.

From the theory section, it was concluded that interactions with HEIs can be explained on the basis of two leading principles: the *absorptive capacity* of the firm and the *entrepreneur's familiarity* with the HEI. These principles are represented in the regression analysis. At the firm level, absorptive capacity is captured by the size (number of employees) and the age of the company. Larger and older firms are expected to have higher levels of absorptive capacity. Also, the location of the firm is considered, because we expect firms in close proximity to interact more easily with the institutes. Finally, the sector of the firm is included as a control variable. At the individual level, we endeavoured to capture the path dependence in communication by including variables for age and the level of education. Entrepreneurs with higher levels of education were expected to contact HEIs more often. Age was expected to correlate negatively with interaction

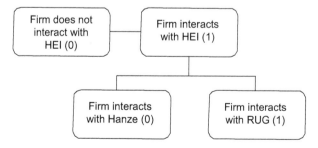

**Figure 3.** The two stages in the regression.

because the link with the education institute was expected to weaken as the number of years following graduation increased. Gender is included as a control, although there was no *a priori* expectation about the propensity for interacting based on gender. Appendix 1 summarizes the descriptive statistics of the variables. The results of the logistic regression are summarized in Table 2.

The firm-level variables show the expected effect of size. Larger firms were more likely to interact with one of the institutes. The coefficient is significant, although the marginal effect is rather small. Company age does not reflect the learning effect expected and there is no significant effect of age. Also, the additional variables proved to be important. Manufacturing firms are least likely to interact with one of the HEIs considered. The marginal effects are quite substantial, business service

firms being more than 30% more likely to interact, with the 'other' category (including government, the health sector and personal services) close to 40%. The difference can probably be attributed to the importance of human capital in these sectors. Attracting students as potential employees is an important goal for these types of firms. This aligns with the previous finding that student-related interactions are an important type of relationship. It also suggests that more attention could be given to the role of service firms in industry–HEI relationships. Although service industries have traditionally been less engaged in formal R&D, it is a growing sector and becoming increasingly important for innovation. In addition, it relies heavily on human capital as an input for production and less so on physical capital and technology.

**Table 2. Determinants of the dependent variable 'interactions with a HEI': logistic regression.**

| Variables in the equation | Coefficient (SE) | dy/dx |
|---|---|---|
| *Firm characteristics* | | |
| Number of employees | 0.12 (0.04)*** | 0.03 |
| Sector (manufacturing) | Ref | Ref |
| Sector (business services) | 1.38 (0.67)** | 0.33 |
| Sector (other) | 1.56 (0.72)** | 0.37 |
| Company age | 0.01 (0.01) | < 0.01 |
| Location (1 = Groningen) | 1.02 (0.44)** | 0.25 |
| *Individual characteristics* | | |
| Gender (1 = female) | −0.11 (0.53) | −0.03 |
| Age respondent | −0.04 (0.02)** | −0.01 |
| Education (no continued education) | Ref | Ref |
| Education (low and middle) | 1.04 (0.78) | 0.25 |
| Education (college) | 1.59 (0.68)** | 0.38 |
| Education (university) | 2.48 (0.72)*** | 0.55 |
| Constant | −2.35 (1.25)** | |
| N = 150 | | |
| Log likelihood = −72.52 Pseudo $R^2$ = 0.30 | | |

*, **, *** Statistically significant at the 10%, 5% and 1% levels respectively.

Finally, proximity has a strong effect. Locating outside the city of Groningen had a strong negative impact on interaction. This confirms the hypothesis that interaction is a localized phenomenon. Also, because we now correct for certain firm characteristics, the effect can be interpreted as a 'real' geographic effect and geographical sorting is less important. It is not a distribution effect in the sense that cities would house different types of firms that may be more inclined to interact with HEIs.

Next, we consider the individual characteristics that are assumed to involve path dependence in the interactions between entrepreneurs and education institutes. The results stress the importance of path dependence. First, there is a negative effect of age. The younger the entrepreneur, the higher the probability that they will interact with an HEI. The idea is that in the years directly following graduation, the link with the university or college is still quite strong, making it easier to interact. This effect then tapers off. When running the same regression with years of graduation as an independent variable (not reported), this result is confirmed. Because both variables are correlated (0.76), they cannot be included in the same model.

The educational attainment of the entrepreneurs also reflects path dependence in the interactions with colleges and universities. There is a strong positive effect for the two categories of higher education compared to the reference category 'no continued education', which includes respondents without any form of education and those with primary and secondary level. The relationship means that the likelihood

of interaction increases when the level of education is higher. Respondents with a lower- to medium-level education do not interact significantly more than entrepreneurs without any secondary education. Indeed, the results suggest that familiarity with the institute is important in managing the expectations concerning the goals and possibilities in the interaction with HEIs. If this is the case, this should also be reflected in the choice between contacting a university or a college.

In order to address this issue, a Heckman probit model with sample selection was used (selection model not reported). This type of model accounts for selection bias in the first step (contacting an HEI, Table 2). The model is limited to those firms

**Table 3. Determinants of interactions: parameter estimates of Heckman Selection Model.**

| Variables in the equation | Coefficient (SE) | dy/dx |
|---|---|---|
| *Firm characteristics* | | |
| Number of employees | −0.05 (0.06) | −0.02 |
| Company age | < 0.01 (0.1) | < 0.01 |
| Location (1 = Groningen) | 0.20 (0.77) | 0.07 |
| *Individual characteristics* | | |
| Gender (1 = female) | 0.13 (0.57) | 0.05 |
| Education (College = 1) | 1.44 (0.60)** | −0.44 |
| Rho | −0.13 (1.16) | |
| Constant | −0.18 (1.93) | |
| N = 131 | | |
| Censored = 93 | | |
| Uncensored = 38 | | |
| Log likelihood = −80.10 | | |

*, **, *** Statistically significant at the 10%, 5% and 1% levels respectively.

that interacted with the college or university only; and this approach excludes redundancy in the cases of SMEs contacting both institutes, which do not add any information regarding the question of whether individual firms contact universities or colleges. As a result, the number of cases in the model is small ($N = 131$ in the selection model and $N = 38$ in the second stage). The results presented in Table 3 should therefore be interpreted with care. The dependent variable is defined in such a way that contacting the university is 1 and contacting the college is 0.

Only one of the explanatory variables has a significant effect. This could indicate that both institutes serve similar markets. Given the small sample size and limited analysis, however, there may be differences that are not identified in the current research set-up. There is, however, one strong result emanating from the analysis: the path-dependent nature of contacts. There is a significant negative relationship with regard to having a college degree: college graduates are not likely to contact the university in favour of the college. The marginal effect is strong, and it suggests that the likelihood of contacting the university rather than the college drops, with 44% doing so if the entrepreneur is a college graduate. From a policy point of view, this is an important finding because it stresses the importance of alumni policies both at the level of the institutes but also, perhaps, at city level. If graduates maintain a link with the university or college, this can lead to increased interactions if the graduates become active as entrepreneurs or employees. Indirectly, this can have important

effects on knowledge dissemination and knowledge spill-overs in local economies.

## Summary and implications of findings

This study analysed interactions between SMEs and colleges and universities. As colleges are increasingly expected to act as knowledge brokers in the Dutch economy, it is important to provide an overview of their activities in terms of interactions with SMEs. From a more general point of view an interesting question is whether or not colleges and universities play distinct roles in knowledge diffusion. Do they, for example, cater for different types of firm? The following main conclusions can be drawn from the study.

First, there are more interactions between colleges and SMEs than there are between universities and SMEs. The interactions with universities are, however, rated slightly higher. This suggests a trade-off between accessibility and the perceived benefits from the interactions. This could further suggest that colleges need to communicate better the possibilities – and limits – of the services they can offer. In general, however, perceived quality is quite high, and the number of contacts shows that colleges are, in the Dutch context, important sources of knowledge and employees for SMEs.

Second, it has been shown that most interactions between SMEs and colleges involve students. Existing literature and policies tend to stress research and R&D-related interactions and cooperation. For colleges, such types represent only a small proportion of all interactions. Labour market issues and employee selection appear to be important reasons for SMEs to interact with colleges. This does not necessarily mean that knowledge transfer as such is not important. Internships and research projects by students can provide valuable knowledge to SMEs. However, it shows that a focus on more institutionalized forms of interaction, including patenting and joint research projects, may obscure knowledge transfer that, for example, takes place through student internships. This, particularly for colleges, may underestimate their importance in the process of knowledge transfer. Policy should therefore allow for a wide variety of channels and avoid singling out a particular link or instrument. In addition, attention needs to be given to different types of firms. Firms are very heterogeneous, especially in the SME sector, and they change depending on their state of development. It therefore seems important to avoid a 'one size fits all' solution.

Third, we found that the interactions between colleges and universities are very localized. There is some evidence that this effect is stronger for universities. Even being located just outside the city that houses the institutes significantly decreases the level of interaction. Also, SMEs in the study area interacted very little with institutes in different regions of the Netherlands. This is in line with existing network studies that find rapid distance decays in interactions and knowledge spill-overs. From a regional economic stance, this finding stresses the importance of housing an HEI in the region. Firms experience substantial difficulties in benefitting from institutes that are located some distance away. The steep distance decay in the likelihood of interaction also suggests that municipal governments are probably the most suitable level at which policy on interactions between businesses and HEIs should be organized.

Finally, with regard to the firms involved in the interactions, the results stress the importance of absorptive capacity and the path-dependent nature of interactions. Absorptive capacity of firms is reflected by their size, and this study confirms earlier findings that larger firms are better able to integrate knowledge and to organize interactions with HEIs. Absorptive capacity is often regarded in relation to knowledge spill-over; however, the significance of attracting students in the interactions with colleges suggests that interactions may also serve as an incentive in trying to attract the best students. Again, larger firms may be more involved with attracting students as a strategic goal than smaller firms. In addition to the size of the firms, the background of the business owner is also important. Entrepreneurs with a specific type of educational attainment are likely to interact with the college or university from which they graduated. There seems to be a high level of path dependence in the interactions between HEIs and entrepreneurs. At a conceptual level, this finding stresses the importance of managing expectations in sustaining network relations. Having an intimate knowledge of the possibilities and limitations of the organizations involved appears crucial in sustaining network contacts. Practically, this finding highlights the relevance of alumni policies. If institutes of learning are able to stay in touch with their graduates, this is also likely to result in interactions with the businesses.

This study has endeavoured to contribute to the literature on knowledge transfer by focusing on one of the mechanisms by which knowledge is disseminated in the economy. Although KT is an important element in recent economic geography thinking, its mechanisms remain under-studied. In the Dutch context it has become clear that colleges should be included in analyses of knowledge spill-overs because they form an integral part of the relationships between businesses and educational institutes. However, the study also calls for a further understanding of what exactly is happening in the interactions between HEIs and firms. Studies that address these issues could complement the general patterns found in this study and would help in unravelling further the mechanisms of knowledge spill-overs.

## Disclaimer

This paper was written as part of the Nicis Institute research programme on 'Economy and innovation'. More specifically, it is part of the research project 'Kenniscirculatie in de regio: de rol van het HBO, relaties met het bedrijfsleven en ondernemerschap' ['Concerning the region: the role of HEI, relations with businesses and entrepreneurship.']

## Notes

[1] There are also private colleges in the Netherlands: these are not included in the present study because they are not subject to the same legislation.

[2] This region includes the municipalities of Assen, Bedum, Groningen, Haren, Hoogezand-Sappemeer, Leek, Noordenveld, Slochteren, Ten Boer, Tynaarlo, Winsum and Zuidhorn. These are all participants in the so-called National Urban Network Groningen-Assen. Internationally, colleges tend to use the term 'university' in their name. The Hanze terms itself a 'university of applied science'.

## References

Agrawal, A. (2001), 'University-to-industry knowledge transfer: literature review and unanswered questions', *International Journal of Management Reviews. Vol 3*, pp 285–302.

Argote, L., and Ingram, P. (2000), 'Knowledge transfer: a basis for competitive advantage in firms', *Organizational Behavior and Human Decision Processes,* Vol 82, pp 150–169.

Brass, D. J., Galaskiewicz, J., Greve, H. R., and Tsai, W. (2004), 'Taking stock of networks and organizations: a multilevel perspective', *Academy of Management Journal,* Vol 47, No 6, pp 795–817.

Bekkers, R., and Bodas Freitas, I. M. (2008), 'Analysing knowledge transfer channels between universities and industry: to what degree do sectors also matter?', *Research Policy*, Vol 37, pp 1837–1853.

Boschma, R. (2005), 'Proximity and innovation: a critical assessment', *Regional Studies,* Vol 39, No 1, pp 61–74.

Bruijn, de, P., and Lagendijk, A. (2005), 'Regional innovation systems in the Lisbon strategy', *European Planning Studies,* Vol 13, pp 1153–1172.

Clark, G., Dawes, F., Heywood, A., and McLaughlin, T. (2008), 'Students as transferors of knowledge: the problem of measuring success', *International Small Business Journal*, Vol 26, No 6, pp 735–758.

Cohen, W. M., and Levinthal, D. A. (1990), 'Absorptive capacity: a new perspective on learning and innovation', *Administrative Science Quarterly,* Vol 35, special issue: 'Technology, Organizations, and Innovation', pp 128–152.

Cohen, W. M., Nelson, R. R., and Walsh, J. P. (2002), 'Links and impacts: the influence of public research on industrial R&D', *Management Science,* Vol 48, pp 1–23.

Cooke, P., and Leydesdorff, L. (2006), 'Regional development in the knowledge based economy: the construction of advantage', *Journal of Technology Transfer,* Vol 31, pp 5–15.

Cornett, A. P. (2009), 'Aims and strategies in regional innovation and growth policy: a Danish perspective', *Entrepreneurship and Regional Development,* Vol 21, pp 399–420.

Cowan, R., Soete, L., and Tchervonnaya, O. (2001), 'Knowledge transfer and the services sector in the context of the new economy', Merit Study, prepared for AWT.

Delfmann, H. S., Koster, S., and Pellenbarg, P. H. (2009), 'Kenniscirculatie in de regio: de rol van het hbo. Relaties met het bedrijfsleven en ondernemerschap', Nicis Institute and Faculty of Spatial Science, University of Groningen.

Ebers, M. (1997), 'Explaining inter-organizational network formation', in Ebers, M., ed, *The Formation of Inter-organizational Networks,* pp 3–40, Oxford University Press, Oxford.

EIM (2007), 'Technologiebedrijven in het MKB; Hoe werken zij samen met kennisinstellingen?', EIM Business and Policy Research, Zoetermeer.

Etzkowitz, H., and Leydesdorff, L. (2000), 'The dynamics of innovation: from national system and 'mode 2' to a Triple Helix of university–industry–government', *Research Policy,* Vol 29, No 2, pp 109–123.

Eurostat CIS 2004–2006 (2009), Stationery Office, Dublin.

Freel, M. (2006), 'Innovation and the characteristics of cooperating and non-cooperating small firm', in *Managing Complexity and Change in SMEs: Frontiers in European Research, 2006,* pp 103–135, Edward Elgar, Cheltenham.

Grant, R. M. (1996), 'Prospering in dynamically competitive environments: organizational capability as knowledge integration', *Organizational Science,* Vol 7, No 4, pp 375–387.

Goldstein, H. and Drucker, J. (2006), 'The economic development impacts of universities on regions: do size and distance matter?', *Economic Development Quarterly,* Vol 20, pp 22–43.

HBO-raad (2010), 'Forse groei studentenaantallen in het hbo', http://www.hbo-raad.nl/onderwiis/609, last accessed on 01 February 2010.

Jong, de, P. J., and Freel, M. (2010), 'Geographical distance of innovation collaborations', *EIM Research Reports, February 2010,* EIM Business and Policy Research, Zoetermeer.

Jong, de, P. J., and Hulsink, W. (2010), 'Patterns of innovation networking in Dutch small firms', *EIM Research Reports, January 2010,* EIM Business and Policy Research, Zoetermeer.

Jonge, de, J., and Berger, J. (2006), 'OECD thematic review of tertiary education: the Netherlands', report prepared for the Ministry of Education, Culture and Science, EIM Onderzoek voor Bedrijf and Beleid.

Knoben, J., and Oerlemans, L.A.G. (2006), 'Proximity and inter-organizational collaboration: a literature review', *International Journal of Management Reviews,* Vol 8, pp 71–89.

MKB-Nederland and VNO-NCW (2006), 'Hogescholen en branches: partners in professie: uitdagingen voor mkb en hbo', Delft.

Malecki, E. J. (2008), 'Higher education, knowledge transfer mechanisms and the promotion of SME innovation', Chapter 9 in *Entrepreneurship and Higher Education,* OECD, Paris.

Muizer A. (2003), 'Knowledge transfer', in *Entrepreneurship in the Netherlands. Knowledge Transfer: Developing High-Tech Ventures,* Ministerie van Economische Zaken.

OECD (2009), 'Amsterdam, Netherlands: self-evaluation report', *OECD Reviews of Higher Education in Regional and City Development,* IMHE, OECD, Paris.

Perkmann, M., and Walsh, K. (2007), 'University–industry relationships and open innovation: towards a research agenda', *International Journal of Management Reviews,* Vol 9, pp 259–280.

Risseeuw, P., and Thurik, R. (2003), *Handboek Ondernemers & Adviseurs: Management en Economie van het Midden-en Kleinbedrijf,* 1st edition, Kluwer, Deventer.

Schartinger, D., Rammer, C., Fischer, M. M., and Fröhlich, J. (2002), 'Knowledge interactions between universities and industry in Austria: sectoral patterns and determinants', *Research Policy,* Vol 31, pp 303–328.

Schmidt, T. (2009), 'Absorptive capacity – one size fits all? A firm-level analysis of absorptive capacity for different kinds of knowledge', *Managerial and Decision Economics,* Vol 31, pp 1–18.

Vermeulen, M. (1996), *Human Capital in the Hinterland: An Analysis of Causes and*

*Consequences of Regional Variation in Educational Participation*, Tilburg University Press, Tilburg.

Veugelers, R., and Cassiman, B. (2005), 'R&D cooperation between firms and universities: some empirical evidence from Belgian manufacturing', *International Journal of Industrial Organization*, Vol 23, pp 355–379.

VSNU (2010), 'Aantal studenten groeit, verdeling over opleidingen blijft ongewijzigd', http://www.vsnu.nl/Media-item/Aantal-studenten-groeit-verdeling-over-opleidingen-blijft-ongewijzigd.htm, Den Haag, 29 January 2010.

WRR (2008), 'Innovatie vernieuwd', in *Opening in Viervoud*, Amsterdam University Press, Den Haag/Amsterdam.

Zahra, S.A., and George, G. (2002), 'Absorptive capacity: a review, reconceptualization and extension', *Academy of Management Review*, Vol 27, pp 185–203.

Zheng, P., and Harris, M. (2007), 'The university in the knowledge economy: the Triple Helix model and its implications', *Industry and Higher Education*, Vol 21, No 4, pp 253–263.

# Appendix 1

## Descriptive statistics: characteristics of firms and individuals (N = 185).

| Variable | Interaction with RUG or Hanze Mean (SD) (min/max) | No interaction Mean (SD) (min/max) |
|---|---|---|
| *Firm characteristics* | | |
| Number of employees | 10.71 (10.30) (1/46) | 4.68 (5.7) (1/35) |
| Sector – service | 55.3% | 39.6% |
| Sector – manufacturing | 9.2% | 34.7% |
| Sector – other | 35.5% | 25.7% |
| Age of organization | 16.67 (18.54) (0/84) | 16.87 (18.54) (0/139) |
| Location – Groningen | 61.0% | 31.3% |
| Location – National Urban Network | 39.0% | 68.7% |
| *Individual characteristics* | | |
| Graduation year respondent | 1988.15 (10.38) (1970/2009) | 1983.07 (11.17) (1957/2006) |
| Gender – men | 76.8% | 79.4% |
| Gender – women | 23.2% | 20.6% |
| Age of respondent | 46.97 (9.69) (22/66) | 50.04 (10.32) (19/78) |
| Education – no continued education | 6.1% | 21.8% |
| Education – lower and middle education | 12.2% | 30.7% |
| Education – college | 42.7% | 33.7% |
| Education – university | 39.0% | 13.9% |

# Organizational transformation to promote knowledge transfer at universities and R&D institutions in Sonora, Mexico

Jorge Inés León Balderrama, Lydia Venecia Gutiérrez Lopez and Cuitláhuac Valdez Lafarga

**Abstract:** Using the results of an empirical study in the State of Sonora, Mexico, this paper reports on an attempt to identify trends and transformations that have taken place in the way knowledge transfer activities are organized and structured in higher education institutions and research centres. The research was designed to provide a characterization of organizational change that captures its complexity in different dimensions: corporate identity, new interface structures, new functions, new forms of human and financial resource management and intellectual property. To achieve this, information was collected and analysed from documentary sources and generated from a series of interviews with key personnel involved with science–industry linkages in the organizations studied.

**Keywords:** organizational change; knowledge transfer; technology transfer; knowledge transfer mechanisms; Mexico

The authors are with Centro de Investigación en Alimentación y Desarrollo AC, Carretera a la Victoria Km 6, Ejido Victoria, CP 83000 Hermosillo, Sonora, Mexico. Dr Jorge Inés León Balderrama (corresponding author) is a Researcher. E-mail: jleon@ciad.mx. Lydia Venecia Gutiérrez López and Cuitláhuac Valdez Lafarga are doctoral students.

In developing nations, there is increasing pressure from government and society in general for universities and public research centres (PRCs) to participate more effectively in knowledge transfer (KT) activities and to engage in the so-called 'Third Mission' with regard to the role of these establishments as promoters of economic and social development.[1] In this context, actions taken by universities and PRCs to promote the transfer of knowledge and technologies generated by staff have gained importance.

Several trends have contributed to the expansion of these activities within universities and research centres: for example, (i) the significant importance that science, technology and innovation as separate activities have each gained as determinants of the competitiveness of companies, territories and nations; (ii) the current constraints on public spending in many countries, forcing higher education institutions (HEIs) and public research centres to generate supplementary income; and (iii) new regulatory frameworks that allow teaching staff and researchers to participate in the ownership of their research results (Geuna and Nesta, 2006). Importantly, the emergence and expansion of activities related to KT in academia are phenomena that have occurred in less-developed nations, inspired by successful experiences in the USA. There, both the increase in the number of university-generated patents and the emergence of high-technology districts – arising from the dynamism of new high-technology companies being linked to academia (spin-offs) – have been significant

and have pioneered successful university–industry collaborations.

The history of academic–business relations is long, but signs of a significant transformation in the way these activities are organized within R&D institutions have recently emerged. There are new 'organizational arrangements' in universities and PRCs that focus on the generalized introduction of technology transfer offices (TTOs), technology parks, university incubators of technology businesses, the creation of spin-offs or the dissemination of activities concerning protection of intellectual property (IP) within scientific institutions. All these changes can be viewed as the emergence of a KT model that is more coordinated and formalized than in the past (Kim, 2009).

Some authors have identified a general shift in scientific systems at a global level, a change from a 'Republic of Science' (Polanyi, 1962) or a Mode 1 of knowledge production to a Mode 2 (Gibbons *et al*, 1994), 'utilitarian science', the 'entrepreneurial university' or the 'Triple Helix of innovation' (Becher and Kogan, 1992; Slaughter and Leslie, 1997; Etzkowitz and Leydesdorff, 1997; Clark, 1998). However, at least two issues connected to this global change should be considered. First, it is too simplistic to assume the notion of change if we consider only the ideological level, because changing beliefs or ideals does not necessarily lead to new practices. To understand the scope of the transformation of scientific institutions beyond the initial ideological change, we need to observe empirically the structures and behaviours within HEIs and PRCs and in different national and regional contexts (Kogan *et al*, 2006). Second, globalization is usually regarded as a homogenization process which, if this is the case, would mean that it is leading *all* HEIs and PRCs into becoming 'entrepreneurial institutions' that would invariably adopt homogeneous organizational arrangements for the commercial exploitation of IP and promotion of the creation of enterprises (spin-offs). This would imply an imminent convergence to a common organizational structure, perhaps that which has proved to be most effective in highly developed countries. Once again, there are reasons to question whether these assumptions are valid in view of the evidence from several national and regional contexts (Bleiklie and Kogan, 2007).

The aim of this study was to identify the trends and transformations that have arisen in the way that KT activities are structured and organized in public institutions which carry out R&D (HEIs and PRCs) by means of an analysis of activities in the State of Sonora in Mexico. To achieve this, a characterization of the organizational changes was carried out, capturing the complexity of these changes through an approach that allowed us to deal with the transformations in different dimensions: changes in institutional identity, new structures or agencies that function as an interface, new flow charts, new functions, new forms of human and financial resource management and new programmes and policies. The data for our analysis were obtained from documentary sources and interviews with people in relevant positions at the institutions included in this study.

The first section of the report contains a review of the main contributions to the field of organizational change associated with knowledge-transfer activities in academic institutions. The second section provides a description of the context of the research system in the State of Sonora and the methodology used. The third section presents the main results which deal with different aspects of organizational change. The final section presents the main conclusions arising from the study.

## Studying organizational change in scientific institutions: the analytical framework

Cortright (2001) emphasizes several trigger factors of organizational change linked to university–enterprise relations: the emergence of a new economy based on knowledge; competitiveness; the liberation of markets; and public policies. Equally, the adoption of the Third Mission has modified the identities of some HEIs, transforming them into 'entrepreneurial universities' (Clark, 1998). The common aspects of this new type of university are:

(1) a diversified funding base;
(2) a reinforced directive nucleus with self-management capacity;
(3) an environment that pushes the university towards a dual structure (traditional and new units);
(4) a stimulated and involved academic community; and
(5) an integrated entrepreneurial culture.

Etzkowitz (2003), adopting an evolutionist perspective, points out that by 'capitalizing' knowledge, the HEIs achieve this mission with regard to an alleged 'second academic revolution', with new structures arising from the co-evolutionary relationships between university and enterprise, but with previous participants being replaced by new ones.

From a different perspective, Geuna and Muscio (2009) analysed the changes in governance of university–industry relations and offer an oversimplified typology of the transition from an 'old' model to a new one (Figure 1). Based on the level of 'institutionalization' of KT in HEIs and PRCs, they argue that in the long term, a clearly identifiable discontinuity has existed in the evolution of the forms of KT governance.

Similarly, other studies have analysed the importance of organizational aspects to the efficiency of KT processes. Bercovitz *et al* (2001), through a comparative analysis of several academic institutions, found that the organizational structure had an important effect on the performance of KT activities. Markman *et al* (2005) point out that the differences in the structures of TTOs have an effect on coordination capacities, the ability to transmit information and the alignment of incentives.

Other authors analyse specific aspects of organizational transformation. Siegel *et al* (2003) and Friedman and Silberman (2003) examined the performance of institutions when changes are implemented in their structures but limited their studies to the description of the implementation process of KT strategies without evaluating the effects of these changes. Operti (2007) maintains that the organizational structure affects different types of KT activities and that when universities increase their participation, they adopt more decentralized, less hierarchical organizational forms, with participative models of governance. Slaughter and Leslie (1997) focus on the diffusion of new values which allow for acceptance of the

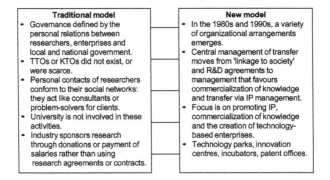

**Figure 1.** Old model–new model transition in KT governance.

*Source:* Based on Geuna and Muscio (2009).

commercialization of knowledge among the academic community, while Bok (2003) typifies the change through his concept of the 'corporate university'. Other aspects, such as the determinants of change in attitudes and motivations of academics towards linkage activities with the entrepreneurial sector, have been studied by Roberts and Malone (1996) and Leon *et al* (2009), while the restructuring of the value and rewards system, such that KT is increasingly incentivized, was studied by Friedman and Silberman (2003) and Mowery *et al* (2004). Arocena and Sutz (2001) and Lockett and Wright (2005) observed that strategies for generating

income have multiplied and noted that new financial instruments are being designed, mainly involving government funding, to boost university–industry relations. Gibb (2005) concurs, pointing out that the sources of funding for HEIs and PRCs have been noticeably diversified in recent years.

With the intention of contributing to the investigation of these aspects, an integral analytical scheme was been designed which allows for a wider examination of organizational change in a specific regional context (Figure 2). This analytical framework includes consideration of additional dimensions of organizational change,

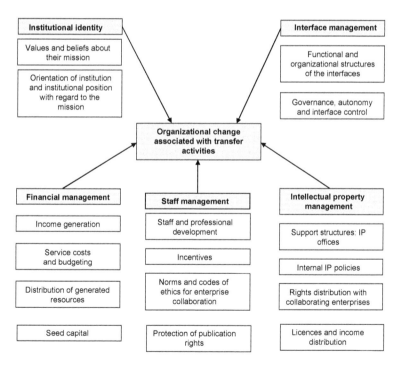

**Figure 2.** Organizational change analysis in R&D institutions.

*Source:* Based on Martin (2000) and Operti (2007).

beyond the mere increase in the number and importance of new structures such as transformations of institutional identity, coordination and governance (Operti, 2007), funding management, human resource management and IP management, amongst others (Martin, 2000).

## Knowledge generation and transfer in Sonora, Mexico

The State of Sonora has consolidated important advances in the creation and development of research capacities in the last few decades. According to Durand (2009) and Sotelo (2008), the development of research in the State has passed through three stages (see Table 1).

(1) Up to 1979, characterized by applied research in commercial fishing and agriculture.
(2) Between 1980 and 2000, dominated by the setting up of PRCs oriented towards local social studies.
(3) Between 2000 and 2010, the emergence of research linked to solving specific problems of industry located in the State.

These changes in the orientation of research activities in the State have been responses to changes in its economic profile. Sonora has been transformed from an economy focused primarily on exploiting natural resources to one based on industrial development and services. Concomitantly, the PRCs and HEIs that undertake research have been adapting and adjusting to the demands of the regional market, with evidence

emerging of a broader approach to business enterprises and other non-academic sectors being adopted.

The R&D infrastructure developed by the State has allowed it to position itself in fifth place, of the country's 32 states, in terms of the number of PRCs. In contrast, Sonora occupies one of the lowest positions with regard to state investment in science and technology: only 0.02% of its total budget is allocated to this. The State is in the middle rankings with regard to investment in the development of human resources and the number of graduates in the population. It is in 15th place with respect to accredited top-quality graduate programmes in the country (data for 2010); 10th place with regard to percentage of the national total graduate enrolment (data for 2008–2009); 17th in national scholarships awarded by the National Council for Science and Technology (CONACyT) for 2009; and 19th for graduate enrolment in areas of science and technology (2008). However, Sonora is better positioned with regard to highly qualified individuals undertaking R&D activities: it is in 5th place in the national ranking of the National Research System (SNI) for the number of researchers per 10,000 of the economically active population (Table 2).[2]

With regard to the dynamics of the Sonora STIS, its accelerating rate of growth since 2001 is especially notable, particularly in the development of suitably competent individuals. Figure 3 shows the increase in enrolment on graduate programmes for the period 1999–2010: it can be seen that the number has almost quintupled. A similar situation

**Table 1.** Historical evolution of the research centres of the State of Sonora.

| Foundation year | Research Centre | Research areas | Location | Graduate programme? |
|---|---|---|---|---|
| 1943 | CIMMYT (CIANO) | Genetic improvement of corn and wheat. | Cajeme | No |
| 1944 | Centro Regional de Investigación Pesquera (CRP) | Marine biology, ecological impact and aquaculture production. | Guaymas | No |
| 1955 | CIANO becomes CIRNO/INIFAP | Agro industry chains, forestry chains, agricultural chains, aquaculture chains, food safety and technology transfer. | Cajeme | No |
| 1955 | Instituto Tecnológico de Sonora (ITSON) | Water quality, hydro systems management, sanity and animal production. | Cajeme | Yes |
| 1963 | CICTUS-UNISON | Desertification, native species agronomy, forestry and renewable natural resources. | Hermosillo | Yes |
| 1969 | Centro de Investigaciones Pecuarias de Sonora (CIPS) | Pasture management, pasture nutrition and watering fodder. | Hermosillo | No |
| 1973 | INAH-Centro Regional Noroeste | Archaeology, anthropology and regional history. | Hermosillo | No |
| 1976 | CIFUS – UNISON | Spectroscopy of insulating materials, semiconducting nanostructures and instruments. | Hermosillo | Yes |
| 1978 | DIPA – UNISON | Nutrition quality, entomology of stored products, quality control of aquaculture products. | Hermosillo | Yes |
| 1981 | CRUNO – UACH | Social organization and rural development. | Cajeme | Yes |
| 1981 | Poli meros y Materiales – UNISON | Nanostructure materials, polymer electro conductors, supramolecular chemistry. | Hermosillo | Yes |
| 1982 | Centro de Investigación en Alimentación y Desarrollo (CIAD) | Nutrition, food science, food technology, regional development. | Hermosillo | Yes |
| 1982 | El Colegio de Sonora (COLSON) | Sociology, development, regional history, sociocultural epidemiology, political studies. | Hermosillo | Yes |
| 1983 | CEDES-State Government of Sonora | Conservation, ecology and natural resources, sustainable development and project promotion. | Hermosillo | No |

(*Continued*)

**Table 1. Continued**

| Foundation year | Research Centre | Research areas | Location | Graduate programme? |
|---|---|---|---|---|
| 1984 | Centro de Investigaciones Biológicas del Noroeste (CIBNOR) | Aquaculture, agriculture in arid zones, fishing ecology, environmental planning and conservation. | Guaymas | Yes |
| 1987 | Instituto Nacional de Astrofísica Óptica y Electron (ENAOE) | Astrophysics, computer science, electronics and optics. | Cananea | No |
| 1987 | Centro Intercultural de Estudios de Desiertos y Océanos (CEDO) | Oceanography biology, desert and marine ecology, wildlife, plants and conservation. | Puerto Peñasco | No |
| 1996 | Estación Regional Noroeste del INE/ UNAM. | Land ecology of Northwestern Mexico. | Hermosillo | Yes |
| 2004 | CI en Educación y Docencia (ITESCA) | Planning and education management, historiography of education. | Cajeme | No |
| 2004 | CI Detección y Prevención de Cáncer | Oncology, cervical-uterine cancer, human papilloma virus. | Hermosillo | No |
| 2004 | Centro de Ahorro de Energía (ITESM) | Electric energy savings. | Hermosillo | No |
| 2004 | Centro de Promócion a la Acuacultura (ITESM) | Aquaculture technologies, aquaculture pathology and safety, shrimp reproducers production. | Hermosillo | No |
| 2005 | CIDIA | Intelligent automation systems, electronic optics of organic semiconductors. | Hermosillo | No |
| 2005 | CIDD | Transparent government, corruption combat, human rights, accountability. | Hermosillo | No |

*Source:* Adapted from Sotelo (2008).

Table 2. Selected indicators and ranking of Sonora's S&T system.

| Indicator | Sonora | Ranking among Mexico's federal States[1] |
|---|---|---|
| PRCs: % of the national total. | 4.30 | 5 |
| S&T budget: % of the total state budget, 2010. | 0.02 | 22 |
| SNI researchers/ 10,000 EAP, 2011. | 3.40 | 9 |
| Quality graduate programmes: % of the national total, 2010. | 2.40 | 15 |
| Graduate students: % of the national total, 2010. | 3.10 | 10 |
| CONACyT scholarships/1,000 graduate students, 2011. | 111.00 | 17 |
| Graduate programme enrolment in S&T areas/10,000 population, 2008. | 2.60 | 19 |
| Scientific articles/10,000 population, 1999–2008. | 11.55 | 9 |
| Patents awarded/1 million population, 2011. | 1.21 | 10 |

[1] Corresponds to the position of Sonora from a total of 32 federal States.

*Source:* FCCT (2012: 43)

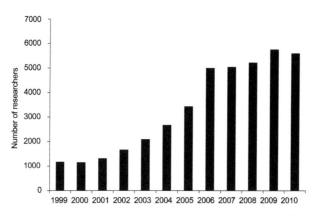

**Figure 3.** Sonora: evolution of graduate programme enrolment, 1999–2010.

*Source:* Based on data from ANUIES (National Association of HEIs).

is observed with regard to the number of SNI researchers, which has tripled in just 10 years (Figure 4).

The growth of the State's STIS capacities in recent years is noteworthy; however, the greater portion of scientific output is concentrated in a small number of institutions, as are most members of the SNI, research projects and graduate programmes. According to the Registry of Scientific and Technological Institutions and Enterprises (RENIECYT), whilst Sonora has 144 R&D establishments (this includes 110 enterprises, 14 Non-Governmental Organizations, 11 HEIs and 2 PRCs) (Durand, 2009), scientific output is mostly generated by two institutions: the University of

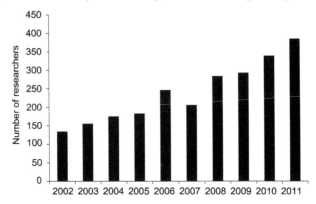

**Figure 4.** Sonora: growth of SNI researchers, 2002–2011.

*Source:* Based on data from CONACyT-SNI.

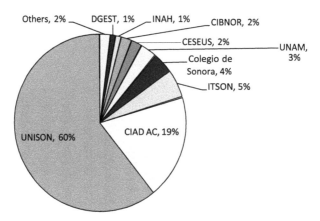

**Figure 5.** Sonora: SNI researchers by institution, 2011(%).

*Source:* Based on data from CONACyT.

Sonora (UNISON) and the Research Centre for Food and Development (CIAD). Other institutions, such as Colegio de Sonora, also participate, but their output is minimal by comparison. In addition, their scientific resources are smaller and less diversified. The Instituto Tecnologico de Sonora (ITSON) and Instituto Tecnologico y de Estudios Superiores de Monterrey (ITESM) have only recently started their programmes of research and therefore lag behind UNISON and CIAD. UNISON is the largest public state university with more than 30,000 students and 3,000 teaching staff: ITSON has a student population of 17,000. Between them, UNISON and CIAD have the largest number of researchers, SNI members, consolidated academic bodies, high-level scientific groups, funded research projects and scientific scholarships and the largest amount of funding for provision of equipment (see Figure 5).

Scientific resources are not evenly distributed in the public state universities because of the consolidation of some disciplines and researchers. For instance, UNISON has three regional units and 11 divisions, with most of the scientific output of the university concentrated in the Central Regional Unit and specifically in the Divisions of Pure and Applied Science and Biological and Health Sciences. CIAD, which is a member of a network of CONACyT public centres, has its head office in Sonora (Hermosillo and Guaymas) and outlying facilities in Sinaloa (Mazatlan, Culiacan) and Chihuahua (Delicias and Ciudad Cuauhtémoc). The Centre has been notable for its research in natural and health sciences.

These two establishments have highly regarded scientific groups that produce state-of-the-art knowledge. These groups have high rates of scientific output; their research is published in prestigious national and international journals; they obtain resources for research projects from national programmes and international sponsors; their members belong to the teaching staffs of high-quality graduate programmes; they maintain collaborative agreements with regional enterprises and other institutions; and, importantly, they have managed to adapt to the standards and demands of the country's scientific policies (Durand, 2009).

## Methodology

An exploratory analysis was undertaken, using interviews and documentary sources to identify changes in the organization of knowledge-transfer activities. The principal aim was to extend current knowledge of the transformations in the context of the evolution of the Sonora R&D system and the new demands for greater impact of R&D institutions on regional development. The study was limited to a sample of research institutions so that, for example, comparisons could be made between public state universities and public research centres. The composition of the sample is shown in Table 3.

The analysis follows the scheme presented in Figure 2. The interviews were based on issues such as the current and past status of relationships between the institution and the enterprise sector and the management of these relationships; a self-evaluation

---

Table 3. R&D institutions selected for the study.

| Type | Name | Location |
|---|---|---|
| Research centre | CIAD, AC | Hermosillo, Son. |
| | CIRNO/ INIFAP | Obregón, Son. |
| Public state university | UNISON | Hermosillo, Son. |
| | ITSON | Obregón, Son. |
| Federal technological institute | Instituto Tecnologico de Hermosillo, ITH | Hermosillo, Son. |
| State technological Institute | Instituto de Estudios Superiores de Cajeme, ITESCA | Obregón, Son. |
| Private university | ITESM, Campus Sonora-Norte | Hermosillo, Son. |

of the benefits and problems; future perspectives and objectives; and the short-, medium- and long-term plans and projects.

# Results: organizational changes for promoting KT in Sonora

The Sonora case study has enabled a series of important changes in the organization and management of knowledge transfer activities between R&D institutions and enterprises to be identified. These changes have been classified under five main headings ('dimensions'):

(1) acknowledgement of knowledge transfer and commercialization as a legitimate and proper function (a Third Mission is assumed);
(2) the rapid increase in the number of new administrative and operational structures for the transfer and commercialization of knowledge;
(3) new trends in financial management;
(4) new trends in human resource management; and
(5) new trends in IP management.

*Universities and PRCs assume an active role in local economic development*

From the interviews with officials and leaders of institutions and examination of the relevant documents, a key factor arising was the change in the perception of the missions of HEIs and PRCs, especially with regard to the importance given to linkages and transfer activities. During the last 10 years, R&D institutions have begun assuming a role in the

economic development of the region, through linkages with the social and productive sectors. This change is most noticeable in the case of HEIs, which now explicitly accept knowledge transfer as one of their main functions, something that was not the case in the past. Driven by reductions in public budgets for higher education and the search for new ways of incorporating their graduates into the labour market, as well as the promotion of entrepreneurism, the HEIs have recently placed greater emphasis on the need to play a more active role in local and regional development. The PRCs, in contrast, formulated a mission to contribute scientific and technological input to the development of the means of local production, especially in the agricultural and fishery sectors.

The institutional development plans and annual reports of HEIs and PRCs show that knowledge transfer has become a strategic issue.[3] ITSON, for example, stands out as a highly enterprising, service-oriented institution, something emphasized repeatedly in its activity reports.[4] Similarly, INIFAP promotes the concept that scientific knowledge and technological innovation generated by research should be disseminated as widely as possible, to benefit the rural sector in particular and society in general.[5] These changes in orientation have gone beyond mere discussion, developing as they have into a series of transformations and innovations, as summarized in Table 4.

*Emergence of new administrative and operational structures*

*New management and coordination bodies.* As the KT activities of

**Table 4. Sonora: new organizational structures for KT in main universities and PRCs.**

| Institution | 1. Administrative structure | 2. Labs and services | 3. Interface structures | 4. Incubators | 5. IP management structures |
|---|---|---|---|---|---|
| UNISON | General office of liaison and diffusion Liaison Council 1999 | Metrologic Assistance Centre (CAM) | Institutional programme of TT (TXTEC) 2004 | Own model incubator 2004 | Innovation Support Unit (UNAIN-TxTec) 2006 |
| ITSON | Office of Services Centre of Evaluation and Education Innovation Centre for Health R&D University Centre for Community Liaison 2005 | Biotech, Agricultural and Environmental Research and Innovation Centre (CIIBAA) Regional Centre of R&D for Water and Energy (CRIDAE) | Experimental Centre of TT (CETT) Technological Centre of Entrepreneurial Integration and Development (CETIDE) 2007 International District of Agribusiness SMEs 2005 | Model transfer incubator 2004 | Patents Office (Centre for institutional customer support) 2009 |
| INIFAP | Office of Innovation and Liaison 2005 | | | | |
| ITH | Liaison Council 2008 | | | Impulse Centre 2006 | |
| ITESCA | Technological Extension and Management Unit 2009 | Advanced Technology Centre 2009 | | Incubator 2009 | Patents Office (Research and Graduate division) 2008 |
| CIAD | Liaison Office 2008 | | Transfer and Innovation Unit (UTI) 2008 | Business Incubator 2008 | Patents Office (Liaison Office) 2009 |
| ITESM | Office of Technology Parks 2008 | | | Own model Incubator 2009 | Patents Office/ decentralized 2006 |

*Source:* Authors.

HEIs and PRCs have intensified and diversified in recent years, the senior executives and management of these organizations have responded by creating structures or agencies with responsibility for facilitating and promoting KT. Perhaps the clearest indication of the extent of the institutionalization of these linkage and transfer activities in HEIs and PRCs is the introduction of management and coordination structures to their organization charts. During the last 10 years, the initial stages of an internal restructuring of institutions in Sonora, to meet their objectives of developing more linkages, have been noted. Around 1999, for example, a 'Liaison Council' was created at UNISON, when a departmental restructuring was initiated in order to support these activities. By 2005, this process had spread to the other institutions: as shown in the first column of Table 4, these coordination structures are usually called 'liaison offices', acting as agencies in charge of managing the relationships between academic researchers and external sectors (that is, a coordination function).

In the 1980s and 1990s, a 'liaison department' was usually responsible for transfer activities and, almost exclusively, for follow-up of agreements with external sectors. However, the new coordination agencies are responsible for new areas of activity: these include business incubation, technology parks and management and commercialization of IP. The Sonora case indicates that HEIs and PRCs follow the same pattern with respect to improving the performance of transfer and linkage practices; this is reflected in the

introduction of new organizational schemes, in which the creation of specialized areas or agencies plays a very important role. There are, of course, differences between the various types of institutions. UNISON, for example, implements a strategy of segmentation and division of labour, and this is expressed in the variety of agencies dealing with the relationships with sectors beyond the academic campus (Table 4). ITESM, in contrast, focuses on coordinating the functions of the business incubator, the IP office and the technology park activities through its Office of Technology Parks. ITSON, one of the institutions that has developed more strategic initiatives, was restructured in 2007 to strengthen the areas of academic planning, extension and services. The PRCs have also undergone structural reorganization; CIAD, for example, created its Liaison Coordination function in 2005 to coordinate all relationships with external sectors.

*New operational structures.* Over the past few years, new support structures have been established to increase and enhance linkages and transfer activities in HEIs and PRCs in Sonora. Some of these structures are internal; others have been formed as external or decentralized departments which operate with their own resources but are managed by the institutions in which they reside. Among the new structures that have emerged are liaison and/or transfer offices, business incubators and science and technology parks.

*Liaison and technology-transfer offices.* The Sonora research institutions have created three offices for the commercialization of knowledge. The technology-transfer offices (TTOs) are responsible for promoting and commercializing the results of research and defining marketing strategies as well as identifying and evaluating the technological and scientific capacities of the institution. The TTOs must also identify market niches and develop strategic contacts in new target markets. These structures are organized in the form of subsidized departments or agencies. UNISON, for example, created a subsidized agency in 2004 called the Institutional Program of Technology Transfer (TxTEC), which, in 2006, secured its own jurisdictional and financial responsibilities. This agency carries out business incubation functions, IP management and technological development consultancy, but on a smaller scale to that of a technology park. In the case of ITSON, some examples of this are the Regional Centre of R&D for Water and Energy (CRIDAE), the Technological Centre of Entrepreneurial Integration and Development (CETIDE), and the Experimental Centre of Technology Transfer (CETT).

With respect to PRCs in Sonora, CIAD is an outstanding example of a centre that has recently followed this trend, creating the Transfer and Innovation Unit (UTI) in 2008 which, as with UNISON, seeks to concentrate several areas of responsibility in one entity: business incubation and acceleration, consultancy and development services and IP.

*Business incubators.* Most of the institutions studied have a technology-based business incubator department based on incubation models recognized by the State Secretary's Office of Economy (SE). The first incubators in Sonora were established in 2004, created by public universities and operated according to their own incubation models and officially recognized by the SE. Later, other HEIs and PRCs also started up incubators by adopting models implemented and tested by other institutions (Table 4). The services offered in the incubators concentrate on consultancy and entrepreneurial training (legal, financial, organizational, production, marketing and human resources) and public resource management support.

*Technology parks.* Technology parks were a new initiative in the most important HEIs in Sonora. The main, distinguishing characteristic of these projects is that they are based on inter-institutional cooperation: that is, academia, industry and government jointly seeking to intensify R&D activities and providing linkages between small and large enterprises. In this study, two established technology parks were identified, ITSON and ITESM, with one more under development at UNISON (Table 5). These technology parks operate according to organizational schemes that vary from one institution to another; however, we found a common feature, that they are agencies aiming to host self-sustainable enterprises. Within the institutions analysed, the internal structures of the park relate to the nature of their administrative offices acting either as intermediate subsidized agencies or constituted as civil associations. This form of

**Table 5. Sonora: technology parks installed by higher education institutions (2007–2011).**

**Sonora Soft Technology Park (ITSON)**

| | |
|---|---|
| *Location:* | Northwest of Cd. Obregón, off campus |
| *Opened:* | 2007 |
| *Areas:* | Software and information technologies service (ISSTE, IMSS, USA enterprises) |
| *Capacity:* | 18 ha, with a 6,327 m building, and another 8,000 m² in construction, parking and green areas. |
| *Investment:* | 1st phase: US$9.615 million (ITSON, State government, federal and local)<br>2nd phase: US$5.219 million added |
| *Services offered:* | Management, update and training programmes, service contracts, business accelerator programmes. |
| *Organizations installed:* | Novutek (main enterprise), SourceCorp, Go-Net, Pinnacle Aerospace, Infemov, 2 incubators (ITESCA and ITSON) |

**Automotive and Aerospace Headquarters for Research and Development of Sonora, STAADIS (ITESM-campus Sonora Norte)**

| | |
|---|---|
| *Location:* | Hermosillo, ITESM Campus Sonora Norte |
| *Opened:* | 2009 |
| *Areas:* | Automotive, aerospace, mechatronics and information technologies |
| *Capacity:* | 3,900 m², of which 2,600 will house high-technology companies and a business incubator. |
| *Investment:* | US$4.447 million (ITESM, Secretary's Office of Economy and State Government) |
| *Services offered:* | Management, update and training programmes, service contracts, business accelerator programmes. |
| *Organizations installed:* | Dunas, Tauvex, Construplan, Tecnologias Automatizadas, Infinity International Engineering and Teknol |

**Renewable Energies Technology Park (TxTec, UNAM, USS Inc.)**

| | |
|---|---|
| *Location:* | Hermosillo, Department of Agriculture and Farming fields (UNISON) |
| *Opened:* | 2011 |
| *Areas:* | Oriented towards research in solar energy use. |
| *Investment:* | First phase, construction of the solar concentration tower of the Campo de Pruebas de Helióstatos. This building will be a part of the Laboratorio Nacional de Concentration Solar y Qui mica; UNAM-Conacyt. |
| *Services offered:* | The Park will be a scientific complex with plans to house enterprises and other research centres (nanotechnology, sustainable development and new materials). |
| *Capacity:* | It will have an extension of 40.5 ha. |
| *Organizations installed:* | Utility Scale Solar, Palo Alto, CA. |

Source: *Expreso Newspaper*, 16 December 2006; Agencia Informativa, 3 November 2009; and, bionero.org, Tuesday 20 April 2010.

organization has created the need for some institutions to establish a specific office responsible for coordinating the activities of the park, and this office provides information to the administrative offices of the university that houses it on goals and objectives that have been reached and achieved.

### New trends in financial management

The manner in which financial resources are managed by HEIs and PRCs has recently been transformed, in response to the increasing relevance of the economic and social linkages of these institutions, within the context of policies characterized by severe financial restraints. The income generated by knowledge-transfer and commercialization activities is becoming an increasingly important component in the budgets of the research institutions. This so-called 'own income' comes primarily from activities linked to externally funded R&D projects, provision of services, commercialization of intellectual property licenses, and so on. In recent years, the importance of these activities as a proportion of the total budgets for HEIs and PRCs has grown, although this applies more to the PRCs. At CIAD, for example, the own income contribution has represented about 30% of the general budget in the past few years. The main sources of income are client enterprises, institutional research funds – amongst which those managed by CONACyT (FOMIX, Sectoral Funds, Basic Science, and others) are particularly important – and some private-sector foundations or associations such as Fundacion

Produce. Similarly, the new structures look for self-sufficient operations. The incubators, for example, regardless of their type of organization, base their income creation on three routes: (a) transfer of their models; (b) commercialization of their services; and (c) the allocation of institutional or public budgets for business projects. Generally, public resources – for example, Fondo PYME of the SE – are directed at building and improving infrastructure, equipment and training, while the use of own income is aimed at maintaining the operation of the interface structure, usually to cover the salaries of staffs.

The payment and allocation of incentives for individuals who collaborate in the new structures is a complex matter due to the absence of well-established mechanisms. Operational personnel receive a fixed salary with benefits established by law and, in some cases, a bonus payment related to annual productivity. In the case of researchers and academics who offer consulting and support services for the development of projects, payment of extra income is based on a formula related to the own incomes of the institutions. UNISON and CIAD, for example, retain 20% of the total budget for projects with external funding, and this is used for paying management expenses, the costs of using the infrastructure, maintenance of facilities and other indirect support approved for the research.[6] It is important to point out that in state universities, as well as PRCs, academic personnel can be paid financial bonuses from this overhead that is retained by the institutions.[7]

*New trends in human resource management*

For research personnel, linkage activities have hitherto been marginal, even voluntary, with regard to their normal activities. However, in recent years, this has changed. The HEIs and PRCs are revising terms and conditions of employment for academic personnel in order to establish linkage and transfer activities as mandatory job requirements for researchers. The trend is towards transforming the profile of the academic from that of teacher-researcher to that of 'teacher-researcher-consultant'.[8]

The systems for evaluating individual academic performance and recognition and incentives have also been revised. The key issue is that, increasingly, linkage and transfer activities are better recognized, valued and rewarded by the research institutions. When first established, the rules governing incentives and bonuses either did not anticipate or allow for these activities or they were regarded as of little importance in comparison with teaching and research activities. Now some institutions such as CIAD give equal weight to the three types of academic activities: research, teaching and linkages.

In contrast, levels of administration and operational staffing in the new KT structures, covering engineering, management and finance, are usually reduced. These personnel deal with human resources, accounting and financial activities; they have responsibility for authorizing consultancy services and, at the same time, act as linkage agents between entrepreneurs and academics. They also support the commercialization of potential products and services, collaborate in the negotiation and budgeting of projects and manage intellectual property rights. The range of competencies that is required by professionals in scientific institutions and involved with enterprise relationships is increasing; as such, the recruitment of personnel and their development in these fields is a very important aspect of personnel management, aimed at facilitating university–enterprise relations.

*New trends in IP management*

In the selected sample of institutions, it was noted that technology transfer by means of the commercialization of patented knowledge remains a minor activity still in its early stages. Whilst an increasing trend regarding the establishment of institutional strategies to increase commercialization of technology with third parties was noted, the results in terms of licensing activity and generating income remain very modest for research institutions in Sonora (see Table 6).

Over the past six to seven years, these institutions have established IP management offices to help with procedures for registering patents, internal administration for their research personnel and external activities. Some of these offices are already in operation; others are still in the planning stages. These offices have been created with support from CONACyT and the Mexican Institute of Intellectual Property (IMPI) by way of inter-institutional collaboration agreements. CONACyT has helped with financial resources, mainly for registering patents and models for implementation; the IMPI also offers support in training administrative

Table 6. Sonora: patents applications and patents granted by HEIs and PRCs, 1995–2011.

| Year | Patent applications | | | Patents granted | | |
|---|---|---|---|---|---|---|
| | Total | Companies and private individuals | HEIs and PRCs | Total | Companies and private individuals | HEIs and PRCs |
| 1995 | 1 | 1 | 0 | 0 | 0 | 0 |
| 1996 | 2 | 2 | 0 | 2 | 2 | 0 |
| 1997 | 1 | 1 | 0 | 3 | 3 | 0 |
| 1998 | 2 | 2 | 0 | 0 | 0 | 0 |
| 1999 | 0 | 0 | 0 | 3 | 3 | 0 |
| 2000 | 2 | 2 | 0 | 1 | 1 | 0 |
| 2001 | 4 | 4 | 0 | 0 | 0 | 0 |
| 2002 | 4 | 4 | 0 | 0 | 0 | 0 |
| 2003 | 1 | 1 | 0 | 0 | 0 | 0 |
| 2004 | 2 | 2 | 0 | 1 | 1 | 0 |
| 2005 | 5 | 1 | 4 | 2 | 2 | 0 |
| 2006 | 10 | 10 | 0 | 1 | 1 | 0 |
| 2007 | 18 | 16 | 2 | 4 | 4 | 0 |
| 2008 | 11 | 8 | 3 | 4 | 3 | 1 |
| 2009 | 10 | 10 | 0 | 4 | 4 | 0 |
| 2010 | 9 | 9 | 0 | 6 | 4 | 2 |
| 2011 | 16 | 14 | 2 | 5 | 3 | 2 |
| Totals, 1995–2011 | 98 | 87 | 11 | 36 | 31 | 5 |

*Source:* Own elaboration based on IMPI, SIGA e-Gaceta: http://siga.impi.gob.mx.

personnel, for instance on details of the IP management process. The services offered by the patent offices, hitherto a State responsibility, consist of assistance and consultancy for research and scientific personnel employed by the institution and external businesses; information and support for completing documentation for registering intellectual property, brands and inventions; management of applications; and developing and drafting contracts and agreements for the commercialization of inventions. The patent offices in HEIs and PRCs have adopted a version of the departmental organizational scheme. The analysis revealed that some of these offices are owned by the established transfer offices; others are part of the structure of technology parks; and still others belong to particular academic divisions (faculties) of the universities. These new arrangements have been developed by university and research centres as a result of the relationships between academia, industry and government.

## Conclusions

This study has shown that the R&D institutions in Sonora that were investigated have followed similar, convergent routes with regard to the creation of new management schemes for knowledge transfer. However, the rate of progress varies from institution to institution and depends on internal policies and the type of system to which the institution belongs as well as the academic culture that prevails among the research staff.

The study confirms that public research centres are increasingly engaged in developing links with society at large, emphasizing and intensifying the 'transfer function'; and this has been especially so during the last 10 years. The results reveal the configuration of a new model for the organization of transfer activities in the region's scientific institutions. The model encompasses organizational changes that go beyond the simple establishment of new structures and considers and anticipates more complex transformations which include aspects of institutional identity, managerial and operational coordination and intellectual property management as well as human and financial resource management. It has been shown that, in the long term, this evolutionary process can be regarded as a transition from non-organized forms – informal, case-specific and non-systematic – to more organized, coordinated and systematic forms.

The analysis has shown that the trend towards the creation of interfaces between the scientific system and the local economy has, in recent years, become more established and strengthened in the State of Sonora. However, it was notable that these operational structures have been subject to increasing diversification and specialization and that the new structures emerging possess different degrees of autonomy.

The new strategies implemented by the institutions may be a reflection of models used in countries such as the USA (Phan and Siegel, 2006), Italy (Corti, 2009), Spain (Cruz *et al*, 2010), Australia (Marginson and Considine, 2000) and elsewhere (Martin, 2000), which have been adopted in Mexico as a consequence of societal or governmental demand, or simply by imitation. However, the institutional characteristics for each case analysed have an impact on the speed and intensity of change – for example, belonging to a centralized or decentralized education system can have an influence, because the size or complexity of the hierarchical systems they maintain is different. These recent initiatives, undertaken by HEIs and PRCs in Sonora, seem to indicate the existence of convergent change, with the adoption of similar structures and practices, following what Dimaggio and Powell (1983) characterized then as the phenomenon of 'isoformism', which, in this case, is expressed as a manifest intention of imitating the innovation model implemented in the USA.

This case study of Sonora contributes new evidence on patterns of change faced by the R&D institutions and emphasizes aspects of organizational transformation. As a final observation, we would argue that future analysis is necessary, for other dimensions such as organizational learning and the efficiency of the transfer activities in different models of organizational structure to be considered on the basis of performance indicators.

## Notes

[1] Knowledge transfer (KT) consists of the array of activities whose objective is to capture and transfer knowledge, abilities and competencies from those who generate them to those who can transform them into economic products or social benefits. It includes commercialization as well as collaboration and has potential benefits for

the participants: higher education institutions, PRCs and entrepreneurial, social and governmental sectors. KT constitutes a key element of the national and regional innovation systems, because it provides for public research to produce an impact on the competitiveness of the economies.

[2]The National Research System (SNI) of Mexico was created in 1984 to recognize the work of those engaged in producing scientific knowledge and technology. The overall purpose of the National Research System is to promote the development of research activities to enhance the quality, performance and efficiency. The award is made on the basis of peer review and is intended to support the appointment of a National Investigator. The award symbolizes the quality and prestige of the scientific contributions. In parallel with the financial incentives, scholarships are offered, the values of which vary according to the level to which they relate.

[3]University of Sonora (2009, 2005); National Council for Science and Technology (2008, 2006, 2005 and 2001) and Technological Institute of Sonora (2010).

[4]Technological Institute of Sonora, ITSON (2004).

[5]National Institute for Forestry, Agricultural and Livestock Research (2006).

[6]Chapter 1, Article 3; Chapter 2, Article 15; Reglamento de Ingresos Propios, UNISON.

[7]In the document *Lineamiento de Recursos Propios de CIAD*, Chapter II, Article 9, it is pointed out that 'surplus of services will be divided among the personnel that participate in the corresponding projects, among which we find research projects, consulting or licensing that links the institutions with the social and productive sectors'.

[8]It is important to keep in mind that the researcher participating in projects such as these must be committed and able to participate in long term activities that require significant personal effort. It is at this point that new tasks emerge for academics who collaborate, in some cases, as consultants, entrepreneurs and even experts in industrial property, where these new activities are marginal, underappreciated and poorly rewarded.

# References

Arocena, R., and Sutz, J. (2001), 'Changing knowledge production and Latin American universities', *Research Policy*, Vol 30, No 1, pp 221–1234.

Becher, T., and Kogan, M. (1992), *Process and Structure in Higher Education*, Open University Press, Milton Keynes.

Bercovitz, J., Feldman, M., Feller, I., and Burton, R. (2001), 'Organizational structure as a determinant of academic patent and licensing behaviour: an exploratory study of Duke, Johns Hopkins and Pennsylvania State Universities', *Journal of Technology Transfer*, Vol 26, No (1–2), pp 21–35.

Bleiklie, I., and Kogan, M. (2007), 'Organization and governance of universities', *Higher Education Policy*, Vol 20, pp 477–493.

Bok, D. (2003), *Universities in the Marketplace: The Commercialization of Higher Education*, Princeton University Press, Princeton, NJ.

Clark, B. (1998), *Creating Entrepreneurial Universities: Organizational Pathways of Transformation*, Pergamon Press, New York.

Consejo Nacional de Ciencia y Tecnologia, Centros Públicos de Investigacion CONACyT, Centro de Investigacion en Alimentacion y Desarrollo A.C. (CIAD), Annual Reports, 2001,2005, 2006 and 2008.

Corti, E., and Riviezzo, A. (2008), 'Hacia la universidad emprendedora: un analisis del compromiso de las universidades italianas en el desarrollo economico y social', *Economia Industrial*, Vol 368, pp 113–124.

Cortright, J. (2001), 'New growth theory, technology and learning: a practitioner's guide', *Reviews of Economic Development Literature and Practice*, No 4, p 35.

Cruz, C., Sanz, M., and Martines, C. (2010), 'Research centers in transition: patterns of convergence and Diversity', *Journal of Technology Transfer*, published online, 06 April 2010, http://springerlink.com/content/01h1556583q24245/, last accessed 25 September 2010.

DiMaggio P. J., and Powell, W. (1983), 'The iron cage revisited: institutional isomorphism and collective rationality in organizational fields', *American Sociological Review*, Vol 48, No 2, pp 147–160.

Durand, J. P. (2008), *El desarrollo de la investigacion en Sonora*, X Congreso nacional de Investigacion Educativa, Consejo Mexicano de Investigacion Educativa, A. C. Veracruz.

Etzkowitz, H. (2003), 'Research groups as "quasi firms": the invention of the entrepreneurial university', *Research Policy*, Vol 32, No 2, pp 109–121.

Etzkowitz, H., and Leydesdorff, L. (1997), *Universities and the Global Knowledge Economy: A Triple Helix of University–Industry–Government Relations*, Cassell, London.

FFCT (2012), *Foro Consultivo Cientifico y Tecnologico: Sonora*, Diagnostico en Ciencia, Tecnologia e Innovacion 2004–2011, Mexico D. F.

Friedman, J., and Silberman, J. (2003), 'University technology transfer: do incentives, management, and location matter?' *Journal of Technology Transfer*, Vol 28, No 1, pp 17–30.

Geuna, A., and Muscio, A. (2009), 'The governance of university knowledge transfer: a critical review of the literature', *Minerva*, Vol 47, No 1, pp 93–114.

Geuna, A., and Nesta, L. (2006), 'University patenting and its effects on academic research: the emerging European evidence', *Research Policy*, Vol 35, pp 790–807.

Gibb, A. (2005), 'Towards the entrepreneurial university: entrepreneurship education as a lever for change', *Report for the National Council for Graduate Entrepreneurship*, NCEE, Coventry, see http://www. ncee.org.uk/publication/towards_the_entrepreneurial_university.pdf.

Gibbons, M., Limoges, C., Nowotny, H., Schwartzman, S., Scott, P., and Trow, M. (1994), *The New Production of Knowledge*, Sage, London.

Instituto Nacional de Investigaciones Forestales, Agricolas y Pecuarias (INIFAP) (2006), *Plan Estratégico de Mediano Plazo dellNiFaP 2006–2011*, Publicacion Especial No 1,27 April.

Instituto Tecnologico de Sonora (2004), *Informe de Actividades 2003–2004*, Rector Mtro Gonzalo Rodriguez Villanueva, Cd-Obregon.

Instituto Tecnologico de Sonora (2010), *Iniciativas Estratégicas*, http:// www.itson.mx/iniciativas/Paginas/ IniciativasEstrategicas.aspx, last accessed 29 August 2010.

Kim, Y. C. (2009), *The Rise of Organized Transfer: Institutional Learning of Technology Transfer in American Research Universities*, VDM Verlag, see http://www.vdmpublishinggroup.com.

Kogan, M., Bauer, M., Bleiklie, I., and Henkel, M., eds (2006), *Transforming*

Higher Education: A Comparative Study, Springer, Dordrecht.

Leon, B., Sandoval G., and Lopez L. (2009), 'Vinculación y transferencia de conocimiento de los investigadores de Sonora: un enfoque basado en la importancia de los factores individuales', *Region y Sociedad*, Vol 21, No 45, pp 65–96.

Lockett, A., and Wright, M. (2005), 'Resources, capabilities, risk capital and the creation of university spin-out companies', *Research Policy*, Vol 34, No 7, pp 1043–1057.

Marginson, S., and Considine, M. (2000), *The Enterprise University: Power, Governance and Reinvention in Australia*, Cambridge University Press, Cambridge.

Markman, G. D., Phan, P. H., Balkin, D. B., and Gianiodis, P. T. (2005), 'Entrepreneurship and university-based technology transfer', *Journal of Business Venturing*, Vol 20, No 2, pp 241–263.

Martin, M. (2000), *Managing University–Industry Relations: A Study of Institutional Practices of 12 different Countries*, International Institute for Educational Planning, Paris.

Mowery, D., Nelson, R., Sampat, B., and Ziedonis, A. (2004), *Ivory Tower and Industrial Innovation: University–Industry Technology Transfer Before and After the Bayh-Dole Act*, Stanford University Press, Palo Alto, CA.

Operti, E. (2007), 'Entrepreneurial universities: organizational change in academic institutions', paper presented at 'Entrepreneurship, Institutions and Policies: The 2007 Ratio Colloquium for Young Social Scientists', 23–25 August, Stockholm.

Phan, P., and Siegel, D. S. (2006), 'The effectiveness of university technology transfer: lessons learned from quantitative and qualitative research in the US and the UK', *Rensselaer Working Papers in Economics*, No 609.

Polanyi, M. (1962), 'The republic of science: its political and economic theory', *Minerva*, No 1, pp 54–73.

Roberts, E. B., and Malone, D. E. (1996), 'Policies and structures for spinning off new companies from research and development organizations', *R&D Management*, Vol 26, No 1, pp 17–48.

Siegel, D., Waldman, D., and Link, A. (2003), 'Assessing the impact of organizational practices on the relative productivity of university technology transfer offices: an exploratory study', *Research Policy*. Vol 32, No 1, pp 27–48.

Slaughter, S., and Leslie, L. (1997), *Academic Capitalism: Politics, Policies, and the Entrepreneurial University*, Johns Hopkins University Press, Baltimore, MD.

Sotelo (2008), *Coyunturas economicas en la produccion del conocimiento en Sonora*, Memoria del Congreso Sistemas de Innovacion y Competitividad (SINNCO), Consejo de Ciencia y Tecnologia del Estado de Guanajuato, Leon, Guanajuato, México.

Universidad de Sonora (2005), *Informes Anual 2004–2005*, Rector Pedro Ortega Moreno, Hermosillo, pp 189–200.

Universidad de Sonora (2009), *Informes Anual 2008–2009*, Rector Pedro Ortega Moreno, Hermosillo, pp 207–216.

# From past to future: where next?

**Jay Mitra and John Edmondson**

There is seemingly no end to either analysis or speculation about the nature, scope, mechanisms and outcomes of knowledge transfer or exchange between universities and industry. As we would expect, the enquiry has now stretched to emerging economies. China invests more in R&D than most countries other than the USA and is fast ramping up its universities. In characteristic style, India appoints various knowledge and innovation commissions to ponder what is possible. Brazil's rapid economic advance is beginning to be matched with growing interest in international collaboration and knowledge cities and zones that stretch from Dubai to Kazakhstan. There is a flurry of highly sophisticated activities in the much smaller countries of Eastern and Central Europe, such as Estonia, to develop technology-based initiatives that change the way young people learn to think and do.

Stronger economies can better afford the allocation of resources and time to engage in the cross-fertilisation of disparate organisations in which knowledge is created, stored, used, retrieved and replenished. Our sweep of strategies, models, good practice, instruments and methods across a wide variety of countries in this book indicates that there is much by way of effort to make university–industry interactions worthwhile and productive. There is also much duplication of institutional effort and sometimes an unfortunate attempt to replicate models and practices that thrive only because of their particular contexts. Contexts matter, and it is the failure to recognize local specificity, local learning and local absorptive capacities that, as Lorentzen argues in this volume, leads to deleterious policy formulations.

So what, then, is the state of play in this interactive world of universities and industry? How best can we evaluate the outcomes of such interactions? If contexts matter, we can judge results only in accordance with their usefulness in the specific context in which they are produced. The level of economic development, the policies and strategies of the institutions that govern practice for and across different stakeholders, the skills quotient and the technology make-up of these contexts, they all shape and mould the nature of the activities. For example, researching the value of mobile telephony in creating new opportunities for work in the poorest regions of the world and using the findings of such research could be deemed more useful in economically poorer countries. But who should do this research, and who could develop the tools, instruments and infrastructure to implement any findings?

## Common and changing contexts

The common, reducible pattern that we search for in the evidence that is presented to or obtained by us is often made impossible by the reality of the empirics and the phenomenon we observe. If the nature and scope of the interaction process are determined by or are expected to reflect certain specific economic, social and institutional factors, then we know that it is virtually impossible to find common ground in the explanations that make sense of the various forms of interactions. Universities are often judged globally using weighted indices and criteria for knowledge creation and usage, including student destinations and job creation, research activities (especially publications), patents filed, numbers of spin-offs and other related measures. These do not, however, necessarily capture the full range of university–industry activity identified in our Introduction to this volume. Neither do they represent a holistic view of the knowledge-exchange process. As we argued in the Introduction, a holistic view is best appreciated on

a case-by-case basis. The knowledge that may be produced in universities in widely different economies may be on a par, but its usefulness for industry in particular environments may not have any traction. This applies as much in developed economies as in less-developed regions. This issue is often put aside by the idea that universities are producers of global knowledge for application anywhere in the world. There is no *a priori* compact that is expected to bind the two together, and there is no requirement anywhere that the production of knowledge in any form must lead to an industrial outcome. Academic science, as Robert Merton (1973) has argued, is an open project.

While industry can undertake scientific and technological activity to safeguard intellectual property and maximise profits emanating from it, academic science seeks discovery and early publication to create a different kind of productive competitiveness (Florida and Cohen, 1999). This difference was chiselled more sharply by Dasgupta and David (1987), who argued for a distinction in terms of fundamental discovery (universities) and proprietary gain (industry). Notions of corporate usurpation and vandalism of research and university work represent the extreme end of views that suggest that the twain should never meet. Judging by recent articles and letters to the editor in, for example, *Times Higher Education* magazine (the weekly paper of the academic community in the UK), the debate flourishes.

In the meantime, universities change, economies grow or decline and industry contributes to the dynamics of change through innovation, new jobs or abysmal performance, leading often to dramatic changes in the economic welfare and the social fabric of communities.

Yet it seems that we cannot find any real theory of the university and especially of the industry–university–government nexus that might help us to navigate through the changes and their meaning. The patchy information and insights we obtain are generally those that come to us from studies done mainly in the West. We have no clear idea or solid empirical data about how universities can or do work with industry and government in the wider arena of development and in the emerging nations of the world. What makes matters worse is that where we need knowledge and its dissemination to work most directly – in less-developed countries of the world – there is scant evidence of either interest or support for pronounced forms of university–industry engagement. There, the deliberations of NGOs, the public sector (mainly governmental) and the aid industry dominate the creation and distribution of resources, including knowledge. Does that mean that universities have no role to play in those environments? We need careful and meaningful answers to such questions – answers that are neither dismissive of efforts occurring locally or through international partnerships nor ignorant of various context-specific initiatives that do not always make headlines. A good example is the work of the National Universities Commission in Nigeria and its strategy for introducing mandatory entrepreneurship programmes in state universities based on a conscious plan for engagement with industry, NGOs and other institutions (Mitra *et al,* 2010). The co-operative approach by decision makers, educators and users to develop a policy and a plan together and then to implement it across the nation at various levels was symptomatic of the need to create a new pathway for change.

## Plurality and convergence

As Shinn notes in this volume, what we may discern from any close observation of the debate and exploration of the subject is that there is at best a plurality of effective university–industry interaction. The advantage of this plurality lies in the diversity of approaches, which is in keeping with the requirements of a specific context and recognition of the importance of different institutions creating and diffusing new knowledge. The disadvantage lies in the difficulties that may arise because of a lack of integrated actions. The Triple Helix model, for example, appears to deflect questions of the need for a new institutional mix of the three players – universities, governments and industry – leaving a form of goodwill and enlightened self-interest to forge relationships. However, as Ranga and Etzkowitz point out in their chapter on the Triple Helix system, the articulation and fostering of non-linear interactions between different spaces of knowledge creation and exchange allow for the generation of new combinations of knowledge that can advance innovation theory and practice. Brioschi and Cassia's chapter on regional competitiveness in the knowledge economy provides direct empirical evidence of 'tri-polar' regional innovation systems embodying the Triple Helix system.

But could the relationships be made any tighter? For instance, do the multiple responsibilities of the UK's Minister for Universities and Science (which include cities and local growth and constitutional reform alongside higher education) enable him to create a new Triple Helix institutional arrangement to foster local economic development (THE, 2014)?

Plurality may indeed be the only outcome that we could consider. The ultimate objective of achieving excellence and eminence in terms of knowledge creation at universities is reflected in the contributions made by academics that are generally embodied in publications. What keeps these publications alive is the quasi-evangelical zealousness of the academic peer group networks that protect the rigour of academic discourse and the methods used to propagate new knowledge. Industry plays little or no part in this endeavour. There is reward and acclaim for such activity, but very little is obtained in its translation through knowledge-transfer activities. Yet in the world of knowledge-based capitalism, two imperatives prevail – the need for funding, especially in continually testing economic conditions, and the capacity to mix diverse approaches to research-based discovery and learning. While the former constraint often leads to the attraction of funds from corporations, the latter ability often involves co-operative activity between universities and corporate bodies.

At the turn of the 20th century, chemistry and engineering departments in the USA played out the tensions between some academics who were keen to pursue applied, industry-specific research and others who did not want basic research to be compromised. MIT became a hotbed of contention, with departments dependent on industry funds losing academic eminence as some well-known researchers left the institution (Florida and Cohen, 1999). As Hessels *et al* indicate in this volume, in their examination of eight different fields of natural sciences, increasing pressure in academic productivity measured in bibliometric terms can adversely affect the practical utility of academic research. The fact that the dynamics of science vary across most scientific fields suggests that pinning down research excellence to a set of common metrics for evaluation can involve the loss of much of the value that is generated in different kinds of knowledge to address varied problems.

## The instruments of excellence: from patenting to economic development

The funding constraint can leave many universities with simple but painful decisions to make, especially about the reduction, merger or closure of departments. In the grand scheme of things, where knowledge is produced in society through a variety of information and communication technologies in different environments, learning too has begun to move out of the classroom to find alternative settings in the workplace and the community (see the paper by Scott in this volume). Technology's rapid advances mean easier acquisition of learning from across institutions raising questions about the nature, scope and even validity of some university departments. There is a greater need to cooperate among learning providers, and many universities have begun to establish cooperative centres of learning and research excellence at both local and international levels. Interestingly, the need for co-operation also drives industry to develop collaborative arrangements between firms and universities. Evidence of such collaboration is found in the growing number of university–industry research centres and in the increase in academic patenting activities.

Patenting represents one way in which universities have become cognizant of their role as exemplary knowledge producers in terms of both public service and the commercialization of such knowledge set against the wider scenario of promotion of both social and economic returns from academic research. Patenting confirms the exclusivity of knowledge, but it encourages universities to generate additional funding for new research, the licensing of any products developed from such research and also business start-up activities. Ever since the Bayh–Dole Act made ownership and licensing of intellectual property possible for universities in the USA, many countries have followed the American dream. Denmark, Japan, Austria and Germany in particular moved swiftly to transfer ownership of patents from academics to the institutions, with the academics

being given a share of the royalty revenue earned. However, the USA continues to lead by a large margin in the revenues earned from academic patenting. At the turn of this century, US universities and federal laboratories received more than 5% of total patenting (or 8,000 patents) and 15% of biotechnology patents. Patents granted to public research institutions ranged from the thousands in German and Korean research laboratories to the hundreds in Japan, Switzerland and the Netherlands. The actual gains are also skewed in favour of a few major inventions, and licensing income remains quite small as a proportion of research budgets. What emerges from this analysis is the fact that the social act of transferring technology to industry far outweighs the profit earned from such activities.

The latest country to join this drive for institutionalization is China as it ramps up its R&D expenditure to become one of the leading players in the global innovation circuit. This development does not suggest uniformity in the development of a framework for or the practice of university research and its commercialization. An added complication is the uncertainty over incentives offered to both institutions and individual academics to protect, exploit and disclose their research and inventions. Neither governments nor institutions have clear policies about royalty income and equity participation in spin-offs. Where the reputation and promotion of academics are predicated almost entirely on publications in selected peer-reviewed academic journals, there is little to offer by way of incentives to those academics who might seek other channels for the development and dissemination of their research. What makes the situation worse is that academics can be penalized for the absence of publications and unrecognized for their work with industry. There are only a few examples of institutions offering incentives such as prizes for the commercialization of inventions, as they do at Tsinghua University in China.

Worries about the negative effects of patenting and commercialization on the quality of public research are not always borne out by the facts. US studies have shown that universities and researchers demonstrating higher levels of patenting have also had the largest gains in academic publishing. However, the decrease in citations of previous academic patents in other patents relative to business patents may suggest a drop in the quality of academic research.

Discussions about patents and intellectual property issues that centre round achievements in science and technology subjects betray a degree of exclusiveness about universities, academics and their industry partners. The relatively low levels of patents and licences reinforce this notion of exclusiveness. Only a few institutions and industry partners reap the harvest from partnerships in critical areas of scientific experimentation, commercialisation and innovation. These institutions are generally located in urban areas and usually in developed countries where the availability of resources drives opportunity creation, which in turn increases the stock of those resources. The result is a skewed picture of university research and development and its benefits for industry in the world.

Take Figure 1. With regard to impact measured in terms of normalized citations to academic publications

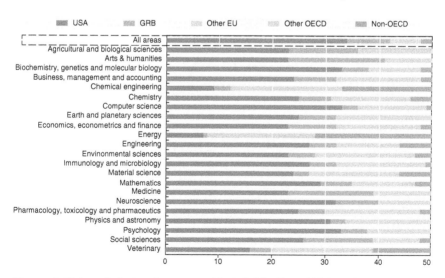

**Figure 1.** University hotspots; geographical distribution of highest impact institutions, 2007–11. Location of the top 50 universities by main subject area.
*Source*: ODCD and SCImages Research Group (CSIC). compendium of bibliometrics Science Indicators 2014, based on Scopus Custom Data, Elsevier MAy 2013. Statlink contains more data.

across all subject areas (output quality per unit of production, not absolute values of high-quality publications), the USA dominates most subject areas apart from energy, chemical engineering and veterinary research. Thirty-four of the top 50 institutions are located in the USA. The UK, which generally runs second in such estimations, excels in medicine and the social sciences. Only two are found outside the OECD area in Chinese Taipei.

If we compare the data in Figure 1 with the data on regions in the world where innovation ranks highly (see Figure 2), we should not be surprised to find spatial correlations between the university hotspots and the innovation magnets, especially in information and communication technology (ICT),

biotechnology and nanotechnology, three of the most important technologies propelling industry and economies forward in this century. Germany probably provides the most circular of ecosystems by connecting businesses, especially mid-sized firms, and their *Fachhochschulen* and *Fraunhofer* institutes to ensure the relevance of skills and technical training and applied research for industry. The top 20 patenting regions in these three technology areas are located in a few countries, with the USA leading on 34% and Japan on 29%. The emergence of Chinese regions, especially Beijing (in biotechnology and nanotechnology) and Guangdong (in ICT) is especially noteworthy.

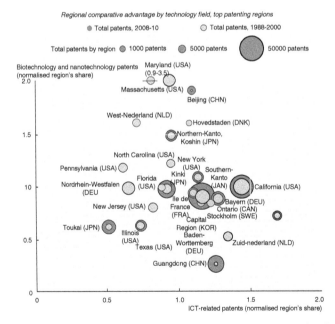

**Figure 2.** Innovation hotspots in ICT, biotechnologies and nanotechnologies, 1998–2000 and 2008–2011.

*Source*: OECD, REGPAT Database, June 2013.

While these two sets of data are not causally connected, there is every reason to infer a close association between the selectivity of regions and the concentration of key technologies involving both university research and industry development.

Outside patenting, universities consider spin-off ventures and licensing as alternatives. Government-funded venture funds, such as the various regional venture funds supported by the European Union, have helped to promote the idea, alongside the growth of entrepreneurship programmes, business incubation centres and accelerators in universities. An alternative is the licensing of research outcomes and new technologies to larger, private firms. In both cases, it is the necessary organization of such activities based on clear strategies for technology development, academic staff incentivisation, and the availability of technical staff to manage these processes – and the genuine integration of such activities in the mission of the university – that can help to establish these forms of knowledge production as legitimate, mainstream functions of universities and their interactions with industry. In fact, what emerges as an outcome is less to do with university–industry interaction and more to do with the university's contribution to the economic development of the region in which it is located. Much of the knowledge creation and exchange can be found to be specific to local contexts. But this raises questions of forms of knowledge, such as tacit and explicit or codified knowledge.

As Lauto *et al* argue in this volume, tacit knowledge creation and dissemination are essentially a function of local contexts in which shared know-how, know-who and experience underpin the augmentation of such knowledge through production processes. Codified knowledge is less a function of local contexts, as it can be shared across different environments through manuals and other written instructions. Large firms in one country with associate or subsidiary firms in other countries are among the strongest purveyors of such knowledge creation and exchange.

## Variable development

What, then, can nations and regions (and their institutions) in less-developed parts of the world do to catch up and, more importantly, to reflect the needs of their economies? The 'catch-up' phenomenon puts pressure on emerging economies to pursue similar trajectories of economic development to their advanced counterparts. Japan's success in doing so, followed by Singapore, South Korea and now China, would suggest that there is value in following the tried and tested path albeit with special Japanese, Singaporean, Korean and Chinese characteristics. In all these countries and especially in the last two, the public sector has played a significant role in determining skills development as the basis of knowledge production and R&D investment. Institutional development at the level of policy formulation, the protection of intellectual property, commercialization and university–industry interaction may not have followed the same pattern of development. However, as Balderrama *et al* point out in their contribution to this volume, there is increasing evidence of a recognition of the value in maximising potential through collaborative effort and across-the-board strategies that cover organisational learning and the creation of new models for knowledge transfer in developing economies such as Mexico.

In her contribution, Kruss identifies the leveraging of value across institutions and partnerships between different tiers of institutions as essential to developing countries such as South Africa. A good starting point for productive partnerships is the creation of a system that gathers pertinent information on curricula, staffing, research, teaching and students on a regular basis, like in the SNIE system in Colombia as described by Lucio-Arias in this volume. Few countries can emulate the rapid advances in catch-up and then take a lead position among the phalanx of developed nations, as the small city-state of Singapore has done. A fine portrait of nation making is provided by Poh-Kam Wong in his contribution, which uses the Triple Helix model to analyse the growth of the life sciences sector.

## Collaboration

A feature of modern forms of R&D and technology transfer is the increasing amount of collaboration between different sets of players and the growing phenomenon of cross-border networks. In the OECD countries, collaboration occurs mainly between higher education institutions and larger firms. Larger firms collaborate two to three times more than do small and medium-sized enterprises. What is interesting is how many of these large firms collaborate in countries such as Finland, Slovenia, Austria and Hungary and how few do so in Mexico and Australia, as shown in Figure 3. Overall, the more R&D oriented a firm is, the more likely it is to collaborate with a range of partners than its non-R&D counterparts. The growth in open innovation systems has created possibilities for higher levels of collaboration but also points to the

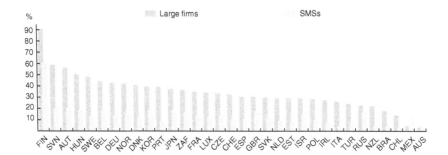

**Figure 3.** Collaboration for innovation.
*Source*: OECD, based on Eurostat (CIS-2010) and national data sources, June 2013.

importance of a variety of players in the innovation value chain, many of which are not necessarily driven by the exclusive R&D agenda of universities.

The increasing levels of collaboration have been made possible by significant advances in new technologies, especially the Internet and mobile telephony. The Global Internet Protocol traffic increased by 20,000 Petabytes a month in 2010 to 55,000 Petabytes in 2013 (OECD, 2013). The widespread commercialization and expansion have meant that the Internet Protocol IPv4 is no longer able to meet the demand for data usage, and the slow progress of its successor IPv6 limits the possibilities of flows of information and knowledge. We live ostensibly in the era of big data: the nature and scope of R&D activity and its commercialization are governed by the volume of data available, the speed with which it is generated and the multiple uses of it made possible through data storage, date crunching, data visualisation and data analysis. The storage and usage of such incomprehensible volumes of data are deemed possible only when multiple players are involved in supporting each other in the value-addition process. Linux's worldwide open-source knowledge platform of people writes 10,923 lines of code or a 300-page book every day. The same team removes 5,547 lines of redundant code and modifies another 2,243 codes (Tapscott and Williams, 2010).

These developments openly challenge the university's privileged position as knowledge producer in today's economy in three distinctive ways. First, there is the use, application and analysis of data for knowledge creation. The sheer volume of data requires significant data-crunching capability. Second, powerful and large data sets are not only used in the context of business operations; they are also embedded in the products and services that customers purchase. Third, established companies such as the Bosch Group in Germany, a 127-year-old manufacturing conglomerate, or Schneider Electric, a 170-year-old French manufacturer of iron, steel and armaments and now involved in energy management, are introducing a range of initiatives that make use of data and analytics to provide intelligent customer offerings. While the former provides for intelligent fleet management and vehicle-charging infrastructure, the latter focuses on energy optimization and smart grid management. So we have data management at the operations level to improve business decisions, data application in product offerings to create better-value propositions for customers and the reorganisation of strategy to enable business to compete on analytics (Davenport, 2013). The new technology of big data and data analytics is demanding a holistic approach to the implementation of business management in technological, operations, strategic and external user-oriented activities, all centred round the use of information.

There is little by way of integrated management learning in universities that will allow us to respond swiftly and in an integrated fashion to the needs of business in this scenario. How universities can compete and collaborate with businesses in making sense of big data remains to be seen.

## More to heaven and earth than science and technology

The attractions of dizzying data and mysterious science overwhelm discussions on university–industry interaction. This dominance often stultifies debates about the future of such interaction. Critics lament the ivory-tower nature of academia or the lack of interest by industry in university research and education while science and technology advance in both spheres. Aficionados see prospects in increasing forms of collaboration but fail to define and elaborate on key strategies or actions. A nuanced, more analytical picture of research, development and other activities reveals that it is worthwhile considering first the type of the activities that actually involve universities and industry and the disciplines most commonly involved.

A recent study in the UK based on a survey of 22,000 academics and 2,500 businesses found that, while basic research was predominant in the science subjects of physics and mathematics (about 40% of respondents), biology, veterinary science and chemistry (around 35%) and, interestingly, the arts and humanities (also around 40%), most of the applied research activity (suggesting industry relevance) took place in the health sciences and in engineering and materials science. User-inspired research (suggesting direct industry involvement) focused on engineering and materials science, physics and mathematics (both around 37%) and biology, chemistry and veterinary science (approximately 35%). Clearly physics and mathematics enjoyed both academic and industry interest. Commercialisation activity by academics has been fairly low (7% for patents, 5% for licences and 4% for spin-offs) over the past three years. Again, engineering and material sciences provided the most fertile commercialization fodder (patenting), and it was mainly senior academics at professorial level who led the patents charge (Hughes *et al*, undated).

A separate study by members of the same academic team found that three categories of activities probably made more of an impact on a variety of external organizations and, therefore, on local economic development (Hughes and Kitson, 2013; 2012). These three categories include:

- people-based activities – training, networks and conferences;
- problem-solving activities – contract research, joint publications, informal advice; and
- community-based activities – lectures for the community, exhibitions and school projects.

In many respects, it is probably through the multiple forms of engagement available that both universities and external organizations are able to afford genuine exchange. In typical scientific projects, there is the greater likelihood of universities generating new knowledge and industry implementing commercial actions. Measuring the impact of these interactions is not easy, but it is incumbent on institutions, governments and industry to do so in order to obtain a full measure of both the intrinsic and extrinsic value of knowledge creation, dissemination and exchange.

Tables 2 and 3 provide a more detailed picture of the diversity of activities in which real forms of engagement occur. Problem-solving and people-based activities are significantly higher than commercialisation and research activities as far as UK academics are concerned. These activities range from direct interactions based on the use of direct scientific and technical expertise to solve problems (prototyping and testing to contract research and informal advice) together with student placement, training and curriculum development activities. Student placements and attending conferences with higher education institutions (HEIs) are high on the list of interactions of UK businesses, but the latter appear to have less of an interest in problem-solving and community-based activities than UK academics think. UK businesses tend to focus more on commercialisation and research activities when it comes to interacting with universities. There is a readiness among academics to engage with the wider community, and contrary to popular opinion, universities may not be the ivory tower that they are imagined to be. It is possible that industry needs to do far more work to reach out to both academic institutions and the wider society to which they belong.

In opening up the wider canvas of engagement, the role of different departments of universities is well worth noting. The data and evidence

Table 1. The wealth of interactions of academia (UK businesses).

| People-based activities | % | Community-based activities | % | Problem-solving activities | % | Commercialisation and research activities | % |
|---|---|---|---|---|---|---|---|
| Giving invited lectures | 65 | Lectures for the community | 38 | Informal advice | 57 | Licensed research | 5 |
| Student placements | 33 | Schools projects | 30 | Research consortia | 35 | Patenting | 7 |
| Participating in networks | 67 | Public exhibitions | 15 | Hosting personnel | 27 | Spun-out company | 4 |
| Standard setting forums | 31 | Community-based sports | 3 | Joint research | 49 | Formed/run consultancy | 14 |
| Enterprise education | 6 | | | Consulting services | 43 | | |
| Curriculum development | 28 | | | Setting of physical facilities | 9 | | |
| Attending conferences | 87 | | | Contract research | 37 | | |
| Sitting on advisory boards | 38 | | | External secondment | | | |
| Employee training | 33 | | | Prototyping and testing | 10 | | |
| | | | | Joint publications | 46 | | |

*Source:* adapted from Kitson (2014).

Table 2. The wealth of interactions of industry (UK businesses).

| People-based activities | % | Community-based activities | % | Problem-solving activities | % | Commercialisation and research activities | % |
|---|---|---|---|---|---|---|---|
| Attending conferences with HEIs | 10 | Lectures for the community | 4 | Hosting academics | 3 | Academic publications | 27 |
| Attending conferences organised by HEIs | 7 | Schools projects | 12 | Consultancy services | 4 | Licences owned by HEIs | 3 |
| Supervising student projects | 6 | Public exhibitions | 3 | Secondment to HEIs | 1 | Spun-out companies | 6 |
| Participation in networks | 7 | Community-based sports | 2 | Joint research | 3 | Licences owned by non-HEIs | 6 |
| Participating in standard-setting forums involving HEIs | 3 | | | Informal advice | 5 | | |
| Sitting on advisory boards | 2 | | | Contract research | 2 | | |
| Training at HEIs | 13 | | | Research consortia | 2 | | |
| Curriculum development | 2 | | | Prototyping and testing | 2 | | |
| Invited lectures | 4 | | | Joint publications | 2 | | |
| Enterprise education | 3 | | | Creation of physical facilities | 1 | | |

*Source:* adapted from Kitson (2014).

referred to previously would indicate that engineering and science departments are probably the key players and the main channels of interaction with industry. Where the very idea of innovation is steeped in technological advancement and where economic progress is predicated upon technological development, it makes sense for strategies and plans at both institutional and governmental levels to give these disciplines premium attention in terms of resource allocation. These disciplines have carved out an economic niche not just because of excellence in research but also because of the seriousness academics attach to teaching. This has implications for both routine forms of knowledge transfer and more direct forms of commercialisation, such as spin-off activities. Chapman *et al*, in their paper in this volume on London HEIs and university spin-offs, show that what is missing from our understanding of their value is their social impact, which can go far beyond the simple economic considerations by which we evaluate them.

History shows us the value of teaching and training in engineering in Germany, which continues to provide excellence. The acclaimed Indian Institutes of Technology are known less for their research output than for the quality of their students. Their eventual success in research, and especially in ICT, biotechnology, advanced manufacturing and service industries, is a testimony to the excellence of their learning environments. Industry seeks out these talents from universities with pronounced interest; governments find in them the best ambassadors for the benefits of immigration (as many a Chinese, Taiwanese, Indian, Israeli and Russian talent in the USA demonstrates year after year).

What do business schools achieve? Where is the wisdom they have lost in knowledge, and where is the knowledge they have lost in research? Are business schools better at analysing disruptive innovation than dealing with it? And does such analysis help industry? 'Schumpeter''s stinging criticism of business schools in a recent article deserves examination:

> In every profession there are people who fail to practise what they preach: dentists with a mouth full of rotten teeth, doctors who smoke 40 a day, accountants who forget to file their tax returns. But it is a rare profession where failure to obey its own rules is practically a condition of entry. Business schools exist to teach the value of management. They impart some basic principles – like setting clear goals and management risk. They also teach how dangerous the business world has become … But when it comes to their own affairs, business schools flout their own rules and ignore their own warnings.
> ('Schumpeter', The Economist, 2014)

'Schumpeter' argues that there is very little incentive for teaching. In maintaining what is often referred to as 'physics envy', the best of academics can perish if they do not publish in the highest-starred peer-reviewed journals. Usable research is of secondary importance. While innovation thrives on connectivity, business school academics excel in cutting up the world, and indeed the word, into tiny, often obscure sub-disciplines. Reams of academic journal papers rarely offer genuine insight, not least because managers seldom bother to read these treasure troves of rarefied knowledge. This ostensible asymmetry does not necessarily affect academic researchers and their career paths, as their creation of a parallel universe of research is judged and rewarded by peers. Teaching and outreach (workshops, seminars, people and community-based together with problem-solving activities) are very rarely accorded any formal recognition or status in terms of performance indicators or measurable outputs.

Yet business schools are probably best placed not only to upgrade and ramp up their teaching, learning and business focused activities, ensuring both rigour and reach, but also to combine with engineering and pure and social science departments to launch integrated research projects and training programmes that reflect the multidisciplinary nature of most activities in business, government and other organizations. The social sciences deserve particular attention. Recent developments in the study of behavioural economics, where economists work with psychologists, and the awarding of the Nobel Prize for Economists to psychologists, indicate that there is hope yet for learning through combinatorial effort cutting across disciplinary silos.

There are other tertiary and higher education institutions, such as technical colleges, whose knowledge-transfer activities may indeed be more relevant to local businesses, and in particular small and medium-sized enterprises, whose search for the resolution of immediate problems and simple technical issues may not fit the exigencies of university researchers and their quest for longer-term enquiry. As Delfmann and Koster show in their contribution, with reference to institutions in the Netherlands, knowledge transfer as practised by colleges is significantly different from that operated by universities.

The SME (small and medium-sized enterprise) question remains a big issue everywhere, not least because SMEs dominate most industrial landscapes. The negative aspect of resource constraints in SMEs is counterbalanced by research evidence that highlights their ability to innovate, especially in sectors dominated by larger firms. Who meets their needs? Large anchor firms in regions and in clusters of industries are often the best sources of support for SMEs. Universities are often not equipped to manage short-term projects aimed at quick but critical problem solving. Major government projects, such as those funded by the European Commission, which demand a strong SME presence, often fail to reach out to that constituency because of the levels of bureaucracy associated with form-filling and administrative reporting. Yet limited engagement with SMEs and especially start-ups in our transformative high-technology world prevents universities from developing a knowledge base over time. Internships with SMEs, or what Varghese *et al* refer to in their contribution as 'cognitive apprenticeship schemes', are often regarded as one of the more effective instruments for improving the self-efficacy of students who can make direct contributions to SMEs and their owner-managers while learning about the SME environment.

## An entrepreneurial approach

How far can universities delve in their search for co-operation? And which institutions should industry choose to work with in the longer term? Excellence in specific fields offers immediate solutions. We know what Imperial College in the UK, Stanford in the USA, Nanyang in Singapore and Kyoto in Japan have to offer to all stakeholders in key technology areas. For many other institutions, there is perhaps a need to look beyond simple trade-offs between specific knowledge inputs and their use. New possibilities could be created through much wider and deeper forms of engagement, in which university students and staff learn together with entrepreneurs and public policy decision makers to develop environments conducive to learning. Gibb, in his contribution on this theme, writes about learning methods and practices based on direct engagement with entrepreneurs and the ways they live and learn.

Entrepreneurship development through education and start-up activities and the necessary engagement with entrepreneurs offers opportunities to universities to become involved in the economic and social change process. These entrepreneurs are change agents, according to Luczkiw (in this volume). Acknowledging the role of change agents and their behaviour can require us to consider new methodologies for research and learning. Mitra argues in his contribution that seeing, observing and then articulating can offer new insights into the creation of ideas, the identification of opportunity and new firm formation, beyond the crunching of macro numbers and case studies. The relationship between what we observe and what we know in entrepreneurship is never settled, but ongoing attention to the dynamics of change helps us to expand our knowledge base and avoid reductionist or formulaic approaches to enquiry.

There is a need for continuous reinvention. A good deal of sustainable entrepreneurial endeavour in universities is made possible when entrepreneurship education and training are supported by physical facilities such as incubation centres and science parks. In Finland in the 1990s, there was a marked effort in regional development in the form of an entrepreneurial approach to networking involving science parks, universities and local agencies. Vartiainen and Viiri in their contribution refer to the salutary example of the Joensuu Science Park, the local university and the North Karelia region of Finland being part of a network supporting international research and education.

## Entrepreneurial talent

Probably the most significant economic and social contribution of universities to industry and to economic development is that of identifying and nurturing talent – not talent as given but talent as scouted for and developed. Talent, often coded by economists as human capital, is a critical factor in the economic production process. It is highly mobile, and its distribution can be highly skewed, especially in scientific and technical fields, as we have seen. Additionally, unlike the general labour market, the market for talent is created around other talent. In other words, talent attracts talent, generating increasing returns on any investment in talent.

This is why universities try to leverage the talent they have in their faculty by recruiting talented students. Moreover, this 'talent breeding' is not restricted to the universities; they contribute to the establishment of technopoles, economic growth habitats which draw in scientists and engineers working in firms and laboratories and who, together with the universities, help to form new spin-off businesses and attract complementary organisations including distributors, suppliers and others in a local ecosystem. There is no suggestion of any linear relationship here – universities may spawn new industries as much as growing businesses can create new founts of knowledge and help to promote higher education institutions. Having Nobel Prize winners on the staff has obvious attractions, but their rarity makes it impossible for many universities to rely on their presence. Rather, the emphasis increasingly is on sets of diverse critical capabilities – theoretical knowledge, empirical awareness and practical experience. One of us, teaching a class of exceptional talent in a leading Chinese university, was once asked if one could demonstrate a capability in business practice as evidence of a meaningful rapport with experienced executive management students. A positive response enabled better communication and a richer environment of learning!

A community of talent in the university becomes a magnet for talent in industry which wants to reach out to them. This is also the reason industry funds scholarships and research institutes, even in other countries. The million-pound funding by Tata Motors of an institute at Warwick University's Warwick Manufacturing Group in the UK is based on the group's reputation as a seat of excellence in the engineering industry. In growth regions such as those identified in Figure 1, we find a dynamic system of talent attraction. There are other legendary examples from the past, such as NEC's Research Institute in Princeton in the USA which, it is claimed, was set up to attract bachelor's-level engineers who trained in a faculty with Nobel Prize-calibre talent (Florida and Cohen, 1999).

Talent creation in universities is a dynamic process in which there is a constant churn, with graduate students moving out to give way to new entrants, along with academics switching jobs. This churn enables the attraction and constant replenishing of the stock of talent, a necessary dynamic in a constantly changing world of scientific and technological advancement. As Walshok notes in her contribution, it is the stock of intellectual capital combining with catalytic enterprises and financial networks plus the high level of skills that make San Diego, California, one of the most innovative regions in the USA.

Enabling this dynamic of talent to work at different levels and across disciplines and in conjunction with different stakeholders is the biggest challenge in all economies. This issue also raises fundamental questions about policy at the level of government and strategies for universities and industry. The assumption that a massive drive towards technological development centred around knowledge creation and innovation in universities would somehow spill over to foster economic growth and social development is at best naïve. This is why the UK government's recent push towards financing STEM (science, technology, engineering and mathematics) in response to the declining levels of achievement in these subjects is perhaps a little myopic in the context of widespread cuts in other subject areas, especially the humanities.

## Arguing for productive change: government, universities and industry

At all times and in all environments, we need strategic and holistic approaches to address complex problems. Strategic selection could, for example, result in the selection and promotion of key technologies and subjects, their scientific and technological advancement, supplemented by critical capability development for their deployment, management and creative advancement, their commercialisation and, crucially, their social adoption and absorption. Without being too deterministic, a strategic approach could help to identify and develop the hard and soft infrastructure of national and local economies centred around a selection of key technologies and their organization. This does not mean a standardized set of technologies or disciplines but a range that reflects local priorities, capabilities and development prospects. Such an approach could entail at the public policy level:

a)  Establishing ecosystem co-ordination networks at the regional level with adequate levels of funding based on choices determined at the local level and with adequate reference to national strategies.

b)  The creation of networks that are not swayed by a form of centralization in the decision-making process, with public funding distributed largely at the behest of one favoured quango. Here, open and transparent governance structures should switch decision-making responsibilities according to the specific actions necessary on a project-by-project basis (for example, education strategies can be developed by schools, colleges and universities together, while apprenticeship training plans can be led by industry and public services by a network of public-sector providers).

c)  Establishing genuine forms of incentivisation of university activities that recognize the significance of excellence in different forms of knowledge creation and knowledge diffusion, breaking down further the notion of a rarefied, ivory-tower environment. Here public policy could tie in funding and other support measures with performance indicators that stretch beyond the traditional role of, for example, research publications as the primary source of knowledge production. Encouraging the setting up of standards and monitoring demonstrations of excellence in establishing spin-off firms, public knowledge dissemination platforms, embedded interactions with industry (industry participation in classrooms, placements, validation of content and pedagogies, involvement in live industry projects, all as part of the mode of assessed learning) could create opportunities for both universities and industry to exchange ideas, knowledge and practice.

If change is going to occur, then our universities will also need to respond to strategic amendments to policy of the kind described. Universities need not always wait for the right signals from government, but they can perhaps demonstrate leadership in curriculum and pedagogic development, research plans and multidisciplinary approaches to the discovery, learning and dissemination of knowledge. This cannot be achieved if they are not complemented by the development of performance indicators which are on a par (in real as opposed to rhetorical terms) or by accommodating education and learning externalities such as jobs.

Take the simple issue of 'employability', high on the agenda of most institutions, especially in a climate of limited or jobless economic growth. Commendable efforts to address this issue are still not resolving the question of how employability is to be embedded in the curriculum and in the pedagogies of courses and modules and in research projects. Or take the other popular question of assessing the impact of research. There is value in projecting the impact of research and projects in terms of commercialisation and development prospects when making research bids, as most public research funding bodies require these days, but this needs to be followed up by monitoring the process *ex-ante*, during and after the completion of research projects.

Being employable does indeed require brushing up CV writing skills, but it also means that students and scholars of science and technology need to be able to reflect on Kuhn's idea of paradigm change, with schoolkids, for example, playing with bits of knowledge using mobile technology, factory workers adopting new technologies and communities absorbing dramatic change as they see a major employer shedding jobs or a private–public partnership building a new airport near precious ecological hotspots. In the past, extra-mural studies addressed such issues, but their demise has left a yawning gap in the exchange of knowledge, which can be filled by using different instruments and partnership arrangements. What can help today is the study of and research into entrepreneurship. In using the word 'entrepreneurship', we do not confine ourselves to its narrow interpretation, principally to do with start-ups and especially the formation of replicative new firms. A larger interpretation of entrepreneurship embraces the identification of opportunities or innovation led by entrepreneurial management in existing organizations, in networked structures of governance in which creating and implementing new ideas in the interstices of connected organizations are the norm rather than the prescription of established patterns of practice and behaviour in silos. Entrepreneurship theory and practice which contribute to the necessary enhancement of the creative mindset across all disciplines reinforce a long-established function of higher education – intellectual and creative enlightenment.

There are more businesses in any economy than there are universities. In a so-called knowledge economy, there are more knowledge workers in industry than in academia. In the ubiquitous world of information and communication technologies, much of what we look at, consume, reflect on and throw away is being determined by industry. The demand for higher levels of consciousness about the environment, human rights, poverty alleviation and meaningful or sustainable economic model building may have brought industry closer to society and its different stakeholders. Against that objective, what we find is the drive for rapid levels of growth to enable higher levels of return on investment for the few to whom capital growth has more value than a nation's overall economic and social development. Universities have produced fodder for relentless, acquisitive growth, often under pressure to meet short-term needs, but they have also been at the forefront of creating environments for knowledge workers, structures of organization and production, for centuries. As the status quo of these institutions is being challenged in the public domain and in a world of Twitter technology, there is an ever-greater need to reinvent the machinery of knowledge production and its exchange among all who sup at its table.

## References

Dasgupta, P. and David, P. (1987), 'Information, disclosure and the economics of science and technology', in Feiwel, G. (ed), *Arrow and the Ascent of Modern Economic Theory*, New York: New York University Press.

Davenport, T. H. (2013), 'Analytics 3.0: In the new era, big data will power consumer products and services', *Harvard Business Review*, Vol 91, No 12, pp 64–72.

Florida, R. and Cohen, W. M. (1999), 'Engine of infrastructure? The university role in economic development', in Branscomb, L. M, Kodama, F. and Florida, R., *Industrialising Knowledge: University–Industry Linkages in Japan and the United States*, Cambridge, MA: MIT Press, pp 589–610.

Hughes, A. and Kitson, M. (2013), *Connecting with the Ivory Tower: The Business Perspective on Knowledge Exchange in the UK*, Cambridge: Centre for Business Research, University of Cambridge.

Hughes, A. and Kitson, M. (2012), cited in Kitson, M. (2014), 'The myth of the ivory tower: the connectivity of UK academia with the business, public and third sector', presentation at Conference on '*Entrepreneurial University, Engaged Industry and Active Government*', University of Surrey, Guildford, 29–30 May.

Hughes, A., Kitson, M., Abreu, M., Grinevich, V., Bullock, A. and Milner, Cambridge Centre for Business Research Survey of Knowledge Exchange Activity by United Kingdom Academics, UK Data, Archive Study Number 6462 (undated), cited in Kitson, M. (2014), 'The myth of the ivory tower: the connectivity of UK academia with the business, public and third sector', presentation at Conference on '*Entrepreneurial University, Engaged Industry and Active Government*', University of Surrey, Guildford, 29–30 May.

Kitson, M. (2014), 'The myth of the ivory tower: the connectivity of UK academia with the business, public and third sector', presentation at Conference on '*Entrepreneurial University, Engaged Industry and Active Government*', University of Surrey, Guildford, 29–30 May.

Merton, R. (1973), *The Sociology of Science*, Chicago, IL: University of Chicago Press.

Mitra, J., Abubakar, Y.A. and Sagagi, M. (2010), 'Knowledge creation and human capital for development: the role of graduate entrepreneurship', *Education and Training Journal*, Vol 53, No 5, pp 462–479.

OECD. (2013), *Science, Technology and Innovation Scoreboard: Innovation for Growth*, Paris: Organisation for Economic Co-operation and Development.

'Schumpeter' (2014), 'Those who can't, teach'; *The Economist*, Vol 410, No 8873, 8 February, p 63.

Tapscott, D. and Williams, A. D. (2010), *MacroWikinomics: Rebooting Business and the World*, London: Atlantic Books.

THE. (2014), 'Call for assurances over Clark's wider remit', *Times Higher Education*, 14–20 August, p 8.

## Original publication dates of papers from *Industry and Higher Education*:

**Chapter 1** (Shinn): Vol 12, No 5, October 1998; **Chapter 2** (Scott): Vol 18, No 5, October 2004; **Chapter 3** (Lorentzen): Vol 19, No 2, April 2005; **Chapter 4** (Mitra): Vol 16, No 3, June 2002; **Chapter 5** (Ranga and Etzkowitz): Vol 27, No 3, August 2013; **Chapter 6** (Lauto *et al*): Vol 27, No 1, February 2013; **Chapter 7** (Gibb): Vol 16, No 3, June 2002; **Chapter 8** (Varghese *et al*): Vol 26, No 5, October 2012; **Chapter 10** (Luczkiw): Vol 21, No 1, February 2007; **Chapter 11** (Hessels *et al*): Vol 25, No 5, October 2011; **Chapter 13** (Brioschi and Cassia): Vol 20, No 6, December 2006; **Chapter 14** (Walshok *et al*): Vol 16, No 1, February 2002; **Chapter 15** (Vartiainen and Viiri) Vol 16, No 2, April 2002; **Chapter 16** (Chapman *et al*): Vol 25, No 6, December 2011; **Chapter 17** (Kruss): Vol 19, No 2, April 2005; **Chapter 18** (Wong): Vol 20, No 4, August 2006; **Chapter 19** (Lucio-Arias): Vol 20, No 4, 2006; **Chapter 20** (Delfmann and Koster): Vol 26, No 1, February 2012; **Chapter 21** (Balderrama *et al*): Vol 27, No 3, June 2013.

# Contributors

*As many of the papers in this volume were originally published in the journal* Industry and Higher Education, *the affiliations on the title pages reflect the authors' affiliations at the time of writing. While some of these remain the same, others have changed. We provide below the current affiliation of the contact author for each paper included.*

*With great sadness we have also to record the very untimely deaths of two of our valued contributors – Eugene Luczkiw and Jo Lorentzen – to whom this book is dedicated.*

Jorge Inés León Balderrama is with CIAD (Centro de Investigación en Alimentación y Desarrollo AC), Sonora, Mexico.

Maria Sole Brioschi is with the Faculty of Engineering at the University of Bergamo, Italy.

Dave Chapman is with the Department of Management Science & Innovation and is Programme Director of the MSc in Technology Entrepreneurship at University College London, UK

Heike Delfmann is with the Department of Economic Geography in the Faculty of Spatial Sciences at the University of Groningen, The Netherlands.

Nathalie Duval-Couetil is Director of the Certificate in Entrepreneurship and Innovation Program, Associate Professor of Technology Leadership and Innovation, and Associate Director of the Burton D. Morgan Center for Entrepreneurship at Purdue University, West Lafayette, IN, USA.

Henry Etzkowitz is President of the International Triple Helix Institute, Palo Alto, CA, USA.

Allan Gibb OBE is Professor Emeritus, University of Durham, UK.

Glenda Kruss is Research Director for Education and Skills Development at the Human Sciences Research Council, Cape Town, South Africa.

Laurens Hessels is a Senior Researcher in the Department of Science System Assessment at the Rathenau Instituut, The Hague, The Netherlands.

Giancarlo Lauto is with the Department of Economics and Statistics at the University of Udine, Italy.

Diana Lucio-Arias is with the Colombian Observatory of Science and Technology, Bogotá, Colombia.

Jonathan Potter is with the Centre for Entrepreneurship, SMEs and Local Development of the Organisation for Economic Co-operation and Development, Paris, France.

Marina Ranga is with the Human Sciences and Technology Advanced Research Institute (H-STAR) at Stanford University, CA, USA.

Peter Scott is Professor of Higher Education Studies at the Institute of Education, University of London, UK.

Terry Shinn is a Director of Research at CNRS, Paris, France.

Mary E. Varghese is with the Discovery Learning Center at Purdue University, West Lafayette, IN, USA.

Perttu Vartiainen is Rector of the University of Eastern Finland, Joensuu, Finland.

Mary L. Walshok is Associate Vice Chancellor for Public Programs and Dean of Extension at the University of California San Diego, CA, USA.

Poh-Kam Wong is with the NUS Entrepreneurship Centre of the NUS Business School, National University of Singapore.

# Index

For Product Safety Concerns and Information please contact our EU
representative  GPSR@taylorandfrancis.com
Taylor & Francis Verlag GmbH, Kaufingerstraße 24, 80331 München, Germany

www.ingramcontent.com/pod-product-compliance
Ingram Content Group UK Ltd.
Pitfield, Milton Keynes, MK11 3LW, UK
UKHW021605240425
457818UK00018B/390